1977

PERSONAL PHILOSOPHY
Perspectives on Living

This book may be kept

PERSPECTIVES ON LIVING

PERSONAL PHILOSOPHY

BURTON F. PORTER

Russell Sage College

Under the general editorship of
Robert J. Fogelin
Yale University

HARCOURT BRACE JOVANOVICH, INC.

New York   Chicago   San Francisco   Atlanta

ISBN: 0-15-569401-4

Library of Congress Catalog Card Number: 75-23923

Printed in the United States of America

For Credits and Acknowledgments see pages 521–23.

to

Susana and Mother
in America

Jean and Andrée
in France

Harold and Rita
in England

NOTE ON THE AUTHOR

Dr. Burton F. Porter earned his undergraduate degree at the University of Maryland and received his graduate education at Oxford University and the University of St. Andrews (Scotland). He is the author of *Deity and Morality: With Regard to the Naturalistic Fallacy* (New York: Humanities Press; London: Allen and Unwin, 1968) and *Philosophy: A Literary and Conceptual Approach* (New York: Harcourt Brace Jovanovich, 1974). At present, he holds the position of Associate Professor of Philosophy at Russell Sage College.

PREFACE

The purpose of this book is to help the reader to develop a personal philosophy of life, which means that technical and remote philosophic problems have not been included. Rather, the emphasis is on those basic philosophic issues that are of immediate concern to us in our lives. In addition, all the issues presented here are not only fundamental ones within the philosophic tradition but are especially meaningful to the contemporary mind. The philosophic portions of the fields of morals, politics, religion, knowledge, and ethics are considered in five sections, and each has been oriented toward the current questions that engage us. The answers that are examined are likewise those that constitute actual life choices for us in the present age.

This is not to say that the more remote and abstract philosophic issues are unimportant or lack all practical value, but we are concentrating here on issues that have more direct significance and immediacy.

If the book is treated as material to be assimilated, the main point will have been lost. Philosophy is never mere information, and the present work, in particular, aims at the personal involvement of the reader in the philosophic dialogue. All the issues discussed are serious ones, affecting the way we lead our lives, and it is important for each of us to reach intelligent decisions regarding them. There is a temptation to be intellectually lazy and timid and to think according to the trends of the times or even not to think deeply at all, but then we live fashionably, not well. In order to exist fully, with maximum awareness, understanding, and choice, the philosophic dimension of existence must be internalized and made real, and philosophic questions must be answered in a deliberate and disciplined way.

Everyone has a personal philosophy of sorts, but that does not mean that one person's opinion is as good as another's. A well-considered idea is more likely to be correct, as well as to be valued more highly, as the result of individual effort. In this book the reader is called upon to confront basic issues and to think them through critically, with the aim of developing or expanding his or her own personal philosophy.

Many persons contributed both directly and indirectly to the creation of this book, but I am particularly indebted to Professor Robert J. Fogelin of the Department of Philosophy at Yale University for his particularly courteous and insightful suggestions. I am also grateful to William A. Pullin, vice-president of Harcourt Brace Jovanovich, Inc., for first suggesting the idea of this book to me and for his support throughout the project. Kathy Barth also deserves my gratitude for her assistance in the preparation of the manuscript.

Burton F. Porter

CONTENTS

III

COMMITTING YOURSELF ON RELIGION

V

DECIDING WHAT TO LIVE FOR   411

EPILOGUE

CONTEMPLATION AND ACTION

PERSONAL PHILOSOPHY
Perspectives on Living

CONFRONTING
MORAL ISSUES

I

ATTEMPTING TO DECIDE moral issues is especially difficult in the contemporary age because we lack a definite moral consensus to use as a reference point. As in certain other turbulent periods in history, the late Hellenic age for example, we are uncertain which standards to apply or whether any standards are applicable other than our personal feelings. Each faction of the society has a different moral outlook, from the blue-collar worker to the intellectuals and artists to the midwestern farmer to the urban black, and each segment defends its position with a virulence that indicates the depth of emotion involved (as well as the insecurity and confusion).

We are tempted to conclude that whatever seems right to a person *is* right, that is, right *to that person*, and not to admit any other sense of moral rightness. However, not only would this approach obliterate the distinction between appearance and reality but all moral conflicts would be attributed to differences in attitude that lie beyond the range of criticism. It would become senseless to speak of moral improvement, deterioration or progress, what is better or what is worse, or to differentiate between the satisfying and the satisfactory, the admired and the admirable. Moreover, conflicting moral positions could only be resolved by emotional persuasion or political coercion, with the individual virtually defenseless against the prevalent fashions or habits of thought.

To resolve disagreements concerning right and wrong it seems preferable to critically examine the validity of the moral position, making sure that the bases of the arguments are sound, that the relevant evidence and experience have been taken into account, and that there are no basic inconsistencies in the reasoning. This is the philosophic approach which aims at maximum objectivity in evaluation and is careful not to assume that even thoroughly considered conclusions are the final and absolute truth. For although there may be absolute truth to be known, we can never be sure that we know it absolutely.

With this approach in mind, we can try to reach our own conclusions about the moral issues of personal relationships, abortion, and euthanasia which are more than an expression of feeling. Although all moral conflicts may not be resolved in this way, a considerable amount of progress can be made—certainly far more than under the slogan *de gustibus non est disputandum*,[1] with ethical positions subsumed under the category of tastes.

Personal relationships, or, more specifically, intimate relationships between human beings, are of particular concern to us today and involve questions of sex, love, marriage, contraception, perversion, and so forth. We are in an age of experimentation in styles of living, and we have seen the emergence (and partial acceptance) of homosexual marriage, pre-

---

1 There is no disputing taste.

marital and extramarital sex, unwed motherhood, lesbian love, group sex, and the extended (communal) family.

In trying to evaluate the worth of current attitudes and conduct, we must ask ourselves whether they contribute to an optimum existence. In what ways should human beings relate to one another so that they are mutually enriched rather than impoverished? Are the new life styles simply novel and daring or genuinely more fulfilling than previous forms of relationships? If we oppose the new freedom, are we simply responding in accordance with our traditional upbringing or perceiving undesirable dimensions of the new ideas that render them unadoptable? Should sex occur only when love is present, and marriage occur as a natural consequence of love? Do contraceptives promote promiscuity and demean the sexual experience by eliminating as its aim the creation of new life, or do they allow a useful separation between gratification and procreation? Is there any sexual expression that can be called perverse: homosexuality, voyeurism, bestiality, exhibitionism, sadism, masochism?

With regard to sex, love, and marriage, the extreme liberal position maintains that sex is a personal matter outside the jurisdiction of society's concerns, particularly now that contraceptives are readily available and sex need not entail children. According to this viewpoint, sex is a pleasurable experience, as natural a function as eating and sleeping, and it should not be hedged round with moral prohibitions and carry a burden of solemnity. People need not be in love (or even have a close relationship) in order to enjoy having sex, and if two people want to live together rather than marry that is their decision and should not carry any social stigma. Marriage is, in general, an outmoded institution that encourages possessiveness, dependency, and dullness and locks people into relationships through legal and religious controls, rather than allowing them to freely decide whether they want to remain together. It may be desirable for people to marry when children are involved, but even then if the couple find they are incompatible it is better for everyone concerned if the child is raised by just one parent.

The extreme conservative position holds that although sex is conducted in private it falls within the public domain of social and sometimes legal regulation, as does suicide, pornography, and drugs.[2] Children can result from sexual relations even when contraceptive measures are taken, and society does have a responsibility to ensure that children are not brought into life irresponsibly and that they are well protected and properly raised. Sex may be natural and enjoyable, but aside from that it is an intimate function which involves the whole person; it should be the highest expression of love and have procreation as its ultimate purpose.

[2] The question of whether a private sin can be a public crime is discussed by Lord Devlin in "Morals and the Criminal Law," *The Enforcement of Morals* (London: Oxford University Press, 1965).

Contraception and sterilization are therefore immoral.[3] Sexual relations should not occur outside marriage even when love is present, and couples who are in love should marry, not live together. Our social and affectional nature, our desires and ambitions, find maximum fulfillment in the institution of marriage and in the family relations that it founds; consequently, marriage is a religious sacrament and a civil contract. Marriage should not be terminated except in extreme cases, especially if the couple have children, since it is best for children to be raised within the family environment.

Obviously there are weaknesses in both positions, and most people will find that their conclusions place them somewhere on the spectrum between the two extremes. For example, sex seems to be accorded far too little weight by the extreme liberal, since human experience indicates that the sex act must have meaning or else one feels degraded and self-betrayed; this is what makes prostitution so unsatisfying for both parties. Rollo May develops this point in the selection from *Love and Will* in this chapter, stressing the mechanical nature of sex today, which has lost contact with meaningfulness (and eros) in its concern with technique and performance. (William Masters and Virginia Johnson echo this point in their recent book *The Pleasure Bond*.)

On the other hand, the extreme conservative seems mistaken in insisting that sex should function only for procreation and that contraceptives should not be used, for surely sex can be said to have a legitimate purpose as the physical expression of mutual love or affection even if its goal is not procreation. Walter Lippmann discusses the separation of these two functions of sex in his article on the following pages, although his conclusions are highly controversial.

With respect to the problem of what constitutes perversion, we have dismissed today a number of criteria that formerly were used to differentiate between deviant and normal, or moral, sex. We know that we cannot use the standard of natural and unnatural because we disapprove of many things that are natural and approve of many unnatural things, for example savagery in men and manners in civilization, respectively. Equally, we cannot claim that perverse sexuality yields less satisfaction and is attended by feelings of guilt and shame, since the social persecution of deviants is probably responsible for these states of feeling, rather than factors innate to the experience. We also cannot use as an indicator the abhorrence and repulsion most people evince toward certain sexual acts, since a minority of people do not react in this way, and truth, in any case, is never established by counting heads.

One interesting recent suggestion is that perversion refers to certain types of attitudes, rather than a category of actions. For example, a de-

[3] For the Roman Catholic position here, see Pope Paul VI, *Humanae Vitae* (Paramus: Paulist Press, 1968).

humanizing attitude toward the other person in a sexual relationship might be termed perverse even if the physical expression fell within the "normal" range. However, one wonders about the wisdom of defining perversion without reference to actions. It would seem that certain acts, such as child molesting, would be perverse regardless of whether the person had an innocent attitude toward those acts. This raises the more profound philosophic issue of whether the intention of the agent or the concrete action is the more important factor to evaluate.

Thomas Nagel, in his essay on sexual perversion in this chapter, offers another standard for normal sexuality, namely, mutual awareness, where individuals interact and are aware of their effect on each other. This would mean that homosexuality, for instance, would not be considered perverse because "reflexive mutual recognition" is present, whereas fetishism and voyeurism would be identified as perversions.[4]

Complementary to the question of personal relationships which we have been discussing is that of abortion. Here too feeling runs high, and there appear polarizing slogans such as "right to life," on the one side, and "abortion on demand," on the other. Each party accuses the other of failing to be humane, the pro-abortion faction being charged with selfishness and the anti-abortion faction being accused of insensitive adherence to doctrine.

One way in which the controversy may be viewed philosophically is as a conflict between two approaches to ethics: the formalistic and the teleological. In *formalistic* ethics the moral quality of an action is judged by the nature of the act itself or, more precisely, by the principle it embodies. Thus exploitation would be considered wrong by the formalist because, as Immanuel Kant said, people should be treated as ends and not only as means.[5] In the *teleological* approach actions are judged by their moral consequences, therefore lying, for instance, could be judged as wrong because it results in distrust that can break down the cohesion of society. Very often the teleologist regards the production of happiness as the general goal of all action and the measure of any action's worth.

Obviously the two approaches are not totally separate, since formalists may consider the consequences of action (even in establishing their principles) and teleologists will judge the results of action as good or bad relative to the values they hold. Nevertheless, there does exist a fundamental difference in ethical perspective.

In terms of the abortion debate, those who oppose abortion generally do so on formalistic grounds. They argue from the alleged sacredness of human life to the indefensibility of abortion even in cases where the consequences appear beneficial, for, it is argued, respect for life must take

[4] For a critical response to Nagel's article, see Robert C. Solomon, "Sexual Paradigms," *The Journal of Philosophy*, Vol. LXXI, No. 11 (June 1974), 336–45.
[5] Kant felt that we treat people as means when we do not allow them the opportunity to offer their consent or to participate in the end of the action.

precedence as a primary humane principle. If anti-abortionists are operating from the standpoint of religion (especially traditional Roman Catholicism), they may add that all human life, including embryonic life, is a miraculous gift from God, which it would be sinful to reject. If they are broadly Christian in outlook, they will speak of the virtue of selfless generosity, particularly toward the weak and defenseless, which should move us to welcome new life even when a considerable amount of sacrifice is entailed. But one need not be religious to believe on formalistic grounds that the foetus possesses the right to be brought into life, or that one should not kill an innocent human being, or that the preservation of life is a basic moral obligation.

The anti-abortionist does pay some attention to the consequences of abortion, as, for example, when it is argued that women who have abortions will be laden with guilt and experience serious emotional disturbances later in life[6] or that society would destroy life with fewer qualms of conscience if abortion became acceptable—the thin-edge-of-the-wedge, or domino, theory. But in general the appeal is to formalistic principles.

The arguments of the pro-abortionists, on the other hand, are largely teleological in character. Abortion is justified, it is asserted, when (1) the physical or mental health of the woman would be gravely impaired by the pregnancy; (2) the child would be born with serious mental or physical defects; (3) the pregnancy is the result of rape or incest; (4) the family is unable to expend adequate amounts of time and money for the child's nurture (e.g., large, impoverished families); or when (5) overpopulation in a region or country necessitates limiting the number of births for the well-being of all. Those who advocate abortion on demand would add that abortion is also warranted (6) whenever the child is unwanted, for, it is argued, rejected and unloved children are a burden to everyone, including themselves; they are doomed to a life of misery.

Sometimes the formalistic argument is offered that a woman should not be forced to bear a child that she does not want—that a person has a right to use his or her own body as he or she pleases—and here the battle lines are drawn over whether the foetus is a separate entity or part of a woman's body. (Does the inability to live outside the womb, for example, mean that the foetus is not an independent being?) On the same level, the political argument is sometimes advanced that denying a woman access to an abortion is a violation of her civil liberties. Here an interesting

[6] In fact, the psychological evidence does not support this assertion; a relatively small percentage of women have suffered any serious psychological aftereffects from having had abortions, even those with a psychiatric history. See J. Ewing and B. Rouse, "Therapeutic Abortion and a Prior Psychiatric History," *American Journal of Psychiatry*, 130, No. 1 (January 1973), 37–40. Ewing and Rouse found no adverse consequences in 92 percent to 96 percent of the cases. For a summary of the literature, including the often cited study by Martin Ekblad, see B. Sarvis and H. Rodman, *The Abortion Controversy* (New York: Columbia University Press, 1973), pp. 107–26.

question arises with regard to where the burden of proof falls: Is the state required to present reasons for refusing abortions (which presupposes that it is a general right) or is the woman obliged to justify requesting an abortion of the state (in which case the right to abortion is not presupposed)?

Distinguishing between the formalistic and the teleological perspectives of the two sides in the abortion controversy can clarify a number of misunderstandings and help reconcile differences as people perceive the extent to which they share the opposite point of view, for few of us are wholly formalistic or teleological in outlook. Beyond that, however, the arguments must be evaluated in themselves and a reasonable assessment made of their individual and collective merit.

Most of what we have discussed about abortion refers to the question of whether and when human life can be sacrificed, but a great deal of the abortion debate centers on the problem of when the foetus actually becomes human.[7] This problem will be left for the reader to investigate through the essays by Paul Ramsey and J. F. Donceel which follow. The essay by Herbert Richardson returns us to the question of the sanctity of life.

The issue of euthanasia is related to that of abortion, since both concern the willful destruction of life, but it provokes less bitterness and controversy, perhaps because we are more concerned with the young than the old or perhaps because the people most affected, the terminally ill, are least able to fight for their beliefs. It also makes a difference that in the case of euthanasia the choice of death is made by the person concerned, and that is considered more acceptable; suicide has never carried the same weight of disapproval as killing. Our present laws still do not permit euthanasia, but at the level of personal morality there is a growing acceptance of the practice as an act of compassion.[8]

The advocates of euthanasia today state their position as follows: euthanasia is justified in the case of a terminally ill person who is in an extreme state of suffering when, in the best opinion of the physician, there exists no hope of cure and when the person, the closest relatives, and the physician all consent to the action. The Roman Catholic proponent of euthanasia would insist that the person be allowed to die (by with-

---

[7] An interesting suggestion concerning the start of human life was made recently by Dr. Dominick Purpura of New York's Albert Einstein College of Medicine. He maintained that human life begins when the structures and nerve cell connections of the brain begin to form, which occurs between the twenty-eighth and thirty-second week of pregnancy. Since human life is now said to end with the cessation of brain activity, this suggestion appears to have some merit.

[8] Bills on euthanasia have been considered by various state legislatures, especially regarding the so-called "living will," whereby individuals can specify in advance the conditions under which they would want their life ended, as, for example, in the case of irreversible coma. Statutes on euthanasia have been proposed before the legislatures of thirteen states, including Delaware, Florida, Hawaii, Idaho, Illinois, Maryland, Massachusetts, Montana, Oregon, Virginia, Washington, West Virginia, and Wisconsin.

drawing artificial support systems) rather than being killed, although the distinction between ending life and not maintaining it is difficult to draw. (How, for example, would one classify withholding insulin from a diabetic?)

Formulating the position this narrowly disarms a number of objections. For one thing, there is no danger of "mercy killing" in curable cases; however acute the suffering might be it is considered endurable for the sake of an eventually healthy life. For another thing, since all three parties must agree—that is, the patient, the closest relatives, and the physician— a variety of possible abuses are prevented from occurring. For instance, the physician could be biased in favor of the patient's death because the equipment being used is needed to help another patient with a greater chance for survival.[9] Setting aside the question of who ought to have priority among patients, the person's relatives would probably act in terms of his or her welfare and refuse consent. Another case would be that of an unscrupulous wife who is anxious for her husband's death so that she can come into an inheritance. In this situation the physician would act as a corrective, and in both cases the patient would probably refuse to give consent. With a system of checks and balances of this type, maximum protection is afforded to the individual.

We might still object to euthanasia on the grounds that the physician may be mistaken in his or her judgment, underestimating the patient's will to live or misdiagnosing the illness. There is also the possibility of a cure being found at the last minute or of a miracle occurring. In any of these cases, the person will have died needlessly.

But the advocates of euthanasia point out that we trust physicians in matters of life and death in other contexts and there is no reason to consider this an exception; if we are uncertain about a diagnosis, we can always request a second or third opinion. As for last minute cures, when medical discoveries are made they only benefit people in the early stages of a fatal disease, not those who are near death. And with regard to miracles, although they may possibly occur, by their very nature they happen extremely rarely, and it seems inhumane to allow a vast number of people to suffer because of our hope that one of them will be miraculously saved.

At this point several of the formalistic arguments of the anti-abortionists can be applied: one should not kill an innocent being,[10] life is in-

---

[9] The physician faces a difficult dilemma in the euthanasia issue because two moral principles of medicine are in direct conflict: the obligation to alleviate suffering and the obligation to preserve life.

[10] The relation between the extinguishing of life and guilt or innocence is an extremely delicate one. Liberals argue that just as we can oppose capital punishment while acknowledging the guilt of the criminal, we can approve of euthanasia and abortion while admitting the innocence of the life we destroy. The real issue, it is argued, in deciding whether we should kill, is not guilt or innocence but whether we are being malicious or humane in our decision. However, such a position would seem to justify

violable from human interference, and so forth. There is also the common fear that if euthanasia and abortion become widespread practices, then the value of life will be depreciated and fearful political repercussions could follow.

But here we have come full circle and the question must be left for the reader to deliberate. The essays by Joseph Fletcher and Anthony Flew which follow should both sharpen and broaden the reader's understanding of the euthanasia issue and, together with the foregoing discussion, should help the reader to reach a well-considered conclusion.

---

killing an innocent person if others would be benefited by the action; this clearly undermines our idea of justice.

1

PERSONAL RELATIONSHIPS

LOVE AND WILL
Rollo May

Rollo May (1909–ㅤ), *existential psychotherapist concerned with the ideals of humanism, personal freedom, and responsibility. In books such as* Man's Search for Himself (1953), Love and Will (1969), *and* Power and Innocence (1972), *May stresses the freedom of individuals to make those choices that maximize their self-realization, but he balances this value against our human responsibility to others for the effects of our actions.*

---

1. PARADOXES OF SEX AND LOVE

There are four kinds of love in Western tradition. One is *sex*, or what we call lust, libido. The second is *eros*, the drive of love to procreate or create —the urge, as the Greeks put it, toward higher forms of being and relationship. A third is *philia*, or friendship, brotherly love. The fourth is *agape* or *caritas* as the Latins called it, the love which is devoted to the welfare of the other, the prototype of which is the love of God for man. Every human experience of authentic love is a blending, in varying proportions, of these four.

We begin with sex not only because that is where our society begins but also because that is where every man's biological existence begins as well. Each of us owes his being to the fact that at some moment in history a man and a woman leapt the gap, in T. S. Eliot's words, "between the desire and the spasm." Regardless of how much sex may be banalized in our society, it still remains the power of procreation, the drive which perpetuates the race, the source at once of the human being's most intense pleasure and his most pervasive anxiety. It can, in its daimonic form, hurl the individual into sloughs of despond, and, when allied with eros, it can lift him out of his despondency into orbits of ecstasy.

The ancients took sex, or lust, for granted just as they took death for granted. It is only in the contemporary age that we have succeeded, on a fairly broad scale, in singling out sex for our chief concern and have required it to carry the weight of all four forms of love. Regardless of Freud's overextension of sexual phenomena as such—in which he is but the voice of the struggle of thesis and antithesis of modern history—it remains true that sexuality is basic to the ongoing power of the race and surely has the *importance* Freud gave it, if not the *extension*. Trivialize sex in our novels and dramas as we will, or defend ourselves from its power by cynicism and playing it cool as we wish, sexual passion remains ready at any moment to catch us off guard and prove that it is still the *mysterium tremendum*.

But as soon as we look at the relation of sex and love in our time, we find ourselves immediately caught up in a whirlpool of contradictions. Let us, therefore, get our bearings by beginning with a brief phenomenological sketch of the strange paradoxes which surround sex in our society.

Sexual wilderness

In Victorian times, when the denial of sexual impulses, feelings, and drives was the mode and one would not talk about sex in polite company, an aura of sanctifying repulsiveness surrounded the whole topic. Males and females dealt with each other as though neither possessed sexual organs. William James, that redoubtable crusader who was far ahead of his time on every other topic, treated sex with the polite aversion characteristic of the turn of the century. In the whole two volumes of his epoch-making *Principles of Psychology*, only one page is devoted to sex, at the end of which he adds, "These details are a little unpleasant to discuss. . . ."[1] But William Blake's warning a century before Victorianism, that "He who desires but acts not, breeds pestilence," was amply demonstrated by the later psychotherapists. Freud, a Victorian who did look at sex, was right in his description of the morass of neurotic symptoms which resulted from cutting off so vital a part of the human body and the self.

[1] William James, *Principles of Psychology* (New York, Dover Publications, 1950; originally published by Henry Holt, 1890), II, p. 439.

Then, in the 1920's, a radical change occurred almost overnight. The belief became a militant dogma in liberal circles that the opposite of repression—namely, sex education, freedom of talking, feeling, and expression—would have healthy effects, and obviously constituted the only stand for the enlightened person. In an amazingly short period following World War I, we shifted from acting as though sex did not exist at all to being obsessed with it. We now placed more emphasis on sex than any society since that of ancient Rome, and some scholars believe we are more preoccupied with sex than any other people in all of history. Today, far from not talking about sex, we might well seem, to a visitor from Mars dropping into Times Square, to have no other topic of communication.

And this is not solely an American obsession. Across the ocean in England, for example, "from bishops to biologists, everyone is in on the act." A perceptive front-page article in *The Times Literary Supplement,* London, goes on to point to the "whole turgid flood of post-Kinsey utilitarianism and post-Chatterley moral uplift. Open any newspaper, any day (Sunday in particular), and the odds are you will find some pundit treating the public to his views on contraception, abortion, adultery, obscene publications, homosexuality between consenting adults or (if all else fails) contemporary moral patterns among our adolescents."[2]

Partly as a result of this radical shift, many therapists today rarely see patients who exhibit repression of sex in the manner of Freud's pre-World War I hysterical patients. In fact, we find in the people who come for help just the opposite: a great deal of talk about sex, a great deal of sexual activity, practically no one complaining of cultural prohibitions over going to bed as often or with as many partners as one wishes. But what our patients do complain of is lack of feeling and passion. "The curious thing about this ferment of discussion is how little anyone seems to be *enjoying* emancipation."[3] So much sex and so little meaning or even fun in it!

Where the Victorian didn't want anyone to know that he or she had sexual feelings, we are ashamed if we do not. Before 1910, if you called a lady "sexy" she would be insulted; nowadays, she prizes the compliment and rewards you by turning her charms in your direction. Our patients often have the problems of frigidity and impotence, but the strange and poignant thing we observe is how desperately they struggle not to let anyone find out they don't feel sexually. The Victorian nice man or woman was guilty if he or she did experience sex; now we are guilty if we *don't*.

One paradox, therefore, is that enlightenment has not solved the sexual problems in our culture. To be sure, there are important positive results of the new enlightenment, chiefly in increased freedom for the individual. Most external problems are eased: sexual knowledge can be

2 *Atlas,* November, 1965, p. 302. Reprinted from *The Times Literary Supplement,* London.
3 *Ibid.*

bought in any bookstore, contraception is available everywhere except in Boston where it is still believed, as the English countess averred on her wedding night, that sex is "too good for the common people." Couples can, without guilt and generally without squeamishness, discuss their sexual relationship and undertake to make it more mutually gratifying and meaningful. Let these gains not be underestimated. External social anxiety and guilt have lessened; dull would be the man who did not rejoice in this.

But *internal* anxiety and guilt have increased. And in some ways these are more morbid, harder to handle, and impose a heavier burden upon the individual than external anxiety and guilt.

The challenge a woman used to face from men was simple and direct —would she or would she not go to bed?—a direct issue of how she stood vis-à-vis cultural mores. But the question men ask now is no longer, "Will she or won't she?" but "Can she or can't she?" The challenge is shifted to the woman's personal adequacy, namely, her own capacity to have the vaunted orgasm—which should resemble a *grand mal* seizure. Though we might agree that the second question places the problem of sexual decision more where it should be, we cannot overlook the fact that the first question is much easier for the person to handle. In my practice, one woman was afraid to go to bed for fear that the man "won't find me very good at making love." Another was afraid because "I don't even know how to do it," assuming that her lover would hold this against her. Another was scared to death of the second marriage for fear that she wouldn't be able to have the orgasm as she had not in her first. Often the woman's hesitation is formulated as, "He won't like me well enough to come back again."

In past decades you could blame society's strict mores and preserve your own self-esteem by telling yourself what you did or didn't do was society's fault and not yours. And this would give you some time in which to decide what you do want to do, or to let yourself grow into a decision. But when the question is simply how you can perform, your own sense of adequacy and self-esteem is called immediately into question, and the whole weight of the encounter is shifted inward to how you can meet the test.

College students, in their fights with college authorities about hours girls are to be permitted in the men's rooms, are curiously blind to the fact that rules are often a boon. Rules give the student time to find himself. He has the leeway to consider a way of behaving without being committed before he is ready, to try on for size, to venture into relationships tentatively—which is part of any growing up. Better to have the lack of commitment direct and open rather than to go into sexual relations under pressure—doing violence to his feelings by having physical commitment without psychological. He may flout the rules; but at least they give some structure to be flouted. My point is true whether he obeys the rule or not.

Many contemporary students, understandably anxious because of their new sexual freedom, repress this anxiety ("one should *like* freedom") and then compensate for the additional anxiety the repression gives them by attacking the parietal authorities for not giving them more freedom!

What we did not see in our short-sighted liberalism in sex was that throwing the individual into an unbounded and empty sea of free choice does not in itself give freedom, but is more apt to increase inner conflict. The sexual freedom to which we were devoted fell short of being fully human.

In the arts, we have also been discovering what an illusion it was to believe that mere freedom would solve our problem. Consider, for example, the drama. In an article entitled "Is Sex Kaput?," Howard Taubman, former drama critic of *The New York Times*, summarized what we have all observed in drama after drama: "Engaging in sex was like setting out to shop on a dull afternoon; desire had nothing to do with it and even curiosity was faint."[4] Consider also the novel. In the "revolt against the Victorians," writes Leon Edel, "the extremists have had their day. Thus far they have impoverished the novel rather than enriched it."[5] Edel perceptively brings out the crucial point that in sheer realistic "enlightenment" there has occurred a *dehumanization* of sex in fiction. There are "sexual encounters in Zola," he insists, "which have more truth in them than any D. H. Lawrence described—and also more humanity."[6]

The battle against censorship and for freedom of expression surely was a great battle to win, but has it not become a new strait jacket? The writers, both novelists and dramatists, "would rather hock their typewriters than turn in a manuscript without the obligatory scenes of unsparing anatomical documentation of their characters' sexual behavior. . . ."[7] Our "dogmatic enlightenment" is self-defeating: it ends up destroying the very sexual passion it set out to protect. In the great tide of realistic chronicling, we forgot, on the stage and in the novel and even in psychotherapy, that imagination is the life-blood of eros, and that realism is neither sexual nor erotic. Indeed, there is nothing *less* sexy than sheer nakedness, as a random hour at any nudist camp will prove. It requires the infusion of the imagination (which I shall later call intentionality) to transmute physiology and anatomy into *interpersonal* experience—into art, into passion, into eros in a million forms which has the power to shake or charm us.

Could it not be that an "enlightenment" which reduces itself to sheer realistic detail is itself an escape from the anxiety involved in the relation of human imagination to erotic passion?

---

[4] Howard Taubman, "Is Sex Kaput?," *The New York Times*, sect. 2, January 17, 1965.
[5] Leon Edel, "Sex and the Novel," *The New York Times*, sect. 7, pt. I, November 1, 1964.
[6] *Ibid.*
[7] See Taubman.

Salvation through technique

A second paradox is that *the new emphasis on technique in sex and love-making backfires.* It often occurs to me that there is an inverse relationship between the number of how-to-do-it books perused by a person or rolling off the presses in a society and the amount of sexual passion or even pleasure experienced by the persons involved. Certainly nothing is wrong with technique as such, in playing golf or acting or making love. But the emphasis beyond a certain point on technique in sex makes for a mechanistic attitude toward love-making, and goes along with alienation, feelings of loneliness, and depersonalization.

One aspect of the alienation is that the lover, with his age-old art, tends to be superseded by the computer operator with his modern efficiency. Couples place great emphasis on bookkeeping and timetables in their love-making—a practice confirmed and standardized by Kinsey. If they fall behind schedule they become anxious and feel impelled to go to bed whether they want to or not. My colleague, Dr. John Schimel, observes, "My patients have endured stoically, or without noticing, remarkably destructive treatment at the hands of their spouses, but they have experienced falling behind in the sexual time-table as a loss of love."[8] The man feels he is somehow losing his masculine status if he does not perform up to schedule, and the woman that she has lost her feminine attractiveness if too long a period goes by without the man at least making a pass at her. The phrase "between men," which women use about their affairs, similarly suggests a gap in time like the *entr'acte.* Elaborate accounting- and ledger-book lists—how often this week have we made love? did he (or she) pay the right amount of attention to me during the evening? was the foreplay long enough?—make one wonder how the spontaneity of this most spontaneous act can possibly survive. The computer hovers in the stage wings of the drama of love-making the way Freud said one's parents used to.

It is not surprising then, in this preoccupation with techniques, that the questions typically asked about an act of love-making are not, Was there passion or meaning or pleasure in the act? but, How well did I perform?[9] Take, for example, what Cyril Connolly calls "the tyranny of the orgasm," and the preoccupation with achieving a simultaneous orgasm, which is another aspect of the alienation. I confess that when people talk

---

[8] John L. Schimel, "Ideology and Sexual Practices," *Sexual Behavior and the Law*, ed. Ralph Slovenko (Springfield, Ill., Charles C. Thomas, 1965), pp. 195, 197.

[9] Sometimes a woman patient will report to me, in the course of describing how a man tried to seduce her, that he cites as part of his seduction line how efficient a lover he is, and he promises to perform the act eminently satisfactorily for her. (Imagine Mozart's Don Giovanni offering such an argument!) In fairness to elemental human nature, I must add that as far as I can remember, the women reported that this "advance billing" did not add to the seducers' chances of success.

about the "apocalyptic orgasm," I find myself wondering, Why do they
have to try so hard? What abyss of self-doubt, what inner void of loneliness, are they trying to cover up by this great concern with grandiose
effects?

Even the sexologists, whose attitude is generally the more sex the
merrier, are raising their eyebrows these days about the anxious over-
emphasis on achieving the orgasm and the great importance attached to
"satisfying" the partner. A man makes a point of asking the woman if
she "made it," or if she is "all right," or uses some other euphemism for
an experience for which obviously no euphemism is possible. We men are
reminded by Simone de Beauvoir and other women who try to interpret
the love act that this is the last thing in the world a woman wants to be
asked at that moment. Furthermore, the technical preoccupation robs the
woman of exactly what she wants most of all, physically and emotionally,
namely the man's spontaneous abandon at the moment of climax. This
abandon gives her whatever thrill or ecstasy she and the experience are
capable of. When we cut through all the rigmarole about roles and performance, what still remains is how amazingly important the sheer fact
of intimacy of relationship is—the meeting, the growing closeness with the
excitement of not knowing where it will lead, the assertion of the self, and
the giving of the self—in making a sexual encounter memorable. Is it not
this intimacy that makes us return to the event in memory again and again
when we need to be warmed by whatever hearths life makes available?

It is a strange thing in our society that what goes into building a
relationship—the sharing of tastes, fantasies, dreams, hopes for the future,
and fears from the past—seems to make people more shy and vulnerable
than going to bed with each other. They are more wary of the tenderness
that goes with psychological and spiritual nakedness than they are of the
physical nakedness in sexual intimacy.

The new puritanism

The third paradox is that our highly-vaunted sexual freedom has
turned out to be a new form of puritanism. I spell it with a small "p"
because I do not wish to confuse this with the original Puritanism. That,
as in the passion of Hester and Dimmesdale in Hawthorne's *The Scarlet
Letter*, was a very different thing.[10] I refer to puritanism as it came down

---

10 That the actual Puritans in the sixteenth and seventeenth centuries were a different
breed from those who represented the deteriorated forms in our century can be seen
in a number of sources. Roland H. Bainton in the chapter "Puritanism and the
Modern Period," of his book *What Christianity Says About Sex, Love and Marriage*
(New York, Reflection Books, Association Press, 1957), writes "The Puritan ideal
for relations of man and wife was summed up in the words, 'a tender respective-
ness.' " He quotes Thomas Hooker: "The man whose heart is endeared to the
woman he loves, he dreams of her in the night, hath her in his eye and apprehen-

via our Victorian grandparents and became allied with industrialism and emotional and moral compartmentalization.

I define this puritanism as consisting of three elements. First, *a state of alienation from the body.* Second, *the separation of emotion from reason.* And third, *the use of the body as a machine.*

In our new puritanism, bad health is equated with sin.[11] Sin used to mean giving in to one's sexual desires; it now means not having full sexual expression. Our contemporary puritan holds that it is immoral *not* to express your libido. Apparently this is true on both sides of the ocean: "There are few more depressing sights," the London *Times Literary Supplement* writes, "than a progressive intellectual determined to end up in bed with someone from a sense of moral duty. . . . There is no more high-minded puritan in the world than your modern advocate of salvation through properly directed passion. . . ."[12] A woman used to be guilty if she went to bed with a man; now she feels vaguely guilty if after a certain number of dates she still refrains; her sin is "morbid repression," refusing to "give." And the partner, who is always completely enlightened (or at least pretends to be) refuses to allay her guilt by getting overtly angry at

---

sion when he awakes, museth on her as he sits at table, walks with her when he travels and parlies with her in each place he comes." Ronald Mushat Frye, in a thoughtful paper, "The Teachings of Classical Puritanism on Conjugal Love," *Studies from the Renaissance,* II (1955), submits conclusive evidence that classical Puritanism inculcated a view of sexual life in marriage as the "Crown of all our bliss," "Founded in Reason, Loyal, Just, and Pure" (p. 149). He believes that "the fact remains that the education of England in a more liberal view of married love in the sixteenth and early seventeenth centuries was in large part the work of that party within English Protestantism which is called Puritan" (p. 149). The Puritans were against lust and acting on physical attraction outside of marriage, but they as strongly believed in the sexual side of marriage and believed it the duty of all people to keep this alive all their lives. It was a later confusion which associated them with the asceticism of continence in marriage. Frye states, "In the course of a wide reading of Puritan and other Protestant writers in the sixteenth and early seventeenth centuries, I have found nothing but opposition to this type of ascetic 'perfection' " (p. 152).

One has only to look carefully at the New England churches built by the Puritans and in the Puritan heritage to see the great refinement and dignity of form which surely implies a passionate attitude toward life. They had the dignity of controlled passion, which may have made possible an actual living with passion in contrast to our present pattern of expressing and dispersing all passion. The deterioration of Puritanism into our modern secular attitudes was caused by the confluence of three trends: industrialism, Victorian emotional compartmentalization, and the secularization of all religious attitudes. The first introduced the specific mechanical model; the second introduced the emotional dishonesty which Freud analyzed so well; and the third took away the depth-dimensions of religion and made the concerns how one "behaved" in such matters as smoking, drinking, and sex in the superficial forms which we are attacking above. (For a view of the delightful love letters between husband and wife in this period, see the two-volume biography of John Adams by Page Smith. See also the writings on the Puritans by Perry Miller.)

[11] This formulation was originally suggested to me by Dr. Ludwig Lefebre.
[12] *Atlas,* November, 1965, p. 302.

her (if she could fight him on the issue, the conflict would be a lot easier for her). But he stands broadmindedly by, ready at the end of every date to undertake a crusade to assist her out of her fallen state. And this, of course, makes her "no" all the more guilt-producing for her.

This all means, of course, that people not only have to learn to perform sexually but have to make sure, at the same time, that they can do so without letting themselves go in passion or unseemly commitment—the latter of which may be interpreted as exerting an unhealthy demand upon the partner. *The Victorian person sought to have love without falling into sex; the modern person seeks to have sex without falling into love.*

. . .

2. EROS IN CONFLICT WITH SEX

. . . The contemporary paradoxes in sex and love have one thing in common, namely *the banalization of sex and love.* By anesthetizing feeling in order to perform better, by employing sex as a tool to prove prowess and identity, by using sensuality to hide sensitivity, we have emasculated sex and left it vapid and empty. The banalization of sex is well-aided and -abetted by our mass communication. For the plethora of books on sex and love which flood the market have one thing in common—they over-simplify love and sex, treating the topic like a combination of learning to play tennis and buying life insurance. In this process, we have robbed sex of its power by sidestepping eros; and we have ended by dehumanizing both.

My thesis . . . is that what underlies our emasculation of sex is the *separation of sex from eros.* Indeed, we have set sex over *against* eros, used sex precisely to avoid the anxiety-creating involvements of eros. In ostensibly enlightened discussions of sex, particularly those about freedom from censorship, it is often argued that all our society needs is full freedom for the expression of eros. But what is revealed beneath the surface in our society, as shown not only in patients in therapy but in our literature and drama and even in the nature of our scientific research, is just the opposite. We are in a flight from eros—and we use sex as the vehicle for the flight.

Sex is the handiest drug to blot out our awareness of the anxiety-creating aspects of eros. To accomplish this, we have had to define sex ever more narrowly: the more we became preoccupied with sex, the more truncated and shrunken became the human experience to which it referred. We fly to *the sensation of sex in order to avoid the passion of eros.*

The return of repressed eros

My thesis was formulated out of several strange phenomena I observed in my patients as well as in our society—psychic eruptions which have a curiously explosive quality. These phenomena occurred in areas in which, from any common-sense point of view, they would be least expected in our day. Most people live in the confidence that our technological developments have largely freed us from the risks of unchosen pregnancy and venereal disease and, therefore, *ipso facto*, the anxiety people used to feel about sex and love is now banished forever to the museum. The vicissitudes about which the novelists of previous centuries wrote—when a woman gave herself to a man, it meant illegitimate pregnancy and social ostracism, as in *The Scarlet Letter*; or the tragic break-up of the family structure and suicide, as in *Anna Karenina*; or venereal disease, as in the market place of social reality—have been outgrown. Now, thank God and science, we tell ourselves, we are rid of all that! The implication is that sex is free and that love is easy and comes in readily procurable packages like what the students call "instant Zen." And any talk of the deeper conflicts which used to be associated with the tragic and daimonic elements is anachronistic and absurd.

But I shall be impolite enough to ask, May there not be a gigantic and extensive repression underlying all this? A repression not of sex, but of something underlying body chemistry, some psychic needs more vital, deeper, and more comprehensive than sex. A repression that is socially sanctioned, to be sure—but just for that reason harder to discern and more effective in its results. I am obviously not questioning contemporary medical and psychological advances as such: no one in his right mind would fail to be grateful for the development of contraceptives, estrogen, and cures for venereal disease. And I count it good fortune indeed to be born into this age with its freedom of possibilities rather than in the Victorian period with its rigid mores. But that issue is fallacious and a red herring. Our problem is more profound and starkly real.

We pick up the morning paper and read that there are a million illegal abortions in enlightened America each year; that premarital pregnancies are increasing on all sides. One girl out of six who is now thirteen will, according to present statistics, become illegitimately pregnant before she is twenty—two and a half times the incidence of ten years ago.[13] The

---

[13] U.S. Department of Health Statistics *Medical World News*, March, 1967, pp. 64–68. These reports also inform us that venereal disease is also increasing 4 per cent a year among adolescents. This increase may have different causes from those for illegitimate pregnancy, but it bears out my general thesis. The second statistic—that this is an increase from one in fifteen of ten years ago—is from a report of the Teamsters Joint Council 16, covered in *The New York Times*, July 1, 1968.

increase is mainly among girls of the proletarian classes, but there is
enough increase among girls of middle and upper classes to prove that this
is not a problem solely of disadvantaged groups. Indeed, the radical increase is not among Puerto Rican or Negro girls but among *white* girls—
the jump of percentage of illegitimate births to all live births being from
1.7 ten years ago to 5.3 last year. We are confronted by the curious situation of *the more birth control, the more illegitimate pregnancies.* As the
reader hastens to cry that what is necessary is to change barbaric abortion
laws and give more sex education, I would not disagree; but I could, and
should, raise a caveat. The blanket advising of more sex education can act
as a reassurance by means of which we escape having to ask ourselves the
more frightening questions. May not the real issue be not on the level of
conscious, rational intentions at all? . . .

. . .

We observe in many of these illegitimate pregnancies—or their equivalent—a defiance of the very socially-ordered system which takes away
affect, where technology is felt to be a substitute for feeling, a society
which calls persons forth to an arid and meaningless existence and gives
them, particularly the younger generation, an experience of depersonalization which is more painful than illegal abortion. No one who has worked
with patients for a long period of time can fail to learn that the psychological and spiritual agony of depersonalization is harder to bear than
physical pain. And, indeed, they often clutch at physical pain (or social
ostracism or violence or delinquency) as a welcome relief. Have we become so "civilized" that we have forgotten that a girl can *yearn* to procreate, and can do so not just for psychobiological reasons but to break up
the arid desert of feelingless existence, to destroy for once if not for all
the repetitive pattern of fucking-to-avoid-the-emptiness-of-despair ("What
shall we do tomorrow?" as T. S. Eliot has his rich courtesan cry, "What
shall we ever do?"). Or that she can yearn to become pregnant because
the heart is never fully converted to passionlessness, and she is driven to
an expression of that which is denied her and which she herself consciously denies in our age of the "cool millennium." At least being pregnant is something *real*, and it proves to the girl and to the man that *they*
are real.

Alienation is felt as a loss of the capacity to be intimately personal.
As I hear these people, they are crying, We yearn to talk but "our dried
voices" are "rats' feet over broken glass."[14] We go to bed because we
cannot hear each other; we go to bed because we are too shy to look in
each other's eyes, and in bed one can turn away one's head.[15]

[14] T. S. Eliot, "The Hollow Men," *Collected Poems* (New York, Harcourt Brace
Jovanovich, 1934), p. 101.
[15] The gripping thing about the movie *La Dolce Vita* was not its sex, but that while
everyone was feeling sexy and emoting all over, no one could *hear* any other

It should not be surprising that a revolt is occurring against the mores which people think cause alienation; a defiance of social norms which promise virtue without trying, sex without risk, wisdom without struggle, luxury without effort—all provided that they agree to settle for love without passion, and soon even sex without feeling. The denial of the daimonic means only that the earth spirits will come back to haunt us in a new guise; Gaea will be heard, and when the darkness returns the black madonna will be present if there is no white.

The error into which we have fallen obviously consists not of our scientific advances and enlightenment as such, but the using of these for a blanket allaying of all anxiety about sex and love. Marcuse holds that in a nonrepressive society, as sex develops it tends to merge with eros. It is clear that our society has done just the opposite: we separated sex from eros and then tried to repress eros. The passion which is one element of the denied eros then comes back from its repression to upset the person's whole existence.

What is eros?

Eros in our day is taken as a synonym for "eroticism" or sexual titillation. *Eros* was the name given to a journal of sexy arcana, containing "Aphrodisiac Recipes" and posing such weighty question-and-answer articles as, "Q: How Do the Porcupines Do It? A: Carefully." One wonders whether everyone has forgotten the fact that eros, according to no less an authority than St. Augustine, is the power which drives men toward God. Such gross misunderstandings would tend to make the demise of eros unavoidable: for in our overstimulated age we have no need for titillation which no longer titillates. It is essential, therefore, that we clarify the meaning of this crucial term.

Eros created life on the earth, the early Greek mythology tells us. When the world was barren and lifeless, it was Eros who "seized his life-giving arrows and pierced the cold bosom of the Earth," and "immediately the brown surface was covered with luxuriant verdure." This is an appealing symbolic picture of how Eros *incorporates* sex—those phallic arrows which pierce—as the instrument by which he creates life. Eros then breathed into the nostrils of the clay forms of man and woman and gave

---

person. From the first scene when the noise of the helicopter blots out the shouting of the men to the women, to the last scene in which the hero strains to hear the girl across the stream but cannot because of the noise of the ocean waves, no one hears another. Just at the moment in the castle when the man and the woman are at the point of declaring authentic love for each other in a communication by echoes, she cannot hear his voice from the other room and immediately drugs herself by promiscuous sexual titillation with a chance passerby. The dehumanizing thing is the so-called emotion without any relatedness; and sex is the most ready drug to hide one's terror at this dehumanization.

them the "spirit of life." Ever since, eros has been distinguished by the function of giving the spirit of life, in contrast to the function of sex as the release of tension. Eros was then one of the four original gods, the others being Chaos, Gaea (mother earth), and Tartarus (the dark pit of Hades below the earth). Eros, says Joseph Campbell, is always, regardless of guise, the progenitor, the original creator from which life comes.[16]

Sex can be defined fairly adequately in physiological terms as consisting of the building up of bodily tensions and their release. Eros, in contrast, is the experiencing of the personal intentions and meaning of the act. Whereas sex is a rhythm of stimulus and response, eros is a state of being. The pleasure in sex is described by Freud and others as the reduction of tension; in eros, on the contrary, we wish not to be released from the excitement but rather to hang on to it, to bask in it, and even to increase it. The end toward which sex points is gratification and relaxation, whereas eros is a desiring, longing, a forever reaching out, seeking to expand.

All this is in accord with the dictionary definitions. *Webster's* defines sex (coming from the Latin *sexus*, meaning "split") as referring to "physiological distinctions. . . . the character of being male or female, or . . . the distinctive functions of male or female."[17] Eros, in contrast, is defined with such terms as "ardent desire," "yearning," "aspiring self-fulfilling love often having a sensuous quality."[18] The Latins and Greeks had two different words for sex and love, as we do; but the curious thing to our ears is how rarely the Latins speak of *sexus*. Sex, to them, was no issue; it was *amor* they were concerned about. Similarly, everyone knows the Greek word *eros*, but practically no one has ever heard of their term for "sex." It is φῦλον, the word from which we derive the zoological term "phylon," tribe or race. This is an entirely different stem from the Greek word *philia*, which means love in the sense of friendship.

Sex is thus a zoological term and is rightly applied to all animals as well as human beings. Kinsey was a zoologist, and appropriately to his profession, he studied human sexual behavior from a zoological point of view. Masters is a gynecologist and studies sex from the viewpoint of sexual organs and how you manage and manipulate them: sex, then, is a pattern of neurophysiological functions and the sexual problem consists of what you do with organs.

Eros, on the other hand, takes wings from human imagination and is forever transcending all techniques, giving the laugh to all the "how to"

---

[16] Joseph Campbell, *Occidental Mythology*, vol. III from *The Masks of God* (New York, Viking Press, 1964), p. 235.

[17] *Webster's Collegiate Dictionary*, 3rd ed. (Springfield, Mass., G. & C. Merriam Company).

[18] *Webster's Third New International Dictionary* (Springfield, Mass., G. & C. Merriam Company, 1961).

books by gaily swinging into orbit above our mechanical rules, making love rather than manipulating organs.

For eros is the power which *attracts* us. The essence of eros is that it draws us from ahead, whereas sex pushes us from behind. This is revealed in our day-to-day language when I say a person "allures" me or "entices" me, or the possibilities of a new job "invite" me. Something in me responds to the other person, or the job, and pulls me toward him or it. I participate in forms, possibilities, higher levels of meaning, on neurophysiological dimensions but also on aesthetic and ethical dimensions as well. As the Greeks believed, knowledge and even ethical goodness exercise such a pull. Eros is the drive toward union with what we belong to—union with our own possibilities, union with significant other persons in our world in relation to whom we discover our own self-fulfillment. Eros is the yearning in man which leads him to dedicate himself to seeking *arête*, the noble and good life.

Sex, in short, is the mode of relating characterized by tumescence of the organs (or which we seek the pleasurable relief) and filled gonads (for which we seek satisfying release). But eros is the mode of relating in which we do not seek release but rather to cultivate, procreate, and form the world. *In eros, we seek increase of stimulation.* Sex is a need, but eros is a desire; and it is this admixture of desire which complicates love. In regard to our preoccupation with the orgasm in American discussions of sex, it can be agreed that the aim of the sex act in its zoological and physiological sense is indeed the orgasm. But the aim of eros is not: eros seeks union with the other person in delight and passion, and the procreating of new dimensions of experience which broaden and deepen the being of both persons. It is common experience, backed up by folklore as well as the testimony of Freud and others, that after sexual release we tend to go to sleep—or, as the joke puts it, to get dressed, go home, and *then* go to sleep. But in eros, we want just the opposite: to stay awake thinking of the beloved, remembering, savoring, discovering ever-new facets of the prism of what the Chinese call the "many-splendored" experience.

It is this urge for union with the partner that is the occasion for human tenderness. For eros—not sex as such—is the source of tenderness. Eros is the longing to establish union, full relationship. This may be, first, a union with abstract forms. The philosopher Charles S. Peirce sat alone in his house in Milford, Connecticut working out his mathematical logic, but this did not prevent his experiencing eros; the thinker must be "animated by a true eros," he wrote, "for the task of scientific investigation." Or it may be a union with aesthetic or philosophical forms, or a union with new ethical forms. But it is most obvious as the pull toward the union of two individuals sexually. The two persons, longing, as all individuals do, to overcome the separateness and isolation to which we all are heir as individuals, can participate in a relationship that, for the moment, is not made up of two isolated, individual experiences, but a genuine union. A sharing takes place which is a new *Gestalt*, a new being, a new field of magnetic force.

We have been led astray by our economic and biological models to think that the aim of the love act is the organism. The French have a saying which, referring to eros, carries more truth: "The aim of desire is not its satisfaction but its prolongation." . . .

. . .

Eros sickening

The Eros we have been discussing is that of the classical age, when he was still the creative power and the bridge between men and gods. But this "healthy" Eros deteriorated. Plato's understanding of Eros is a middle form of the concept, standing between Hesiod's view of Eros as the powerful and original creator and the later deteriorated form in which Eros becomes a sickly child. These three aspects of Eros are also accurate reflections of psychological archetypes of human experience: each of us at different times has the experience of Eros as creator, as mediator, and as banal playboy. Our age is by no means the first to experience the banalization of love, and to find that without passion, love sickens.

In the charming story quoted at the beginning of this chapter, we saw that the ancient Greeks had put ino the quintessential language of myth the insights which spring from the archetypes of the human psyche. Eros, the child of Ares and Aphrodite, "did not grow as other children, but remained a small, rosy, chubby child, with gauzy wings and rougish, dimpled face." After telling us that the alarmed mother was informed, "Love cannot grow without Passion," the myth goes on:

> In vain the goddess strove to catch the concealed meaning of this answer. It was only revealed to her when Anteros, god of passion, was born. When with his brother, Eros grew and flourished, until he became a handsome slender youth; but when separated from him, he invariably resumed his childish form and mischievous habits.[19]

Within these disarmingly naïve sentences, with which the Greeks were wont to clothe their most profound wisdom, lie several points which are crucial for our problems now. One is that Eros is the child of *Ares* as well as Aphrodite. This is to say that love is inseparably connected with aggression.

Another is that the Eros which had been the powerful creator in

---

[19] Helene A. Guerber, *Myths of Greece and Rome* (London, British Book Centre, 1907), p. 86.

Hesiod's time, causing the barren earth to spring up with green trees and breathing the spirit of life into man, has now deteriorated into a child, a rosy, chubby, playful creature, sometimes a mere fat infant playing with his bow and arrows. We see him represented as an effete Cupid in so many of the paintings of the seventeenth and eighteenth centuries as well as in ancient times. "In archaic art Eros is represented as a beautiful winged youth and tends to be made younger and younger until by the Hellenistic period he is an infant." In Alexandrine poetry, he degenerates into a mischievous child.[20] There must be something within Eros' own nature to cause this deterioration, for it is present already in the myth which, while later than the Hesiod version, still dates from long before Greek civilization disintegrated.

This brings us to the very heart of what has also gone wrong in our day: eros has lost passion, and has become insipid, childish, banal.

As is so often the case, the myth reveals a critical conflict in the roots of human experience, true for the Greeks and true for us: we engage in a flight from eros, the once powerful, original source of being, to sex, the mischievous plaything. Eros is demoted to the function of a pretty bartender, serving grapes and wine, a stimulator for dalliance whose task is to keep life endlessly sensuous on a bank of soft clouds. He stands not for the creative use of power—sexual, procreative, and other—but for the immediacy of gratification. And, *mirabile dictu*, we discover that the myth proclaims exactly what we have seen happening in our own day: *eros, then, even loses interest in sex.* In one version of the myth, Aphrodite tries to find him to get him up and about his business of spreading love with his bow and arrows. And, teen-age loafer that he has become, he is off gambling with Ganymede and cheating at the cards.

Gone is the spirit of the life-giving arrows, gone the creature who could breathe spirit into man and woman, gone the powerful Dionysian festivals, gone the frenzied dancing and the mysteries that moved the initiates more than the vaunted drugs of our mechanical age, gone even the bucolic intoxication. Eros now playboy indeed! Bacchanal with Pepsi-Cola.

Is this what civilization always does—tames Eros to make him fit the needs of the society to perpetuate iself? Changes him from the power that brings to birth new being and ideas and passion, weakens him till he is no longer the creative force that breaks old forms asunder to make new ones? Tames him until he stands for the goal of perpetual ease, dalliance, affluence, and, ultimately, apathy?[21]

---

20 "Eros," *Encyclopaedia Britannica*, vol. VIII (1947), p. 695.
21 Rollo May, in a review of Vance Packard's *The Sexual Wilderness: The Contemporary Upheaval in Male-Female Relationships* (New York, David McKay Company, 1968), appearing in *The New York Times Book Review*, October 13, 1968: "Packard here cites J. D. Unwin's massive, if almost forgotten, 'Sex and Culture' (1934), a study of 80 uncivilized societies and also a number of historically advanced cultures. Unwin sought to correlate various societies' sexual permissiveness

In this respect we confront a new and specific problem in our Western world—*the war between eros and technology*. There is no war between *sex* and technology: our technical inventions help sex to be safe, available, and efficient as demonstrated from birth-control pills all the way to the how-to-do-it books. Sex and technology join together to achieve "adjustment"; with the full release of tension over the weekend, you can work better in the button-down world on Monday. Sensual needs and their gratification are not at war with technology, at least in any immediate sense (whether they are in the long run is another question).

But it is not at all clear that technology and *eros* are compatible, or can even live without perpetual warfare. The lover, like the poet, is a menace on the assembly line. Eros breaks existing forms and creates new ones and that, naturally, is a threat to technology. Technology requires regularity, predictability, and runs by the clock. The untamed eros fights against all concepts and confines of time.

Eros is the impetus in building civilizations. But the civilization then turns on its progenitor and disciplines the erotic impulses. This can still work toward the increase and expansion of consciousness. The erotic impulses can and should have some discipline: the gospel of the free expression of every impulse disperses experience like a river with no banks, its water spilled and wasted as it flows in every direction. The discipline of eros provides *forms* in which we can develop and which protect us from unbearable anxiety. Freud believed that the disciplining of eros was necessary for a culture, and that it was from the repression and sublimation of erotic impulses that the power came out of which civilizations were built. De Rougement, for one of the few times, here agrees with Freud; he does not forget

> that without the sexual discipline which the so-called puritanical tendencies have imposed on us since Europe first existed, there would be nothing more in our civilization than in those nations known as underdeveloped, and no doubt less: there would be neither work, organized effort nor the technology which has created the present world. There would also not be the problem of eroticism! The erotic authors forget this fact quite naively, committed as they are to their poetic or moralizing passion, which too often alienates them from the true nature of

---

with their energy for civilized advancement. He concluded that the 'amount of cultural ascent of the primitive societies closely paralleled the amount of limitation they placed upon the nonmarital sexual opportunity.' Virtually all the civilized societies Unwin examined—the Babylonians, Athenians, Romans, Anglo-Saxons, and English—began their historical careers in a 'state of absolute monogamy.' The one exception was the Moors, where a specific religious sanction supported polygamy. 'Any human society,' Unwin writes, 'is free to choose either to display great energy or to enjoy sexual freedom; the evidence is that it cannot do both for more than one generation.' Packard points out that this is supported in different ways by other historians and anthropologists, such as Carl C. Zimmerman, Arnold J. Toynbee, Charles Winick and Pitirim A. Sorokin."

the "facts of life," and their complex links with economy, society, and culture.[22]

But there comes a point (and this is the challenge facing modern technological Western man) when the cult of technique destroys feeling, undermines passion, and blots out individual identity. The technologically efficient lover, defeated in the contradiction which is copulation without eros, is ultimately the impotent one. He has lost the power to be carried away; he knows only too well what he is doing. At this point, technology diminishes consciousness and demolishes eros. Tools are no longer an enlargement of consciousness but a substitute for it and, indeed, tend to repress and truncate it.

Must civilization always tame eros to keep the society from breaking up again? Hesiod lived in the strongly fomenting, archaic sixth century, closer to the sources of culture and the moments of gestation and birth, when the procreative powers were at work, and man *had* to live with chaos and form it into something new. But then, with the growing need for stabilization, the daimonic and tragic elements tended to be buried. Insight into the downfall of civilizations is revealed here. We see effete Athens set up for the more primitive Macedonians, they in turn for the Romans, and the Romans in turn for the Huns. And we for the yellow and black races?

Eros is the center of the vitality of a culture—its heart and soul. And when release of tension takes the place of creative eros, the downfall of the civilization is assured.

[22] From Denis de Rougement's *The Myths of Love* (New York, Pantheon Books, 1963), quoted in *Atlas*, November, 1965, p. 306.

LOVE IN THE GREAT SOCIETY

Walter Lippmann

Walter Lippmann (1889–1974), journalist, social commentator, and political pundit whose columns appeared in the New Republic, *the* New York World, *and the* New York Herald Tribune *for over forty years. He wrote some twenty-five books, including* A Preface to Politics (1913), The Good Society (1937), Essays in the Public Philosophy (1955), *and the extremely influential work* Public Opinion (1922, 1956, 1965).

1. THE EXTERNAL CONTROL
OF SEXUAL CONDUCT

While the changes which modernity implies affect the premises of all human conduct, the problem as a whole engages the attention of relatively few persons. The larger number of men and women living within the orbit of the Great Society are no doubt aware that their inherited beliefs about religion, politics, business, and sex do not square entirely with the actual beliefs upon which they feel compelled to act. But the fundamental alterations in political and economic ideals which the machine technology is inducing come home to each man only indirectly and partially. The consequences are subtle, delayed, and what is even more important, they are outside the scope of the ordinary man's personal decision. There is little that is urgent, immediate, or decisive which he can do, even if he understands them, about the changes in the structure and purpose of industry and the state. Most men can manage, therefore, to live without ever attempting to decide for themselves any fundamental question about business or politics. But they can neither ignore changes in sexual relations nor do they wish to. It is possible for a man to be a socialist or an individualist without ever having to make one responsible decision in which his theories play any part. But what he thinks about divorce and contraception, continence and license, monogamy, prostitution, and sexual experience outside of marriage, are matters that are bound at some point in his life to affect his own happiness immediately and directly. It is possible to be hypocritical about sex. But it is not possible for any adult who is not anæsthetic to be indifferent. The affairs of state may be regulated by leaders. But the affairs of a man and a woman are inescapably their own.

That obviously is the reason why in the popular mind it is immediately assumed that when morals are discussed it is sexual morals that are meant. The morals of the politician and the voter, of the shareholder and executive and employee, are only moderately interesting to the general public: thus they almost never supply the main theme of popular fiction. But the relation between boy and girl, man and woman, husband and wife, mistress and lover, parents and children, are themes which no amount of repetition makes stale. The explanation is obvious. The modern audience is composed of persons among whom only a comparatively negligible few are serenely happy in their personal lives. Popular fiction responds to their longings: to the unappeased it offers some measure of vicarious satisfaction, to the prurient an indulgence, to the worried, if not a way out, then at least the comfort of knowing that their secret despair is a common, and not a unique, experience.

Yet in spite of this immense preoccupation with sex it is extraordinarily difficult to arrive at any reliable knowledge of what actual change in human behavior it reflects. This is not surprising. In fact this is the very essence of the matter. The reason it is difficult to know the actual facts about sexual behavior in modern society is that sexual behavior eludes observation and control. We know that the old conventions have lost most of their authority because we cannot know about, and therefore can no longer regulate, the sexual behavior of others. It may be that there is, as some optimists believe, a fine but candid restraint practiced among modern men and women. It may be that incredible licentiousness exists all about us, as the gloomier prophets insist. It may be that there is just about as much unconventional conduct and no more than there has always been. Nobody, I think, really knows. Nobody knows whether the conversation about sex reflects more promiscuity or less hypocrisy. But what everybody must know is that sexual conduct, whatever it may be, is regulated personally and not publicly in modern society. If there is restraint it is, in the last analysis, voluntary; if there is promiscuity, it can be quite secret.

The circumstances which have wrought this change are inherent in modern ways of living. Until quite recently the main conventions of sex were enforced first by the parents and then by the husband through their control over the life of the woman. The main conventions were: first, that she must not encourage or display any amorous inclinations except where there was practical certainty that the young man's intentions were serious; second, that when she was married to the young man she submitted to his embraces only because the Lord somehow failed to contrive a less vile method of perpetuating the species. All the minor conventions were subsidiary to these; the whole system was organized on the premise that procreation was the woman's only sanction for sexual intercourse. Such control as was exercised over the conduct of men was subordinate to this control over the conduct of women. The chastity of women before marriage was guarded; that meant that seduction was a crime, but that relations with "lost" or unchaste women were tolerated. The virtuous man, by popular standards, was one who before his marriage did not have sexual relations with a virtuous woman. There is ample testimony in the outcries of moralists that even in the olden days these conventions were not perfectly administered. But they were sufficiently well administered to remain the accepted conventions, honored even in the breach. It was possible, because of the way people lived, to administer them.

The woman lived a sheltered life. That is another way of saying that she lived under the constant inspection of her family. She lived at home. She worked at home. She met young men under the zealous chaperonage of practically the whole community. No doubt, couples slipped away occasionally and more went on than was known or acknowledged. But even then there was a very powerful deterrent against an illicit relationship. This deterrent was the fear of pregnancy. That in the end made it almost certain that if a secret affair were consummated it could not be kept secret and that terrible penalties would be exacted. In the modern world effective chaperonage has become impracticable and the fear of pregnancy has been virtually eliminated by the very general knowledge of contraceptive methods.

The whole revolution in the field of sexual morals turns upon the fact that external control of the chastity of women is becoming impossible.

·   ·   ·

2. BIRTH CONTROL

. . . Liberal reformers . . . have been arguing for the removal of the prohibitory laws, and they have built their case on two main theses. They have argued, first, that the limitation of births was sound public policy for economic and eugenic reasons; and second, that it was necessary to the happiness of families, the health of mothers, and the welfare of children. All these reasons may be unimpeachable. I think they are. But it was idle to pretend that the dissemination of this knowledge, even if legally confined to the instruction of married women by licensed physicians, could be kept from the rest of the adult population. Obviously that which all married couples are permitted to know every one is bound to know. Human curiosity will make that certain. Now this is what the Christian churches, especially the Roman Catholic, which oppose contraception on principle, instantly recognized. They were quite right. They were quite right, too, in recognizing that whether or not birth control is eugenic, hygienic, and economic, it is the most revolutionary practice in the history of sexual morals.

For when conception could be prevented, there was an end to the theory that woman submits to the embrace of the male only for purposes of procreation. She had to be persuaded to co-operate, and no possible reason could be advanced except that the pleasure was reciprocal. She had to understand and inwardly assent to the principle that it is proper to have sexual intercourse with her husband and to prevent conception. She had, therefore, to give up the whole traditional theory which she may have only half-believed anyway, that sexual intercourse was an impure means to a noble end. She could no longer believe that procreation alone mitigated the vileness of cohabiting with a man, and so she had to change her valuation and accept it as inherently delightful. Thus by an inevitable process the practice of contraception led husbands and wives to the conviction that they need not be in the least ashamed of their desires for each other.

But this transvaluation of values within the sanctity of the marital chamber could hardly be kept a secret. What had happened was that married couples were indulging in the pleasures of sex because they had learned how to isolate them from the responsibilities of parenthood. When we talk about the unconventional theories of the younger generation we might in all honesty take this fact into account. They have had it demonstrated to them by their own parents, by those in whom the administering of the conventions is vested, that under certain circumstances it is legitimate and proper to gratify sexual desire apart from any obligation to the family or to the race. They have been taught that it is possible to do this, and that it may be proper. Therefore, the older generation could no longer argue that sexual intercourse as such was evil. It could no longer argue that it was obviously dangerous. It could only maintain that the psychological consequences are serious if sexual gratification is not made incidental to the enduring partnership of marriage and a home. That may be, in fact, I think it can be shown to be, the real wisdom of the matter. Yet if it is the wisdom of the matter, it is a kind of wisdom which men and women can acquire by experience alone. They do not have it instinctively. They cannot be compelled to adopt it. They can only learn to believe it.

That is a very different thing from submitting to a convention upheld by all human and divine authority.

3. THE LOGIC OF BIRTH CONTROL

With contraception established as a more or less legitimate idea in modern society, a vast discussion has ensued as to how the practice of it can be rationalized. In this discussion the pace is set by those who accept the apparent logic of contraception and are prepared boldly to revise the sexual conventions accordingly. They take as their major premise the obvious fact that by contraception it is possible to dissociate procreation from gratification, and therefore to pursue independently what Mr. Have-lock Ellis calls the primary and secondary objects of the sexual impulse. They propose, therefore, to sanction two distinct sets of conventions: one designed to protect the interests of the offspring by promoting intelligent, secure, and cheerful parenthood; the other designed to permit the freest and fullest expression of the erotic personality. They propose, in other words, to distinguish between parenthood as a vocation involving public responsibility, and love as an art, pursued privately for the sake of happiness.

As a preparation for the vocation of parenthood it is proposed to educate both men and women in the care, both physical and psychological, of children. It is proposed further that mating for parenthood shall become an altogether deliberate and voluntary choice: the argument here is that the duties of parenthood cannot be successfully fulfilled except where both parents cheerfully and knowingly assume them. Therefore, it is proposed, in order to avert the dangers of love at first sight and of mating under the blind compulsion of instinct, that a period of free experimentation be allowed to precede the solemn engagement to produce and rear children. This engagement is regarded as so much a public responsibility that it is even proposed, and to some extent has been embodied in the law of certain jurisdictions, that marriages for parenthood must be sanctioned by medical authority. In order, too, that no compulsive considerations may determine what ought to be a free and intelligent choice, it is argued that women should be economically independent before and during marriage. As this may not be possible for women without property of their own during the years when they are bearing and rearing children, it is proposed in some form or other to endow motherhood. This endowment may take the form of a legal claim upon the earnings of the father, or it may mean a subsidy from the state through mothers' pensions, free medical attention, day nurseries, and kindergartens. The principle that successful parenthood must be voluntary is maintained as consistently as possible. Therefore, among those who follow the logic of their idea, it is proposed that even marriages deliberately entered into for procreation shall be dissoluble at the will of either party, the state intervening only to insure the economic security of the offspring. It is proposed, furthermore, that where women find the vocation of motherhood impracticable for one reason or another, they may be relieved of the duty of rearing their children.

Not all of the advanced reformers adopt the whole of this program, but the whole of this program is logically inherent in the conception of parenthood as a vocation deliberately undertaken, publicly pursued, and motivated solely by the parental instincts.

The separate set of conventions which it is proposed to adopt for the development of love as an art have a logic of their own. Their function is not to protect the welfare of the child but the happiness of lovers. It is very easy to misunderstand this conception. Mr. Havelock Ellis, in fact, describes it as a "divine and elusive mystery," a description which threatens to provide a rather elusive standard by which to fix a new set of sexual conventions. But baffling as this sounds, it is not wholly inscrutable, and a sufficient understanding of what is meant can be attained by clearing up the dangerous ambiguity in the phrase "love as an art."

There are two arts of love and it makes a considerable difference which one is meant. There is the art of love as Casanova, for example, practiced it. It is the art of seduction, courtship, and sexual gratification: it is an art which culminates in the sexual act. It can be repeated with the same lover and with other lovers, but it exhausts itself in the moment of ecstasy. When that moment is reached, the work of art is done, and the lover as artist "after an interval, perhaps of stupor and vital recuperation" must start all over again, until at last the rhythm is so stale it is a weariness to start at all; or the lover must find new lovers and new resistances to conquer. The aftermath of romantic love—that is, of love that is consummated in sexual ecstasy—is either tedium in middle age or the compulsive adventurousness of the libertine.

Now this is not what Mr. Ellis means when he talks about love as an art. "The act of intercourse," he says, "is only an incident, and not an essential in love." Incident to what? His answer is that it is an incident to an "exquisitely and variously and harmoniously blended" activity of "all the finer activities of the organism, physical and psychic." I take this to mean that when a man and woman are successfully in love, their whole activity is energized and victorious. They walk better, their digestion improves, they think more clearly, their secret worries drop away, the world is fresh and interesting, and they can do more than they dreamed that they could do. In love of this kind sexual intimacy is not the dead end of desire as it is in romantic or promiscuous love, but periodic affirmation of the inward delight of desire pervading an active life. Love of this sort can grow: it is not, like youth itself, a moment that comes and is gone and remains only a memory of something which cannot be recovered. It can grow because it has something to grow upon and to grow with; it is not contracted and stale because it has for its object, not the mere relief of physical tension, but all the objects with which the two lovers are concerned. They desire their worlds in each other, and therefore their love is as interesting as their worlds and their worlds are as interesting as their love.

It is to promote unions of this sort that the older liberals are proposing a new set of sexual conventions. There are, however, reformers in the field who take a much less exalted view of the sexual act, who regard it, indeed, not only as without biological or social significance, but also as without any very impressive psychological significance. "The practice of birth control," says Mr. C. E. M. Joad, for example, "will profoundly modify our sexual habits. It will enable the pleasures of sex to be tasted without its penalties, and it will remove the most formidable deterrent to irregular intercourse." For birth control "offers to the young . . . the prospect of shameless, harmless, and unlimited pleasure." But whether the reformers agree with Mr. Ellis that sexual intimacy is, as he says, a sacrament signifying some great spiritual reality, or with Mr. Joad that it is a harmless pleasure, they are agreed that the sexual conventions should be revised to permit such unions without penalties and without any sense of shame.

They ask public opinion to sanction what contraception has made feasible. They point out that "a large number of the men and women of to-day form sexual relationships outside marriage—whether or not they ultimately lead to marriage—which they conceal or seek to conceal from the world." These relationships, says Mr. Ellis, differ from the extra-marital manifestations of the sexual life of the past in that they do not derive from prostitution or seduction. Both of these ancient practices, he adds, are diminishing, for prostitution is becoming less attractive and, with the education of women, seduction is becoming less possible. The novelty of these new relations, the prevalence of which is conceded though it cannot be measured, lies in the fact that they are entered into voluntarily, have no obvious social consequences, and are altogether beyond the power of law or opinion to control. The argument, therefore, is that they should be approved, the chief point made being that by removing all stigma from such unions, they will become candid, wholesome, and delightful. The objection of the reformers to the existing conventions is that the sense of sin poisons the spontaneous goodness of such relationships.

The actual proposals go by a great variety of fancy names such as free love, trial marriage, companionate marriage. When these proposals are examined it is evident they all take birth control as their major premise, and then deduce from it some part or all of the logical consequences. Companionate marriage, for example, is from the point of view of the law, whatever it may be subjectively, nothing but a somewhat roundabout way of saying that childless couples may be divorced by mutual consent. It is a proposal, if not to control, then at least to register, publicly all sexual unions, the theory being that this public registration will abolish shame and furtiveness and give them a certain permanence. Companionate marriage is frankly an attempt at a compromise between marriages that are difficult to dissolve and clandestine relationships which have no sanction whatever.

The uncompromising logic of birth control has been stated more clearly, I think, by Mr. Bertrand Russell than by anyone else. Writing to Judge Lindsey during the uproar about companionate marriage, Mr. Russell said:

> I go further than you do: the things which your enemies say about you would be largely true of me. My own view is that the state and the law should take no notice of sexual relations apart from children, and that no marriage ceremony should be valid unless accompanied by a medical certificate of the woman's pregnancy. But when once there are children, I think that divorce should be avoided except for very grave cause. I should not regard physical infidelity as a very grave cause and should teach people that it is to be expected and tolerated, but should not involve the begetting of illegitimate children—not because illegitimacy is bad in itself, but because a home with two parents is best for children. I do not feel that the main thing in marriage is the feeling of the parents for each other; the main thing is cooperation in bearing children.

In this admirably clear statement there is set forth a plan for that complete separation between the primary and secondary function of sexual intercourse which contraception makes possible.

4. THE USE OF CONVENTION

It is one thing, however, to recognize the full logic of birth control and quite another thing to say that convention ought to be determined by that logic. One might as well argue that because automobiles can be driven at a hundred miles an hour the laws should sanction driving at the rate of a hundred miles an hour. Birth control is a device like the automobile, and its inherent possibilities do not fix the best uses to be made of it.

What an understanding of the logic of birth control does is to set before us the limits of coercive control of sexual relations. The law can, for example, make divorce very difficult where there are children. It could, as Mr. Bertrand Russell suggests, refuse divorce on the ground of infidelity. On the other hand the law cannot effectively prohibit infidelity, and as a matter of fact does not do so to-day. It cannot effectively prohibit fornication though there are statutes against it. Therefore, what Mr. Russell has done is to describe accurately enough the actual limits of effective legal control.

But sexual conventions are not statutes, and it is important to define quite clearly just what they are. In the older world they were rules of conduct enforceable by the family and the community through habit, coercion, and authority. In this sense of the word, convention tends to lose force and effect in modern civilization. Yet a convention is essentially a theory of conduct and all human conduct implies some theory of conduct. Therefore, although it may be that no convention is any longer coercive, conventions remain, are adopted, revised, and debated. They embody the considered results of experience: perhaps the experience of a lonely pioneer or perhaps the collective experience of the dominant members of a community. In any event they are as necessary to a society which recognizes no authority as to one which does. For the inexperienced must be offered some kind of hypothesis when they are confronted with the necessity of making choices: they cannot be so utterly open-minded that they stand inert until something collides with them. In the modern world, therefore, the function of conventions is to declare the meaning of experience. A good convention is one which will most probably show the inexperienced the way to happy experience.

Just because the rule of sexual conduct by authority is dissolving, the need of conventions which will guide conduct is increasing. That, in fact, is the reason for the immense and urgent discussion of sex throughout the modern world. It is an attempt to attain an understanding of the bewilderingly new experiences to which few men or women know how to adjust themselves. The true business of the moralist in the midst of all this is not to denounce this and to advocate that, but to see as clearly as he can into the meaning of it, so that out of the chaos of pain and happiness and worry he may help to deliver a usable insight.

It is, I think, to the separation of parenthood as a vocation from love as an end in itself that the moralist must address himself. For this is the heart of the problem: to determine whether this separation, which birth control has made feasible and which law can no longer prevent, is in harmony with the conditions of human happiness.

5. THE NEW HEDONISM

Among those who hold that the separation of the primary and secondary functions of the sexual impulse is good and should constitute the major premise of modern sexual conventions, there are, as I have already pointed out, two schools of thought. There are the transcendentalists who believe with Mr. Havelock Ellis that "sexual pleasure, wisely used and not abused, may prove the stimulus and liberator of our finest and most exalted activities," and there are the unpretentious hedonists who believe that sexual pleasure is pleasure and not the stimulus or liberator of anything important. Both are, as we say, emancipated: neither recognizes the legitimacy of objective control unless a child is born, and both reject as an evil the traditional subjective control exercised by the sense of sin. Where they differ is in their valuation of love.

Hedonism as an attitude toward life is, of course, not a new thing in the world, but it has never before been tested out under such favorable conditions. To be a successful hedonist a man must have the opportunity to seek his pleasures without fear of any kind. Theodorus of Cyrene, who taught about 310 B.C., saw that clearly, and therefore to release men from fear openly denied the Olympian gods. But the newest hedonism has had an even better prospect than the classical: it finds men emancipated not only of all fear of divine authority and human custom but of physical and social consequences as well. If the pursuit of pleasure by carefree men were the way to happiness, hedonism ought, then, to be proving itself triumphantly in the modern world. Possibly it is too early to judge, but the fact is nevertheless highly significant, I think, that the new hedonists should already have arrived at the same conclusion as the later hedonists in the classical world. Hegesias, for example, wrote when hedonism had already had a great vogue: he was called, rather significantly, the "persuader to die." For having started from the premise that pleasure is the end of life, he concluded that, since life affords at least as much pain as pleasure, the end of life cannot be realized. There is now a generation in the world which is approaching middle age. They have exercised the privileges which were won by the iconoclasts who attacked what was usually called the Puritan or Victorian tradition. They have exercised the privileges without external restraint and without inhibition. Their conclusions are reported in the latest works of fiction. Do they report that they have found happiness in their freedom? Well, hardly. Instead of the gladness which they were promised, they seem, like Hegesias, to have found the wasteland.

"If love has come to be less often a sin," says that very discerning critic of life and letters, Mr. Joseph Wood Krutch, "it has come also to be less often a supreme privilege. If one turns to the smarter of those novelists who describe the doings of the more advanced set of those who are experimenting with life—to, for example, Mr. Aldous Huxley or Mr. Ernest Hemingway,—one will discover in their tragic farces the picture of a society which is at bottom in despair because, though it is more completely absorbed in the pursuit of love than in anything else, it has lost the sense of any ultimate importance inherent in the experience which preoccupies it; and if one turns to the graver of the intellectual writers,—to, for example, Mr. D. H. Lawrence, Mr. T. S. Eliot, or Mr. James Joyce,—one will find both explicitly and implicitly a similar sense that the transcendental value of love has become somehow attenuated, and that, to take a perfectly concrete example, a conclusion which does no more than bring a man and woman into complete possession of one another is a mere bathos which does nothing except legitimately provoke the comment,

'Well, what of it?' One can hardly imagine them concerned with what used to be called, in a phrase which they have helped to make faintly ridiculous, 'the right to love.' Individual freedom they have inherited and assumed as a right, but they are concerned with something which their more restricted forefathers assumed—with, that is to say, the value of love itself. No inhibitions either within or without restrain them, but they are asking themselves, 'What is it worth?' and they are certainly no longer feeling that it is obviously and in itself something which makes life worth the living . . ."

This "generally devaluated world," of which Mr. Krutch speaks, what is it after all, but a world in which nothing connects itself very much with anything else? If you start with the belief that love is the pleasure of a moment, is it really surprising that it yields only a momentary pleasure? For it is the most ironical of all illusions to suppose that one is free of illusions in contracting any human desire to its primary physiological satisfaction. Does a man dine well because he ingests the requisite number of calories? Is he freer from illusions about his appetite than the man who creates an interesting dinner party out of the underlying fact that his guests and he have the need to fill their stomachs? Would it really be a mark of enlightenment if each of them filled his stomach in the solitary and solemn conviction that good conversation and pleasant companionship are one thing and nutrition is another?

This much the transcendentalists understand well enough. They do not wish to isolate the satisfaction of desire from our "finest and most exalted activities." They would make it "the stimulus and the liberator" of these activities. They would use it to arouse to "wholesome activity all the complex and interrelated systems of the organism." But what are these finest and most exalted activities which are to be stimulated and liberated? The discovery of truth, the making of works of art, meditation and insight? Mr. Ellis does not specify. If these are the activities that are meant, then the discussion applies to a very few of the men and women on earth. For the activities of most of them are necessarily concerned with earning a living and managing a household and rearing children and finding recreation. If the art of love is to stimulate and liberate activities, it is these prosaic activities which it must stimulate and liberate. But if you idealize the logic of birth control, make parenthood a separate vocation, isolate love from work and the hard realities of living, and say that it must be spontaneous and carefree, what have you done? You have separated it from all the important activities which it might stimulate and liberate. You have made love spontaneous but empty, and you have made home-building and parenthood efficient, responsible, and dull.

What has happened, I believe, is what so often happens in the first enthusiasm for a revolutionary invention. Its possibilities are so dazzling that men forget that inventions belong to man and not man to his inventions. In the discussion which has ensued since birth control became generally feasible, the central confusion has been that the reformers have tried to fix their sexual ideals in accordance with the logic of birth control instead of the logic of human nature. Birth control does make feasible this dissociation of interests which were once organically united. There are undoubtedly the best of reasons for dissociating them up to a point. But how completely it is wise to dissociate them is a matter to be determined not by saying how completely it is possible to dissociate them, but how much it is desirable to dissociate them.

All the varieties of the modern doctrine that man is a collection of separate impulses, each of which can attain its private satisfaction, are in fundamental contradiction not only with the traditional body of human wisdom but with the modern conception of the human character. Thus in one breath it is said in advanced circles that love is a series of casual episodes, and in the next it transpires that the speaker is in process of having himself elaborately psychoanalyzed in order to disengage his soul from the effects of apparently trivial episodes in his childhood. On the one hand it is asserted that sex pervades everything and on the other that sexual behavior is inconsequential. It is taught that experience is cumulative, that we are what our past has made us and shall be what we are making of ourselves now, and then with bland indifference to the significance of this we are told that all experiences are free, equal, and independent.

6. MARRIAGE AND AFFINITY

It is not hard to see why those who are concerned in revising sexual conventions should have taken the logic of birth control rather than knowledge of human nature as their major premise. Birth control is an immensely beneficent invention which can and does relieve men and women of some of the most tragic sorrows which afflict them: the tragedies of the unwanted child, the tragedies of insupportable economic burdens, the tragedies of excessive child bearing and the destruction of youth and the necessity of living in an unrelenting series of pregnancies. It offers them freedom from intolerable mismating, from sterile virtue, from withering denials of happiness. These are the facts which the reformers saw, and in birth control they saw the instrument by which such freedom could be obtained.

The sexual conventions which they have proposed are really designed to cure notorious evils. They do not define the good life in sex; they point out ways of escape from the bad life. Thus companionate marriage is proposed by Judge Lindsey not as a type of union which is inherently desirable, but as an avenue of escape from corrupt marriages on the one hand and furtive promiscuity on the other. The movement for free divorce comes down to this: it is necessary because so many marriages are a failure. The whole theory that love is separate from parenthood and home-building is supported by the evidence in those cases where married couples are not lovers. It is the pathology of sexual relations which inspires the reformers of sexual conventions.

There is no need to quarrel with them because they insist upon remedies for manifest evils. Deep confusion results when they forget that these remedies are only remedies, and go on to institute them as ideals. It is better, without any doubt, that incompatible couples should be divorced and that each should then be free to find a mate who is compatible. But the frequency with which men and women have to resort to divorce because they are incompatible will be greatly influenced by the notions they have before and during marriage of what compatibility is, and what it involves. The remedies for failure are important. But what is central is the conception of sexual relations by which they expect to live successfully.

They cannot—I am, of course, speaking broadly—expect to live successfully by the conception that the primary and secondary functions of sex are in separate compartments of the soul. I have indicated why this conception is self-defeating and why, since human nature is organic and experience cumulative, our activities must, so to speak, engage and imply each other. Mates who are not lovers will not really cooperate, as Mr. Bertrand Russell thinks they should, in bearing children; they will be distracted, insufficient, and worst of all they will be merely dutiful. Lovers who have nothing to do but love each other are not really to be envied; love and nothing else very soon is nothing else. The emotion of love, in spite of the romantics, is not self-sustaining; it endures only when the lovers love many things together, and not merely each other. It is this understanding that love cannot successfully be isolated from the business of living which is the enduring wisdom of the institution of marriage. Let the law be what it may be as to what constitutes a marriage contract and how and when it may be dissolved. Let public opinion be as tolerant as it can be toward any and every kind of irregular and experimental relationship. When all the criticisms have been made, when all supernatural sanctions have been discarded, all subjective inhibitions erased, all compulsions abolished, the convention of marriage still remains to be considered as an interpretation of human experience. It is by the test of how genuinely it interprets human experience that the convention of marriage will ultimately be judged.

The wisdom of marriage rests upon an extremely unsentimental view of lovers and their passions. Its assumptions, when they are frankly exposed, are horrifying to those who have been brought up in the popular romantic tradition of the Nineteenth Century. These assumptions are that, given an initial attraction, a common social background, common responsibilities, and the conviction that the relationship is permanent, compatibility in marriage can normally be achieved. It is precisely this that the prevailing sentimentality about love denies. It assumes that marriages are made in heaven, that compatibility is instinctive, a mere coincidence, that happy unions are, in the last analysis, lucky accidents in which two people who happen to suit each other happen to have met. The convention of marriage rests on an interpretation of human nature which does not confuse the subjective feeling of the lovers that their passion is unique, with the brutal but objective fact that, had they never met, each of them would in all probability have found a lover who was just as unique. "Love," says Mr. Santayana, "is indeed much less exacting than it thinks itself. Nine-tenths of its cause are in the lover, for one-tenth that may be in the object. Were the latter not accidentally at hand, an almost identical passion would probably have been felt for some one else; for, although with acquaintance the quality of an attachment naturally adapts itself to the person loved, and makes that person its standard and ideal, the first assault and mysterious glow of the passion is much the same for every object."

This is the reason why the popular conception of romantic love as the meeting of two affinities produces so much unhappiness. The mysterious glow of passion is accepted as a sign that the great coincidence has occurred; there is a wedding and soon, as the glow of passion cools, it is discovered that no instinctive and preordained affinity is present. At this point the wisdom of popular romantic marriage is exhausted. For it proceeds on the assumption that love is a mysterious visitation. There is nothing left, then, but to grin and bear a miserably dull and nagging fate, or to break off and try again. The deep fallacy of the conception is in the failure to realize that compatibility is a process and not an accident, that it depends upon the maturing of instinctive desire by adaptation to the whole nature of the other person and to the common concerns of the pair of lovers.

The romantic theory of affinities rests upon an immature theory of desire. It springs from an infantile belief that the success of love is in the satisfactions which the other person provides. What this really means is that in childlike fashion the lover expects his mistress to supply him with happiness. But in the adult world that expectation is false. Because nine-tenths of the cause, as Mr. Santayana says, are in the lover for one-tenth that may be in the object, it is what the lover does about that nine-tenths which is decisive for his happiness. It is the claim, therefore, of those who uphold the ideal of marriage as a full partnership, and reject the ideal which would separate love as an art from parenthood as a vocation, that in the home made by a couple who propose to see it through, there are provided the essential conditions under which the passions of men and women are most likely to become mature, and therefore harmonious and disinterested.

7. THE SCHOOLING OF DESIRE

They need not deny, indeed it would be foolish as well as cruel for them to underestimate, the enormous difficulty of achieving successful marriages under modern conditions. For with the dissolution of authority and compulsion, a successful marriage depends wholly upon the capacity of the man and the woman to make it successful. They have to accomplish wholly by understanding and sympathy and disinterestedness of purpose what was once in a very large measure achieved by habit, necessity, and the absence of any practicable alternative. It takes two persons to make a successful marriage in the modern world, and that fact more than doubles its difficulty. For these reasons alone the modern state ought to do what it would none the less be compelled to do: it ought to provide decent ways of retreat in case of failure.

But if it is the truth that the convention of marriage correctly interprets human experience, whereas the separatist conventions are self-defeating, then the convention of marriage will prove to be the conclusion which emerges out of all this immense experimenting. It will survive not as a rule of law imposed by force, for that is now, I think, become impossible. It will not survive as a moral commandment with which the elderly can threaten the young. They will not listen. It will survive as the dominant insight into the reality of love and happiness, or it will not survive at all. That does not mean that all persons will live under the convention of marriage. As a matter of fact in civilized ages all persons never have. It means that the convention of marriage, when it is clarified by insight into reality, is likely to be the hypothesis upon which men and women will ordinarily proceed. There will be no compulsion behind it except the compulsion in each man and woman to reach a true adjustment of his life.

It is in this necessity of clarifying their love for those who are closest to them that the moral problems of the new age come to a personal issue. It is in the realm of sexual relations that mankind is being schooled amidst pain and worry for the novel conditions which modernity imposes. It is there, rather than in politics, business, or even in religion, that the issues are urgent, vivid, and inescapable. It is there that they touch most poignantly and most radically the organic roots of human personality. And it is there, in the ordering of their personal attachments, that for most men the process of salvation must necessarily begin.

For disinterestedness in all things, as Dean Inge says, is a mountain track which the many are likely in the future as in the past to find cold, bleak, and bare: that is why "the road of ascent is by personal affection for man." By the happy ordering of their personal affections they may establish the type and the quality and the direction of their desires for all things. It is in the hidden issues between lovers, more than anywhere else, that modern men and women are compelled, by personal anguish rather than by laws and preachments or even by the persuasions of abstract philosophy, to transcend naive desire and to reach out towards a mature and disinterested partnership with their world.

SEXUAL PERVERSION
Thomas Nagel

Thomas Nagel (1937–   ), Professor of Philosophy at Princeton University primarily concerned with ethics, the concept of mind, and ancient philosophy. In addition to his contributions to professional journals, he is the author of The Possibility of Altruism *(1969).*

There is something to be learned about sex from the fact that we possess a concept of sexual perversion. I wish to examine the concept, defending it against the charge of unintelligibility and trying to say exactly what about human sexuality qualifies it to admit of perversions. Let me make some preliminary comments about the problem before embarking on its solution.

Some people do not believe that the notion of sexual perversion makes sense, and even those who do disagree over its application. Nevertheless I think it will be widely conceded that, if the concept is viable at all, it must meet certain general conditions. First, if there are any sexual perversions, they will have to be sexual desires or practices that can be plausibly described as in some sense unnatural, though the explanation of this natural/unnatural distinction is of course the main problem. Second, certain practices will be perversions if anything is, such as shoe fetishism, bestiality, and sadism; other practices, such as unadorned sexual intercourse, will not be; about still others there is controversy. Third, if there are perversions, they will be unnatural sexual *inclinations* rather than merely unnatural practices adopted not from inclination but for other reasons. I realize that this is at variance with the view, maintained by some Roman Catholics, that contraception is a sexual perversion. But although contraception may qualify as a deliberate perversion of the sexual and reproductive functions, it cannot be significantly described as a *sexual* perversion. A sexual perversion must reveal itself in conduct that expresses an unnatural *sexual* preference. And although there might be a form of fetishism focused on the employment of contraceptive devices, that is not the usual explanation for their use.

I wish to declare at the outset my belief that the connection between sex and reproduction has no bearing on sexual perversion. The latter is a concept of psychological, not physiological interest, and it is a concept that we do not apply to the lower animals, let alone to plants, all of which have reproductive functions that can go astray in various ways. (Think of seedless oranges.) Insofar as we are prepared to regard higher animals as perverted, it is because of their psychological, not their anatomical similarity to humans. Furthermore, we do not regard as a perversion every deviation from the reproductive function of sex in humans: sterility, miscarriage, contraception, abortion.

Another matter that I believe has no bearing on the concept of sexual perversion is social disapprobation or custom. Anyone inclined to think that in each society the perversions are those sexual practices of which the community disapproves, should consider all the societies that have frowned upon adultery and fornication. These have not been regarded as unnatural practices, but have been thought objectionable in other ways. What is regarded as unnatural admittedly varies from culture to culture, but the classification is not a pure expression of disapproval or distaste. In fact it is often regarded as a *ground* for disapproval, and that suggests that the classification has an independent content.

I am going to attempt a psychological account of sexual perversion, which will depend on a specific psychological theory of sexual desire and human sexual interactions. To approach this solution I wish first to consider a contrary position, one which provides a basis for skepticism about the existence of any sexual perversions at all, and perhaps about the very significance of the term. The skeptical argument runs as follows:

"Sexual desire is simply one of the appetites, like hunger and thirst. As such it may have various objects, some more common than others perhaps, but none in any sense 'natural'. An appetite is identified as sexual by means of the organs and erogenous zones in which its satisfaction can be to some extent localized, and the special sensory pleasures which form the core of that satisfaction. This enables us to recognize widely divergent goals, activities, and desires as sexual, since it is conceivable in principle that anything should produce sexual pleasure and that a nondeliberate, sexually charged desire for it should arise (as a result of conditioning, if nothing else). We may fail to empathize with some of these desires, and some of them, like sadism, may be objectionable on extraneous grounds, but once we have observed that they meet the criteria for being sexual, there is nothing more to be said on *that* score. Either they are sexual or they are not: sexuality does not admit of imperfection, or perversion, or any other such qualification—it is not that sort of affection."

This is probably the received radical position. It suggests that the cost of defending a psychological account may be to deny that sexual desire is an appetite. But insofar as that line of defense is plausible, it should make us suspicious of the simple picture of appetites on which the skepticism depends. Perhaps the standard appetites, like hunger, cannot be classed as pure appetites in that sense either, at least in their human versions.

Let us approach the matter by asking whether we can imagine anything that would qualify as a gastronomical perversion. Hunger and eating are importantly like sex in that they serve a biological function and also play a significant role in our inner lives. It is noteworthy that there is little temptation to describe as perverted an appetite for substances that are not nourishing. We should probably not consider someone's appetites as *perverted* if he liked to eat paper, sand, wood, or cotton. Those are merely rather odd and very unhealthy tastes: they lack the psychological complexity that we expect of perversions. (Coprophilia, being already a sexual perversion, may be disregarded.) If on the other hand someone liked to eat cookbooks, or magazines with pictures of food in them, and preferred these to ordinary food—or if when hungry he sought satisfaction by fondling a napkin or ashtray from his favorite restaurant—then the concept of perversion might seem appropriate (in fact it would be natural to describe this as a case of gastronomical fetishism). It would be natural to describe as gastronomically perverted someone who could eat only by having food forced down his throat through a funnel, or only if the meal were a living animal. What helps in such cases is the peculiarity of the desire itself, rather than the inappropriateness of its object to the biological function that the desire serves. Even an appetite, it would seem, can have perversions if in addition to its biological function it has a significant psychological structure.

In the case of hunger, psychological complexity is provided by the activities that give it expression. Hunger is not merely a disturbing sensation that can be quelled by eating; it is an attitude toward edible portions of the external world, a desire to relate to them in rather special ways. The method of ingestion: chewing, savoring, swallowing, appreciating the texture and smell, all are important components of the relation, as is the passivity and controllability of the food (the only animals we eat live are helpless mollusks). Our relation to food depends also on our size: we do not live upon it or burrow into it like aphids or worms. Some of these features are more central than others, but any adequate phenomenology of eating would have to treat it as a relation to the external world and a way of appropriating bits of that world, with characteristic affection. Displacements or serious restrictions of the desire to eat could then be described as perversions, if they undermined that direct relation between man and food which is the natural expression of hunger. This explains why it is easy to imagine gastronomical fetishism, voyeurism, exhibitionism, or even gastronomical sadism and masochism. Indeed some of these perversions are fairly common.

If we can imagine perversions of an appetite like hunger, it should be possible to make sense of the concept of sexual perversion. I do not wish to imply that sexual desire is an appetite—only that being an appetite is no bar to admitting of perversions. Like hunger, sexual desire has as its characteristic object a certain relation with something in the external world; only in this case it is usually a person rather than an omelet, and the relation is considerably more complicated. This added complication allows scope for correspondingly complicated perversions.

The fact that sexual desire is a feeling about other persons may tempt us to take a pious view of its psychological content. There are those who believe that sexual desire is properly the expression of some other attitude, like love, and that when it occurs by itself it is incomplete and unhealthy —or at any rate subhuman. (The extreme Platonic version of such a view is that sexual practices are all vain attempts to express something they cannot in principle achieve: this makes them all perversions, in a sense.) I do not believe that any such view is correct. Sexual desire is complicated enough without having to be linked to anything else as a condition for phenomenological analysis. It cannot be denied that sex may serve various functions—economic, social, altruistic—but it also has its own content as a relation between persons, and it is only by analyzing that relation that we can understand the conditions of sexual perversion.

I believe it is very important that the object of sexual attraction is a particular individual, who transcends the properties that make him attractive. When different persons are attracted to a single person for different reasons: eyes, hair, figure, laugh, intelligence—we feel that the object of their desire is nevertheless the same, namely that person. There is even an inclination to feel that this is so if the lovers have different sexual aims, if they include both men and women, for example. Different specific attractive characteristics seem to provide enabling conditions for the operation of a single basic feeling, and the different aims all provide expressions of it. We approach the sexual attitude toward the person through the features that we find attractive, but these features are not the objects of that attitude.

This is very different from the case of an omelet. Various people may desire it for different reasons, one for its fluffiness, another for its mushrooms, another for its unique combination of aroma and visual aspect; yet we do not enshrine the transcendental omelet as the true common object of their affections. Instead we might say that several desires have accidentally converged on the same object: any omelet with the crucial characteristics would do as well. It is not similarly true that any person with the same flesh distribution and way of smoking can be substituted as object for a particular sexual desire that has been elicited by those characteristics. It may be that they will arouse attraction whenever they recur, but it will be a new sexual attraction with a new particular object, not merely a transfer of the old desire to someone else. (I believe this is true even in cases where the new object is unconsciously identified with a former one.)

The importance of this point will emerge when we see how complex a psychological interchange constitutes the natural development of sexual attraction. This would be incomprehensible if its object were not a particular person, but rather a person of a certain *kind*. Attraction is only the beginning, and fulfillment does not consist merely of behavior and contact expressing this attraction, but involves much more.

The best discussion of these matters that I have seen appears in part III of Sartre's *Being and Nothingness*.[1] Since it has influenced my own views, I shall say a few things about it now. Sartre's treatment of sexual desire and of love, hate, sadism, masochism, and further attitudes toward others, depends on a general theory of consciousness and the body which we can neither expound nor assume here. He does not discuss perversion, and this is partly because he regards sexual desire as one form of the perpetual attempt of an embodied consciousness to come to terms with the existence of others, an attempt that is as doomed to fail in this form as it is in any of the others, which include sadism and masochism (if not certain of the more impersonal deviations) as well as several nonsexual attitudes. According to Sartre, all attempts to incorporate the other into my world as another subject, i.e., to apprehend him at once as an object for me and as a subject for whom I am an object, are unstable and doomed to collapse into one or other of the two aspects. Either I reduce him entirely to an object, in which case his subjectivity escapes the possession or appropriation I can extend to that object; or I become merely an object for him, in which case I am no longer in a position to appropriate his subjectivity. Moreover, neither of these aspects is stable; each is continually in danger of giving way to the other. This has the consequence that there can be no such thing as a *successful* sexual relation, since the deep aim of sexual desire cannot in principle be accomplished. It seems likely, therefore, that the view will not permit a basic distinction between successful or complete and unsuccessful or incomplete sex, and therefore cannot admit the concept of perversion.

I do not adopt this aspect of the theory, nor many of its metaphysical underpinnings. What interests me is Sartre's picture of the attempt. He says that the type of possession that is the object of sexual desire is carried out by "a double reciprocal incarnation" and that this is accomplished, typically in the form of a caress, in the following way: "I make myself flesh in order to impel the Other to realize *for-herself* and *for me* her own flesh, and my caresses cause my flesh to be born for me in so far as it is for the Other *flesh causing her to be born as flesh*" (italics Sartre's). The incarnation in question is described variously as a clogging or troubling of consciousness, which is inundated by the flesh in which it is embodied.

The view I am going to suggest, I hope in less obscure language, is related to this one, but it differs from Sartre's in allowing sexuality to

[1] Translated by Hazel E. Barnes (New York: Philosophical Library: 1956).

achieve its goal on occasion and thus in providing the concept of perver-
version with a foothold.

Sexual desire involves a kind of perception, but not merely a single
perception of its object, for in the paradigm case of mutual desire there
is a complex system of superimposed mutual perceptions—not only perceptions of the sexual object, but perceptions of oneself. Moreover, sexual
awareness of another involves considerable self-awareness to begin with—
more than is involved in ordinary sensory perception. The experience is
felt as an assault on oneself by the view (or touch, or whatever) of the
sexual object.

Let us consider a case in which the elements can be separated. For
clarity we will restrict ourselves initially to the somewhat artificial case of
desire at a distance. Suppose a man and a woman, whom we may call
Romeo and Juliet, are at opposite ends of a cocktail lounge, with many
mirrors on the walls which permit unobserved observation, and even
mutual unobserved observation. Each of them is sipping a martini and
studying other people in the mirrors. At some point Romeo notices Juliet.
He is moved, somehow, by the softness of her hair and the diffidence with
which she sips her martini, and this arouses him sexually. Let us say that
X *senses* Y whenever X regards Y with sexual desire. (Y need not be a
person, and X's apprehension of Y can be visual, tactile, olfactory, etc., or
purely imaginary; in the present example we shall concentrate on vision.)
So Romeo senses Juliet, rather than merely noticing her. At this stage he
is aroused by an unaroused object, so he is more in the sexual grip of his
body than she of hers.

Let us suppose, however, that Juliet now senses Romeo in another
mirror on the opposite wall, though neither of them yet knows that he is
seen by the other (the mirror angles provide three-quarter views). Romeo
then begins to notice in Juliet the subtle signs of sexual arousal: heavy-
lidded stare, dilating pupils, faint flush, et cetera. This of course renders
her much more bodily, and he not only notices but senses this as well. His
arousal is nevertheless still solitary. But now, cleverly calculating the line
of her stare without actually looking her in the eyes, he realizes that it is
directed at him through the mirror on the opposite wall. That is, he
notices, and moreover senses, Juliet sensing him. This is definitely a new
development, for it gives him a sense of embodiment not only through his
own reactions but through the eyes and reactions of another. Moreover,
it is separable from the initial sensing of Juliet; for sexual arousal might
begin with a person's sensing that he is sensed and being assailed by the
perception of the other person's desire rather than merely by the perception of the person.

But there is a further step. Let us suppose that Juliet, who is a little
slower than Romeo, now senses that he senses her. This puts Romeo in a

position to notice, and be aroused by, her arousal at being sensed by him. He senses that she senses that he senses her. This is still another level of arousal, for he becomes conscious of his sexuality through his awareness of its effect on her and of her awareness that this effect is due to him. Once she takes the same step and senses that he senses her sensing him, it becomes difficult to state, let alone imagine, further iterations, though they may be logically distinct. If both are alone, they will presumably turn to look at each other directly, and the proceedings will continue on another plane. Physical contact and intercourse are perfectly natural extensions of this complicated visual exchange, and mutual touch can involve all the complexities of awareness present in the visual case, but with a far greater range of subtlety and acuteness.

Ordinarily, of course, things happen in a less orderly fashion—sometimes in a great rush—but I believe that some version of this overlapping system of distinct sexual perceptions and interactions is the basic framework of any full-fledged sexual relation and that relations involving only part of the complex are significantly incomplete. The account is only schematic, as it must be to achieve generality. Every real sexual act will be psychologically far more specific and detailed, in ways that depend not only on the physical techniques employed and on anatomical details, but also on countless features of the participants' conceptions of themselves and of each other, which become embodied in the act. (It is a familiar enough fact, for example, that people often take their social roles and the social roles of their partners to bed with them.)

The general schema is important, however, and the proliferation of levels of mutual awareness it involves is an example of a type of complexity that typifies human interactions. Consider aggression, for example. If I am angry with someone, I want to make him feel it, either to produce self-reproach by getting him to see himself through the eyes of my anger, and to dislike what he sees—or else to produce reciprocal anger or fear, by getting him to perceive my anger as a threat or attack. What I want will depend on the details of my anger, but in either case it will involve a desire that the object of that anger be aroused. This accomplishment constitutes the fulfillment of my emotion, through domination of the object's feelings.

Another example of such reflexive mutual recognition is to be found in the phenomenon of meaning, which appears to involve an intention to produce a belief or other effect in another by bringing about his recognition of one's intention to produce that effect. (That result is due to H. P. Grice,[2] whose position I shall not attempt to reproduce in detail.) Sex has a related structure: it involves a desire that one's partner be aroused by the recognition of one's desire that he or she be aroused.

It is not easy to define the basic types of awareness and arousal of which these complexes are composed, and that remains a lacuna in this

[2] "Meaning," *Philosophical Review*, LXVI, 3 (July 1957): 377–388.

discussion. I believe that the object of awareness is the same in one's own case as it is in one's sexual awareness of another, although the two awarenesses will not be the same, the difference being as great as that between feeling angry and experiencing the anger of another. All stages of sexual perception are varieties of identification of a person with his body. What is perceived is one's own or another's *subjection* to or *immersion* in his body, a phenomenon which has been recognized with loathing by St. Paul and St. Augustine, both of whom regarded "the law of sin which is in my members" as a grave threat to the dominion of the holy will.[3] In sexual desire and its expression the blending of involuntary response with deliberate control is extremely important. For Augustine, the revolution launched against him by his body is symbolized by erection and the other involuntary physical components of arousal. Sartre too stresses the fact that the penis is not a prehensile organ. But mere involuntariness characterizes other bodily processes as well. In sexual desire the involuntary responses are combined with submission to spontaneous impulses: not only one's pulse and secretions but one's actions are taken over by the body; ideally, deliberate control is needed only to guide the expression of those impulses. This is to some extent also true of an appetite like hunger, but the takeover there is more localized, less pervasive, less extreme. One's whole body does not become saturated with hunger as it can with desire. But the most characteristic feature of a specifically sexual immersion in the body is its ability to fit into the complex of mutual perceptions that we have described. Hunger leads to spontaneous interactions with food; sexual desire leads to spontaneous interactions with other persons, whose bodies are asserting their sovereignty in the same way, producing involuntary reactions and spontaneous impulses in *them*. These reactions are perceived, and the perception of them is perceived, and that perception is in turn perceived; at each step the domination of the person by his body is reinforced, and the sexual partner becomes more possessible by physical contact, penetration, and envelopment.

Desire is therefore not merely the perception of a preexisting embodiment of the other, but ideally a contribution to his further embodiment which in turn enhances the original subject's sense of himself. This explains why it is important that the partner be aroused, and not merely aroused, but aroused by the awareness of one's desire. It also explains the sense in which desire has unity and possession as its object: physical possession must eventuate in creation of the sexual object in the image of one's desire, and not merely in the object's recognition of that desire, or in his or her own private arousal. (This may reveal a male bias: I shall say something about that later.)

To return, finally, to the topic of perversion: I believe that various deviations constitute truncated or incomplete versions of the complete

[3] See Romans, VII, 23; and the *Confessions*, Book 8, v.

configuration, and may therefore be regarded as perversions of the central impulse.

In particular, narcissistic practices and intercourse with animals, infants, and inanimate objects seem to be stuck at some primitive version of the first stage. If the object is not alive, the experience is reduced entirely to an awareness of one's own sexual embodiment. Small children and animals permit awareness of the embodiment of the other, but present obstacles to reciprocity, to the recognition by the sexual object of the subject's desire as the source of his (the object's) sexual self-awareness.

Sadism concentrates on the evocation of passive self-awareness in others, but the sadist's engagement is itself active and requires a retention of deliberate control which impedes awareness of himself as a bodily subject of passion in the required sense. The victim must recognize him as the source of his own sexual passivity, but only as the active source. De Sade claimed that the object of sexual desire was to evoke involuntary responses from one's partner, especially audible ones. The infliction of pain is no doubt the most efficient way to accomplish this, but it requires a certain abrogation of one's own exposed spontaneity. All this, incidentally, helps to explain why it is tempting to regard as sadistic an excessive preoccupation with sexual technique, which does not permit one to abandon the role of agent at any stage of the sexual act. Ideally one should be able to surmount one's technique at some point.

A masochist on the other hand imposes the same disability on his partner as the sadist imposes on himself. The masochist cannot find a satisfactory embodiment as the object of another's sexual desire, but only as the object of his control. He is passive not in relation to his partner's passion but in relation to his nonpassive agency. In addition, the subjection to one's body characteristic of pain and physical restraint is of a very different kind from that of sexual excitement: pain causes people to contract rather than dissolve.

Both of these disorders have to do with the second stage, which involves the awareness of oneself as an object of desire. In straightforward sadism and masochism other attentions are substituted for desire as a source of the object's self-awareness. But it is also possible for nothing of that sort to be substituted, as in the case of a masochist who is satisfied with self-inflicted pain or of a sadist who does not insist on playing a role in the suffering that arouses him. Greater difficulties of classification are presented by three other categories of sexual activity: elaborations of the sexual act; intercourse of more than two persons; and homosexuality.

If we apply our model to the various forms that may be taken by two-party heterosexual intercourse, none of them seem clearly to qualify as perversions. Hardly anyone can be found these days to inveigh against oral-genital contact, and the merits of buggery are urged by such respectable figures as D. H. Lawrence and Norman Mailer. There may be something vaguely sadistic about the latter technique (in Mailer's writings it seems to be a method of introducing an element of rape), but it is not obvious that this has to be so. In general, it would appear that any bodily contact between a man and a woman that gives them sexual pleasure, is a possible vehicle for the system of multi-level interpersonal awareness that I have claimed is the basic psychological content of sexual interaction. Thus a liberal platitude about sex is upheld.

About multiple combinations, the least that can be said is that they are bound to be complicated. If one considers how difficult it is to carry on two conversations simultaneously, one may appreciate the problems of multiple simultaneous interpersonal perception that can arise in even a small-scale orgy. It may be inevitable that some of the component relations should degenerate into mutual epidermal stimulation by participants otherwise isolated from each other. There may also be a tendency toward voyeurism and exhibitionism, both of which are incomplete relations. The exhibitionist wishes to display his desire without needing to be desired in return; he may even fear the sexual attentions of others. A voyeur, on the other hand, need not require any recognition by his object at all: certainly not a recognition of the voyeur's arousal.

It is not clear whether homosexuality is a perversion if that is measured by the standard of the described configuration, but it seems unlikely. For such a classification would have to depend on the possibility of extracting from the system a distinction between male and female sexuality; and much that has been said so far applies equally to men and women. Moreover, it would have to be maintained that there was a natural tie between the type of sexuality and the sex of the body, and also that two sexualities of the same type could not interact properly.

Certainly there is much support for an aggressive-passive distinction between male and female sexuality. In our culture the male's arousal tends to initiate the perceptual exchange, he usually makes the sexual approach, largely controls the course of the act, and of course penetrates whereas the woman receives. When two men or two women engage in intercourse they cannot both adhere to these sexual roles. The question is how essential the roles are to an adequate sexual relation. One relevant observation is that a good deal of deviation from these roles occurs in heterosexual intercourse. Women can be sexually aggressive and men passive, and temporary reversals of role are not uncommon in heterosexual exchanges of reasonable length. If such conditions are set aside, it may be urged that there is something irreducibly perverted in attraction to a body anatomically like one's own. But alarming as some people in our culture may find such attraction, it remains psychologically unilluminating to class it as perverted. Certainly if homosexuality is a perversion, it is so in a very different sense from that in which shoe-fetishism is a perversion, for some version of the full range of interpersonal perceptions seems perfectly possible between two persons of the same sex.

In any case, even if the proposed model is correct, it remains implausible to describe as perverted every deviation from it. For example, if the partners in heterosexual intercourse indulge in private heterosexual fantasies, that obscures the recognition of the real partner and so, on the theory, constitutes a defective sexual relation. It is not, however, generally regarded as a perversion. Such examples suggest that a simple dichotomy between perverted and unperverted sex is too crude to organize the phenomena adequately.

I should like to close with some remarks about the relation of perversion to good, bad, and morality. The concept of perversion can hardly fail to be evaluative in some sense, for it appears to involve the notion of an ideal or at least adequate sexuality which the perversions in some way fail to achieve. So, if the concept is viable, the judgment that a person or practice or desire is perverted will constitute a sexual evaluation, implying that better sex, or a better specimen of sex, is possible. This in itself is a very weak claim, since the evaluation might be in a dimension that is of little interest to us. (Though, if my account is correct, that will not be true.)

Whether it is a moral evaluation, however, is another question entirely —one whose answer would require more understanding of both morality and perversion than can be deployed here. Moral evaluation of acts and of persons is a rather special and very complicated matter, and by no means all our evaluations of persons and their activities are moral evaluations. We make judgments about people's beauty or health or intelligence which are evaluative without being moral. Assessments of their sexuality may be similar in that respect.

Furthermore, moral issues aside, it is not clear that unperverted sex is necessarily *preferable* to the perversions. It may be that sex which receives the highest marks for perfection *as sex* is less enjoyable than certain perversions; and if enjoyment is considered very important, that might outweigh considerations of sexual perfection in determining rational preference.

That raises the question of the relation between the evaluative content of judgments of perversion and the rather common *general* distinction between good and bad sex. The latter distinction is usually confined to sexual acts, and it would seem, within limits, to cut across the other: even someone who believed, for example, that homosexuality was a perversion could admit a distinction between better and worse homosexual sex, and might even allow that good homosexual sex could be better *sex* than not very good unperverted sex. If this is correct, it supports the position that, if judgments of perversion are viable at all, they represent only one aspect of the possible evaluation of sex, even *qua sex*. Moreover it is not the only important aspect: certainly sexual deficiencies that evidently do not constitute perversions can be the object of great concern.

Finally, even if perverted sex is to that extent not so good as it might be, bad sex is generally better than none at all. This should not be controversial: it seems to hold for other important matters, like food, music, literature, and society. In the end, one must choose from among the available alternatives, whether their availability depends on the environment or on one's own constitution. And the alternatives have to be fairly grim before it becomes rational to opt for nothing.

2

THE ABORTION QUESTION

REFERENCE POINTS IN DECIDING ABOUT ABORTION

Paul Ramsey

Paul Ramsey (1937–   ), Professor of Theology at Princeton University principally involved with questions of religion and ethics, including biomedical ethics. His publications include Basic Christian Ethics (1950), The Just War: Force and Political Responsibility (1968), Nine Modern Moralists (1962), Who Speaks for the Church (1967), and The Patient as Person (1970).

IMPLANTATION, SEGMENTATION, AND THE GENOTYPE

If we are to ask when a new life has a sanctity that claims protection, and if scientific findings have anything to do with the answer to that question, we must ponder four different possibilities of such a beginning: the moment of origin of the genotype, the time of implantation, the time of segmentation, and the development of the fetus in the first 4-8 weeks. Compared to any one of these determinations, the difference made by capacities later discernible in the fetus, by its quickening or by birth, would seem to be lesser disjunctions in the total course of the transmission of life disclosed to us by modern knowledge. These latter, common-sense tests are as crude or gross determinations, even if not as speculative, as the Mediterranean world's old measure of forty and eighty days.

One could say that human life begins with the implantation of the fertilized egg in the uterus seven or eight days after ovulation. Such a definition is a questionable apology for the "morning after" pill now being experimentally developed. Embracing this view, Gregory Pincus, who with John Rock developed the antiovulant pill, declared that "the new pill is not an abortifacient."[1] The basis for the theoretical assertion that life begins with implantation is the merely practical consideration that the "union of sperm and ovum cannot be detected clinically unless implantation occurs." If this is the case, one might correctly draw the conclusion that a scientist's clinical knowledge that life has started begins with implantation. We could say that *pregnancy* begins with implantation, if to say this is not a redundancy. However, to declare categorically that new life begins with implantation is to make oneself by definition ignorant of the first six or seven days. This proposal can only be set down as self-serving. As a layman, I can only express surprise if it is a statement of scientific fact that fertilized ova before implantation have not been "clinically detected."[2] Such a working definition of the origin of life can only mean: our knowledge that implanted life has begun can only begin with implantation.

The segmentation of the sphere of developing cells in the case of identical twins (who have the same genotype) is entitatively distinct from implantation as a process, though this is completed at about the same time as implantation. A "primitive streak" across the hollow cluster of developing cells (the blastocyst) signals the separation of the same genotype into identical twins. This occurs by about the time of implantation, that is, on the seventh or eighth day after ovulation. It might be asserted that it is at the time of segmentation, not earlier, that life comes to be the individual human being it is ever thereafter to be. The religious word for that process would be to say that then germinating matter becomes "animate," or is informed by, or constituted, a unique human "soul."

There is a species of biological life close to us in evolution, though not in gross physical form, whose reproduction takes place in every case by, so to speak, quadruple identical "twins." Each individual of the species armadillo has the same genotype with three others arising from segmentation. Let us imagine that, similarly, every case of human reproduction resulted in identical twins. Then I suggest that, upon acquiring our modern knowledge of segmentation explaining this phenomenon, the minds of men would be strongly drawn to locate at that point, and not

---

[1] Lawrence Lader, "There Men Who Made A Revolution," in the *New York Times Magazine*, April 10, 1966, p. 8, at p. 55. On this Dr. Rock disagrees with his colleague.

[2] Dr. John Rock's report of the experiments carried out at the Free Hospital for Women in Brookline, Mass., from 1938 to 1954 seems plainly to assert that fertilized ova were secured from "a two-day, two-cell egg to a 17-day ovum already implanted in the uterus" (*The Time Has Come*, New York: Alfred A. Knopf, 1963, pp. 184–185).

earlier or later, the first origins of nascent individual human life that places upon us the claims we may acknowledge to be due to any individual of our kind. If there is a moment in the development of these nascent lives of ours subsequent to fertilization and prior to birth (or graduation from college) at which it would be reasonable to believe that an individual human life begins and therefore begins to be inviolate, that moment is arguably at the stage when segmentation may or may not take place.

The argument from genotype is, to say the least, a remarkable one. The unique, never-to-be-repeated individual human being comes into existence first as a minute informational speck, and this speck has been drawn at random from still more minute informational specks his parents possessed out of the common human gene pool. Arguably, he began to be at the moment of impregnation. There was a virtually unimaginable number of combinations of the specks on his paternal and maternal chromosomes that did not come to be when these were refused and he began his life. No one else (with the single exception of an identical twin if segmentation happens seven days later) in the entire history of the human race has ever had or ever will have exactly the same genotype. Thus it might be said that in all essential respects the individual is whoever he is going to become from the moment of impregnation. He already is this while not knowing this or anything else. Thereafter, his subsequent development cannot be described as his becoming someone he now is not. It can only be described as a process of achieving, a process of becoming the one he already is. Genetics teaches that we were from the beginning what we essentially still are in every cell and in every generally human attribute and in every individual attribute. There are formal principles constituting us from the beginning. Thus genetics seems to have provided an approximation to the religious belief that there is a soul animating and forming a man's bodily being from the very beginning. That far, theological speculation never dared to go with theoretical certainty.

What is this but to say that we are all fellow fetuses? From impregnation to the tomb ours is a nascent and a dying life; we are bound together as congeners from our Mendelian beginnings. Any unique sanctity or dignity we may have cannot be because we are any larger than the period at the end of a sentence. Although we know only in the light of our particular span of conscious existence, this light and that darkness from which we came and toward which we go are both alike to the One who laid his hand upon us, covered us in the womb, and by whom we were fearfully and wonderfully made. We will never be anything more or anything other than the beings we always were in every cell and attribute.

In a remarkable way, modern genetics seems to teach—with greater precision and assurance than theology could ever muster—that there are "formal causes," immanent principles or constitutive elements long before there is any shape or motion of discernible size or subjective consciousness or rationality in a human being—not merely potency for these things that later supervene, but in some sense the present, operative actuality of these powers and characteristics. These minute formal elements are already determining the organic life to be not only generally "human" but also *the* unique *individual* human being it is to be. It is now not unreasonable to assert, for the first time in the history of scientific speculation upon this question, that who one is and is ever going to be came about at the moment an ovum was impregnated.

The teachings of genetics here is about as close as science is likely to come to the doctrine of creation ex nihilo. This doctrine affirms the radical contingency of the whole created world; the world need not have been or might have been wholly otherwise. Such also, genetics seems to tell us, is the nature of that lottery by which any human creature comes to be. There were no compelling reasons, no substance simply emanating or drawn forth by necessary laws from generation to generation, no causal predetermination requiring or even making for the conception of this particular individual and not one of a myriad other possibilities. It is true, of course, that once a unique combination of informational specks comes to be science can then give an account of him as an understandable resultant of the genes of his maternal and paternal chromosomes. Genetic clinics can unfold the pre-existent factors in laws of probability; but none of these factors reaches the individual who is actualized. There can never be an account of why *he* had to be the who and what he is rather than some other individual being. In this sense, *he* was procreated "out of nothing."

So generally with the doctrine of creation ex nihilo. Any creature or the whole creation might have been quite otherwise, or might not have been and some other creation have been instead. The creation did not emanate from the divine substance, nor can we ask what necessity the recalcitrance of pre-existing matter imposed on the Creator. If either of these world views were tenable, it would be theoretically possible to forecast the nature of the creature. To the contrary, creation ex nihilo means that if one wants to know who or what the creature is, one must look to see. This doctrine was a main source of the empiricism of science in the western world; it placed upon man's way of knowing a requirement stemming from the radical contingency of the entire creation, from the fact that nothing about creation could be deduced from anything.

So with regard to the individual human being. He cannot be predictably "traduced" out from the being of his mother and father. There is no necessity, rational or nonrational, why as a particular individual he should be; nor is there any prior propensity toward his emanation from among myriad possibilities. *That* he is may be explained scientifically or romantically, but not why he is this particular one and not one of those many, many others who might have been. Once he, that is, his genotype, *is* and once his individual "determiners" *are* in the land of the living, a sort of explanation can be proffered by specifying the genes. Still there is no explaining why he who has these characteristics and not someone else having another set of characteristics came to be. There is no explaining why he who was conceived on the particular occasion has these characteristics and not others that might just as well have been. This is the nature of our strange passage from being only a gleam in one father's eye or only an informational genetic possibility; from this nonbeing we became the actuality of the genotype each of us is for the entirety of nascent and conscious life. Some call this process the genetic "lottery." Others call it *procreation*, the transmission of life by a mechanism that serves as the occasion upon which from things that are not God calls into being the things that are.

IMPLANTATION AND THE
DEVELOPMENT OF THE FETUS

Given our present knowledge of reproductive biology, there is also some evidence to support us if we take the development of the fetus, as distinct from the activity of implantation, to be the span of time in which there comes to be a human being in the womb. The signal stages in the development of the fetus take place, as we shall see, quite early. Development of the fetus is entitatively distinct from the blastocyst's activity in implanting itself in the wall of the uterus. Both lines of development, both capacities—to implant and to grow into the fetus—were contained, it can reasonably be argued, in the mere "outline" of the person or the "formal principles" contained in the genotype and in the sphere or spheres of cells. A moral "argument" based on the signal importance of the early development of the fetus, is, therefore, a kind of rebuttal of the arguments from genotype or from the time of identical twinning which we have reviewed.

This is a strong argument precisely because of the separation between the activity of implantation and the activity of development of the fetus, both of which are activities of the new life (of the blastocyst) and not of the mother-to-be. After six or seven days of cell division in the tube, if all goes well the sphere of cells enters the uterus. The blastocyst buries itself in the wall of the uterus like a parasite. More now begins to take place than the cell's single-minded self-reproduction and differentiation into the organic life to come. A "beachhead" must first be secured in this new environment. That now is crucial. The uterus alone is no place to live; and, without the preparation of a separate "system" within which the new life can live for the next nine months, the self-reproductive power of the cells and their destiny to become the differentiated organs of a human being could not proceed. If the activity of both poles of the sphere of cells proceed simultaneously, one of these—implantation—is now fundamental to the success of the other: further embryonic development. It has to be stressed that it is the sphere of cells that accomplishes both tasks, not the mother. The original "outline" contained a determination toward the execution of the task of implantation, the growth of the placental system and amniotic sac, and not solely a determination toward the human being (the fetus) in the womb and beyond.

One pole of the sphere of cells, called the trophoblast, burrows its way into the lining of the uterus.[3] This pole is later to become the placenta, which, it is important to emphasize, is a fetal and not a maternal system for sustaining the life of the fetus. The opposite pole becomes the embryo, then the fetus. In other words, the sphere of cells (the blastocyst that has grown by division of cells having the same, original genotype) now devotes some of its foreordained cellular powers to throwing out a lifeline by which it can be attached to the life of the mother. Having made the catch, the system in which the fetus is to live must then be developed in a remarkable way. This activity of implantation and development of the placenta, it can reasonably be argued, and not only the development of the fetus, was contained in the directions the original cells contained. Thus it could be argued that "the person in the womb" (I would prefer to say, the human being in the womb, who later becomes personal) comes to be with the early development of the fetus following or entitatively distinct from the blastocyst's activity in implantation. In terms of development, the fetus is more than genotype or blastocyst. Yet in a sense it is less, because implantation and placenta sprang also from the original cells.

The sphere of cells can throw out its lifeline, in rare cases, in the tubes or, in rarer cases, in the abdominal cavity. The mother's uterus is simply the appropriate place for its activity of nidation or "nesting," where the fetal blood system can be connected with that of the mother and there is room for 9 months' fetal growth. The placental system and amniotic sac are *not* to be compared with the rope that links two mountain climbers together. The rope "belongs" to both those lives. But the placental system and amniotic bag "belongs" to the unborn child. This, I suppose, is the reason that the procedure of amniocentesis, that is, taking a sample from the amniotic sac, discloses to a medical investigator information about the genetic make-up or chromosomal difficulties of the unborn child, rather than those of the mother.

[3] For the following account of fetal development, except for footnoted references and for some of the references, I draw upon a paper by Dr. André Hellegers, "Fetal Development," prepared for the Conference on Abortion sponsored by the Harvard Divinity School in cooperation with the Joseph P. Kennedy, Jr., Foundation at the Washington Hilton Hotel, Washington, D.C., Sept. 5–8, 1967. Dr. Hellegers' paper has also been published in *Theological Studies* (March 1970).

At the time one side of the sphere "nests" or implants, it may have become a hollow mass of several hundred cells. The decision whether there is to be one or two or more individuals (segmentation) may still be somewhat uncertain. In any case, shelter and supply lines come first. The trophoblast burrows into the lining of the upper wall of the uterus, creating for itself a small nutritive bath of blood and broken cells for its immediately future needs. The part of the sphere of cells later to become the placenta also produces hormones. These hormones enter the mother's blood system and serve the critical function of preventing menstruation. The time interval from ovulation to menstruation is approximately 14 days, and the developing cells have already been alive 7 days in the tubes. Therefore, the implanting trophoblast has only about 7 days to produce enough hormones to stop the mother from menstruating. Otherwise, the new life will be flushed out. (These hormones are also the basis for chemical tests determining pregnancy.)

The patch of cells buried in the uterine wall has work to do which it is difficult to follow. There apparently takes place a branching, finger-like process growing larger and more numerous, to create the whole mechanism of support and sustenance (the placenta, a rather large organ) that will take care of the nutritional and chemical needs of embryo and fetus by drawing upon the mother "until birth do them part." The placenta "acts aggressively toward the tissues of the mother, takes what it needs and on the whole only what it needs, and passes out to the mother's system whatever products of its own that can be considered waste."[4] Thus the navel which is supposed to be an external mark of the dependence of everyone since Adam and Eve is actually a sign of an independent and entitatively distinct activity of the germinating cells. Such also is the barrier between the mother's blood and nutritional system and the fetal blood system which the original implanting patch of cells has created around the developing embryo. "These appurtenances," whose design came from the cells everyone was from conception, to be discarded later as the afterbirth, are "as truly a part of each of us as were our milk teeth."[5]

Meantime, back at the patch of cells at the opposite pole from the burrowing, hormone-producing, placenta-forming trophoblast, another line of development takes place. At the end of the second week, the patch of cells that protrudes into the uterine cavity is no longer spherical; it has stretched along one axis and has ends and sides. This aspect of the blastocyst or original sphere is now called the "embryonic plate."

At the end of the third or fourth week following fertilization (or the second or third week after implantation), when the woman begins to wonder whether she is pregnant, the *embryo* is said to be present. This is an exceedingly crucial stage in development. While the embryo is only an

[4] N. J. Berrill, *The Person in the Womb* (New York: Dodd, Mead & Co., 1968), pp. 42, 43.
[5] *Ibid.*, p. 44.

elongated mass about one-third of an inch long, scientists can recognize more. "All the most important decisions and events have been made by the end of the first month."[6] There is a head, rudimentary eyes, ears and brain, a body with digestive tract, heart and bloodstream, simple kidneys and liver, two pairs of bulges where future arms and legs will grow. The differentiation is sufficient for heart pumping to occur,[7] although the human heart reaches its final four-chamber configuration later on.

Certainly by the end of six weeks all the internal organs are present in rudimentary formation. At the end of seven weeks the fetus will flex its neck if tickled on the nose. After eight weeks the embryo ceases to be called an embryo and becomes known as a fetus, to emphasize the completion of an important phase of its existence. After the end of eight weeks there is growth, not crucial development, yet to take place, although the fetus is only one inch in length. Here at eight weeks there is readable electrical activity coming from the fetal brain.[8] Fingers and toes are now recognizable. "By the end of the second month, therefore, we can say with some assurance that the person in the womb is present, with all the basic equipment and some sensitivity, although with a long, long way to go to be fully human."[9]

By the end of the ninth or tenth week the child has local reflexes such as swallowing, squinting, and movement of the tongue. By the tenth week he is capable of spontaneous movement, without any outside stimulation. By the eleventh week thumb sucking has been observed. After twelve weeks brain structure is complete, although the fetus is only 3½ inches long, and growth of structure and organs (including the brain) will continue. By twelve weeks, also, a fetal heartbeat has been monitored by modern electrocardiographic techniques, via the mother.

Between the 12th and 16th weeks, "quickening" will occur. This means that fetal movements are felt by the mother—an event long considered important in human sentiment and in law. "Quickening," however, "is a phenomenon of maternal perception rather than a fetal achievement."[10] The child quickens or is the source of its own motion two weeks or more earlier, at ten weeks.

Between the 18th and 20th week it is possible to hear the fetal heart by simple stethoscope, not by refined ECG.

A delivery before the 20th week is called an *abortion*; after this date it will be called a *premature delivery* in medical terminology, since a fetus one pound or more in weight and from 20 to 28 weeks of gestational life

[6] Berrill, *The Person in the Womb*, p. 45.

[7] J. W. C. Johnson, "Cardio-Respiratory Systems," *Intrauterine Development*, ed. A. C. Barnes (Philadelphia: Lea and Febiger, 1968).

[8] D. Goldblatt, "Nervous System and Sensory Organs," *Intrauterine Development*, ed. A. C. Barnes (Philadelphia: Lea and Febiger, 1968).

[9] Berrill, *The Person in the Womb*, pp. 45–46. "We are all there in every important way" (p. 51).

[10] Hellegers, "Fetal Development."

has 10 percent chance of survival. The dividing line in former days was 28 weeks. However, *current* possible "viability" determines for medical practice (though often not for the law) the distinction between an abortus and a premature infant. Later on, we shall return to the significance for the morality of abortion of the fact that "viability" is bound in the future to be pushed further back in the development of the fetus which we have sketched. The difference between an abortus and a premature infant is a phenomenon of medical achievement and not of medicine's perception of the fetus' actual development. The law also lags behind medicine in that a certificate of death is required for an abortus or a miscarriage only at 20 weeks and after; before that the abortus can be treated as a pathological specimen. Since 10 percent viability now begins at this point, this could mean the erasure of a class of *infants* born dead or quite nonviable. At the same time, this lag may account for a pedagogy in the law toward justifying abortion as late as 20 weeks, that is, on the border of viability, because before that the fetus is only a pathological specimen.

Albert Rosenfeld, science writer for *Life* magazine, reports that "Many readers of *Life* who saw Lennart Nilsson's marvelous photographs of fetuses in their sacs, especially in the later stages of development, wrote in to say that they could never again think of their *babies* as disposable *things*. Such sentiment might well increase as fetuses become visible from the outset. And if the day of conception were to become a person's official birth date, then the act of aborting a fetus would be ending a baby of a given age."[11] Good morality, however, ought not to depend on "visual aids." Ethical judgments are not constructed out of sentiment or emotions or feelings of identification stimulated by pictures. The latter, of course, and a sympathetic imagination grasping the facts of fetal development which we have reviewed, help to sustain in us an appropriate respect for human life hitherto hidden from view. Doubtless it is our fellow-feeling and identification with children that accounts for the fact that people generally tend to *perceive* that human life begins at birth.

Ethics, however, is based on the nature of things and not on heightened imagination or feelings, however important these may be in strengthening moral behavior. Medical science knows the babies to be present in all essential respects earlier in fetal development than the women who wrote in to *Life* magazine perceived them in the pictures. It is the rational account of the nature of fetal development that matters most.

We have, then, three stages at which it is reasonable to believe that human life begins: conception, when the unique genotype originates; segmentation, or when it is irreversibly settled whether there will be one, two, or more individuals; and the early development of the fetus when

11 *The Second Genesis: The Coming Control of Life* (Englewood Cliffs, N.J.: Prentice-Hall, 1969), pp. 125–126. Nilsson's photographs were published in *Life*, April 30, 1965; and are reprinted in *The Terrible Choice: The Abortion Dilemma* (Bantam Books, 1968).

the "outline" the cells contained is actualized in all essential respects, with only growth to come. By comparison, with the achievements already made by the unborn life, quickening refers to no change and birth to less significant change in the human life that is present in the womb. By "When does human life begin?" we, of course, mean to ask and possibly to answer this question in the medical-ethical context and not in the evolutionary context of the continuity of three billion years. We mean to ask and possibly to answer the question, When is there human life deserving respect and protection like any other? The fact that nascent life is minute and vulnerable and "incapable of independent existence" does not matter in determining its worth. Certainly, a religious ethics will have special regard for the near-neighbor beneath a woman's heart and the distant-neighbor in foreign lands, for the alien resident or sojourner in the womb no less than for the alien resident or sojourner in the land of Israel—for we know the heart of the stranger, the weak and the vulnerable, and God's special redemptive care for every one of us in like circumstances. As Professor Ralph Potter of the Harvard Divinity School has written, "The fetus symbolizes you and me and our tenuous hold upon a future here at the mercy of our fellow men."[12]

Anyone who seeks a clearer or better place to light upon in answering the question, When in nascent life is there a right of life in exercise? than genotype (conception), segmentation, or the early stages of fetal development will have to wait for the development of personal self-consciousness. That would be at about age one in an infant's life, when it begins to exercise the power of speech; before that, an infant is likely only potentially human by the standard of self-awareness or incipient rationality. Indeed, there is scientific confirmation of such a choice, in the fact that at about this time *full* cortical brain activity is achieved, as evidenced by the appearance of *rhythmical* markings on an electroencephalogram. Otherwise, brain and heart activity as signs of life have been evident long before birth.

These and other indices of life (except for autonomous breathing) are all present in the morphologically human, the organically complete and interrelatedly functioning fetus in its early development. Only the growth of what the individual already is, plus breathing on its own, locomotion by crawling and by walking upright, and the final completion of cortical brain activity (at about age one) are yet to come. Every one of these achievements, indeed, may be described better as further growth, not as additional stages in development.

One may remark in passing upon the oddity of an age in which we are elevating the importance of evidences of brain activity and rejecting the singular significance of heart or lung activity when we are dealing with men in the last of life, while we seem willing to settle every question

12 "The Abortion Debate," *The Religious Situation* 1968, ed. Dwight Culver (Boston: Beacon Press, 1968), p. 157.

of their moral claims upon our common humanity in the continuum of life's first beginnings by reference solely to the start of spontaneous respiration which a physician evoked from every one of us (or inflicted upon us) in the birthroom, taking little or no account of the early evidence of heartbeat and brain activity in the unborn child.[13] The "breath of life" is today taken to be the sole evidence that a woman has a child or that a man and a woman have become parents, while the "breath of life" is more and more minimized among the tests for whether that same child grown-up and now terminal is still alive. A proper comment upon this must be that we can indulge in many a sophisticated inconsistency if we too quickly address ourselves to the solution of the serious social problem of abortion, without an adequate concept of what the life is that claims respect and protection that can cohere with our notion of what the death is that brings these claims to an end.

To conclude this section, the timetable for the important stages in fetal development, given above, should be compared with the time limits suggested in the Model Abortion Law Reform Bill, and with the time limits in the legislation that has been passed by several of the states and proposed in many others. At most it may be said that the Model Penal Code proposed by the draftsmen of the American Law Institute "suggested" a time limit, by the mention of *twenty-six weeks* in its definition of "unjustified abortion" in sec. 230.3(1): "A person who purposely and unjustifiably terminates the pregnancy of another otherwise than by a live birth commits a felony of the third degree or, where the pregnancy has continued beyond the twenty-sixth week, a felony of the second degree." When the Commissioners came to the definition of "justifiable abortion," however, nothing was said about the time abortion could rightfully be performed. Only the "indications" were specified, in sec. 230.3(2): "A licenced physician is justified in terminating a pregnancy if he believes there is substantial risk that continuation of the pregnancy would gravely impair the physical and mental health of the mother or that the child would be born with grave physical or mental defect, or that the pregnancy resulted from rape, incest, or other felonious intercourse." On one interpretation, the Commissioners may have wanted abortion upon these approved indications to be open-ended as to time.

On another interpretation, however, they may have meant to leave it to the state legislatures to determine the time limits upon the abortions to be justified for these reasons. In fact this is what has happened. The California law, for example, stipulates a sliding scale of acceptability, by stating that the abortions must be performed in the first 12 weeks, by

---

[13] In an article by Dr. Hannibal Hamlin of Boston, notably entitled "Life or Death by EEG," one finds the following significant description of the EEG of an unborn child: "The intra-uterine fetal brain responds to biochemical changes associated with oxygen deprivation by abnormal EEG activity similar to that produced in the adult brain. Thus at an early prenatal stage of life, the EEG reflects *a distinctly individual pattern that soon becomes truly personalized.*"

requiring that between 12 and 20 weeks an abortion must receive the *unanimous* approval of a committee of at least three doctors, and that no abortion can be legally done after 20 weeks. Of several bills Assemblyman Albert H. Blumenthal has introduced in New York, the first required that no more than 24 weeks have passed since conception; to meet criticism this was lowered to 20 weeks; then raised again to 24.

At this point the reader may compare these times with the account of fetal development given above. There we saw that heart pumping starts by the end of 4 weeks; there is readable electrical activity in the fetal brain at 8 weeks and all essential organic formations; the fetus is capable of spontaneous movement at 10 weeks; heart beat can be monitored via the mother at 12 weeks; "quickening" may occur to the mother's perception between the 12th and 16th week; and the heart beat can be heard by stethoscope between the 16th and the 20th.

Fetal development might lend some support to limiting permissible abortion to 8 weeks—at most, perhaps 10 weeks—of gestational life. No such laws have been proposed.[14] Why?

Searching for an explanation of this strange discrepancy, we must simply conclude that the proposed liberalization of abortion law is in no way based rationally on concern for the fetus and the nature of its development. The proposed laws are rather statements about the mother, or based upon the assumed safety of the operation upon her.

Some scientists may have an interest in obtaining later abortuses for research purposes. Some medical practitioners may have an interest in doing abortion for the sake of the fetus if its impairment is discoverable only late in pregnancy. Still the earlier time limits are the ones realistically to consider. The time limits that are being enacted have, as we have seen, no basis in the nature of fetal development nor in the current alternative methods of performing an abortion. These limits are based on the danger to the woman of one method only—curettage—and, of course, on the general psychological and emotional desirability of early abortion, if this is to be done.

Finally, the time limits being enacted are quite unenforceable. On the most optimistic expectation, one more month of fetal development must be added to them. A physician may easily mistake by one month the length of the pregnancy. In statistically improbable numbers doctors record that women report that they last menstruated on the fifteenth of the month. In about 20 percent of women, bleeding occurs prior to the 20th week of pregnancy; and this bleeding may be mistaken for the last menstrual period although the woman was pregnant before the bleeding

14 *The Christian Science Monitor* reported on July 22, 1969, a poll of 5,000 British doctors showed that nearly two-thirds of them wanted the Abortion Law modified or repealed. The modifications would allow *no abortions after 12 weeks' gestation*, and provide that the "social grounds"—certainly not a medical matter—be assessed by local committees or authorities.

episode. Where a physician errs by one month in estimating the age of the fetus, the baby is exceedingly likely to die of pulmonary insufficiency if born prematurely.

Therefore, the reader may want to compare the time limits upon legalized abortion in any statute or proposed legislation *plus one month* with the timetable of important stages in fetal development, given above.[15] This he will do if he believes that morality should be rationally based on the nature of things and if he believes that morality has anything to do with the laws he should favor in the matter of abortion.

[15] As to the laws being enacted, see David W. Louisell and John T. Noonan, Jr., "Constitutional Balance," sec. III, *infra*.

A LIBERAL CATHOLIC'S VIEW

Joseph F. Donceel

J. F. Donceel (1906–   ), Roman Catholic priest who is a member of the Society of Jesus; he is currently Professor of Philosophy at Fordham University. Donceel's publications include Philosophical Psychology *(1955, 1961) and* Elements of Natural Theology *(1962). He is cofounder and coordinating editor of the* International Philosophic Quarterly, *which provides a forum for the interchange of philosophic ideas between Europe and the Americas and between East and West.*

I fully agree with the basic Catholic principle that we are never allowed to kill an innocent human being. Therefore, if there is a real human being from the moment of conception, abortion would have to be considered immoral at any stage of pregnancy. The majority Catholic opinion holds nowadays that there is indeed a real human being from the first moment of conception, or, at least, that we cannot be certain that such is not the case. But there is also a minority Catholic opinion, which has good standing in the church, which was the opinion of her greatest theologian, Thomas Aquinas,[1] and which is now slowly regaining favor among Catholic thinkers. This minority opinion holds that there is certainly no human being during the early stages of pregnancy. I would like to show you briefly why Thomas held this position, how it was given up by his successors on account of erroneous scientific theories, and how, even after these theories had been given up, the Catholic church did not return to her traditional view because of a philosophy which was at variance with her official doctrine of the nature of man.

Traditional Catholic philosophy holds that what makes an organism a human being is the spiritual soul and that this soul starts to exist at the moment of its "infusion" into the body. When is the human soul infused into the body? Nowadays the majority of Catholic thinkers would not hesitate to answer: at the moment of conception. This is known as the *theory of immediate animation.* However, during long centuries Catholic

---

[1] See *Summa contra Gentiles,* II, 88–89; *De Potentia,* Q. 3, Art. 9–12; *Summa Theologica,* I, Q. 118, Art. 1–3.

philosophy and theology held that the human soul was infused into the
body only when the latter began to show a human shape or outline and
possessed the basic human organs. Before this time, the embryo is alive,
but in the way in which a plant or an animal is alive. It possesses, as the
traditional terminology puts it, a vegetative or an animal soul, not yet a
human soul. In more modern terms we might say that it has reached the
physiological or the psychological, not yet the spiritual level of existence.
It is not yet a human person; it is evolving, within the womb, toward
hominization. This is the *theory of mediate or delayed animation*.

Why did Thomas and the great medieval thinkers favor this theory?
Because they held the doctrine of hylomorphism, according to which the
human soul is the substantial form of man, while the human body is the
result of the union of this soul with materiality, with undetermined cosmic
stuff, with what was then known as prime matter. Hylomorphism holds
that the human soul is to the body somewhat as the shape of a statue is
to the actual statue. The shape of a statue cannot exist before the statue
exists. It is not something which the sculptor first makes and subsequently
introduces into a block of marble. It can exist only in the completed
statue. Hylomorphism holds that, in the same way, the human soul can
exist only in a real human body.

Although Thomas knew nothing about chromosomes, genes, DNA, or
the code of life, he knew that whatever was growing in the mother's womb
was not yet, early in pregnancy, a real human body. Therefore he held that
it could not be animated by a human soul, any more than a square block
of marble can possess a human shape. The medieval thinkers knew very
well that this growing organism would develop into a human body, that
virtually, potentially, it was a human body. But they did not admit that
an actual human soul could exist in a virtual human body. The Catholic
church, which had officially adopted the hylomorphic conception of
human nature at the Council of Vienne, in 1312, was so strongly convinced of this position that, for centuries, her law forbade the faithful to
baptize any premature birth which did not show at least some human
shape or outline.

Under the influence of erroneous scientific reports, however, Catholic
thinkers gave up this traditional doctrine. In the early seventeenth century, as
a result of a combination of poor microscopes and lively imaginations, some
physicians saw in embryos which were only a few days old a tiny human
being, a homunculus, with microscopic head, legs, and arms.[2] This view of
the fetus implied the *preformation theory*, which held that organic development simply consists of the gradual increase in size of organs and
structures which are fully present from the very start. If there really were
from the beginning a human body, be it ever so small, there might also

[2] See H. de Dorlodot, "A Vindication of the Mediate Animation Theory," in E. C.
Messenger (ed.), *Theology and Evolution*, pp. 273–83, London, 1949.

from the start exist a human soul. Even a microscopic statue must have a shape. Granted the preformation theory, immediate animation was compatible with the hylomorphic conception of man.

The theory of preformation was eventually replaced by the *theory of epigenesis,* which maintains that the organism, far from being microscopically preformed from the start, develops its organs through a complex process of growth, cleavage, differentiation, and organization.

Why did the Christian thinkers not return to the delayed animation theory, which seems to be demanded by their hylomorphic theory of man? The main reason seems to have been the influence of Cartesian dualism. For Descartes, both man's soul and his body are each a complete substance. The soul is a thinking substance, the body an extended substance. This is no longer hylomorphism. To express it in nontechnical language, this is no longer a "shape in the statue" conception, but rather a "ghost in the machine" conception of the human soul. A full-fledged ghost can manage very well with a microscopic machine. If the soul is no longer the formal cause, the constitutive idea of the body, it might well become its efficient cause, that which produces the ovum's development from the start. Instead of being the idea incarnated in the body, it has turned into the architect and the builder of the body. Just as the architect exists before the first stone of the building is laid, so there can be a real human soul from the first moment of conception, before the emergence of a real human body.[3]

This way of explaining embryogeny is not absurd. The Cartesian outlook, although quite unfashionable nowadays, has been held by many great thinkers. This kind of philosophy calls for immediate animation, which is clearly in conflict with the hylomorphic doctrine of man, solemnly endorsed by the Catholic church at the Council of Vienne.

There have been other influences which explain the shift in Catholic opinion. One of them may have been the long-standing opposition of the church to the idea of evolution. Thomas admitted some kind of evolution of the embryo and the fetus in the mother's womb. How could the church admit this evolution in the womb and reject it in the race? Since the Catholic church has finally come around to admitting the evolution of the human body, it might also be willing to return to Thomas's idea of evolution in the womb.[4]

[3] The anonymous author of an article in Latin, "De Animatione Foetus" (*Nouvelle Revue Théologique,* 11:163–86, 268–89 [1879]), quotes a certain Michael Alberti Germaniae Medicus, who wrote in 1725 "quod a primis conceptionis initiis anima rationalis in foetu adsit, eo quod sine anima illa conceptio fieri nequeat, quae tanquam artifex et architecta sui corporis praesto est; a qua deinde actus formationis dependet" (that the rational soul is present in the fetus from the first beginnings of conception, because the conception cannot take place without this soul, which is there *like the maker and the architect of its body;* hence the act of formation depends on it) (my italics). This sounds like pure Cartesianism.
[4] "For the evolutionistic way of thinking it is more probable that hominization occurs not at the moment of conception, but at a later time of embryonic development,"

Moreover, once we give up the idea of immediate animation, we can no longer say when the human soul is infused, when the embryo or the fetus becomes a human person. That is why those who want to play it absolutely safe claim that the human soul is present from the moment of conception. They seem to take it for granted that, since we do not know when the human soul is present, we neither can know for sure when it is not yet present. This assumption is false. Let us consider another case, where we do not know when a certain factor is present, while knowing very well when it is not yet present. Nobody can tell with certitude when a child is capable of performing his first free moral choice, but all of us are quite certain that, during the first months or years of his life, a human baby is not yet a free moral agent. Likewise, I do not know when the human soul is infused, when the embryo becomes human. But I feel certain that there is no human soul, hence no human person, during the first few weeks of pregnancy, as long as the embryo remains in the vegetative stage of its development.

Some people make much of the following objection to my position. They say that from the very first the fertilized ovum possesses forty-six human chromosomes, all the human genes, its code of life—that it is a human embryo. This is undeniable. But it does not make it a human person. When a heart is transplanted, it is kept alive, for a short while, outside of the donor. It is a living being, a human heart, with the human chromosomes and genes. But it is not a human being; it is not a person.

The objection may be pressed. Not only does the fertilized human ovum possess the human chromosomes; unlike the heart, it will, if circumstances are normal, develop into a human being. It is virtually a human being. I admit this, but it does not affect my position. The fertilized human ovum, the early embryo, is virtually a human body, not actually. Correctly understood, the hylomorphic conception of human nature, the official Catholic doctrine, cannot admit the presence of an actual human soul in a virtual human body. Let me use a comparison again. A deflated rubber ball is virtually round; when inflated, it can assume no other shape than the spherical shape. Yet it does not actually possess any roundness or sphericity. In the same way, the early embryo does not actually possess a human soul; it is not a human person.

Experimental embryology tells us that every single cell of the early embryo, of the morula, is virtually a human body. It does not follow that each of these cells possesses a human soul. When embryologists carefully separate the cells of a morula in lower organisms, each one of these cells may develop into a complete organism. Starting with the pioneering attempts of Hans Driesch, such an experiment has been performed on many animal species. We do not see why it might not eventually succeed with

---

writes J. Feiner in the most recent comprehensive treatise of dogmatic theology, *Mysterium Fidei*, edited by J. Feiner and M. Löhrer, vol. II, p. 581, Einsiedeln, 1967.

the human embryo. As a matter of fact, nature frequently performs it on human ova. Identical twins derive from one ovum fertilized by one spermatozoon. This ovum splits into two at an early stage of pregnancy and gives rise to two human beings. In this case the defenders of immediate animation must admit that one person may be divided into two persons. This is a metaphysical impossibility.

Throughout my exposition I have taken for granted the hylomorphic conception of human nature. This is in line with the purpose of my essay, which is not only to present a liberal Catholic's view of fetal animation, but also to show that this view seems to be the only one which agrees with the official Catholic conception of human nature. In other words, I submit that Catholics should give up the immediate animation theory, because it implies a Cartesian, dualistic conception of man, which conflicts with the doctrine endorsed by the Council of Vienne.

In conclusion I would like to say a few words about the standing of hylomorphism among contemporary philosophers. Very few non-Catholic philosophers hold the doctrine of hylomorphism today. Even among Catholics it has fallen into disrepute, although personally I cannot see how one may avoid dualism without this theory or some theory which resembles it. Hylomorphism is radically opposed to dualism, to the doctrine which considers both the soul and the body as complete substances. Contemporary philosophy, as a rule, is also strongly opposed to this kind of dualism. In this sense, negatively, the doctrine I have defended continues to live; it is stronger than ever, although it may be known by other names.

Both linguistic analysis, the leading philosophy in the English-speaking countries, and existential phenomenology, which tends to dominate the field elsewhere, reject any form of Cartesian dualism.[5] Gilbert Ryle, a leading British analyst, has strongly attacked what he calls "the dogma of the ghost in the machine." And Maurice Merleau-Ponty, possibly France's greatest phenomenologist, defended a doctrine which looks very much like an updated form of hylomorphism. For him there are three kinds of behavior: the syncretic, the amovable, and the symbolic. We might perhaps put it more simply and speak of three levels in man: the level of reflex activity and of instincts, the level of learning, and the level of symbolic thinking. Or again, the physiological, the psychic, and the spiritual level. Each lower level stands to the next higher one in the same relation as data stand to their meaning, as materiality stands to the idea embodied in it. The data are not data if they do not possess some meaning, and there can be no meaning which is not embedded in some data. Each higher level presupposes the lower one; there can be no mind before the organism is ready to carry one and no spirit before the mind is

---

[5] Among the few exceptions we must mention J.-P. Sartre, whose dualism constitutes one of the weakest and most controversial aspects of his philosophy.

capable of receiving it. I submit that this clearly implies delayed animation.

In my opinion there is a great amount of agreement between the contemporary antidualistic trend of philosophy and the hylomorphic conception of man. It is wise therefore to return to this conception or, at least, to accept the conclusions which follow from it. One of these conclusions is that the embryo is certainly not a human person during the early stages of pregnancy, and that, consequently, it is not immoral to terminate pregnancy during this time, provided there are serious reasons for such an intervention.

Let me insist on this restriction: the opinion which I have defended may lead to abuses, to abortions performed under flimsy pretexts. I would be among the first to deplore and condemn such abuses. Although a prehuman embryo cannot demand from us the absolute respect which we owe to the human person, it deserves a very great consideration, because it is a living being, endowed with a human finality, on its way to hominization. Therefore it seems to me that only very serious reasons should allow us to terminate its existence. Excesses will unavoidably occur, but they should not induce us to overlook the instances where sufficiently serious reasons exist for performing an abortion during the early stages of pregnancy.

WHAT IS THE VALUE OF LIFE?

Herbert W. Richardson

Herbert Richardson (1932–   ) is Associate Professor of Theology at St. Michael's College, University of Toronto. He is the author of Toward an American Theology *(1967).*

What is the value of life? Reverse the question: When is life utterly without value? When is life worthless?

A man lies in a hospital bed. His heartbeat is maintained by artificial stimulation and his brain has by now lost all reactive power. His illness is irreversible. He will never again regain consciousness. Why do we hesitate to pull the switch?

A fetus is growing beneath the heart of a woman who dreams of imminent motherhood. But her dreams will become nightmares. The baby growing inside her is defective. It will never learn to say "Mama"; it will never learn to tie its shoes; it will never know it is a human person. What value can such life have? Why not abort it before we look upon its face?

The lives of the patient in the hospital and the defective fetus seem to be valueless because they lack all capacity to enjoy even minimum human fulfillment. They will never experience the happiness of joys remembered, of love shared, of things hoped for and attained. *The first value of life, then, is in all those things that contribute to human happiness.*

But there is something more in life than happiness and its pursuit.

Imagine that you are a doctor engaged in cancer research. You care for a ward of patients, now elderly and senile, who are in the last stages of various terminal illnesses. Their lives are as good as over. They shall experience no further human fulfillment and shall bring no more joy into the lives of their friends or family. But you could use them in such a way that mankind might benefit. You could inject cells into their bodies in order to study the effects. Such an experiment would probably not shorten their lives and might lead to immense good.

Several years ago such an experiment was performed on terminal patients in a New York hospital. The doctors involved were not discharged for appreciably shortening the lives of their patients. They were discharged because they violated a basic human value, a value which conflicted with the desire to increase the happiness of all mankind. They were discharged for performing this experiment upon their patients without the patients' consent—a basic ethical principle governing medical research.

The principle of informed consent was formulated at Nuremburg after the Second World War as a specification of the wrong done by German doctors who used concentration camp prisoners for medical experimentation. These doctors reasoned in a humanitarian way. They knew that the prisoners were marked for an early death and that they themselves were utterly helpless to prevent this or ameliorate their condition. In principle, the prisoners were as good as dead and, separated from all friends and family, now experienced only the torment of anticipating their doom. Since these prisoners were going to die anyway, the doctors reasoned, why not take advantage of the situation to benefit all mankind? Why not use them for medical experimentation?

Why not? Because there is another value to life besides the happiness of mankind and its increase; because the greatest happiness of the greatest number cannot justify to any individual the denial of the right to decide about the use of his body; because if all the happiness in the world could be bought for the price of selling even one person into involuntary servitude, that happiness would be immoral. To reject the right of a man to choose his own fate is to sacrifice a value that outweighs happiness itself.

We see, then, that the endurance of suffering may be right when the alleviation of that unhappiness can only be accomplished by violating human dignity, by sacrificing human freedom and truth. This was the heroic affirmation of the portrait of Thomas More in *A Man For All Seasons*. He shows us a second basic value of life, *the value of human freedom*.

But what about those who lack the capacity to decide for themselves? Isn't this precisely the situation of the terminally ill patient or the human fetus? Someone else must decide for them as well as for all minors who because of youth, illness, or other incapacity are unable to understand their situations and are without the ability to choose. Minors are fully human, but need our special care. Because of their minority, their weakness, we must choose in their behalf. Moreover, because of their weakness, it is always presumed that *the caring exercise of choice on behalf of a minor always will involve some special advantage to him and some special disadvantage to the one who is stronger and is responsible for acting on his behalf.*

Suppose, for example, you know a parent whose choices respecting his children always work out to his own advantage rather than to theirs.

Is he really caring for them or is he taking advantage of their weakness and using them as things? Or suppose you are a wife who must decide whether your incurably ill husband should continue to be kept alive. If your decision is to your own advantage, then how can you be sure that you are really caring for *him*?

It is because of this disequilibrium of advantage characteristic of true caring that we especially revere, protect, even "uselessly prolong" the lives of the weak: the terminally ill patient, the mentally retarded, the little child. The mark of a caring person or society is the protection and special advantage it accords to the weak, to those unable to fend for themselves.

The life for which we care is the life whose destiny we regard as intertwined with our own. When we identify with others we suffer with them in their place. This feeling of identification with others is the foundation of all compassion (*compassio*, to suffer together) and moral action. It is alluded to in the Great Commandment and in the golden rule of every religion: "Do unto others as you would have them do unto you." That is, imagine yourself in their place, identify with them, feel how you participate together in a single life.

The "golden rule" feeling of identification is the presupposition of all ethical behavior. This is because we only treat with respect that life which we first acknowledge, or recognize, as bound up with our own. Because of this feeling of identification, we act towards others as if they were ourselves. This is why every moral obligation is both an obligation to another and an obligation to oneself. More exactly, every moral obligation is a single obligation towards one whole reality to which I and others belong.

REVERENCE FOR LIFE

The feeling of unity, or sense of participation with others in a larger whole, is technically called reverence for life. Some people seem to have very little of this reverence for life or fellow feeling. They identify only with a small group of others—sometimes only with their family or racial group, sometimes only with a somewhat more abstract social unit such as their nation. And it may be that there are some people who identify with nothing outside of themselves, having absolutely no fellow feeling. In this case they will be called amoral. For they do not experience that motivational reality on which all particular ethical actions depend. Because reverence for life is the root of all particular ethical actions, it therefore must be enumerated among the values of life.

Hence we now enumerate three: (1) *the value of happiness* (including all the things we use to make us happy), (2) *the value of freedom* (including the intellectual understanding that makes choice possible), and (3) *the value of reverence for life* (including the care that expresses it).

Reverence for life is a matter of both extensiveness and intensiveness. It relates not only to the number of beings for whom we care, but also to the degree of care we feel for each of them. Most of us care more about those to whom we are related by ties of blood than to all others; next we care more about those we know in person than those we do not know personally. This is why we are more grieved by injuries that befall our family and acquaintances than by injuries that befall persons whom we know only through the newspapers. For even though we may feel some small compassion for those we have never met, we usually identify with them less and so care about them less.

For most of us, therefore, the feeling of reverence for life can be diagrammed as a circular area that is very intense at the center (ourselves, family, close friends) while becoming increasingly less intense toward the edges where it shades off almost indiscernibly into that area of life with which we feel absolutely no identification and for which we do not care at all. On the penumbral fringes of this circle, huddled just barely within it, are many of the weak: the mentally retarded, the physically disabled, the genetically defective, the seriously ill, primitive and aboriginal peoples, and even our enemies. They all seem to lack certain characteristics that we feel are essential to ourselves and so we identify with them only slightly —and sometimes not at all.

Today we should recall that many of those who huddle in this penumbra of humanity have, until recently, been regarded as nonsacred expendable life. In fact, it is only within the last two hundred years that members of other races, women, and even children have been regarded as more than property. And though we seem, at last, to have agreed about their status as fully human beings, we argue still about the status of the terminally ill and the human fetus. When a patient's brain is no longer reactive, then may we use the rest of his body as a mine from which to obtain transplant organs? And what of the fetus? Should we care for it as a weaker human life, accepting the fact that such choosing in its behalf always must involve a disequilibrium of advantage in its favor?

The difficulty of settling these questions arises from a conflict among the values of happiness, freedom, and reverence for life. Apart from this conflict between our happiness and our continued care for the life of a human fetus or someone terminally ill, we would find no special difficulty in allowing such weaker life to exist. For apart from this conflict, the continued existence of such life would in no way disadvantage us or limit our freedom. But when there is such a conflict, we are pressed to a

choice among the competing values. Should we accept disadvantage and
limit our freedom by the continued preservation of such life or should
we limit our fellow feeling and sense of identification with such life in
order to enhance our happiness and opportunities for choice?

A conflict of values can take place both within an individual self and
within a larger society of persons. Such a conflict threatens to disintegrate
them and hence must be resolved in order for there to be a personal or
social unity and identity. The right resolution of a potential conflict
among several values is called justice. Justice is both the harmonizing
power of the several tendencies of the inner spirit of a man (a just man)
and the ordering principle of an entire society (a just society).

Because justice aims at the maximization of values through their
harmonization, it is a value in itself. Hence, to the list we have been
enumerating we now add: (4) *the value of justice* (including all the
ordering resources of life).

Notice that justice is not simply an ordering of external relations
and behavior. It is also an ordering of various values, attitudes, and
tendencies within the inner person. Such "psychological justice" is the
principle that seeks to harmonize and actualize the full range of valuings
that a person feels—his desire for maximal happiness, his desire for maximal freedom, and his desire for maximal unity with other beings.

Justice is rooted in the demand of the self (or of a society, if we
think of social justice) for integration. A person's inner life is ordered
and oriented in a definite way, whether he accomplishes this himself or
passively accepts the person-forming influences from his society and culture. The conflict of values at stake in any particular problem (e.g.,
abortion) is not, therefore, simply a conflict that exists between persons,
but is also a conflict of feelings that exists within a person.

Someone who claims that the fetus is simply a tumorous blob of
tissue having no right to life is ordering his own inner feelings and his
psychological life in a definite way. Such a claim could only be made by
a certain kind of person. Whether abortion is right or not is therefore not
simply a question about social justice, but a question about psychological
justice. It is a question about the kinds of people we want to be. Are persons most just as persons, have they maximally actualized and harmonized
the full range of values when they order their inner life by refusing to
identify with and reverence fetal life? The same question can be raised
with regard to persons who achieve psychological integration by refusing
to identify with persons of other races, or nationalities, or even of the
opposite sex. Are such persons as truly persons when they achieve their
psychological integration by diminishing the range of values they affirm?
Don't persons who achieve psychological integration in this way not only
lack justice in their actions, but also in their very soul? Aren't they somewhat less as persons than a person ought to be?

Justice is rooted in the demand of any self or society for order and integration and it must fulfill this demand. But merely to order and to integrate is not, ipso facto, justice. There can be law and order that is unjust. Justice must not only order the values of life (including all the behavior that expresses value), but must order them in such a way that all value claims are maximally and simultaneously coaffirmed.

RELATIVE JUSTICE

Justice always aims at perfect harmony, that is, at a simultaneous affirmation of value claims in such a way that none must be sacrificed. This perfect justice is so difficult to achieve, however, that we usually must compromise for the best possible combination of compatible values. Such a compromise order is called "relative justice." *Because it always involves the rejection of some values for the sake of affirming others, a relatively just compromise is also relatively unjust. For the sake of justice, therefore, men and societies are frequently required to tolerate injustice.*

It may be relatively just to organize society in terms of a reverence for the sanctity of all life. But in India, where sacred cows are fed while children starve, it is also relatively unjust. It may be relatively just for a benevolent dictatorship to deny freedom to its citizens while seeking to promote and increase their happiness; but this denial of freedom is also an injustice. And it may be relatively just, in American society, to organize life in terms of a maximization of the value of freedom. But we should also see how this identification of justice with freedom has provided the rhetoric used to justify a disregard for the lives of the weak. In the name of freedom America has decimated the Indian, the Negro, the ghetto dweller, the Appalachian poor, and most recently, the people of Vietnam. By focusing our ethical rhetoric on the justification for the destruction of these peoples, we have failed to see how the "justice of freedom" perpetrates vast injustice and violence to the sanctity of life. For a relative justice is also an injustice.

We should ask ourselves, in view of America's traditional disregard for the sanctity of life as a part of the value mix, whether our present willingness to exclude the human fetus and the terminally ill patient from that community of life with which we feel we are a part is not one more manifestation of our national pathology. It is a pathological state of affairs when a person or society has so identified its particular compromise of value claims with perfect justice that it no longer sees the injustice which it perpetrates in the name of justice.

Injustice can and usually does seek to justify itself by adducing as its legitimate reason for existing the correlative values affirmed in the compromise of a value conflict. It can always do this. Since no values are ever repudiated and overruled except for the sake of maintaining or increasing other values, injustice is always found in conjunction with relative justice and is always perpetrated out of a desire to attain some good. This leads to *a consistent rhetoric of injustice* wherein persons constantly call attention to the positive values in any given compromise and suggest that the evil which this compromise accepts is actually the cause of the positive values therein attained. In this way, evil is "rhetorically transformed" into the cause of good and a good in itself.

The fact that all injustice is perpetrated for the sake of attaining other values explains why those who do evil frequently fail to see themselves as acting unjustly. Concerned to excuse and justify their actions (thereby relieving the disintegrative effect of an accusing conscience), they see only the positive values they are seeking to attain and for whose sake they do such harm. Hence we find the strange anomaly that sinners regard themselves as relatively upright persons while saints, who are concerned not to justify themselves before an accusing conscience but to measure themselves against perfect justice, often feel themselves to be great malefactors.

When we consider such acts as abortion or capital punishment or the termination of the lives of the hopelessly ill, it is a pathological concern for self-justification that makes us insensitive to the degree to which these acts violate the sanctity of life. This self-justification is pathological because it aims to excuse and reinforce the will of men for their private happiness rather than exposing human action to the requirements of perfect justice. The effect of self-justification, therefore, is to close men off from the very things that make possible moral growth.

The only way we can be delivered from this pathological condition is to measure our acts against perfect justice, whether or not we can actually accomplish what such perfection requires. Perfect justice aims, as we have seen, at the simultaneous co-affirmation and co-actualization of happiness, freedom, and reverence for the sanctity of life. It is not perfect justice, therefore, when one person feels he must sacrifice another because of interference with the former's own happiness or freedom. Rather, we can have perfect justice only when one person feels his happiness is identical with the maximization of the happiness, freedom, and the life of others.

Happiness, freedom, and the reverence of life can coincide only if our fellow feeling is expanded to include all life. When this expansion occurs, our self is no longer to be diagrammed as a point within a circle that gradually shades off towards something of which it has no part. The self might now be diagrammed as a centerless area of infinite extent and of equal intensity throughout. The self now includes all beings and it cares equally about each and all. The "expanded self" with its infinitely expanded fellow feelings is, of course, something mystical and spiritual, for the spiritual man no longer identifies himself with his body, his flesh, his blood, and his five senses. Now he feels as close to those who are far away and whom he has never met as he does to those whom he sees and hears daily. Every living being is *already* felt to be his friend, his brother. He knows no strangers. When he sees a new face or hears a voice for the first time, he exclaims in his soul "At last!"

Filled with this spirit which is the unity of all life, a man's greatest happiness can be care (agape). Because there can be an identity between his personal happiness and his seeking and delighting in the happiness of others, he is able to act in a perfectly just way by simultaneously affirming every value of life. The act of the spiritual man is peaceful for he himself is filled with peace. Peace is the greatest of the virtues and values of life since, as we have seen, it alone makes both justice and care (agape) possible. We should add, therefore, to the list of values: (5) *the value of peace* (including the instrumentalities of spiritualization).

EVOLUTION OF VALUES

The five values discriminated above are not "natural" in the sense that one could examine any society and find them all differentiated as they have been in this essay. Rather, I suggest that the discrimination of values presented here presupposes the historical evolution of several stages of human culture. For example, classical Greek ethical reflection focused on the value of happiness and its attainment. It did not know the value of freedom precisely because it had no experience of genuine autonomy. Within classical culture, therefore, slavery was not regarded as an ethical problem.

The European discovery of human freedom, i.e., that the will can legislate values by itself when it adheres strictly to the demands of reason, gave man power over his appetites and established a new basis for ethics. Once this freedom was experienced, the prerequisite of every moral action was then seen to be that it conform to the rule of autonomy. It was in European Christianity that freedom emerged. The struggle to reconcile this value with happiness (and with the classical ethical tradition) has set the problematic of European moral reflection to this day. This concern still animates contemporary academic ethics on both sides of the Atlantic (i.e., the teleological/deontological debate).

In the United States, there was still another ethical development: the discrimination of justice as a pragmatic value-optimizing and harmonizing procedure. This constructive or pragmatic justice is distinct from mere right reason in two respects. (In the European tradition justice and reason/freedom were inseparable.) First, American society allocated a sphere of life to freedom alone. In this sphere persons were said to have "rights" and justice could not intrude upon these rights, but only seek from outside to harmonize the choices of men. Second, American society increasingly harnessed theoretical reason and elective freedom to serve man's constructive visions. Rather than accepting situations and asking what is right (what should a free rational being choose), Americans increasingly sought to construct new kinds of situations in which more things could be right.

The particular scheme of values presented in this essay suggests, therefore, a social evolution. For example, only one who has experienced the distinction between justice and rights can make sense out of it. And one experiences such a distinction only in societies that operate in terms of it, that is, in cultures that are more highly differentiated and evolved. In such cultures persons learn and internalize such value discriminations in the course of their education and social experience. This is why the American youth who boldly protests police brutality as a violation of his rights is, I suggest, more developed morally *in this respect* than even Socrates in his cell.

By discriminating among several values, therefore, I am hoping to explain why within the evolution of human morality a new value orientation is emerging. It is an orientation towards peace and spiritualization. Considerations that reflect this new orientation must increasingly influence our experience of and arguments from freedom and justice. And peace must increasingly become the central category in terms of which we rethink all ethical questions. From this new perspective, therefore, abortion is seen to be a morally insensitive act.

However, I know many persons who read this essay will not find its argument persuasive. *This is because they know that in the biological sphere of life women have not yet experienced genuine freedom.* In the past, woman's sexuality has been discussed almost exclusively in terms of happiness. Through motherhood she has been said to fulfill her nature and find satisfaction. For her to refuse motherhood, at any point, has been called "unnatural." Refusal of motherhood has not been interpreted until very recently as woman's gaining freedom over the biological dimensions of her life. It is because the question of abortion is for the first time being articulated in terms of the value of freedom—of woman's right to control her own body, of her freedom to decide whether or not to bear a child— that the desire for abortion law reform can be regarded as a moral step forward. This does not mean that the action of abortion itself must be judged morally right. It means only that a person's demand to decide for himself whether he will or will not do what is right is an evidence of moral maturation. It is never good for a person to do something that violates perfect justice. But at a certain stage in human moral development it is actually more unjust to require people (through the institution of law) to choose the thing that perfect justice requires than to permit people (through the removal of law) to reject it.

We must be clear about this point: that the legal prohibition of abortion is *relatively unjust* because it sacrifices the value of freedom to the value of reverence for life. Opponents of abortion law reform tend to be insensitive to *this* injustice. On the other hand, an abortion freely chosen (whether in defiance of existing law or in consequence of its abolition) is relatively unjust because it affirms the value of freedom while denying the value of reverence for life.

In this situation, therefore, we must choose between two relatively unjust solutions. Our choice must not be the cynical one that denies the relevance of perfect justice, but must be one that leaves open and affirms the possibility of *further moral growth* toward it.

With these considerations in mind, it would seem that the best solution to the abortion dilemma in the United States is the removal of all laws proscribing it. Such a solution is not perfectly just, but it maximizes the largest number of human values and offers a better way to regulate this matter, i.e., by allowing the persons involved to regulate themselves.

The strongest impediment to the attainment of such personal responsibility, in the present situation, is the very abortion laws that prohibit persons from accepting it. This does not mean, of course, that abortions *will decrease* immediately following the removal of such laws. Quite the contrary is to be expected. This is because personal freedom, limited by a threatening law, can only keep itself alive by imaginations of disobedience and through threats of rebellion. The removal of law may well lead to the actual doing of that which was imagined and threatened beforehand.

Even if this occurs, however, the situation is relatively as just as one that eliminates both abortion and freedom together. This is because the elimination of abortion laws is not simply for the sake of affirming the value of freedom, but also because the attainment of freedom is the "next step" in persons growing toward more perfect justice. At present, the laws bar the way to this maturation.

Those who have lived only under the law cannot believe that persons would freely choose the good that the law prescribes *after that law* has been removed. They depend on something outside themselves to compensate for a moral deficiency within themselves. By now we have had enough experience in dealing with other social problems to know how deficient is the psychology that legalistic morality supposes to be "normal." Free persons, following the first moments of excess and disorientation once the law is removed, then begin voluntarily to do what is good.

3
EUTHANASIA

EUTHANASIA: OUR RIGHT TO DIE

Joseph Fletcher

Joseph Fletcher (1905—   ), Episcopal minister and moral theologian who is primarily known for his advocacy of "situational ethics"—a theory which asserts that love of others is the only norm for Christian decision, transcending all laws and codes of conduct. His publications include Situation Ethics: The New Morality (1966) *and* Moral Responsibility (1967).

Euthanasia, the deliberate easing into death of a patient suffering from a painful and fatal disease, has long been a troubling problem of conscience in medical care. For us in the Western world the problem arises, *pro forma,* out of a logical contradiction at the heart of the Hippocratic Oath. Our physicians all subscribe to that oath as the standard of their professional ethics. The contradiction is there because the oath promises two things: first, to relieve suffering, and second, to prolong and protect life. When the patient is in the grip of an agonizing and fatal disease, these two promises are incompatible. Two duties come into conflict. To prolong life is to violate the promise to relieve pain. To relieve the pain is to violate the promise to prolong and protect life.

Ordinarily an attempt is made to escape the dilemma by relieving the pain with an analgesic that does not induce death. But this attempt to evade the issue fails in many cases for the simple reason that the law of diminishing returns operates in narcosis. Patients grow semi-immune to its effects, for example in some forms of osteomyelitis, and a dose which first produces four hours of relief soon gives only three, then two, then almost none. The dilemma still stands: the choice between euthanasia or suffering. Euthanasia may be described, in its broadest terms, as a "theory that in certain circumstances, when owing to disease, senility or the like, a person's life has permanently ceased to be either agreeable or useful, the sufferer should be painlessly killed, either by himself or by another."[1] More simply, we may call euthanasia merciful release from incurable suffering.

Our task . . . is to put the practice under examination in its strictly medical form, carefully limiting ourselves to cases in which the patient himself chooses euthanasia and the physician advises against any reasonable hope of recovery or of relief by other means. Yet even in so narrowly defined an application as this, there are conscientious objections, of the sort applied to broader concepts or usages. In the first place it is claimed that the practice of euthanasia might be taken as an encouragement of suicide or of the wholesale murder of the aged and infirm. Again, weak or unbalanced people may more easily throw away their lives if medical euthanasia has approval. Still another objection raised is that the practice would raise grave problems for the public authority. Government would have to overcome the resistance of time-honored religious beliefs, the universal feeling that human life is too sacred to be tampered with, and the problem of giving euthanasia legal endorsement as another form of justifiable homicide. All of this could lead to an appalling increase of crimes such as infanticide and geronticide. In short, in this problem as in others which we have been analyzing there is a common tendency to cry abuse and to ignore *abusus non tollit usum.**

Prudential and expedient objections to euthanasia quickly jump to mind among many people confronted with the issue. There are few, presumably, who would not be moved by such protests as this one from the *Linacre Quarterly:* "Legalized euthanasia would be a confession of despair in the medical profession; it would be the denial of hope for further progress against presently incurable maladies. It would destroy all confidence in physicians, and introduce a reign of terror. . . . [Patients] would turn in dread from the man on whose wall the Hippocratic Oath proclaims, 'If any shall ask of me a drug to produce death I will not give it, nor will I suggest such counsel.' "[2]

However, it is the objection that euthanasia is inherently wrong, that the disposition of life is too sacred to be entrusted to human control, which calls for our closest analysis. . . . Here . . . we shall be dealing with the *personal* dimensions of morality in medical care. The social ethics of medical care, as it is posed to conscience by proposals to use euthanasia

---

* That is, to ignore the rule that an abuse is not elevated by usage.
[1] H. J. Rose, "Euthanasia," *Encyc. of Rel. and Ethics,* v, 598–601.
[2] Hilary R. Werts, S.J., in April, 1947, 19.2, p. 33.

for eugenic reasons, population control, and the like, have to be left for another time and place.

Not infrequently the newspapers carry stories of the crime of a spouse, or a member of the family or a friend, of a hopelessly stricken and relentlessly tortured victim of, let us say, advanced cancer. Desperate people will sometimes take the law into their own hands and administer some lethal dose to end it all. Sometimes the euthanasiast then commits suicide, thus making two deaths instead of one. Sometimes he is tried for murder in a court of law, amid great scandal and notoriety. But even if he is caught and indicted, the judgment never ends in conviction, perhaps because the legalism of the charge can never stand up in the tested conscience of a sympathetic jury.

For the sake of avoiding offense to any contemporaries, we might turn to literary history for a typical example of our problem. Jonathan Swift, the satirist and Irish clergyman, after a life of highly creative letters ended it all in a horrible and degrading death. It was a death degrading to himself and to those close to him. His mind crumbled to pieces. It took him eight years to die while his brain rotted. He read the third chapter of Job on his birthday as long as he could see. "And Job spake, and said, Let the day perish when I was born, and the night in which it was said, There is a man child conceived." The pain in Swift's eye was so acute that it took five men to hold him down, to keep him from tearing out his eye with his own hands. For the last three years he sat and drooled. Knives had to be kept entirely out of his reach. When the end came, finally, his fits of convulsion lasted thirty-six hours.[3] Now, whatever may be the theological meanings of St. Paul's question, "O death, where is thy sting?"[4] the moral meaning—in a word, the evil—of a death like that is only too plain.

We can imagine the almost daily scene preceding Swift's death. (Some will say we should not imagine such things, that it is not fair to appeal to emotion. Many good people cannot willingly accept the horrendous aspects of reality as a factor of reasoning, especially when reality cuts across their customs and commitments. The relative success with which we have repressed the reality of atomic warfare and its dreadful prospects is an example on a wider scale.) We can easily conceive of Dean Swift grabbing wildly, madly, for a knife or a deadly drug. He was *demoralized*, without a vestige of true self-possession left in him. He wanted to commit what the law calls suicide and what vitalistic ethics calls sin. Standing by was some good doctor of physick, trembling with sympathy and frustration. Secretly, perhaps, he wanted to commit what the law calls murder. Both had full knowledge of the way out, which is half the foundation of moral integrity, but unlike his patient the physician felt he had no

[3] Virginia Moore, *Ho for Heaven*, New York, 1946, pp. 180–182.
[4] I Cor. 15:55.

freedom to act, which is the other half of moral integrity. And so, meanwhile, necessity, blind and unmoral, irrational physiology and pathology,
made the decision. It was in reality no decision at all, no moral behavior
in the least, unless submission to physical ruin and spiritual disorganiza-
tion can be called a decision and a moral choice. For let us not forget
that in such tragic affairs there is a moral destruction, a spiritual disorder,
as well as a physical degeneration. As Swift himself wrote to his niece
fully five years before the end: "I am so stupid and confounded that I
cannot express the mortification I am under both of body and soul."[5]

The story of this man's death points us directly to the broad problem
of suicide, as well as to the more particular problem of euthanasia. We
get a glimpse of this paradox in our present customary morality, that it
sometimes condemns us to live or, to put it another way, destroys our
moral being for the sake of just *being*. This aspect of suicide makes it
important for us to distinguish from the outset between voluntary and
involuntary euthanasia. They are by no means the same, either in policy
or ethical meaning. Those who condemn euthanasia of both kinds would
call the involuntary form murder and the voluntary form a compounded
crime of murder and suicide if administered by the physician, and suicide
alone if administered by the patient himself. As far as voluntary euthanasia goes, it is impossible to separate it from suicide as a moral category;
it is, indeed, a form of suicide. In a very proper sense, the case for medical
euthanasia depends upon the case for the righteousness of suicide, given
the necessary circumstances. And the justification of its administration by
an attending physician is therefore dependent upon it too, under the time-
honored rule that what one may lawfully do another may help him to do.

. . .

PRO AND CON

It is at this point that we can turn to the definitely moral arguments
for and against euthanasia. Our aim here is to be as orderly as possible
in the discussion, and to forsake any *argumentum ad misericordiam*. We
must try to avoid the penny-dreadful type of treatment Richard Cabot had
in mind when he spoke of euthanasia as "that ancient and reliable novelty
. . . which the newspapers trick out afresh each year in August when
politics are dull and there is a dearth of copy."[6] In a limited space, perhaps
the best procedure will be to speak directly to the ten most common and

[5] Quoted by Richard Garnett, "Jonathan Swift" in *Encyc. Brit.*, 11th ed.
[6] *Adventures on the Borderlands of Ethics*, New York, 1926, p. 34.

most important objections. Therefore, suppose we deal with them as if they stood one by one in a bill of particulars.

1. It is objected that euthanasia, when voluntary, is really suicide. If this is true, and it would seem to be obviously true, then the proper question is: have we ever a right to commit suicide? Among Catholic moralists the most common ruling is that "it is never permitted to kill oneself intentionally, without explicit divine inspiration to do."[7] Humility requires us to assume that divine inspiration cannot reasonably be expected to occur either often or explicitly enough to meet the requirements of medical euthanasia. A plea for legal recognition of "man's inalienable right to die" is placed at the head of the physicians' petition to the New York State Assembly. Now, has man any such right, however limited and imperfect it may be? Surely he has, for otherwise the hero or martyr and all those who deliberately give their lives are morally at fault. It might be replied that there is a difference between the suicide, who is directly seeking to end his life, and the hero or martyr, who is seeking directly some other end entirely, death being only an undesired by-product. But to make this point is only to raise a question as to what purposes are sufficient to justify the loss of one's life. If altruistic values, such as defense of the innocent, are enough to justify the loss of one's life (and we will all agree that they are), then it may be argued that personal integrity is a value worth the loss of life, especially since, by definition, there is no hope of relief from the demoralizing pain and no further possibility of serving others. To call euthanasia egoistic or self-regarding makes no sense, since in the nature of the case the patient is not choosing his own good rather than the good of others.

Furthermore, it is important to recognize that there is no ground, in a rational or Christian outlook, for regarding life itself as the *summum bonum*. As a ministers' petition to buttress the New York bill puts it, "We believe in the sacredness of *personality*, but not in the worth of mere existence or 'length of days.' . . . We believe that such a sufferer has the right to die, and that society should grant this right, showing the same mercy to human beings as to the sub-human animal kingdom." (The point might be made validly in criticism of this statement that society can only recognize an "inalienable right," it cannot confer it. Persons are not mere creatures of the community, even though it is ultimately meaningless to claim integrity for them unless their lives are integrated into the community.) In the personalistic view of man and morals, asserted throughout these pages, personality is supreme over mere life. To prolong life uselessly, while the personal qualities of freedom, knowledge, self-possession and control, and responsibility are sacrificed is to attack the moral status of a person. It actually denies morality in order to submit to fatality. And in

7 Henry Davis, *Moral and Pastoral Theology*, New York, 1943, vol. II, p. 142. This author explains that Jerome and Lessius excused suicide in defense of chastity, but that Aquinas opposed even this exception to the prohibition.

addition, to insist upon mere "life" invades religious interests as well as moral values. For to use analgesic agents to the point of depriving sufferers of consciousness is, by all apparent logic, inconsistent even with the practices of sacramentalist Christians. The point of death for a human person *in extremis* is surely by their own account a time when the use of reason and conscious self-commitment is most meritorious; it is the time when a responsible competence in receiving such rites as the viaticum and extreme unction would be most necessary and its consequences most invested with finality.

2. It is objected that euthanasia, when involuntary, is murder. This is really an objection directed against the physician's role in medical euthanasia, assuming it is administered by him rather than by the patient on his own behalf. We might add to what has been said above about the word "murder" in law and legal definition by explaining that people with a moral rather than a legal interest—doctors, pastors, patients, and their friends—will never concede that malice means only premeditation, entirely divorced from the motive and the end sought. These factors are entirely different in euthanasia from the motive and the end in murder, even though the means—taking life—happens to be the same. If we can make no moral distinction between acts involving the same means, then the thrifty parent who saves in order to educate his children is no higher in the scale of merit than the miser who saves for the sake of hoarding. But, as far as medical care is concerned, there is an even more striking example of the contradictions which arise from refusing to allow for anything but the consequences of a human act. There is a dilemma in medication for terminal diseases which is just as real as the dilemma posed by the doctor's oath to relieve pain while he also promises to prolong life. As medical experts frequently point out, morphine, which is commonly used to ease pain, also shortens life, i.e., it induces death. Here we see that the two promises of the Hippocratic Oath actually conflict at the level of means as well as at the level of motive and intention.

3. What of the common religious opinion that God reserves for himself the right to decide at what moment a life shall cease? Koch-Preuss says euthanasia is the destruction of "the temple of God and a violation of the property rights of Jesus Christ."[8] As to this doctrine, it seems more than enough just to answer that if such a divine-monopoly theory is valid, then it follows with equal force that it is immoral to lengthen life. Is medical care, after all, only a form of human self-assertion or a demonic pretension, by which men, especially physicians, try to put themselves in God's place? Prolonging life, on this divine-monopoly view, when a life appears to be ending through natural or physical causes, is just as much an interference with natural determinism as mercifully ending a life before physiology does it in its own amoral way.

[8] *Ibid.*, 11, 76. He cites texts such as I Cor. 3:16–17.

This argument that we must not tamper with life also assumes that physiological life is sacrosanct. But as we have pointed out repeatedly, this doctrine is a form of vitalism or naturalistic determinism. Dean Sperry of the Harvard Divinity School, who is usually a little more sensitive to the scent of anti-humane attitudes, wrote recently in the *New England Journal of Medicine* that Albert Schweitzer's doctrine of "reverence for life," which is often thought to entail an absolute prohibition against taking life, has strong claims upon men of conscience.[9] Perhaps so, but men of conscience will surely reject the doctrine if it is left unqualified and absolute. In actual fact, even Schweitzer has suggested that the principle is subject to qualification. He has, with apparent approval, explained that Gandhi "took it upon himself to go beyond the letter of the law against killing. . . . He ended the sufferings of a calf in its prolonged death-agony by giving it poison."[10] It seems unimaginable that either Schweitzer or Gandhi would deny to a human being what they would render, with however heavy a heart, to a calf. Gandhi did what he did in spite of the special sanctity of kine in Hindu discipline. In any case Dr. Schweitzer in his African hospital at Lambaréné is even now at work administering death-inducing-because-pain-relieving drugs. As William Temple once pointed out, "The notion that life is absolutely sacred is Hindu or Buddhist, not Christian." He neglected to remark that even those Oriental religionists forget their doctrine when it comes to *suttee* and *hara-kiri*. He said further that the argument that it cannot ever be right to kill a fellow human being will not stand up because "such a plea can only rest upon a belief that life, physiological life, is sacrosanct. This is not a Christian idea at all; for, if it were, the martyrs would be wrong. If the sanctity is *in* life, it must be wrong to give your life for a noble cause as well as to take another's. But the Christian must be ready to give life gladly for his faith, as for a noble cause. Of course, this implies that, *as compared with some things*, the loss of life is a small evil; and if so, then, *as compared with some other things*, the taking of life is a small injury."[11]

Parenthetically we should explain, if it is not evident in these quotations themselves, that Dr. Temple's purpose was to justify military service. Unfortunately for his aim, he failed to take account of the ethical factor of free choice as a right of the person who thus loses his life at the hands of the warrior. We cannot put upon the same ethical footing the ethical right to take our own lives, in which case our freedom is not invaded, and taking the lives of others in those cases in which the act is done against the victim's will and choice. The true parallel is between self-sacrifice and a merciful death provided at the person's request; there is none between self-sacrifice and violent or coercive killing. But the relevance of what Dr.

---

[9] Dec. 23, 1948. Incorporated in William Sperry, *The Ethical Basis of Medical Care*, New York, 1950, p. 160 sq.

[10] *Indian Thought and Its Development*, London, 1930, pp. 225–238.

[11] *Thoughts in War Time*, London, 1940, pp. 31–32. Italics in original.

Temple has to say and its importance for euthanasia is perfectly clear. The non-theological statement of the case agrees with Temple: "Are we not allowing ourselves to be deceived by our self-preservative tendency to rationalize a merely instinctive urge and to attribute spiritual and ethical significance to phenomena appertaining to the realm of crude, biological utility?"[12]

4. It is also objected by religious moralists that euthanasia violates the Biblical command, "Thou shalt not kill." It is doubtful whether this kind of Biblicism is any more valid than the vitalism we reject. Indeed, it is a form of fundamentalism, common to both Catholics and reactionary Protestants. An outspoken religious opponent of euthanasia is a former chancellor to Cardinal Spellman as military vicar to the armed forces, Monsignor Robert McCormick. As presiding judge of the Archdiocesan Ecclesiastical Tribunal of New York, he warned the General Assembly of that state in 1947 not to "set aside the commandment 'Thou shalt not kill.' "[13] In the same vein, the general secretary of the American Council of Christian Churches, an organization of fundamentalist Protestants, denounced the fifty-four clergymen who supported the euthanasia bill, claiming that their action was "an evidence that the modernistic clergy have made further departure from the eternal moral law."[14]

Certainly those who justify war and capital punishment, as most Christians do, cannot condemn euthanasia on this ground. We might point out to the fundamentalists in the two major divisions of Western Christianity that the beatitude "Blessed are the merciful" has the force of a commandment too! The medical profession lives by it, has its whole *ethos* in it. But the simplest way to deal with this Christian text-proof objection might be to point out that the translation "Thou shalt not kill" is incorrect. It should be rendered, as in the responsive decalogue of the *Book of Common Prayer*, "Thou shalt do no murder," i.e., unlawful killing. It is sufficient just to remember that the ancient Jews fully allowed warfare and capital punishment. Lawful killing was also for hunger-satisfaction and sacrifice. Hence, a variety of Hebrew terms such as *shachat*, *harag*, *tabach*, but *ratsach* in the Decalogue (both Exodus 20:13 and Deut. 5:17), clearly means *unlawful* killing, treacherously, for private vendetta or gain. Thus it is laid down in Leviticus 24:17 that "he who kills a man shall be put to death," showing that the lawful forms of killing may even be used to punish the unlawful! In the New Testament references to the prohibition against killing (e.g., Matt. 5:21, Luke 18:20, Rom. 13:9) are an endorsement of the commandments in the Jewish law. Each time, the verb *phoneuo* is used and the connotation is *unlawful* killing, as in the Decalogue. Other verbs connote simply the fact of killing, as *apokteino*

---

[12] H. Roberts, "Two Essays on Medicine," in *Living Age*, Oct. 1934, 347.159–162.
[13] Quoted H. N. Oliphant, *Redbook Magazine*, Sep. 1948.
[14] *Ibid*.

(Luke 12:4, "Be not afraid of them that kill the body") and *thuo* which is used interchangeably for slaughter of animals for food and for sacrifice. We might also remind the Bible-bound moralists that there was no condemnation either of Abimelech, who chose to die, or of his faithful swordbearer who carried out his wish for him.[15]

5. Another common objection in religious quarters is that suffering is a part of the divine plan for the good of man's soul, and must therefore be accepted. Does this mean that the physicians' Hippocratic Oath is opposed to Christian virtue and doctrine? If this simple and naive idea of suffering were a valid one, then we should not be able to give our moral approval to anesthetics or to provide any medical relief of human suffering. Such has been the objection of many religionists at every stage of medical conquest, as we pointed out in the first chapter in the case of anesthetics at childbirth. Here is still another anomaly in our mores of life and death, that we are, after much struggle, now fairly secure in the righteousness of easing suffering at birth but we still feel it is wrong to ease suffering at death! Life may be begun without suffering, but it may not be ended without it, if it happens that nature combines death and suffering.

Those who have some acquaintance with the theological habit of mind can understand how even the question of euthanasia may be colored by the vision of the Cross as a symbol of redemptive suffering in Christian doctrine. As Emil Brunner has said of the crucifix, "it is not without its significance that the picture of a dying man is the sacred sign of Christendom."[16] But when it is applied to suffering in general it becomes, of course, a rather uncritical exemplarism which ignores the unique theological claims of the doctrine of the Atonement and the saving power of the Cross as a singular event. It is, at least, difficult to see how any theological basis for the suffering argument against medical euthanasia would be any different or any more compelling for keeping childbirth natural and "as God hath provided it."

It is much more realistic and humble to take as our regulative principle the rule that "Blessed are the merciful, for they shall see mercy," since this moral standard gives more recognition in actual fact to the motive of compassion, which, according to the theology of Atonement, lies behind the crucifixion of Jesus and gave it its power and its *ethos*. "All things whatsoever you would that men should do unto you, do you even so unto them." Mercy to the suffering is certainly the point of Psalm 102, vs. 12: "As a father hath compassion on his children, so hath the Lord compassion on them that fear him: for he knoweth our frame." Let the Biblicist take his position on the story of Job! Job explored the problem of human suffering and left it a mystery for the man of faith. Some have tried to find a recommendation of suicide in Job's wife's advice, but it is

[15] Judges 9:54.
[16] *Man in Revolt*, New York, 1939, pp. 388–389.

hardly more than a warning that he must not curse God.[17] In Job 7:15 there may be a thought of suicide, but nothing more than that. Our point here is that even Job never hinted that euthanasia was wrong; he only wondered, as we all do sometimes, why such a thing is ever needed or desired. The patience of Job is proverbial, but this is the Job of the prose part of the book. The poetry has another Job, a most rebellious and morally disturbed one. He could come to no other conclusion but that suffering is a mystery, as far as God's will and power are concerned. He did not give much attention to man's part in its control, nor to its particular aspect in incurable illness.

6. It is frequently pointed out, as an objection to euthanasia, that patients pronounced incurable might recover after all, for doctors can and do make mistakes. This seems, frankly, like a fundamentally obstructionist argument. It takes us back to the evasion based on fallibility with which we had to deal in the question of truth-telling. Doctors are indeed finite creatures. So they may also err in recommending and carrying out operations, or in other forms of treatment. As far as the accuracy of their advice is concerned, we have to trust them, although it is always our right to doubt their advice and to change doctors. If reluctance to trust them were a common attitude pervading medical relationships generally, it would spell the doom of medical care. Also, it is sometimes added that if we will just hang on something may turn up, perhaps a new discovery which will save us after all. Although this objection really evades the point at issue, it has a very great importance when seen in its own perspective. We always have ground for hope that many of the conditions which have called for euthanasia in the past will no longer do so. Not long ago crippling arthritis was thought almost hopeless, but cortisone and ACTH have offered new hope and success. Medical science is also continuously making discoveries which narrow the range of cases in which the conditions of justifiable euthanasia are apt to occur. Improved narcosis, new healing drugs and treatments, surgical relief of pain by new techniques of chordotomy and lobotomy—these things make news constantly.

And there are, of course, occasional incidents of totally unexpected, last-minute recovery from "hopeless" illnesses. An actual case would be that of the hospital chaplain who once stood by at a "certain" death and a horrible one from pemphigus. The doctors had even advised that the patient's family be called in for a last visit. Then, at the last moment, a new penicillin drug was flown in from another city, and the patient was saved. Such things happen, yes. But all we need to say to this objection to euthanasia is that by no stretch of the imagination, in a typical situation, can we foresee a discovery that will restore health to a life already running out. A patient dying of metastatic cancer may be considered already dead,

---

[17] Job 2:9–10.

though still breathing. In advanced cases, even if a cure were to be found, toxemia has in all likelihood damaged the tissues and organs fatally.

7. It is said, with some truth, that patients racked by pain might make impulsive and ill-considered requests for euthanasia, if it were morally and legally approved. To this there are two rejoinders: first, that a careful law, such as that of the Euthanasia Society, would provide that there must be medical advice that death is certain, which rules out any hasty euthanasia in non-fatal illnesses; and, second, that the law would provide an interval between application and administration. The law should not permit euthanasia to be done on the spur of the moment, and the patient should be free to withdraw his request at any time. The requirement that the disease must be of a fatal character is needed to guard against unconscious wishes for destruction which are to be seen sometimes, although rarely, in patients. The confirmation of the patient's and the attending physician's decisions by disinterested parties is a sufficient bulwark against impulsive action. This might also be the place to emphasize that a doctor is always free to refuse to administer medical euthanasia, as a patient ought to be free to request it. In a wide search of the literature, incidentally, only one really *medical* objection to the practice was found, although there are frequent moral objections. Dr. A. A. Brill, of the International Psychoanalytical Association, has declared that *although doctors are actually doing it they should stop*, because for reasons of depth psychology the practice will demoralize both patients and doctors, fill them with fear that inhibits healing relationships and lowers vitality.[18] As we have already seen, Dr. Brill's colleague in the Association, Dr. Ernest Jones, does not regard this as a real objection to euthanasia, if we may draw that conclusion from his support of it before the United Nations.

Connected with this is this further objection: what if the patient can no longer speak or even gesture intelligibly? Can we be sure we always understand the patient's real desire, his choice for or against death, especially in cases where his condition is nearly unconscious or comatose? We all know that communication is not solely verbal. The provision that the request must come from the patient in a documentary form is introduced in proposals like that of the Euthanasia Society out of great caution, presumably in the fear that a gesture or other sign might be misinterpreted. A restriction like this will also exclude the possibility of a doctor's carrying out euthanasia when the patient had expressed a desire for it but the formalities could not be fulfilled before his physical powers to apply had failed. This would be tragic, but perhaps it is the necessary price exacted for legalization. There is also, of course, the reverse possibility that a patient might make the proper application, then change his mind after his powers of communication had failed. But these seem unreal problems,

[18] *Journ. of Nervous and Mental Diseases*, July 1936, p. 84.

purely logical in character, if it is held, as we indeed do hold, that a patient who has completely lost the power to communicate has passed into a submoral state, outside the forum of conscience and beyond moral being. Being no longer responsive, he is no longer responsible.

Conscience and consciousness are inseparable and presuppose each other. Their interdependence has always been recognized, since the Stoics first explored the cognitive aspect of conscience as distinct from the judicial, and recognized that to act with *conscientia*, with knowledge, requires consciousness. The Stoics predicated awareness or consciousness of Natural Law insight; the Christians have predicated Natural Law insight plus communion with God and the voice of the Holy Spirit. Some have held that the moral factor in consciousness is innate; others, acquired. Some have thought it to be reason; others, intuition; still others, emotion. In any case, these faculties are parts of consciousness, without which personality is gone and there is no longer a "person" to fulfill even the minimum requirements of moral status, i.e., freedom and knowledge.

8. Sometimes we hear it said that the moral and legal approval of euthanasia would weaken our moral fiber, tend to encourage us to minimize the importance of life. Hence such well-known witticisms as G. K. Chesterton's, that the proponents of euthanasia now seek only the death of those who are a nuisance to themselves, but soon it will be broadened to include those who are a nuisance to others.[19] It is very hard to find any real hope of taking hold of an objection like this, with its broad value-terms such as "moral fiber" and "the importance of life." It could just as easily be reasoned that to ask for euthanasia, to leave voluntarily for the unknown, would call for courage and resolution and faith, and would encourage us to live with faith and without fear of the unknown. There is great wisdom and moral assurance in the decision of Charlotte Perkins Gilman, one of America's greatest women, who chose self-euthanasia rather than endure a degenerative death by cancer. These were her last words, typed by her own hand: "A last duty. Human life consists in mutual service. No grief, no pain, misfortune or 'broken heart' is excuse for cutting off one's life while any power of service remains. But when all usefulness is over, when one is assured of an imminent and unavoidable death, it is the simplest of human rights to choose a quick and easy death in place of a slow and horrible one. Public opinion is changing on this subject. The time is approaching when we shall consider it abhorrent to our civilization to allow a human being to lie in prolonged agony which we should mercifully end in any other creature. Believing this choice to be of social service in promoting wider views on this question, I have preferred chloroform to cancer."[20]

Our attention should be given particularly to one sentence here: "No

---

[19] Symposium, "Pro and Con," in *The Digest*, Oct. 23, 1937, 124.22–23.
[20] Quoted by A. L. Woolbarst, *Medical Record*, May 17, 1939.

grief, no pain, no misfortune or 'broken heart' is excuse for cutting off one's life while any power of service remains." It is a cause for joy that many avenues of service are open, or could be opened, to properly diagnosed terminal patients. Because of its psychological effects, genuine service, or being needed, will postpone the unendurable stages of pain or collapse. Enlightened hospital procedure is making great advances in this respect. One of the most significant services open to terminal patients is willingness to submit to drugs and cures and narcotics of an experimental kind, aimed at eliminating *the very pain and demoralization which is a major justification for euthanasia.* This consideration is certainly a welcome one to the advocates of euthanasia, and is always kept in mind by them. For them the best possible news would be that medicine has at last deprived euthanasia of its *raison d'être.*

Sometimes it is suggested by advocates of euthanasia that those who insist that the suffering go on are unconscious sadists, moved by the wish to make others suffer, or in a voyeurist version actually eager to see them suffer. This is an extremely problematical ground upon which to enter in the discussion, and it tends to "psychologize" all ethical reason out of the picture. It is true, theoretically, that the idea of noble suffering may be, deep down, a reaction-formation to rationalize sadistic or masochistic sentiments. But on the other hand, opponents of euthanasia could charge that the advocates are the victims of a death instinct or destruction-wishes; or even a sado-masochist syndrome, sadist in the friends of the patient, masochist in the patient. To this, in their turn, the advocate could reply that if they were sadistic in their drives they would *want* the suffering to go on. There are hardly any limits to the kind of wool-gathering that could develop along these lines, with little or no possibility of contributing to a solution ethically.

9. It is objected that the ethics of a physician forbids him to take life. We have already recognized that fact *as a fact,* but the issue is raised precisely because there are cases when the doctor's duty to prolong and protect life is in conflict with his equal duty to relieve suffering. As a matter of fact, this dilemma is actually inescapable and inherent in the medical care of many terminal illnesses anyway, at the technical as well as the moral level. If the physician's obligation is both to relieve pain and prolong life, how then can he use analgesics, which bring relief but have the necessary effect of hastening death? Great strides in non-toxemic medications are being made, but it remains true that, for example, prolonged morphine has a lethal effect, especially when finally there is a failure of natural functions such as breathing, salivation, and heat regulation, and when it no longer works intravenously because circulation is ceasing and it has to be injected directly into the heart. Everyone concerned in the care of the sick knows quite well that the medication itself is euthanasia. We hear constantly of overdoses somehow or other taken in terminal cases. There are many cases indeed in which actions are carried

out by patients or attendants in the spirit of Socrates, drinking the cup of hemlock, who cried to Crito, "We owe a cock to Aesculapius. . . . Pay the debt and do not forget it."[21]

The dilemma of the physician who takes a contradictory oath could hardly be more evident than in the words of an article in *The New England Journal of Medicine* entitled "The Theology [sic] of Medicine." The author, a physician, declared, "I feel as Dr. Woodward did when he said, 'I have no sympathy with the man who would shorten the death agony of a dog but prolong that of a human being.' "[22] Dr. Woodward had himself advised a class of medical students, "I hold it to be your duty to smooth as much as possible the pathway to the grave even if life is somewhat shortened. Nor is it necessary to talk it over with friends and relatives, nor need you expect them to formally countenance either neglect or expedition. Let that be your affair, settled with your own conscience."[23] It is a dilemma. The only real problem in conscience is not whether the mystique of vitalism or an ethic of mercifulness should reign, but whether the decision should rest upon the lonely conscience of the doctor without honest approval or responsibility shared fully with patient and family. Dr. Woodward is correct ethically to show mercy, but he is not justified in being so god-like about it. He should be man-like about it, and so should the students to whom he was giving his advice. As long as doctors continue, as at present, making unilateral decisions, they are in the position of needing something stronger than a Rule of Double Effect of their own, whereby they can convince themselves that it is right to do a good thing if they do not intend the evil consequences. Under these circumstances, can they sort out their emotions and motives, and make sure that they do not *want* the luckless patient to reach an end to his sufferings? Under these circumstances, what of the Hippocratic Oath?

Our defense of the right to die, with the doctor's aid, is not made in any kind of illness except the fatal and demoralizing ones. Besides, as we have seen in other questions already discussed, there are common exceptions to the rule against medical homicide. If one can be made at the beginning of life (abortion) why not also at the end of life (euthanasia)? The one situation is no more absolute than the other. There is no more stigma in the one than in the other. On personalistic grounds we could say that there is less question morally in euthanasia, for in euthanasia a merciful death is chosen in cooperation with a person whose integrity is threatened by disintegration, whereas an embryo in therapeutic abortion has no personal value or development at stake and cannot exercise the moral qualities of freedom and knowledge.

10. Finally, it is objected that doctors do not want euthanasia made

---

[21] *Phaedo*, conclusion.
[22] R. E. Osgood, M.D., 210.4, 182–192, Jan. 25, 1934.
[23] *Ibid.*, 202.18, 843–853.

legal.[24] It is not at all uncommon to hear doctors admit that they generally engage in the practice, in one way or another. Lest any reader be skeptical, he should examine the Cumulative Book Index and the index of periodicals for medical opinion on the subject, and he will find several places in which the admission is candidly made.[25] From time to time there are reports, undocumentable but from usually reliable sources, of medical meetings such as one recently in the Middle West at which a speaker asked for a show of hands from those who have never administered euthanasia. Not a hand was raised.[26] In 1935 great excitement was caused by a doctor's public confession in a London newspaper that he had been practicing euthanasia, and in *Time Magazine* an article reported, "Pungent, voluble Dr. Morris Fishbein, editor of the American Medical Association's *Journal*, observed that the average doctor frequently faces the problem, that when it is a matter between him and his patient he may decide it in his own way without interference."[27] Many are the uses which we may be sure are made of drugs such as bichloride of mercury, potassium cyanide, and some of the barbiturates. In 1947, when an English doctor publicly announced he too engaged in medical euthanasia, a spokesman for the British Medical Association, in a very oblique but patent *non dixit*, said, "I think a good many doctors feel as Dr. Barton does, that euthanasia ought to be legalized. The association has no objection to doctors saying what they think about law."[28]

There are three other objections closely allied to these we have examined. They may deserve just a word or two. First, it is said that medical euthanasia would weaken medical research, that it would take away the incentive to find cures for painful maladies. This is nonsense because doctors are already practicing euthanasia and yet their fight against fatal diseases is mounting, not flagging. As cancer and malignant tumors, for example, increase (nearly 200,000 Americans will die of them this year) the research in that field increases too. The motive behind medical research is the elimination or control of disease, not merely the avoidance of suffering.[29] Second, it is objected that the heirs or enemies of an invalid

---

[24] Cf. G. E. Byers, *Ohio Med. Journ.*, 1936, 32.342; J. S. Manson, *Brit. Med. Journ.*, 1936, 1.86; W. W. Gregg, *North Amer. Rev.*, 1934, 237.239; J. J. Walsh, *The Forum*, Dec. 1935, 333–334. The Council of the World Medical Association, at Copenhagen, Apr. 24–28, 1950, *recommended* that "the practice of euthanasia be condemned." Cf. *Journal of the Amer. Med. Assoc.*, June 10, 1950, 143–6, p. 561.

[25] E.g., cf. Frank Hinman, M.D., *Journ. of Nervous and Mental Diseases*, 99, 1944.

[26] Cf. H. N. Oliphant, *op. cit.*

[27] Nov. 18, 1935, 26.21, pp. 53–54.

[28] *New York Herald Tribune*, May 23, 1947.

[29] See the thrilling story of vigorous medical progress in an account by the Secretary of the American Medical Association, Stephen M. Spencer, *Wonders of Modern Medicine*, New York, 1953. Between 1900 and 1952 the average life span of Americans has risen from 49 to 69 years, and Louis I. Dublin of the Metropolitan Life Insurance Company estimates it will be 73 within this generation, thus exceeding the threescore and ten allotted in the Bible.

might use euthanasia to hasten his death. To this we reply that the legal requirements of a written application by the sufferer, and of both legal and medical investigations, would be a safeguard. He would have far more protection than is provided for many patients now committed for treatment of mental disorder. He would, indeed, have a great deal more protection than he now receives under the present system of clandestine euthanasia being widely practiced. Third, it is claimed that once we legalize mercy deaths the application of the principle will be widened disastrously to cover non-fatal illnesses. But why is it, then, that although legal killing by capital punishment has been in vogue a long time, yet it has been narrowed rather than extended in scope? In fact it has been narrowed a great deal from the days when people were hanged for stealing a few shillings. This alarmist objection is the old red herring against which we have had to aim the rule of *abusus non tollit usum* time and again. It is drawn across many ethical trails.

A TIME TO PLANT, A TIME TO PLUCK

To draw our thinking together, we ought to repeat that there are three schools of thought favoring euthanasia. First, there are those who favor voluntary euthanasia, a personalistic ethical position. Second, there are those who favor involuntary euthanasia for monstrosities at birth and mental defectives, a partly personalistic and partly eugenic position.[30] Third, there are those who favor involuntary euthanasia for all who are a burden upon the community, a purely eugenic position. It should be perfectly obvious that we do not have to endorse the third school of thought just because we favor either the first or the second, or both. Our discussion has covered only the first one—voluntary medical euthanasia— as a means of ending a human life enmeshed in incurable and fatal physical suffering. The principles of right based upon selfhood and moral being favor it.

Defense of voluntary medical euthanasia, it should be made plain, does not depend upon the superficial system of values in which physical evil (pain) is regarded as worse than moral evil (sin) or intellectual evil (error). On the contrary, unless we are careful to see that pain is the least of evils, then our values would tie us back into that old attitude of taking the material or physical aspects of reality so seriously that we put nature or things as they are *out there* in a determinant place, subordinating the ethical and spiritual values of freedom and knowledge and upholding, in

---

[30] It has always been a quite common practice of midwives and, in modern times, doctors, simply to fail to respirate monstrous babies at birth.

effect, a kind of naturalism. C. S. Lewis has described it by saying that, "Of all evils, pain only is sterilized or disinfected evil."[31] Pain cannot create moral evil, such as a disintegration or demoralization of personality would be, unless it is submitted to in brute fashion as opponents of euthanasia insist we should do.

We repeat, the issue is not one of life or death. The issue is which kind of death, an agonized or peaceful one. Shall we meet death in personal integrity or in personal disintegration? Should there be a moral or a demoralized end to mortal life? Surely . . . we are not as persons of moral stature to be ruled by ruthless and unreasoning physiology, but rather by reason and self-control. Those who face the issues of euthanasia with a religious faith will not, if they think twice, submit to the materialistic and animistic doctrine that God's will is revealed by what nature does, and that life, qua life, is absolutely sacred and untouchable. All of us can agree with Reinhold Niebuhr that "the ending of our life would not threaten us if we had not falsely made ourselves the center of life's meaning."[32] One of the pathetic immaturities we all recognize around us is stated bluntly by Sigmund Freud in his *Reflections on War and Death*: "In the subconscious every one of us is convinced of his immortality." Our frantic hold upon life can only cease to be a snare and delusion when we objectify it in some religious doctrine of salvation, or, alternatively, agree with Sidney Hook that "the romantic pessimism which mourns man's finitude is a vain lament that we are not gods."[33] At least, the principles of personal morality warn us not to make physical phenomena, unmitigated by human freedom, the center of life's meaning. There is an impressive wisdom in the words of Dr. Logan Clendenning: "Death itself is not unpleasant. I have seen a good many people die. To a few death comes as a friend, as a relief from pain, from intolerable loneliness or loss, or from disappointment. To even fewer it comes as a horror. To most it hardly comes at all, so gradual is its approach, so long have the senses been benumbed, so little do they realize what is taking place. As I think it over, death seems to me one of the few evidences in nature of the operation of a creative intelligence exhibiting qualities which I recognize as mind stuff. To have blundered onto the form of energy called life showed a sort of malignant power. After having blundered on life, to have conceived of death was a real stroke of genius."[34]

As Ecclesiastes the Preacher kept saying in first one way and then another, "The living know that they shall die" and there is "a time to be born and a time to die, a time to plant and a time to pluck up that which is planted."[35] And in the New Covenant we read that "all flesh is as grass"

---

[31] *The Problem of Pain*, London, 1943, p. 104.
[32] *Human Destiny*, New York, 1943, 11, 293.
[33] Quoted by Corliss Lamont, *The Illusion of Immortality*, New York, 1950, p. 191.
[34] *The Human Body*, New York, 1941, 3rd ed., pp. 442–443.
[35] Eccl. 9:5 and 3:2.

and "the grass withereth, and the flower thereof falleth away." Nevertheless, "who is he that will harm you, if ye be followers of that which is
good?"[36]

Medicine contributes too much to the moral stature of men to persist
indefinitely in denying the ultimate claims of its own supreme virtue and
ethical inspiration, mercy. With Maeterlinck, we may be sure that "there
will come a day when Science will protest its errors and will shorten our
sufferings."[37]

[36] I Pet. 1:24 and 3:13.
[37] Quoted by G. W. Jacoby, *Physician, Pastor and Patient*, New York, 1936, p. 206.

THE PRINCIPLE
OF EUTHANASIA

Anthony Flew

Anthony Flew (1923–), Professor of Philosophy at the University of Keele, Staffordshire, England. His writings include A New Approach to Psychical Research *(1953),* Hume's Philosophy of Belief *(1961),* God and Philosophy *(1966), and* Evolutionary Ethics *(1967). He also edited the book* Logic and Language *(1951) and was coeditor with A. E. MacIntyre of* New Essays in Philosophical Theology *(1955).*

1

My particular concern here is to deploy a general moral case for the establishment of a legal right to voluntary euthanasia. The first point to emphasize is that the argument is about *voluntary* euthanasia. Neither I nor any other contributor to the present volume* advocates the euthanasia of either the incurably sick or the miserably senile except in so far as this is the strong, constant, and unequivocally expressed wish of the afflicted candidates themselves. Anyone, therefore, who dismisses what is in fact being contended on the gratuitously irrelevant grounds that he could not tolerate compulsory euthanasia, may very reasonably be construed as thereby tacitly admitting inability to meet and to overcome the case actually presented.

Second, my argument is an argument for the establishment of legal right. What I am urging is that any patient whose condition is hopeless and painful, who secures that it is duly and professionally certified as such, and who himself clearly and continuously desires to die should be enabled to do so: and that he should be enabled to do so without his incurring, or his family incurring, or those who provide or administer the means of

* This paper appeared in *Euthanasia and the Right to Die*, ed. A. B. Downing (London: Peter Owen, Ltd., 1969).

death incurring, any legal penalty or stigma whatsoever. To advocate the establishment of such a legal right is not thereby to be committed even to saying that it would always be morally justifiable, much less that it would always be morally obligatory, for any patient to exercise this right if he found himself in a position so to do. For a legal right is not as such necessarily and always a moral right; and hence, *a fortiori*, it is not necessarily and always a moral duty to exercise whatever legal rights you may happen to possess.

This is a vital point. It was—to refer first to an issue now at last happily resolved—crucial to the question of the relegalization in Great Britain of homosexual relations between consenting male adults. Only when it was at last widely grasped, and grasped in its relation to this particular question, could we find the large majorities in both Houses of Parliament by which a liberalizing bill was passed into law. For presumably most members of those majorities not only found the idea of homosexual relations repugnant—as most of us do—but also believed such relations to be morally wrong—as I for one do not. Yet they brought themselves to recognize that neither the repugnance generally felt towards some practice, nor even its actual wrongness if it actually is wrong, by itself constitutes sufficient reason for making or keeping that practice illegal. By the same token it can in the present instance be entirely consistent to urge, both that there ought to be a legal right to voluntary euthanasia, and that it would sometimes or always be morally wrong to exercise that legal right.

Third, the case presented here is offered as a moral one. In developing and defending such a case I shall, of course, have to consider certain peculiarly religious claims. Such claims, however, become relevant here only in so far as they either constitute, or may be thought to constitute, or in so far as they warrant, or may be thought to warrant, conclusions incompatible with those which it is my primary and positive purpose to urge.

Fourth, and finally, this essay is concerned primarily with general principles, not with particular practicalities. I shall not here discuss or— except perhaps quite incidentally—touch upon any questions of comparative detail: questions, for instance, of how a Euthanasia Act ought to be drafted; of what safeguards would need to be incorporated to prevent abuse of the new legal possibilities by those with disreputable reasons for wanting someone else dead; of exactly what and how much should be taken as constituting an unequivocal expression of a clear and constant wish; of the circumstances, if any, in which we ought to take earlier calculated expressions of a patient's desires as constituting still adequate grounds for action when at some later time the patient has become himself unable any longer to provide sufficiently sober, balanced, constant and unequivocal expressions of his wishes; and so on.

I propose here as a matter of policy largely to ignore such particular and practical questions. This is not because I foolishly regard them as unimportant, or irresponsibly dismiss them as dull. Obviously they could become of the most urgent interest. Nor yet is it because I believe that my philosophical cloth disqualifies me from contributing helpfully to any down-to-earth discussions. On the contrary, I happen to be one of those numerous academics who are convinced, some of them correctly, that they are practical and businesslike men! The decisive reason for neglecting these vital questions of detail here in, and in favour of, a consideration of the general principle of the legalization of voluntary euthanasia is that they are all secondary to that primary issue. For no such subordinate question can properly arise as relevantly practical until and unless the general principle is conceded. Some of these practical considerations are in any event dealt with by other contributors to this volume.

2

So what can be said in favour of the principle? There are two main, and to my mind decisive, moral reasons. But before deploying these it is worth pausing for a moment to indicate why the onus of proof does not properly rest upon us. It may seem as if it does, because we are proposing a change in the present order of things; and it is up to the man who wants a change to produce the reasons for making whatever change he is proposing. This most rational principle of conservatism is in general sound. But here it comes into conflict with the overriding and fundamental liberal principle. It is up to any person and any institution wanting to prevent anyone from doing anything he wishes to do, or to compel anyone to do anything he does not wish to do, to provide positive good reason to justify interference. The question should therefore be: *not* 'Why should people be given this new legal right?'; *but* 'Why should people in this matter be restrained by law from doing what they want?'

Yet even if this liberal perspective is accepted, as it too often is not, and even if we are able to dispose of any reasons offered in defence of the present legal prohibitions, still the question would arise, whether the present state of the law represents a merely tiresome departure from sound liberal principles of legislation, or whether it constitutes a really substantial evil. It is here that we have to offer out two main positive arguments.

(1) First, there are, and for the foreseeable future will be, people afflicted with incurable and painful diseases who urgently and fixedly want to die quickly. The first argument is that a law which tries to prevent such sufferers from achieving this quick death, and usually thereby forces other people who care for them to watch their pointless pain helplessly, is a very cruel law. It is because of this legal cruelty that advocates of eutha-

nasia sometimes speak of euthanasia as 'mercy-killing.' In such cases the sufferer may be reduced to an obscene parody of a human being, a lump of suffering flesh eased only by intervals of drugged stupor. This, as things now stand, must persist until at last every device of medical skill fails to prolong the horror.

(2) Second, a law which insists that there must be no end to this process —terminated only by the overdue relief of 'death by natural causes'—is a very degrading law. In the present context the full force of this second reason may not be appreciated immediately, if at all. We are so used to meeting appeals to 'the absolute value of human personality', offered as the would-be knock-down objection to any proposal to legalize voluntary euthanasia, that it has become hard to realize that, in so far as we can attach some tolerably precise meaning to the key phrase, this consideration would seem to bear in the direction precisely opposite to that in which it is usually mistaken to point. For the agonies of prolonged terminal illness can be so terrible and so demoralizing that the person is blotted out in ungovernable nerve reactions. In such cases as this, to meet the patient's longing for death is a means of showing for human personality that respect which cannot tolerate any ghastly travesty of it. So our second main positive argument, attacking the present state of the law as degrading, derives from a respect for the wishes of the individual person, a concern for human dignity, an unwillingness to let the animal pain disintegrate the man.

Our first main positive argument opposes the present state of the law, and of the public opinion which tolerates it, as cruel. Often and appositely this argument is supported by contrasting the tenderness which rightly insists that on occasion dogs and horses must be put out of their misery, with the stubborn refusal in any circumstances to permit one person to assist another in cutting short his suffering. The cry is raised, 'But people are not animals!' Indeed they are not. Yet this is precisely not a ground for treating people worse than brute animals. Animals are like people, in that they too can suffer. It is for this reason that both can have a claim on our pity and our mercy.[1]

But people are also more than brute animals. They can talk and think and wish and plan. It is this that makes it possible to insist, as we do, that there must be no euthanasia unless it is the firm considered wish of the person concerned. People also can, and should, have dignity as human beings. That is precisely why we are urging that they should be helped and not hindered when they wish to avoid or cut short the often degrading miseries of incurable disease or, I would myself add, of advanced senile decay.

[1] Thus Jeremy Bentham, urging that the legislator must not neglect animal sufferings, insists that the 'question is not "Can they *reason?*" nor "Can they *talk?*" but "Can they *suffer?*" ' (*Principles of Morals and Legislation*, Chap. XVII, *n.*)

3

In the first section I explained the scope and limitations of the present chapter. In the second I offered—although only after suggesting that the onus of proof in this case does not really rest on the proposition—my two main positive reasons in favour of euthanasia. It is time now to begin to face, and to try to dispose of, objections. This is the most important phase in the whole exercise. For to anyone with any width of experience and any capacity for compassion the positive reasons must be both perfectly obvious and strongly felt. The crucial issue is whether or not there are decisive, overriding objections to these most pressing reasons of the heart. (1) Many of the objections commonly advanced, which are often mistaken to be fundamental, are really objections only to a possible specific manner of implementing the principle of voluntary euthanasia. Thus it is suggested that if the law permitted doctors on occasion to provide their patients with means of death, or where necessary to do the actual killing, and they did so, then the doctors who did either of these things would be violating the Hippocratic Oath, and the prestige of and public confidence in the medical profession would be undermined.

As to the Hippocratic Oath, this makes two demands which in the special circumstances we have in mind may become mutually contradictory. They cannot both be met at the same time. The relevant section reads: 'I will use treatments to help the sick according to my ability and judgment, but never with a view to injury and wrong-doing. I will not give anyone a lethal dose if asked to do so, nor will I suggest such a course.'[2] The fundamental undertaking 'to help the sick according to my ability and judgment' may flatly conflict with the further promise not to 'give anyone a lethal dose if asked to do so.' To observe the basic undertaking a doctor may have to break the further promise. The moral would, therefore, appear to be: not that the Hippocratic Oath categorically and unambiguously demands that doctors must have no dealings with voluntary euthanasia; but rather that the possible incompatibility in such cases of the different directives generated by two of its logically independent clauses constitutes a reason for revising that Oath.

As to the supposed threat to the prestige of and to our confidence in the medical profession, I am myself inclined to think that the fears expressed are—in more than one dimension—disproportionate to the realities. But whatever the truth about this whole objection would bear only

---

[2] The Greek text is most easily found in *Hippocrates and the Fragments of Heracleitus,* ed. W. H. S. Jones and E. T. Withington for the Loeb series (Harvard Univ. Pr. and Heinemann), Vol. 1, p. 298. The translation in the present essay is mine.

against proposals which permitted or required doctors to do, or directly to assist in, the actual killing. This is not something which is essential to the whole idea of voluntary euthanasia, and the British Euthanasia Society's present draft bill is so formulated as altogether to avoid this objection. It is precisely such inessential objections as this which I have undertaken to eschew in this essay, in order to consider simply the general principle.

(2) The first two objections which do really bear on this form a pair. One consists in the contention that there is no need to be concerned about the issue, since in fact there are not any, or not many, patients who when it comes to the point want to die quickly. The other bases the same complacent conclusion on the claim that in fact, in the appropriate cases, doctors already mercifully take the law into their own hands. These two comfortable doctrines are, like many other similarly reassuring bromides, both entirely wrong and rather shabby.

(a) To the first the full reply would probably have to be made by a doctor, for a medical layman can scarcely be in a position to make an estimate of the number of patients who would apply and could qualify for euthanasia.[3] But it is quite sufficient for our immediate purposes to say two things. First, there can be few who have reached middle life, and who have not chosen to shield their sensibilities with some impenetrable carapace of dogma, who cannot recall at least one case of an eager candidate for euthanasia from their own experience—even from their own peacetime experience only. If this statement is correct, as my own inquiries suggest that it is, then the total number of such eager candidates must be substantial. Second, though the need for enabling legalization becomes progressively more urgent the greater the numbers of people personally concerned, I wish for myself to insist that it still matters very much indeed if but one person who would have decided for a quick death is forced to undergo a protracted one.

(b) To the second objection, which admits that there are many cases where euthanasia is indicated, but is content to leave it to the doctors to defy the law, the answer is equally simple. First, it is manifestly not true that all doctors are willing on the appropriate occasions either to provide the means of death or to do the killing. Many, as they are Roman Catholics, are on religious grounds absolutely opposed to doing so. Many others are similarly opposed for other reasons, or by force of training and habit. And there is no reason to believe that among the rest the proportion of potential martyrs is greater than it is in any other secular occupational group. Second, it is entirely wrong to expect the members of one profession as a regular matter of course to jeopardize their whole careers by breaking the criminal law in order to save the rest of us the labour and embarrassment of changing that law.

[3] See Downing, pp. 20–1; also pp. 23–4 for his reference to Professor Hinton's work, *Dying* (Pelican, 1967).

Here I repeat two points made to me more than once by doctor friends. First, if a doctor were convinced he ought to provide euthanasia in spite of the law, it would often be far harder for him to do so undetected than many laymen think, especially in our hospitals. Second, the present attitude of the medical establishment is such that if a doctor did take the chance, was caught and brought to trial, and even if the jury, as they well might, refused to convict, still he must expect to face complete professional disaster.

(3) The next two objections, which in effect bear on the principle, again form a pair. The first pair had in common the claim that the facts were such that the question of legislative action need not arise. The second pair are alike in that whereas both might appear to be making contentions of fact, in reality we may have in each a piece of exhortation or of metaphysics masquerading as an empirical proposition.

(a) Of this second relevant pair the first suggests that there is no such thing as an incurable disease. This implausible thesis becomes more intelligible, though no more true, when we recall how medical ideologues sometimes make proclamations: 'Modern medicine cannot recognize any such thing as a disease which is incurable'; and the like. Such pronouncements may sound like reports on the present state of the art. It is from this resemblance that they derive their peculiar idiomatic point. But the advance of medicine has not reached a stage where all diseases are curable. And no one seriously thinks that it has. At most this continuing advance has suggested that we need never despair of finding cures *some day*. But this is not at all the same thing as saying, what is simply not true, that *even now* there is no condition which is at any stage incurable. This medical ideologue's slogan has to be construed as a piece of exhortation disguised for greater effect as a paradoxical statement of purported fact. It may as such be instructively compared with certain favourite educationalists' paradoxes: 'We do not teach subjects, we teach children!'; or 'There are no bad children, only bad teachers!'

(b) The second objection of this pair is that no one can ever be certain that the condition of any particular patient is indeed hopeless. This is more tricky. For an objection of this form might be given two radically different sorts of content. Yet it would be easy and is common to slide from one interpretation to the other, and back again, entirely unwittingly.

Simply and straightforwardly, such an objection might be made by someone whose point was that judgments of incurability are, as a matter of purely contingent fact, so unreliable that no one has any business to be certain, or to claim to know, that anyone is suffering from an incurable affliction. This contention would relevantly be backed by appealing to the alleged fact that judgments that 'this case is hopeless, *period*' are far more frequently proven to have been mistaken than judgments that, for instance, 'this patient will recover fully, *provided that* he undergoes the appropriate operation.' This naïve objector's point could be made out, or decisively refuted, only by reference to quantitative studies of the actual relative reliabilities and unreliabilities of different sorts of medical judgments. So unless and until such quantitative empirical studies are actually made, and unless and until their results are shown to bear upon the question of euthanasia in the way suggested, there is no grounded and categorical objection here to be met.

But besides this first and straightforwardly empirical interpretation there is a second interpretation of another quite different sort. Suppose someone points to an instance, as they certainly could and well might, where some patient whom all the doctors had pronounced to be beyond hope nevertheless recovers, either as the result of the application of new treatment derived from some swift and unforeseen advance in medical science, or just through nature taking its unexpected course. This happy but chastening outcome would certainly demonstrate that the doctors concerned had on this occasion been mistaken; and hence that, though they had sincerely claimed to know the patient's condition to have been incurable, they had not really known this. The temptation is to mistake it that such errors show that no one ever really knows. It is this perfectly general contention, applied to the particular present case of judgments of incurability, which constitutes the second objection in its second interpretation. The objector seizes upon the point that even the best medical opinion turns out sometimes to have been wrong (as here). He then urges, simply because doctors thus prove occasionally to have been mistaken (as here) and because it is always—theoretically if not practically—possible that they may be mistaken again the next time, that therefore none of them ever really knows (at least in such cases). Hence, he concludes, there is after all no purchase for the idea of voluntary euthanasia. For this notion presupposes that there are patients recognizably suffering from conditions known to be incurable.

The crux to grasp about this contention is that, notwithstanding that it may be presented and pressed as if it were somehow especially relevant to one particular class of judgments, in truth it applies—if it applies at all —absolutely generally. The issue is thus revealed as not medical but metaphysical. If it follows that if someone is ever mistaken then he never really knows, and still more if it follows that if it is even logically possible that he may be mistaken then he never really knows, then, surely, the consequence must be that none of us ever does know—not *really*. (When a metaphysician says that something is never really such and such, what he really means is that it very often is, *really*.) For it is of the very essence of our cognitive predicament that we do all sometimes make mistakes; while always it is at least theoretically possible that we may. Hence the argument, if it holds at all, must show that knowledge, *real* knowledge, is for all us mortal men forever unattainable.

What makes the second of the present pair of objections tricky to handle is that it is so easy to pass unwittingly from an empirical to a metaphysical interpretation. We may fail to notice, or noticing may fail convincingly to explain, how an empirical thesis has degenerated into metaphysics, or how metaphysical misconceptions have corrupted the medical judgment. Yet, once these utterly different interpretations have been adequately distinguished, two summary comments should be sufficient.

First, in so far as the objection is purely metaphysical, to the idea that *real* knowledge is possible, it applies absolutely generally; or not at all. It is arbitrary and irrational to restrict it to the examination of the principle of voluntary euthanasia. If doctors never really know, we presumably have no business to rely much upon any of their judgments. And if, for the same metaphysical reasons, there is no knowledge to be had anywhere, then we are all of us in the same case about everything. This may be as it may be, but it is nothing in particular to the practical business in hand.

Second, when the objection takes the form of a pretended refusal to take any decision in matters of life and death on the basis of a judgment which theoretically might turn out to have been mistaken, it is equally unrealistic and arbitrary. It is one thing to claim that judgments of incurability are peculiarly fallible: if that suggestion were to be proved to be correct. It is quite another to claim that it is improper to take vital decisions on the basis of sorts of judgment which either are in principle fallible, or even prove occasionally in fact to have been wrong. It is an inescapable feature of the human condition that no one is infallible about anything, and there is no sphere of life in which mistakes do not occur. Nevertheless we cannot as agents avoid, even in matters of life and death and more than life and death, making decisions to act or to abstain. It is only necessary and it is only possible to insist on ordinarily strict standards of warranted assertability, and on ordinarily exacting rather than obsessional criteria of what is beyond reasonable doubt.

Of course this means that mistakes will sometimes be made. This is in practice a corollary of the uncontested fact that infallibility is not an option. To try to ignore our fallibility is unrealistic, while to insist on remembering it only in the context of the question of voluntary euthanasia is arbitrary. Nor is it either realistic or honourable to attempt to offload the inescapable burdens of practical responsibility, by first claiming that we never really *know*, and then pretending that a decision not to act is somehow a decsion which relieves us of all proper responsibility for the outcome.

(4) The two pairs of relevant objections so far considered have both been attempts in different ways to show that the issue does not, or at any rate need not, arise as a practical question. The next concedes that the question does arise and is important, but attempts to dispose of it with the argument that what we propose amounts to the legalization, in certain

circumstances, of murder, or suicide, or both; and that this cannot be right because murder and suicide are both gravely wrong always. Now even if we were to concede all the rest it would still not follow, because something is gravely wrong in morals, that there ought to be a law against it; and that we are wrong to try to change the law as it now subsists. We have already urged that the onus of proof must always rest on the defenders of any restriction.

(a) In fact the rest will not do. In the first place, if the law were to be changed as we want, the present legal definition of 'murder' would at the same time have to be so changed that it no longer covered the provision of euthanasia for a patient who had established that it was his legal right. 'Does this mean,' someone may indignantly protest, 'that right and wrong are created by Acts of Parliament?' Emphatically, yes: and equally emphatically, no. Yes indeed, if what is intended is *legal* right and *legal* offence. What is meant by the qualification 'legal' if it is not that these rights are the rights established and sanctioned by the law? Certainly not, if what is intended is *moral* right and *moral* wrong. Some moral rights happen to be at the same time legal rights, and some moral wrongs similarly also constitute offences against the law. But, notoriously, legislatures may persist in denying moral rights; while, as I insisted earlier, not every moral wrong either is or ought to be forbidden and penalized by law.

Well then, if the legal definition of 'murder' can be changed by Act of Parliament, would euthanasia nevertheless be murder, morally speaking? This amounts to asking whether administering euthanasia legally to someone who is incurably ill, and who has continually wanted it, is in all relevant respects similar to, so to speak, a standard case of murder; and whether therefore it is to be regarded morally as murder. Once the structure of the question is in this way clearly displayed it becomes obvious that the cases are different in at least three important respects. First, whereas the murder victim is (typically) killed against his will, a patient would be given or assisted in obtaining euthanasia only if he steadily and strongly desired to die. Second, whereas the murderer kills his victim, treating him usually as a mere object for disposal, in euthanasia the object of the exercise would be to save someone, at his own request, from needless suffering, to prevent the degradation of a human person. Third, whereas the murderer by his action defies the law, the man performing euthanasia would be acting according to law, helping another man to secure what the law allowed him.

It may sound as if that third clause goes back on the earlier repudiation of the idea that moral right and wrong are created by Act of Parliament. That is not so. For we are not saying that this action would now be justifiable, or at least not murder morally, simply because it was now permitted by the law; but rather that the change in the law would remove one of possible reasons for moral objection. The point is this: that although the fact that something is enjoined, permitted, or forbidden by law does not necessarily make it right, justifiable, or wrong morally, never-theless the fact that something is enjoined or forbidden by a law laid down by established authority does constitute one moral reason for obedi-ence. So a doctor who is convinced that the objects of the Euthanasia Society are absolutely right should at least hesitate to take the law into his own hands, not only for prudential but also for moral reasons. For to defy the law is, as it were, to cast your vote against constitutional proce-dures and the rule of law, and these are the foundations and framework of any tolerable civilized society. (Consider here the injunction posted by some enlightened municipal authorities upon their public litter bins: 'Cast your vote here for a tidy New York!'—or wherever it may be.)

Returning to the main point, the three differences which we have just noticed are surely sufficient to require us to refuse to assimilate legalized voluntary euthanasia to the immoral category of murder. But to insist on making a distinction between legalized voluntary euthanasia and murder is not the same thing as, nor does it by itself warrant, a refusal to accept that both are equally immoral. What an appreciation of these three differ-ences, but crucially of the first, should do is to suggest that we ought to think of such euthanasia as a special case not of murder but of suicide. Let us therefore examine the second member of our third pair of relevant objections.

(b) This objection was that to legalize voluntary euthanasia would be to legalize, in certain conditions, the act of assisting suicide. The ques-tion therefore arises: 'Is suicide always morally wrong?'

The purely secular considerations usually advanced and accepted are not very impressive. First, it is still sometimes urged that suicide is unnatural, in conflict with instinct, a breach of the putative law of self-preservation. All arguments of this sort, which attempt directly to deduce conclusions about what *ought* to be from premises stating, or mis-stating, only what *is* are—surely—unsound: they involve what philosophers label, appropriately, the 'Naturalistic Fallacy'. There is also a peculiar viciousness about appealing to what is supposed to be a descriptive law of nature to provide some justification for the prescription to obey that supposed law. For if the law really obtained as a description of what always and unavoid-ably happens, then there would be no point in prescribing that it should; whereas if the descriptive law does not in fact hold, then the basis of the supposed justification does not exist.[4] Furthermore, even if an argument of this first sort could show that suicide is always immoral, it could scarcely provide a reason for insisting that it ought also to be illegal.

Second, it is urged that the suicide by his act deprives other people of the services which he might have rendered them had he lived longer. This can be a strong argument, especially where the suicide has a clear,

[4] I have argued this kind of point more fully in *Evolutionary Ethics* (London: Mac-millan, 1967). See Chap. IV, 'From *Is to Ought.*'

positive family or public obligation. It is also an argument which, even in a liberal perspective, can provide a basis for legislation. But it is irrelevant to the circumstances which advocates of the legalization of voluntary euthanasia have in mind. In such circumstances as these, there is no longer any chance of being any use to anyone, and if there is any family or social obligation it must be all the other way—to end your life when it has become a hopeless burden both to yourself and to others.

Third, it is still sometimes maintained that suicide is in effect murder —'self-murder.' To this, offered in a purely secular context, the appropriate and apparently decisive reply would seem to be that by parity of reasoning marriage is really adultery—'own-wife-adultery.' For, surely, the gravamen of both distinctions lies in the differences which such paradoxical assimilations override. It is precisely because suicide is the destruction of oneself (by one's own choice), while murder is the destruction of somebody else (against his wishes), that the former can be, and is, distinguished from the latter.

Yet there is a counter to this own-wife-adultery-move. It begins by insisting, rightly, that sexual relations—which are what is common to both marriage and adultery—are not in themselves wrong: the crucial question is, 'Who with?' It then proceeds to claim that what is common to both murder and suicide is the killing of a human being; and here the questions of 'Which one?' or 'By whom?' are not, morally, similarly decisive. Finally appeal may be made, if the spokesman is a little old-fashioned, to the Sixth Commandment, or if he is in the contemporary swim, to the Principle of the Absolute Sanctity of Human Life.

The fundamental difficulty which confronts anyone making this counter move is that of finding a formulation for his chosen principle about the wrongness of all killing, which is both sufficiently general not to appear merely question-begging in its application to the cases in dispute, and which yet carries no consequences that the spokesman himself is not prepared to accept. Thus, suppose he tries to read the Sixth Commandment as constituting a veto on any killing of human beings. Let us waive here the immediate scholarly objections: that such a reading involves accepting the mistranslation 'Thou shalt not kill' rather than the more faithful 'Thou shalt do no murder'; and that neither the children of Israel nor even their religious leaders construed this as a law forbidding all war and all capital punishment.[5] The question remains whether our spokesman himself is really prepared to say that all killing, without any exception, is morally wrong.

It is a question which has to be pressed, and which can only be answered by each man for himself. Since I cannot give your answer, I can only say that I know few if any people who would sincerely say 'Yes'. But

---

[5] See, f.i., Joseph Fletcher, *Morals and Medicine* (1954; Gollancz, 1955), pp. 195–6. I recommend this excellent treatment by a liberal Protestant of a range of questions in moral theology too often left too far from liberal Roman Catholics.

as soon as any exceptions or qualifications are admitted, it becomes excessively difficult to find any presentable principle upon which these can be admitted while still excluding suicide and assistance to suicide in a case of euthanasia. This is not just because, generally, once any exceptions or qualifications have been admitted to any rule it becomes hard or impossible not to allow others. It is because, particularly, the case for excluding suicide and assisting suicide from the scope of any embargo on killing people is so strong that only some absolutely universal rule admitting no exceptions of any sort whatever could have the force convincingly to override it.

Much the same applies to the appeal to the Principle of the Absolute Sanctity of Human Life. Such appeals were continually made by conservatives—many of them politically not Conservative but Socialist—in opposition to the recent efforts to liberalize the British abortion laws. Such conservatives should be, and repeatedly were, asked whether they are also opponents of all capital punishment and whether they think that it is always wrong to kill in a 'just war'. (In fact none of those in Parliament could honestly have answered 'Yes' to both questions.) In the case of abortion their position could still be saved by inserting the qualification 'innocent', a qualification traditionally made by cautious moralists who intend to rest on this sort of principle. But any such qualification, however necessary, must make it almost impossible to employ the principle thus duly qualified to proscribe all suicide. It would be extraordinarily awkward and far-fetched to condemn suicide or assisting suicide as 'taking an innocent life.'

Earlier in the present subsection I described the three arguments I have been examining as secular. This was perhaps misleading. For all three are regularly used by religious people: indeed versions of all three are to be found in St Thomas Aquinas's *Summa Theologica*, the third being there explicitly linked with St Augustine's laboured interpretation of the Sixth Commandment to cover suicide.[6] And perhaps the incongruity of trying to make the amended Principle of the Absolute Sanctity of Innocent Human Life yield a ban on suicide is partly to be understood as a result of attempting to derive from secularized premises conclusions which really depend upon a religious foundation. But the next two arguments are frankly and distinctively religious.

The first insists that human beings are God's property: 'It is our duty to take care of God's property entrusted to our charge—our souls and bodies. They belong not to us but to God';[7] 'Whoever takes his own life sins against God, even as he who kills another's slave sins against that

---

[6] Part II: Q. 64, A5. The Augustine reference is to *The City of God*, 1, 20. It is worth comparing, for ancient Judaic attitudes, E. Westermarck's *Origin and Development of the Moral Ideas*, Vol. 1, pp. 246–7.

[7] See the Rev. G. J. MacGillivray, 'Suicide and Euthanasia', p. 10; a widely distributed Catholic Truth Society pamphlet.

slave's master';[8] and 'Suicide is the destruction of the temple of God and a violation of the property rights of Jesus Christ.'[9]

About this I restrict myself to three comments here. First, as it stands, unsupplemented by appeal to some other principle or principles, it must apply, if it applies at all, equally to *all* artificial and intentional shortening *or* lengthening of any human life, one's own *or* that of anyone else. Alone and unsupplemented it would commit one to complete quietism in all matters of life and death; for all interference would be interference with someone else's property. Otherwise one must find further particular moral revelations by which to justify capital punishment, war, medicine, and many other such at first flush impious practices. Second, it seems to presuppose that a correct model of the relation between man and God is that of slave and slave-master, and that respect for God's property ought to be the fundamental principle of morals. It is perhaps significant that it is to this image that St Thomas and the pagan Plato, in attacking suicide, both appeal. This attempt to derive not only theological but all obligations from the putative theological fact of Creation is a commonplace of at least one tradition of moral theology. In this derivation the implicit moral premise is usually that unconditional obedience to a Creator, often considered as a very special sort of owner, is the primary elemental obligation.[10] Once this is made explicit it does not appear to be self-evidently true; nor is it easy to see how a creature in absolute ontological dependence could be the genuinely responsible subject of obligations to his infinite Creator.[11] Third, this objection calls to mind one of the sounder sayings of the sinister Tiberius: 'If the gods are insulted let them see to it themselves.' This remark is obviously relevant only to the question of legalization, not to that of the morality or the prudence of the action itself.

The second distinctively religious argument springs from the conviction that God does indeed see to it Himself, with a penalty of infinite severity. If you help someone to secure euthanasia, 'You are sending him from the temporary and comparatively light suffering of this world to the eternal suffering of hell.' Now if this appalling suggestion could be shown to be true it would provide the most powerful moral reason against helping euthanasia in any way, and for using any legislative means which might save people from suffering a penalty so inconceivably cruel. It would also be the strongest possible prudential reason against 'suiciding oneself'.[12] (Though surely anyone who knowingly incurred such a penalty

---

[8] Aquinas, loc. cit.

[9] Koch-Preuss, *Handbook of Moral Theology*, Vol. II, p. 76. This quotation has been taken from Fletcher, op. cit., p. 192.

[10] Cf., for convenience, MacGillivray, loc. cit.; and for a Protestant analogue the Bishop of Exeter quoted by P. Nowell-Smith in *Ethics* (Penguin, 1954), pp. 37–8 *n*.

[11] I have developed this contention in *God and Philosophy* (Hutchinson, 1966), §§ 2.34 ff.

[12] This rather affected-sounding gallicism is adopted deliberately: if you believe, as I do,

would by that very action prove himself to be genuinely of unsound mind; and hence not *justly* punishable at all. Not that a Being contemplating such unspeakable horrors could be expected to be concerned with justice!)

About this second, peculiarly religious, argument there is, it would seem, little to be done except: either simply to concede that for anyone holding this belief it indeed is reasonable to oppose euthanasia, and to leave it at that; or, still surely conceding this, to attempt to mount a general offensive against the whole system of which it forms a part.

(5) The final objection is one raised, with appropriate modifications, by the opponents of every reform everywhere. It is that even granting that the principle of the reform is excellent it would, if adopted, lead inevitably to something worse; and so we had much better not make any change at all. Thus G. K. Chesterton pronounced that the proponents of euthanasia now seek only the death of those who are a nuisance to themselves, but soon it will be broadened to include those who are a nuisance to others.[13] Such cosy arguments depend on two assumptions: that the supposedly inevitable consequences are indeed evil and substantially worse than the evils the reform would remove; and that the supposedly inevitable consequences really are inevitable consequences.

In the present case we certainly can grant the first assumption, if the consequence supposed is taken to be large-scale legalized homicide in the Nazi manner. But whatever reason is there for saying that this would, much less inevitably must, follow? For there are the best of reasons for insisting that there is a world of difference between legalized voluntary euthanasia and such legalized mass-murder. Only if public opinion comes to appreciate their force will there be any chance of getting the reform we want. Then we should have no difficulty, in alliance doubtless with all our present opponents, in blocking any move to legalize murder which might conceivably arise from a misunderstanding of the case for voluntary euthanasia. Furthermore, it is to the point to remind such objectors that the Nazi atrocities they probably have in mind were in fact not the result of any such reform, but were the work of people who consciously repudiated the whole approach to ethics represented in the argument of the present essay. For this approach is at once human and humanitarian. It is concerned above all with the reduction of suffering; but concerned at the same time with other values too, such as human dignity and respect for the wishes of the individual person. And always it is insistent that

---

that suicide is not always and as such wrong, it is inappropriate to speak of 'committing suicide'; just as correspondingly if you believe, as I do not, that (private) profit is wrong, it becomes apt to talk to those who 'commit a profit.'

13 I take this quotation, too, from Fletcher, op. cit., p. 201: it originally appeared in *The Digest* (Dec. 23, 1937). Another, much more recent specimen of this sort of obscurantist flim-flam may be found in Lord Longford's speech to the House of Lords against Mr David Steel's Abortion Bill as originally passed by the Commons. Lord Longford (formerly Pakenham) urged that if that bill were passed, we might see the day when senile members of their lordships' House were put down willy-nilly.

morality should not be 'left in the dominion of vague feeling or inexplicable internal conviction, but should be . . . made a matter of reason and calculation.'[14]

[14] J. S. Mill's essay on Bentham quoted in F. R. Leavis, *Mill on Bentham and Coleridge* (Chatto & Windus, 1950), p. 92.

Selected bibliography

Personal Relationships
Bieber, I., et al. *Homosexuality: A Psychoanalytic Study.* New York: Basic Books, 1962.
Calverton, V. F., and Schmaulhausen, S. D., eds. *Sex in Civilization.* New York: Macaulay, 1929.
Daly, C. B. *Morals, Law and Life.* Chicago: Scepter Publishers, 1966.
Ellis, Albert. *The Art and Science of Love.* New York: Dell, 1965.
Ellis, Havelock. *Studies in the Psychology of Sex.* Philadelphia: Davis, 1923.
Freud, S. *Three Contributions to the Theory of Sex.* New York: Dutton, 1962.
Fromm, Erich. *The Art of Loving.* New York: Harper & Row, 1956.
Heider, Fritz. *The Psychology of Interpersonal Relations.* New York: Wiley, 1958.
Karlen, A. *Sexuality and Homosexuality.* New York: Norton, 1971.
Laing, R. D., and Esterson, A. *Sanity, Madness, and the Family.* New York: Basic Books, 1964.
Lewis, C. S. *The Four Loves.* New York: Harcourt Brace Jovanovich, 1960.
Masters, William, and Johnson, Virginia. *Human Sexual Response.* Boston: Little, Brown, 1966.
Mead, Margaret. *Male and Female.* New York: Morrow, 1949.
Menninger, Karl. *Love Against Hate.* New York: Harcourt Brace Jovanovich, 1959.
Montagu, A. *Sex, Man and Society.* New York: Tower Publications, 1969.
Neubeck, G., ed. *Extramarital Relations.* Englewood Cliffs, N.J.: Prentice-Hall, 1969.
Neumann, Erich. *Amor and Psyche.* Princeton: Princeton University Press, 1956.
Nygren, Anders. *Agape and Eros.* Philadelphia: Westminster Press, 1953.
Ortega y Gasset, José. *On Love, Aspects of a Single Theme.* New York: Meridian Books, 1957.
Reik, T. *Of Love and Lust.* New York: Farrar, Straus & Giroux, 1970.
Rosenbaum, S., and Alger, I., eds. *The Marriage Relationship: Psychoanalytic Perspectives.* New York: Basic Books, 1968.
Russell, Bertrand. *Marriage and Morals.* New York: Bantam Books, 1968.
Stendahl [Beyle, Marie-Henri]. *On Love.* New York: Liveright, 1947.
Westermarck, Edward. *A Short History of Human Marriage.* New York: Macmillan, 1926.
————. *The Future of Marriage in Western Civilization.* London: Macmillan, 1936.

Abortion
Callahan, Daniel. *Abortion: Law, Choice and Morality.* New York: Macmillan, 1970.

Cutler, Donald R., ed. *Updating Life and Death: Essays in Ethics and Medicine*. Boston: Beacon Press, 1969.

Feinberg, Joel, ed. *The Problem of Abortion*. Belmont, Calif.: Wadsworth, 1973.

Granfield, David. *The Abortion Decision*. New York: Doubleday, 1971.

Grisez, Germain G. *Abortion: The Myths, the Realities, and the Arguments*. New York: Corpus Books, 1970.

Guttmacher, Alan F., ed. *The Case for Legalized Abortion Now*. Berkeley: Diablo Press, 1967.

Hall, R. E., ed. *Abortion in a Changing World*. New York: Columbia University Press, 1970.

Horden, Anthony. *Legal Abortion: The English Experience*. Oxford: Pergamon, 1971.

Labby, Daniel H., ed. *Life or Death: Ethics and Options*. Seattle: University of Washington Press, 1968.

Lader, Lawrence. *Abortion*. Indianapolis: Bobbs-Merrill, 1966.

———. *Abortion II*. Boston: Beacon Press, 1973.

Noonan, John T., ed. *The Morality of Abortion: Legal and Historical Perspectives*. Cambridge: Harvard University Press, 1970.

Reiterman, Carl, ed. *Abortion and the Unwanted Child*. New York: Springer, 1971.

St. John-Stevas, Norman. *The Right to Life*. New York: Holt, Rinehart & Winston, 1964.

Smith, D. T., ed. *Abortion and the Law*. Cleveland: Case Western Reserve University Press, 1967.

Walbert, David F., and Butler, J. D., eds. *Abortion, Society and the Law*. Cleveland: Case Western Reserve University Press, 1973.

Euthanasia

Choron, Jacques. *Suicide*. New York: Charles Scribner's, 1972.

Crane, Diana. *The Social Aspects of the Prolongation of Life*. New York: Russell Sage Foundation, 1969.

Dedek, John F. *Human Life: Some Moral Issues*. New York: Sheed, 1972.

Downing, A. B., ed. *Euthanasia and the Right to Life*. London: Peter Owen, 1971.

Epictetus. *Discourses*. Oxford: Oxford University Press, 1928.

Fletcher, Joseph. *Morals and Medicine*. Boston: Beacon Press, 1954.

Gould, Jonathan, and Craigmyle, Lord, eds. *Your Death Warrant? The Implications of Euthanasia*. New York: Arlington House, 1973.

Hadas, Moses. *The Stoic Philosophy of Seneca*. New York: Doubleday, 1958.

Healy, Edwin F. *Medical Ethics*. Chicago: Loyola University Press, 1956.

Kohl, Marvin. *Beneficent Euthanasia*. Buffalo: Prometheus Books, 1974.

Maguire, Daniel C. *Death by Choice*. New York: Doubleday, 1974.

McFadden, Charles J. *Medical Ethics*. Philadelphia: F. A. Davis, 1967.

Ramsey, Paul. *The Patient as Person*. New Haven: Yale University Press, 1970.

Roberts, Harry. *Euthanasia and Other Aspects of Life and Death*. Ann Arbor: Finch Press, 1936.

Shneidman, Edwin S., ed. *On the Nature of Suicide*. San Francisco: Jossey-Bass, 1969.

Torrey, E. F., ed. *Ethical Issues in Medicine*. Boston: Little, Brown, 1968.

Trubo, Richard. *An Act of Mercy: Euthanasia Today*. Freeport, N.Y.: Nash Publications, 1973.

Visscher, Maurice B., ed. *Humanistic Perspectives in Medical Ethics*. Buffalo:
    Prometheus Books, 1972.
Williams, Glanville. *Sanctity of Life and the Criminal Law*. New York: Knopf,
    1957.

JUSTIFYING YOUR POLITICAL POSITION

II

THE POLITICAL PROBLEMS considered in this section on war and violence, the equality of women, and privacy and surveillance are highly contemporary yet perennial in character. The question of woman's status has received considerable attention recently, but it was also a point of difference between Athens and Sparta discussed by Plato in the fifth century B.C. War and violence are as old as the human race, but the nuclear dimension and the forms of political blackmail and urban terrorism are peculiarly modern, and although the invasion of privacy is nothing novel in history, the development of electronic surveillance equipment and computer databanks has added a new dimension to the problem.

Let us begin with the issue of war and violence. Having undergone two world wars and the Korean and Vietnam wars thus far this century (in addition to various "brush fires," incursions, invasions, cold wars, and so forth), we are disillusioned about the prospect of lasting peace, and if we consider the repeated warfare that has characterized human history, we may be tempted to adopt the pessimistic position that war is inevitable. Nevertheless, that which has always been need not always be. In the eighteenth century, slavery was thought to be inherent to the human condition because (until that time) there had always been slaves; but slavery has since been virtually eliminated. In the same way, various diseases thought to be ineradicable torments of mankind have moved from the incurable to the curable or cured categories, for instance, typhoid fever and diphtheria. Even death may not be inevitable since people always die of specific medical problems which, in principle, are conquerable.

War too may be a temporary phenomenon characteristic of man's early development and not intrinsic to human interaction. It is encouraging to consider the fact that although men have always fought, in the same sense they have always been at peace; that is, there has always been peace in some areas of the world while war occurred elsewhere. In the balance, peace has predominated, but the point is that *both* characterize our past, and we can hope to increase the periods of peace and reduce or eliminate the incidence of war.[1]

Why should it strike us as utopian and unrealistic to consider a world without war? Probably because we are impressed with the aggressive tendencies in human beings, which we feel must erupt periodically in violent acts. War is collective, organized violence, but the newspapers supply us with evidence every day of individual aggression—from brutal muggings to horrible murders. We may be led to conclude that if a point is reached when people no longer fight over economic, political, religious, or ideological issues, they will find other excuses for venting their aggression; that is, that human beings are simply aggressive by nature.

[1] The evidence from nature also furnishes greater cause for hope than despair, for there are many herd and community creatures, such as bees, wasps, ants, and deer, which fight in a chiefly ritualistic manner; and few creatures destroy their own kind.

This question, of course, involves our theories about human nature and the causes of aggression, on which there is a vast literature,[2] but the psychological evidence so far indicates that aggression is not an innate but a learned response. However, even if aggression were innate, there is no necessity for it to be expressed in destructive ways; it could be channeled toward useful and creative purposes and function as a positive survival mechanism. The usual (ironic) example is that of a surgeon, but any occupation—from construction worker to corporation executive—could operate to express (displace) aggression in productive ways for the maintenance and enhancement of life. Hostility can also be expressed through sports; although violent contact sports, such as football and boxing, tend to incite rather than dispell aggression.

Whether innate or learned, violent and destructive acts do not have to continually occur and war is not inevitable because of human nature. To achieve peace, the task would be to create a social environment that minimizes the need for violent responses and harnesses aggression in the service of human welfare. Bringing these conditions about is a gigantic undertaking, but at least we need not be undermined in our efforts by the assumption that the problem lies in the incorrigible nature of human beings.

Apart from the question of whether people *must* fight is the question of whether they *should* fight. Are there any conditions under which, in our present imperfect world, reason can dictate violence and the use of force be justified? Can there be a just war?

A. Campbell Garnett provides some interesting insights into this question through a discussion of how philosophic ideas affect our willingness to make war in his essay "Philosophical Ideas and World Peace" in this section. The extreme position, of course, is that we should never offer force, but be pacifist in outlook and behavior, and this alternative is examined by Gordon C. Zahn in his paper "Violence and Pacifism." Zahn is willing to allow defensive action in the form of passive resistance, but he is unwilling to endorse aggression, especially the threat or use of nuclear weapons.

It is an open question whether this more sophisticated version of pacifism saves it from the charges of naiveté and impracticality which are usually leveled at it. Pacifists are in a difficult position, perhaps because of the profundity of their thought, but if they fail to oppose force with force, they may be encouraging it by default, and if they use violence, even as a temporary measure, they oppose their own principles and come to re-

---

[2] Hostility has been variously attributed to the death instinct (turned outwards), to a constant aggressive energy, to repeated frustration, to instinctive targets of aggression (for the cat, mice; and for human beings, other people), and to purposelessness and boredom, to mention just a few. See especially S. Freud, *Civilization and Its Discontents*; H. Marcuse, *Eros and Civilization*; K. Lorenz, *On Aggression*; and E. Fromm, *The Anatomy of Human Destructiveness*.

semble those they criticize. This was the dilemma of socialist pacifists in Italy at the time of the fascist takeover, to use Reinhold Niebuhr's example. Perhaps passive resistance can work as it did in India, but governments with less conscience than the British, and especially tyrants and despots, would welcome the absence of militancy in a people.

Another dimension of the war and violence issue is the possible desirability of war for the economic or spiritual good of a nation or of civilization itself. It has been argued that war unifies the people of a country in a common purpose, improves the economy, and purifies the race by ensuring that only the fittest will survive.[3] John Ruskin expressed the position very persuasively:

> . . . all the pure and noble arts of peace are founded on war; no great art ever yet arose on earth, but among a nation of soldiers. . . . I tell you that war is the foundation of all the arts (and) also that it is the foundation of all the high virtues and faculties of men. . . .
> It was very strange to me to discover this; and very dreadful—but I saw it to be quite an undeniable fact. The common notion that peace and the virtues of civilization flourished together, I found, to be wholly untenable. Peace and the *vices* of civil life only flourish together. We talk of peace and learning, and of peace and plenty, and of peace and civilization; but I found that those were not the words which the Muse of History coupled together; that on her lips, the words were—peace and sensuality, peace and selfishness, peace and corruption, peace and death. I found, in brief, that all great nations learned their truth of word, and strength of thought, in war; that they were nourished in war, and wasted by peace; taught by war, and deceived by peace; trained by war, and betrayed by peace;—in a word, that they were born in war, and expired in peace.[4]

Ruskin reminds us here of the virtues that follow from war, nevertheless, we do not necessarily need to have war in order to obtain these virtues; there are other, more humane means to reach the same end. William James, in his essay "The Moral Equivalent of War" (which follows), shows us how equal benefits can accrue to civilization without the awful cost in suffering and death. War may sometimes be necessary, but if so, it is a necessary evil not a good; it does not provide unique advantages to humankind and is not something to be welcomed.

With regard to the question of the equality of women, we are all familiar with the issues of the woman's movement today: equal pay for equal work, liberation from the traditional female roles of wife and mother, the elimination of discrimination in hiring practices, participation in the higher levels of government and industry, equal status as a human being rather than a sex object, partnership not male domination in marriage, and so forth.

---

[3] Actually, war is only economically beneficial over the short-run, and it is the young and strong of a nation that are most likely to be killed in battle.
[4] *Crown of Wild Olive* (London, 1866), Lecture III, pp. 66–67, 70.

Underlying all these issues is the question "What is a woman?" and depending upon our answer, we will be more or less sympathetic to demands for equality. Obviously, there are physical differences that distinguish men from women in their skeletal structure, sexual organs, secondary sexual characteristics, body size, proportion of muscle tissue, weight distribution, and so forth. However, the moot point today is whether there are other natural differences of a social and psychological kind, and whether they necessarily follow from the physical factors. Even within the woman's movement there is radical disagreement, some feminists insisting that no essential differences exist beyond anatomy and that we all belong to the single category of human beings,[5] while others want to be equal to men *as women*, retaining what they regard as their distinctive femininity.

Beyond the question of differences between the sexes lies the question of whether women are inherently inferior. Most people would immediately answer "no," yet the treatment of women now and in the past suggests that both sexes have presupposed women to be inferior to men. If we give intellectual assent to the proposition that women are qualitatively equal to men (while not necessarily being the same), then a great deal of our social structure will have to change.

Simone de Beauvoir, in the selection from *The Second Sex* that follows, has written what is probably the definitive feminist statement on the issue of equality. Although she acknowledges basic differences between the sexes, she does not feel that any inferior status is thereby implied or that women are therefore consigned to certain "natural" roles, such as wife, cook, housekeeper, laundress, nurse, temptress, mother, secretary, or waitress. Her analysis of woman as "the Other" is extremely insightful, sharing features in common with Jean-Paul Sartre's description in *Being and Nothingness*, and her book is now regarded as something of a classic.

In the selection by Lionel Tiger and Robin Fox evidence from anthropology and primatology is used to challenge feminist righteousness. The central thesis of *The Imperial Animal* is that comradeship is the basic social bond and that it is exclusively male in character. Comradeship among men occurred first in hunting parties, then in the political organization of society, and then in the professions and in war. Social evolution, it is claimed, depends upon the retention of male bonding, and the intrusion of women into historically male fields can only be disruptive and lead to social deterioration.

Women, consequently, should accept the traditional division of functions, particularly the role of mother. The mother-infant bond, in fact, occurred first in time and is of critical importance; it must be maintained

---

[5] Some feminists even minimize or reject the physical differences between the sexes and see, instead of two categories, a continuum with the extremes of what are now regarded as masculine and feminine types at either end.

to allow the development of male bonding on which social progress depends.

The layman is not in any position to assess the validity of the scientific evidence that is employed, but questions can be raised about the logical propriety of arguing from "fact" to "value," or "is" to "ought." That is to say, even if the analysis is correct and the mother-infant and male-male bonds do characterize our anthropological development, it is a leap in reasoning to conclude that this arrangement has been valuable, that it ought to continue, or that men and women find these bonds fundamentally satisfying. Perhaps in the contemporary age we ought to resist the pull of our early and primate past and aim at fulfillment in human life, not the perpetuation of anthropological trends.

But, again, the question must be referred to the reader at this point, and we must turn to the political issue of privacy and surveillance.

Two recent events have increased public consciousness of the problems surrounding privacy, confidentiality, disclosure, and surveillance: the publication by the press of the classified "Pentagon Papers," an action which allegedly violated the government's right to confidentiality, and the Watergate scandal, in which the privacy of individuals was invaded by the government.[6] Most people were far more concerned about the latter, and in the last years of the Nixon administration that was the more serious problem. However, the right to confidentiality on the institutional level corresponds to the right to privacy on the personal level, and the loss of respect for either principle is a matter for serious reflection.

Let us look first at disclosure and confidentiality in government. In a democratic state we try to maximize the openness of communication so that citizens are informed about governmental operations and, consequently, are in a position to make sound electoral decisions and to judge government policy. Judgments are always made relative to information received, and it is therefore a truism to say that an informed electorate is essential to popular rule. One of the shoddiest devices recently used was the Nixon administration's claim that only those with access to private information could assess the wisdom of our foreign policy, while at the same time withholding the information on the grounds that it was too sensitive to share with the public. Here the appeal to classified information and expertise was used to circumvent the democratic system and to increase centralized control of the state.

Nevertheless, a government secrecy system can function for purposes other than self-promotion and self-protection. Even within a totally democratic system secrecy may be necessary and legitimate, as, for example, in diplomatic affairs. Secrecy could well be required while negotiations are in progress, if not with regard to the results of those negotiations, and the

---

[6] The recent admissions of domestic surveillance activities by the Central Intelligence Agency have also dramatized the privacy issue.

formula of "open covenants secretly arrived at" is perfectly consistent with democratic procedure. We would also not question the appropriateness of secrecy in the field of intelligence and the need for secrecy about military strategy, weaponry, and so forth, most particularly during time of war. Also exempt from public scrutiny would be government plans which, if disclosed, would lead to speculation on the part of private investors and consequently higher government costs, as in the case of imminent land purchases or government contracts. And we would want to exclude from public access any information given to the government by individuals who presumed that confidentiality pertained, such as income tax information. In all these cases, few people would challenge a policy of official secrecy and insist on absolute openness.[7]

The danger that has been impressed upon us recently, of course, is that the government can overextend the application of the principle and, exploiting the classification system to its own advantage, deny the public access to important information. Manipulation of the right to secrecy does not invalidate this right, but secrecy seems so susceptible to abuse that careful public monitoring is constantly needed. Whenever government information is classified, we must ask ourselves "Is secrecy really necessary in this case for legitimate purposes such as diplomacy, national security, or confidential communication, or is the classification category merely being used as a ploy to gain political advantage and escape accountability and embarrassment?" Any governmental secrecy must take place in an atmosphere of credibility, and if we are in doubt in a given situation as to whether secrecy or disclosure should be operative, the democratic bias is always in favor of disclosure to the public.

In contrast to this position, individual privacy, rather than maximum openness, has always held a high place among democratic values. It has been asserted as a legal right covered under common law that the individual shall have full protection in his or her person and property; the "right to be let alone," it has been argued, is an extension of the legal prohibitions against physical interference, now applied to the intangibles of thought and emotion.[8] The Fourth Amendment to the Constitution is also cited quite often as our guarantee against the invasion of privacy, for it proclaims the right of the people to be secure in their persons, houses, papers, and effects against unreasonable searches and seizures.

Philosophically, the right to privacy is often viewed as a moral entitlement relating to the respect that should be accorded to persons. When our private space is invaded we feel that contempt has been shown toward us in our status as a person, that we are not worth respecting, and

---

[7] We also allow the legitimacy of executive privilege (despite its recent abuses), and privileged communications between lawyer and client, priest and penitent, doctor and patient, husband and wife, and journalist and informant (the last is currently under legal debate).

[8] See Samuel Warren and Louis Brandeis, "The Right to Privacy," *Harvard Law Review* IV (1890), 193–220.

when we limit the knowledge others have of ourselves by secrecy, we are protecting our private selves from violation. By the same token, we can elect to surrender a great deal of our privacy to another person in an intimate relationship, and this is a characteristic of love; intimacy, in fact, does not mean having sexual relations (which can occur without intimacy), but the sharing of personal matters.

Privacy, therefore, is related to the respect due to us as persons; it can be surrendered but not invaded without loss of dignity, liberty, and self-esteem. We must retain the right and the power to grant or deny access to personal information about ourselves. The amount of information that is gathered about us is far less important than the kind, for we do not mind if general facts are public knowledge, but we do feel depreciated if certain details are known. Privacy, then, does not mean being anonymous, but controlling what is known about oneself.

In the light of this analysis, one can see why the invasion of privacy presents a considerable threat to the person and why we would not want the kind of surveillance that is a feature of totalitarian regimes. Nevertheless, our privacy has been eroded to an alarming extent through the use of sophisticated technology. Alan F. Westin, in his writings on the privacy issue (a selection from which appears in this chapter), has distinguished three types of contemporary surveillance methods: physical, psychological, and data surveillance. In each area sophisticated technology has made it possible to penetrate the individual's privacy more easily and more completely.

For example, in physical surveillance it is possible today to photograph people with long range cameras at a distance of one thousand yards (or several miles with military equipment used by "spy satellites"). It is also possible to plant in a room miniature television, movie, or still cameras that are radio controlled from locations a mile away; photographs can even be made through walls if special panels are used that allow infrared light to pass through. Eavesdropping on private conversations can be accomplished by secreting transmitters the size of a button on a person's clothing or by using spike microphones in an adjoining room; when windows have been treated with transparent radar-reflecting coating, conversations can be recorded from buildings across the street. Locating and following a person can now be done by planting in a person's eyeglasses, wristwatch, or pills a radio transmitter which emits signals that can be followed at a range of several city blocks; alternately, radioactive substances that are visible by means of ultraviolet light can be applied to a person's clothing. (This last type of monitoring has been suggested for parolees.)[9]

The examples of physical surveillance techniques could be compounded, and the capabilities of data technology affect all of us daily, for

---

[9] For a complete description of surveillance technology and the consequent problem of maintaining privacy, see Alan F. Westin, "Science, Privacy, and Freedom: Issues and Proposals for the 1970's," *Columbia Law Review* 66 (1966), 1003–50.

computers and databanks can gather, record, and share information that the individual is often forced to supply on birth and marriage records, census data, school records, passport data, military records, employment records, banking and credit information, health and hospital records, income tax and social security records, driving license applications, and a great deal more. Mere possession of a person's social security number can yield all of the above information. But knowing the technological capabilities for surveillance is only a first step in evaluating the privacy issue. The main question concerns the use to which our surveillance techniques should be put.

Most people would acknowledge that some degree of surveillance is essential in society for the purposes of law enforcement, but the development and widespread use of technical surveillance equipment makes it imperative to define the limits. We must have a clear understanding of why privacy is valued and what constitutes an unconscionable intrusion into our private lives. In recent years the balance between privacy and surveillance has been upset, and to restore it we need to think through the various cases in which surveillance is claimed as necessary. For example, are cameras permissible on highways to monitor traffic, in banks and federal office buildings, in stores and factories to prevent theft, or on street corners in high-crime neighborhoods? Should psychological personality tests be required for political office, employment by corporations and the government, admission to colleges and universities, or as a routine part of counseling services in the schools? Who has the right to demand your social security number: a hospital, a credit company, a state motor vehicle agency, a hotel?

A well-considered, personal decision must be made with regard to these questions, and the criteria for privacy carefully defined. The selections by H. J. McCloskey and Alan F. Westin in this chapter should help the reader in forming a judgment.

4

WAR AND VIOLENCE

PHILOSOPHICAL IDEAS
AND WORLD PEACE

A. Campbell Garnett

A. Campbell Garnett (1894–   ), American philoso-
pher principally concerned with questions of ethical value, morality and
religion, and the perception of reality. His writings range from Reality
and Value (1938) *to* Religion and the Moral Life (1955) *to* The Perceptual Process (1965).

Widely held ideologies affect mass behavior. They are factors in the
making of war and peace. They are not the only factors. Economic conditions, institutions, outstanding personalities, and other factors are often
more influential. This paper is not concerned with an attempt to weigh
and compare the relative importance of philosophical ideas and other
factors in their influence on peace and war. The relative importance of the
various factors constantly changes and such an attempt could only have
validity with reference to a specific situation. Ideologies played their part
along with other factors in the making of the present war* and will play
their part, along with other factors, in the maintaining of the peace after
the war, or in the making of a new war. But I am not concerned to
attempt an assessment of the relative importance of ideological and other
factors in either case. I conceive my task, in this paper, to be an assessment of the tendencies and effects upon war and peace of various types of

* This article appeared during World War II.

philosophical ideas. Space will not permit a full discussion of the truth of these ideas. I am chiefly concerned to assess the war-and-peace value of various types of philosophical ideas that are, or have been, sufficiently widely held to affect mass behavior in ways leading to war or peace.

1. *Ideas that directly promote aggression.*   In the past one of the direct causes of aggression has been religious fanaticism. Strong religious belief stimulates defense against aggression when liberty of religious faith is attacked. On the whole this acts as a deterrent to aggression. But when religion so far misunderstands its own true nature as to seek to propagate or defend its particular faith by force, instead of simply by logical and moral suasion, it becomes a direct incentive to war. Such wars are fought nominally for the glory of God, but actually for the glory of the "true believers," whose ego is inflated by the conviction that they possess a peculiar revelation of divine truth and who enjoy a further inflation of the ego in imposing its acceptance upon others. This motive has, fortunately, almost ceased to be an important cause of war. It survives only as a means of securing support from certain sections of the community for aggressive policies otherwise motivated. Thus Mussolini's adventure into Abyssinia received justification in certain quarters as a means of bringing the blessings of true Christianity and civilization to a barbarous people.

In the present time the philosophical idea most actively promoting aggression is an ethic of devotion to the state as the supreme moral law, the state itself being exalted above all law. This is especially dangerous when linked with ideas of racial superiority and more or less mystical notions of manifest destiny. In Japan this set of ideas is supported by the ancient Shinto religion. But the aggressions of Japan are not religious wars in the sense with which we are familiar in Occidental civilization. They are not aimed at making or keeping converts to Shinto. Shinto is merely a part of a set of ideas exalting the state and the race and thus justifying and encouraging the expansion of its power.

Ideas of national superiority, of course, are common. Most nations entertain such pleasant fantasies, not least our own. But such ideas do not lead directly to aggression. A superior nation may even be "too proud to fight." Still oftener it may be too much concerned with individual welfare to risk that welfare in war. The danger lies in concepts that ignore the fact that the individual is the ultimate vehicle of the good and see a good greater than individual good in an alleged good of a particular state or race as such, a good conceived as the power and glory of institutions and societies, in abstraction from the immediate experience of individuals.

Such ideas are dangerous because in one vitally important feature they are genuinely ethical and superior to philosophies that place the emphasis on the self-interest of the individual. They call for devotion of the individual to something conceived as greater and worthier than himself.

The self can only fulfill itself by finding ends that are beyond itself. Such ends are found in the service of some social group, of humanity, of institutions, and of God. Such objectives can become objects of high devotion that integrate all discordant factors within the personality of the devotee and call forth the best that is in him in fullest degree. Their power is great, and their effect is good just so far as the pursuit of the high goal involves the pursuit of individual welfare as its specific content or means. The service of a God Whose nature is love and Who wills the good of all is thus thoroughly wholesome. But the service of a state the good of which consists in power and glory rather than the welfare of individuals, and which owes no obligations to individuals or groups outside itself, is dangerous in the extreme.

In answer to all such concepts our value theory must nail up one fundamental statement of fact so that none can lose sight of it. The ultimate test of all good and evil is the value that is actually felt in individual (human and animal) experience. No earthly thing has value except as object of individual enjoyment, or instrument of individual welfare. And only in the service of such individual good is there service of God. A god or a state whose good can be served at the cost of a net loss of experienceable, individual, human good is an idol and a devil.

2. *Ideas that disturb peace by encouraging fear and suspicion.*   Fear and suspicion are, for the most part, specific, and are conditioned by practical experience and traditions based on practical experience. However, they are, inevitably, also somewhat affected by general philosophical ideas concerning human nature. A low view of human nature in general is bound to create an atmosphere in which fear and suspicion of one's neighbors easily grow. In particular, a low view of human nature militates against the development of self-governing institutions and the growth of liberty. Who will "trust the people" if the people in general are regarded as brutish, selfish, and lazy? Such views of human nature make those already in positions of power and privilege adopt measures of repressive control. They justify aristocracies, slavery, dictatorships, class ascendancies, imperialism, and restrictions on civil liberties. And these things in turn lead to revolutions and wars.

Philosophies teaching a low view of human nature fall into two main types. The first is the religious type which emphasizes the sinfulness of man, the outstanding example being Augustinianism. It is, I believe, the Augustinian emphasis on the sinfulness of man that accounts for the ambiguous and contradictory elements in the political effects of Protestantism. The fathers of Protestantism were Christians and the Christian ethic is one of neighbor love, and the Christian philosophy asserts that all men are brethren. In England they were also the leaders of a revolt against secular and religious tyranny in the name of the freedom of the individual conscience and the right of private judgment on matters of doctrine. Yet when they gained power they refused to others the religious liberty they had claimed for themselves. They imposed repressive blue laws to force upon sinners the rectitude they feared could be secured in no other way. They fought for their own independence, but they allowed the lead in the democratic process of broadening human liberties to be taken from them by thinkers of less intense religious convictions. Even today conservative theology and conservative politics usually go together. And the main reason, I believe, is that the surviving influence of Augustinianism in orthodox Protestant circles still leads to such distrust of human nature as to create fear of changes which would enlarge human freedom. This spirit of generalized fear and distrust of one's fellow men leads to war in two ways. Sometimes it leads to the effort to mend by force, under the conviction that there is no other way, conditions that could, with patience, be mended in time without force. Such an unbelief in the possibility of peaceful reform was certainly one of the factors leading to the American civil war. Again, this distrust leads to extreme actions that bring about counterreaction. This happened in England when the reaction from Puritan rule plunged the country into a moral retrogression from which it did not recover until the time of the Wesleys, and a political reaction to monarchy and class rule from which it has not yet entirely recovered and which was certainly responsible for the revolt of the American colonies.

The second type of philosophy that presents a low view of human nature is reductionism—various types of philosophy that explain human behavior in terms of categories that are infrahuman. Typical examples are Thomas Hobbes's explanation of man in terms of mechanical appetitions and aversions, the Nietzschean explanation in terms of will to power, the Neo-Darwinian in terms of the struggle for existence, and the Marxian in terms of dialectic materialsm. None of these does justice to the moral element in human nature. Their typical effect is most vividly seen in that of the last named. Its doctrines of economic determinism and the class war lead to the belief that the maldistribution of wealth can never be remedied by peaceful democratic action, that the workers therefore must be prepared for violent struggle with their masters, and that a period of dictatorship of the proletariat must intervene before an era of equalitarian justice can be established. These effects have occurred in spite of the fact that Marx himself did not advocate violence but rather emphasized respect for personality. This doctrine has introduced much unnecessary violence into the industrial struggle. It led to the overthrow of an incipient democracy in Russia and has caused unnecessary violence and repression in the subsequent history of that revolution. Above all, it has been a major factor in producing the countermovement known as Fascism, which is, in its simplest terms, a violent reaction of the privileged classes, induced by fear of their violent overthrow by the disciples of those who have preached class war. How unnecessary is this preaching of class war is shown by the remarkably rapid development of legislation in the direction of Socialism in democratic countries during the past quarter of a century—in spite of the fact that even that development has been held back by fears induced by the taint of Communism in the ranks of labor. Thus, lack of a reasonable faith in human nature, whether due to a religious and upper-class philosophy or to a nonreligious and lower-class philosophy, has a similar effect. It creates distrust and suspicion and thus contributes strongly to those forces that disturb the peace. It leads both to civil and to international war.

3. Ideas that facilitate aggression by weakening resistance to it.   Just as the unduly pessimistic views of human nature tend to unleash the dogs of war by creating fear and suspicion, so, on the other hand, unduly optimistic views of human nature create an unrealistic overconfidence in the friends of peace that puts them off their guard and betrays them to the aggressor. Liberalism has always suffered from overoptimism. The older economic liberalism of *laissez faire* was led astray by the optimistic assumption that private enterprise, in pursuing its own interests, would always find itself compelled to serve public interests. Before the First World War, liberalism was betrayed by a facile confidence in the inevitability of progress, induced by the discovery of the evolutionary ascent of man. In the last few decades overoptimism has been induced by the prevalent social theory of mind. The fact that motivation is chiefly determined by socially developed habits and that society inculcates in the individual habits that are in accord with social interests, so far as society knows its own interests, has been taken as indicating that the trouble with society is not lack of good will, but lack of an intelligent understanding of how best to attain those ends which the socially induced habits of thought set before us as goals. It has therefore been believed that education and the cultivation of the spirit of free critical inquiry are all that is needed to set individuals in general on the path toward socially valuable goals; i.e., toward the satisfaction of social, rather than merely private, interests.[1]

---

[1] John Dewey, *Human Nature and Conduct*, Henry Holt & Co., pp. 326–327. "For Right is only an abstract name for the multitude of concrete demands in action which they impress upon us, and of which we are obliged, if we would live, to take some account . . . If we had desires, judgments, plans, in short a mind, apart from social connections, then the latter would be external and their action might be regarded as that of a non-moral force. But we live mentally as physically only *in* and *because* of our environment. Social pressure is but a name for the interactions which are always going on and in which we participate, living so far as we partake and dying so far as we do not. . . . Accordingly failure to recognize the authority of right means defect in effective apprehension of the realities of human association, not an arbitrary exercise of free will."

For further statement to the same effect we may refer to C. W. Morris's intro-

In so far as the facts concerning the social influences that shape the development of human minds are presented in refutation of earlier theories assuming the essential egoism of all human motives, this argument is pertinent and important. Man is not merely an egoist and cannot possibly become one, short of insanity. His motivation is predominantly socially induced. But that does not mean that it need only be intelligent and it will be socially valuable. Society is not a single unit, with a unified set of goals. It is divided into groups with conflicting goals. And it is these narrow groups, with their partisan ends, that shape the habits of the growing individual. They inculcate in him the special interest of his own family, class, gang, tribe, state, nation, and race. They drive him to war in the interests of the group as well as to peace. Intelligence and the free spirit of inquiry, unless guided by something higher than these socially induced ends, merely make a more efficient partisan so long as he is true to those ends. Sometimes, because he also has private interests, biologically developed, intelligence and critical inquiry lead him to desert the interests of his social groups for his own egoistic ends. On the other hand, intelligence and critical inquiry lead him sometimes to rise above his narrow, socially induced goals to objectives of wider, or even universal, scope. But this must be taken as indicative of a further needed qualification of the social theory of mind. It indicates that there are sources of motivation in man that cannot be explained as induced by the interests of any of the special groups of which he is a part, motives not explicable as products of social conditioning.

This further weakness of the social theory of mind can best be indicated by reference to its treatment by G. H. Mead. Mead is well aware of the fact that it is narrow and antagonistic social groups that frame our habitual interests. The following quotations from his *Mind, Self and Society* (pp. 154–156) will briefly indicate his position.

> The organized community or social group which gives to the individual his unity of self may be called "the generalized other." The attitude of the generalized other is the attitude of the whole community (p. 154).
> It is in the form of the generalized other that the social process influences the behavior of the individuals involved in it (p. 155).
> But only by taking the attitude of the generalized other toward himself . . . can the individual think at all; for only thus can thinking—or the internalized conversation of gestures which constitutes thinking—occur (p. 156).

duction (p. xxxii) to G. H. Mead, *Mind, Self and Society*, The University of Chicago Press, p. xxxii. "For Mead, moral ends are social ends because in the first place the only standard for impulse that impulse makes possible resides in the answer as to whether the impulse in question feeds or dies on its own satisfaction, and whether it expands and harmonizes, or narrows and defeats, other impulses; and second, because the self, as a social being, must be concerned within and without with a social harmony of impulses."

The self-conscious human individual, then, takes or assumes the organized social attitudes of the given social group or community (or of some one section thereof) to which he belongs, toward the social problems of various kinds which confront that group or community at any given time (p. 156).

It should be noticed that Mead, here, clearly recognizes that it is only the particular, habitual interests of his own narrow group that are thus transmitted to the individual. This raises the question as to how we are to account for ethical progress. Mead offers the following explanation.

The attitudes involved are gathered from the group, but the individual in whom they are organized has the opportunity of giving them an expression which perhaps has never taken place before (p. 198).

An individual of the type to which we are referring arises always with reference to a form of society or social order which is implied but not adequately expressed. Take the religious genius, such as Jesus or Buddha, or the reflective type, such as Socrates. What has given them their unique importance is that they have taken the attitude of living with reference to a larger society. That larger state was one which was already more or less implied in the institutions of the community in which they lived. Such an individual is divergent from the point of view of what we could call the prejudices of the community; but in another sense he expresses the principles of the community more completely than any other (p. 217).

Jesus generalized the conception of the community in terms of the family in such a statement as that of the neighbor in the parables (p. 216).

But the weakness of this explanation of ethical progress is only too obvious. On the social theory of mind all that the ethical genius can do is to work out what is already implied in the habits or institutions of the society that shaped his own mind; and it is said that Jesus did this when he generalized the conception of the community in terms of the family. The obvious reply is that only if one first accepts the doctrine of the Fatherhood of God does the principle of good will found in the institution of the family have any logical implication whatever with regard to the whole human race. On any other view it is a simple fallacy of false analogy. But the concept of ethical universalism is already implied in that of the Fatherhood of God. It means that God loves all the human race. And this concept depends on the prior conviction that one *ought* to love them all. If this were not the case, then, when people give up the idea of the Fatherhood of God, they should also, logically, give up their conviction that they ought to show good will to all men. The moral conviction of our obligation to our fellow men is the foundation of the religious conception of the universal love of God, not *vice versa*. The religious conception is a logical completion and psychological reinforcement of the moral conviction, but no more. To make it the foundation of the moral conviction would be to take a position that Mead would be the first to repudiate.

But, when this is recognized, what becomes of the assertion that ethical universalism is an implication of institutions already established? It is shown to have no foundation. We must conclude that the social theory of mind has failed to explain the development of the higher moral ideas —those that go beyond the individual's concern for his own interest and that of the particular narrow groups to which he belongs.

What we started out to show, however, was not merely the theoretical inadequacy of the social theory of mind, but that it has an unfortunate effect in inducing a false optimism. It suggests that scientific intelligence alone can solve our moral and social problems, both internal and international. It thus leads us to ignore the dangers arising from the decay of belief in objective moral standards. And it leads to the placing of too great faith in nations and classes that obviously have intelligence, as do the German aristocracy and the Japanese, while ignoring the power of fixed traditions, narrow pride, and selfish interests by which they are dominated. Believing, as Morris says, that "the self, as a social being, must be concerned within and without with a social harmony of impulses," it concludes that scientific and educational progress must sooner or later counteract any serious social evils.

This confidence has been one factor lulling to sleep many liberals, especially in America, in the face of the menace of Fascism. It has enabled them to persuade themselves that even a triumphant Fascism could not maintain its ascendancy long in the face of a growing human enlightenment. It thus suggested that a merely temporary triumph of Fascism in some parts of the world is not very important; and this belief helped to maintain the spirit of isolationism which facilitated the drift into the present war. And its influence is still present, encouraging a return to isolationism when the present conflict is over, thus opening the way for developments which may lead to yet another world war.

Exponents of the social theory of mind are usually relativists in ethics. Believing that values are determined by interest—and interest by social conditioning—they see the ethical problem as merely one of finding the best means for these socially conditioned interests to work their way through to their socially determined goals. The choice of the right means is, of course, relative to the specific situation and the goal unfolds of itself so long as, and so far as, it is intelligently pursued. Questions of right and wrong are not qustions of *ends* to be judged by some ultimate standard; they are simply questions of the best *means* of solving life's problems, of fulfilling life's interests. This complete rejection of any ultimate standard for our choice of ends is, I am convinced, an error, for the reason above stated; *i.e.*, because even those of our ends that are socially determined are apt to be narrow and conflicting. Nevertheless, relativism avoids an error common to much religious ethics—that of making absolute certain general principles concerning specific modes of behavior. It is this error that underlies another of those philosophical ideas that facilitate aggression by weakening resistance to it; namely, the traditional and common form of pacifism.

Specific principles may, and often do, apply over large ranges of human affairs. But they are bound to come into conflict in exceptional situations. Then resort has to be made to casuistry. And casuistry flounders unless it can find some more general principle above those that are in conflict. This process can end only in the discovery of some principle of supreme generality, which can be stated as the ultimate goal, a goal to which specific principles are merely tentative instrumentalities. Such an absolute goal is commonly found in the ideal of universal welfare, so far as obtainable, *i.e.*, the greatest good of all concerned. Here the question of what constitutes the greatest good, or welfare, is left for empirical discovery. The principle simply states the obligation of *each* to be concerned, so far as he can, with the good of *all*. Ideals of this kind are intended by the utilitarian principle of the greatest happiness of the greatest number, the Kantian conception of a kingdom of ends, and the Golden Rule of Christianity.

Because of the very vagueness of such an ideal goal, it is necessary in practice to recognize guiding principles of a more specific character as having a certain validity. But these, if made absolute, become impractical and lead to disaster. This is the case with traditional pacifism. It erects the principle of respect for human life into a specific absolute. It makes an ultimate end of a guiding principle which has general, but not universal, validity as a means. If it becomes widespread in any community it weakens the power of that community to resist aggression that threatens human life and values that are more important than life. Or it weakens the will of that community to go to the aid of others thus threatened. Thus pacifism must also be reckoned among those ideas that facilitate aggression by weakening resistance to it. There can be no doubt that American pacifism did much to strengthen our disastrous isolationism, and that British pacifism contributed to the unilateral disarmament, appeasement, and vacillating foreign policy that encouraged the Axis powers to attempt their conquests.

4. Ideas that promote peace by removing causes of friction. We have seen that pacifism does not promote peace, that low views of human nature stimulate aggression and that blindly optimistic views facilitate it. We need a theory of human nature that is realistic enough to recognize that social forces are at work for evil that can be kept in check only by force, and a theory that, at the same time, has sufficient faith in the goodness of normal human nature not to create unnecessary fear and suspicion. Unduly pessimistic views of human nature are positively vicious, in that they actually stimulate the tendencies to aggression. Unduly optimistic views of human nature are dangerous in that they fail to guard against them. To maintain peace we need a *true* view of human nature. The biological and mechanical theories contain some truth that should not be forgotten. Man does have passions and instincts akin to the animals. The social theory of mind contains truth that is very important. Our habits of thought and action are subject to the molding influences of society and these influences do, very largely, offset and control our animal passions and infantile egoisms. But neither one, nor both, of these views contains the whole truth.

Now low views of human nature lead to social pessimism. High views lead to optimism. The social theory of mind is a higher view of human nature than the biological theory. It leads, as we have seen, to an unjustifiable optimism. But its undue optimism is not due to its being too high a view of human nature, but to a certain blindness which leaves it not high enough. It recognizes two sources of human motivation. These are (a) blind biological impulses such as the appetites, which tend in general to the survival of the individual and the herd, but which often lead to destruction and conflict; (b) social conditioned interests marked by foresight and developed by social communication. These latter include the intellectual and aesthetic interests, the interest in personal advancement and interests in social welfare. They are often egoistic but predominantly reflect the *common* interests of the group, because the interests of the group as a whole, or interests commonly manifested within the group, are sure to be communicated to, and thus developed within, each individual. And among interests developed by communication such common and, in general, socially valuable, interests, are sure to predominate.

There is no need to deny the reality of both these sources of interest and impulse. But, as has already been shown, if these were man's *only* sources of interest and impulse, then man would forever be dominated by the common interests of the narrow social groups to which he belongs, modified only by his blind biological impulses and egoistic infantile habits. Yet he is not so dominated. He rises above these narrow interests to pursue the good of those beyond his social group. His narrow family, class, national, and racial interests set themselves against the expanding interest in the good of all mankind; but it grows in spite of them. It is impossible to explain this expansion as a process of conditioning the individual to feel the interests that his society feels, for it grows in single individuals, living in societies that do not feel it. In so far as there is transmission of this interest it is from the outstanding individual, who has acquired the higher and wider interest in spite of society, to the society, which is moved to acknowledge the higher interest as higher, in spite of its own traditions to the contrary.

When we inquire how the individuals in a society that has only limited interests in other persons come to acquire these wider interests in human welfare, we see that it is through imaginative reflection on the value-experience of other persons in the light of their own. We find that, in spite of our egoisms and tribalisms, we human beings, when we imaginatively reflect upon the joys and sorrows of strangers and aliens, find ourselves concerned for their welfare. It is simply human nature to be so concerned. The simple aboriginal tribesman finding a white explorer, of a race he has never before seen, dying of thirst in the desert, gives him water and food and leads him back along the tracks whence he came. Only if tradition or bitter experience have made him fear such strangers, or if pressed by some other need, does he injure him. The *natural* human impulse is to care for the poor, incompetent stranger's welfare. He acts from no recognized traditional obligation, such as obtains with regard to his fellow tribesman and is maintained by social conditioning. He has simply recognized a human need, a human value at stake, and he responds with interest in its preservation.

Here is the secret of the whole thing. Human beings are interested in human values. They are interested in values, as such, not merely in values recognized as values-for-me or values-for-my-group. Experience creates *special* and *habitual* interests in certain values-for-me. And social conditioning creates special and habitual interests in certain values-for-my-group. But human nature, as such, is interested in value, as such. Will *is* a positive tendency to respond to value, whether immediately felt or anticipated, whether seen as a value-for-me or as a value-for-some-other-person-though-not-for-me. This general tendency of will gets canalized by habits into special tendencies to attend to special cases of value, of the ego and the group. But its *essential* nature is simply to respond to value. It is not necessary to invoke specific, inherited, biological drives, or social conditioning, to explain all altruistic interests. Will is naturally concerned with all values, both egoistic *and* altruistic. The young child cannot manifest concern with the value-experience of other persons until it has developed intelligence and imagination enough to recognize the existence of other selves as distinct centers of value-experience. But as soon as it does recognize the existence of such centers of value-experience external to itself, it responds to the thought of them and manifests an interest in the production of such value-experience. The young child, as soon as it can be made to understand that "baby brother likes candy," responds to this thought with a spontaneous interest in the production of such satisfying experience for baby brother. No unbiased observer who has watched those spontaneous, generous responses on the part of the child could easily persuade himself that they are merely an imitative response conditioned by similar manifestations of interest on the part of adults.

Recognition of the fact that man is naturally interested in human values as such, that altruism is spontaneous and naturally universal, gives us a much more hopeful view of human nature. At the same time it leads to no unrealistic optimism. For we have to recognize that "habit is second nature," and habit, through narrow social influences, conditions human minds to form bias and prejudice. It is these products of history and vicious environment with which we have to deal in the production of a better world and a world at peace. But what one type of history and environment can produce, another type of history and environment can change. The vice of violence and aggression is not essential to human nature. It is an incidental product of the conditions of the childhood and adolescence of the human race, the product of early history and incomplete social order. In many areas of human life it has already been decisively overcome. The essential nature of man as will, a will that responds to the good as such, presses constantly toward the overcoming of these vices. And there is, therefore, no reason why every national borderline in the world should not eventually become as defenseless and as peaceful as that of Canada and these United States. This holds out hope for the maintenance of peace, and directs attention to the nature of the danger factors that need to be removed. It removes unnecessary fears and suspicions that come from false and low views of human nature and at the same time guards against an unrealistic optimism that would fail to erect and maintain the necessary safeguards of world law and order.

VIOLENCE AND PACIFISM
Gordon C. Zahn

G. C. Zahn (1918–   ), *sociologist, educator, and author whose professional life has been devoted to the cause of world peace. He has written and edited numerous books on the themes of war and pacifism, including* German Catholics and Hitler's Wars (1962), In Solitary Witness (1964), *and* Thomas Merton on Peace (1971). *He also contributed to the volumes* Morality and Modern Warfare (1960) *and* Breakthrough to Peace (1962), *as well as writing the influential pamphlet* An Alternative to War (1963).

At a time when military policies and technology have achieved eschatological potentiality, if not imminence, one frequently hears friendly references to the pacifist alternative. True, the tendency—as is amply illustrated in some recent articles and editorials of *Worldview*—is still abruptly to dismiss this alternative from serious consideration as a practical solution to present or threatening world dilemmas. For what satisfaction it brings, the pacifist notes that even this abrupt dismissal is usually couched in wistful, somewhat longing, "how nice if it could be, but . . ." terms; there is little or none of the old indignation, seldom the old imputations of treason or subversion that formerly accompanied the closing of the mind to all pacifist argumentation.

But the satisfaction is slight. The new aura of "almost" respectability brings with it a new source of impatient annoyance in the utter refusal of others to recognize and respect certain distinctions which previously were more or less academic in view of the offhand rejection of the whole pacifist package. This essay will try to bring these distinctions to a more explicit statement.

Learned scholars and journalists in discussing foreign policy and defense alternatives consistently equate all pacifism with an extreme position of passive compliance involving the complete denial or waiver of all right to mount any kind of defense against aggression, no matter how unjust. Of course, there are such pacifist extremists—just as there are extremists who rashly advocate all-out nuclear war as the response to any national affront, whether such affront be actually sustained, merely threatened or suspected, or even nothing more than a fearful possibility. The same critical judgment that carefully discriminates between such advocates of preventive, preemptive, defensive, and retaliatory war should serve to separate the total submissionists from other pacifists who not only accept the legitimacy of defense but actually insist that their alternative to violence offers the only real possibility of an effective and ultimately successful defense against aggression.

Whether they base their position upon a formal religious creed or hold to a more generalized code of humanitarian values, such pacifists would insist that any acceptable defense must be *effective* (offering at least some sound assurances of success) and *moral* (conformable to the basic norms deriving from and safeguarding human decency and the dignity of the person). They would argue that a policy based on either the actual intent or the implied threat to use nuclear arms simply cannot meet either test.

With respect to the first, the generalization that "everyone loses in war" is no longer to be taken as a pacifist cliché; instead, most competent scientific authority can document the horrible but conservative expectation that nuclear war will bring virtually certain destruction to all, contesting nations and would be neutrals alike. A charred and radioactive planet, peopled with some monstrously deformed remnant of mankind, has come to represent the brightest hope the scientist can offer as the aftermath of such a war. A "defense" program which offers such as its likely outcome is, to the pacifist, no defense at all.

Of at least equal importance, the tendency of all modern war—and in this respect nuclear war is merely the logical product of a long-developing and now well-established trend—is to become ever more dehumanized, seeking to reduce the person to nothing more than a standardized and wholly mechanical unit of destruction (or, if he be "the enemy," a quite identical unit to be destroyed). And, in a parallel and probably related development, it has become ever more total in scope and now threatens to eliminate all remaining distinctions between the guilty aggressor, the helpless conscript, and the innocent noncombatant. On both counts, it should be evident to all, the requirement that a defense be moral is clearly violated.

For these reasons, then, because nuclear war involves the near-certainty of mutual destruction and passes far beyond all limits of human decency, any statement of the pacifist position must begin with a negative —the outright repudiation of nuclear war as a conceivable defense option. It demands, further, that the "unthinkable" be absolutely excluded from the realm of possibility, even accidental possibility; and in this it does not reject unilateral action if international agreements cannot be negotiated. The logic of this position rests upon a recognition of the psychological fact that man's mental processes are such that what is "unthinkable" in one context can become "thinkable" (albeit regretfully) in another and even "morally obligatory" in still another.

The pacifist, it follows, is not greatly impressed by the intricate formulations favoring "limited war" or "nuclear deterrence." With regard to the former, he would insist that the "limits" will always prove flexible enough to permit whatever course of action the military may propose as the only remaining alternative to defeat. Thus most pacifists did not experience the surprise that greeted reports that one of our leading generals had seriously proposed a nuclear attack at a preliminary stage of the conflict in Laos. There may have been some mild surprise that the proposal had come so early in the struggle and from so high a level of military authority; but that such proposals will always be advanced by some trigger-happy or efficiency-minded or battle-pressed military or political leader, however "limited" a war may be at its inception, may be taken as a foregone conclusion. So, too, with deterrence. An empty threat with no intent to follow through with the use of nuclear weapons under any conceivable circumstances simply will not deter. Yet any intention, however faint or however simulated, necessarily opens the way to the same grim progression just described; for we cannot hope to convince the potential enemy that we will actually use the bombs "as a last resort" without convincing ourselves as well. And that "last resort" will always prove to be more imminent than we thought.

The second basis for the pacifist's insistence that the unthinkable be absolutely excluded from all possibility leads into the more positive aspect of pacifism as a policy option. As long as a nation places all or even most of its reliance upon violent means, even though the demands of effectiveness and morality will not permit their use, it will neither seek nor develop whatever other capabilities and means might hold promises of being both moral and effective. I refer particularly to the possibilities offered by organized nonviolent resistance as a program of action, any serious consideration of which is usually blocked by a whole complex of essentially specious arguments purporting to prove that such means "would not work" in the Western world. While massive volumes are written and batteries of computers are programmed in an effort to discover some thin margin of survival potential under all conceivable situations of violent assault and violent reprisal, the polite smile and the impatient shrug are all we can spare for any serious proposal that the only real hope for survival lies in a tactical surrender followed by an altogether different kind of "second strike" incorporating planned and disciplined civil disobedience, the general strike—in short, the complete refusal of all cooperation with the "victors." In place of the motivations furnished by the particularist national prides and sentiments which are so essential to a defense based on violence potential, the pacifist alternative would be keyed to a universalistic identity with, and regard for, the humanity inherent in all men, including the would-be oppressor. And this, in turn, would be expected to trigger a reciprocal response in the opponent; to fan, so to speak, the spark of human decency, which, no matter how low it may burn in individual men for a time, cannot be extinguished completely or forever.

There is, of course, a world of difference between such "passive resistance" and the defeatist compliance usually attributed to the pacifist position. The difference rests primarily upon the note of discipline and the kind of power such action calls into being. Realistically, one must acknowledge that, given the nature of the present world order and its long-time commitment to violence, such a program of nonviolent resistance would take a fearful toll in terms of human suffering and death—though these would probably not equal, much less exceed, that contemplated as the cost of nuclear war. It must even be assumed that this spark of human decency may be especially faint in individuals formed under the repressive controls available to our current totalitarian systems and that, therefore, such individuals would be far more callous (and for a considerably longer period) in their efforts to break a campaign of nonviolent resistance than were, for example, the British faced with Gandhi's revolution. One must reckon, then, with the fact that there would be many more victims, that the trains would be driven over many more protesting demonstrators, that many more hostages would be executed.

But ultimately the trains and the reprisals would have to stop, if only because the men who gave the orders realized the futility of the situation or, far more likely, because they and the men who received the orders had reached the point at which they could no longer force themselves to order further slaughter or to comply. Describing the execution of Jehovah's Witnesses at Auschwitz (and significantly enough, comparing them to the early Christian martyrs who converted a pagan empire quite as ruthless as our modern totalitarians), Rudolf Hess noted: "All who saw them die were deeply moved, and even the execution squad itself was affected." If these master exterminators, specially selected and trained for their inhuman task, could be "moved" and "affected" by a handful of religious activists, what might have been the effect upon less committed agents of the Nazi power had they been faced with organized nonviolent resistance on the part of great masses of inhabitants in the lands overrun by that power?

That the necessary organization and discipline would require a program of preparation and training every bit as intensive as that now provided the armed forces is obvious. Gandhi had his *ashrams*; any serious attempt to prepare for the pacifist's "second strike" would involve the full use of all facilities designed to mold the nation into a readiness to become "a community of sacrifice." But it is clear that the development of any such training program or even the recognition of its need and possible value, is out of the question as long as we delude ourselves into continued reliance upon an ever-expanding capacity for violent resistance and reprisal. Needless to say, we shall remain locked in this delusion until we are at least willing to contemplate the possibility that an alternative exists, that it may be the *only* alternative to a "peace" which, in the words of C. Wright Mills, is nothing more than "a mutual fright, a balance of armed fear."

In the last analysis, though, the pacifist alternative depends not upon the disciplined readiness for self-sacrifice but, rather, upon the kind of power which alone would make such sacrifice possible and successful. Even Mills, in his biting analysis of the drift of our day, too lightly accepts the untested premise that the "ultimate kind of power" is violence. If this were really true, then the logic of the ultramilitarist would become unchallengeable: the greater the capacity for violence, the greater the power; the greater the power, the more certain the victory; the more certain the victory, the more perfect the defense. If, however, it is not true; if there is a "more ultimate" kind of power, this logical sequence comes to naught. And it is the pacifist's contention that there *are* other kinds of power ranging above and beyond the limits of violence. Gandhi and his followers called it "soul force"; the Christian pacifist speaks of the "power of love," of the "charity" that overcomes the world.

The pacifist alternative of nonviolent resistance would lift these principles above the level of easily mouthed platitudes and convert them into a program of action in the firm confidence that action based on these principles represents the true ultimate of power. There is a logic for this position, too. The purpose of any exercise of power is to obtain behavior conforming to the pattern set by the one exerting the power. Since, in the last analysis, a fixed and unwavering refusal to comply with these demands cannot be overcome by violence, it is clear that the power of violence is not ultimate. Of course, it is always possible to destroy by violence the man who persists in his refusal, but this represents the final defeat of violence in that it abandons all further attempts to obtain the compliance the power-wielder sought in the first place.

Superficially, since the man is destroyed, this logic may appear every bit as callously indifferent in its attitude toward the loss of human life as are the cold calculations of those who define the "permissible levels" of civilian deaths to be "allowed for" in their advocacy of nuclear war as a defense option. But I would insist that there is a crucial difference: the man who makes the refusal and accepts the consequences does so in a responsible exercise of the ultimate power at his disposal, something vastly different from the meaningless death of the nameless and faceless cipher who just happens to be in the wrong place at the wrong time.

The practical question remains: Is the pacifist alternative, even granting its "second strike" potentiality, a real policy option today? Obviously not, if by this we mean that the nation is psychologically ready to abandon its reliance upon violence as the ultimate source of security—or that, even if it were, we could now hope to "screw our courage to the sticking point" and mount a successful campaign of nonviolent resistance, should the occasion present itself. But in another sense it must be viewed as a real option, even the only option holding promise of ultimate success; for if even one nation could be awakened to this promise and be prepared to pursue it, the world could finally be freed from the vicious circle of violence in which it is now locked and the way opened to a security based on those greater and surer kinds of power that until now we have not dared to consider, much less exploit.

We are dealing with something far more profound than a difference in policy options. Our question ultimately concerns our basic conceptions of man. Is man, after all is said and done, a creature whose behavior is finally controlled through promises of physically satisfying rewards and threats of violence-induced pain; or is he something greater, the deepest wellsprings of whose behavior contain forces responsive only to the power of love and recognition of common identity? If we deny the latter, we deny many of the core values upon which we base our claims to a preferable way of life and, indeed, our hopes for any future advance for humankind. The pacifist alternative takes these values seriously to the point of proposing them as the foundation of our defense action. The belief that all men share a common humanity which cannot be totally or permanently suppressed; the corollary that every man (including the Roman tyrant, the Buchenwald guard, the Soviet oppressor, yes, even the indifferent RAND theorist at his computer) has a "breaking point" beyond which his participation in patterned inhumanity cannot be forced; and, finally, the confidence that a disciplined, large-scale exercise of the moral power of sacrificial "love" or "soul force" will most surely bring him to that breaking point and thereby negate whatever power of violence he may have at his disposal—these deserve a far more receptive hearing than they have received on the part of those supposedly committed to the defense of the West and its Judeo-Christian foundations. If, as history has demonstrated, the way of violence demands an ever more thorough-going renunciation of this common humanity and its implications for our own behavior, coupled with a callous ignoring of the humanity of the "enemy," it—and not pacifism—should be rejected as a policy option not worthy of consideration. Otherwise, in the process of "defending" these most cherished values, we may find ourselves forced to abandon and betray them in our total surrender to the inevitably destructive logic of violence.

THE MORAL EQUIVALENT OF WAR

William James

William James (1842–1910), American philosopher and psychologist chiefly associated with the early beginnings of behaviorism in psychology and the philosophic movement of Pragmatism. His two-volume work The Principles of Psychology (1893) *contributed to establishing psychology as a science, and* The Varieties of Religious Experience (1902) *still stands as a definitive study of the philosophy and psychology of religion. James's distinctively philosophic works include* The Will to Believe (1897) *and* Pragmatism (1925).

The war against war is going to be no holiday excursion or camping party. The military feelings are too deeply grounded to abdicate their place among our ideals until better substitutes are offered than the glory and shame that come to nations as well as to individuals from the ups and downs of politics and the vicissitudes of trade. There is something highly paradoxical in the modern man's relation to war. Ask all our millions, north and south, whether they would vote now (were such a thing possible) to have our war for the Union expunged from history, and the record of a peaceful transition to the present time substituted for that of its marches and battles, and probably hardly a handful of eccentrics would say yes. Those ancestors, those efforts, those memories and legends, are the most ideal part of what we now own together, a sacred spiritual possession worth more than all the blood poured out. Yet ask those same people whether they would be willing in cold blood to start another civil war now to gain another similar possession, and not one man or woman would vote for the proposition. In modern eyes, precious though wars may be, they must not be waged solely for the sake of the ideal harvest. Only when forced upon one, only when an enemy's injustice leaves us no alternative, is a war now thought permissible.

It was not thus in ancient times. The earlier men were hunting men, and to hunt a neighboring tribe, kill the males, loot the village and possess the females, was the most profitable, as well as the most exciting, way of living. Thus were the more martial tribes selected, and in chiefs and people a pure pugnacity and love of glory came to mingle with the more fundamental appetite for plunder.

Modern war is so expensive that we feel trade to be a better avenue to plunder; but modern man inherits all the innate pugnacity and all the love of glory of his ancestors. Showing war's irrationality and horror is of no effect upon him. The horrors make the fascination. War is the *strong* life; it is life *in extremis*; war-taxes are the only ones men never hesitate to pay, as the budgets of all nations show us.

History is a bath of blood. The Iliad is one long recital of how Diomedes and Ajax, Sarpedon and Hector *killed*. No detail of the wounds they made is spared us, and the Greek mind fed upon the story. Greek history is a panorama of jingoism and imperialism—war for war's sake, all the citizens being warriors. It is horrible reading, because of the irrationality of it all—save for the purpose of making "history"—and the history is that of the utter ruin of a civilization in intellectual respects perhaps the highest the earth has ever seen.

Those wars were purely piratical. Pride, gold, women, slaves, excitement, were their only motives. In the Peloponnesian war for example, the Athenians ask the inhabitants of Melos (the island where the "Venus of Milo" was found), hitherto neutral, to own their lordship. The envoys meet, and hold a debate which Thucydides gives in full, and which, for sweet reasonableness of form, would have satisfied Matthew Arnold. "The powerful exact what they can," said the Athenians, "and the weak grant what they must." When the Meleans say that sooner than be slaves they will appeal to the gods, the Athenians reply: "Of the gods we believe and of men we know that, by a law of their nature, wherever they can rule they will. This law was not made by us, and we are not the first to have acted upon it; we did but inherit it, and we know that you and all mankind, if you were as strong as we are, would do as we do. So much for the gods; we have told you why we expect to stand as high in their good opinion as you." Well, the Meleans still refused, and their town was taken. "The Athenians," Thucydides quietly says, "thereupon put to death all who were of military age and made slaves of the women and children. They then colonized the island, sending thither five hundred settlers of their own."

Alexander's career was piracy pure and simple, nothing but an orgy of power and plunder, made romantic by the character of the hero. There was no rational principle in it, and the moment he died his generals and governors attacked one another. The cruelty of those times is incredible. When Rome finally conquered Greece, Paulus Aemilius was told by the Roman Senate to reward his soldiers for their toil by "giving" them the old kingdom of Epirus. They sacked seventy cities and carried off a hundred and fifty thousand inhabitants as slaves. How many they killed I know not; but in Etolia they killed all the senators, five hundred and fifty in number. Brutus was "the noblest Roman of them all," but to reanimate his soldiers on the eve of Philippi he similarly promises to give them the cities of Sparta and Thessalonica to ravage, if they win the fight.

Such was the gory nurse that trained societies to cohesiveness. We inherit the warlike type; and for most of the capacities of heroism that the human race is full of we have to thank this cruel history. Dead men tell no tales, and if there were any tribes of other type than this they have left no survivors. Our ancestors have bred pugnacity into our bone and marrow, and thousands of years of peace won't breed it out of us. The popular imagination fairly fattens on the thought of wars. Let public opinion once reach a certain fighting pitch, and no ruler can withstand it. In the Boer war both governments began with bluff but couldn't stay there, the military tension was too much for them. In 1898 our people had read the word "war" in letters three inches high for three months in every newspaper. The pliant politician McKinley was swept away by their eagerness, and our squalid war with Spain became a necessity.

At the present day, civilized opinion is a curious mental mixture. The military instincts and ideals are as strong as ever, but are confronted by reflective criticisms which sorely curb their ancient freedom. Innumerable writers are showing up the bestial side of military service. Pure loot and mastery seem no longer morally avowable motives, and pretexts must be found for attributing them solely to the enemy. England and we, our army and navy authorities repeat without ceasing, arm solely for "peace," Germany and Japan it is who are bent on loot and glory. "Peace" in military mouths today is a synonym for "war expected." The word has become a pure provocative, and no government wishing peace sincerely should allow it ever to be printed in a newspaper. Every up-to-date dictionary should say that "peace" and "war" mean the same thing, now *in posse*, now *in actu*. It may even reasonably be said that the intensely sharp competitive *preparation* for war by the nations *is the real war*, permanent, unceasing; and that the battles are only a sort of public verification of the mastery gained during the "peace"-interval.

It is plain that on this subject civilized man has developed a sort of double personality. If we take European nations, no legitimate interest of any one of them would seem to justify the tremendous destructions which a war to compass it would necessarily entail. It would seem as though common sense and reason ought to find a way to reach agreement in every conflict of honest interests. I myself think it our bounden duty to believe in such international rationality as possible. But, as things stand, I see how desperately hard it is to bring the peace-party and the war-party together, and I believe that the difficulty is due to certain deficiencies in the program of pacificism which set the militarist imagination strongly, and to a certain extent justifiably, against it. In the whole discussion both sides are on imaginative and sentimental ground. It is but one utopia against another, and everything one says must be abstract and hypothetical. Subject to this criticism and caution, I will try to characterize in abstract strokes

the opposite imaginative forces, and point out what to my own very
fallible mind seems the best utopian hypothesis, the most promising line
of conciliation.

In my remarks, pacificist though I am, I will refuse to speak of the
bestial side of the war-*régime* (already done justice to by many writers)
and consider only the higher aspects of militaristic sentiment. Patriotism
no one thinks discreditable; nor does any one deny that war is the romance
of history. But inordinate ambitions are the soul of every patriotism, and
the possibility of violent death the soul of all romance. The militarily
patriotic and romantic-minded everywhere, and especially the professional
military class, refuse to admit for a moment that war may be a transitory
phenomenon in social evolution. The notion of a sheep's paradise like
that revolts, they say, our higher imagination. Where then would be the
steeps of life? If the war had ever stopped, we should have to re-invent
it, on this view, to redeem life from flat degeneration.

Reflective apologists for war at the present day all take it religiously.
It is a sort of sacrament. Its profits are to the vanquished as well as to the
victor; and quite apart from any question of profit, it is an absolute good,
we are told, for it is human nature at its highest dynamic. Its "horrors" are
a cheap price to pay for rescue from the only alternative supposed, of a
world of clerks and teachers, of co-educational and zo-ophily, of "con-
sumer's leagues" and "associated charities," of industrialism unlimited, and
feminism unabashed. No scorn, no hardness, no valor any more! Fie upon
such a cattleyard of a planet!

So far as the central essence of this feeling goes, no healthy minded
person, it seems to me, can help to some degree partaking of it. Militarism
is the great preserver of our ideals of hardihood, and human life with no
use for hardihood would be contemptible. Without risks or prizes for the
darer, history would be insipid indeed; and there is a type of military
character which every one feels that the race should never cease to breed,
for every one is sensitive to its superiority. The duty is incumbent on mankind, of keeping military characters in stock—of keeping them, if not for
use, then as ends in themselves and as pure pieces of perfection—so that
Roosevelt's weaklings and mollycoddles may not end by making everything
else disappear from the face of nature.

This natural sort of feeling forms, I think, the innermost soul of army-
writings. Without any exception known to me, militarist authors take a
highly mystical view of their subject, and regard war as a biological or
sociological necessity, uncontrolled by ordinary psychological checks and
motives. When the time of development is ripe the war must come, reason
or no reason, for the justifications pleaded are invariably fictitious. War is,
in short, a permanent human *obligation*. General Homer Lea, in his recent
book *The Valor of Ignorance*, plants himself squarely on this ground.
Readiness for war is for him the essence of nationality, and ability in it
the supreme measure of the health of nations.

Nations, General Lea says, are never stationary—they must necessarily expand or shrink, according to their vitality or decrepitude. Japan now is culminating; and by the fatal law in question it is impossible that her statesmen should not long since have entered, with extraordinary foresight, upon a vast policy of conquest—the game in which the first moves were her wars with China and Russia and her treaty with England, and of which the final objective is the capture of the Philippines, the Hawaiian Islands, Alaska, and the whole of our Coast west of the Sierra Passes. This will give Japan what her ineluctable vocation as a state absolute forces her to claim, the possession of the entire Pacific Ocean; and to oppose these deep designs we Americans have, according to our author, nothing but our conceit, our ignorance, our commercialism, our corruption, and our feminism. General Lea makes a minute technical comparison of the military strength which we at present could oppose to the strength of Japan, and concludes that the islands, Alaska, Oregon, and Southern California, would fall almost without resistance, that San Francisco must surrender in a fortnight to a Japanese investment, that in three or four months the war would be over, and our republic, unable to regain what it had heedlessly neglected to protect sufficiently, would then "disintegrate," until perhaps some Cæsar should arise to weld us again into a nation.

A dismal forecast indeed! Yet not unplausible, if the mentality of Japan's statesmen be of the Cæsarian type of which history shows so many examples, and which is all that General Lea seems able to imagine. But there is no reason to think that women can no longer be the mothers of Napoleonic or Alexandrian characters; and if these come in Japan and find their opportunity, just such surprises as *The Valor of Ignorance* paints may lurk in ambush for us. Ignorant as we still are of the innermost recesses of Japanese mentality, we may be foolhardy to disregard such possibilities.

Other militarists are more complex and more moral in their considerations. The *Philosophie des Krieges*, by S. R. Steinmetz is a good example. War, according to this author, is an ordeal instituted by God, who weighs the nations in its balance. It is the essential form of the State, and the only function in which peoples can employ all their powers at once and convergently. No victory is possible save as the resultant of a totality of virtues, no defeat for which some vice or weakness is not responsible. Fidelity, cohesiveness, tenacity, heroism, conscience, education, inventiveness, economy, wealth, physical health and vigor—there isn't a moral or intellectual point of superiority that doesn't tell when God holds his assizes and hurls the peoples upon one another. *Die Weltgeschichte ist das Weltgericht*; and Dr. Steinmetz does not believe that in the long run chance and luck play any part in apportioning the issues.

The virtues that prevail, it must be noted, are virtues anyhow, superiorities that count in peaceful as well as in military competition; but the strain on them, being infinitely intenser in the latter case, makes war infinitely more searching as a trial. No ordeal is comparable to its winnow-ings. Its dread hammer is the welder of men into cohesive states, and no-where but in such states can human nature adequately develop its capac-ity. The only alternative is "degeneration."

Dr. Steinmetz is a conscientious thinker, and his book, short as it is, takes much into account. Its upshot can, it seems to me, be summed up in Simon Patten's word, that mankind was nursed in pain and fear, and that the transition to a "pleasure-economy" may be fatal to a being wielding no powers of defence against its disintegrative influences. If we speak of the *fear of emancipation from the fear-régime*, we put the whole situation into a single phrase; fear regarding ourselves now taking the place of the ancient fear of the enemy.

Turn the fear over as I will in my mind, it all seems to lead back to two unwillingnesses of the imagination, one aesthetic, and the other moral; unwillingness, first to envisage a future in which army-life, with its many elements of charm, shall be forever impossible, and in which the destinies of peoples shall nevermore be decided quickly, thrillingly, and tragically, by force, but only gradually and insipidly by "evolution"; and, secondly, unwillingness to see the supreme theatre of human strenuousness closed, and the splendid military aptitudes of men doomed to keep always in a state of latency and never show themselves in action. These insistent unwillingnessess, no less than other aesthetic and ethical insistencies, have, it seems to me, to be listened to and respected. One cannot meet them effectively by mere counter-insistency on war's expensiveness and horror. The horror makes the thrill; and when the question is of getting the extremest and supremest out of human nature, talk of expense sounds ignominious. The weakness of so much merely negative criticism is evi-dent—pacificism makes no converts from the military party. The military party denies neither the bestiality nor the horror, nor the expense; it only says that these things tell but half the story. It only says that war is *worth* them; that, taking human nature as a whole, its wars are its best protection against its weaker and more cowardly self, and that mankind cannot *afford* to adopt a peace-economy.

Pacifists ought to enter more deeply into the aesthetical and ethical point of view of their opponents. Do that first in any controversy, says J. J. Chapman, *then move the point*, and your opponent will follow. So long as anti-militarists propose no substitute for war's disciplinary function, no *moral equivalent* of war, analogous, as one might say, to the mechanical equivalent of heat, so long they fail to realize the full inwardness of the situation. And as a rule they do fail. The duties, penalties, and sanctions pictured in the utopias they paint are all too weak and tame to touch the military-minded. Tolstoï's pacificism is the only exception to this rule, for it is profoundly pessimistic as regards all this world's values, and makes the fear of the Lord furnish the moral spur provided elsewhere by the fear of the enemy. But our socialistic peace-advocates all believe absolutely in this

world's values; and instead of the fear of the Lord and the fear of the
enemy, the only fear they reckon with is the fear of poverty if one be lazy.
This weakness pervades all the socialistic literature with which I am
acquainted. Even in Lowes Dickinson's exquisite dialogue, high wages and
short hours are the only forces invoked for overcoming man's distaste for
repulsive kinds of labor. Meanwhile men at large still live as they always
have lived, under a pain-and-fear economy—for those of us who live in an
ease-economy are but an island in the stormy ocean—and the whole atmosphere of present-day utopian literature tastes mawkish and dishwatery to
people who still keep a sense for life's more bitter flavors. It suggests, in
truth, ubiquitous inferiority.

Inferiority is always with us, and merciless scorn of it is the keynote
of the military temper. "Dogs, would you live forever?" shouted Frederick
the Great. "Yes," say our utopians, "let us live forever, and raise our level
gradually." The best thing about our "inferiors" today is that they are as
tough as nails, and physically and morally almost as insensitive. Utopian-
ism would see them soft and squeamish, while militarism would keep their
callousness, but transfigure it into a meritorious characteristic, needed by
"the service," and redeemed by that from the suspicion of inferiority. All
the qualities of a man acquire dignity when he knows that the service of
the collectivity that owns him needs them. If proud of the collectivity, his
own pride rises in proportion. No collectivity is like an army for nourishing
such pride; but it has to be confessed that the only sentiment which the
image of pacific cosmopolitan industrialism is capable of arousing in countless worthy breasts is shame at the idea of belonging to *such* a collectivity.
It is obvious that the United States of America as they exist today impress
a mind like General Lea's as so much human blubber. Where is the
sharpness and precipitousness, the contempt for life, whether one's own,
or another's? Where is the savage "yes" and "no," the unconditional duty?
Where is the conscription? Where is the blood-tax? Where is anything
that one feels honored by belonging to?

Having said thus much in preparation, I will now confess my own
utopia. I devoutly believe in the reign of peace and in the gradual advent
of some sort of a socialistic equilibrium. The fatalistic view of the war-
function is to me nonsense, for I know that war-making is due to definite
motives and subject to prudential checks and reasonable criticisms, just
like any other form of enterprise. And when whole nations are the armies,
and the science of destruction vies in intellectual refinement with the
sciences of production, I see that war becomes absurd and impossible from
its own monstrosity. Extravagant ambitions will have to be replaced by
reasonable claims, and nations must make common cause against them. I
see no reason why all this should not apply to yellow as well as to white
countries, and I look forward to a future when acts of war shall be formally
outlawed as between civilized peoples.

All these beliefs of mine put me squarely into the antimilitarist party. But I do not believe that peace either ought to be or will be permanent on this globe, unless the states pacifically organized preserve some of the old elements of army-discipline. A permanently successful peace-economy cannot be a simple pleasure-economy. In the more or less socialistic future towards which mankind seems drifting we must still subject ourselves collectively to those severities which answer to our real position upon this only partly hospitable globe. We must make new energies and hardihoods continue the manliness to which the military mind so faithfully clings. Martial virtues must be the enduring cement; intrepidity, contempt of softness, surrender of private interest, obedience to command, must still remain the rock upon which states are built—unless, indeed, we wish for dangerous reactions against commonwealths fit only for contempt, and liable to invite attack whenever a centre of crystallization for military-minded enterprise gets formed anywhere in their neighborhood.

The war-party is assuredly right in affirming and reaffirming that the martial virtues, although originally gained by the race through war, are absolute and permanent human goods. Patriotic pride and ambition in their military form are, after all, only specifications of a more general competitive passion. They are its first form, but that is no reason for supposing them to be its last form. Men now are proud of belonging to a conquering nation, and without a murmur they lay down their persons and their wealth, if by so doing they may fend off subjection. But who can be sure that *other aspects of one's country* may not, with time and education and suggestion enough, come to be regarded with similarly effective feelings of pride and shame? Why should men not some day feel that it is worth a blood-tax to belong to a collectivity superior in *any* ideal respect? Why should they not blush with indignant shame if the community that owns them is vile in any way whatsoever? Individuals, daily more numerous, now feel this civic passion. It is only a question of blowing on the spark till the whole population gets incandescent, and on the ruins of the old morals of military honor, a stable system of morals of civic honor builds itself up. What the whole community comes to believe in grasps the individual as in a vise. The war-function has grasped us so far; but constructive interests may some day seem no less imperative, and impose on the individual a hardly lighter burden.

Let me illustrate my idea more concretely. There is nothing to make one indignant in the mere fact that life is hard, that men should toil and suffer pain. The planetary conditions once for all are such, and we can stand it. But that so many men, by mere accidents of birth and opportunity, should have a life of *nothing else* but toil and pain and hardness and inferiority imposed upon them, should have *no* vacation, while others natively no more deserving never get any taste of this campaigning life at all—*this* is capable of arousing indignation in reflective minds. It may end by seeming shameful to all of us that some of us have nothing but campaigning, and others nothing but unmanly ease. If now—and this is my idea—there were, instead of military conscription a conscription of the whole youthful population to form for a certain number of years a part of the army enlisted against *Nature*, the injustice would tend to be evened out, and numerous other goods to the commonwealth would follow. The military ideals of hardihood and discipline would be wrought into the growing fibre of the people; no one would remain blind as the luxurious classes now are blind, to man's relations to the globe he lives on, and to the permanently sour and hard foundations of his higher life. To coal and iron mines, to freight trains, to fishing fleets in December, to dishwashing, clothes-washing, and window-washing, to road-building and tunnel-making, to foundries and stoke-holes, and to the frames of skyscrapers, would our gilded youths be drafted off, according to their choice, to get the childishness knocked out of them, and to come back into society with healthier sympathies and soberer ideas. They would have paid their blood-tax, done their own part in the immemorial human warfare against nature; they would tread the earth more proudly, the women would value them more highly, they would be better fathers and teachers of the following generation.

Such a conscription, with the state of public opinion that would have required it, and the many moral fruits it would bear, would preserve in the midst of a pacific civilization the manly virtues which the military party is so afraid of seeing disappear in peace. We should get toughness without callousness, authority with as little criminal cruelty as possible, and painful work done cheerily because the duty is temporary, and threatens not, as now, to degrade the whole remainder of one's life. I spoke of the "moral equivalent" of war. So far, war has been the only force that can discipline a whole community, and until an equivalent discipline is organized, I believe that war must have its way. But I have no serious doubt that the ordinary prides and shames of social man, once developed to a certain intensity, are capable of organizing such a moral equivalent as I have sketched, or some other just as effective for preserving manliness of type. It is but a question of time, skillful propagandism, and of opinion-making men seizing historic opportunities.

The martial type of character can be bred without war. Strenuous honor and disinterestedness abound elsewhere. Priests and medical men are in a fashion educated to it, and we should all feel some degree of it imperative if we were conscious of our work as an obligatory service to the state. We should be *owned*, as soldiers are by the army, and our pride would rise accordingly. We could be poor, then, without humiliation, as army officers now are. The only thing needed henceforward is to inflame the civic temper as past history has inflamed the military temper. H. G. Wells, as usual, sees the centre of the situation. "In many ways," he says, "military organization is the most peaceful of activities. When the contemporary man steps from the street, of clamorous insincere advertisement, push, adulteration, underselling and intermittent employment into the barrack-yard, he steps on to a higher social plane, into an atmosphere of service and coöperation and of infinitely more honorable emulations. Here at least men are not flung out of employment to degenerate because there is no immediate work for them to do. They are fed and drilled and trained for better services. Here at least a man is supposed to win promotion by self-forgetfulness and not by self-seeking. And beside the feeble and irregular endowment of research by commercialism, its little short-sighted snatches at profit by innovation and scientific economy, see how remarkable is the steady and rapid development of method and appliances in naval and military affairs! Nothing is more striking than to compare the progress of civil conveniences which has been left almost entirely to the trader, to the progress in military apparatus during the last few decades. The house-appliances of today, for example, are little better than they were fifty years ago. A house of today is still almost as ill-ventilated, badly heated by wasteful fires, clumsily arranged and furnished as the house of 1858. Houses a couple of hundred years old are still satisfactory places of residence, so little have our standards risen. But the rifle or battle-ship of fifty years ago was beyond all comparison inferior to those we possess; in power, in speed, in convenience alike. No one has a use now for such superannuated things."[1]

Wells adds[2] that he thinks that the conceptions of order and discipline, the tradition of service and devotion, of physical fitness, unstinted exertion, and universal responsibility, which universal military duty is now teaching European nations, will remain a permanent acquisition, when the last ammunition has been used in the fireworks that celebrate the final peace. I believe as he does. It would be simply preposterous if the only force that could work ideals of honor and standards of efficiency into English or American natures should be the fear of being killed by the Germans or Japanese. Great indeed is Fear; but it is not, as our military enthusiasts believe and try to make us believe, the only stimulus known for awakening the higher ranges of men's spiritual energy. The amount of alteration in public opinion which my utopia postulates is vastly less than the difference between the mentality of those black warriors who pursued Stanley's party on the Congo with their cannibal war-cry of "Meat! Meat!" and that of the "general staff" of any civilized nation. History has seen the latter interval bridged over: the former one can be bridged over much more easily.

1 *First and Last Things*, 1908, p. 215.
2 *Ibid.*, p. 226.

5

THE EQUALITY
OF WOMEN

THE SECOND SEX

Simone de Beauvoir

(*trans. by H. M. Parshley*)

Simone de Beauvoir (1908–   ), existential philosopher whose novels, essays, and philosophic works deal with the basic themes of freedom versus responsibility, the relationship between conscience and "the other," the status of women, and the meaning that ageing and death impart to life. Her most celebrated book is The Second Sex *(1953), but she is also well known for her novels* She Came to Stay *(1954),* The Blood of Others *(1948), and, most particularly,* The Mandarins *(1954). De Beauvoir is also the author of* The Ethics of Ambiguity *(1948), which is a strong essay in existentialism.*

. . .

. . . First we must ask: what is a woman? "*Tota mulier in utero,*" says one, "woman is a womb." But in speaking of certain women, connoisseurs declare that they are not women, although they are equipped with a uterus like the rest. All agree in recognizing the fact that females exist in the human species; today as always they make up about one half of humanity. And yet we are told that femininity is in danger; we are exhorted to be women, remain women, become women. It would appear, then, that every female human being is not necessarily a woman; to be so considered she must share in that mysterious and threatened reality known as femininity. Is this attribute something secreted by the ovaries? Or is it a Platonic essence, a product of the philosophic imagination? Is a rustling petticoat enough to bring it down to earth? Although some women try zealously to incarnate this essence, it is hardly patentable. It is frequently described in vague and dazzling terms that seem to have been borrowed from the vocabulary of the seers, and indeed in the times of St. Thomas it was considered an essence as certainly defined as the somniferous virtue of the poppy.

But conceptualism has lost ground. The biological and social sciences no longer admit the existence of unchangeably fixed entities that determine given characteristics, such as those ascribed to woman, the Jew, or the Negro. Science regards any characteristic as a reaction dependent in part upon a *situation*. If today femininity no longer exists, then it never existed. But does the word *woman*, then, have no specific content? This is stoutly affirmed by those who hold to the philosophy of the enlightenment, of rationalism, of nominalism; women, to them, are merely the human beings arbitrarily designated by the word *woman*. Many American women particularly are prepared to think that there is no longer any place for woman as such; if a backward individual still takes herself for a woman, her friends advise her to be psychoanalyzed and thus get rid of this obsession. In regard to a work, *Modern Woman: The Lost Sex*, which in other respects has its irritating features, Dorothy Parker has written: "I cannot be just to books which treat of woman as woman. . . . My idea is that all of us, men as well as women, should be regarded as human beings." But nominalism is a rather inadequate doctrine, and the anti-feminimists have had no trouble in showing that women simply *are not* men. Surely woman is, like man, a human being; but such a declaration is abstract. The fact is that every concrete human being is always a singular, separate individual. To decline to accept such notions as the eternal feminine, the black soul, the Jewish character, is not to deny that Jews, Negroes, women exist today—this denial does not represent a liberation for those concerned, but rather a flight from reality. Some years ago a well-known woman writer refused to permit her portrait to appear in a series of photographs especially devoted to women writers; she wished to be counted among the men. But in order to gain this privilege she made use of her husband's influence! Women who assert that they are men lay claim none the less to masculine consideration and respect. I recall also a young Trotskyite standing on a platform at a boisterous meeting and getting ready to use her fists, in spite of her evident fragility. She was denying her feminine weakness; but it was for love of a militant male whose equal she wished to be. The attitude of defiance of many American women proves that they are haunted by a sense of their femininity. In truth, to go for a walk with one's eyes open is enough to demonstrate that humanity is divided into two classes of individuals whose clothes, faces, bodies, smiles, gaits, interests, and occupations are manifestly different. Perhaps these differences are superficial, perhaps they are destined to disappear. What is certain is that right now they do most obviously exist.

If her functioning as a female is not enough to define woman, if we decline also to explain her through "the eternal feminine," and if nevertheless we admit, provisionally, that women do exist, then we must face the question: what is a woman?

To state the question is, to me, to suggest, at once, a preliminary answer. The fact that I ask it is in itself significant. A man would never get the notion of writing a book on the peculiar situation of the human male.[1] But if I wish to define myself, I must first of all say: "I am a woman"; on this truth must be based all further discussion. A man never begins by presenting himself as an individual of a certain sex; it goes without ·saying that he is a man. The terms *masculine* and *feminine* are used symmetrically only as a matter of form, as on legal papers. In actuality the relation of the two sexes is not quite like that of two electrical poles, for man represents both the positive and the neutral, as is indicated by the common use of *man* to designate human beings in general; whereas woman represents only the negative, defined by limiting criteria, without reciprocity. In the midst of an abstract discussion it is vexing to hear a man say: "You think thus and so because you are a woman"; but I know that my only defense is to reply: "I think thus and so because it is true," thereby removing my subjective self from the argument. It would be out of the question to reply: "And you think the contrary because you are a man," for it is understood that the fact of being a man is no peculiarity. A man is in the right in being a man; it is the woman who is in the wrong. It amounts to this: just as for the ancients there was an absolute vertical with reference to which the oblique was defined, so there is an absolute human type, the masculine. Woman has ovaries, a uterus; these peculiarities imprison her in her subjectivity, circumscribe her within the limits of her own nature. It is often said that she thinks with her glands. Man superbly ignores the fact that his anatomy also includes glands, such as the testicles, and that they secrete hormones. He thinks of his body as a direct and normal connection with the world, which he believes he apprehends objectively, whereas he regards the body of woman as a hindrance, a prison, weighed down by everything peculiar to it. "The female is a female by virtue of a certain *lack* of qualities," said Aristotle; "we should regard the female nature as afflicted with a natural defectiveness." And St. Thomas for his part pronounced woman to be an "imperfect man," an "incidental" being. This is symbolized in Genesis where Eve is depicted as made from what Bossuet called "a supernumerary bone" of Adam.

Thus humanity is male and man defines woman not in herself but as relative to him; she is not regarded as an autonomous being. Michelet writes: "Woman, the relative being. . . ." And Benda is most positive in his *Rapport d'Uriel:* "The body of man makes sense in itself quite apart from that of woman, whereas the latter seems wanting in significance by itself. . . . Man can think of himself without woman. She cannot think

[1] The Kinsey Report [Alfred C. Kinsey and others: *Sexual Behavior in the Human Male* (W. B. Saunders Co., 1948)] is no exception, for it is limited to describing the sexual characteristics of American men, which is quite a different matter.

of herself without man." And she is simply what man decrees; thus she is called "the sex," by which is meant that she appears essentially to the male as a sexual being. For him she is sex—absolute sex, no less. She is defined and differentiated with reference to man and not he with reference to her; she is the incidental, the inessential as opposed to the essential. He is the Subject, he is the Absolute—she is the Other.[2]

The category of the *Other* is as primordial as consciousness itself. In the most primitive societies, in the most ancient mythologies, one finds the expression of a duality—that of the Self and the Other. This duality was not originally attached to the division of the sexes; it was not dependent upon any empirical facts. It is revealed in such works as that of Granet on Chinese thought and those of Dumézil on the East Indies and Rome. The feminine element was at first no more involved in such pairs as Varuna-Mitra, Uranus-Zeus, Sun-Moon, and Day-Night than it was in the contrasts between Good and Evil, lucky and unlucky auspices, right and left, God and Lucifer. Otherness is a fundamental category of human thought.

Thus it is that no group ever sets itself up as the One without at once setting up the Other over against itself. If three travelers chance to occupy the same compartment, that is enough to make vaguely hostile "others" out of all the rest of the passengers on the train. In small-town eyes all persons not belonging to the village are "strangers" and suspect; to the native of a country all who inhabit other countries are "foreigners"; Jews are "different" for the anti-Semite, Negroes are "inferior" for American racists, aborigines are "natives" for colonists, proletarians are the "lower class" for the privileged.

Lévi-Strauss, at the end of a profound work on the various forms of primitive societies, reaches the following conclusion: "Passage from the state of Nature to the state of Culture is marked by man's ability to view biological relations as a series of contrasts; duality, alternation, opposition, and symmetry, whether under definite or vague forms, constitute not so much phenomena to be explained as fundamental and immediately given

---

2 E. Lévinas expresses this idea most explicitly in his essay *Temps et l'Autre.* "Is there not a case in which otherness, alterity [*altérité*], unquestionably marks the nature of a being, as its essence, an instance of otherness not consisting purely and simply in the opposition of two species of the same genus? I think that the feminine represents the contrary in its absolute sense, this contrariness being in no wise affected by any relation between it and its correlative and thus remaining absolutely other. Sex is not a certain specific difference . . . no more is the sexual difference a mere contradiction. . . . Nor does this difference lie in the duality of two complementary terms, for two complementary terms imply a pre-existing whole. . . . Otherness reaches its full flowering in the feminine, a term of the same rank as consciousness but of opposite meaning."

I suppose that Lévinas does not forget that woman, too, is aware of her own consciousness, or ego. But it is striking that he deliberately takes a man's point of view, disregarding the reciprocity of subject and object. When he writes that woman is mystery, he implies that she is mystery for man. Thus his description, which is intended to be objective, is in fact an assertion of masculine privilege.

data of social reality."[3] These phenomena would be incomprehensible if in fact human society were simply a *Mitsein* or fellowship based on solidarity and friendliness. Things become clear, on the contrary, if, following Hegel, we find in consciousness itself a fundamental hostility toward every other consciousness; the subject can be posed only in being opposed—he sets himself up as the essential, as opposed to the other, the inessential, the object.

But the other consciousness, the other ego, sets up a reciprocal claim. The native traveling abroad is shocked to find himself in turn regarded as a "stranger" by the natives of neighboring countries. As a matter of fact, wars, festivals, trading, treaties, and contests among tribes, nations, and classes tend to deprive the concept *Other* of its absolute sense and to make manifest its relativity; willy-nilly, individuals and groups are forced to realize the reciprocity of their relations. How is it, then, that this reciprocity has not been recognized between the sexes, that one of the contrasting terms is set up as the sole essential, denying any relativity in regard to its correlative and defining the latter as pure otherness? Why is it that women do not dispute male sovereignty? No subject will readily volunteer to become the object, the inessential; it is not the Other who, in defining himself as the Other, establishes the One. The Other is posed as such by the One in defining himself as the One. But if the Other is not to regain the status of being the One, he must be submissive enough to accept this alien point of view. Whence comes this submission in the case of woman?

There are, to be sure, other cases in which a certain category has been able to dominate another completely for a time. Very often this privilege depends upon inequality of numbers—the majority imposes its rule upon the minority or persecutes it. But women are not a minority, like the American Negroes or the Jews; there are as many women as men on earth. Again, the two groups concerned have often been originally independent; they may have been formerly unaware of each other's existence, or perhaps they recognized each other's autonomy. But a historical event has resulted in the subjugation of the weaker by the stronger. The scattering of the Jews, the introduction of slavery into America, the conquests of imperialism are examples in point. In these cases the oppressed retained at least the memory of former days; they possessed in common a past, a tradition, sometimes a religion or a culture.

The parallel drawn by Bebel between women and the proletariat is valid in that neither ever formed a minority or a separate collective unit of mankind. And instead of a single historical event it is in both cases a historical development that explains their status as a class and accounts for the membership of *particular individuals* in that class. But proletarians have not always existed, whereas there have always been women. They are women in virtue of their anatomy and physiology. Throughout history

[3] See C. Lévi-Strauss: *Les Structures élémentaires de la parenté*. My thanks are due to C. Lévi-Strauss for his kindness in furnishing me with the proofs of his work, which, among others, I have used liberally in Part II.

they have always been subordinated to men, and hence their dependency is not the result of a historical event or a social change—it was not something that *occurred*. The reason why otherness in this case seems to be an absolute is in part that it lacks the contingent or incidental nature of historical facts. A condition brought about at a certain time can be abolished at some other time, as the Negroes of Haiti and others have proved; but it might seem that a natural condition is beyond the possibility of change. In truth, however, the nature of things is no more immutably given, once for all, than is historical reality. If woman seems to be the inessential which never becomes the essential, it is because she herself fails to bring about this change. Proletarians say "We"; Negroes also. Regarding themselves as subjects, they transform the bourgeois, the whites, into "others." But women do not say "We," except at some congress of feminists or similar formal demonstration; men say "women," and women use the same word in referring to themselves. They do not authentically assume a subjective attitude. The proletarians have accomplished the revolution in Russia, the Negroes in Haiti, the Indo-Chinese are battling for it in Indo-China; but the women's effort has never been anything more than a symbolic agitation. They have gained only what men have been willing to grant; they have taken nothing, they have only received.

The reason for this is that women lack concrete means for organizing themselves into a unit which can stand face to face with the correlative unit. They have no past, no history, no religion of their own; and they have no such solidarity of work and interest as that of the proletariat. They are not even promiscuously herded together in the way that creates community feeling among the American Negroes, the ghetto Jews, the workers of Saint-Denis, or the factory hands of Renault. They live dispersed among the males, attached through residence, housework, economic condition, and social standing to certain men—fathers or husbands—more firmly than they are to other women. If they belong to the bourgeoisie, they feel solidarity with men of that class, not with proletarian women; if they are white, their allegiance is to white men, not to Negro women. The proletariat can propose to massacre the ruling class, and a sufficiently fanatical Jew or Negro might dream of getting sole possession of the atomic bomb and making humanity wholly Jewish or black; but woman cannot even dream of exterminating the males. The bond that unites her to her oppressors is not comparable to any other. The division of the sexes is a biological fact, not an event in human history. Male and female stand opposed within a primordial *Mitsein*, and woman has not broken it. The couple is a fundamental unity with its two halves riveted together, and the cleavage of society along the line of sex is impossible. Here is to be found the basic trait of woman: she is the Other in a totality of which the two components are necessary to one another.

One could suppose that this reciprocity might have facilitated the liberation of woman. When Hercules sat at the feet of Omphale and helped with her spinning, his desire for her held him captive; but why did she fail to gain a lasting power? To revenge herself on Jason, Medea killed their children; and this grim legend would seem to suggest that she might have obtained a formidable influence over him through his love for his offspring. In *Lysistrata* Aristophanes gaily depicts a band of women who joined forces to gain social ends through the sexual needs of their men; but this is only a play. In the legend of the Sabine women, the latter soon abandoned their plan of remaining sterile to punish their ravishers. In truth woman has not been socially emancipated through man's need—sexual desire and the desire for offspring—which makes the male dependent for satisfaction upon the female.

Master and slave, also, are united by a reciprocal need, in this case economic, which does not liberate the slave. In the relation of master to slave the master does not make a point of the need that he has for the other; he has in his grasp the power of satisfying this need through his own action; whereas the slave, in his dependent condition, his hope and fear, is quite conscious of the need he has for his master. Even if the need is at bottom equally urgent for both, it always works in favor of the oppressor and against the oppressed. That is why the liberation of the working class, for example, has been slow.

Now, woman has always been man's dependent, if not his slave; the two sexes have never shared the world in equality. And even today woman is heavily handicapped, though her situation is beginning to change. Almost nowhere is her legal status the same as man's, and frequently it is much to her disadvantage. Even when her rights are legally recognized in the abstract, long-standing custom prevents their full expression in the mores. In the economic sphere men and women can almost be said to make up two castes; other things being equal, the former hold the better jobs, get higher wages, and have more opportunity for success than their new competitors. In industry and politics men have a great many more positions and they monopolize the most important posts. In addition to all this, they enjoy a traditional prestige that the education of children tends in every way to support, for the present enshrines the past—and in the past all history has been made by men. At the present time, when women are beginning to take part in the affairs of the world, it is still a world that belongs to men—they have no doubt of it at all and women have scarcely any. To decline to be the Other, to refuse to be a party to the deal—this would be for women to renounce all the advantages conferred upon them by their alliance with the superior caste. Man-the-sovereign will provide woman-the-liege with material protection and will undertake the moral justification of her existence; thus she can evade at once both economic risk and the metaphysical risk of a liberty in which ends and aims must be contrived without assistance. Indeed, along with the ethical urge of each individual to affirm his subjective existence, there is also the temptation to forgo liberty and become a thing. This is an inauspicious road, for he who takes it—passive, lost, ruined—becomes henceforth the creature of another's will, frustrated in his transcendence and deprived of every value. But it is an easy road; on it one avoids the strain involved in undertaking an authentic existence. When man makes of woman the *Other*, he may, then, expect her to manifest deep-seated tendencies toward complicity. Thus, woman may fail to lay claim to the status of subject because she lacks definite resources, because she feels the necessary bond that ties her to man regardless of reciprocity, and because she is often very well pleased with her role as the *Other*.

But it will be asked at once: how did all this begin? It is easy to see that the duality of the sexes, like any duality, gives rise to conflict. And doubtless the winner will assume the status of absolute. But why should man have won from the start? It seems possible that women could have won the victory; or that the outcome of the conflict might never have been decided. How is it that this world has always belonged to the men and that things have begun to change only recently? Is this change a good thing? Will it bring about an equal sharing of the world between men and women?

These questions are not new, and they have often been answered. But the very fact that woman *is the Other* tends to cast suspicion upon all the justifications that men have ever been able to provide for it. These have all too evidently been dictated by men's interest. A little-known feminist of the seventeenth century, Poulain de la Barre, put it this way: "All that has been written about women by men should be suspect, for the men are at once judge and party to the lawsuit." Everywhere, at all times, the males have displayed their satisfaction in feeling that they are the lords of creation. "Blessed be God . . . that He did not make me a woman," say the Jews in their morning prayers, while their wives pray on a note of resignation: "Blessed be the Lord, who created me according to His will." The first among the blessings for which Plato thanked the gods was that he had been created free, not enslaved; the second, a man, not a woman. But the males could not enjoy this privilege fully unless they believed it to be founded on the absolute and the eternal; they sought to make the fact of their supremacy into a right. "Being men, those who have made and compiled the laws have favored their own sex, and jurists have elevated these laws into principles," to quote Poulain de la Barre once more.

Legislators, priests, philosophers, writers, and scientists have striven to show that the subordinate position of woman is willed in heaven and advantageous on earth. The religions invented by men reflect this wish for domination. In the legends of Eve and Pandora men have taken up arms against women. They have made use of philosophy and theology, as the quotations from Aristotle and St. Thomas have shown. Since ancient times satirists and moralists have delighted in showing up the weaknesses of women. We are familiar with the savage indictments hurled against women throughout French literature. Montherlant, for example, follows the tradition of Jean de Meung, though with less gusto. This hostility may at times be well founded, often it is gratuitous; but in truth it more or less successfully conceals a desire for self-justification. As Montaigne says, "It is easier to accuse one sex than to excuse the other." Sometimes what is going on is clear enough. For instance, the Roman law limiting the rights of woman cited "the imbecility, the instability of the sex" just when the weakening of family ties seemed to threaten the interests of male heirs. And in the effort to keep the married woman under guardianship, appeal was made in the sixteenth century to the authority of St. Augustine, who declared that "woman is a creature neither decisive nor constant," at a time when the single woman was thought capable of managing her property. Montaigne understood clearly how arbitrary and unjust was woman's appointed lot. "Women are not in the wrong when they decline to accept the rules laid down for them, since the men make these rules without consulting them. No wonder intrigue and strife abound." But he did not go so far as to champion their cause.

It was only later, in the eighteenth century, that genuinely democratic men began to view the matter objectively. Diderot, among others, strove to show that woman is, like man, a human being. Later John Stuart Mill came fervently to her defense. But these philosophers displayed unusual impartiality. In the nineteenth century the feminist quarrel became again a quarrel of partisans. One of the consequences of the industrial revolution was the entrance of women into productive labor, and it was just here that the claims of the feminists emerged from the realm of theory and acquired an economic basis, while their opponents became the more aggressive. Although landed property lost power to some extent, the bourgeoisie clung to the old morality that found the guarantee of private property in the solidity of the family. Woman was ordered back into the home the more harshly as her emancipation became a real menace. Even within the working class the men endeavored to restrain woman's liberation, because they began to see the women as dangerous competitors—the more so because they were accustomed to work for lower wages.

In proving woman's inferiority, the antifeminists then began to draw not only upon religion, philosophy, and theology, as before, but also upon science—biology, experimental psychology, etc. At most they were willing to grant "equality in difference" to the *other* sex. That profitable formula is most significant; it is precisely like the "equal but separate" formula of the Jim Crow laws aimed at the North American Negroes. As is well known, this so-called equalitarian segregation has resulted only in the most extreme discrimination. The similarity just noted is in no way due to chance, for whether it is a race, a caste, a class, or a sex that is reduced to a position of inferiority, the methods of justification are the same. "The eternal feminine" corresponds to "the black soul" and to "the Jewish character." True, the Jewish problem is on the whole very different from the other two—to the anti-Semite the Jew is not so much an inferior as he is an enemy for whom there is to be granted no place on earth, for whom annihilation is the fate desired. But there are deep similarities between the situation of woman and that of the Negro. Both are being emancipated today from a like paternalism, and the former master class wishes to "keep them in their place"—that is, the place chosen for them. In both cases the former masters lavish more or less sincere eulogies, either on the virtues of the good Negro with his dormant, childish, merry soul—the submissive Negro—or on the merits of the woman who is "truly feminine"—that is, frivolous, infantile, irresponsible—the submissive woman. In both cases the dominant class bases its argument on a state of affairs that it has itself created. As George Bernard Shaw puts it, in substance, "The American white relegates the black to the rank of shoe-shine boy; and he concludes from this that the black is good for nothing but shining shoes." This vicious circle is met with in all analogous circumstances; when an individual (or a group of individuals) is kept in a situaton of inferiority, the fact is that he *is* inferior. But the significance of the verb *to be* must be rightly understood here; it is in bad faith to give it a static value when it really has the dynamic Hegelian sense of "to have become." Yes, women on the whole *are* today inferior to men; that is, their situation affords them fewer possibilities. The question is: should that state of affairs continue?

. . .

. . . If we survey some of the works on woman, we note that one of the points of view most frequently adopted is that of the public good, the general interest; and one always means by this the benefit of society as one wishes it to be maintained or established. For our part, we hold that the only public good is that which assures the private good of the citizens; we shall pass judgment on institutions according to their effectiveness in giving concrete opportunities to individuals. But we do not confuse the idea of private interest with that of happiness, although that is another common point of view. Are not women of the harem more happy than women voters? Is not the housekeeper happier than the working-woman? It is not too clear just what the word *happy* really means and still less what true values it may mask. There is no possibility of measuring the happiness of others, and it is always easy to describe as happy the situation in which one wishes to place them.

In particular those who are condemned to stagnation are often pronounced happy on the pretext that happiness consists in being at rest. This notion we reject, for our perspective is that of existentialist ethics. Every subject plays his part as such specifically through exploits or projects that serve as a mode of transcendence; he achieves liberty only through a continual reaching out toward other liberties. There is no justification for present existence other than its expansion into an indefinitely open future. Every time transcendence falls back into immanence, stagnation, there is a degradation of existence into the "*en-soi*"—the brutish life of subjection to given conditions—and of liberty into constraint and contingence. This downfall represents a moral fault if the subject consents to it; if it is inflicted upon him, it spells frustration and oppression. In both cases it is an absolute evil. Every individual concerned to justify his existence feels that his existence involves an undefined need to transcend himself, to engage in freely chosen projects.

Now, what peculiarly signalizes the situation of woman is that she—a free and autonomous being like all human creatures—nevertheless finds herself living in a world where men compel her to assume the status of the Other. They propose to stabilize her as object and to doom her to immanence since her transcendence is to be overshadowed and forever transcended by another ego (*conscience*) which is essential and sovereign. The drama of woman lies in this conflict between the fundamental aspirations of every subject (ego)—who always regards the self as the essential —and the compulsions of a situation in which she is the inessential. How can a human being in woman's situation attain fulfillment? What roads are open to her? Which are blocked? How can independence be recovered in a state of dependency? What circumstances limit woman's liberty and how can they be overcome? These are the fundamental questions on which I would fain throw some light. This means that I am interested in the fortunes of the individual as defined not in terms of happiness but in terms of liberty.

Quite evidently this problem would be without significance if we were to believe that woman's destiny is inevitably determined by physiological, or economic forces. . . .

. . .

Marriage is the destiny traditionally offered to women by society. It is still true that most women are married, or have been, or plan to be, or suffer from not being. The celibate woman is to be explained and defined with reference to marriage, whether she is frustrated, rebellious, or even indifferent in regard to that institution. We must therefore continue this study by analyzing marriage.

Economic evolution in woman's situation is in [the] process of upsetting the institution of marriage: it is becoming a union freely entered upon by the consent of two independent persons; the obligations of the two contracting parties are personal and reciprocal; adultery is for both a breach of contract; divorce is obtainable by the one or the other on the same conditions. Woman is no longer limited to the reproductive function, which has lost in large part its character as natural servitude and has come to be regarded as a function to be voluntarily assumed; and it is compatible with productive labor, since, in many cases, the time off required by a pregnancy is taken by the mother at the expense of the State or the employer. In the Soviet Union marriage was for some years a contract between individuals based upon the complete liberty of the husband and wife; but it would seem that it is now a duty that the State imposes upon them both. Which of these tendencies will prevail in the world of tomorrow will depend upon the general structure of society, but in any case male guardianship of woman is disappearing. Nevertheless, the epoch in which we are living is still, from the feminist point of view, a period of transition. Only, a part of the female population is engaged in production, and even those who are belong to a society in which ancient forms and antique values survive. Modern marriage can be understood only in the light of a past that it tends to perpetuate in part.

Marriage has always been a very different thing for man and for woman. The two sexes are necessary to each other, but this necessity has never brought about a condition of reciprocity between them; women, as we have seen, have never constituted a caste making exchanges and contracts with the male caste upon a footing of equality. A man is socially an independent and complete individual; he is regarded first of all as a producer whose existence is justified by the work he does for the group; we have seen why it is that the reproductive and domestic role to which woman is confined has not guaranteed her an equal dignity. Certainly the male needs her; in some primitive groups it may happen that the bachelor, unable to manage his existence by himself, becomes a kind of outcast; in agricultural societies a woman coworker is essential to the peasant; and for most men it is of advantage to unload certain drudgery upon a mate; the individual wants a regular sexual life and posterity, and the State requires him to contribute to its perpetuation. But man does not make his appeal directly to woman herself; it is the men's group that allows each of its members to find self-fulfillment as husband and father; woman, as slave or vassal, is integrated within families dominated by fathers and brothers, and she has always been given in marriage by certain males to other males. In primitive societies the paternal clan, the gens, disposed of woman almost like a thing: she was included in deals agreed upon by two groups. The situation is not much modified when marriage assumes a contractual form in the course of its evolution;[4] when dowered or having her share in inheritance, woman would seem to have civil standing as a person, but dowry and inheritance still enslave her to her family. During a long period the contracts were made between father-in-law and son-in-law, not between wife and husband; only widows then enjoyed economic independence.[5] The young girl's freedom of choice has always been much restricted; and celibacy—apart from the rare cases in which it bears a sacred character— reduced her to the rank of parasite and pariah; marriage is her only means of support and the sole justification of her existence. It is enjoined upon her for two reasons.

The first reason is that she must provide the society with children;

---

[4] This evolution proceeded in discontinuous fashion, being repeated in Egypt, Rome, and modern civilization.

[5] Hence the special place of the young widow in erotic literature.

only rarely—as in Sparta and to some extent under the Nazi regime—does the State take woman under direct guardianship and ask only that she be a mother. But even the primitive societies that are not aware of the paternal generative role demand that woman have a husband, for the second reason why marriage is enjoined is that woman's function is also to satisfy a male's sexual needs and to take care of his household. These duties placed upon woman by society are regarded as a *service* rendered to her spouse: in return he is supposed to give her presents, or a marriage settlement, and to support her. Through him as intermediary, society discharges its debt to the woman it turns over to him. The rights obtained by the wife in fulfilling her duties are represented in obligations that the male must assume. He cannot break the conjugal bond at his pleasure; he can repudiate or divorce his wife only when the public authorities so decide, and even then the husband sometimes owes her compensation in money: the practice even becomes an abuse in Egypt under Bocchoris or, as the demand for alimony, in the United States today. Polygamy has always been more or less openly tolerated: man may bed with slaves, concubines, mistresses, prostitutes, but he is required to respect certain privileges of his legitimate wife. If she is maltreated or wronged, she has the right—more or less definitely guaranteed—of going back to her family and herself obtaining a separation or divorce.

Thus for both parties marriage is at the same time a burden and a benefit; but there is no symmetry in the situations of the two sexes; for girls marriage is the only means of integration in the community, and if they remain unwanted, they are, socially viewed, so much wastage. . . .

· · ·

[There are] two currently accepted preconceptions [about motherhood]. The first of these preconceptions is that maternity is enough in all cases to crown a woman's life. It is nothing of the kind. There are a great many mothers who are unhappy, embittered, unsatisfied. Tolstoy's wife is a significant example; she was brought to childbed more than twelve times and yet writes constantly in her journal about the emptiness and uselessness of everything, including herself. She tells of calm and happy moments, when she enjoyed being indispensable to her children, and she speaks of them as her sole weapon against the superiority of her husband; but all this was absolutely insufficient to give meaning to her boresome existence. At times she felt capable of anything, but there was nothing for her beyond caring for the children, eating, drinking, sleeping; what should have brought happiness made her sad. She wished ardently to bring her children up well, but the eternal struggle with them made her impatient and angry.

The mother's relation with her children takes form within the totality of her life; it depends upon her relations with her husband, her past, her occupation, herself; it is an error as harmful as it is absurd to regard the child as a universal panacea. This is also Helene Deutsch's conclusion in the work, often quoted above, in which she examines the phenomena of maternity in the light of her psychiatric experience. She gives this function a high importance, believing that through it woman finds complete self-realization—but on condition that it is freely assumed and *sincerely* wanted; the young woman must be in a psychological, moral, and material situation that allows her to bear the effort involved; otherwise the consequences will be disastrous. In particular, it is criminal to recommend having a child as a remedy for melancholia or neurosis; that means the unhappiness of both mother and child. Only the woman who is well balanced, healthy, and aware of her responsibilities is capable of being a "good" mother.

As we have seen, the curse which lies upon marriage is that too often the individuals are joined in their weakness rather than in their strength—each asking from the other instead of finding pleasure in giving. It is even more deceptive to dream of gaining through the child a plenitude, a warmth, a value, which one is unable to create for oneself; the child brings joy only to the woman who is capable of disinterestedly desiring the happiness of another, to one who without being wrapped up in self seeks to transcend her own existence. To be sure, the child is an enterprise to which one can validly devote oneself; but it represents a ready-made justification no more than any other enterprise does; and it must be desired for its own sake, not for hypothetical benefits. As Stekel well says:[6]

> Children are not substitutes for one's disappointed love, they are not substitutes for one's thwarted ideal in life, children are not mere material to fill out an empty existence. Children are a responsibility and an opportunity. Children are the loftiest blossoms upon the tree of untrammeled love. . . . They are neither playthings, nor tools for the fulfillment of parental needs or ungratified ambitions. Children are obligations; they should be brought up so as to become happy human beings.

There is nothing *natural* in such an obligation: nature can never dictate a moral choice; this implies an engagement, a promise to be carried out. To have a child is to undertake a solemn obligation; if the mother shirks this duty subsequently, she commits an offense against an existent, an independent human being; but no one can impose the engagement upon her. The relation between parent and offspring, like that between husband and wife, ought to be freely willed. And it is not true, even, that having a child is a privileged accomplishment for woman, primary in relation to all others; it is often said of a woman that she is coquettish, or amorous, or lesbian, or ambitious, "for lack of a child"; her sexual life, the aims, the values she pursues, would in this view be substituted for a child. In fact, the matter is originally uncertain, indeterminate: one can say as well that a woman wants a child for lack of love, for lack of occupation,

[6] *Frigidity in Woman*, Vol. II, pp. 305, 306.

for lack of opportunity to satisfy homosexual tendencies. A social and artificial morality is hidden beneath this pseudo-naturalism. That the child is the supreme aim of woman is a statement having precisely the value of an advertising slogan.

The second false preconception, directly implied by the first, is that the child is sure of being happy in its mother's arms. There is no such thing as an "unnatural mother," to be sure, since there is nothing natural about maternal love; but, precisely for that reason, there are bad mothers. And one of the major truths proclaimed by psychoanalysis is the danger to the child that may lie in parents who are themselves "normal." The complexes, obsessions, and neuroses of adults have their roots in the early family life of those adults; parents who are themselves in conflict, with their quarrels and their tragic scenes, are bad company for the child. Deeply scarred by their early home life, their approach to their own children is through complexes and frustrations; and this chain of misery lengthens indefinitely. In particular, maternal sado-masochism creates in the daughter guilt feelings that will be expressed in sado-masochistic behavior toward her children, and so on without end.

There is an extravagant fraudulence in the easy reconciliation made between the common attitude of contempt for women and the respect shown for mothers. It is outrageously paradoxical to deny woman all activity in public affairs, to shut her out of masculine careers, to assert her incapacity in all fields of effort, and then to entrust to her the most delicate and the most serious undertaking of all: the molding of a human being. There are many women whom custom and tradition still deny the education, the culture, the responsibilities and activities that are the privilege of men, and in whose arms, nevertheless, babies are put without scruple, as earlier in life dolls were given them to compensate for their inferiority to little boys. They are permitted to play with toys of flesh and blood.

Woman would have to be either perfectly happy or a saint to resist the temptation to abuse her privileges. Montesquieu was perhaps right when he said that it would be better to turn over to women the government of the State rather than that of the family; for if she is given opportunity, woman is as rational, as efficient, as a man; it is in abstract thought, in planned action, that she rises most easily above her sex. It is much more difficult, *as things are*, for her to escape from her woman's past, to attain an emotional balance that nothing in her situation favors. Man, also, is much more balanced and rational at work than at home; he makes his business calculations with mathematical precision, but he becomes illogical, lying, capricious, at home with his wife, where he "lets down." In the same way she "lets down" with her child. And her letting down is more dangerous because she can better defend herself against her husband than can the child against her. It would clearly be desirable for the good of the child if the mother were a complete, unmutilated person, a woman finding in her work and in her relation to society a self-realization that she would not seek to attain tyrannically through her offspring; and it would also be desirable for the child to be left to his parents infinitely less than at present, and for his studies and his diversions to be carried on among other children, under the direction of adults whose bonds with him would be impersonal and pure.

Even when the child seems a treasure in the midst of a happy or at least a balanced life, he cannot represent the limits of his mother's horizon. He does not take her out of her immanence; she shapes his flesh, she nourishes him, she takes care of him. But she can never do more than create a situation that only the child himself as an independent being can transcend; when she lays a stake on his future, her transcendence through the universe and time is still by proxy, which is to say that once more she is doomed to dependency. Not only her son's ingratitude, but also his failure will give the lie to all her hopes: as in marriage or love, she leaves it to another to justify her life, when the only authentic course is freely to assume that duty herself.

We have seen that woman's inferiority originated in her being at first limited to repeating life, whereas man invented reasons for living more essential, in his eyes, than the not-willed routine of mere existence; to restrict woman to maternity would be to perpetuate this situation. She demands today to have a part in that mode of activity in which humanity tries continually to find justification through transcendence, through movement toward new goals and accomplishments; she cannot consent to bring forth life unless life has meaning; she cannot be a mother without endeavoring to play a role in the economic, political, and social life of the times. It is not the same thing to produce cannon fodder, slaves, victims, or, on the other hand, free men. In a properly organized society, where children would be largely taken in charge by the community and the mother cared for and helped, maternity would not be wholly incompatible with careers for women. On the contrary, the woman who works—farmer, chemist, or writer—is the one who undergoes pregnancy most easily because she is not absorbed in her own person; the woman who enjoys the richest individual life will have the most to give her children and will demand the least from them; she who acquires in effort and struggle a sense of true human values will be best able to bring them up properly. If too often, today, woman can hardly reconcile with the best interests of her children an occupation that keeps her away from home for hours and takes all her strength, it is, on the one hand, because feminine employment is still too often a kind of slavery, and, on the other, because no effort has been made to provide for the care, protection, and education of children outside the home. This is a matter of negligence on the part of society; but it is false to justify it on the pretense that some law of nature, God, or man requires that mother and child belong exclusively to one another; this restriction constitutes in fact only a double and baneful oppression.

THE IMPERIAL ANIMAL
Lionel Tiger and Robin Fox

*Lionel Tiger (1937–   ) and Robin Fox (1934–   )
are Canadian anthropologists who have attempted to combine the findings of the biological and social sciences in order to understand man as a
species and to promote human survival. Aside from their collaboration in
writing the celebrated book* The Imperial Animal *(1971),* Lionel Tiger is
the author of *Men in Groups *(1969), and Robin Fox has written such
works as* The Keresan Bridge: A Problem in Pueblo Ethnology *(1967)
and* Kinship and Marriage *(1967).*

. . .

Our proposal is that the mother-infant bond precedes all others in time—
which is obvious—and is the basis for the development of the other bonds
that humans are "programmed" to be likely to have. What is the evidence
for a statement both so simple and so portentous of complexities to come?

The maladjusted adult has frequently been traced back to the disturbed child, and the disturbed child to the unloved infant. Psychoanalysts
argue among themselves about the most vulnerable period of the mother-
child relationship.[1] Some favor a late date, some argue for the first few
months, some stress the moment of birth itself with its attendant traumas,
while still others look into the darkness of the womb—which does in fact
contain a living child capable of psychic upset. In any event; the child *is*
born in a very "fetal" state—one of the means of extending its dependency
and hence its maturation period. But all agree that basic disturbances in
the early stages will adversely affect proper passage through the later ones.
Many of these explanations and arguments seem overelaborate. A con-
vergence of work in child psychiatry and the study of animal behavior
suggests that something rather simple is behind all this, even if the simplicity is disguised by the jargon term "separation trauma."[2] Nature intended mother and child to be together. It is at once as simple and as
profound as that. If they are separated when the bond should be forming,
it forms imperfectly, if at all. The child suffers a deep sense of loss and

---

[1] Psychoanalytic interpretations, *see* e.g.: Freud 1949; Horney 1945; Klein 1949.
[2] For general treatments of separation: Ainsworth 1962; Bowlby 1953; 1958; 1960;
1961a; 1961b; 1963; 1969; Cassler 1961; Mead 1962.

even physical distress. And though the mother may not be clear about what has happened to her, she too may suffer—from feelings of depression and inadequacy.

The mother is totally essential to the well-being of the child. Remove her, and its world collapses. This dependence is based on the suckling tendency of mammals, but it does not wholly hinge on food. It is largely a matter of emotional security, of which food is but a part. The human mother is a splendid mammal—the epitome of her order. Her physiology is more highly developed for suckling behavior—with permanent breasts, for example—than any of her cousins, except domesticated ungulates bred specially for milk-giving. But more than this, she is, like any other mammal, emotionally programmed to be responsive to the growing child. Her whole physiology from the moment she conceives is changed not only to accommodate the sheer business of parturition but also to cope with this physical extension of her body for years after the event. Animal experiments have shown that the softness and texture of the mother—and even her smell—are more important to the child than simply her milk supply, although without the latter, in most "wild" conditions, it would not live. Primate infants deprived of real mothers will adapt best to mechanical substitutes that are alike in *texture* to their real parent, in preference to those that simply provide milk but no warmth.[3]

Whatever the value of the substitute, the young animal, psychically, is permanently damaged by the separation.[4] The male may never learn to relate to females, with the consequence that his sexual identity will be confused.[5] The female will almost certainly fail in her task as a mother by ignoring her own offspring, as she was ignored herself.[6] Anyone who has seen the grief, the listlessness, the obvious and heart-rending despair of infant monkeys deprived, in an experiment, of maternal care, will echo the sentiments of the man who performed the experiment. He declared: "Thank God we only have to do it once to prove the point."[7]

The point is proved time and time again in human society. Brief separations of mother and child are bad enough, but excessive separations are devastating. Nature is ruthless about this. In the case of some animals, if the mother is not able to find the child immediately at birth, respond to its cries, and above all, lick it from head to foot, she will treat it as a

[3] On texture: Harlow 1958; 1959. On smell: Brill 1932; Kalogerakis 1963.
[4] Social development in monkeys and apes: Hinde, Rowell, and Spencer-Booth 1964; Hinde and Spencer-Booth 1967; Mason 1965a; 1965b. Primate mothers and young: DeVore 1963; Harlow 1962a; Harlow, Harlow, and Hansen 1963; Harlow and Zimmerman 1959; Lawick-Goodal 1967a.
[5] Effects of deprivation on sexual behavior: Harlow 1962b; Harlow and Harlow 1965.
[6] Effects of deprivation on maternal behavior: Hansen 1966; Seay, Alexander, and Harlow 1964.
[7] Effects of deprivation on primates generally: Griffin and Harlow 1966; Harlow and Harlow 1962; Kaufman and Rosenblum 1967a; Mason and Sponholz 1963; Nissen 1956; Seay, Hansen, and Harlow 1962. Critique: Meier 1965.

stranger and refuse to suckle it when it is later presented to her.[8] Yet in the name of sanitation we risk tampering with this delicate system by taking babies away from their mothers on the maternity wards moments after they are born. Monkey infants that lose their mothers develop all the characteristics of autistic children, even to the endless rocking and crouching—with little chance of becoming fully functioning adults. Our orphanages and nurseries are full of children wholly or partly so deprived who also rock and grieve and make only painfully insecure adjustments to the adult world.

The practice of taking infants from their mothers during the first five days of life is an example of the acceptance of hygiene and comfort as of greater importance than the possibility of behavior disruption—if this is even considered. In some of the most sophisticated and admirable places on earth—the wards of excellent hospitals—newborn organisms emerge from their mothers' wombs in a demanding and exciting process to face a suddenly novel environment containing unmuted sounds, swirls of unfamiliar air, and the impressive movements of hands and bodies. Often the mother of such a confused and needy creature is drugged and will sleep for many hours after this first potential social encounter with her child. The neonate itself may be somewhat under the influence of her drugs and in any event will be quickly removed in a plastic basket from her presence to a ward of a dozen or two similar creatures, many crying, all under high light, and all handled by skilled nurses—part of whose professional skill must be that denial of the special treatment which seems to mark how women treat their own children as opposed to the children of others. The child will be labeled by a card on its container, and some mothers will confuse their own child with another, and the more naïve among them will question their competence as mothers: if they cannot even recognize their child, how can they possibly cope with it?

This plight has to be seen in the context of the improved health of mothers and infants. It is probably true that there are important advantages to having the mother rest after the single most trying of all predictable human actions. The question here is about the effects of systems— which are perhaps useful for mothers and certainly efficient for hospitals— on the essential bond between mother and infant. On theoretical and empirical grounds there is a real and disturbing possibility that—with effects difficult to measure—some human babies and their mothers encounter in the act of birth a fact of technology and custom that may make more uncertain the elaboration of a bond begun *in utero,* a bond severely interrupted at just that point when presumably some forceful re-creation of the certainty and strength of uterine environment is most necessary.

The mother-child bond is the basic instruction in the human bonding program, and the ground rule of the human biogrammar. If this rule is

[8] Mammalian mothers at parturition: Count 1967; Hediger 1955, chap. 7.

not learned, the human may not learn to "speak" behaviorally, just as, if he does not learn the difference between subject and predicate, he will never be able to handle the verbal grammar. What he "learns," essentially, is the ability to make successful bonds in general. Bonds depend on feelings, and the mother-deprived child is most commonly described as "affectless"—lacking the motive power to love or care. It is here that the groundwork for "emotional maturity" is laid: that the child will eventually become an adult capable of the full sexual experience and of complete parental behavior. In general, he learns to be confident in his own ability to explore; he develops self-confidence and security. Young monkeys with mothers will move off to enjoy the pleasures of curiosity, whereas maternally deprived monkeys will be afraid to. Successful bonding in later life depends to a great extent on this tendency to explore. This program of security/exploration is so easily interfered with—especially in "advanced" societies—that a large number of people end up by making only partial adjustments in all these areas, to the detriment of their social relationships.[9]

It is just as important to note that the instructions are also quite precise about the termination of the bond—which begins with the gross physiological act of weaning and ends with the transference of emotional ties onto peers and mates.[10] If the mother ignores the instructions to terminate the bond, the results can be just as disastrous as if the child continues to talk baby talk into adulthood: its chances of communicating effectively with other adults are severely curtailed. "Maternal overprotection"—the continuation into adolescence of the relationship appropriate to childhood—extends the mother-child program to a time when the "child-child" and "child-other-adult" programs should be coming into play.

It is not necessary here to pursue the *content* of the mother-child bond, once it has been established as the basic bond. Whatever else a linguistic system does, it has to have some means of sorting out subject from object. Whatever else a social system does, it has to have some means of ensuring the security of the relationship between mother and infant until at least that point when the infant is independently mobile and able to survive with a reasonable chance of reaching adulthood. There are many and various ways of doing this. Within any animal species they tend to be uniform, but across species, as has been seen, they are very diverse. Within the human species, given the biological adaptation of culture, there is also diversity—but within very narrow limits. And the diversity revolves around this basic dyad as a fixed point in a changing social universe. The languages are exotically different, but the basic grammar is always the same.

The mother-child bond offers a model for other bonded relationships in which humans and other social animals engage. The model implies that

9 Exploration and curiosity in infants: Rheingold 1961; 1963.
10 Termination of bond: Kaufman and Rosenblum 1969.

social responses of a surprisingly complicated kind involve genetic pro-
gramming. These patterns, far from reflecting simple "instinctive" needs,
are directly social; their stimulus, operation, and consummation depend
upon the existence of other members of the species and their actions. This
is really the heart of the ethological approach; social interactions reveal
the evolutionary history and biology of an animal as much as its digestive
processes and means of movement do.

In this context we can reexamine some of the more common human
relationships. Perhaps this will clarify the limits of variation and the
intricacy of the special process of affiliation that marks us as the particular
animal we are. So let us turn to some of the other strategic bonds between
members of our species, in order to understand better how these "social
organs" have worked in our history and how they are expressed today.

The claim that the mother-child bond is the basic one might appear
paradoxical, if not repetitious; after all, it is preceded by sexual intercourse
—which implies that the mating bond preceded *it*. But the answer to this
is that the mating "bond" may or may *not* have preceded it—it does not
have to. A simple act of copulation which need last only ninety seconds is
all that is necessary to start the mother-child process.

But a mating bond is convenient to ensure food and protection for
the mother and child at a later stage. Protection is what the whole business is about. In other species and many human societies, the mating
bond as such is not activated to this end. There are many alternatives.
Among deer, as we have seen, a group of self-sufficient females provides
this envelope of provision and protection.[11] Even when the "harems"
form during the rutting season, the stag does not in any sense control the
group—he is preoccupied with repeated copulation on the one hand and
driving off rival males on the other. The harem generally responds to the
leadership of the old female; once his inseminating function is completed,
the male leaves for the rest of the year. Sometimes the mother and young
can survive without any help at all—as with the hamster. In other cases
a troop organization takes over as the envelope or shell, as with elephants
or trooping monkeys. Here the whole group is responsible for the mother-
child units within it. All the males and mature childless females surround
and protect the nursing mothers. Many bonds are activated in this way,
but in none of these cases is the mating bond more than a brief episode.

The bond, once activated, can take a number of forms. With some
carnivores, such as wolves, pairs form for life, develop "packs" with the
offspring, and enter a cycle of family development.[12] Alternatively, as
with hamadryas baboons, "harems" (each male may have four or five
females) are collected, which last for a lifetime and not just a rutting

[11] Deer: Darling 1937.
[12] Wolves: Mowat 1963; Murie 1944.

season.[13] Among the anthropoid apes there is the unique case of the gibbon, which lives in treetops and defends territories. On each territory a mated pair jointly repels intruders and disperses its young as soon as they are mature.[14] In all these primate groups the mother-child unit is a "constant." What varies is the degree of involvement of the mate. In most cases of pair formation the key determinants are ecological—the unit of male-plus-female (or females) and offspring is the optimum unit for survival. Where these ecological conditions do not hold, a species is unlikely to make much of the mating bond.

What is true across the range of mammalian species is true across different populations of the human species. Because of the brilliant biological adaptation of culture, human societies can create different rules. They can adapt various customs to fit different ecological niches, and need not wait for natural selection to program them genetically. They have to observe a number of grammatical ground rules—one of which has already been explored here—but they can use a variety of languages. Each human population protects and provides for its mother-child units; but whether or not the father stays "home" is another and highly variable matter. The strategy of the father staying home has been commonly adopted because human cultures can capitalize on the powerful motivations aroused by courtship, especially during the volatile and intense period of puberty. These motivations can then be changed into powerful bonding patterns associated with parenthood. The combination can produce a relatively lasting set of bonds that make up what we commonly refer to as the "family."

But it is revealing that societies always seem to find it necessary to surround these "natural" bonds with a host of legal provisions and sanctions to make them stick. This is not the case with many consanguine bonds: people do not have to enter into contractual obligations to be made someone's sister, but they do have to have a "contract" to become someone's husband or wife. It is arguable that without all the legal safeguards a much more fluid mating and family system would prevail; indeed, there are many instances where this is so.

This is a central point. Many social scientists want to maintain that the "family" is in some sense a "natural" unit like the "family" of the gibbon and is based on a similar "pairing-for-life" instinct.[15] When people persistently behave differently, they are accused of failing to live up to their natural obligations, and we speak of breakdown, neuroses, the crisis in the family, etc. Our interpretation is exactly the opposite.[16] What the "family" as a unit does is artificially to cement together, with social con-

---

[13] Hamadryas: Kummer 1968.

[14] Gibbons: Carpenter 1940.

[15] On family as a "natural" unit, see e.g.: Bell and Vogel 1960; Goode 1964; Murdock 1949; Westermarck 1903. On "pairing instinct": Morris 1967a; 1970.

[16] For similar dissident views: Adams 1960; Bohannan 1963; Goodenough 1970; Linton 1936; Spiro 1954.

ventions and legal rules, one subset of the possible sets of bonds that can
be used as the envelope for the mother-child unit.[17] In many senses this
parental bond is the most fragile, even if the most common, of such
arrangements, since it involves bringing together two people not previously
related and predicating the success of their relationship on the relatively
temporary emotional ties that flood through them and between them in
the courtship stage. Most societies that use mated pairs as the basic units
do not dare to leave the necessary stability of the family to the vagaries
of adolescent emotion. They "arrange" marriages without regard to such
emotion, but with the continuity and stability of the unit in mind.

It is nonsense to assume that the only kind of "parental" bond possible in the human species is between sexual partners. Yes, the mother
has to be impregnated, but her impregnator need not be the male who
provides the provision and protection for her and her young. There is
another bond more fundamental in some ways, and just as logical—the
bond between brother and sister. This is an asexual bond that grows up
over the years and is in some sense ready-made for the task of parental
care. It does not involve the setting up of a new and risky contractual
relationship, but can draw on already existing trust and deeply developed
obligations. In some human societies, the weight of responsibility for a
woman and her children rests with her brothers. Her sex life is separate
from her parental role. Usually she has a series of lovers more or less attached to her. To call such systems exceptional is to beg the question:
they represent a logical and viable alternative that, while relatively rare,
works well in certain circumstances. The mating relationship and the
security relationship are simply not allowed to coincide.[18]

In other cases the two types of bond—blood ties and mating ties—
may both be partly activated. Some aspects of security can be associated
with the mating bond, and so shared with the brother-sister tie.[19] The
most common arrangement here is for groups of related women to live
together and to depend for some things on their brothers and sons, and
for other things on their husbands and sons-in-law. Again the brother-sister
tie is permanent and continuous (one cannot divorce a brother), while the
husband-wife tie is relatively loose. . . .

. . .

. . . Given the current arrangement of politics in nearly all countries
—and women have failed to find their places in these so far—it may be
statistically unlikely that anything significant will change unless our con-

[17] For a survey of patterns of attachment of males to mother-child units in man: Fox
1967a; 1970.
[18] Examples of activation of brother-sister bond: deMoubray 1931; Gough 1959; 1961;
Nakane 1963; Williamson 1962.
[19] Examples of "sharing" between brother-sister and husband-wife ties: Eggan 1950;
Malinowski 1929.

sciousness changes first. In other words, we must begin to understand the nature of sexual difference and come to terms with it and operate within it, not against it, and to use it constructively and not deny it in the name of equality. Probably equality can be realized only if men become sufficiently understanding of their own peacock enterprises to accept that they have not actually made provision for full female participation in politics. It is hardly enough simply to solicit the votes of females; this is, after all, just another way of keeping power in the hands of candidates who are nearly always male. For men to understand that they are socially different from females, and how, may induce them more effectively to invite women to genuine colleagueship in the places where power is manipulated. On their part, females may more rapidly and happily achieve political goals by asserting the value of specifically female skills and interests rather than by denying the reality of any differences and insisting that all social tasks are performed in the same way by males and females.[20]

This is the place to explore the chief characteristics of the social relations in the "block" of females. Undoubtedly it is women who have borne most of the effects of change in human technology. Nearly all females for most of their adult lives in nearly all places throughout virtually all of human history have been involved with childbearing and child-rearing. Nothing less than the very survival of the group in which they lived depended upon their successful gestation and raising of a child until it could manage on its own. Because learning and maturation are so important to humans, this is a long process; indeed, it remains the most time-consuming and labor-intensive of all major human tasks. It is also very difficult to mechanize, and even to bureaucratize in some efficient and personal fashion. This has plainly meant that women have had to spend much time with children, one direct consequence of which is that they have also spent much time with other women—their own friends, and mothers of their children's friends.

There are some general questions about the biogrammar of female bonding that must be answered: What patterns may we have inherited from our history as prehumans? What could we do with this inheritance to bend it to our new conditions and to our new ability to impose will between ourselves and nature? And what social relationships among females would fit, influence, and conflict with the patterns among males, and the relations between males and females that we have some reason to believe actually marked our evolution?

Primate females are intensely interested in newborn infants. Mothers

[20] Political goals of feminist movements: Friedan 1963; Morgan 1970. Historical account of feminism: O'Neill 1967. See also: Bird 1968. For a complementary statement of male difficulties: Bednarik 1970. For a review of sex differences as reflected in reading matter: White 1970.

have high status among the other females; so do those who are pregnant; childless females will plead to hold an infant, and, as a favor, they will be allowed to.[21] Among humans the situation becomes more complex, though the basic emotional patterns the primates display seem to persist, in however attenuated and modified form. The new complexity stems from the importance of the child as both a measure and as a property of the kinship structure. The matter of what happens to infants is therefore of considerable concern to the males, and the social career of the child is carefully worked out in the context of the overall pattern of social bonds. The net effect of this concern is to bind females into the social structure in a much more demanding, elaborate, and persistent way than is possible among the nonhuman primates where the cycles of estrus rather than the long-term cycle of life govern how males and females interact.

The act of having a child is thus for the human female not only a new event biologically and emotionally but also a contract with her community—a contract perhaps not always formalized but certainly always palpable. The conditions of motherhood are real: mothers must attend to their children, must not leave them alone, must not injure them, and must give them that care and tutelage thought seemly by their fellow citizens. In return females are offered protection, welfare, tax advantages if they have children, and a generalized claim on the resources of time and property of the dominants—both male and female—of the community. (The responsibility of the community to mothers is relatively clear, though with the development in industrial societies of mechanical forms of welfare, women with children but without male supporters are often treated harshly in relation to the difficulty of their task and the scarcity of their resources.)

. . . Males bond to help one another gain power, defend groups, and acquire animal protein. Females bond too, but in different ways, for significantly different purposes, and with different results for the overall social structure. To put it as economically as possible, males bond for reasons of macrostructure, females for reasons of microstructure—that is, in general, females occupy themselves with interpersonal matters involving face-to-face encounters and focusing upon subjects that have to do with the bearing, nurturing, and training of the young, and with the establishment and management of dwellings and other immediate surroundings. By contrast, males involve themselves with groups and activities that extend directly to the whole community. Here again the primate biogrammar emerges from a variety of possible patterns. The females are at the center of the group; they are concerned chiefly with what happens there and with their relations to the males and young. The males are at the center too, but only after they have served a period of apprenticeship at the periphery, and in some cases only after, in bands of two or three, they

---

[21] Primate females and newborn infants: Hinde 1965; Rowell, Hinde, and Spencer-Booth 1964.

have explored some strange terrain and become accustomed to seeing their local place in terms of its wider setting.

This pattern corresponds with a tediously conventional view of the distinction between what men and women do. The important point remains that throughout selection, as we became human, we retained many of the emphases and predispositions of our primate colleagues. We have already noted how significant it was that, alone among the primates, man divided labor between males and females, and that this division depended on males forming effective and cooperative groups for hunting. Females too formed groups, but were best adapted for groups that did different things, and in a different perspective, and with a different set of challenges and satisfactions. This is quite another thing from saying "a woman's place is in the home." If a woman's place is anywhere at all, it is precisely not in the home but in an arena of great interpersonal activity, a place from which brief excursions for purposes of gathering may be undertaken, and a place in which—because of the kinship breakthrough—the lives of individuals are articulated, structured, and blended in concern and competition with the lives of others.

Our concern at this point is with groups, not individuals, because groups of females seem to do different things from groups of males, and have different ways of doing the different things they do. Of course, individual females can perform as well as individual males, and many males can perform tasks usually taken to be the special province of females. But predictably in a gregarious species, male-male bonds differ from male-female bonds, and female-female bonds differ from both.

What are some of these differences? One of the most characteristic and consequential is that the status of females depends on their mates far more than the other way around, and on their reproductive situation. For example, males very rarely take their wives' names at marriage, and this reflects the reality that social placement normally occurs in terms of the occupational and ritual status of the chief male in the female's life.

Females have more to gain and lose by their marriage arrangements than males do. For all males' remarkable concern with status differences, females are capable of even greater interest in the thrust of a snub and the refinement of a pretension. In a real sense this is because females are more committed to the intimate sphere and more dependent on the implications of their personal encounters for their income and satisfaction than males, who may contrive relatively impersonal items of work or group antagonism on which to focus their energy and concern. It is important not to confuse these differences of emphasis and activity with the evaluation of status and importance. To do so is to devalue that intimate sphere in which all people must live, enjoy, and grow, and to glorify activities— often the prerogative of males—that may be destructive, exploitative, crass, and pointless.

We have already noted the significant phenomenon among some

primates that although females formed groups of mother-child units (plus interested childless or pregnant females), the groups were totally unstable unless a male joined them as a focus of attention and an agent of social control. This need not seem strange. The female is primarily concerned with the survival of her own little unit—and rightly so. Insofar as other females may help, they are tolerated, but this is at best a tenuous and short-term toleration. Once the child is old enough to fend for itself, the female is interested in getting herself pregnant again and once again is in competition with the other females as the directs her attention toward the mature males.

The human mother is likewise caught in these two intensive activities —looking after her child and maintaining a relationship with a supportive male. In the first instance other women may be useful; in the second, however, they are a direct threat. Coping with the eternal round of birth, copulation, and child-rearing does not leave any primate mother with much time for the great affairs of state, and this has been the lot of the human mother for virtually our whole history as a species. On the other hand, the male, who is not constrained in this way, can exercise these functions and hold the group together—particularly as the attention of the females becomes fixed on him as a source to which they can turn for pro-tection and sexual satisfaction. The male, then, is concerned with the whole community of mothers, mates, and children, while the female tends to be more narrowly occupied. Thus she cannot act as focus of cohesion, nor can she effectively form the kinds of bonds males form to achieve those male ends that affect the interests of whole communities.

Both females and males enter into sexual competition with others of their sex, and to some extent their status depends on the outcome, but men have always had something over and above this competition for which they must bond and from which they could derive status, while women have rarely had any other source from which to gain a sense of personal worth and social superiority than their position in the reproduc-tive struggle—measured in terms of their mate and their offspring. Women have had little opportunity or reason (in these terms) to bond or form groups for macrostructural purposes. This, then, is the primate situation, and it has been the basic human situation for most of our history. It can be—and is being—mitigated and changed in ways which allow women greater opportunity for involvement in the macrosystem. But these women carry with them a considerable evolutionary burden which may demand more energy and enthusiasm from them than from men to seek these opportunities, and which makes their task more difficult once they become involved in the intricacies of the program they wish to follow.

In one vital and all but unexplored respect the relationships between females differ from those between men. Young males, human and primate, have in a real sense to go to the peripheries of the group before they regain internal status; the distance they go and the length of time it takes them to get back can be considerable. Young females, on the other hand, except in those countries where their education is deliberately fashioned on the male model (but even to some extent in these), are never "peripheralized" to the same extent. Physically they may never move from their mothers until they marry; their base is always "home." Their peripheralization is metaphorical rather than real, in the sense that between puberty and marriage they have a transitional status. But this is usually brief; on marriage the girl automatically joins the ranks of "married women" with all the status implications this carries and often becomes a mother almost immediately. She does not have to win her way back to the center in the same way as a boy; the transition is not so severe; very few will ever fail to make it. She proves herself in a simple biological way—by being fertile; she continues with tasks that she has already been performing anyway in her mother's household. The affluent and technologically advanced nation that peripheralizes females in the same way that it does males may find (and often does find) itself in some difficulty. It reverses the natural trend, breaks the evolutionary continuity which has insisted on a continuing and close bond between older women and young potential wives. Educated young women in particular find the transition to household chores unbearably difficult and uncongenial, not only because they feel they are wasting their education, but because they have suffered a bond disruption and a minor separation trauma. An adolescent female is just not a substitute adolescent male.

Neither is a mother simply a father who has children. But what about the postmenopausal female? In some sense she is a biological anomaly. What use to a species is a female who can no longer reproduce and who is consuming valuable food that might well go to youngsters, mothers, and warriors? In most species the female life span is the reproductive life span, and no more. It occasionally happens that an older female past childbearing will take on some role. The most spectacular example is in the red deer, where an old hind becomes the leader of the group of hinds. She is their focus of attention, and even when the stag has gathered her little group together as a harem during the rutting season, she remains the leader. The stag does not control the movement of the hinds—he simply focuses on the activities of his male rivals. Otherwise he follows the harem about rather ineffectively. Here the experience and sagacity of the older female are called into play very successfully. But this is in a situation where males do not form the focus of the attention structure.

When they do, what role is there for the older female to play? Clearly her usefulness in the human primate society should lie in the area of economic activity. The demands the dependent human infant makes on the young mother inhibit her contribution. But the old woman can make up for this loss in the labor force. Her knowledge of the terrain—of the roots and berries and grains—is incomparably greater, and she can teach all this to her daughters. If they always had to learn it from scratch, it would be an insufferably inefficient system. She is also a store of knowledge and help on the subject of child-rearing. After all, in primitive conditions not that many women live beyond their reproductive period anyway. Certainly in times of food shortage they are often the first to go—along with female infants. (The death of the one conserves food supplies; the death of the other prevents an increase in future population.)

With the remarkable increase in the life span of recent years, we are faced with the problem of a vast expansion of the numbers of post-reproductive females. These women may not be integrated into the female world of their daughters made independent by machinery and often callous by social mobility or change in generation life style. But the old women are not really making their way into the man's world, either, where they are, logically at least, most likely to fit, since they are through with the essentially female business of child-rearing. For example, from a simple-minded point of view it remains curious that such females do not take a more active role in formal politics, since of all the groups in the population they have probably the most time and the most money with which to support their effort. What in fact do they do?

One important activity, at least in industrialized communities, which they can undertake successfully and with some contentment, is a set of voluntary activities that support other sections of the community. They may be welfare workers, canvassers, fund-raisers for worthwhile causes. The women who tend toward volunteer work are usually well-off; they have none of the need for a job that poor women, even with husbands, have. It is a comment on the impracticality and anti-feminism of most communities that they are more willing to accommodate their otherwise rigid schedules to suit the free time of volunteer workers than of women who need money as well as want to accomplish something outside their home and in their community.

Of course, this varies considerably in many communities. In the Soviet Union many grandmothers live with their daughters or sons; it is the *babushka* who minds the child while the mother is at work. Even in such a committed and self-consciously revolutionary society, there is nothing approaching an adequate number of day-care centers; as usual, it is to old primate bonds that we turn when we want to take part in even post-industrial activity. In a society like ours, the solution is far more complex, because in part the mother-daughter bond is disrupted by education, by mobility, and by the rapidity of social change which makes the mother seem irrelevant to the practices and ideals of the daughter. Indeed, there is often bleak antipathy between mother and daughter, if only because they share households; perhaps one reason for the declining age at which females marry is that girls cannot abide their mothers and must leave their houses and their implicitly supervised bedrooms. And yet, tragically, psychiatric records tell of many girls who bear children earlier than they openly want them or are married or can afford them, in good part because they want to affirm themselves against their mothers.

Once again, then, we see that the fruits of the industrial revolution were most sour for females; it was they who had their important bond earliest threatened and first broken. In school they lost their mothers' philosophy, and in mobility their presence. In the factory they lost the dependence out of which reciprocity is made. With puberty arriving earlier and earlier—four months sooner every ten years—the transitional period described above was extended at the same time as the demand for schooling and for skills increased the time it took the capacities of their bodies to make themselves manifest in their behavior. And it is even possible that the earlier arrival of puberty is in part the result of competition among younger and younger girls to stimulate men to bear them off and away from home.[22] As bodily changes may affect behavior, so different pressures from behavior may (as with psychosomatic diseases) speed up or slow down bodily processes.

Females bond; but in quantity, quality, direction, purpose and even aesthetic, their bonding processes and procedures differ considerably from those of the male block in direct proportion to the difference in life cycle, life style, and life chance of males and females. Their long-lasting bonds are largely kinship bonds. Outside these, their bonding is more tenuous, more episodic, and less productive of groupings that affect the macrostructure than in the case of the male. But the female bonds are as crucial and heroic as the more political male bonds. If they fail, the system collapses, and no amount of male solidarity will be able to hold it together.

[22] Decrease of age at puberty: Tanner 1960.

6
PRIVACY AND SURVEILLANCE

PRIVACY AND FREEDOM
Alan F. Westin

  Alan F. Westin, lawyer and political scientist, is currently Professor of Public Law and Government at Columbia University and Director of the Center for Research and Education in American Liberties at Columbia University and Teachers College. His writings include The Supreme Court: Views from Inside *(1961),* The Centers of Power *(1963, with others),* Freedom Now: The Civil Rights Struggle in America *(1964), and* Privacy and Freedom *(1967). He has frequently participated in television discussion programs, and his articles have appeared in numerous journals, including* Harper's, *the* Nation, *and the* New Republic.

· · ·

It is obvious that the political system in each society will be a fundamental force in shaping its balance of privacy, since certain patterns of privacy, disclosure, and surveillance are functional necessities for particular kinds of political regime. This is shown most vividly by contrasting privacy in the democratic and the totalitarian state.

  The modern totalitarian state relies on secrecy for the regime, but high surveillance and disclosure for all other groups.[1] With their demand for a complete commitment of loyalties to the regime, the literature of both fascism and communism traditionally attacks the idea of privacy as

---

[1] For writing relating the anti-privacy measures of Soviet totalitarianism to aspects of Russian national character and culture, see Margaret Mead and Elena Calas, "Child-training Ideas in a Postrevolutionary Context: Soviet Russia," in Margaret Mead and Martha Wolfenstein (eds.), *Childhood in Contemporary Cultures* (Chicago, 1955), 179, 190–91; Henry V. Dicks, "Observations on Contemporary Russian Behavior," 5 *Human Relations*, 111, 140, 159, 163–64 (1952).

"immoral," "antisocial," and "part of the cult of individualism." This attitude is most strongly expressed in the consolidation phase of a new totalitarian regime.[2] Autonomous units are denied privacy, traditional confidential relationships are destroyed, surveillance systems and informers are widely installed, and thorough dossiers are compiled on millions of citizens. Most important, the individual is not allowed to gain security by conforming without opposition and quietly doing his job. The regime demands active and positive loyalty.[3] These policies, by creating fear and distrust, tend to foster a sense of loneliness and isolation in the citizen; for relief, he turns to identification with the state and its programs so that he may find the satisfactions of affiliation and achievement.

Once the regime has consolidated its power and a new generation has grown up under totalitarian rule, some of the anti-privacy measures are relaxed. A degree of privacy is allowed to families, churches, science, and the arts, and police terror is reduced. However, the public has been well conditioned by the old methods, and occasional punishment of those who use their new privacy too aggressively is sufficient to restore the required amount of regime control. Furthermore, the primary surveillance systems of paid and volunteer spies, eavesdropping and watching devices, and strict records control are retained to keep the regime on its guard.

Just as a social balance favoring disclosure and surveillance over privacy is a functional necessity for totalitarian systems, so a balance that ensures strong citadels of individual and group privacy and limits both disclosure and surveillance is a prerequisite for liberal democratic societies. The democratic society relies on publicity as a control over government, and on privacy as a shield for group and individual life. The reasons for protecting privacy tend to be familiar to citizens of liberal democracies; thus the specific functions that privacy performs in their political systems are often left unexpressed.[4] The discussion that follows will treat these functions briefly.

Liberal democratic theory assumes that a good life for the individual must have substantial areas of interest apart from political participation —time devoted to sports, arts, literature, and similar non-political pursuits. These areas of individual pursuit prevent the total politicizing of life and

2 For a discussion of this phenomenon in Communist China today, see P. J. Hollander, "Privacy: A Bastion Stormed," in "Mores and Morality in Communist China," 12 *Problems of Communism* No. 6, Nov-Dec., 1963, 1–9.

3 See Sidney Hook, *The Hero in History* (Beacon ed., Boston, 1955), 6; R. J. Lifton, *Thought Reform and the Psychology of Totalism* (New York, 1963), 426.

4 For discussion of privacy in terms of democratic political theory, see Hannah Arendt, *The Human Condition* (Anchor ed., New York, 1959), 23–69; H. M. Roelofs, *The Tension of Citizenship: Private Man and Public Duty* (New York, 1957); H. D. Lasswell, "The Threat to Privacy," in R. M. MacIver (ed.), *Conflict of Loyalties* (New York, 1952), 121–40; Clinton Rossiter, "The Pattern of Liberty," in M. R. Konvitz and Clinton Rossiter (eds.), *Aspects of Liberty* (Ithaca, N.Y., 1958), 15–32; Monroe Berger *et al.*, *Freedom and Control in Modern Society* (New York, 1964), 190.

permit other models of success and happiness to serve as alternatives to the political career and the citizenship role. Personal retreats for securing perspective and critical judgment are also significant for democratic life. A liberal democratic system maintains a strong commitment to the family as a basic and autonomous unit responsible for important educational, religious, and moral roles, and therefore the family is allowed to assert claims to physical and legal privacy against both society and the state. As a result of religious diversity and ideas of toleration, most democratic systems make religious choice a "private" concern; both law and custom forbid government controls over the nature and legitimacy of religious affiliations and allow maximum privacy for religious observance and for religious examination of public policy issues.

Because of the central role played by groups in a democratic society —they provide opportunities for sociability, expression of independent ideas, resolution of community conflicts, criticism of government, and formation of a consensus on public policy—citizens are given wide freedom to join associations and participate in group affairs. To this end, privacy of membership and intra-group action are protected. Associations themselves are given substantial organizational privacy to achieve their objectives efficiently and responsibly. Liberal democracy recognizes the special needs of scholars and scientists to be free of constant community and government examination so that paths to truth and discovery can be pursued even in directions that offend dominant opinion. Liberal democratic systems ensure maximum freedom for political choice by providing a secret ballot to protect the voting process and by forbidding governmental inquiries into a citizen's past voting record. Through a network of constitutional, legal, and political restraints, democratic societies protect the individual's person and personality from improper police conduct such as physical brutality, compulsory self-incrimination, and unreasonable searches and seizures. Finally, liberal democratic societies set a balance between government's organizational needs for preparatory and institutional privacy and the need of the press, interest groups, and other governmental agencies for the knowledge of government operations required to keep government conduct responsible.

The functions of privacy in liberal systems do not require that it be an absolute right. The exercise of privacy creates dangers for a democracy that may call for social and legal responses. Private-life commitments can produce such indifference to political and governmental needs on the part of citizens that society must work to bring its members back to participating responsibility. In some situations claims to organizational privacy can give rise to anonymous influences over public life, can overweigh the organized sectors of the citizenry, and can foster the growth of conspiracies that will threaten the democracy's survival. Persons who venture into public debates or civic life sometimes claim an unjustified right to privacy from fair reply or fair criticism. Rules protecting the privacy of the person by forbidding new but not necessarily unreasonable law-enforcement methods can seriously impede protection of the public from crime and lessen the nation's internal security. Privacy may also frustrate the public's "need to know," important behavioral research, and effective administration of government and business. An overly strict cloak of privacy for governmental affairs can cover manipulation of the public, misuse of office, and aggrandizement of power by government agencies. Thus the constant search in democracies must be for the proper boundary line in each specific situation and for an over-all equilibrium that serves to strengthen democratic institutions and processes.

No one has written more sensitively on this problem than the political sociologist, Edward Shils:

> Democracy requires the occasional political participation of most of its citizenry some of the time, and a moderate and dim perceptiveness—as if from the corner of the eye—the rest of the time. It could not function if politics and the state of the social order were always on everyone's mind. If most men, most of the time, regarded themselves as their brother-citizens' keepers, freedom, which flourishes in the indifference of privacy, would be abolished.[5]

Shils sees the "first principle of individualist democracy" to be "the partial autonomy of individuals and of corporate bodies or institutions."

> Autonomy involves the right to make decisions, to promulgate rules of action, to dispose over resources and to recruit associates in accordance with criteria which the individual or organization deems appropriate to its tasks. The principle of partial autonomy assumes that, by and large, an individual's or a corporate group's life is its own business, that only marginal circumstances justify intrusion by others, and that only more exceptional circumstances justify enforced and entire disclosure, to the eyes of the broader public, of the private affairs to the corporate body or individual.[6]

Shils makes an important distinction between privacy and secrecy. In secrecy, he notes, law forbids the disclosure of information. In privacy, disclosure "is at the discretion of the possessor, and such sanctions as laws provide are directed only against coercive acquisition" by persons to whom the individual does not want to disclose.[7]

In over-all terms, the goal of a liberal society is to achieve a state of political "civility," which Shils defines as a condition in which there is

[5] Edward A. Shils, *The Torment of Secrecy* (Glencoe, Ill., 1956), 21–22.
[6] *Ibid.*, 22.
[7] Edward Shils, "Privacy: Its Constitution and Vicissitudes," 31 *Law and Contemporary Problems* (Spring, 1962), 281, 283n.

enough privacy to nourish individual creativity and group expression; enough publicity of government affairs to let the public know the facts necessary to form judgments in political matters; and a small area of secrecy for government to preserve the integrity of certain secret information and the privacy of internal policy-making processes.

. . .

Recognizing the differences that political and sensory cultures make in setting norms of privacy among modern societies, it is still possible to describe the general functions that privacy performs for individuals and groups in Western democratic nations. Before describing these, it is helpful to explain in somewhat greater detail the four basic states of individual privacy . . . : solitude, intimacy, anonymity, and reserve.

The first state of privacy is solitude; here the individual is separated from the group and freed from the observation of other persons. He may be subjected to jarring physical stimuli, such as noise, odors, and vibrations. His peace of mind may continue to be disturbed by physical sensations of heat, cold, itching, and pain. He may believe that he is being observed by God or some supernatural force, or fear that some authority is secretly watching him. Finally, in solitude he will be especially subject to that familiar dialogue with the mind or conscience. But, despite all these physical or psychological intrusions, solitude is the most complete state of privacy that individuals can achieve.

In the second state of privacy, intimacy, the individual is acting as part of a small unit that claims and is allowed to exercise corporate seclusion so that it may achieve a close, relaxed, and frank relationship between two or more individuals. Typical units of intimacy are husband and wife, the family, a friendship circle, or a work clique. Whether close contact brings relaxed relations or abrasive hostility depends on the personal interaction of the members, but without intimacy a basic need of human contact would not be met.[8]

The third state of privacy, anonymity, occurs when the individual is in public places or performing public acts but still seeks, and finds, freedom from identification and surveillance. He may be riding a subway, attending a ball game, or walking the streets; he is among people and knows that he is being observed; but unless he is a well-known celebrity, he does not expect to be personally identified and held to the full rules of behavior and role that would operate if he were known to those observing him. In this state the individual is able to merge into the "situational landscape." Knowledge or fear that one is under systematic observation in public places destroys the sense of relaxation and freedom that men seek in open spaces and public arenas.

[8] On the need for interpersonal intimacy, see H. S. Sullivan, *The Interpersonal Theory of Psychiatry* (New York, 1953), 290.

Anonymous relations give rise to what Georg Simmel called the "phenomenon of the stranger," the person who "often received the most surprising openness—confidences which sometimes have the character of a confessional and which would be carefully withheld from a more closely related person."[9] In this aspect of anonymity the individual can express himself freely because he knows the stranger will not continue in his life and that, although the stranger may give an objective response to the questions put to him, he is able to exert no authority or restraint over the individual.

Still another kind of anonymity is the publication of ideas anonymously. Here the individual wants to present some idea publicly to the community or to a segment of it, but does not want to be universally identified at once as the author—especially not by the authorities, who may be forced to take action if they "know" the perpetrator. The core of each of these types of anonymous action is the desire of individuals for times of "public privacy."

Reserve, the fourth and most subtle state of privacy, is the creation of a psychological barrier against unwanted intrusion; this occurs when the individual's need to limit communication about himself is protected by the willing discretion of those surrounding him. Most of our lives are spent not in solitude or anonymity but in situations of intimacy and in group settings where we are known to others. Even in the most intimate relations, communication of self to others is always incomplete and is based on the need to hold back some parts of one's self as either too personal and sacred or too shameful and profane to express. This circumstance gives rise to what Simmel called "reciprocal reserve and indifference," the relation that creates "mental distance" to protect the personality.[10] This creation of mental distance—a variant of the concept of "social distance"—takes place in every sort of relationship under rules of social etiquette; it expresses the individual's choice to withhold or disclose information—the choice that is the dynamic aspect of privacy in daily interpersonal relations. Simmel identified this tension within the individual as being between "self-revelation and self-restraint" and, within society, between "trespass and discretion." The manner in which individuals claim reserve and the extent to which it is respected or disregarded by others is at the heart of securing meaningful privacy in the crowded, organization-dominated settings of modern industrial society and urban life, and varies considerably from culture to culture.[11]

.   .   .

[9] *The Sociology of Georg Simmel*, tr. and ed. by Kurt Wolff (New York, 1950), 402–408. See also the discussion of the stranger in J. S. Plant, *Personality and the Cultural Pattern* (Oxford, 1937), 121–23; Robert Merton, "Selected Problems of Field Work in the Planned Community," 12 *American Sociological Review*, 305 (1947).
[10] Georg Simmel, *op. cit.*, 320–29.
[11] See Hall, *The Hidden Dimension*, 108–12, 131.

Just as individuals need privacy to evaluate what is happening to them and to decide how to respond, so organizations need privacy to plan their courses of action.

Planning by organizations involves both periods of reflection for considering long-range implications of organizational policies and the frank process of internal debate needed to reach day-to-day decisions. In both situations privacy is essential if the individuals involved are to be able to contemplate and to express their views with primary loyalty to the organization. If all written memos and policy discussions were subject to immediate publication, or if private organizations knew themselves to be under continuous monitoring by government agents, much of the debate would automatically become formalized. Gradual accommodation of divergent views within the organization would be hampered.

It is useful to recall that the Constitution of the United States was itself written in a closed meeting in Philadelphia; press and outsiders were excluded, and the participants were sworn to secrecy. Historians are agreed that if the convention's work had been made public contemporaneously, it is unlikely that the compromises forged in private sessions could have been achieved, or even that their state governments would have allowed the delegates to write a new constitution. Once the constitution had been drafted, of course, it was made public and its merits were freely debated and discussed as part of the ratification process. A generation later Madison's notes of the debates within the convention appeared and the record of who said what was finally disclosed.

The privacy involved in the writing of the American Constitution suggests the importance of confidentiality of organizational decisions until agreement has been reached, and confidentiality for a reasonable time thereafter of the way in which they were reached. Today this issue is most often discussed in terms of the federal executive branch and the question of legislative power to compel disclosure of policy positions taken by executive officials. President Eisenhower expressed the view of chief executives since Washington's time when he wrote in 1954:

> [I]t is essential to efficient and effective administration that employees of the executive branch be in a position to be completely candid in advising with each other on official matters. . . . [I]t is not in the public interest that any of their conversations or communications, or any documents or reproductions, concerning such advice be disclosed.[12]

In one of the recent public debates over the propriety of publishing

[12] Francis Rourke, *Secrecy and Publicity: Dilemmas of Democracy* (Baltimore, 1961), p. 72. For criticism of executive claims to privacy, see, for example, Harold Cross, *The People's Right to Know—Legal Access to Public Records and Proceedings* (New York, 1953); Rourke, *op. cit.*; J. R. Wiggins, *Freedom or Secrecy* (New York, 1956); *Second Report by the House Committee on Government Operations,* 85th Cong., 1st Sess., 157 (1957).

former presidential aides' accounts of recent intra-executive positions, Adolf A. Berle, Jr., has written:

> A President must talk to his staff. He can get the best from them—and they can best function—only when exchange is wholly candid. In the reviewer's experience, great decision-making usually boils down to a tired chief of state on one side of the desk and a trusted friend or aide on the other. If at that point the chief of state must consider not only the decision involved but also the possible effect of revelation of himself, his emotions and his thinking—concerning men, political effects of possible measures, his personal hopes and fears—frankness will necessarily be inhibited.[13]

Obviously, the issue has its counterpart in the staff relations of law clerks to judges, of military aides to commanding officers, and of legislative assistants to Senators and Representatives. What law there is on the matter remains confused, because at heart the question is usually one of reasonableness, the nature of the issue involved, and the give-and-take of the checks-and-balances system.[14] Time is obviously an important factor in striking the practical balances, since what is an invasion of a former superior's privacy in a memoir today may not be so five or ten years from now. Staff advice must, in the usual case, be kept private for a reasonable time if men are to make government work.

The other aspect of privacy for organizational decision making is the issue of timing—when and how to release the decision—which corresponds to the individual's determination whether and when to communicate about himself to others. Groups obviously have a harder time keeping decisions secret. The large number of persons involved increases the possibility of leaks, and the press, competitors, and opponents often seek energetically to discover the decision before the organization is ready to release it. Since most organizational decisions will become known eventually, privacy is a temporary claim—a claim of foundations, university administrations, political parties, and government agencies to retain the power of deciding for themselves when to break the seal of privacy and "go public."

. . .

The basic point is obvious: privacy in government decision making is a functional necessity for the formulation of responsible policy, especially in a democratic system concerned with finding formulas for reconciling differences and adjusting majority-minority interests. Nevertheless, drawing the line between what is proper privacy and what becomes dan-

---

[13] A. A. Berle, Jr., "The Protection of Privacy," 79 *Political Science Quarterly*, 162–68, 164 (1964).
[14] See J. W. Bishop, Jr., "The Executive's Right of Privacy: An Unresolved Constitutional Question," 66 *Yale Law Journal*, 477 (1957).

gerous "government secrecy" is a difficult task. Critics have complained that the public often has a right to know what policies are being considered and, after a decision is taken, to know who influenced the result and what considerations moved the governmental leaders. Apart from the broad jockeying for position that underlies privacy conflicts between the legislature and the executive or between elected and appointed branches of government, there is also the problem of manipulation of the privacy claim by government agencies to secure what is really unfair advantage. An effective legislative or press campaign may be needed to compel responsibility when an agency makes a partial disclosure of information to advance its own interests or invokes the privacy principle to shield wrong-doing by public officials. . . .

The organization's need to communicate in confidence with its outside advisors and sources of information and to negotiate privately with other organizations corresponds to the individual's need for protected communication. At the governmental level this necessity ranges from the so-called "informer privilege" (by which American law recognizes the need of the executive branches, especially the law-enforcement and security services, to keep secret the identities of persons who report wrongdoings in confidence) to the situation of private persons who give confidential advice to the President and to executive departments. For example, in refusing to release a private citizen group's confidential report on the adequacy of national defenses, President Eisenhower in 1958 explained that the willingness of citizens to give advice to the government was heavily dependent on protecting the privacy of these communications. Society sets limits on this privacy for informational sources, such as the requirement that informers be produced if the government wants to use their statements in criminal prosecutions or that information "volunteered" to executive and regulatory agencies by private citizens—when it is really advocacy of their economic interests—be placed on the record.

Another aspect of privacy for confidential communication involves the information that organizations acquire from individuals and other organizations. Private agencies such as life-insurance companies, credit bureaus, employers, and many others collect reams of personal information, sometimes under the compulsion that the benefits offered by the organization cannot be had unless the information is provided. Government departments, in their capacities as law-enforcement, regulatory, money-granting, and employment agencies, collect even more personal data, and much of this, too, is compelled—by a legal duty to respond to the government inquiry. Normally, this issue is discussed as a matter of individual rather than of organizational privacy, because of the individual's interest in ensuring that personal information which he gave for one purpose is not used for another without his consent. But organizations also need to protect such information against many of the claims to access made by the press and other private and public agencies if they are to continue to get frank and full information from reporting sources. This fact makes confidential treatment of the data an independent organizational need, not an assertion of privacy solely on behalf of those furnishing the information.

Many private organizations have developed confidentiality policies to govern this issue. Government usually tries to safeguard confidential information through statutes or regulations prohibiting unauthorized disclosures by government employees of information acquired in their official capacities or contained in government files. Census data, for example, are legally restricted to the statistical purposes for which they were acquired and no other government officials may examine the census returns. Income-tax data are also restricted; they may be used beyond revenue purposes only for limited governmental inquiries.[15] Pressures on the privacy of governmentally obtained data arise when business, the press, or other governmental agencies claim the right of "the people" to have access to such information, creating an important area of struggle over executive privacy.

. . .

Surveillance is obviously a fundamental means of social control. Parents watch their children, teachers watch students, supervisors watch employees, religious leaders watch the acts of their congregants, policemen watch the streets and other public places, and government agencies watch the citizen's performance of various legal obligations and prohibitions. Records are kept by authorities to organize the task of indirect surveillance and to identify trends that may call for direct surveillance. Without such surveillance, society could not enforce its norms or protect its citizens, and an era of ever increasing speed of communication, mobility of persons, and coordination of conspiracies requires that the means of protecting society keep pace with the technology of crime. Yet one of the central elements of the history of liberty in Western societies since the days of the Greek city-state has been the struggle to install limits on the power of economic, political, and religious authorities to place individuals and private groups under surveillance against their will. The whole network of American constitutional rights—especially those of free speech, press, assembly, and religion; forbidding the quartering of troops in private homes; securing "persons, houses, papers and effects" from unreasonable search and seizure; and assuring the privilege against self-incrimination— was established to curtail the ancient surveillance claims of governmental authorities. Similar rules have evolved by statute, common law, and judicial decision to limit the surveillance powers of corporations, unions, and other private agencies.

15 See Internal Revenue Code of 1954, Sect. 6103.

Though this general principle of civil liberty is clear, many governmental and private authorities seem puzzled by the protest against current or proposed uses of new surveillance techniques. Why should persons who have not committed criminal acts worry whether their conversations might be accidentally overheard by police officers eavesdropping on public telephone booths or at public places used by suspected criminals? Why should truthful persons resist verifying their testimony through polygraph examination? Shouldn't anyone who appreciates the need for effective personnel placement accept personality testing? And aren't fears about subliminal suggestion or increased data collection simply nervous responses to the new and the unknown? In all these instances, authorities point to the fact that, beyond the benefits of the surveillance for the organization or the community, the individual himself can now prove his innocence, virtue, or talents by "science" and avoid the unjust assumptions frequently produced by "fallible" conventional methods.

The answer, of course, lies in the impact of surveillance on human behavior. This impact can best be understood by distinguishing three main types of modern surveillance. First is surveillance by observation. Writings by leading social scientists[16] have made it clear that observation by listening or watching which is known to the subject necessarily exercises a restrictive influence over him. In fact, in most situations this is exactly why the observational surveillance is set up—to enforce the rules. When a person knows his conduct is visible, he must either bring his actions within the accepted social norms in the particular situation involved or decide to violate those norms and accept the risk of reprisal. Sociological writing has stressed that there are degrees of observation in various types of groups (work forces, government agencies, and the like) which will prevent the particular group's members from performing effectively. Robert Merton has explained this phenomenon as follows:

> Few groups, it appears, so fully absorb the loyalties of members that they will readily accept unrestricted observability of their role-performance. . . . Resistance to full visibility of one's behavior appears . . . to result from structural properties of group life. *Some* measure of leeway in conforming to role-expectations is presupposed in all groups. To have to meet the strict requirements of a role at all times, without some degree of deviation, is to experience insufficient allowances for individual differences in capacity and training and for situational exigencies which make strict conformity extremely difficult.[17]

Even though the authorities may accept evasion of the rules, the experience will be "psychologically taxing" on both the observed person and

---

[16] See Robert Merton, *Social Theory and Social Structure* (Glencoe, Ill., 1957), 341–53; Simmel, *op. cit.*, 330–61; Hans Zetterberg, "Complaint Actions," 2 *Acta Sociologica*, 179 (1957).

[17] Merton, *Social Theory and Social Structure* (Rev. Ed., Glencoe, Ill., 1957), 343.

the authorities, since the latter must decide whether or not to act against the non-complying person and must measure the effects of not acting on the group perception of authority.

> What is sometimes called "the need for privacy"—that is, insulation of actions and thought from surveillance by others—is the individual counterpart to the functional requirement of social structure that some measure of exemption from full observability be provided for. Otherwise, the pressure to live up to the details of all (and often conflicting) social norms would become literally unbearable; in a complex society, schizophrenic behavior would become the rule rather than the formidable exception it already is. "Privacy" is not merely a personal predilection; it is an important functional requirement for the effective operation of social structure. Social systems must provide for some appropriate measure, as they would say in France, of *quant-à-soi*—a portion of the self which is kept apart, immune from social surveillance.[18]

Though the destructive effect of near total observation and compulsory public confessions is associated in the public mind with totalitarian systems, as depicted with chilling effect in Huxley's *Brave New World* and Orwell's *1984*, the histories of utopian community experiments also document the disintegrative effect of complete observation over individual and group life. Robert Owen's famous community of New Lanark contained what Owen called a "silent monitor" system to watch the conduct of workers.[19] This feature of life in several utopian communist communities of England and America in the nineteenth century led Charles Nordhoff to observe in 1875 that the absence of the "precious" thing called "solitude" was one of the key factors in the failure of these experiments.[20] In his leading work on the Israeli kibbutz, Melford Spiro has noted that the early settlers' deliberate rejection of personal privacy gave way in the established kibbutz, and especially among the second kibbutz generation, to a demand for privacy in family and living arrangements that had to be satisfied to keep the loyalty of the kibbutz members.[21] It is revealing that the attempt to use total observational surveillance and to require total self-revelation to the group or to authorities takes place either as part of efforts to run perfect societies, such as utopias, or perfect sub-societies, such as monasteries or convents. In the Jesuit order, for example, brothers in training must keep themselves under a total monitor, keep a record of their improper thoughts and actions, and report themselves each day to their superior. In addition, each week all the brothers must report anything they have heard their fellow brothers say or do that breaches the rules. Only those who can sustain an absolute

---

[18] *Ibid.*, 375.
[19] *Ibid.*, 343–44.
[20] See Charles Nordhoff, *The Communistic Societies of the United States* (New York, 1875), 399–418.
[21] M. E. Spiro, *Kibbutz: Venture in Utopia* (New York, 1963), xiii, 5, 9, 21, 30–33, 65–69, 203–211, 216, 221, 246.

commitment to the ideal of perfection can survive total surveillance. This is not the condition of men in ordinary society.

Sociological analysis of observability explains why the prospect of total physical surveillance is so psychologically shattering to the individual. If a factory is wired completely with listening and watching devices, workers know that every station cannot be monitored all the time. Yet no individual has any way of knowing when he is under observation and when not. The particularly dehumanizing feature of this situation is not the fact that the surveillance is done by machine techniques rather than by direct human observation, but that the person-to-person factor in observation—with its softening and "game" aspects—has been eliminated. The same element is present in data surveillance—the maintenance of such detailed daily and cumulative records of each individual's personal transactions that computerized systems can reconstruct his acts and use such data for social control even without direct physical surveillance.

On the other hand, surveillance may be such a vital means of providing physical security, as in our public places, that properly controlled use of new watching and listening devices may be desirable. This point was made by Margaret Mead in a recent essay. After noting that city life offers "extraordinary possibilities" for anonymity from neighbors, relatives, and community controls, Mead stated that the desire for "personal privacy" is being confused with a notion of "privacy from the law." This confusion is based on the erroneous assumption that there is no obligation to create institutions of social protection in cities to replace the public safety provided by social surveillance of known persons in small communities. New listening, watching, and recording devices in apartment buildings, police street monitoring, and similar situations are to be welcomed. "[T]he devices we have rejected because they can be (and have been) used to invade individual privacy can also be used to ensure the public safety, without which privacy itself becomes a nightmare isolation."[22]

A second main type of surveillance is extraction—entry into a person's psychological privacy by requiring him to reveal by speech or act those parts of his memory and personality that he regards as private. Earlier discussion of the individual's need for autonomy explains the threat this procedure poses to the individual in a free society. American society has understood well that such extraction through torture, test oaths, self-incrimination, and governmental inquiries into religious belief is antithetical to civil liberty, and our law has forbidden such official surveillance.

It is not such traditional methods of extraction that are causing the present debate over privacy, of course, but less direct methods, such as

[22] Margaret Mead, "Margaret Mead Re-Examines Our Right to Privacy," *Redbook*, April, 1965, 15, 16. See also Jane Jacobs, *The Death and Life of Great American Cities* (Vintage ed., New York, 1962), 43, 57–67.

polygraphs and personality testing. The issue of personality testing for personnel selection by industry and government provides a useful subject for studying the social effect of extraction.

The basic objection on privacy grounds to the typical personality test used in personnel selection today—with its questions on such topics as sex and political values—is that many individuals do not want to be sorted and judged according to standards that rest on the unexplained evaluations of professional psychologists in the employ of "institutional" clients. Liberals fear that a government or industrial psychologist will enforce conformist or elitist norms. Conservatives fear that school or government testing might not only "reward" liberal ideology and penalize conservative ideas but also "implant" ideas through the testing process itself. Negroes are concerned that psychologists might enforce standards of personality that penalize minority groups and that the personality test might enable the "white structure" to accomplish covertly discrimination it can no longer carry out openly. In all these situations the assertion of privacy serves to say to those in power: "If you make evaluative decisions openly, questioning me directly and justifying your decisions openly, I can fight out publicly your right to judge me in a certain way, and American society will decide our conflicting claims. But if you invoke 'science' and 'expertise' and evaluate me through personality tests, the issue becomes masked and the public cannot judge the validity and morality of these evaluative decisions. Thus, where such basic issues as political ideology, religion, and race are at stake, the selection process must be objective and public, and I assert my right of privacy to close my emotions, beliefs, and attitudes to the process of job evaluation in a free society."

. . .

A third type of surveillance, which has not yet been studied by social scientists because of its recent development, is what I would call reproducibility of communication. Through the new recording and camera devices, it is now simple to obtain permanent pictorial and sound recordings of subjects without their knowledge. This may be done by the person with whom the subject is talking or acting, or a secret recording may be made by a third party. The special character of this surveillance is that it gives the person who conducted the surveillance the power to reproduce, at will, the subject's speech or acts. When a person writes a letter or files a report, he knows that he is communicating a record and that there is a risk of circulation; thus he exercises care and usually tries to say what he really means. But in speech that is overheard and recorded, all the offhand comments, sarcastic remarks, indiscretions, partial observations, agreements with statements to draw out a partner in conversation or to avoid argument, and many similar aspects of informal private intercourse are capable of being "turned on" by another for his own purposes. The right of individuals and organizations to decide when, to whom, and in what way they will "go public" has been taken away from them. It is almost as if we were witnessing an achievement through technology of a risk to modern man comparable to that primitive men felt when they had their photographs taken by visiting anthropologists: a part of them had been taken and might be used to harm them in the future.

When surreptitious recording and filming was limited primarily to security or law-enforcement agencies or to private investigations into misconduct such as employee pilfering, the risk to society may not have been great. Now that such recording devices have become general commodities—and are spreading so rapidly into the business, governmental, and personal worlds—we must consider the impact of their use on our freedom of private expression, and the widespread public assumption that important conversations are being recorded, whether they are in fact or not. Secret recordings *are* being made by federal executive agencies (wholly apart from security matters) and other government bodies, and such recordings *are* being used to exert pressure on individuals by playing back to them comments which would be embarrassing if revealed publicly. Such use in corporate life is not yet as widespread, but if the history of surveillance practices teaches us anything, it is that business will not lag far behind government for long.

·   ·   ·

. . . Let me restate the main conclusions that have been presented:

1. A technological breakthrough in techniques of physical surveillance now makes it possible for government agents and private persons to penetrate the privacy of homes, offices, and vehicles; to survey individuals moving about in public places; and to monitor the basic channels of communication by telephone, telegraph, radio, televsion, and data line. Most of the "hardware" for this physical surveillance is cheap, readily available to the general public, relatively easy to install, and not presently illegal to own. As of the 1960's, the new surveillance technology is being used widely by government agencies of all types and at every level of government, as well as by private agents for a rapidly growing number of businesses, unions, private organizations, and individuals in every section of the United States. Increasingly, permanent surveillance devices have been installed in facilities used by employees or the public. While there are defenses against "outside" surveillance, these are so costly and complex and demand such constant vigilance that their use is feasible only where official or private matters of the highest security are to be protected. Finally, the scientific prospects for the next decade indicate a continuing increase in the range and versatility of the listening and watching devices, as well as the possibility of computer processing of recordings to identify automatically the speakers or topics under surveillance. These advances will come just at the time when personal contacts,

business affairs, and government operations are being channeled more and more into electronic systems such as data-phone lines and computer communications.

2. In the field of psychological surveillance, techniques such as polygraphing and personality testing that probe the intimate thought processes of their subjects have swept into widespread use since World War II. Because they are supposed to offer "scientific" examination of individuals, these techniques have become commonplace in the personnel-selection system of many corporations, private organizations, and government agencies, and are used for a variety of other purposes as well. At the same time, advances in drug research indicate that we may be approaching the point at which the administration of a drug (with or without the subject's knowledge) may render him a truthful person under questioning; already, arguments in favor of such narco-analysis under new drugs have appeared in police and legal journals. Finally, research in brain-wave analysis establishes that "reading" certain signals of the brain is now possible; if in the coming decades this progresses to the ability to distinguish the more complex messages involved in thoughts and emotions, direct interrogation of the mind may become the "ultimate weapon" in penetration of privacy.

3. In the area I have called data surveillance, the rapid pace of computer development and usage throughout American society means that vast amounts of information about individuals and private groups in the nation are being placed in computer-usable form. More and more information is being gathered and used by corporations, associations, universities, public schools, and governmental agencies. And as "life-long dossiers" and interchange of information grow steadily, the possibilities increase that agencies employing computers can accomplish heretofore impossible surveillance of individuals, businesses, and groups by putting together all the now-scattered pieces of data. This danger is augmented by current proposals from some private and government spokesmen who advocate the adoption of a fully-computerized and automatic credit system to replace cash transactions, a single-identifying-number system for every person in his dealings with public authorities, and similar "total" computer systems.

4. In each of these areas of surveillance, most of the scientific advances did not arise through efforts to develop instruments for invading the privacy of the citizenry. Rather, they grew out of research to solve broad problems of American society—space travel and communication, medical research, diagnosis and treatment of mental illness, mobile television broadcasts, rapid analysis and use of general data, and a host of similar purposes. Once the scientific advances were made, however, often at levels of cost that only government could supply in the stages of basic research and prototype development, many of the techniques were then adopted swiftly by both government agencies and private interests for

purposes of physical, psychological, or data surveillance. The technology we have been discussing has thus been "socially useful" in origin, and potentially "neutral" in relation to privacy. Yet the ease with which the new techniques have been used for penetration of privacy, their relatively low cost in relation to the resources of those wishing to employ these techniques for surveillance, and the ready accessibility of the "parts" or "processes" indicate that existing legal and social rules for policing the borderline between "proper" and "improper" use have proved inadequate. Furthermore, the test psychologists and computer scientists involved in applying the new surveillance techniques have often been so sure of their own purposes and ethics that they have been insufficiently sensitive to the issues of privacy created by the uses of these processes. This preoccupation with scientific solutions to social problems has sometimes tended to place the professionals in various fields in opposition to what they regard as "unscientific" and "emotional" positions asserting "new" claims of privacy.

5. The response of American society to these technological and scientific developments since 1945 has been uneven and often without the consistency that comes with self-consciousness. But the studies of civic reactions to five key problems—subliminal suggestion, electronic eavesdropping, polygraphs, personality testing, and the computer—show steadily growing sensitivity to privacy claims in the press and among national civic groups. Group positions vary, depending on who is doing the surveillance, who is being surveyed, and the purpose for intruding. But so many areas have been affected by the new techniques and so many group interests have been directly threatened that statements deploring the erosion of privacy and the tactics of "Big Brother" have been issuing steadily from every position along the ideological spectrum, from extreme right to radical left. While some might read the record differently, I conclude from the five depth-studies that a "minimum position" in support of privacy is emerging. This unites both liberal and conservative camps, and awaits only a clear enunciation of basic standards and the development of a creative evaluative process before it becomes a national consensus which can be drawn upon by legislators, judges, and private authorities to deal with the specific problems of privacy under technological pressure.

6. In probing the functions which privacy serves in democratic systems—its psychological, sociological, and political utility—we [find] that privacy is an irreducibly critical element in the operations of individuals, groups, and government in a democratic system with a liberal culture. For the individual, there is a need to keep some facts about himself wholly private, and to feel free to decide for himself who shall know other facts, at what time, and under what conditions. At the same time, there is an equally powerful need in each person to disclose "personal" or "private" matters to others, as well as a strong impulse to penetrate the privacy of others, not only in terms of his peers and local gossip but

also by "eavesdropping" on the activities of leading elites of the society through exposés by the press, government investigations, court trials, etc. While some aspects of this urge for penetration of another's privacy can be considered "voyeuristic" in the personal sense and "populistic" in their political aspect, this is so clearly a fact of behavior, and serves such a key role in a mass society, that its presence must be noted by anyone seriously concerned with privacy norms in our society. There is also a close correlation between the availability of privacy from hostile surveillance and the achievement of creativity, mental health, and ethical self-development, though there is always a shifting standard of balance in these matters and a heavy layer of cultural relativism.

Privacy as a need in organizational life [is] amply demonstrated in considering the internal affairs of businesses, civic groups, and ideological protest movements. Without time for preparation and internal rationalization of views and differences, private groups cannot fulfill the independent role envisaged for them by the values of a pluralistic, democratic society. Whether to allow such nutritive privacy for a particular group, and how much, are always policy questions for law and government. Thus a scale of privacy depending on the social prestige and assumed social contributions of groups has been a standard feature of our society, with the major religious organizations placed at one end of the scale and "subversive" groups at the other. In addition to the need of individual groups for privacy, there is also a need for privacy in negotiations *between* private groups, such as labor-management bargaining sessions, intercorporate negotiations, and a variety of similar relations in the civic and political sphere.

A core area of privacy is also essential to the successful conduct of democratic government, whether the setting is the private conference of the Supreme Court, meetings of the White House staff with the President, executive sessions of legislative committees, the conference-committee stage of legislation in Congress, exploratory negotiations with foreign governments, or "frank" sessions behind the scenes at international conferences or at the U.N. In situations of all types, privacy is a critical ingredient for the process of accommodation and resolution upon which peaceful settlement of conflicting interests rests. In most instances, the privacy required is a temporary one, and the interests of a democratic society in knowing what its elected and appointed officials are doing can be properly served by pulling back the curtain of privacy after the bargains have been struck and implemented. At that stage, democratic statesmen are held responsible for their acts. . . .

THE
POLITICAL IDEAL
OF PRIVACY
H. J. McCloskey

H. J. McCloskey is Professor of Philosophy at La Trobe University in Australia. In addition to his articles in professional journals, he is the author of Meta-ethics and Normative Ethics (1969).

Privacy is a value or ideal in our society, in the Western World, and in liberal thought generally. By this I mean at least, and perhaps only, that *ceteris paribus* we think much more highly of a society which respects privacy and much less highly of one in which privacy is exposed to invasions. Privacy is therefore in some sense a basic contemporary liberal value. We liberals abhor the thought of a society in which there is censorship of letters, unrestricted phone tapping, bugging of private homes and of offices, searching, compulsory questionnaires by the government, employers, etc. Indeed, much of the force of novels such as *Brave New World* and *1984* rests on the total loss of privacy portrayed in the imagined new society. We value privacy, and we believe ourselves to have a right to privacy; and the right is thought of as not simply a negative right, the basis of which consists in the lack of rights in others to invade our privacy, but as a positive right in the enjoyment of which we may, by virtue of it, demand the help of the state, society, and other persons. The right to privacy, like all other rights, is of course seen to be a *prima facie* right. It may legitimately be overridden and is so overridden in situations such as those of national emergency. However, it is generally believed that there must be very good reasons for overriding this right, for invading privacy. This too is part of what I mean by saying that privacy is a value or ideal of our society, namely, that it is generally believed that there must be positive, powerful, justificatory reasons for invading a person's privacy. The U.N. acknowledged this. In its declaration concerning human rights it noted in its *International Covenants of Human Rights*, Article 17, that:

"1. No one shall be subjected to arbitrary or unlawful interference with his privacy, family, home or correspondence, nor to unlawful attacks on his honour or reputation."

"2. Everyone has the right to the protection of the law against such interference or attacks."[1]

This, unfortunately, has the customary equivocation of U.N. statements about rights. Of course individuals are entitled to protection by the law from unlawful interference. The problem is, as this statement brings out, that of defining and determining what ought to be made to be unlawful interferences with privacy. This involves discussing three distinct issues, namely: (i) How is privacy to be characterised, defined, or explained? What properly counts as protecting and what as losing one's privacy? What relates to privacy and what to other ideals and rights, ideals such as liberty, rights such as property rights? To say that privacy relates to that which is of private concern to the person, and which is no business of anyone else, circumscribes the area of privacy too narrowly, whilst at the same time leaving unresolved the different but equally difficult problem concerning what is and what is not of purely private concern to the individual. (ii) There is also the issue concerning how privacy as an ideal, or the right to privacy as a right, is to be defended, i.e., there is the question concerning what are the grounds upon which the ideal or right is based. The obvious line of defence in the terms of the lack of right of others to invade my privacy may prove to be the only line of defence available. However, judging by the role played by the demand for protection of privacy in our society, a more positive, stronger line of defence would seem generally to be assumed to be available. (iii) Another distinct issue concerns what constitute legitimate and what illegitimate losses or invasions of privacy. Clearly, there are occasions on which a person may legitimately be deprived of some or all of his privacy. The right to privacy is not an absolute, inviolable right, but one which may legitimately be overridden and even lost for long periods of time. It is important that consideration be given to the general principles relevant to determining when the right is overridden, forfeited, or yielded up.

WHAT IS PRIVACY?

What relates to privacy, and what to other ideals and rights? Although privacy has been an important liberal value for a considerable time now, few political philosophers have addressed themselves to this question. Indeed, the only discussion of privacy prior to 1950 known to me as being

---

[1] Quoted by S. H. Hofstadter and G. Horowitz in *The Right to Privacy* (New York, 1964), p. 3.

by a philosopher is that of James Fitzjames Stephen who was a lawyer *cum* philosopher. Stephen wrote:

"Legislation and public opinion ought in all cases whatever scrupulously to respect privacy. To define the province of privacy distinctly is impossible, but it can be described in general terms. All the more intimate and delicate relations of life are of such a nature that to submit them to unsympathetic observation, or to observation which is sympathetic in the wrong way, inflicts great pain, and may inflict lasting moral injury. Privacy may be violated not only by the intrusion of a stranger, but by compelling or persuading a person to direct too much attention to his own feelings and to attach too much importance to their analysis. The common usage of language affords a practical test which is almost perfect upon this subject. Conduct which can be described as indecent is always in one way or another a violation of privacy."[2]

The absence of serious discussion of privacy is one of the most remarkable features of the writings of such British liberals as J. S. Mill, Spencer, Hobhouse, and Tawney. It has been suggested in the writings of lawyers that the relatively recent emergence of recognition of privacy in the law has in a large measure been due to the development of such threats to privacy as the camera and the many electronic bugging devices. This may well be true in respect of the development of laws restricting invasions of privacy, but it would seem not to be the explanation of the absence of philosophical discussion of the ideal. The latter appears rather to have resulted from a confusion of thought, privacy and negative liberty being identified as one and the same thing. Both have been explained and characterized as consisting in "being let alone," and a notable legal work on privacy, that by M. L. Ernst and A. U. Schwartz, is entitled *Privacy: The Right To Be Let Alone*.[3] Although the two things are closely related, they are nonetheless distinct.

Two considerations are available which provide clear grounds for distinguishing negative liberty and privacy as separate notions, and hence, as relating to separate, distinct, political ideals. First, the greater the extent of the interference with a person's liberty, the more inclined we are to think of him as being rendered incapable of being a full person; complete interference in the form of complete control over his decisions and actions during the whole of his life is incompatible with his remaining a full *person*, in the Kantian sense of 'person.' Further, usually although not necessarily, such lengthy, extensive interference or control would be known to the person concerned. By contrast, a person's privacy can be totally invaded during the whole of his life without his knowledge, and without his freedom being in any way restricted or curtailed, and without his being any less a person, qua *person*. Here I need only invite you to

---

[2] *Liberty, Equality, Fraternity* (Cambridge, 1967), p. 160 (1st ed., 1873).
[3] New York, 1962.

enter the world of philosophy-science-fiction, and to imagine the material-ist theory of mind to be proven philosophically and scientifically true, and that science so advances that bugging devices not merely for bugging private homes but for bugging minds are invented (Brain-Mind-Bugs as they may come to be called) which can publish the contents of their victims' minds without their knowledge. In this case, there *need* be no interference with the individual's freedom of action, nor with his freedom of thought and expression; yet there would be a total loss of privacy. Secondly, there may be a conflict between the right of privacy and the right to liberty, even where liberty is conceived of as negative liberty. Part of the right to liberty is the right to observe, to know, to report, and to publish. The ideal society from the point of view of the exponent of nega-tive liberty, the kind of society one finds commended as such, as in the writings of Humboldt and Spencer, is that in which there is as little inter-ference by way of coercion as possible, where the only coercion which is justified, is coercion directed against coercive interference. Nonetheless, privacy can be invaded by members of such a community, who at the same time respect the liberty of their fellows by not interfering with them. Privacy would be invaded by the person who eavesdrops on her neighbour, by someone who used his binoculars to watch a distant person working in his garden, or hanging out her washing, etc. Yet these are not forms of interference in the sense relevant to negative or other kinds of liberty. To seek to justify coercion of the eavesdropper and the spy as coercion di-rected against coercion would be utterly implausible, and would involve gross distortion of the concept of interference. The contrast with privacy is publicity. Privacy is something which is to be respected, which may be forgone, lost, forfeited, or invaded. The contrasts with negative liberty are interference and coercion; negative liberty may be lost by interference and coercion. With positive liberty, the contrasts are more various—coercion, interference, and lack of facilities are the more obvious contrasts. Positive liberty is something which may have to be brought into being; privacy, on the other hand, typically needs only to be protected.

It has been the lawyers, particularly the lawyers of the U.S.A., rather than the philosophers, who have engaged in useful discussions of privacy, and to such good effect that there are laws defining the right to privacy in the U.S.A., although not in Great Britain and Australia (unless such laws have been introduced in the immediate past few years). In Britain and in Australia attempts are made to deal with grosser invasions of privacy under property-type laws such as those relating to trespass, breach of con-tract, copyright, defamation, or libel. However, useful though the U.S. legal discussions are, they are of less value philosophically than might be hoped, and this for two reasons. The legal concept is distinct from the political concept as most of us conceive it. It is in some respects broader, covering such things as using a person's photo without his consent, and in some states, even the writing about a relative who is now dead. It is in other respects narrower, allowing as not invasions of privacy "accidental" or non-deliberate photographs of individuals in the private pursuit of their pleasures, as in newscasts. The legal approach has, by and large, been by way of making invasion of privacy a civil offence (in some cases, and in important areas, a criminal offence), and the concern of lawyers and legislators has been to define what are illegitimate invasions of privacy for which damages can reasonably be sought and awarded, rather than to define what constitute losses and invasions of privacy. The legal discussions are nonetheless worthy of very serious consideration. The most famous is the article, "The Right to Privacy," by Samuel D. Warren and Louis D. Brandeis in the *Harvard Law Review*, IV, 1890. A key passage runs:

"These considerations lead to the conclusion that the protection afforded to thoughts, sentiments, and emotions, expressed through the medium of writing or of the arts, so far as it consists in preventing publication, is merely an instance of the enforcement of the more general right to be let alone. . . . The principle which protects personal writing and all other personal productions, not against theft and physical appropriation, but against publication in any form, is in reality not the principle of private property, but that of an inviolate personality." (p. 206)

They then go on to list applications and exceptions, namely:

"1. The right of privacy does not prohibit any publication of matter which is of public or general interest." (p. 215)

"2. The right to privacy does not prohibit the communication of any matter, though in its nature private, when the publication is made under circumstances which would render it a privileged communication according to the law of slander and libel." (p. 217)

"3. The law would probably not grant any redress for the invasion of privacy by oral publication in the absence of special damage." (p. 218)

"4. The right to privacy ceases upon the publication of the facts by the individual, or with his consent." (p. 219)

"5. The truth of the matter does not afford a defence." (p. 219)

"6. The absence of 'malice' in the publisher does not afford a defence." (p. 219)

The Warren-Brandeis article was a key step in the development of the law relating to the right to privacy in the U.S.A. Since then the law has so developed that it can be briefly summed up, as by S. H. Hofstadter and G. Horowitz in *The Right to Privacy* thus:

"The diversity of the situations and of the cases in which the right of privacy may be involved precludes precise delimitation. It may be described broadly as the right against the unwarranted appropriation or exploitation of one's personality; or the publicizing of one's private affairs with which the public has no legitimate concern; or the wrongful intrusion into one's private activities in such manner as to outrage a person of ordinary sensibilities or cause him mental suffering, shame or humiliation."

The authors then represent Prosser's classification of the four broad groups of acts against which the right offers protection in the following way:

"1. Intrusion upon the plaintiff's seclusion or solitude, or into his private affairs.

2. Public disclosure of embarrassing private facts about the plaintiff.

3. Publicity which places the plaintiff in a false light in the public eye.

4. Appropriation for the defendant's advantage, of the plaintiff's name or likeness."[4]

Such accounts are no doubt very useful in law; they are less useful as philosophical elucidations of the concept of privacy, and this chiefly because they are concerned with marking off illegitimate invasions of privacy rather than with what in general counts as an invasion and what as a loss of privacy. However, the initial, general formula has important considerations to offer which bear on this, in particular the suggestion that one suffers a loss or an invasion of privacy if one's private activities and concerns are intruded into in such a manner as to outrage a person of ordinary sensibilities or cause him mental suffering, shame or humiliation. A modification has been suggested along the lines of writing in the clause 'cause or may reasonably cause.'

Such an account, modified in the suggested way, might seem to accommodate most types of losses and invasions of privacy—phone-tapping, eavesdropping, peeping, spying, prying, bugging, etc. In fact, it does not come near to doing so, and this for two reasons. First, as noted above, the key notion of "private" has to be explained further; and secondly, the section of the formula relating to outraging, paining, shaming, or humiliating, actually or potentially, a person of ordinary sensibilities, needs modification to guard against the dangerous degree of relativity of which it admits.

It is of course true that we suffer a loss of privacy if our private activities are intruded upon, but the major problem with privacy is that of determining what activities and concerns may properly be deemed to be purely private activities and concerns. Attempts to explain this by contrast with what is of public or general concern, that is, in terms of their relation to the general interest, will not do. Something may still be in the area of privacy and yet relate to the general interest, for example, whether one has venereal disease. Here the general interest provides a justification for invading a person's privacy. Other private acts, for example a planned suicide by the country's leading scientist, may be relevant to the general interest, and yet not justify invading his privacy as by spying on him to

---

[4] *Op. cit.*, pp. 7, 8. See W. L. Prosser, *The Law of Torts* (St. Paul, 1964).

see how advanced his plans are before acting to interfere with his liberty by thwarting the suicide. Further, others, besides the state, society, or the community, may have genuine interests in what otherwise would be private acts or concerns of the individual. People are thought to have a right to privacy in respect of the *affaires* they have, unless one or other party to the *affaire* is married. Yet, I suggest that if the girl involved in the *affaire* is a minor, a father who spied on the pair could not be charged with an improper invasion of their privacy; and if the man involved knew that she was a minor, he could not complain that he had suffered a loss of privacy as a result of the father's spying, because, by his actions he had put that area of his life outside the area of privacy. A better case illustrating the latter might be that of a single woman who is supporting her illegitimate child and who is seeking marriage with a man who suspects this but who has not been told the facts. The woman's intentions here would render it no invasion of her privacy for the man to check up on her. (His doing so may make his approach to marriage less romantic than romanticists would like approaches to marriage to be.) Another case would be that of a divorcee who is seeking to marry a devout Roman Catholic, and from whom she is seeking to conceal the fact that she has been married and divorced. The man would not be invading her privacy if he made the relevant inquiries. The test here would seem to consist in whether the person has a right to know, i.e., whether the individual whose privacy is said to be involved has, by her actions, rendered this aspect of her life public for the person with a right to know. If, as I suggest is the case in respect of the father of the minor, the prospective husband, and the Roman Catholic, those concerning whom they obtained information had not suffered a loss of privacy thereby, then the right to know would seem to be very relevant to determining the area which relates to privacy.

Unfortunately, things are not as simple and straightforward as that. There is an element of arbitrariness in our usage here, for there can be cases in which others possess the right to know facts about us (for example, the taxation department) and yet we suffer a loss and an invasion of privacy in their gaining this knowledge, albeit a justifiable loss or invasion. Here the fact that we have no choice but to enter into the situation seems relevant—the mother of the illegitimate child, the divorcee, and the seducer of the minor freely put themselves into the position of making certain areas of their lives properly knowable by certain other people. This is why we should deem it a lack of respect for privacy for those who have a right to know, to pass on what they learn to those who lack the right to know. The persons have freely chosen to act in such a way that *for some*, their lives are less in the area of the right to privacy than for others. With respect to matters relating to taxation, for most of us in respect of most such matters, we have no choice. An interesting, inbetween kind of case which suggests that the element of arbitrariness in our usage is slighter than first appearances suggest, is that of the news film of a race, which at the same time takes in the spectators, these including malingerers, men with their mistresses, and the like, and a criminal in the pursuit of his calling, picking pockets. It is certainly a loss, and I should suggest, an invasion of privacy for the malingerers, and others who wish not to be observed, to have the film shown on the TV; often it would be a loss or invasion which could be justified in terms of the general interest, and the fact that those concerned knew the risks they were running. However, I suggest that the criminal pickpocket, who is filmed whilst actually picking pockets, cannot reasonably object that the film ought not to be shown publicly on the grounds that such publicity involved a loss or even an invasion of his privacy. It would involve neither an illegitimate invasion of his privacy, nor even an invasion of it; indeed, I suggest that we should be disinclined to say even that he had suffered a loss of privacy as a result of the showing of the film.

Thus, in so far as both the right to know and freely entering into activities in ways and under conditions which confer the right to know on others are relevant to privacy, our problem resolves itself, to that extent, into determining who have rights to know, and on what occasions, as a result of the individual's free actions. No doubt many people would dispute certain of my examples, but I suggest that other examples could easily be produced which would be acceptable as illustrations that there are personal "private" acts and concerns which are such that other individuals, or society, or the state have the right to knowledge of them, and in such a way that we should not describe their taking steps to obtain this knowledge as depriving the individual of his privacy. This being so, it would follow that it is impossible to mark off certain areas or certain concerns as those which are the peculiar concern of privacy. Any concern, any activity, no matter how personal, may fall outside the area of privacy. Further, it is impossible to mark out the area of privacy in terms of those areas concerning which others lack the right to knowledge, for many non-personal matters are of such a character, for example, such trivial matters as concern the brand of soap I use, the grade of oil I use in my car, the barber I use, and the like. No one has the right to obtain this knowledge *from me, ceteris paribus*, yet it is knowledge which does not relate to privacy although in certain circumstances it, like almost any other knowledge relating to me, could do so.

The second important issue here relates to the clause concerning invasions which may actually or reasonably outrage, hurt, shame, or humiliate a person of ordinary sensibilities. This clause results from an attempt to take note of the relativity between societies and within societies concerning what are judged to be losses and invasions of privacy. Different societies judge different things to be or to involve losses and invasions of privacy. Subject to certain qualifications, one's sexual arrangements other than *via* marriage are matters appertaining to privacy in our society. One may voluntarily consent to a loss of privacy by making one's arrangements publicly known, but this is nonetheless seen as a forgoing of one's right to privacy. It is unlikely that this would in the eighteenth and nineteenth centuries have been seen to be so in Tahiti and the Trobriand Islands even if the natives could have grasped the concept of privacy; and it would seem to be much less the case in Moslem than in Christian countries to-day. On the other hand, whether one drinks alcoholic beverages may well be a matter relating to privacy in Moslem countries but less so in ours. Within any one society there are changing standards. Matters such as the nature of the work done by one's forebears, one's salary, one's wealth and possessions, the diseases one has or has had, used formerly to be con-sidered matters of purely private concern, but now are not generally re-garded as such. The formula goes a long way towards accommodating this relativity by making the effect or emotional reaction a vital part of the characterization of privacy being lost. However, it does this at the cost of denying to be losses or invasions of privacy what are the grossest and most objectionable ones.

Part of our objection to totalitarian regimes is that they render per-sons of ordinary sensibilities no longer outraged, hurt, shamed, or humili-ated by invasions of privacy. The invasions become so frequent, so com-monplace, the emotional reactions and hurts cease to follow. This is true even of the losses and invasions of privacy experienced in the armed ser-vices, for example, during a war. Persons of ordinary sensibilities become used to all their affairs being common knowledge, to their letters being read by prying censors, and the like, so that, before very long, only the hy-persensitive are outraged, hurt, shamed, or humiliated. (Those involved in the last world war would confirm this.) Yet any account of privacy, more especially of what constitute losses and invasions of privacy, must be such as to explain life under Nazism and life in the armed services as life with little privacy. To attempt to save the formula by adding some such clause as 'under normal circumstances,' or 'for the natural rather than normal man' will not do. Cultural relativity does need to be accommodated at least to some extent. Further, privacy is not tied to some vague philo-sophical concept of a natural man, but relates to men as they are, and hence to a concept of a normal rather than of a natural man. There are obvious difficulties in the way of elucidating satisfactory and relevantly the concept of normality here.

I suggest, therefore, that there are two types of problems in character-izing the concept or notion of privacy, namely, the basic one of cutting off that which is the individual's private concern or activity from that which is legitimately the concern of others. That an individual may so act as to give another or others a right to know is relevant here, but seems to fall short of being the complete story. In any case, much work needs to be done on what does and what does not give another a right to know, and in this context, what kinds of freely chosen conduct give rise to such a right. Secondly, there is the problem of characterizing the losses and invasions of privacy in such a way that relativity is acknowledged in the right ways and only in the right ways.

PRIVACY AS AN IDEAL: ITS GROUNDS

Privacy is so very highly valued in our society that we are prepared to render some invaders of privacy criminals, with all that that involves, in order to protect the individual's privacy. Individuals such as Peeping-Toms, those who phone-tap, listen-in on crossed lines, those who bug private homes, and the like, where they are prosecuted may not always be prosecuted under the label or crime of being violators of privacy. However, support for such laws as exist and under which they are prosecuted, and the demand for laws banning such activities, spring in a large measure from a concern for privacy as a value in this society. My concern now is to consider why privacy is so valued, and whether it is rightly so valued.

There are obvious reasons for looking upon such invasions of privacy as undesirable, dangerous activities which ought to be discouraged as such. The information obtained by those who act in these ways may be used to harm the individuals whose privacy is invaded. Private individuals may use the information to blackmail, intimidate, hurt, or interfere with others; the police and/or others may harass and persecute individuals on the basis of their prying and thereby make the lives of the legally blameless, miserable. Invasions of privacy may also lead to thefts and other losses of property rights, or of rights closely associated with property rights. The Peeping-Tom may photograph the girl and sell her photo; the business spy may learn his competitor's plans and thwart them, or use discoveries not yet patented, and the like. Further, there will often be the loss of private pleasures. Most people in our society enjoy freedom from involuntary loss of privacy. They prefer to converse and act in contexts where the only privacy they have lost is that to which they have voluntarily consented.

Yet there remains the problem of explaining the very great stress attached to the value of privacy. The loss of pleasure and private enjoyment which comes with a sudden loss of privacy seems not to be the explanation, for we soon adjust and adapt to such losses, and the loss of pleasure and contentment is only temporary. Indeed, slum dwellers who, against their wishes, are given good housing which affords them a degree of privacy they never formerly enjoyed, frequently loathe the privacy which is forced upon them. It has often been suggested that privacy is an essential context for the emergence and development of sensitive feelings, that gross invasions of privacy as in prying in love-making, reading love

letters, observing the intimacies of private life, are inimical to the development, and even the survival of such delicate, valuable human feelings.[5]
This seems to be empirically untrue. Human beings seem to have an unlimited capacity to adapt to publicity, provided that the publicity is not
connected with interference. It is of course true in our society that publicity is commonly associated with interference by way of social, legal, or
simply personal pressures. Where it is not so associated, it seems not to
be the case that these civilized emotions and relations wither; on the
contrary, they appear to thrive.

It has been argued by S. I. Benn in a paper, "Privacy, Freedom, and
Respect for Persons,"[6] that the duty of respect for persons entails respect
for privacy. This is associated with the view that invasions of privacy
consist in knowing what is desired by the individual concerned not to be
known. (All knowledge of facts about another person, it would seem on
this view, involve a loss, although not necessarily an invasion of privacy.)
The suggestion seems to be that invading privacy is a kind of forcing of or
opposing the will of another, and that the right to privacy is a right to
secrecy. Privacy and secrecy are related but distinct concepts.

In reply to this kind of argument, I suggest that respect for persons
may dictate repudiating privacy so construed. The relation of lover to
lover is similar to that of the respecters of persons. Yet love, and like it
respect for persons, may dictate invasions of privacy. The lover, because of
his love, wants to know all about his loved one, because he loves her, and
he wants to know her more fully as the person she is. Indeed, love involves
knowledge, extensive, ideally, complete knowledge of the loved one. So
too, real respect for persons must be for real persons, persons as they
really are, as concrete individuals with certain traits, weaknesses, vices.
Love, and equally respect for persons, may dictate the seeking of knowledge against the wishes of the person concerned. The lover may be distressed at the unhappiness of his loved one, and rightly and reasonably
seek, without her permission, to learn the cause; or he may suspect that
she has a serious disease and is afraid to have it diagnosed and treated,
and know that if it is diagnosed and treated soon it will not be fatal. Love,
and respect for persons, lead to attempts to obtain the knowledge relevant
to such situations. They would also lead to attempts to persuade the diseased person to accept the treatment. Love, and respect for persons, involve an attitude of concern for others or another; concern involves knowledge, even undesired, unwanted knowledge.

Nonetheless, there are considerations which suggest that the duty of
respect for persons is relevent to the ideal of privacy. Consider the individual who takes pleasure in encouraging girls to reveal details of their
intimate, private lives (usually but not only sexual aspects). If both parties

---

[5] C. Fried in "Privacy," Yale Law Journal 77, 1967–8, pp. 475–493 so argues in respect
of trust, love and friendship as requiring privacy.
[6] Forthcoming in Nomos.

take pleasure in the exercise and thereby knowingly debase themselves, then I suggest that the individual is showing lack of respect for the girl as a person, and he and she for themselves as persons. Respect for persons involves living up to certain standards as persons, a treating of oneself and of others not merely as animals in a scientific experiment but as persons. Needlessly and deliberately to reveal certain aspects of one's intimate, personal life would seem to offend against this principle.

Further, to invade privacy is often to show lack of respect for persons. Without good reason, to ignore a person's wishes to conceal, pretend, or hide facts about himself, is to show lack of respect.[7] Nonetheless, the duty need not, and often does not, give rise to a corresponding right. Rights and duties are not correlative in this sense.[8]

Nevertheless, I wish to suggest that the case for privacy is basically an ideal utilitarian one, grounded on values such as human happiness, justice, and, to an extent, liberty. (Elsewhere I have argued that the case for liberty is, in turn, founded on goods such as happiness, knowledge, justice and fraternity.) Hence, to answer the third question noted in the introductory discussion concerning what constitute legitimate and what illegitimate invasions and losses of privacy, it may here be argued that a serious case could be made out for accepting invasions of privacy where these goods are not jeopardized, and where no great evils result, for example, in the cases of Peeping-Toms who are proven to be simply harmless observers.

It is relevant here to compare harmless invasions of privacy, and the hurt, outrage, shame, and humiliation they may cause, with offensive and indecent behaviour which may shock, offend, or hurt the bystander. I suggest that the truly liberal response to offensive and indecent persons (and behaviour) is not that of attempting to curtail the liberty of all who would be offensive and indecent, by making offenders criminals, but that of tolerating the offences and putting up with the temporary inconvenience of a readjustment of one's feeling reactions. This is because, on the one hand, it is important that we avoid curtailing liberty and rendering individuals criminals when we can do so without any hardship to anyone, and, on the other hand, because of the adaptability of human beings and human feelings. (Also some account must be taken of good manners— most people most of the time are reluctant needlessly to shock or hurt others.) So much that would have shocked, outraged, offended, and hurt people fifty years ago, clothing such as bikinis, mini-skirts, see-through clothing, and activities such as extensive public sexual conduct, talks concerning whether Christ was a homosexual, and the like, arouse, at the time of writing this paper, no unfavourable reaction. Many members of the community have found the period of adjustment difficult and un-

---

[7] For this and the preceding point I am in large measure indebted to Miss Christina Bell.

[8] See my discussion in "Rights," this journal [*Philosophical Quarterly*], Vol. 15, 1965.

pleasant, but this is a small price to pay for the liberty enjoyed, and the absence of the harm done in rendering some individuals criminals. I hope the time will come when there will be no such crimes as those of offensive and indecent behaviour. I suggest that, if and when we can be sure that the ideal utilitarian considerations for restricting invasions of privacy do not apply, it is a better and a more liberal position to adopt to accept the loss of privacy or, alternatively, to make private arrangements to prevent this, rather than to curtail the freedom of many and to render some persons criminals and many more exposed to costly legal actions. Our feelings soon adapt themselves as they have in respect of so-called offensive and indecent behaviour.

Selected bibliography

War and Violence
Addison, James T. *War, Peace, and the Christian Mind: A Review of Recent Thought.* New York: Seabury Press, 1953.
Arendt, Hannah. *On Revolution.* New York: Viking, 1965.
Aron, Raymond. *On War.* New York: Norton, 1968.
Bernal, J. D. *World Without War.* London: Routledge & Kegan Paul, 1958.
Bramson, Leon, and Goethals, George W., eds. *War: Studies From Psychology, Sociology, Anthropology.* New York: Basic Books, 1968.
Clancy, William, ed. *The Moral Dilemma of Nuclear Weapons: Essays from Worldview.* New York: Council on Religion and International Affairs, 1961.
Clark, Grenville. *A Plan for Peace.* New York: Harper Brothers, 1950.
Clausewitz, Karl von. *On War.* New York: Modern Library, 1943.
Center for the Study of Democratic Institutions. *A Constitution for the World.* Santa Barbara, Calif., 1965.
Cordier, Andrew W., and Foote, Wilder, eds. *The Quest for Peace.* New York: Columbia University Press, 1965.
Ewing, A. C. *The Individual, the State, and World Government.* New York: Macmillan, 1947.
Falk, Richard A. *Law, Morality, and War in the Contemporary Era.* New York: Praeger, 1963.
Freud, S. *Why War?* London: Hogarth Press, 1948.
Friedrich, Carl J. *Inevitable Peace.* Cambridge: Harvard University Press, 1948.
Ginsberg, Robert. *The Critique of War.* Chicago: Henry Regnery, 1969.
Hoffmann, Stanley. *The State of War.* New York: Praeger, 1965.
Hutchins, Robert Maynard. *The Atomic Bomb Versus Civilization.* Washington: Human Events, 1945.
Jaspers, Karl. *The Future of Mankind.* Chicago: University of Chicago Press, 1961.
Kahn, Hermann. *On Thermonuclear War.* Princeton: Princeton University Press, 1960.
Lorenz, Konrad. *On Aggression.* New York: Harcourt Brace Jovanovich, 1966.
Martin, Kingsley. *War, History and Human Nature.* New York: Asia Publishing House, 1959.
Mills, C. Wright. *The Causes of War.* New York: Simon & Schuster, 1958.

Mumford, Lewis. *Atomic War: The Way Out*. London: National Peace Council, 1948.
Niebuhr, R. *The Structure of Nations and Empires*. New York: Charles Scribner's, 1959.
Pear, T. H., ed. *Psychological Factors of Peace and War*. New York: Philosophical Library, 1950.
Ramsey, Paul. *The Just War*. New York: Charles Scribner's, 1968.
Russell, Bertrand. *Common Sense and Nuclear Warfare*. London: Allen & Unwin, 1959.
————. *Why Men Fight*. New York: The Century Company, 1920.
Somerville, John. *The Philosophy of Peace*. New York: Liberty, 1954.
Storr, Anthony. *Human Aggression*. New York: Atheneum, 1968.
Thomas, Norman. *The Prerequisites for Peace*. New York: Norton, 1959.
Toynbee, Arnold J. *War and Civilization*. New York: Oxford University Press, 1950.
Wallace, Victor H., ed. *Paths to Peace*. Carlton, Australia: Melbourne University Press, 1957.
Waltz, Kenneth N. *Man, the State, and War*. New York: Columbia University Press, 1965.
Wright, Quincy. *A Study of War*. Chicago: University of Chicago Press, 1965.

The Equality of Women

Adams, Mildred. *The Right to Be People*. New York: Lippincott, 1967.
Beauvoir, Simone de. *The Second Sex*. New York: Knopf, 1953.
Bird, Caroline. *Born Female*. New York: McKay, 1968.
Bonaparte, Marie. *Female Sexuality*. New York: Grove Press, 1965.
Briffault, Robert. *The Mothers*. London: Allen & Unwin, 1959.
Cade, Toni. *The Black Woman*. New York: New American Library, 1970.
Dector, Midge. *The New Chastity and Other Arguments Against Women's Liberation*. New York: Coward, McCann & Geoghegan, 1972.
Deutsch, Helene. *The Psychology of Women*. New York: Grune & Stratton, 1945.
Ellman, Mary. *Thinking About Women*. New York: Harcourt Brace Jovanovich, 1968.
Farber, S., and Wilson, Roger H. L., eds. *The Potential of Woman*. New York: McGraw-Hill, 1963.
Friedan, Betty. *The Feminine Mystique*. New York: Norton, 1963.
Hays, H. R. *The Dangerous Sex, The Myth of Feminine Evil*. New York: Putnam, 1964.
Hernton, Calvin C. *Sex and Racism in America*. New York: Grove Press, 1965.
Huber, Jean. *Changing Woman in a Changing Society*. Chicago: University of Chicago Press, 1973.
Janeway, Elizabeth. *Man's World, Woman's Place*. New York: Morrow, 1971.
Krich, Aron, ed. *The Sexual Revolution*. New York: Dell, 1965.
Lifton, Robert J., ed. *The Woman in America*. Boston: Beacon Press, 1964.
Mead, Margaret. *Sex and Temperament*. New York: Morrow, 1935.
Mill, John Stuart. *The Subjection of Women*. London: Oxford University Press, 1966.
Millett, Kate. *Sexual Politics*. New York: Doubleday, 1970.
Pankhurst, Sylvia. *The Suffragette Movement*. New York: Longmans Green, 1931.
Patai, Raphael, ed. *Women in the Modern World*. New York: Free Press, 1967.

Reich, Wilhelm. *The Sexual Revolution.* New York: Farrar, Straus & Giroux, 1945.
Reik, Theodor. *The Creation of Woman.* New York: Braziller, 1960.
Sinclair, Andrew. *The Emancipation of the American Woman.* New York: Harper & Row, 1965.
Tiger, Lionel. *Men in Groups.* New York: Random House, 1969.
Wollstonecraft, Mary. *A Vindication of the Rights of Woman.* London: J. M. Dent, 1791.

*Privacy and Surveillance**

Armer, Paul. *Social Implications of the Computer Utility.* Santa Monica, Calif.: Rand Corporation, 1967.
Brenton, Myron. *The Privacy Invaders.* New York: Fawcett, 1964.
Brown, R. M. *The Electronic Invasion.* New York: John F. Rider, 1967.
Chartrand, R. L. *Information Concerning the Proposed Federal Data Center.* Washington, D.C.: Library of Congress, 1966.
Cook, F. J. *The FBI Nobody Knows.* New York: Macmillan, 1964.
Dash, S., Knowlton, R. E., and Schwartz, R. F. *The Eavesdroppers.* New Brunswick: Rutgers University Press, 1959.
Ernst, M. L., and Schwartz, A. U. *Privacy: The Right to Be Let Alone.* New York: Macmillan, 1962.
Fanwick, Charles. *Maintaining Privacy of Computerized Data.* Santa Monica, Calif.: System Development Corporation, 1966.
Garrison, O. V. *Spy Government: The Emerging Police State in America.* New York: L. Stuart, 1967.
Hofstadtler, S. H., and Horowitz, G. *The Right of Privacy.* Brooklyn: Central Book Co., 1964.
Lamoreux, Stephen. *The Right of Privacy: A Bibliography.* Washington, D.C.: Pullman, 1962.
Long, E. V. *The Intruders: The Invasion of Privacy by Government and Industry.* New York: Praeger, 1967.
Lowi, T. J. *Private Life and Public Order.* New York: Norton, 1968.
Madgwick, Donald. *Privacy Under Attack.* London: National Council for Civil Liberties, 1968.
Marchetti, Victor, and Marks, John D. *The CIA and the Cult of Intelligence.* New York: Knopf, 1974.
Murphy, W. F. *Wiretapping on Trial.* New York: Random House, 1965.
Packard, Vance. *The Naked Society.* New York: McKay, 1964.
Rosenberg, J. M. *The Death of Privacy.* New York: Random House, 1969.
Shils, E. A. *The Torment of Secrecy.* Glencoe, Ill.: The Free Press, 1956.
Westin, Alan F. *Privacy and Freedom.* New York: Atheneum, 1967.
Westin, Alan F., and Baker, Michael A. *Databanks in a Free Society: Computers, Record-Keeping and Privacy.* New York: Quadrangle Books, 1972.
Wise, David. *The Politics of Lying: Government Deception, Secrecy and Power.* New York: Random House, 1973.
Zelermyer, William. *Invasion of Privacy.* Syracuse: Syracuse University Press, 1959.

* See also the reports and hearings of the 90th Congress, 1967–68, Washington, D.C.

COMMITTING YOURSELF ON RELIGION

III

A FTER CENTURIES OF verbal and physical warfare between religious factions, each of which was sincerely convinced of the truth of its beliefs, we have now come to experience widespread uncertainty about the truth of any and all religion. We may acknowledge the social and psychological value of religion as a cohesive force and a source of personal strength (although Marxists and Freudians regard it otherwise), but we wonder whether the term "God" refers to any real being and whether the elaborate theologies that have been constructed are not merely ingenious mythological systems. In short, we have come to seriously question the existence of that spiritual realm which religion claims to be the fundamental reality.

The reasons for the contemporary scepticism are various. In part it is due to the emphasis on science, which generally rejects religious assertions as contradicting scientific facts or as theoretically unverifiable, lying beyond the range of empirical tests. In either case, to the scientific mind religion falls in the category of superstition, and in the warfare between religion and a scientific world view it is religion that has continually retreated throughout history. Despite the attempts of theologians to show that science and religion do not conflict but operate on different levels, the scientific interpretation of reality has held sway. At best, the religious perspective is allowed as an additional interpretation of events, but usually it is excluded altogether, for the principle of parsimony (or Occam's Razor)[1] dictates that explanations should not be compounded beyond what is required. Thus the argument that God is ultimately responsible for DNA or electromagnetic force is considered superfluous and unacceptable.

The decline in religious belief is also due to a number of other factors of varying degrees of importance. For one thing, as people become better educated their faith tends to diminish, for religious belief varies inversely with education (which is not to say that there are no educated theists). This fact may be viewed as an indictment of religion, that it appeals mainly to ignorance, or as a criticism of modern education, that it leads people astray.

Another cause of disbelief is our current standard of living, which, in general, is quite high, for when people struggle to survive they are likely to be more religious than during times of prosperity. We seem to turn to God most often in times of trouble when, from a logical standpoint, there is the least evidence of a benevolent God existing; but psychological and logical requirements are often at variance.[2] In any case, we are not inclined to praise God for our current well-being.

---

[1] Named after William of Occam to whom it is (erroneously) attributed.
[2] Petitionary prayer is another case in point. When instances of success are few the hypothesis that "God provides" is logically weak, but on the psychological level, intermittent reinforcement is extremely strong, so that when prayers are answered infrequently, religious belief tends to be strengthened.

Still another cause is our concern with the present, rather than the distant future, which makes religion less appealing in its promise of a life to come and in its call for a certain self-denial in this life in order to achieve heaven hereafter. Perhaps we have reversed cause and effect here, and it is loss of belief in immortality that has resulted in our concentration on the here and now. Whichever the truth might be, without sufficient interest or belief in a future life religion is deprived of one of its main supports.

In addition, one could point to the incongruity many people feel between the modern age of nuclear reactors, supersonic jets, and space travel, and the traditional conception of God contained in Scripture; the way in which doctors, psychologists, and social workers have usurped the functions of priests, ministers, and rabbis; and the commonly observed fact that institutional religion has failed to meet the needs of contemporary man. With regard to the last point, religious institutions are in an impossible dilemma, for if they maintain their traditional articles of belief, they lose their followers by being anachronistic, and if they change with the times, they are accused of betraying basic principles in order to gain popularity. What this double-bind illustrates is that a rather inelastic structure is being applied to a rapidly changing society, and as a result considerable tension is generated for the believer.

All of these causes of disbelief are, strictly speaking, outside the province of philosophy, which is concerned with evaluating reasons rather than describing causes. However, on the philosophic level, religion has also been on the defensive as intellectual demands increased for the justification of its claims to truth. Unlike the scientist, most philosophers do not insist on empirical verification to support religious assertions, but they do ask for sound arguments that establish the alleged truths of religion. It simply will not do to protest that God is beyond logic and that transcendental reality surpasses all understanding, for on those grounds every absurd idea could be asserted as true. We must have some criterion for distinguishing between nonsense and good sense, otherwise the search for knowledge becomes futile. The presentation of good reasons, therefore, is necessary to substantiate belief in God and a spiritual reality. The case for religious belief need not be complete, and one can make a leap of faith from partial grounds, but not without any grounds.

There are three traditional arguments for the existence of God: the cosmological, the teleological, and the ontological; although each still claims its adherents, most philosophers and theologians have serious reservations about the validity of all three. Let us examine each in turn.

The cosmological argument generally carries the subtitle of "the argument from first cause," or, more properly, to first cause, and is one of the proofs of God's existence used by St Thomas Aquinas in his *Summa Theologica* (the teleological argument is another).[3] In the cosmological

[3] See Part One, Question II, Third Article, the famous "five ways" of St Thomas.

argument the point is stressed that the world is arranged in cause and effect sequences, so that for any event it is legitimate to ask "What was the cause?" But, the argument runs, the cause-effect chain cannot stretch back infinitely in time, with every cause the effect of some still prior cause. There had to be a first cause to the sequence, a cause that is itself uncaused, and this, of course, is God.

The argument gains its force from the idea that the world must have begun sometime and only God is sufficient to have created it. The child's question "Where did flowers come from?" leads us back to the primary source of life itself, the *primum mobile* (i.e., prime mover) ultimately responsible for producing the universe.

But we could ask why there had to be a beginning; why is an infinite regress of effects and causes impossible to contemplate? It seems entirely conceivable that the universe did not begin but always was, just as God is thought of as having existed eternally rather than beginning at some point in time. That is to say, if God is an exception to the rule that everything has a cause, then the universe may well be an exception too, and if there are no exceptions to the rule, then we can legitimately ask who or what caused God. Another way of stating the objection is that if God is outside the cause-effect network, then He cannot be considered to have caused it, and if He is within the causal system, He too must have been caused.[4]

Another criticism of the cosmological argument is that even if it were valid, it would not establish the existence of a God who sustains life and intervenes in human existence, but only of a God who started life initially. We might want to claim that the God who began the universe is also an active force in it, but that is not proven by the argument. At best, only the God of eighteenth-century deism is established—a God who does not interfere with the natural laws of the universe—not the immanent or all-pervasive being of theism.

To make matters worse, the first cause need not be a personal God, but could equally well be an abstract force or physical power. That is, even if there had to be a beginning to the universe (which is questionable), that initial movement could be accounted for in physical terms, for example by the so-called "big bang theory" of the explosion of the primal atom; we need not have reference to God for an explanation.

As a final objection, it has been charged that the cosmological argument is essentially an argument from ignorance, for its advocates are saying "How could the world have originated if God did not create it?" or "We do not know how the world originated, therefore it must be attributed to God." But all that can be concluded from "we do not know"

---

[4] Some philosophers have tried to rebut this criticism by distinguishing between God as "efficient cause," that is, the agent producing an effect, and the subsequent series of "instrumental causes," but we cannot pursue this point here. For further information, see F. Copleston, *A History of Philosophy*, Vol. II, Part II, Ch. 34.

is "we do not know," not "therefore God is responsible." It is doubtful that even the most zealous theologian would want to maintain an argument of this type, for not only is it invalid but the term 'God' is functioning as a word for the unknown; thus the more we know, the less often would we call on God. As science advanced, God would be edged out of the universe.

There is a more sophisticated version of the cosmological argument that should be mentioned since most Thomists[5] identify with it, although most of the criticisms mentioned above apply equally well. This version of the argument relies upon the concepts of contingency and necessity—both of which can be difficult to grasp.

When we say that the world is contingent, we mean that neither the world itself nor anything in the world can account for its own existence; the fact that it exists depends upon something else. For example, plants grow, flourish, and wither; rocks are formed, crumble, and become dust; people are born, mature, and die. There is nothing in the nature of any of these things that requires their continued existence or makes it necessary that they come into being; their existence or non-existence is contingent upon something else. But that which they are contingent upon does not carry the necessity for its own existence within itself; it too is contingent upon something else which, in turn, is contingent upon something further. Now, it is argued, we cannot go on forever explaining one thing in terms of another; eventually something must be assumed to exist by necessity, something that, by its very nature, must exist and does not depend upon anything else for its being. God is that necessarily existent entity on whom everything else in the universe depends.

The weak link in the argument, of course, is the assumption that the contingent implies the necessary when, in fact, everything could conceivably be contingent. Logicians today use the term "necessary" only in connection with a proposition that must logically follow from another; it is considered as illegitimately employed when applied to reality. However, a discussion of these objections would take us too far afield. It is sufficient to say that the contingency version of the cosmological proof suffers from many of the same weaknesses as the version stated in terms of first cause.[6]

The teleological argument is often referred to as the argument from design, and the Greek word *telos*, from which it is derived, means purpose, order, plan, design, or system. It is an argument from analogy and has been the most psychologically persuasive of all the alleged proofs.

The basis of the argument is that orderliness and regularity charac-

---

[5] Followers of the theology of St Thomas Aquinas (1225–1274).
[6] The second law of thermodynamics, the law of entropy, is also used in a version of the cosmological proof. The argument is that if energy is constantly being transformed and rendered unavailable, it must have been provided by a being initially; but the same criticisms apply, translated to this context.

terize our world, from the movements of the planets to the balance of
nature to the complex organization of the human body. Wherever we
look we are impressed with pattern, arrangement, and harmonious systems. The temperature fluctuations on earth are perfect for sustaining
life, and if the planet were closer to the sun or in a wider orbit away from
the sun we could not survive. The fauna and flora of the earth are edible
by human beings, and there is water to drink, natural fuels for warmth,
and building materials for shelter. Animals possess the exact equipment
that they need to exist: deer are camouflaged in their coloration so that
they escape detection in the forest; porcupines are equipped with sharp
quills and would be defenseless without them; giraffes need to feed off
of leaves at the tops of trees and have long necks that enable them to do
so; lions and tigers have the sharp teeth and claws that they need for a
carnivorous life. Man too is perfectly suited for survival by virtue of a
highly developed brain, and the systems of the body are astonishingly intricate and mutually integrated.

An endless number of illustrations exist, but the point is that orderliness cannot be denied, and if there is order there must be an orderer,
if design is present there must exist a designer. It would make no sense,
the argument runs, to assert that all of the arrangement we see came
about by chance; there had to be an intelligent mind behind everything
and a mind of cosmic scope. In short, God must be acknowledged to
exist from the undeniable evidence of order and design in the universe.
The famous analogy by the eighteenth-century philosopher William Paley
is that if we found a watch on an island, we would have to assume it was
made by a watchmaker; we would never presume that the parts came together accidentally in perfect combination. In the same way, when we
perceive the vast mechanism of the universe, we must infer a divine intelligence behind it.

The teleological argument makes a strong appeal to common sense,
nevertheless, certain basic flaws can be seen in the reasoning. The principal
objection turns on the Darwinian theory of evolution. We now know that
a gradual evolution of organisms took place over millions of years and
that there was not an instantaneous creation of species with their various
attributes. This evolutionary process operated in terms of natural selection,
whereby those creatures that were suited for survival were able to survive
and produce offspring and those creatures that did not possess the necessary equipment perished in the struggle for survival.

Thus it is not surprising that the creatures that exist possess the
means for survival; if they had not, they would not have continued to
exist. Many species did, in fact, become extinct along the road of evolution (which, incidentally, raises questions in itself about design), and the
surviving species naturally have the adaptations necessary for survival.

To be amazed, therefore, that creatures possess various necessary
qualities is to fail to appreciate the nature of evolution. It would be like

saying "Isn't it marvelous that all Olympic winners are good athletes" or "How miraculous that there are so many navigable rivers by large cities." If the athletes had not been good, they would not have won, and if the rivers were not navigable, the cities would never have arisen there. The same failure in logic is responsible for our being impressed with the balance of nature or with the position of the earth in relation to the sun, seeing these things as evidence of divine design.

In brief, there is a natural explanation for the regularity and orderliness that exists, and we need not have recourse to the supernatural in order to account for it. Natural selection does not rule out the possibility of inherent purpose in nature, but it renders such reasoning superfluous.

Another objection to the teleological argument is that, like the cosmological, it fails to give us the kind of God that we want to establish. Even if the argument were sound, it would only prove the existence of a God who designed the universe, not one who created it. As in the watchmaker analogy, we can only claim that some intelligent being arranged the materials in an orderly way so that the mechanism functioned well, but we cannot, on the strength of the teleological argument alone, claim that this being also created the materials. To establish the existence of a God who is both creator and sustainer of the universe, both the cosmological and the teleological arguments would have to be valid.

Several other criticisms may be briefly mentioned. Some philosophers (most notably the eighteenth-century philosopher David Hume) have pointed out that manifold natural evils exist in the world in the form of earthquakes, typhoons, volcanic eruptions, tidal waves, disease, sickness, and so forth, and they have argued that we cannot infer the existence of the traditional God of love from a plan of this character. Or if God is claimed to be the designer, then we are faced with the problem of explaining why He would include evil in the design.

It has also been charged that, in keeping with the analogy with human productions, it would be more likely that a number of gods designed the universe, rather than one; that there is as much empirical evidence of disorder as of order in the world; that the human machine is not perfectly designed for it continually breaks down; and that the universe resembles an organic growth rather than a mechanism for which there was a blueprint.

Because of all of these criticisms, particularly the first concerning evolution, the teleological argument is not generally considered to be valid.

The ontological argument is usually associated with St Anselm, although the seventeenth-century French philosopher René Descartes also employed it.[7] St Anselm argued that he had in his mind the idea of a

---

[7] See St Anselm's *Proslogium*, Chaps. II and III, and René Descartes' *Meditations on First Philosophy*, Meditation III. Versions of the ontological proof were also put forward by St Bonaventura, G. W. Leibniz, and G. W. F. Hegel.

being "than which nothing greater can be conceived," which is, of course, the supreme being God. It follows from this assertion (which no one can deny) that this being must possess the attributes of omnipotence, omniscience, eternality, omnipresence, absolute love, and so forth, since a being that lacked any of these properties would not be one "than which nothing greater can be conceived." This being would also have to possess the attribute of existence, since a being who had existence would be greater than one who lacked it. Or as St Anselm stated it, "if that, than which nothing greater can be conceived, exists in the understanding alone, the very being, than which nothing greater can be conceived, is one, than which a greater can be conceived." Therefore, from the idea of God we can infer His necessary existence.

A more modern way of phrasing the argument is to say that if we conceive of a perfect being (or one as nearly perfect as we can conceive), with all possible properties, that being would also have to exist because existence must be included as part of perfection. An allegedly perfect being that did not possess existence would not be perfect. Therefore, from the very idea of a perfect God we must conclude that God exists.

The logical defect in the ontological argument is the confusion between a concept and that to which it refers. The concept of a perfect God (or one than which nothing greater can be conceived) certainly must include the notion of existence or it would be incomplete *as a concept*, but that is not to say that the being referred to by the concept therefore exists.

Another way of stating the objection is to say, as the seventeenth-century German philosopher Immanuel Kant did, that existence is not an attribute along with omnipotence, omniscience, and so forth. Rather, when something is said to exist, it is being posited with its attributes. Therefore, existence cannot be tacked onto a list of God's properties in developing the concept of a perfect being. The fact that the concept of God includes the attribute of existence does not stand as proof of God's existence.

For these reasons, the ontological argument is generally rejected along with the teleological and cosmological.[8] There are other arguments for the existence of God, such as the claim that moral laws require a moral lawgiver, but they are relatively minor and do not stand up well to criticism either.

When faced with the failure of the traditional arguments of God's existence, theologians and philosophers respond in various ways. Some try to present the same arguments in more refined and sophisticated ways that avoid a certain number of the criticisms. Some insist on the logical point that the existence of God has not been disproven by the criticisms, but only the *arguments* for His existence have been shown to be faulty; there-

---

[8] There are philosophers of some sophistication who do defend the ontological argument, for example A. Plantinga and C. Hartshorn, but it has generally fallen into disrepute.

fore, faith can be maintained on other grounds, such as an immediate religious experience.

In the selections that follow, three additional (and major) responses are presented—responses both to the intellectual difficulties of religious belief just described and to the more general causes of disbelief sketched earlier.

First, many people, particularly the young, have sought an alternative to Western Protestantism, Catholicism, and Judaism in Eastern beliefs of various types. Alan Watts, in his selection "The Art of Feeling," effectively expresses the orientation and appeal of Eastern religion and contrasts it with the philosophic assumptions of the European tradition. D. T. Suzuki focuses on an exposition of one Eastern religion, Zen Buddhism, and explains its essential principles insofar as they are capable of conceptualization. Both Watts and Suzuki are leading interpreters of Eastern philosophy and religion.

Second, there has been a strong movement recently within Christianity to redefine the idea of God and to reinterpret the fundamentals of the faith. This response is represented by Paul Tillich and Dietrich Bonhoeffer in selections from their works. Both theologians are extremely influential (especially Tillich), and their writings offer an unconventional and contemporary view of Christianity.

Third, there is the response that "God is dead." This phrase can be taken to mean, at one extreme, that God does not exist and people must be mature enough to accept the fact and assume responsibility for their own existence. At the other extreme, it can be interpreted as a rallying cry that the archaic conception of (and language about) God is no longer credible and must be abandoned in order for us to reach the contemporary, living God. The selection by William Hamilton presents the latter view, and the essays by Ernest Nagel and Bertrand Russell deal with the former atheistic position. It should be noted that the "God is dead" theologians, such as J. J. Altizer, Mark van Buren, G. Vahanian, and William Hamilton, feel a much greater kinship with contemporary theism than with atheism.

After reading these selections and the foregoing analysis, the reader should be in a position to evaluate his or her own religious ideas and either reformulate them, abandon them, or achieve a deeper sense of their significance. Additional reading is strongly recommended for increased understanding of this issue. (See the bibliography at the end of this section.)

7

EASTERN BELIEFS

THE ART OF FEELING
Alan Watts

Alan Watts (1915–1973), British-born American philoso-pher who has been one of the major interpreters of Eastern religion to the West. Among his many books are The Spirit of Zen (1936), Behold the Spirit (1947), Nature, Man, and Woman (1958), Psychotherapy East and West (1961), *and* The Joyous Cosmology (1962).

The words which one might be tempted to use for a silent and wide-open mind are mostly terms of abuse—thoughtless, mindless, unthinking, empty-headed, and vague. Perhaps this is some measure of an innate fear of releasing the chronic cramp of consciousness by which we grasp the facts of life and manage the world. It is only to be expected that the idea of an awareness which is something other than sharp and selective fills us with considerable disquiet. We are perfectly sure that it would mean going back to the supposedly confused sensitivity of infants and animals, that we should be unable to distinguish up from down, and that we should certainly be run over by a car the first time we went out on the street.

Narrowed, serial consciousness, the memory-stored stream of impres-sions, is the means by which we have the sense of ego. It enables us to feel that behind thought there is a thinker and behind knowledge a knower—an individual who stands aside from the changing panorama of experience to order and control it as best he may. If the ego were to disappear, or rather, to be seen as a useful fiction, there would no longer be the duality of subject and object, experiencer and experience. There would simply be a continuous, self-moving stream of experiencing, without the sense either of an active subject who controls it or of a passive subject who suffers it. The thinker would be seen to be no more than the series of thoughts, and the feeler no more than the feelings. As Hume said in the *Treatise of Human Nature*:

> For my part, when I enter most intimately into what I call *myself*, I always stumble on some particular perception or other, of heat or cold, light or shade, love or hatred, pain or pleasure. I never can catch *myself* at any time without a perception, and never can observe any thing but the perception. . . . [We are] nothing but a bundle or collection of different perceptions, which succeed each other with an inconceivable rapidity, and are in a perpetual flux and movement.[1]

Now this is just what we fear—the loss of human identity and integrity in a transient stream of atoms. Hume, arguing against the notion of the self as a metaphysical or mental substance, had of course no alternative conception other than the "bundle or collection" of intrinsically separate perceptions, for he was translating his experience into the disjointed terms of linear thought. He maintained that all our impressions are "different, and distinguishable, and separable from each other, and may be separately consider'd, and may exist separately, and have no need of any thing to support their existence." Having seen the fiction of the separate ego-substance, he failed to see the fiction of separate things or perceptions which the ego, as a mode of awareness, abstracts from nature. As we have seen, inherently separate things can be ordered only mechanically or politically, so that without a real ego in which impressions are integrated and ordered, human experience is delivered over to mechanism or chaos.

If the world of nature is neither things seen by an ego nor things, some of which are sensations, bundled mechanically together, but a field of "organic" relations, there is no need to fear that disorder is the only alternative to political order or to mechanism. The stream of human experience would then be ordered neither by a transcendental ego nor by a transcendental God but by itself. Yet this is what we usually mean by a mechanical or automatic order, since the machine is what "goes by itself." We have seen, however, that there is a profound difference of operation between organism and mechanism. An organism can be represented in terms of a mechanical model just as "formless" shapes can be approximated by geometric models and as the movements of the stars can be translated into the figures in an almanac. But as the celestial bodies are other than and infinitely more than numerical relations and schedules, organisms and natural forms must never be confused with their mechanical representations.

Once again, because the order of thought is a linear, bit-by-bit series, it can approximate but never comprehend a system of relations in which everything is happening simultaneously. It would be as if our narrowed

[1] Hume (1), p. 252.

consciousness had to take charge of all the operations of the body so that, unless it took thought of them, the glands and nerves and arteries could not do their work. As language, both written and spoken, so eloquently shows, the order of thought must be strung out in a line. But nature is not strung out in a line. Nature is, at the very least, a volume, and at most an infinitely dimensioned field. We need, then, another conception of natural order than the logical, than the order of the Logos or word based on bit-by-bit awareness.

As Needham has shown, Chinese philosophy provides this in the Neo-Confucian (and Buddhist) conception of *li*, for which there has been no better English equivalent than "principle." *Li* is the universal principle of order, but in this case the principle or principles cannot be stated in terms of law (*tse*). The root meaning of *li* is the markings in jade, the grain in wood, or the fiber in muscle. The root meaning of *tse* is the writing of imperial laws upon sacrificial caldrons.[2] Now the markings in jade are "formless." That is to say, they are unsymmetrical, fluid, and intricate patterns which appeal highly to the Chinese sense of beauty. Thus when it is said that the Tao has "no shape"[3] we are not to imagine a uniform blank so much as a pattern without clearly discernible features, in other words, just exactly what the Chinese painter admires in rocks and clouds, and what he sometimes conveys in the texture of black ink applied with bold strokes of a rather dry brush. In the words of the *Huai Nan Tzu*:

> The Tao of Heaven operates mysteriously and secretly; it has no fixed shape; it follows no definite rules (*tse*); it is so great that you can never come to the end of it; it is so deep that you can never fathom it.[4]

At the same time the order of the Tao is not so inscrutable that man can see it only as confusion. When the artist handles his material, perfection consists in knowing how to follow its nature, how to follow the grain in carving wood, and how to employ the sound-textures of various musical instruments. The nature of the material is precisely *li*. He discovers it, however, not by logical analysis but by *kuan*,[5] to which we have already referred as "silent contemplation," or looking at nature without *thinking* in the sense of narrowed attention. Speaking of the hexagram *kuan* in the *Book of Changes*, Wang Pi writes:

> The general meaning of the *tao* of "Kuan" is that one should not govern by means of punishments and legal pressure, but by looking forth

---

[2] For the characters see Mathews' *Chinese-English Dictionary* 3864 (*li*) and 6746 (*tse*). For the original forms, see Karlgren's *Grammata Serica* 978 and 906. Since the Romanized forms of Chinese words give little clue to the actual written term, we shall hereinafter identify Chinese terms with their numbers in the Mathews *Dictionary*, e.g., M 3864.
[3] *Yung*, M 7560.
[4] *Huai Nan Tzu*, 9. Tr. Needham (1), vol. 2, p. 561.
[5] M 3575.

one should exert one's influence so as to change all things. Spiritual power can no man see. We do not see Heaven command the four seasons, and yet they never swerve from their course. So also we do not see the sage ordering people about, and yet they obey and spontaneously serve him.[6]

The point is that things are brought into order through regarding them from a viewpoint unrestricted by the ego, since their *li* or pattern cannot be observed while looking and thinking piecemeal, nor when regarding them as objects apart from oneself, the subject. The Chinese character for *kuan* shows the radical sign for "seeing" beside a bird which is probably a heron, and although Needham feels that it may originally have had something to do with watching the flight of birds for omens, I am inclined to think that the root idea was taken from the way in which a heron stands stock-still at the edge of a pool, gazing into the water. It does not seem to be looking *for* fish, and yet the moment a fish moves it dives. *Kuan* is, then, simply to observe silently, openly, and without seeking any particular result. It signifies a mode of observation in which there is no duality of seer and seen: there is simply the seeing. Watching thus, the heron is all pool.

In some respects this is what we mean by *feeling*, as when one learns to dance by watching and "getting the feel of it" rather than following a diagram of the steps. Similarly the bowler in cricket or the pitcher in baseball develops his skill by "feel" rather than by studying precise technical directions. So, too, it is by feeling that the musician distinguishes the styles of composers, that the wine taster identifies vintages, that the painter determines compositional proportions, that the farmer foretells the weather, and that the potter throws and shapes his clay. Up to a point these arts have communicable rules, but there is always something indefinable which distinguishes true mastery: As the wheelwright says in the *Chuang-tzu*:

> Let me take an illustration from my own trade. In making a wheel, if you work too slowly, you can't make it firm; if you work too fast, the spokes won't fit in. You must go neither too slowly nor too fast. There must be co-ordination of mind and hand. Words cannot explain what it is, but there is some mysterious art herein. I cannot teach it to my son; nor can he learn it from me. Consequently, though seventy years of age, I am still making wheels in my old age.[7]

Analytically studied, these skills appear at first sight to be the result of "unconscious thinking," the brain acting as an extremely complex electronic computer which delivers its results to the consciousness. In other words, they are the consequence of a thinking process which differs merely in quantity from conscious thought: it is faster and more complex.

[6] Tr. Needham (1), vol. 2, pp. 561–62.
[7] H. A. Giles (1), p. 171.

But this tells us not so much about what the brain does as about the way in which it has been studied and the model to which it has been approximated. The brain may be represented in terms of quantitative measurement, but it does not follow that it works in these terms. On the contrary, it does not work in terms at all, and for this reason can respond intelligently to relations which can be termed only approximately, slowly, and laboriously.

But if we pursue the question, "How, then, does feeling work?" recognizing that an answer in terms is no answer, we shall have to say that it works as it feels from the inside, in the same way that we feel how to move our legs. We easily forget that this is a more intimate knowledge of our nature than objective description, which is of necessity superficial, being knowledge of surfaces. Thus it is of relatively little use to the scientist to know, in terms, how his brain operates, for in practice he gets his best results when he resorts to feeling or intuition, when his research is a kind of puttering without any specific result in mind. He must, of course, have a knowledge of terms which will enable him to recognize a result when he sees it. But these enable him to communicate the result to himself and to others; they do not supply the result any more than the dictionary and the rules of prosody supply the poet with poetry. *Kuan* as feeling without seeking, or open awareness, is therefore as essential to the scientist, for all his analytic rigor, as to the poet. The attitude is marvellously described by Lin Ching-hsi in his *Poetical Remains of the Old Gentleman of Chi Mountain* as follows:

> Scholars of old time said that the mind is originally empty, and only because of this can it respond [resonate][8] to natural things without prejudices (lit. traces, *chi*,[9] left behind to influence later vision). Only the empty mind can respond to the things of Nature. Though everything resonates with the mind, the mind should be as if it had never resonated, and things should not remain in it. But once the mind has received (impressions of) natural things, they tend to remain and not to disappear, thus leaving traces in the mind. It should be like a river gorge with swans flying overhead; the river has no desire to retain the swan, yet the swan's passage is traced out by its shadow without any omission. Take another example. All things, whether beautiful or ugly, are reflected perfectly in a mirror; it never refuses to show anything, nor retains anything afterwards.[10]

Kuan is no more a mind that is merely empty than *li*, the pattern of the Tao, is a featureless blank. Indeed, *kuan* is not so much a mind empty of contents as a mind empty of mind. It is mind or "experiencing" at work

___

[8] *Ying*, M 7477. Needham points out that this is the technical term for "resonance," an idea basic to the Chinese philosophy of the relations between events, derived from the *Book of Changes*. Cf. Eckhart, "If my eye is to discern color, it must itself be free from color."

[9] M 502. Also "effects" or "searching out."

[10] *Chi Shan Chi*, 4. Tr. Needham (1), vol. 2, p. 89.

without the sense of the seeking and staring subject, for the sensation of the ego is the sensation of a kind of effort of consciousness, of a confusion of nerves with muscles. But as glaring and staring do not clarify the eyesight, and as straining to hear does not sharpen the ears, mental "trying" does not enhance understanding. Nevertheless the mind is constantly making efforts to fight off the sense of boredom or depression, to stop being afraid, to get the most out of a pleasure, or to compel itself to be loving, attentive, patient, or happy. On being told that this is wrong, the mind will even make efforts not to make efforts. This can come to an end only as it is clearly seen that all these efforts are as futile as trying to leap into the air and fly, as struggling to sleep, or as forcing an erection of the sexual member. Everyone is familiar with the contradiction of trying to recollect a forgotten name, and though it happens again and again, we never seem to trust the memory to supply the information spontaneously. Yet this is one of the most common forms of what is known in Zen Buddhism as *satori*—the effortless, spontaneous, and sudden dawning of a realization. The difficulty is of course that the mind strains itself by force of habit, and that until it loses the habit it must be watched—gently—all the time.[11]

In saying that the ego is a sensation of mental strain, we must not overlook the fact that the words "ego" and "I" are sometimes used simply to denote *this* organism as distinct from its soul or from one of its psychological functions. In this sense, of course, "I" does not necessarily denote a state of strain or a psychological excrescence. But the sensation of the ego as a part function of the whole organism, or rather, as an inner entity which owns and inhabits the organism, is the result of an excess of activity in the use of the senses and of certain muscles. This is the habit of using more energy than is necessary to think, see, hear, or make decisions. Thus even when lying flat on the floor most people will continue to make totally needless muscular efforts to retain their position, almost as if they were afraid of the organism losing its shape and dissolving into a jelly. All this

[11] The habitual straining of the mind can be relaxed temporarily by the use of certain drugs, such as alcohol, mescalin, and lysergic acid. Whereas alcohol dulls the clarity of awareness, mescalin and lysergic acid do not. Consequently these two, and sometimes also nitrous oxide and carbon dioxide, will induce states of consciousness in which the individual feels his relational identity with the whole realm of nature. Although these states appear to be similar to those realized through more "natural" means, they differ in the sense that being able to swim with a life jacket differs from swimming unaided. From personal, though limited, experimentation with a research group working with lysergic acid, I would judge that the state of consciousness induced is confused with a mystical state because of similarities of language used in describing the two. The experience is multidimensional, as if everything were inside, or implied, everything else, requiring a description which is paradoxical from the standpoint of ordinary logic. But whereas the drug gives a vision of nature which is infinitely complex, the mystical state is clarifying, and gives a vision which is as infinitely simple. The drug seems to give the intelligence a kaleidoscopic quality which "patterns" the perception of relations in accordance with its own peculiar structure.

arises from anxiety acquired in learning control and co-ordination, for under social pressure the child tries to speed up his neural skills by sheer muscle-power.

For all that has been said, we are so convinced of the necessity of mental strain that the dropping of the habit will hardly be acceptable until certain theoretical objections are answered. The "mental strain" deplored by conventional psychology is, of course, highly excessive strain, but it is not generally recognized that there is a contradiction in mental strain as such and in any degree. The two principal objections are, I think, firstly, that an absence of strain would encourage a view of the world characterized by mystical and pantheistic vagueness which is both demoralizing and uncritical; and, secondly, that since mental strain is essential to any self-control, its absence will result in being completely swept away by one's feelings.

In theological circles "pantheism" has long been a definitively damning label, and those who like their religious and philosophical opinions to be robust and definite are also inclined to use the word "mysticism" with the same kind of opprobrium. They associate it with "mist," with vagueness, with clouding of issues and blurring of distinctions. Therefore from this standpoint nothing could be more ghastly than "mystical pantheism" or "pantheistic nature mysticism," which is just what the attitude of *kuan* appears to produce. However much the contrary may be pointed out, such people continue to insist that Taoist and Buddhist mysticism reduces the interesting and significant distinctions of the world to a miasma of uniform oneness.[12] I am God, you are God, everything is God, and God is a boundless and featureless sea of dimly conscious tapioca pudding. The mystic is thus a feeble-minded fellow who finds in this boring "undifferentiated aesthetic continuum" (Northrop) a source of enthusiasm, because, somehow or other, it unifies the conflicts and evils of the world into a transcendental Goodness.

While this is obviously an ignorant caricature, there is something to be said in defense of philosophical vagueness. Strangely assorted people join forces in making fun of it—Logical Positivists and Catholic Neo-Thomists, Dialectical Materialists and Protestant Neo-Orthodoxists, Behaviorists and Fundamentalists. Despite intense differences of opinion among themselves, they belong to a psychological type which takes special glee in having one's philosophy of life clear-cut, hard, and rigid. They range from the kind of scientist who likes to lick his tongue around the

---

[12] In my *Supreme Identity* I put forward a view of the Vedanta which very carefully explained its difference from pantheism and from all those types of "acosmistic" mysticism which seem to idealize the complete disappearance of the natural world from consciousness. Nevertheless, it was criticized by Reinhold Niebuhr in *The Nation* for advocating exactly those views which it opposed, an interesting example of the fact that Christian polemicists spend a good deal of energy attacking points of view which exist only in their own minds.

notion of "brute" facts to the kind of religionist who fondles a system of "unequivocal dogma." There is doubtless a deep sense of security in being able to say, "The clear and authoritative teaching of the Church is . . . ," or to feel that one has mastered a logical method which can tear other opinions, and especially metaphysical opinions, to shreds. Attitudes of this kind usually go together with a somewhat aggressive and hostile type of personality which employs sharp definition like the edge of a sword. There is more in this than a metaphor, for, as we have seen, the laws and hypotheses of science are not so much discoveries as instruments, like knives and hammers, for bending nature to one's will. So there is a type of personality which approaches the world with an entire armory of sharp and hard instruments, by means of which it slices and sorts the universe into precise and sterile categories which will not interfere with one's peace of mind.

There is a place in life for a sharp knife, but there is a still more important place for other kinds of contact with the world. Man is not to be an intellectual porcupine, meeting his environment with a surface of spikes. Man meets the world outside with a soft skin, with a delicate eyeball and eardrum, and finds communion with it through a warm, melting, vaguely defined, and caressing touch whereby the world is not set at a distance like an enemy to be shot, but embraced to become one flesh, like a beloved wife. After all, the whole possibility of clear knowledge depends upon sensitive organs which, as it were, bring the outside world into our bodies, and give us knowledge of that world precisely in the form of our own bodily states.

Hence the importance of opinions, of instruments of the mind, which are vague, misty, and melting rather than clear-cut. They provide possibilities of communication, of actual contact and relationship with nature more intimate than anything to be found by preserving at all costs the "distance of objectivity." As Chinese and Japanese painters have so well understood, there are landscapes which are best viewed through half-closed eyes, mountains which are most alluring when partially veiled in mist, and waters which are most profound when the horizon is lost, and they are merged with the sky.

> Through the evening mist a lone goose is flying;
> Of one tone are wide waters and sky.

Or consider Po Chü-i's lines on "Walking at Night in Fine Rain," translated, I think, by Arthur Waley:

> Autumn clouds, vague and obscure;
> The evening, lonely and chill.
> I felt the dampness on my garments,
> But saw no spot, and heard no sound of rain.

Or Lin Yutang's version of Chia Tao's "Searching for the Hermit in Vain":

> *I asked the boy beneath the pines.*
> *He said, "The Master's gone alone.*
> *Herb-picking somewhere on the mount,*
> *Cloud-hidden, whereabouts unknown."*

Images of a rather similar mood are strung together by Seami when he tries to suggest what the Japanese mean by *yugen*, a subtle order of beauty whose origin is dark and obscure: "To watch the sun sink behind a flower-clad hill, to wander on and on in a huge forest with no thought of return, to stand on the shore and gaze after a boat that goes hid by far-off islands, to ponder on the journey of wild geese seen and lost among the clouds."[13] But there is a kind of brash mental healthiness ever ready to rush in and clean up the mystery, to find out just precisely where the wild geese have gone, what herbs the master is picking and where, and that sees the true face of a landscape only in the harsh light of the noonday sun. It is just this attitude which every traditional culture finds utterly insufferable in Western man, not just because it is tactless and unrefined, but because it is blind. It cannot tell the difference between the surface and the depth. It seeks the depth by cutting into the surface. But the depth is known only when it reveals itself, and ever withdraws from the probing mind. In the words of Chuang-tzu:

> Things are produced around us, but no one knows the whence. They issue forth, but no one sees the portal. Men one and all value that part of knowledge which is known. They do not know how to avail themselves of the unknown in order to reach knowledge. Is not this misguided?[14]

We fail so easily to see the difference between fear of the unknown and respect for the unknown, thinking that those who do not hasten in with bright lights and knives are deterred by a holy and superstitious fear. Respect for the unknown is the attitude of those who, instead of raping nature, woo her until she gives herself. But what she gives, even then, is not the cold clarity of the surface but the warm inwardness of the body—a mysteriousness which is not merely a negation, a blank absence of knowledge, but that positive substance which we call wonderful.

> "The highest that man can attain in these matters," said Goethe, "is wonder; if the primary phenomenon causes this, let him be satisfied; more it cannot bring; and he should forbear to seek for anything further behind it: here is the limit. But the sight of a prime phenomenon is

[13] Waley (1), pp. 21–22.
[14] H. A. Giles (1), p. 345.

generally not enough for people. They think they must go still further; and are thus like children, who, after peeping into a mirror, turn it round directly to see what is on the other side."[15]

For as Whitehead said:

> When you understand all about the sun and all about the atmosphere and all about the rotation of the earth, you may still miss the radiance of the sunset. There is no substitute for the direct perception [*kuan*] of the concrete achievement of a thing in its actuality.[16]

This is, surely, a true materialism, or perhaps it would be better to say a true substantialism, since matter is really cognate to "meter" and properly designates not the reality of nature but nature in terms of measures. And "substance" in this sense would not be the gross notion of "stuff," but what is conveyed by the Chinese *t'i*[17]—the wholeness, the *Gestalt*, the complete field of relations, which escapes every linear description.

The natural world therefore reveals its content, its fullness of wonder, when respect hinders us from investigating it in such a way as to shatter it to abstractions. If I *must* cross every skyline to find out what is beyond, I shall never appreciate the true depth of sky seen between trees upon the ridge of a hill. If I must map the canyons and count the trees, I shall never enter into the sound of a hidden waterfall. If I must explore and investigate every trail, that path which vanishes into the forest far up on the mountainside will be found at last to lead merely back to the suburbs. To the mind which pursues every road to its end, every road leads nowhere. To abstain is not to postpone the cold disillusionment of the true facts but to see that one arrives by staying rather than going, that to be forever looking beyond is to remain blind to what is here.

To know nature, the Tao, and the "substance" of things, we must know it as, in the archaic sense, a man "knows" a woman—in the warm vagueness of immediate contact. As the *Cloud of Unknowing* says of God, "By love he may be gotten and holden, but by thought never." This implies, too, that it is also mistaken to think of it as *actually* vague, like mist or diffused light or tapioca pudding. The image of vagueness implies that to know nature, outside ourselves as within, we must abandon every idea, every thought and opinion, of what it is—and look. If we must have some idea of it, it must be the most vague imaginable, which is why, even for Westerners, such formless conceptions as the Tao are to be preferred to the idea of God, with its all too definite associations.

The danger of the "pantheistic" and mystical attitude to nature is, of course, that it may become exclusive and one-sided, though there seem to be few historical instances of this. There is no real reason why it should

---

[15] Eckermann (1). February 18th, 1829.
[16] Whitehead (1), p. 248.
[17] M 6246.

become so, for its advantage is precisely that it gives us a formless background against which the forms of everyday, practical problems may be
seen more clearly. When our idea of the background, of God, is highly
formal, practical conduct is as tortuous as trying to write upon a printed
page. Issues cannot be seen clearly because it is not seen that matters of
right and wrong are like the rules of grammar—conventions of communication. By grounding right and wrong in the Absolute, in the background,
not only do the rules become too rigid, but they are also sanctioned by too
weighty an authority. As a Chinese proverb says, "Do not swat a fly upon
your friend's head with a hatchet." By grounding the rules of action in
God, the West has not succeeded in fostering any unusual degree of
morality. On the contrary, it has invited just those violent ideological
revolutions against intolerable authority which are so characteristic of its
history. The same would apply to a rigid scientific dogma as to what is
natural and what is not.

In practice a mysticism which avoids all rigid formulations of both
nature and God has usually been favorable to the growth of science.[18] For
its attitude is empirical, emphasizing concrete experience rather than
theoretical construction or belief, and its frame of mind is contemplative
and receptive. It is unfavorable to science to the degree that science confuses abstract models with nature, and to the degree that science, as technology, interferes with nature myopically, or upon the basis of prescientific
views of man from which it has not recovered. Furthermore, it provides a
basis for action which is not a cumbersome linear and legal view either of
God's will or of laws of nature based on an accumulation of *past* experiment.

The attitude of *kuan* is peculiarly sensitive to the conditions of the
immediate moment in all their changeful interrelatedness, and, as we have
seen, one of the difficulties of scientific knowledge is that its linear complexity makes it hard to apply to swift decisions, especially when "circumstances alter cases." Thus in discussing the secrets of successful drama
Seami wrote:

> If you look deeply into the ultimate essentials of this art, you will
> find that what is called "the flower" [of *yugen*] has no separate existence.
> Were it not for the spectator who reads into the performance a thousand
> excellences, there would be no "flower" at all. The Sutra says, "Good and
> ill are one; villainy and honesty are of like kind." Indeed, what standard
> have we whereby to discern good from bad? We can only take what suits
> the need of the moment and call it good."[19]

Such an attitude would be short-sighted indeed if it were based on the
linear and punctive view of the moment, where each "thing" is not seen

[18] On which see Needham (1), vol. 2, pp. 89–98.
[19] Waley (1), p. 22.

in its relation to the whole.[20] For example, those whom we hate most violently are often those we love most deeply, and if we are insensitive to this interrelation we may confuse the part feeling with the whole, and destroy someone we love or marry someone we are going to hate.

This brings us, then, to the second theoretical objection: that the mental strain of the controlling ego is necessary if we are not to be carried away by naturally undisciplined feelings and emotions. The objection is, once again, based on a political instead of an organic view of human nature. Human psychology is seen as composed of separate parts, functions, or faculties, as if the Lord God had made him by grafting the soul of an angel to the body of an animal. Man is then conceived as a collection of powers, urges, and appetites to be governed by the ego-soul. It is obvious at once that this view has had a profound influence upon modern psychology, which, though advising the ego to govern with kindness rather than violence, still treats it as the responsible boss.

But if we think of the total course of a man's experience, inner and outer, together with its unconscious psychophysical bases, as a system regulated organically, the principle of control must be entirely different.

> Joy and anger, sorrow and happiness, caution and remorse, come upon us by turns, with ever-changing mood. They come like music from hollows (in wood, when played upon by the wind), or like mushrooms from the damp. Daily and nightly they alternate within us, but we cannot tell whence they spring. . . .
> But for these emotions I should not be. But for me, they would have no scope. So far we can go: but we do not know what it is that brings them into play. If there is really a governor [*tsai*, M 6655], we find no evidence of its being. One could believe that it might be active, but we do not see its form. It would have to have feeling without form.
> The hundred bones, the nine orifices, and the six internal organs are all complete in their places. Which of them should one prefer? Do we like them all equally, or some more than others? Are they all the servants [of another]? Are these servants unable to govern one another mutually, or do they take the parts of ruler and servant alternately?[21]

Taking up this theme in his commentary on Chuang-tzu, Kuo Hsiang says:

[20] An excellent example of sensitivity to the moment is found in the application of Zen to *kendo*, or swordsmanship. No amount of drilled-in rules or reflexes can prepare the swordsman for the infinity of different attacks which he may have to face, especially when confronted with more than one opponent. He is taught, therefore, never to make any specific preparation for attack nor to expect it from any particular direction. Otherwise, to meet an unusual attack he will have to retreat from one stance before being able to adopt another. He must be able to spring immediately from a relaxed center of rest to the direction required. This relaxed openness of sensitivity in every direction is precisely *kuan*, or, as it is more commonly called in Zen, *mushin*, which is to say no "mind," no strain of the mind to watch for a particular result.

[21] *Chuang-tzu*, ii. Cf. H. A. Giles (1), p. 14, Lin Yutang (2), p. 235, and Needham (1), vol. 2, p. 52.

The hands and feet differ in their duties; the five internal organs differ in their functions. They never associate with one another, yet the hundred parts (of the body) are held together by them in a common unity. This is the way in which they associate through non-association. They never (deliberately) cooperate, and yet, both internally and externally, all complete one another. This is the way in which they cooperate through non-cooperation.[22]

In other words, all parts of the organism regulate themselves spontaneously (*tzu-jan*), and their order is confused when the changing panorama of feelings seems to be confronted by a controlling ego, which attempts to retain the positive (*yang*) and to reject the negative (*yin*).

According to Taoist philosophy, it is just this attempt to regulate the psyche from outside and to wrest the positive from the negative which is at the root of all social and moral confusion. What needs, then, to be controlled is not so much the spontaneous flow of human passions as the ego which exploits them—in other words, the controller itself. This has likewise been evident to such highly perceptive Christians as St. Augustine and Martin Luther, who realized so keenly that mere *self*-control was in no sense a remedy for the ills of man since it was precisely in the self that evil had taken its root. But they never abandoned the political idea of control, since their solution was to have the self empowered and regenerated by the grace of God—the ego of the universe. They did not see that the difficulty lay, not in the good or ill will of the controller, but in the whole rationale of control which they were attempting to use. They did not realize that the problem for God was the same as the problem for the human ego. For even God's universe had spawned the Devil, who arises not so much from his own independent malice as from God's "arrogance" in assuming omnipotent kingship and identifying himself with unalloyed goodness. The Devil is God's unconsciously produced shadow. Naturally, God is not allowed to be responsible for the origin of evil, for the connection between the two lies in the unconscious. Man says, "I didn't mean to hurt you, but my temper got the better of me. I shall try to control it in future." And God says, "I didn't mean there to be any evil, but my angel Lucifer brought it up of his own free will. In the future I will shut him up safely in hell."[23]

A problem of evil arises as soon as there is a problem of good, that is, as soon as there is any thought of what may be done to make the present situation "better," under whatever nomenclature the idea may be concealed. Taoist philosophy may easily be misunderstood as saying that it is better to let an organic system regulate itself than to meddle in it from without, and better to recognize that good and evil are correlative than to wrest the one from the other. And yet Chuang-tzu says plainly:

[22] *Chuang-tzu Chu, iii,* 25. Tr. Bodde in Fung Yu-lan (1), vol. 2, p. 211.
[23] For a fuller discussion of this theme see Jung (1), and Watts (2), ch. 2.

> Those who would have right without its correlative, wrong; or good government without its correlative, misrule,—they do not apprehend the great principles of the universe nor the conditions to which all creation is subject. One might as well talk of the existence of heaven without that of earth, or of the negative principle without the positive, which is clearly absurd. Such people, if they do not yield to argument, must be either fools or knaves.[24] *xvii*

Yet, if this be true, must there not be fools and knaves as the correlatives of sages and saints, and does not the fallacy attacked simply reappear in the attack?

If the positive and the negative, the good and the evil, are indeed correlative, no course of action can be recommended, including even the course of inaction. Nothing will make anything better which will not also make it worse. But this is exactly the predicament of the human ego as Taoist philosophy sees it. It is always wanting to control its situation so as to improve it, but neither action nor, with the motive of improvement, inaction will succeed. Recognizing the trap in which it finds itself, the mind has no alternative but to surrender that "straining after the good" which constitutes the ego. It does not surrender cunningly, with the thought that this will make things better. It surrenders unconditionally— not because it is good to do nothing, but because nothing can be done. All at once there descends upon it, quite spontaneously, a profound and completely uncontrived stillness—a quietude that envelops the world like the first fall of heavy snow, or like a windless afternoon in the mountains, where silence makes itself known in the undisturbed hum of insects in the grass.

In this stillness there is no sense of passivity, of submitting to necessity, for there is no longer any differentiation between the mind and its experience. All acts, one's own and others', seem to be happening freely from a single source. Life keeps moving on, and yet remains profoundly rooted in the present, seeking no result, for the present has spread out from its constriction in an elusive pin-point of strained consciousness to an all-embracing eternity. Feelings both positive and negative come and go without turmoil, for they seem to be simply observed, though there is no one observing. They pass trackless like birds in the sky, and build up no resistances which have to be dissipated in reckless action.

Clearly this state is, in retrospect, "better" than the seeking and staring strain of the mind which came before. But its goodness is of another order. Because it came unsought, it is not the kind of goodness which is in relation to evil, not the fantasy of peace which is conceived in the midst of turmoil. Furthermore, since nothing is done to retain it, it is not in relation to the memory of the former state, which otherwise would move one to fortify and protect it against change. For now there is no one left to

[24] H. A. Giles (1), pp. 207–8.

build the fortifications. Memories rise and fall like other feelings, ordered perhaps better than before, but no longer congealing around an ego to build its illusion of continued identity.

From this standpoint it can be seen that intelligence is not a separate, ordering faculty of the mind, but a characteristic of the whole organism-environment relationship, the field of forces wherein lies the reality of a human being. For as Macneile Dixon said in his *Human Situation*, "Tangible and visible things are but the poles, or terminations of these fields of unperceived energy. Matter, if it exists at all in any sense, is a sleeping partner in the firm of Nature." Between subject and object, organism and environment, *yang* and *yin*, is the balancing or homeostatic relationship called Tao—intelligent not because it has an ego but because it has *li*, organic pattern. The spontaneous flow of feeling, rising and falling in its mood, is an essential part of this balancing process, and is not, then, to be regarded as the disordered play of blind passions. Thus it is said that Lieh-tzu attained the Tao by "letting the events of the heart go just as they liked."[25] As a good sailor gives himself to the motion of a ship and does not fight it with his stomach muscles, the man of Tao gives himself to the motion of his moods.

Surprisingly, perhaps, this is not at all the same thing as is ordinarily meant by "giving in to one's feelings"—always a symptom of resistance rather than "give." For when we think about our feelings we tend to represent them as fixed states. Such words as anger, depression, fear, grief, anxiety, and guilt suggest uniform states which tend to persist if no action is taken to change or release them. As fever was once considered a disease instead of a natural healing process, we still think of negative feelings as disorders of the mind which need to be cured. But what needs to be cured is the inner resistance to those feelings which moves us to dissipate them in precipitate action. To resist the feeling is to be unable to contain it long enough for it to work itself out. Anger, for example, is not a fixed state but a motion, and unless compressed by resistance into unusual violence, like boiling water in a sealed vessel, it will adjust itself spontaneously. For anger is not a separate, autonomous demon rushing up from time to time from his quarters in the unconscious. Anger is simply a direction or pattern of psychic action. There is thus no anger; there is only acting angrily, or feeling angrily. Anger is feeling in motion to some other "state," for as Lao-tzu said:

> A swishing wind does not outlast the morning; pelting rain does not outlast the day. Who makes these things but heaven and earth? If heaven and earth cannot maintain them for long, how can man? *xxiii*

[25] *Lieh-tzu*, 2. L. Giles (1), p. 41, translates this passage, "my mind (*hsin*) gave free rein to its reflections (*nien*)," but this is rather too intellectual since *hsin* (M 2735) is not so much the thinking mind as the totality of psychic functioning, conscious and unconscious, and *nien* (M 4716) is not so much cortical thought as any event of psychic experience.

To give free rein to the course of feeling is therefore to observe it without interference, recognizing that because feeling is motion it is not to be understood in terms which imply not only static states but judgments of good and bad. Watched without naming, feelings become simply neuro-muscular tensions and changes, palpitations and pressures, tinglings and twitchings, of enormous subtlety and interest. This is, however, not quite the same thing as the psychotherapeutic gambit of "accepting" negative feelings *in order* to change them, that is, with the intention of effecting a shift of the whole tone of feeling in the direction of the positive and "good." "Acceptance" of this kind still implies the ego, standing apart from the immediate feeling or experience, and waiting for it to change—however patiently and submissively.

So long as the sense of the observing subject remains, there is the effort, however indirect, to control feeling from the outside, which is resistance setting up turmoil in the stream. Resistance disappears and the balancing process comes into full effect not by intention on the part of the subject, but only as it is seen that the feeling of being the subject, the ego, is itself part of the stream of experience and does not stand outside it in a controlling position. In the words of Chuang-tzu:

> Only the truly intelligent understand this principle of the identity of all things. They do not view things as apprehended by themselves, subjectively, but transfer themselves into the position of the things viewed. And viewing them thus they are able to comprehend them, nay, to master them.[26]

However, the point might be expressed more exactly by saying that the subject is treated not as an object but as the inseparable pole or term of a subject-object identity. The dividedness of the knower and the known becomes, without being simply obliterated, the plainest sign of their inner unity.

This is, indeed, the crucial point of the whole unitive philosophy of nature as it is set forward in Taoism and Buddhism, and which distinguishes it from a merely monistic pantheism. Distinct and unique events, whether external objects or the internal subject, are seen to be "one with nature" by virtue of their very distinctness, and not at all by absorption into a featureless uniformity. Once again, it is the mutual distinction of figure and ground, subject and object, and not their merging which reveals their inner identity. A Zen master was asked, "I have heard that there is one thing which cannot be named. It has not been born; it will not die when the body dies. When the universe burns up it will not be affected. What is that one thing?" The master answered, "A sesame bun."

In addition, then, to the mood of *yugen*, of mysterious and pregnant vagueness, which haunts Far Eastern painting, there is also an immensely

[26] *Chuang-tzu*, 2. Tr. H. A. Giles (1), p. 20.

forceful delineation of the unique event—the single bird, the spray of
bamboo, the solitary tree, the lonely rock. Hence the sudden awakening
to this "inner identity" which in Zen is called *satori* is usually precipitated
by, or bound up with, some such simple fact as the sound of a berry falling
in the forest or the sight of a piece of crumpled paper in the street. There
is thus a double meaning in Suzuki's translation of the poem:

> *Oh, this one rare occurrence,*
> *For which would I not be glad to give ten thousand pieces of gold!*
> *A hat is on my head, a bundle round my loins;*
> *And on my staff the refreshing breeze and the full moon I carry!*

For the "one rare occurrence" is at once the *satori* experience and the
unique event to which it is attached—one implying all, moment implying
eternity. But to *state* the implication is, in a way, to say too much, especially if it were taken to mean that the perception of the particular ought
to make us think about the universal. On the contrary, the universality of
the unique event and the eternity of the moment come to be seen only
as the straining of the mind is released and the present event, whatever it
may be, is regarded without the slightest attempt to get anything from it.
However, this attempt is so habitual that it can hardly be stopped, so that
whenever anyone tries to accept the moment just as it is he becomes aware
only of the frustration of himself trying to do so. This seems to present
an unbreakable vicious circle—unless he realizes that the moment which
he was trying to accept has now moved on and is presenting itself to him
as his own sensation of strain! If he feels it to be voluntary, there is no
problem in accepting it, for it is his own immediate act. If he feels it to
be involuntary, he must perforce accept it, for he can do no other. Either
way, the strain is accepted and it dissolves. But this is also the discovery
of the inner identity of the voluntary and the involuntary, the subjective
and the objective. For when the object, the moment to be accepted, presented itself as the sensation of the strain of trying to accept, this was the
subject, the ego itself. In the words of the Zen master P'u-yen, "Nothing
is left to you at this moment but to burst out into a loud laugh. You have
accomplished a final turning and in very truth know that 'when a cow in
Kuai-chou grazes the herbage, a horse in I-chou finds its stomach filled.' "[27]

In sum, then, the realization that nature is ordered organically rather
than politically, that it is a field of relationships rather than a collection
of things, requires an appropriate mode of human awareness. The habitual
egocentric mode in which man identifies himself with a subject facing a
world of alien objects does not fit the physical situation. So long as it remains, our inward feeling is at variance with reality. Based on this feeling,
our efforts to control ourselves and the surrounding world become viciously
circular entanglements of ever-growing complexity. More and more the in-

[27] Suzuki (3), p. 80.

dividual feels himself frustrated and impotent in the midst of a mechanical world order which has become an irresistible "march of progress" toward ends of its own. Therapies for the frustrated individual, whether religious or psychological, merely complicate the problem in so far as they assume that the separate ego is the very reality toward which their ministrations are directed. For, as Trigant Burrow saw, the source of the trouble is social rather than individual: that is to say, the ego is a social convention foisted upon human consciousness by conditioning. The root of mental disorder is not therefore a malfunctioning peculiar to this or that ego; it is rather that the ego-feeling as such is an error of perception. To placate it is only to enable it to go on confusing the mind with a mode of awareness which, because it clashes with the natural order, breeds the vast family of psychological frustrations and illnesses.

An organic natural order has its proper correspondence in a mode of consciousness which is a total feeling or experiencing. Where feeling is broken up into the feeler and the feeling, the knower and the known, what lies between the two is not relationship but mere juxtaposition. Identified with one of its terms alone, consciousness feels "out on a limb" facing an alien world which it controls only to find it more and more uncontrollable, and which it exploits only to find it more and more ungratifying.

ZEN BUDDHISM
D. T. Suzuki

D. T. Suzuki (1870–1966), Japanese scholar and thinker best known for rendering the philosophy of Zen Buddhism highly intelligible to the Western mind. In books such as Outline of Mahayana Buddhism (1907), Essays in Zen Buddhism (1961), and The Essentials of Zen Buddhism (1962), Suzuki argues against the Western duality of subject and object, self and others, good and bad; reality, he maintains, is essentially One.

In more than two centuries' quiet and steady development, since its introduction into China by Bodhidharma from the West, that is, from Southern India, where he was born as son of a royal family, Zen Buddhism established itself firmly, in the land of Confucianism and Taoism, as a teaching which claims to be,

> A special transmission outside the Scripture;
> No dependence on words or letters;
> Direct pointing at the Mind of man;
> Seeing into one's Nature and the attainment of Buddhahood.

By whom and exactly when this declaration in four lines was formulated to characterize the teaching of Zen Buddhism is not known. Tentatively, it was during the early part of the T'ang dynasty when Zen really began to take hold of the Chinese mind. The laying of its foundation is to be historically ascribed to Bodhidharma, but it was by Enō and his followers that it came to be recognized as a great spiritual power throughout the T'ang and all the following dynasties. They emphasized a great deal Zen's non-dependence upon the letter, that is, intellection, and its directly seizing upon the Mind itself which is Reality.

I now propose to analyze this four-line declaration and see what constitutes the essentials of Zen teaching.

In "A special transmission outside the Scripture" there are no implications whatever that point to the existence of an esoteric teaching in Buddhism, which came to be known as Zen. The phrase is simply identical with the following one which states Zen's non-dependence on the letter.

Here "the letter" or "the Scripture" stands for conceptualism and all that
the term implies—Zen abhors words and concepts and reasoning based
on them. It thinks that we have been misled from the first rising of consciousness to resort to ratiocination. We generally make too much of ideas
and words thinking them to be facts themselves. They have so deeply
entered, indeed, into the constitution of our being and we imagine that
when we have them there is nothing more to be taken hold of in our
experience. That is to say, words are everything, and experience is nothing,
or at best secondary; and this is the way we have come to interpret life
and consequently thereby to drain the sources of creative imagination.

Zen upholds, as every true religion does, direct experience of Reality.
It aspires to drink from the fountain of life instead of merely listening to
roundabout remarks concerning it. A Zen follower is not satisfied until he
scoops with his own hands the living water of Reality which alone, he
knows, will quench his thirst. The idea is well expressed in the *Gan-
davyūha-sūtra* (the Chinese version known as the forty-volume *Kegon*),
thus:

"Sudhana asked: How does one come to this emancipation face to
face? How does one get this realization?

"Sucandra answered: A man comes to this emancipation face to face
when his mind is awakened to Prajñāpāramitā and stands in a most intimate relationship to it; for then he attains self-realization in all that he
perceives and understands.

"Sudhana: Does one attain self-realization by listening to the talks
and discourses on Prajñāpāramitā?

"Sucandra: That is not so. Why? Because Prajñāpāramitā sees intimately into the truth and reality of all things.

"Sudhana: Is it not that thinking comes from hearing and that by
thinking and reasoning one comes to perceive what suchness is? And is this
not self-realization?

"Sucandra: That is not so. Self-realization never comes from mere
listening and thinking. O son of a good family, I will illustrate the matter
by analogy. Listen! In a great desert there are no springs or wells; in the
springtime or in the summer when it is warm, a traveller comes from the
west going eastward; he meets a man coming from the east and asks him:
I am terribly thirsty; pray tell where I can find a spring and a cool refreshing shade where I may drink, bathe, rest, and get thoroughly revived?

"The man from the east gives the traveller, as desired, all the information in detail, saying: When you go further east the road divides itself
into two, right and left. You take the right one, and going steadily further
on you will surely come to a fine spring and a refreshing shade. Now, son
of a good family, do you think that the thirsty traveller from the west,
listening to the talk about the spring and the shady trees, and thinking
of going to that place as quickly as possible, can be relieved of thirst and
heat and get refreshed?

"Sudhana: No, he cannot; because he is relieved of thirst and heat and gets refreshed only when, as directed by the other, he actually reaches the fountain and drinks of it and bathes in it.

"Sucandra: Son of a good family, even so with the Bodhisattva. By merely listening to it, thinking of it, and intellectually understanding it, you will never come to the realization of any truth. Son of a good family, the desert means birth and death; the man from the west means all sentient beings; the heat means all forms of confusion; thirst is greed and lust; the man from the east who knows the way is the Buddha or the Bodhisattva, who abiding in all-knowledge has penetrated into the true nature of all things and the reality of sameness; to quench the thirst and to be relieved of the heat by drinking of the refreshing fountain means the realization of the truth by oneself.

"Again, son of a good family, I will give you another illustration. Suppose the Tathāgata had stayed among us for another kalpa and used all kinds of contrivance, and, by means of fine rhetoric and apt expressions, had succeeded in convincing people of this world as to the exquisite taste, delicious odor, soft touch, and other virtues of the heavenly nectar; do you think that all the earthly beings who listened to the Buddha's talk and thought of the nectar, could taste its flavor?

"Sudhana: No, indeed; not they.

"Sucandra: Because mere listening and thinking will never make us realize the true nature of Prajñāpāramitā.

"Sudhana: By what apt expressions and skilful illustrations, then, can the Bodhisattva lead all beings to the true understanding of Reality?

"Sucandra: The true nature of Prajñāpāramitā as realized by the Bodhisattva—this is the true definite principle from which all his expressions issue. When this emancipation is realized he can aptly give expression to it and skilfully illustrate it."

From this it is evident that whatever apt expressions and skilful contrivances the Bodhisattva can make in his work among us, they must come out of his own experiences and also that, how believing we may be, we cannot cherish real faith until we experience it in our own lives and make it grow out of them.

Again, we read in the Laṅkāvatāra-sūtra: "The ultimate truth (paramārtha) is a state of inner experience by means of Noble Wisdom (āryajñāna), and as it is beyond the realm of words and discriminations it cannot be adequately expressed by them. Whatever is thus expressible is the product of conditional causation subject to the law of birth and death. The ultimate truth transcends the antithesis of self and not-self, and words are the products of antithetical thinking. The ultimate truth is Mind itself which is free from all forms, inner and outer. No words can therefore describe Mind, no discriminations can reveal it."

Discrimination is a term we quite frequently come across in Buddhist philosophy. It corresponds to intellection or logical reasoning. According to Buddhism, the antithesis of "A" and "not-A" is at the bottom of our ignorance as to the ultimate truth of existence, and this antithesis is discrimination. To discriminate is to be involved in the whirlpool of birth and death, and as long as we are thus involved, there is no emancipation, no attainment of Nirvana, no realization of Buddhahood.

We may ask: "How is this emancipation possible? And does Zen achieve it?"

When we say that a thing exists, or, rather, that we live, it means that we live in this world of dualities and antitheses. Therefore, to be emancipated from this world may mean to go out of it, or to deny it by some means if possible. To do either of these, is to put ourselves out of existence. Emancipation is then, we can say, self-destruction. Does Buddhism teach self-destruction? This kind of interpretation has often been advanced by those who fail to understand the real teaching of Buddhism.

But the fact is that this interpretation is not yet an "emancipated" one and fails to grasp the Buddhist logic of non-discrimination. This is where Zen properly comes in, asserting its own way of being "outside the Scripture" and "independent of the letter." The following *mondō* will illustrate my point.

Sekisō asked Dōgo: "After your passing, if somebody asks me about the ultimate truth of Buddhism, what should I say to him?"

Dōgo made no answer but called out to one of his attendants. The attendant answered, "Yes, master"; and the master said, "Have that pitcher filled with water." So ordering, he remained silent for a while, and then turning to Sekisō said, "What did you ask me about just now?" Sekisō repeated his question. Whereupon the master rose from his seat and walked away.

Sekisō was a good Buddhist student and no doubt understood thoroughly the teaching as far as his intellectual understanding went. What he wanted to know when he questioned his master concerning the ultimate truth of Buddhism was how to grasp it in the Zen way. The master was well aware of the situation. If he wished to explain the matter for Sekisō along the philosophical line of thought, he could of course give many citations from the Scripture and enter into the wordy explanations of them. But he was a Zen master, he knew the uselessness and fruitlessness of such a procedure. He called out his attendant, who immediately responded. He ordered him to fill the pitcher and the deed was immediately executed. He was silent for a while, for he had nothing further to say or to do. The ultimate truth of Buddhism could not go beyond this.

But Dōgo was kindhearted, indeed too kindhearted, and asked Sekisō what his question was. Sekisō was, however, not intelligent enough to see into the meaning of the entire transaction which had taken place right before his eyes. He stupidly repeated his question which was already answered. Hence the master's departure from the room. In fact, this abrupt departure itself told Sekisō all that the latter wished to know.

Some may say that this kind of answering leads the questioner no-where, for he remains ignorant just as much as before, perhaps even worse than before. But does a philosophical or explanatory definition give the questioner any better satisfaction, that is, put him in any better position, as to the real understanding of the ultimate truth? He may in all likeli-hood have his conceptual stock of knowledge much augmented, but this augmentation is not the clearing up of his doubt, that is, the confirmation of his faith in Buddhism. Mere amassing of knowledge, mere stocking of timeworn concepts, is really suicidal in so far as real emancipation is taken into consideration. We are too used to so-called explanations, and have come to think when an explanation of a thing or a fact is given there is nothing more to ask about it. But the point is that there is no better explanation than actual experience and that actual experience is all that is needed in the attainment of Buddhahood. The object of the Buddhist life is to have it in actual actuality and in full abundance and this not loaded with explanatory notes.

To give another Zen way of treating this problem: Tokusan once remarked, "To ask is an error, but not to ask is also faulty." This is tanta-mount to saying: "To be or not to be—that is the question." This ques-tioning has indeed been the curse or the blessing of human consciousness ever since it came into existence. A monk came out of the congregation and proceeded to bow before Tokusan, as was customary for a disciple to do before he was about to ask instruction of the master. But Tokusan struck him without even waiting for him to finish his bowing. The monk naturally failed to understand him and made this protest, "I am just begin-ning to bow before you, O master, and why this striking?" The master lost no time in giving him this, "If I wait for your mouth to open it's too late."

From the so-called "religious" point of view, there is nothing in this, and for that matter in the previous *mondō*, that savors of piety, faith, grace, love, and so on. Where then is the religiosity of Zen Buddhism? I am not, however, going to discuss this question here. I only wish to remark that Buddhism, including Zen and all other schools, has a different set of terms wherewith its followers express their spirtual experience in accordance with their psychology and habits of thinking and feeling.

We now come to the second two lines of the Zen declaration: "Direct pointing at the Mind of man"; and "Seeing into one's Nature and the attainment of Buddhahood." What are "Mind," "Nature," and "Bud-dha?"

"Mind" here does not refer to our ordinarily functioning mind—the mind that thinks according to the laws of logic and feels according to the psychology described by the professors, but the Mind that lies underneath all these thoughts and feelings. It is *cittamātra*, the subject of talk in the *Lankāvatāra-sūtra*. This Mind is also known as Nature, i.e., Reality (*svābhāva*), that which constitutes the basis of all things. The Mind may be regarded as the last point we reach when we dig down psychologically into the depths of a thinking and feeling subject, while Nature is the limit of objectivity beyond which our ontology cannot go. The ontological limit is the psychological limit, and vice versa; for when we reach the one, we find ourselves in the other. The starting point differs: in the one we retreat inwardly as it were, but in the other we go on outwardly, and in the end we arrive at what might be called the point of identity. When we have the Mind, we have Nature: when Nature is understood, the Mind is understood; they are one and the same.

The one who has a thoroughgoing understanding of the Mind and whose every movement is in perfect accordance with Nature is the Buddha—he who is enlightened. The Buddha is Nature personified. Thus we can say that all these three terms—Nature, Mind, and Buddha—are different points of reference; as we shift our positions, we speak in terms of respective orders. The ideal of Zen as expressed in its four-line declaration is directly to take hold of Reality without being bothered by any interrupting agency, intellectual, moral, ritualistic, or what not.

This direct holding of Reality is the awakening *prajñā*, which may be rendered as transcendental wisdom. *Prajñā* awakened or attained is *prajñāpāramitā* (in Japanese *hannya-haramitsu*). This transcendental wisdom gives the solution to all the questions we are capable of asking about our spiritual life. Wisdom is not, therefore, the intellect in the ordinary sense; it transcends dialectics of all kinds. It is not the analytical process of reasoning, it does not work step by step, it leaps over the abyss of contradiction and mutual checking. Hence *pāramitā*, "reaching the other shore."

As the awakening of *prajñā* is the leaping over an intellectual impasse, it is an act of Will. Yet as it sees into Nature itself, there is a noetic quality in it. *Prajñā* is both Will and Intuition. This is the reason why Zen is associated strongly with the cultivation of the will power. To cut asunder the bonds of ignorance and discrimination is no easy task; unless it is done with the utmost exertion of the will, it can never be accomplished. To let go the hold of a solitary branch of the tree, called intellect, which outstretches over a precipice, and to allow ourselves to fall into a supposedly bottomless abyss—does this not require a desperate effort on the part of one who attempts to sound the depths of the Mind? When a Zen Buddhist monk was asked as to the depths of the Zen River while he was walking over a bridge, he at once seized the questioner and would have thrown him down into the rapids had not his friends hurriedly interceded for him. The monk wanted to see the questioner himself go down to the bottom of Zen and survey its depths according to his own measure. The leaping is to be done by oneself, all the help outsiders can offer is to let the one concerned realize the futility of such help. Zen in this respect is harsh and merciless, at least superficially so.

The monk just referred to as trying to throw the questioner overboard was a disciple of Rinzai, one of the greatest masters in the T'ang history of Zen in China. When this monk asked the master what was the ultimate teaching of Buddhism, the master came right down from his seat and taking hold of the monk, exclaimed, "Speak out! Speak out!" How could the poor bewildered novice in the study of Zen speak, so unceremoniously seized by the throat and violently shaken? In fact he wanted to see the master "speak out" instead of his "speaking out," in regard to this question. He never imagined his master to be so "direct." He did not know what to say or what to do. He stood as if in ecstasy. It was only when he was about to perform the deed of bowing before the master, reminded by his fellow-monks, that a realization came over him as to the meaning of the Scripture and the demand to "speak out."

Even when an intellectual explanation is given, the understanding is an inner growth and not an external addition. This must be much more the case with the Zen understanding. The basic principle, therefore, underlying the whole fabric of Zen is directed towards the growth or self-maturing of inner experience. Those who are used to intellectual training or moral persuasion or devotional exercises would no doubt find in Zen discipline something extraordinarily going against their expectations. But this is where Zen is unique in the whole history of religion. Zen has indeed developed along this line ever since the T'ang era when Baso and Sekitō brought out fully the characteristic features of the Zen form of Buddhism. The main idea is to live within the thing itself and thus to understand it. What we in most cases do in order to understand a thing, is to describe it from outside, to talk about it objectively as the philosopher would have it, and try to carry out this method from every possible point of observation except that of inner assimilation or sympathetic merging. The objective method is intellectual and has its field of useful application. Only let us not forget the fact that there is another method which really gives the key to an effective and all-satisfying understanding. The latter is the method of Zen.

The following few examples will illustrate what the Zen method is in the understanding of Buddhism. Zen, being a form of Buddhism, has no specific philosophy of its own except what is usually accepted by the Buddhists of the Mahayana school. What makes Zen so peculiarly outstanding is its method, while the latter is the inevitable growth of Zen's own attitude towards life and truth.

Shōdai Erō who wished to know Zen came to Baso, and Baso asked, "What made you come here?"

"I wish to have Buddha-knowledge."

"No knowledge can be had of him, knowledge belongs to the Devil."

As the monk failed to grasp the meaning of this, the master directed him to go to Sekitō, a contemporary leader of Zen, who he suggested might enlighten the knowledge-seeking monk. When he came to Sekitō, he asked, "Who is the Buddha?"

"You have no Buddha-nature," the master gave his verdict.

"How about the animals?" demanded the monk.

"They have."

"Why not I?" Which was the natural question issuing from an extremely puzzled mind.

"Just because you ask."

This, it is said, opened the mind of Erō to the truth asserted by both Sekitō and Baso.

Superficially considered, there is no logical consistency in the remarks of these masters. Why does knowledge belong to the Devil? Why is not the monk endowed with the Buddha-nature when, according to Buddhist philosophy, it is taught that all beings are in possession of the Buddha-nature and that because of this fact they are all ultimately destined to attain Buddahood. But that we are all Buddhas or that we are endowed with the Buddha-nature is the statement of a fact and not at all the inference reached by means of logical reasoning. The fact comes first and the reasoning follows, and not conversely. This being so, the Zen master desires to see his disciples come in actual personal touch with the fact itself and then to build up if they wish any system of thought based on their experience.

Shinrō, another monk, came to Sekitō and asked, "What is the idea of Bodhidharma's coming over to China from the west (that is, from India)?" This question was asked frequently in the early days of Zen history in China. The meaning is the same as asking, "What is the truth of Buddhism?"

Said Sekitō, "Ask the post standing there."

The monk confessed, "I fail to understand."

"My ignorance exceeds yours," said Sekitō.

The last remark made the monk realize the purport of the whole dialogue.

One or two more instances on ignorance follow. When Sekitō saw Tokusan absorbed in meditation, Sekitō asked, "What are you doing there?"

"I am not doing anything," replied Tokusan.

"If so, you are sitting in idleness."

"Sitting in idleness is doing something."

"You say you are not doing anything," Sekitō pursued further; "but what is that anything which you are not doing?"

"Even the ancient sages know not," was the conclusion given by Tokusan.

Sekitō was one of the younger disciples of Enō and finished his study of Zen under Gyōshi, of Seigen. He was once asked by his monk, Dōgo, "Who has attained to the understanding of Enō's doctrine?"

"One who understands Buddhism."

"Have you then attained it?"

"No, I do not understand Buddhism."

The strange situation created by Zen is that those who understand it do not understand it, and those who do not understand it understand it—a great paradox, indeed, which runs throughout the history of Zen.

"What is the essential point of Buddhism?"

"Unless you have it, you do not understand."

"Is there any further turning when one thus goes on?"

"A white cloud is free to float about anywhere it lists—infinitely vast is the sky!"

To explain this in a more rational manner suited to our mortal intelligence, I may add: what Buddhism teaches is that all is well where it is; but as soon as one steps out to see if he is all right or not, an error is committed leading to an infinite series of negations and affirmations. To Eckhart every morning is "Good Morning" and every day a blessed day. This is our personal experience. When we are saved, we know what it is. However much we inquire about it, salvation never falls upon us.

A monk asks Sekitō, "What is emancipation?" "Who has ever put you in bondage?"

"What is the Pure Land?" "When did you ever get stained?"

"What is Nirvana?" "From whom did you get birth-and-death?"

The Mind, Nature, Buddha, or Buddha-nature—all these are so many ways of giving expression to the one idea, which is Great Affirmation. Zen proposes to bring it to us.

8

CONTEMPORARY CHRISTIANITY

DYNAMICS OF FAITH

Paul Tillich

Paul Tillich (1886–1965), theologian and philosopher who updated traditional Christianity to a contemporary form through a reinterpretation of the ideas of faith, reason, anxiety, and God. Although he wrote numerous books, such as The Religious Situation *(1948),* Love, Power and Justice *(1954),* Dynamics of Faith *(1957), and, his major opus,* Systematic Theology *(1951), he is best known for* The Courage to Be *(1952), in which he asserts that "the affirmation of one's essential being in spite of desires and anxieties creates joy."*

---

1. FAITH AS ULTIMATE CONCERN

Faith is the state of being ultimately concerned: the dynamics of faith are the dynamics of man's ultimate concern. Man, like every living being, is concerned about many things, above all about those which condition his very existence, such as food and shelter. But man, in contrast to other living beings, has spiritual concerns—cognitive, aesthetic, social, political. Some of them are urgent, often extremely urgent, and each of them as well as the vital concerns can claim ultimacy for a human life or the life of a social group. If it claims ultimacy it demands the total surrender of him who accepts this claim, and it promises total fulfillment even if all other claims have to be subjected to it or rejected in its name. If a national group makes the life and growth of the nation its ultimate concern, it demands that all other concerns, economic well-being, health and life, family, aesthetic and cognitive truth, justice and humanity, be sacrificed. The extreme nationalisms of our century are laboratories for the study of what ultimate concern means in all aspects of human existence, including the smallest concern of one's daily life. Everything is centered in the only god, the nation—a god who certainly proves to be a demon, but who shows clearly the unconditional character of an ultimate concern.

But it is not only the unconditional demand made by that which is one's ultimate concern, it is also the promise of ultimate fulfillment which is accepted in the act of faith. The content of this promise is not necessarily defined. It can be expressed in indefinite symbols or in concrete symbols which cannot be taken literally, like the "greatness" of one's nation in which one participates even if one has died for it, or the conquest of mankind by the "saving race," etc. In each of these cases it is "ultimate fulfillment" that is promised, and it is exclusion from such fulfillment which is threatened if the unconditional demand is not obeyed.

An example—and more than an example—is the faith manifest in the religion of the Old Testament. It also has the character of ultimate concern in demand, threat and promise. The content of this concern is not the nation—although Jewish nationalism has sometimes tried to distort it into that—but the content is the God of justice, who, because he represents justice for everybody and every nation, is called the universal God, the God of the universe. He is the ultimate concern of every pious Jew, and therefore in his name the great commandment is given: "You shall love the Lord your God with all your heart, and with all your soul, and with all your might" (Deut. 6:5). This is what ultimate concern means and from these words the term "ultimate concern" is derived. They state unambiguously the character of genuine faith, the demand of total surrender to the subject of ultimate concern. The Old Testament is full of commands which make the nature of this surrender concrete, and it is full of promises and threats in relation to it. Here also are the promises of symbolic indefiniteness, although they center around fulfillment of the national and individual life, and the threat is the exclusion from such fulfillment through national extinction and individual catastrophe. Faith, for the men of the Old Testament, is the state of being ultimately and unconditionally concerned about Jahweh and about what he represents in demand, threat and promise.

Another example—almost a counter-example, yet nevertheless equally revealing—is the ultimate concern with "success" and with social standing and economic power. It is the god of many people in the highly competitive Western culture and it does what every ultimate concern must do: it demands unconditional surrender to its laws even if the price is the sacrifice of genuine human relations, personal conviction, and creative *eros*. Its threat is social and economic defeat, and its promise—indefinite as all such promises—the fulfillment of one's being. It is the breakdown of this kind of faith which characterizes and makes religiously important most contemporary literature. Not false calculations but a misplaced faith is revealed in novels like *Point of No Return*. When fulfilled, the promise of this faith proves to be empty.

Faith is the state of being ultimately concerned. The content matters infinitely for the life of the believer, but it does not matter for the formal definition of faith. And this is the first step we have to make in order to understand the dynamics of faith.

2. FAITH AS A CENTERED ACT

Faith as ultimate concern is an act of the total personality. It happens in the center of the personal life and includes all its elements. Faith is the most centered act of the human mind. It is not a movement of a special section or a special function of man's total being. They all are united in the act of faith. But faith is not the sum total of their impacts. It transcends every special impact as well as the totality of them and it has itself a decisive impact on each of them.

Since faith is an act of the personality as a whole, it participates in the dynamics of personal life. These dynamics have been described in many ways, especially in the recent developments of analytic psychology. Thinking in polarities, their tensions and their possible conflicts, is a common characteristic of most of them. This makes the psychology of personality highly dynamic and requires a dynamic theory of faith as the most personal of all personal acts. The first and decisive polarity in analytic psychology is that between the so-called unconscious and the conscious. Faith as an act of the total personality is not imaginable without the participation of the unconscious elements in the personality structure. They are always present and decide largely about the content of faith. But, on the other hand, faith is a conscious act and the unconscious elements participate in the creation of faith only if they are taken into the personal center which transcends each of them. If this does not happen, if unconscious forces determine the mental status without a centered act, faith does not occur, and compulsions take its place. For faith is a matter of freedom. Freedom is nothing more than the possibility of centered personal acts. The frequent discussion in which faith and freedom are contrasted could be helped by the insight that faith is a free, namely, centered act of the personality. In this respect freedom and faith are identical.

Also important for the understanding of faith is the polarity between what Freud and his school call ego and superego. The concept of the superego is quite ambiguous. On the one hand, it is the basis of all cultural life because it restricts the uninhibited actualization of the always-driving libido; on the other hand, it cuts off man's vital forces, and produces disgust about the whole system of cultural restrictions, and brings about a neurotic state of mind. From this point of view, the symbols of faith are considered to be expressions of the superego or, more concretely, to be an expression of the father image which gives content to the superego. Responsible for this inadequate theory of the superego is Freud's naturalistic negation of norms and principles. If the superego is not established through valid principles, it becomes a suppressive tyrant. But real faith, even if it uses the father image for its expression, transforms this image into a principle of truth and justice to be defended even against the "father." Faith and culture can be affirmed only if the superego represents the norms and principles of reality.

This leads to the question of how faith as a personal, centered act is related to the rational structure of man's personality which is manifest in his meaningful language, in his ability to know the true and to do the good, in his sense of beauty and justice. All this, and not only his possibility to analyze, to calculate and to argue, makes him a rational being. But in spite of this large concept of reason we must deny that man's essential nature is identical with the rational character of his mind. Man is able to decide for or against reason, he is able to create beyond reason or to destroy below reason. This power is the power of his self, the center of self-relatedness in which all elements of his being are united. Faith is not an act of any of his rational functions, as it is not an act of the unconscious, but it is an act in which both the rational and the nonrational elements of his being are transcended.

Faith as the embracing and centered act of the personality is "ecstatic." It transcends both the drives of the nonrational unconscious and the structures of the rational conscious. It transcends them, but it does not destroy them. The ecstatic character of faith does not exclude its rational character although it is not identical with it, and it includes nonrational strivings without being identical with them. In the ecstasy of faith there is an awareness of truth and of ethical value; there are also past loves and hates, conflicts and reunions, individual and collective influences. "Ecstasy" means "standing outside of oneself"—without ceasing to be oneself —with all the elements which are united in the personal center.

A further polarity in these elements, relevant for the understanding of faith, is the tension between the cognitive function of man's personal life, on the one hand, and emotion and will, on the other hand. In a later discussion I will try to show that many distortions of the meaning of faith are rooted in the attempt to subsume faith to the one or the other of these functions. At this point it must be stated as sharply and insistently as possible that in every act of faith there is cognitive affirmation, not as the result of an independent process of inquiry but as an inseparable element in a total act of acceptance and surrender. This also excludes the idea that faith is the result of an independent act of "will to believe." There is certainly affirmation by the will of what concerns one ultimately, but faith is not a creation of the will. In the ecstasy of faith the will to accept and to surrender is an element, but not the cause. And this is true also of feeling. Faith is not an emotional outburst: this is not the meaning of ecstasy. Certainly, emotion is in it, as in every act of man's spiritual life. But emotion does not produce faith. Faith has a cognitive content and is an act of the will. It is the unity of every element in the centered self. Of course, the unity of all elements in the act of faith does not prevent one or the other element from dominating in a special form of faith. It dominates the character of faith but it does not create the act of faith.

This also answers the question of a possible psychology of faith. Everything that happens in man's personal being can become an object of psychology. And it is rather important for both the philosopher of religion and the practical minister to know how the act of faith is embedded in the totality of psychological processes. But in contrast to this justified and desirable form of a psychology of faith there is another one which tries to derive faith from something that is not faith but is most frequently fear. The presupposition of this method is that fear or something else from which faith is derived is more original and basic than faith. But this presupposition cannot be proved. On the contrary, one can prove that in the scientific method which leads to such consequences faith is already effective. Faith precedes all attempts to derive it from something else, because these attempts are themselves based on faith.

3. THE SOURCE OF FAITH

We have described the act of faith and its relation to the dynamics of personality. Faith is a total and centered act of the personal self, the act of unconditional, infinite and ultimate concern. The question now arises: what is the source of this all-embracing and all-transcending concern? The word "concern" points to two sides of a relationship, the relation between the one who is concerned and his concern. In both respects we have to imagine man's situation in itself and in his world. The reality of man's ultimate concern reveals something about his being, namely, that he is able to transcend the flux of relative and transitory experiences of his ordinary life. Man's experiences, feelings, thoughts are conditioned and finite. They not only come and go, but their content is of finite and conditional concern—unless they are elevated to unconditional validity. But this presupposes the general possibility of doing so; it presupposes the element of infinity in man. Man is able to understand in an immediate personal and central act the meaning of the ultimate, the unconditional, the absolute, the infinite. This alone makes faith a human potentiality.

Human potentialities are powers that drive toward actualization. Man is driven toward faith by his awareness of the infinite to which he belongs, but which he does not own like a possession. This is in abstract terms what concretely appears as the "restlessness of the heart" within the flux of life.

The unconditional concern which is faith is the concern about the unconditional. The infinite passion, as faith has been described, is the passion for the infinite. Or, to use our first term, the ultimate concern is concern about what is experienced as ultimate. In this way we have turned from the subjective meaning of faith as a centered act of the personality to its objective meaning, to what is meant in the act of faith. It would not help at this point of our analysis to call that which is meant in the act of faith "God" or "a god." For at this step we ask: What in the idea of God constitutes divinity? The answer is: It is the element of the unconditional and of ultimacy. This carries the quality of divinity. If this is seen, one can understand why almost every thing "in heaven and on earth" has received ultimacy in the history of human religion. But we also can understand that a critical principle was and is at work in man's religious consciousness, namely, that which is really ultimate over against what claims to be ultimate but is only preliminary, transitory, finite.

The term "ultimate concern" unites the subjective and the objective side of the act of faith—the *fides qua creditur* (the faith through which one believes) and the *fides quae creditur* (the faith which is believed). The first is the classical term for the centered act of the personality, the ultimate concern. The second is the classical term for that toward which this act is directed, the ultimate itself, expressed in symbols of the divine. This distinction is very important, but not ultimately so, for the one side cannot be without the other. There is no faith without a content toward which it is directed. There is always something meant in the act of faith. And there is no way of having the content of faith except in the act of faith. All speaking about divine matters which is not done in the state of ultimate concern is meaningless. Because that which is meant in the act of faith cannot be approached in any other way than through an act of faith.

In terms like ultimate, unconditional, infinite, absolute, the difference between subjectivity and objectivity is overcome. The ultimate of the act of faith and the ultimate that is meant in the act of faith are one and the same. This is symbolically expressed by the mystics when they say that their knowledge of God is the knowledge God has of himself; and it is expressed by Paul when he says (I Cor. 13) that he will know as he is known, namely, by God. God never can be object without being at the same time subject. Even a successful prayer is, according to Paul (Rom.

8), not possible without God as Spirit praying within us. The same experience expressed in abstract language is the disappearance of the ordinary subject-object scheme in the experience of the ultimate, the unconditional. In the act of faith that which is the source of this act is present beyond the cleavage of subject and object. It is present as both and beyond both.

This character of faith gives an additional criterion for distinguishing true and false ultimacy. The finite which claims infinity without having it (as, e.g., a nation or success) is not able to transcend the subject-object scheme. It remains an object which the believer looks at as a subject. He can approach it with ordinary knowledge and subject it to ordinary handling. There are, of course, many degrees in the endless realm of false ultimacies. The nation is nearer to true ultimacy than is success. Nationalistic ecstasy can produce a state in which the subject is almost swallowed by the object. But after a period the subject emerges again, disappointed radically and totally, and by looking at the nation in a skeptical and calculating way does injustice even to its justified claims. The more idolatrous a faith the less it is able to overcome the cleavage between subject and object. For that is the difference between true and idolatrous faith. In true faith the ultimate concern is a concern about the truly ultimate; while in idolatrous faith preliminary, finite realities are elevated to the rank of ultimacy. The inescapable consequence of idolatrous faith is "existential disappointment," a disappointment which penetrates into the very existence of man! This is the dynamics of idolatrous faith: that it is faith, and as such, the centered act of a personality; that the centering point is something which is more or less on the periphery; and that, therefore, the act of faith leads to a loss of the center and to a disruption of the personality. The ecstatic character of even an idolatrous faith can hide this consequence only for a certain time. But finally it breaks into the open.

4. FAITH AND THE DYNAMICS
OF THE HOLY

He who enters the sphere of faith enters the sanctuary of life. Where there is faith there is an awareness of holiness. This seems to contradict what has just been said about idolatrous faith. But it does not contradict our analysis of idolatry. It only contradicts the popular way in which the word "holy" is used. What concerns one ultimately becomes holy. The awareness of the holy is awareness of the presence of the divine, namely of the content of our ultimate concern. This awareness is expressed in a grand way in the Old Testament from the visions of the patriarchs and Moses to the shaking experiences of the great prophets and psalmists. It is a presence which remains mysterious in spite of its appearance, and it exercises both an attractive and a repulsive function on those who encounter it. In his classical book, *The Idea of the Holy*, Rudolph Otto has described these two functions as the fascinating and the shaking character of the holy. (In Otto's terminology: *mysterium fascinans et tremendum.*) They can be found in all religions because they are the way in which man always encounters the representations of his ultimate concern. The reason for these two effects of the holy is obvious if we see the relation of the experience of the holy to the experience of ultimate concern. The human heart seeks the infinite because that is where the finite wants to rest. In the infinite it sees its own fulfillment. This is the reason for the ecstatic attraction and fascination of everything in which ultimacy is manifest. On the other hand, if ultimacy is manifest and exercises its fascinating attraction, one realizes at the same time the infinite distance of the finite from the infinite and, consequently, the negative judgment over any finite attempts to reach the infinite. The feeling of being consumed in the presence of the divine is a profound expression of man's relation to the holy. It is implied in every genuine act of faith, in every state of ultimate concern.

This original and only justified meaning of holiness must replace the currently distorted use of the word. "Holy" has become identified with moral perfection, especially in some Protestant groups. The historical causes of this distortion give a new insight into the nature of holiness and of faith. Originally, the holy has meant what is apart from the ordinary realm of things and experiences. It is separated from the world of finite relations. This is the reason why all religious cults have separated holy places and activities from all other places and activities. Entering the sanctuary means encountering the holy. Here the infinitely removed makes itself near and present, without losing its remoteness. For this reason, the holy has been called the "entirely other," namely, other than the ordinary course of things or—to refer to a former statement—other than the world which is determined by the cleavage of subject and object. The holy transcends this realm; this is its mystery and its unapproachable character. There is no conditional way of reaching the unconditional; there is no finite way of reaching the infinite.

The mysterious character of the holy produces an ambiguity in man's ways of experiencing it. The holy can appear as creative and as destructive. Its fascinating element can be both creative and destructive (referring again to the fascinating character of the nationalistic idolatry), and the terrifying and consuming element can be destructive and creative (as in the double function of Siva or Kali in Indian thought). This ambiguity, of which we still find traces in the Old Testament, is reflected in the ritual or quasi-ritual activities of religions and quasi religions (sacrifices of others or one's bodily or mental self) which are strongly ambiguous. One can call this ambiguity divine-demonic, whereby the divine is characterized by the victory of the creative over the destructive possibility of the holy, and the demonic is characterized by the victory of the destructive over the creative possibility of the holy. In this situation, which is most profoundly understood in the prophetic religion of the Old Testament, a fight has been waged against the demonic-destructive element in the holy. And this fight was so successful that the concept of the holy was changed. Holiness becomes justice and truth. It is creative and not destructive. The true sacrifice is obedience to the law. This is the line of thought which finally led to the identification of holiness with moral perfection. But when this point is reached, holiness loses its meaning as the "separated," the "transcending," the "fascinating and terrifying," the "entirely other." All this is gone, and the holy has become the morally good and the logically true. It has ceased to be the holy in the genuine sense of the word. Summing up this development, one could say that the holy originally lies below the alternative of the good and the evil; that it is both divine and demonic; that with the reduction of the demonic possibility the holy itself becomes transformed in its meaning; that it becomes rational and identical with the true and the good; and that its genuine meaning must be rediscovered.

These dynamics of the holy confirm what was said about the dynamics of faith. We have distinguished between true and idolatrous faith. The holy which is demonic, or ultimately destructive, is identical with the content of idolatrous faith. Idolatrous faith is still faith. The holy which is demonic is still holy. This is the point where the ambiguous character of religion is most visible and the dangers of faith are most obvious: the danger of faith is idolatry and the ambiguity of the holy is its demonic possibility. Our ultimate concern can destroy us as it can heal us. But we never can be without it.

5. FAITH AND DOUBT

We now return to a fuller description of faith as an act of the human personality, as its centered and total act. An act of faith is an act of a finite being who is grasped by and turned to the infinite. It is a finite act with all the limitations of a finite act, and it is an act in which the infinite participates beyond the limitations of a finite act. Faith is certain in so far as it is an experience of the holy. But faith is uncertain in so far as the infinite to which it is related is received by a finite being. This element of uncertainty in faith cannot be removed, it must be accepted. And the element in faith which accepts this is courage. Faith includes an element of immediate awareness which gives certainty and an element of uncertainty. To accept this is courage. In the courageous standing of uncertainty, faith shows most visibly its dynamic character.

If we try to describe the relation of faith and courage, we must use a larger concept of courage than that which is ordinarily used.[1] Courage as an element of faith is the daring self-affirmation of one's own being in spite of the powers of "nonbeing" which are the heritage of everything finite. Where there is daring and courage there is the possibility of failure. And in every act of faith this possibility is present. The risk must be taken. Whoever makes his nation his ultimate concern needs courage in order to maintain this concern. Only certain is the ultimacy as ultimacy, the infinite passion as infinite passion. This is a reality given to the self with his own nature. It is as immediate and as much beyond doubt as the self is to the self. It *is* the self in its self-transcending quality. But there is not certainty of this kind about the content of our ultimate concern, be it nation, success, a god, or the God of the Bible: They all are contents without immediate awareness. Their acceptance as matters of ultimate concern is a risk and therefore an act of courage. There is a risk if what was considered as a matter of ultimate concern proves to be a matter of preliminary and transitory concern—as, for example, the nation. The risk to faith in one's ultimate concern is indeed the greatest risk man can run. For if it proves to be a failure, the meaning of one's life breaks down; one surrenders oneself, including truth and justice, to something which is not worth it. One has given away one's personal center without having a chance to regain it. The reaction of despair in people who have experienced the breakdown of their national claims is an irrefutable proof of the idolatrous character of their national concern. In the long run this is the inescapable result of an ultimate concern, the subject matter of which is not ultimate. And this is the risk faith must take; this is the risk which is unavoidable if a finite being affirms itself. Ultimate concern is ultimate risk and ultimate courage. It is not risk and needs no courage with respect to ultimacy itself. But it is risk and demands courage if it affirms a concrete concern. And every faith has a concrete element in itself. It is concerned about something or somebody. But this something or this somebody may prove to be not ultimate at all. Then faith is a failure in its concrete expression, although it is not a failure in the experience of the unconditional itself. A god disappears; divinity remains. Faith risks the vanishing of the concrete god in whom it believes. It may well be that with the vanishing of the god the believer breaks down without being able to re-establish his centered self by a new content of his ultimate concern. This risk cannot be taken away from any act of faith. There is only one point which is a matter not of risk but of immediate certainty and herein lies the greatness and the pain of being human; namely, one's standing between one's finitude and one's potential infinity.

All this is sharply expressed in the relation of faith and doubt. If faith is understood as belief that something is true, doubt is incompatible with

[1] Cf. Paul Tillich, *The Courage to Be.* Yale University Press.

the act of faith. If faith is understood as being ultimately concerned, doubt is a necessary element in it. It is a consequence of the risk of faith.

The doubt which is implicit in faith is not a doubt about facts or conclusions. It is not the same doubt which is the lifeblood of scientific research. Even the most orthodox theologian does not deny the right of methodological doubt in matters of empirical inquiry or logical deduction. A scientist who would say that a scientific theory is beyond doubt would at that moment cease to be scientific. He may believe that the theory can be trusted for all practical purposes. Without such belief no technical application of a theory would be possible. One could attribute to this kind of belief pragmatic certainty sufficient for action. Doubt in this case points to the preliminary character of the underlying theory.

There is another kind of doubt, which we could call skeptical in contrast to the scientific doubt which we could call methodological. The skeptical doubt is an attitude toward all the beliefs of man, from sense experiences to religious creeds. It is more an attitude than an assertion. For as an assertion it would conflict with itself. Even the assertion that there is no possible truth for man would be judged by the skeptical principle and could not stand as an assertion. Genuine skeptical doubt does not use the form of an assertion. It is an attitude of actually rejecting any certainty. Therefore, it can not be refuted logically. It does not transform its attitude into a proposition. Such an attitude necessarily leads either to despair or cynicism, or to both alternately. And often, if this alternative becomes intolerable, it leads to indifference and the attempt to develop an attitude of complete unconcern. But since man is that being who is essentially concerned about his being, such an escape finally breaks down. This is the dynamics of skeptical doubt. It has an awakening and liberating function, but it also can prevent the development of a centered personality. For personality is not possible without faith. The despair about truth by the skeptic shows that truth is still his infinite passion. The cynical superiority over every concrete truth shows that truth is still taken seriously and that the impact of the question of an ultimate concern is strongly felt. The skeptic, so long as he is a serious skeptic, is not without faith, even though it has no concrete content.

The doubt which is implicit in every act of faith is neither the methodological nor the skeptical doubt. It is the doubt which accompanies every risk. It is not the permanent doubt of the scientist, and it is not the transitory doubt of the skeptic, but it is the doubt of him who is ultimately concerned about a concrete content. One could call it the existential doubt, in contrast to the methodological and the skeptical doubt. It does not question whether a special proposition is true or false. It does not reject every concrete truth, but it is aware of the element of insecurity in every existential truth. At the same time, the doubt which is implied in faith accepts this insecurity and takes it into itself in an act of courage. Faith includes courage. Therefore, it can include the doubt about itself.

Certainly faith and courage are not identical. Faith has other elements besides courage and courage has other functions beyond affirming faith. Nevertheless, an act in which courage accepts risk belongs to the dynamics of faith.

This dynamic concept of faith seems to give no place to that restful affirmative confidence which we find in the documents of all great religions, including Christianity. But this is not the case. The dynamic concept of faith is the result of a conceptual analysis, both of the subjective and of the objective side of faith. It is by no means the description of an always actualized state of the mind. An analysis of structure is not the description of a state of things. The confusion of these two is a source of many misunderstandings and errors in all realms of life. An example, taken from the current discussion of anxiety, is typical of this confusion. The description of anxiety as the awareness of one's finitude is sometimes criticized as untrue from the point of view of the ordinary state of the mind. Anxiety, one says, appears under special conditions but is not an ever-present implication of man's finitude. Certainly anxiety as an acute experience appears under definite conditions. But the underlying structure of finite life is the universal condition which makes the appearance of anxiety under special conditions possible. In the same way doubt is not a permanent experience within the act of faith. But it is always present as an element in the structure of faith. This is the difference between faith and immediate evidence either of perceptual or of logical character. There is no faith without an intrinsic "in spite of" and the courageous affirmation of oneself in the state of ultimate concern. This intrinsic element of doubt breaks into the open under special individual and social conditions. If doubt appears, it should not be considered as the negation of faith, but as an element which was always and will always be present in the act of faith. Existential doubt and faith are poles of the same reality, the state of ultimate concern.

.   .   .

6. FAITH AND THE INTEGRATION
OF THE PERSONALITY

. . . If faith is the state of being ultimately concerned, all preliminary concerns are subject to it. The ultimate concern gives depth, direction and unity to all other concerns and, with them, to the whole personality. A personal life which has these qualities is integrated, and the power of a personality's integration is his faith. It must be repeated at this point that such an assertion would be absurd if faith were what it is in its distorted meaning, the belief in things without evidence. Yet the assertion is not absurd, but evident, if faith is ultimate concern.

Ultimate concern is related to all sides of reality and to all sides of the human personality. The ultimate is one object beside others, and the ground of all others. As the ultimate is the ground of everything that is, so ultimate concern is the integrating center of the personal life. Being without it is being without a center. Such a state, however, can only be approached but never fully reached, because a human being deprived completely of a center would cease to be a human being. For this reason one cannot admit that there is any man without an ultimate concern or without faith.

The center unites all elements of man's personal life, the bodily, the unconscious, the conscious, the spiritual ones. In the act of faith every nerve of man's body, every striving of man's soul, every function of man's spirit participates. But body, soul, spirit, are not three parts of man. They are dimensions of man's being, always within each other; for man is a unity and not composed of parts. Faith, therefore, is not a matter of the mind in isolation, or of the soul in contrast to mind and body, or of the body (in the sense of animal faith), but is the centered movement of the whole personality toward something of ultimate meaning and significance.

Ultimate concern is passionate concern; it is a matter of infinite passion. Passion is not real without a bodily basis, even if it is the most spiritual passion. In every act of genuine faith the body participates, because genuine faith is a passionate act. The way in which it participates is manifold. The body can participate both in vital ecstasy and in asceticism leading to spiritual ecstasy. But whether in vital fulfillment or vital restriction, the body participates in the life of faith. The same is true of the unconscious strivings, the so-called instincts of man's psyche. They determine the choice of symbols and types of faith. Therefore, every community of faith tries to shape the unconscious strivings of its members, especially of the new generations. If the faith of somebody expresses itself in symbols which are adequate to his unconscious strivings, these strivings cease to be chaotic. They do not need repression, because they have received "sublimation" and are united with the conscious activities of the person. Faith also directs man's conscious life by giving it a central object of "con-centration." The disrupting trends of man's consciousness are one of the great problems of all personal life. If a uniting center is absent, the infinite variety of the encountered world, as well as of the inner movements of the human mind, is able to produce or complete disintegration of the personality. There can be no other uniting center than the ultimate concern of the mind. There are various ways in which faith unites man's mental life and gives it a dominating center. It can be the way of discipline which regulates the daily life; it can be the way of meditation and contemplation; it can be the way of concentration on the ordinary work, or on a special aim or on another human being. In each case, faith is presupposed; none of it could be done without faith. Man's spiritual function, artistic creation, scientific knowledge, ethical formation and political organization are consciously or unconsciously expressions of an ultimate concern which gives passion and creative *eros* to them, making them inexhaustible in depth and united in aim.

. . .

CONCLUSION: THE POSSIBILITY AND NECESSITY OF FAITH TODAY

Faith is real in every period of history. This fact does not prove that it is an essential possibility and necessity. It could be—like superstition— an actual distortion of man's true nature. This is what many people who reject faith believe. The question raised by this book is whether such belief is based on insight or on misunderstanding, and the answer is unambiguously that the rejection of faith is rooted in a complete misunderstanding of the nature of faith. Many forms of this misunderstanding, many misrepresentations and distortions of faith have been discussed. Faith is a concept—and a reality—which is difficult to grasp and to describe. Almost every word by which faith has been described—also on the preceding pages—is open to new misinterpretations. This cannot be otherwise, since faith is not a phenomenon beside others, but the central phenomenon in man's personal life, manifest and hidden at the same time. It is religious and transcends religion, it is universal and concrete, it is infinitely variable and always the same. Faith is an essential possibility of man, and therefore its existence is necessary and universal. It is possible and necessary also in our period. If faith is understood as what it centrally is, ultimate concern, it cannot be undercut by modern science or any kind of philosophy. And it cannot be discredited by its superstitions or authoritarian distortions within and outside churches, sects and movements. Faith stands upon itself and justifies itself against those who attack it, because they can attack it only in the name of another faith. It is the triumph of the dynamics of faith that any denial of faith is itself an expression of faith, of an ultimate concern.

LETTERS AND PAPERS FROM PRISON

Dietrich Bonhoeffer

(trans. by Reginald Fuller and Frank Clark)

Dietrich Bonhoeffer (1906–1945), German theologian who is noted for his support of ecumenism and his efforts to unite Christians and non-Christians in a common secular responsibility. Among his many writings are The Communion of Saints *(1930),* The Cost of Discipleship *(1937),* Life Together *(1939), and the posthumous* Letters and Papers from Prison *(1951). Bonhoeffer was an active opponent of Nazism from its inception and participated in an attempt to assassinate Hitler in 1944. He could have escaped to the United States when his life was endangered, but he chose to remain in Germany and share in the struggle of the Church. He was imprisoned by the Nazis and subsequently hanged, thereby suffering a martyr's death at the age of thirty-nine.*

. . .

NO GROUND UNDER OUR FEET

One may ask whether there have ever before in human history been people with so little ground under their feet—people to whom every available alternative seemed equally intolerable, repugnant, and futile, who looked beyond all these existing alternatives for the source of their strength so entirely in the past or in the future, and who yet, without being dreamers, were able to await the success of their cause so quietly and confidently. Or perhaps one should rather ask whether the responsible thinking people of any generation that stood at a turning-point in history did not feel much as we do, simply because something new was emerging that could not be seen in the existing alternatives.

WHO STANDS FAST?

The great masquerade of evil has played havoc with all our ethical concepts. For evil to appear disguised as light, charity, historical necessity,

or social justice is quite bewildering to anyone brought up on our traditional ethical concepts, while for the Christian who bases his life on the
Bible it merely confirms the fundamental wickedness of evil.

The *'reasonable'* people's failure is obvious. With the best intentions
and a naïve lack of realism, they think that with a little reason they can
bend back into position the framework that has got out of joint. In their
lack of vision they want to do justice to all sides, and so the conflicting
forces wear them down with nothing achieved. Disappointed by the
world's unreasonableness, they see themselves condemned to ineffective-
ness; they step aside in resignation or collapse before the stronger party.

Still more pathetic is the total collapse of moral *fanaticism*. The
fanatic thinks that his single-minded principles qualify him to do battle
with the powers of evil; but like a bull he rushes at the red cloak instead
of the person who is holding it; he exhausts himself and is beaten. He
gets entangled in non-essentials and falls into the trap set by cleverer
people.

Then there is the man with a *conscience*, who fights single-handed
against heavy odds in situations that call for a decision. But the scale of
the conflicts in which he has to choose—with no advice or support except
from his own conscience—tears him to pieces. Evil approaches him in so
many respectable and seductive disguises that his conscience becomes nervous and vacillating, till at last he contents himself with a salved instead
of a clear conscience, so that he lies to his own conscience in order to
avoid despair; for a man whose only support is his conscience can never
realize that a bad conscience may be stronger and more wholesome than
a deluded one.

From the perplexingly large number of possible decisions, the way of
duty seems to be the sure way out. Here, what is commanded is accepted
as what is most certain, and the responsibility for it rests on the com-
mander, not on the person commanded. But no one who confines himself
to the limits of duty ever goes so far as to venture, on his sole responsibility, to act in the only way that makes it possible to score a direct hit
on evil and defeat it. The man of duty will in the end have to do his duty
by the devil too.

As to the man who asserts his complete *freedom* to stand four-square
to the world, who values the necessary deed more highly than an unspoilt
conscience or reputation, who is ready to sacrifice a barren principle for
a fruitful compromise, or the barren wisdom of a middle course for a
fruitful radicalism—let him beware lest his freedom should bring him
down. He will assent to what is bad so as to ward off something worse,
and in doing so he will no longer be able to realize that the worse, which
he wants to avoid, might be the better. Here we have the raw material
of tragedy.

Here and there people flee from public altercation into the sanctuary
of private *virtuousness*. But anyone who does this must shut his mouth

and his eyes to the injustice around him. Only at the cost of self-deception can he keep himself pure from the contamination arising from responsible action. In spite of all that he does, what he leaves undone will rob him of his peace of mind. He will either go to pieces because of this disquiet, or become the most hypocritical of Pharisees.

Who stands fast? Only the man whose final standard is not his reason, his principles, his conscience, his freedom, or his virtue, but who is ready to sacrifice all this when he is called to obedient and responsible action in faith and in exclusive allegiance to God—the responsible man, who tries to make his whole life an answer to the question and call of God. Where are these responsible people?

CIVIL COURAGE?

What lies behind the complaint about the dearth of civil courage? In recent years we have seen a great deal of bravery and self-sacrifice, but civil courage hardly anywhere, even among ourselves. To attribute this simply to personal cowardice would be too facile a psychology; its background is quite different. In a long history, we Germans have had to learn the need for and the strength of obedience. In the subordination of all personal wishes and ideas to the tasks to which we have been called, we have seen the meaning and the greatness of our lives. We have looked upwards, not in servile fear, but in free trust, seeing in our tasks a call, and in our call a vocation. This readiness to follow a command from 'above' rather than our own private opinions and wishes was a sign of legitimate self-distrust. Who would deny that in obedience, in their task and calling, the Germans have again and again shown the utmost bravery and self-sacrifice? But the German has kept his freedom—and what nation has talked more passionately of freedom than the Germans, from Luther to the idealist philosophers?—by seeking deliverance from self-will through service to the community. Calling and freedom were to him two sides of the same thing. But in this he misjudged the world; he did not realize that his submissiveness and self-sacrifice could be exploited for evil ends. When that happened, the exercise of the calling itself became questionable, and all the moral principles of the German were bound to totter. The fact could not be escaped that the German still lacked something fundamental: he could not see the need for free and responsible action, even in opposition to his task and his calling; in its place there appeared on the one hand an irresponsible lack of scruple, and on the other a self-tormenting punctiliousness that never led to action. Civil courage, in fact, can grow only out of the free responsibility of free men. Only now are the Germans beginning to discover the meaning of free responsibility. It depends on a God who demands responsible action in a bold venture of faith, and who promises forgiveness and consolation to the man who becomes a sinner in that venture.

OF SUCCESS

Although it is certainly not true that success justifies an evil deed and shady means, it is impossible to regard success as something that is ethically quite neutral. The fact is that historical success creates a basis for the continuance of life, and it is still a moot point whether it is ethically more responsible to take the field like a Don Quixote against a new age, or to admit one's defeat, accept the new age, and agree to serve it. In the last resort success makes history; and the ruler of history repeatedly brings good out of evil over the heads of the history-makers. Simply to ignore the ethical significance of success is a short-circuit created by dogmatists who think unhistorically and irresponsibly; and it is good for us sometimes to be compelled to grapple seriously with the ethical problem of success. As long as goodness is successful, we can afford the luxury of regarding it as having no ethical significance; it is when successs is achieved by evil means that the problem arises. In the face of such a situation we find that it cannot be adequately dealt with, either by theoretical dogmatic arm-chair criticism, which means a refusal to face the facts, or by opportunism, which means giving up the struggle and surrendering to success. We will not and must not be either outraged critics or opportunists, but must take our share of responsibility for the moulding of history in every situation and at every moment, whether we are the victors or the vanquished. One who will not allow any occurrence whatever to deprive him of his responsibility for the course of history—because he knows that it has been laid on him by God—will thereafter achieve a more fruitful relation to the events of history than that of barren criticism and equally barren opportunism. To talk of going down fighting like heroes in the face of certain defeat is not really heroic at all, but merely a refusal to face the future. The ultimate question for a responsible man to ask is not how he is to extricate himself heroically from the affair, but how the coming generation is to live. It is only from this question, with its responsibility towards history, that fruitful solutions can come, even if for the time being they are very humiliating. In short, it is much easier to see a thing through from the point of view of abstract principle than from that of concrete responsibility. The rising generation will always instinctively discern which of these we make the basis of our actions, for it is their own future that is at stake.

OF FOLLY

Folly is a more dangerous enemy to the good than evil. One can protect against evil; it can be unmasked and, if need be, prevented by force. Evil always carries the seeds of its own destruction, as it makes people, at the least, uncomfortable. Against folly we have no defence. Neither protests nor force can touch it; reasoning is no use; facts that contradict personal prejudices can simply be disbelieved—indeed, the fool can counter by criticizing them, and if they are undeniable, they can just be pushed aside as trivial exceptions. So the fool, as distinct from the scoundrel, is completely self-satisfied; in fact, he can easily become dangerous, as it does not take much to make him aggressive. A fool must therefore be treated more cautiously than a scoundrel; we shall never again try to convince a fool by reason, for it is both useless and dangerous.

If we are to deal adequately with folly, we must try to understand its nature. This much is certain, that it is a moral rather than an intellectual defect. There are people who are mentally agile but foolish, and people who are mentally slow but very far from foolish—a discovery that we make to our surprise as a result of particular situations. We thus get the impression that folly is likely to be, not a congenital defect, but one that is acquired in certain circumstances where people *make* fools of themselves or allow others to make fools of them. We notice further that this defect is less common in the unsociable and solitary than in individuals or groups that are inclined or condemned to sociability. It seems, then, that folly is a sociological rather than a psychological problem, and that it is a special form of the operation of historical circumstances on people, a psychological by-product of definite external factors. If we look more closely, we see that any violent display of power, whether political or religious, produces an outburst of folly in a large part of mankind; indeed, this seems actually to be a psychological and sociological law: the power of some needs the folly of the others. It is not that certain human capacities, intellectual capacities for instance, become stunted or destroyed, but rather that the upsurge of power makes such an overwhelming impression that men are deprived of their independent judgment, and—more or less unconsciously—give up trying to assess the new state of affairs for themselves. The fact that the fool is often stubborn must not mislead us into thinking that he is independent. One feels in fact, when talking to him, that one is dealing, not with the man himself, but with slogans, catchwords, and the like, which have taken hold of him. He is under a spell, he is blinded, his very nature is being misused and exploited. Having thus become a passive instrument, the fool will be capable of any evil and at the same time incapable of seeing that it is evil. Here lies the danger of a diabolical exploitation that can do irreparable damage to human beings.

But at this point it is quite clear, too, that folly can be overcome, not by instruction, but only by an act of liberation; and so we have come to terms with the fact that in the great majority of cases inward liberation must be preceded by outward liberation, and that until that has taken place, we may as well abandon all attempts to convince the fool. In this state of affairs we have to realize why it is no use our trying to find out what 'the people' really think, and why the question is so superfluous for the man who thinks and acts responsibly—but always given these particular circumstances. The Bible's words that 'the fear of the Lord is the beginning of wisdom' (Ps. 111.10) tell us that a person's inward liberation to live a responsible life before God is the only real cure for folly.

But there is some consolation in these thoughts on folly: they in no way justify us in thinking that most people are fools in all circumstances. What will really matter is whether those in power expect more from people's folly than from their wisdom and independence of mind.

CONTEMPT FOR HUMANITY?

There is a very real danger of our drifting into an attitude of contempt for humanity. We know quite well that we have no right to do so, and that it would lead us into the most sterile relation to our fellow-men. The following thoughts may keep us from such a temptation. It means that we at once fall into the worst blunders of our opponents. The man who despises another will never be able to make anything of him. Nothing that we despise in the other man is entirely absent from ourselves. We often expect from others more than we are willing to do ourselves. Why have we hitherto thought so intemperately about man and his frailty and temptability? We must learn to regard people less in the light of what they do or omit to do, and more in the light of what they suffer. The only profitable relationship to others—and especially to our weaker brethren—is one of love, and that means the will to hold fellowship with them. God himself did not despise humanity, but became man for men's sake.

IMMANENT RIGHTEOUSNESS

It is one of the most surprising experiences, but at the same time one of the most incontrovertible, that evil—often in a surprisingly short time—proves its own folly and defeats its own object. That does not mean that punishment follows hard on the heels of every evil action; but it does mean that deliberate transgression of the divine law in the supposed interests of worldly self-preservation has exactly the opposite effect. We learn this from our own experience, and we can interpret it in various ways. At least it seems possible to infer with certainty that in social life there are laws more powerful than anything that may claim to dominate them, and that it is therefore not only wrong but unwise to disregard them. We can understand from this why Aristotelian-Thomist ethics made wisdom one of the cardinal virtues. Wisdom and folly are not ethically indifferent, as Neo-protestant motive-ethics would have it. In the fullness of the concrete situation and the possibilities which it offers, the wise man at the same time recognizes the impassable limits that are set to all action by the permanent laws of human social life; and in this knowledge the wise man acts well and the good man wisely.

It is true that all historically important action is constantly overstepping the limits set by these laws. But it makes all the difference whether such overstepping of the appointed limits is regarded in principle as the superseding of them, and is therefore given out to be a law of a special kind, or whether the overstepping is deliberately regarded as a fault which is perhaps unavoidable, justified only if the law and the limit are re-established and respected as soon as possible. It is not necessarily hypocrisy if the declared aim of political action is the restoration of the law, and not mere self-preservation. The world *is*, in fact, so ordered that a basic respect for ultimate laws and human life is also the best means of self-preservation, and that these laws may be broken only on the odd occasion in case of brief necessity, whereas anyone who turns necessity into a principle, and in so doing establishes a law of his own alongside them, is inevitably bound, sooner or later, to suffer retribution. The immanent righteousness of history rewards and punishes only men's deeds, but the eternal righteousness of God tries and judges their hearts.

A FEW ARTICLES OF FAITH ON THE SOVEREIGNTY OF GOD IN HISTORY

I believe that God can and will bring good out of evil, even out of the greatest evil. For that purpose he needs men who make the best use of everything. I belive that God will give us all the strength we need to help us to resist in all time of distress. But he never gives it in advance, lest we should rely on ourselves and not on him alone. A faith such as this should allay all our fears for the future. I believe that even our mistakes and shortcomings are turned to good account, and that it is no harder for God to deal with them than with our supposedly good deeds. I believe that God is no timeless fate, but that he waits for and answers sincere prayers and responsible actions.

CONFIDENCE

There is hardly one of us who has not known what it is to be betrayed. The figure of Judas, which we used to find so difficult to understand, is now fairly familiar to us. The air that we breathe is so polluted by mistrust that it almost chokes us. But where we have broken through the layer of mistrust, we have been able to discover a confidence hitherto undreamed of. Where we trust, we have learnt to put our very lives into the hands of others; in the face of all the different interpretations that have been put on our lives and actions, we have learnt to trust unreservedly. We now know that only such confidence, which is always a venture, though a glad and positive venture, enables us really to live and work. We know that it is most reprehensible to sow and encourage mistrust, and that our duty is rather to foster and strengthen confidence wherever we can. Trust will always be one of the greatest, rarest, and happiest blessings of our life in community, though it can emerge only on the dark background of a necessary mistrust. We have learnt never to trust a scoundrel an inch, but to give ourselves to the trustworthy without reserve.

THE SENSE OF QUALITY

Unless we have the courage to fight for a revival of wholesome reserve between man and man, we shall perish in an anarchy of human values. The impudent contempt for such reserve is the mark of the rabble, just as inward uncertainty, haggling and cringing for the favour of insolent people, and lowering oneself to the level of the rabble are the way of becoming no better than the rabble oneself. When we forget what is due to ourselves and to others, when the feeling for human quality and the power to exercise reserve cease to exist, chaos is at the door. When we tolerate impudence for the sake of material comforts, then we abandon our self-respect, the flood-gates are opened, chaos bursts the dam that we were to defend; and we are responsible for it all. In other times it may have been the business of Christianity to champion the equality of all men; its business today will be to defend passionately human dignity and reserve. The misinterpretation that we are acting for our own interests, and the cheap insinuation that our attitude is anti-social, we shall simply have to put up with; they are the invariable protests of the rabble against decency and order. Anyone who is pliant and uncertain in this matter does not realize what is at stake, and indeed in his case the reproaches may well be justified. We are witnessing the levelling down of all ranks of society, and at the same time the birth of a new sense of nobility, which is binding together a circle of men from all former social classes. Nobility arises from and exists by sacrifice, courage, and a clear sense of duty to oneself and society, by expecting due regard for itself as a matter of course; and it shows an equally natural regard for others, whether they are of higher or of lower degree. We need all along the line to recover the lost sense of quality and a social order based on quality. Quality is the greatest enemy of any kind of mass-levelling. Socially it means the renunciation of all place-hunting, a break with the cult of the 'star', an open eye both upwards and downwards, especially in the choice of one's more intimate friends, and pleasure in private life as well as courage to enter public life. Culturally it means a return from the newspaper and the radio to the book, from feverish activity to unhurried leisure, from dispersion to concentration, from sensationalism to reflection, from virtuosity to art, from snobbery to modesty, from extravagance to moderation. Quantities are competitive, qualities are complementary.

SYMPATHY

We must allow for the fact that most people learn wisdom only by personal experience. This explains, first, why so few people are capable of taking precautions in advance—they always fancy that they will somehow or other avoid the danger, till it is too late. Secondly, it explains their insensibility to the sufferings of others; sympathy grows in proportion to the fear of approaching disaster. There is a good deal of excuse on ethical grounds for this attitude. No one wants to meet fate head-on; inward calling and strength for action are acquired only in the actual emergency. No one is responsible for all the injustice and suffering in the world, and no one wants to set himself up as the judge of the world. Psychologically, our lack of imagination, of sensitivity, and of mental alertness is balanced by a steady composure, an ability to go on working, and a great capacity for suffering. But from a Christian point of view, none of these excuses can obscure the fact that the most important factor, large-heartedness, is lacking. Christ kept himself from suffering till his hour had come, but when it did come he met it as a free man, seized it, and mastered it. Christ, so the scriptures tell us, bore the sufferings of all humanity in his own body as if they were his own—a thought beyond our comprehension —accepting them of his own free will. We are certainly not Christ; we are not called on to redeem the world by our own deeds and sufferings, and we need not try to assume such an impossible burden. We are not lords, but instruments in the hand of the Lord of history; and we can share in other people's sufferings only to a very limited degree. We are not Christ, but if we want to be Christians, we must have some share in Christ's large-heartedness by acting with responsibility and in freedom when the hour of danger comes, and by showing a real sympathy that springs, not from fear, but from the liberating and redeeming love of Christ for all who suffer. Mere waiting and looking on is not Christian behaviour. The Christian is called to sympathy and action, not in the first place by his own sufferings, but by the sufferings of his brethren, for whose sake Christ suffered.

OF SUFFERING

It is infinitely easier to suffer in obedience to a human command than in the freedom of one's own responsibility. It is infinitely easier to suffer with others than to suffer alone. It is infinitely easier to suffer publicly and honourably than apart and ignominiously. It is infinitely easier to suffer through staking one's life than to suffer spiritually. Christ suffered as a free man alone, apart and in ignominy, in body and spirit; and since then many Christians have suffered with him.

PRESENT AND FUTURE

We used to think that one of the inalienable rights of man was that he should be able to plan both his professional and his private life. That is a thing of the past. The force of circumstances has brought us into a situation where we have to give up being 'anxious about tomorrow' (Matt. 6.34). But it makes all the difference whether we accept this willingly and in faith (as the Sermon on the Mount intends), or under continual constraint. For most people, the compulsory abandonment of planning for the future means that they are forced back into living just for the moment, irresponsibly, frivolously, or resignedly; some few dream longingly of better times to come, and try to forget the present. We find both these courses equally impossible, and there remains for us only the very narrow way, often extremely difficult to find, of living every day as if it were our last, and yet living in faith and responsibility as though there were to be a great future: 'Houses and fields and vineyards shall again be bought in this land' proclaims Jeremiah (32.15), in paradoxical contrast to his prophecies of woe, just before the destruction of the holy city. It is a sign from God and a pledge of a fresh start and a great future, just when all seems black. Thinking and acting for the sake of the coming generation, but being ready to go any day without fear or anxiety— that, in practice, is the spirit in which we are forced to live. It is not easy to be brave and keep that spirit alive, but it is imperative.

OPTIMISM

It is wiser to be pessimistic; it is a way of avoiding disappointment and ridicule, and so wise people condemn optimism. The essence of optimism is not its view of the present, but the fact that it is the inspiration of life and hope when others give in; it enables a man to hold his head high when everything seems to be going wrong; it gives him strength to sustain reverses and yet to claim the future for himself instead of abandoning it to his opponent. It is true that there is a silly, cowardly kind of optimism, which we must condemn. But the optimism that is will for the future should never be despised, even if it is proved wrong a hundred times; it is health and vitality, and the sick man has no business to impugn it. There are people who regard it as frivolous, and some Christians think it impious for anyone to hope and prepare for a better earthly future. They think that the meaning of present events is chaos, disorder, and catastrophe; and in resignation or pious escapism they surrender all responsibility for reconstruction and for future generations. It may be that the day of judgment will dawn tomorrow; in that case, we shall gladly stop working for a better future. But not before.

INSECURITY AND DEATH

In recent years we have become increasingly familiar with the thought of death. We surprise ourselves by the calmness with which we hear of the death of one of our contemporaries. We cannot hate it as we used to, for we have discovered some good in it, and have almost come to terms with it. Fundamentally we feel that we really belong to death already, and that every new day is a miracle. It would probably not be true to say that we welcome death (although we all know that weariness which we ought to avoid like the plague); we are too inquisitive for that—or, to put it more seriously, we should like to see something more of the meaning of our life's broken fragments. Nor do we try to romanticize death, for life is too great and too precious. Still less do we suppose that danger is the meaning of life—we are not desperate enough for that, and we know too much about the good things that life has to offer, though on the other hand we are only too familiar with life's anxieties and with all the other destructive effects of prolonged personal insecurity. We still love life, but I do not think that death can take us by surprise now. After what we have been through during the war, we hardly dare admit that we should like death to come to us, not accidentally and suddenly through some trivial cause, but in the fullness of life and with everything at stake. It is we ourselves, and not outward circumstances, who make death what it can be, a death freely and voluntarily accepted.

ARE WE STILL OF ANY USE?

We have been silent witnesses of evil deeds; we have been drenched by many storms; we have learnt the arts of equivocation and pretence; experience has made us suspicious of others and kept us from being truthful and open; intolerable conflicts have worn us down and even made us cynical. Are we still of any use? What we shall need is not geniuses, or cynics, or misanthropes, or clever tacticians, but plain, honest, straightforward men. Will our inward power of resistance be strong enough, and our honesty with ourselves remorseless enough, for us to find our way back to simplicity and straightforwardness?

THE VIEW FROM BELOW

There remains an experience of incomparable value. We have for once learnt to see the great events of world history from below, from the perspective of the outcast, the suspects, the maltreated, the powerless, the oppressed, the reviled—in short, from the perspective of those who suffer. The important thing is that neither bitterness nor envy should have gnawed at the heart during this time, that we should have come to look with new eyes at matters great and small, sorrow and joy, strength and weakness, that our perception of generosity, humanity, justice and mercy should have become clearer, freer, less corruptible. We have to learn that personal suffering is a more effective key, a more rewarding principle for exploring the world in thought and action than personal good fortune. This perspective from below must not become the partisan possession of those who are eternally dissatisfied; rather, we must do justice to life in all its dimensions from a higher satisfaction, whose foundation is beyond any talk of 'from below' or 'from above'. This is the way in which we may affirm it.

9

THE DEATH
OF GOD

BELIEF IN A TIME
OF THE DEATH OF GOD

William Hamilton

William Hamilton (1924–), contemporary theologian and a founder of the new "God is dead" theology. In books such as The Christian Man *(1956),* The New Essence of Christianity *(1961), and* Radical Theology and the Death of God *(1966, with J. J. Altizer), Hamilton argues for a "Christian atheism" in which the idea and language of God are radically reformulated.*

We cannot objectify God, but we must speak about him. So we get into trouble, our words become distorted, and we raise questions about his location and behavior that we cannot answer. If we objectify him, we make him part of the world, but a part we cannot see. We make him part of the causal sequences of the world, and try to fit him into the order and disorder that we see. But then we find that we must say that he made the world or that he caused the evil and suffering of the world, or we refuse to say this. And so we have on our hands either a capricious tyrant causing evil as well as good, or an ineffectual thing, impotent before evil and causing only the good. We seek for words that express God as something other than personal, and we fall into the danger of making him less than personal. The God seen as a person, making the world, manipulating some people towards good, condemning other people to damnation—the objectified God, in other words—this is the God many have declared to be dead today. This is the God who must disappear, so that we may remake our thinking and our speaking about him. "The courage to be," Dr. Tillich writes in one of his most elusive and profound statements, "is rooted in the God who appears when God has disappeared in the anxiety of doubt."[1]

These two affirmations suggest the contours of the rediscovered Augustinian-Reformed portrait of God in our time. They point to what might be called a recovery of God's divinity, his holiness, his separateness from men. Each of the two basic statements we used to describe this portrait carried a positive and a negative component. The first declared that we cannot know God, but that he has made himself known to us. The second stated that God cannot be properly spoken of or treated as an object, but that we can still praise, adore, speak to him. Put technically, the generally received portrait of God today supports the Reformed insistence that the finite cannot contain the infinite (*finitum non capax infiniti*) and rejects the Lutheran tradition which declares that in the humanity of Jesus the finite has received, and thus can contain, the infinite (*finitum capax infiniti*).[2]

There is a great deal to be said for this rediscovery of the divinity of God, but it may be that we are beginning to pay too dear a price for it. Are we not, perhaps, beginning to lose the delicate balance between negation and affirmation that this position requires? We have come to find it far easier to say "we cannot know" than to say "he can make himself known." His holiness and separateness are beginning to look like an indifference. Now it comes as no great surprise to remind ourselves that the most scrupulously correct theological statements have their own built-in difficulties. One of the reasons why theological moods change is that men come to a time when they want to live with new kinds of difficulties. Theology is always like having six storm windows to cover eight windows. One is quite free to choose which six windows to keep the cold air from entering, and you can live pretty well for a while in the protected rooms. But the uncovered windows will let the cold air in sooner or later, and the whole house will feel it. This contemporary portrait of God is serving well at many points, but some leakage is beginning to be felt.

THE PROBLEM OF SUFFERING

I am convinced that the most serious leakage caused by this traditional and correct portrait of God today is at the point of the problem of

---

[1] *The Courage to Be* (New Haven: Yale University Press, 1952), p. 190.

[2] Eberhard Bethge has recently noted that the Lutheran *finitum capax infiniti* was very close to the center of Bonhoeffer's thought:

"While other dialectial theologians thought of the sovereignty of revelation as gloriously manifest in its freedom and its intangibility, Bonhoeffer, quite after Lutheran fashion, thought of it as apparent in its self-disclosure. Bonhoeffer differed from the other dialectical theologians of those years in his emphasis on the *finitum capax infiniti*." "The Editing and Publishing of the Bonhoeffer Papers," *The Andover Newton Bulletin*, LII, No. 2 (December, 1959), p. 20. See also Bonhoeffer, *Gesammelte Schriften*, II (Munich: Kaiser Verlag, 1959), p. 278.

suffering. There is something in this correct doctrine of God that keeps it from dealing responsibly with the problem, and therefore, because of this silence and carelessness, one can claim today that the problem of suffering has become a major barrier to faith for many sensitive unbelievers.[3]

It is not that the theology dominated by this doctrine of God does not mention the problem. It does, but when it does it is just not good enough. It may, for example, make much of the mystery of iniquity and ask us to shy away from questions about suffering on the grounds that we have no right to put impious questions to the holy God. It may speak of the ontological impossibility of evil; it may say that we are not asked to understand, but only to fight evil; it may say that God is the source of all, good and evil alike, and this is what it means to affirm the divinity of God, and if we don't like it we don't need to affirm him.

Now this kind of evasion may be correct, may even be true, and is certainly very safe. But we miss something: we miss the curious fact that participation in the reality of suffering sometimes destroys the very possibility of faith. The special power of the problem of suffering is that it can really dry up in a man any capacity or wish to call out for the presence of God. If theology cannot reshape its statements about God to face this fact, many men will continue to prefer some sort of humanism without answers to a correct doctrine of God without answers. . . .

THE DEATH OF GOD

I am not here referring to a belief in the nonexistence of God.[4] I am talking about a growing sense, in both non-Christians and Christians, that

---

[3] "The insurmountable barrier to Christianity does seem to me to be the problem of evil. But it is also a real obstacle for traditional humanism. There is the death of children, which means a divine reign of terror, but there is also the killing of children, which is an expression of a human reign of terror. We are wedged between two kinds of arbitrary law," Albert Camus, quoted by John Cruickshank, *Albert Camus and the Literature of Revolt* (New York: Galaxy Books, Oxford University Press, 1960), pp. xii–xiii.

[4] "The world has become an entity rounded off in itself, which is neither actually open at certain points where it merges into God, nor undergoes at certain observable points the causal impact of God . . . but it points to God as its presupposition only as a whole, and even so not very obviously. . . . We are experiencing today that we can make no image of God that is not carved from the wood of this world. The educated man of our time has the duty, painful though fruitful, to accept this experience. He is not to suppress it by a facile, anthropomorphic 'belief in God,' but interpret it correctly, realizing that, in fact, it has nothing in common with atheism." Karl Rahner, "Wissenschaft als Confession?" *Wort und Wahrheit*, November, 1954, pp. 812–13. Quoted by Hans Urs von Balthasar, *Science, Religion and Christianity* (London: Burns & Oates, 1958), p. 95. Published in America by The Newman Press, Westminster, Md.

God has withdrawn, that he is absent, even that he is somehow dead. Elijah taunted the false prophets and suggested that their god may have gone on a journey, since he could not be made to respond to their prayers.[5] Now, many seem to be standing with the false prophets, wondering if the true God has not withdrawn himself from his people. This feeling ranges from a sturdy unbelieving confidence in God's demise to the troubled believer's cry that he is no longer in a place where we can call upon him. Arthur Koestler represents the confident mood:

> God is dethroned; and although the incognisant masses are tardy in realising the event, they feel the icy draught caused by that vacancy. Man enters upon a spiritual ice age; the established churches can no longer provide more than Eskimo huts where their shivering flock huddles together.[6]

The patronizing and confident tone of this announcement reminds us of both Feuerbach and Nietzsche. In the famous passage in "The Gay Science" where the idea of the death of God is put forward by Nietzsche, a madman is portrayed as searching for God, calling out for him, and finally concluding that he and all men have killed him. The man's hearers do not understand his words, and he concludes that he has come with his message too early. He goes on to wander about the city's churches, calling out, "What are these churches now if they are not the tombs and sepulchers of God?" Koestler's igloos and Nietzsche's tombs are spiritually, if not architecturally, related. But in spite of Nietzsche's statement that the madman had come too soon, his declaration of God's death was heard and believed. And in the nineteenth century, as De Lubac writes, "man is getting rid of God in order to regain possession of the human greatness which, it seems to him, is being unwarrantably withheld by another. In God he is overthrowing an obstacle in order to gain his freedom."[7] Freud shared something of this Nietzschean conviction that God must be dethroned and killed to make way for the proper evaluation and freedom of man. And of course, as against many forms of religion, even this strident cry bears some truth.

But Koestler's confident assurance of God's dethronement and death is not the only way modern man describes his sense of God's absence or disappearance. When Dr. Tillich refers to the death of God he usually means the abolition of the idea of God as one piece of being alongside others, of God as a big person. Death of God for him is thus the death of

---

[5] I Kings 18:27.
[6] "The Trail of the Dinosaur," *Encounter* (London), May, 1955. One should add that Koestler never seems to stand still, and that at the close of his recent book *The Lotus and the Robot* (London: Hutchinson & Co., Ltd., 1960), he has a very modest word of praise for Christianity, and, if not for dogma, at least for "the tenets of Judeo-Christian ethics."
[7] Henri de Lubac, *The Drama of Atheist Humanism* (New York: Sheed & Ward, 1949), p. 6.

the idols, or the false gods. The novels of Albert Camus, on the other hand, portray not only a world from which the false gods, and the holy God of the theological revival, have departed, but a world from which any and all gods have silently withdrawn. The world of these novels is a world in which the word God simply refuses to have any meaning. This is not treated as a good thing or a terrible thing; it is just a fact that is ruefully assumed. It is the God described by the best and most sophisticated theologians of our time, who seems to many today to have withdrawn from his world. When we feel this, we do not feel free or strong, but weak, unprotected, and frightened.[8]

We seem to be those who are trying to believe in a time of the death of God. Just what do we mean when we say this? We mean that the Augustinian-Reformed portrait of God itself is a picture of a God we find more and more elusive, less and less for us or with us. And so we wonder if God himself is not absent. When we speak of the death of God, we speak not only of the death of the idols or the falsely objectivized Being in the sky; we speak, as well, of the death in us for any power to affirm any of the traditional images of God. We mean that the world is not God and that it does not point to God.[9] Since the supports men have always depended on to help them affirm God seem to be gone, little wonder that many take the next step and wonder whether God himself has gone. Little wonder that Lent is the only season when we are at home, and that that cry of dereliction from the cross is sometimes the only biblical word that can speak to us. If Jesus can wonder about being forsaken by God, are we to be blamed if we wonder?

BEYOND THE DEATH OF GOD

Now, a believing Christian can face without distress any announcement about the disappearance of the idols from the religious world of

---

[8] "Men are frightened at the absence of God from the world, they feel that they can no longer realize the Divine, they are terrified at God's silence, at his withdrawal into his own inaccessibility. . . . This experience which men think they must interpret theoretically as atheism, is yet a genuine experience of the most profound existence . . . with which popular Christian thought and speech will not have finished for a long time." Rahner, *op. cit.*, p. 812, quoted by Von Balthasar, *op. cit.*, p. 96.

[9] The classical Reformation conception of Providence depended for its formulation on the presence of a whole series of orders that were self-evident to sixteenth-century man: the order of the celestial bodies, the order of the political realm, the order and predictability of the natural world, the order and inner coherence of the self. Men as diverse as Calvin and Shakespeare drew on this experience of order in their own work. In the *Institutes*, I. 5., Calvin used this external orderliness as a means of illuminating the sovereign care of God over the world. Tragedy, for Shakespeare, was the unusual and odd breakdown of the natural order of human life. Hamlet's perception that "the time is out of joint" is a perception of a disorder that is the basis of Shakespeare's sense of tragedy. See also Ulysses' speech on order in *Troilus and Cressida*, Act I, Scene 3.

man, but he cannot live as a Christian for long with the suspicion that God himself has withdrawn. How is it possible to turn this difficult corner, and to move from an acknowledgment of God's disappearance to a sense of some kind of reappearance and presence? This sense of the separation of God from the world, Ronald Gregor Smith writes,

> does not lead to mere or sheer undialectical atheism. Any assertion of the absence of God and even further of his nonexistence among the phenomena of the world is dialectically confronted by the equal assertion of his presence. I am sorry if this sounds like a mere verbal trick, but it cannot be helped.[10]

There is something disarming about Gregor Smith's unwillingness to look carefully at the connections between the sense of disappearance of God and the problem of his reappearance. But his way of putting it does indeed sound like a verbal trick, and we must try to discover if there are not ways of moving from the one state to the other.

One of the favorite contemporary attempts to do this might be called the Augustinian doubt maneuver. Augustine noted that he overcame his temptation toward skepticism by observing that even skepticism implied some affirmation of truth, the truth at least of the skeptical position.

> Everyone who knows that he is in doubt about something knows a truth, and in regard to this that he knows he is certain. Therefore he is certain about a truth. Consequently everyone who doubts if there be a truth has in himself a true thing on which he does not doubt.[11]

This may or may not be a convincing way to overcome radical skepticism. But it certainly cannot be used to mean that we can, by a kind of interior maneuver, affirm that we know the very thing we doubt. Augustine did not use it thus; we may doubt one truth, but that implies, he tells us, that we know another thing in our act of doubt, namely, that we are doubters. But some Christians have tried to claim that somehow doubt implies faith. God's existence, we are often told, is most profoundly proven in the very experience of doubting or denying him. Of course, passionate doubt has a resemblance to passionate faith. Both have a deep concern for the problem of truth; both real doubt and real faith deeply care. But it is not good enough to suggest that "There is no God" or "I cannot know that there is a God" really bears the same meaning as "Thou art my God." Let us continue to say that doubt is a necessary way for many of us to faith; that faith never overcomes doubt finally and completely; that lively faith can bear a good deal of doubt around the edges. But the depth of doubt is not the depth of faith; these are two places, not one, and a choice must finally

---

[10] "A Theological Perspective of the Secular," *The Christian Scholar*, XLIII, No. 1 (March, 1960), p. 22.
[11] *On True Religion*, XXIX. 73.

be made between them. We cannot evade such a problem by a trick of redefinition.

This confusion of doubt and faith obscures the problem of moving from an affirmation about the disappearance of God to an affirmation of his presence. I wonder if the following, and quite beautiful, passage from Dr. Tillich, is not also obscure in its apparent identification of having with not-having.

> To the man who longs for God and cannot find Him; to the man who wants to be acknowledged by God and cannot even believe that He is; to the man who is striving for a new and imperishable meaning of his life and cannot discover it—to this man Paul speaks. We are each such a man. Just in this situation, where the Spirit is far from our consciousness, where we are unable to pray or to experience any meaning in life, the Spirit is working quietly in the depth of our souls. In the moment when we feel separated from God, meaningless in our lives, and condemned to despair, we are not left alone. The Spirit, sighing and longing in us and with us, represents us. It manifests what we really are. In feeling this against feeling, in believing this against belief, in knowing this against knowledge, we like Paul, possess all.[12]

Now this is less specious than the doubt-equals-faith position. And it points to a profound truth. Faith is never the claim to own or possess. God comes to us finally when we confess that we have nothing in our hands to bring. Our not-knowing alone leads to knowing; our not-having is the only way to possession. All this is true, and very close to the Protestant conviction that God's access is to sinners and not to saints. But it will not do. Such a word as Dr. Tillich's can do much. It can persuade the man who struggles for God that there is a sense in which he has been found. It can portray the Christian tradition attractively as one which knows, welcomes, and lives with the experience of struggle and not-knowing. But it will not serve to transform an experience of not-having into an experience of having. For all of our verbalizing, these remain two different experiences, and we are not finally helped by those who do not face openly the distinctions.

The curious thing about this matter of God's disappearance is that even in those moments when we are most keenly aware of God's absence we still, somehow, find it possible to pray for his return. Perhaps we ought to conclude that the special Christian burden of our time is the situation of being without God. There is, for some reason, no possession of God for us, but only a hope, only a waiting.[13] This is perhaps part of

---

[12] *The Shaking of the Foundations* (New York: Scribner's, 1958), p. 139.

[13] Perhaps one of the reasons why Samuel Beckett's *Waiting for Godot* has fascinated us is that Beckett has portrayed so many of the ambiguities in our feeling about God today. Godot, for whom Vladimir and Estragon wait, seems to stand for the traditional God for whom all of us think we are waiting. This Godot has a white beard (p. 59), he punishes those who reject him (p. 60), he saves (pp. 48, 61), he is the one to whom Vladimir and Estragon offer a "kind of prayer," a "vague

the truth: to be a Christian today is to stand, somehow, as a man without God but with hope. We know too little to know him now; we only know enough to be able to say that he will come, in his own time, to the broken and contrite heart, if we continue to offer that to him. Faith is, for many of us, we might say, purely eschatological. It is a kind of trust that one day he will no longer be absent from us. Faith is a cry to the absent God; faith is hope.

An identification of faith with hope is possible, but a little more can be said. The absent one has a kind of presence; the one for whom the Christian man waits still makes an impact on us. W. H. Auden has described this presence very accurately.

> In our anguish we struggle
> To elude Him, to lie to Him, yet His love observes
> His appalling promise; His predilection
> As we wander and weep is with us to the end.
> Minding our meanings, our least matter dear to Him. . . .
> It is where we are wounded that is when He speaks
> Our creaturely cry, concluding His children
> In their mad unbelief to have mercy on them all
> As they wait unawares for His world to come.[14]

In this there is waiting, but also something else. God is also the one whom we struggle to elude; as Augustine says, "Thou never departest from us, and yet only with difficulty do we return to thee."[15] He speaks to us at the point where we are wounded. And even though our wound is our separation from him, the separation is not absolute. The reflections of Psalm 139 and Genesis 32:24–25 in this fragment from Auden remind us of part of our situation.

Thus, neither "death of God," "absence of God," nor "disappearance of God" is wholly adequate to describe the full meaning of our religious situation. Our experience of God is deeply dissatisfying to us, even when we are believers. In one sense God seems to have withdrawn from the world and its sufferings, and this leads us to accuse him of either irrelevance or cruelty. But in another sense, he is experienced as a pressure and a wounding from which we would love to be free. For many of us who

---

supplication" (p. 13). In Godot there is a combination of absence and harshness. He is always postponing his visit; yet he is said to beat the young boy's brother (p. 34). Vladimir asks the boy, Godot's messenger, "What does he do, Mr. Godot?" And the boy replies, "He does nothing, Sir" (p. 59). At the close of the play, when Godot still has not arrived, Estragon asks if they should not drop Godot altogether. To this Vladimir replies, "He'd punish us" (p. 60). Finally, is the Christian critic being over-eager when he notes that the waiting takes place by a tree—the only part of the landscape that has not died (pp. 60–61)? (The page references are to the Grove Press edition, New York, 1954.)

14 From The Age of Anxiety, by W. H. Auden. (New York: Random House).

15 Confessions, VIII. 8.

call ourselves Christians, therefore, believing in the time of the "death of God" means that he is there when we do not want him, in ways we do not want him, and he is not there when we do want him.

The rediscovery of the divinity of God which we described at the start of this chapter seems defective on two counts. It gives us a portrait of God that does not seem able to receive honestly the threat posed by the problem of suffering, and it does not accurately enough describe the curious mixture of the disappearance and presence of God that is felt by many today. I am not sure just what ought to be our proper response to this curious mixture. There seems to be some ground for terror here, so that we can partly agree with Ingmar Bergmann when he said recently that "if God is not there, life is an outrageous terror."[16] Yet in another sense we face the special texture of our unsatisfactory religious situation with calmness. Most of us are learning to accept these things: the disappearance of God from the world, the coming of age of the world, as it has been called, the disappearance of religion as a lively factor in modern life, the fact that there are men who can live both without God and without despair. We are coming to accept these calmly as events not without their advantages. Perhaps our calmness will disappear when we face the possibility that God will even more decisively withdraw—that he will withdraw from our selves as he has already withdrawn from the world, that not only has the world become sheer world but that self will become sheer self. For if there are men today who can do without God, it still seems to be true that we cannot do so. We are afraid of ourselves without him, even though what we know of him may be only a pressure and a wounding.

Finally, this portrait of the situation between man and God today, in the time (as we have called it) of the death of God, is not satisfactory if this is all we know. We have really described a bondage, not a freedom; a disturbance and very little else. If this were all there were to the Christian faith, it would not be hard to reject it. Is there, then, a deliverance from this absent-present disturber God? There is, and the deliverance will somehow be connected with another image of God—what we have already referred to as the impotent God—that emerges when we try to take our next step and saying something about Jesus the Lord.[17] But I have not

16 *Time*, March 14, 1960, p. 66.
17 In a recent debate on the BBC, Professor Gregor Smith tried to bring together the sense of the disappearance of God from the world and a Christian affirmation about Jesus.

"I recognize in that situation that you describe, for yourself and for us all, what you might call the reappearance of God, a veiled reappearance certainly, and I should focus this in the life of Christ, in his life of being for other people, which is how you can sum it up—just being for other people absolutely. I should focus it there, and also in the constellation of events that gather round that particular bit of human history both before and after. I find it almost impossible to say more than this, just because I recognize at once that though I see here action of God, it is, of course, ambiguous. It is still possible to say: 'Well, I just don't see it.' " *The Listener* (London), January 21, 1960.

stated, and I do not want to state, that we can know nothing of God apart from Jesus. We can and do know something, and it is just this unsatisfactory mixture of his presence and absence, his disturbance.[18] As we move towards the center of the Christian faith, Jesus Christ, will we be able to overcome the instability of our belief in a time of the death of God or, even reckoning with Jesus, will something of this experience remain?

.   .   .

JESUS THE LORD

Lordship as humiliation answers the questions

Jesus and the knowledge of God.   If one begins his reflections on this problem with the statement that Jesus is Lord, a first consequence may be some uneasiness with the formula "divinity of Christ," though not with the meaning behind the formula. Uneasiness, not because the phrase points to something false, but rather because it seems difficult to understand how either an affirmation or denial of it could make any sense. Let us assume you are asked, "Do you believe in the divinity of Christ?" It makes no difference whether the questioner is impeccably orthodox and suspects you are not, or wildly unitarian and suspects you of dogmatism. The question implies a comparison between two clearly known categories: one, called the divine or divinity; the other, the man Jesus. And the questioner wishes to know whether or not you find these two known categories commensurable. But the point is this: we do not have two known categories at all. We have Jesus the man. Of him we know something; not enough to satisfy, not enough to provide answers to our ethical

18 At this point the Jew—both ancient Israel and the modern Jew—becomes significant for Christian theological reflection. Jewish existence is an important part of the evidence we cite for our conviction that God is the one who leaves us alone and the one who disturbs us. The Jew is the one who knows what it is to be disturbed by both God and men, and in this sense the Christian never ceases being a Jew when he is a Christian. The reality and integrity of Jewish existence are what prevent the Christian from holding too rigid a Christological definition of God. "Apart from Christ I am an atheist" is false; "apart from Christ I am a Jew" would be closer to the truth. This close theological dependence of the Christian on the Jew (which is a mutual dependence for some Jewish thinkers, but not for others) is one reason why we ought to be deeply disturbed by the lack of really effective theological conversation between Christianity and Judaism today. It is arguable that there is more real theological affinity between Protestantism and some forms of Judaism than between Protestantism and Roman Catholicism. The latter is a Christian heresy, whereas Judaism is in some way a theological necessity. The Protestant needs to learn what it means to stand with the Jew, even when the Jew is not willing to stand with him.

problems, but enough to be able to say what was characteristic of him and his way with men. And we have further a decision of faith that Jesus is the Lord, the one through whom God meets us. But we do not know any separate category of divinity, a separate divine essence by means of which we can define Jesus.[19] [Previously] we described man's situation before God today, and what we found there was a "divinity" quite perplexing, dissatisfying, even intolerable. That kind of divinity was both an absence and a wounding presence: an absence or disappearance from the world, and a presssure or presence in the heart of the individual. In this sense, Jesus is not divine; as the suffering Lord he is a protest against this kind of divinity, or, in better terms, he is a correction and a transformation of divinity as seen in that way.

If there is divinity apart from Jesus, it is a form of divinity that Jesus as suffering Lord corrects, destroys, transforms. In Jesus the Lord we see for the first time what Christian "divinity" must be taken to be: it is God withdrawing from all claims to power and authority and sovereignty, and consenting to become himself the victim and subject of all that the world can do. The afflicting God of our previous chapter becomes now the afflicted God. Divinity in Jesus is not withdrawal from the world; it is a full consent to abide in the world, and to allow the world to have its ways with it.

This is why we can't be content with the traditional way of formulating the question of the divinity of Jesus. "Divinity, divine essence?" we say. "Yes, we know a little of what this means, and what we know of it haunts and disturbs us, both because of its abdication from the world and because of its wounding presence in our hearts. But what we know of it by itself leads us to reject it, not to welcome it at all. In Jesus the Lord, the whole meaning of what it is to be God is so radically transformed that we can no longer move from divinity to Jesus (and thus to assert the divinity of Christ) but from Jesus to divinity, and to affirm that our picture of God is ultimately determined by seeing him as the one who has come in the lowliness of Jesus the Lord."

If it is true that "Luther limited our knowledge of God to our individual experience of temptation and our identification in prayer with the passion of God's son,"[20] then there are some affinities between our position here and Luther's. God himself, Luther would say, is the remote one

---

[19] "Jesus Christ . . . is not God in a self-evident and explainable manner, but only in faith. This divine being does not exist. If Jesus Christ is to be described as God, then one must not speak about his divine essence, his omnipotence or his omniscience, but only about this weak man among sinners, about his cradle and his cross. If we are dealing with the divinity of Jesus we must speak especially of his weakness." From a reconstructed version of Bonhoeffer's 1933 Berlin lectures on Christology, Gesammelte Schriften. Vol. 3 (Munich: Kaiser Verlag, 1960), p. 233. Compare the passage from Letters and Papers from Prison, pp. 163–64, quoted [in the complete The New Essence of Christianity], pp. 54–55.

[20] Erik H. Erikson, Young Man Luther (New York: W. W. Norton & Co., 1958), p. 253.

who comes to us directly only as law and demand. This is the terrible God
whom man cannot abide or compass, for he is hidden from man's knowing. But, Luther went on, God has made himself small, and has willed to
enter wholly into the lives of men in the humanity of Jesus. Here he is not
hidden; he is manifest. Here the infinite one has put himself completely
into the finite space of Jesus the man.

Two passages, characteristic of hundreds more, might be cited to remind us of Luther's powerful, and perhaps even dangerous, concentration
of the lowly humanity of Jesus. The first is from the early lectures on the
Epistle to the Hebrews, 1516–17:

> It is to be noted that he (i.e., the author of the epistle) speaks of the
> humanity of Christ before he names his deity, and by this approves that
> rule of knowing God by faith. For his humanity is our holy ladder, by
> which we ascend to the knowledge of God. . . . Who wishes safely to
> ascend to the love and knowledge of God, let him leave human and
> metaphysical rules for knowing the deity, and let him first exercise
> himself in the humanity of Christ. For it is the most impious of all te-
> merities when God himself has humbled himself in order that he might
> be knowable, that a man should seek to climb up some other way, through
> his own ingenious devices.[21]

The second is from the lectures on Galatians, delivered in 1531:

> But true Christian divinity (as I give you often warning) setteth not
> God forth unto us in his majesty, as Moses and other doctrines do. It
> commandeth us not to search out the nature of God; but to know his
> will set out to us in Christ, whom he would have to take our flesh upon
> him, to be born and to die for our sins. . . . Wherefore . . . there is
> nothing more dangerous than to wander with curious speculations in
> heaven, and there to search out God in his incomprehensible power, wis-
> dom and majesty, how he created the world, and how he governeth it.
> . . . Therefore begin thou there where Christ began, namely, in the
> womb of the Virgin, in the manger, and at his mother's breasts. . . .
> For to this end he came down, was born, was conversant among men,
> suffered, was crucified and died, that by all means he might set forth
> himself plainly before our eyes, and fasten the eyes of our hearts upon
> himself, that he thereby might keep us from climbing up into heaven,
> and from the curious searching of the divine majesty. . . . Then know
> thou that there is no other God besides this man Christ Jesus. . . . I
> know by experience what I say.[22]

In our day, Karl Barth, in the first part of his treatment of the doctrine of reconciliation, insists over and over that we must allow Jesus'
lowliness and humiliation to determine what we mean by God. Here are
some of his comments:

[21] Weimar edition, 57.99.1.
[22] From Philip S. Watson's revision of the 1575 English translation (London: James
Clarke & Co., 1953), pp. 43–44.

How the freedom of God is constituted, in what character He is the Creator and Lord of all things, distinct from and superior to them, in short, what is to be understood by "Godhead," is something which—watchful against all imported ideas, ready to correct them and perhaps to let them be reversed and renewed in the most astonishing way—we must always learn from Jesus Christ (p. 129).

God shows Himself to be the great and true God in the fact that He can and will let His grace bear this cost, that He is capable and willing and ready for this condescension, this act of extravagance, this far journey (p. 159).

The meaning of His deity—the only true deity in the New Testament sense—cannot be gathered from any notion of supreme, absolute, nonworldly being. It can be learned only from what took place in Christ (p. 177).

Has He really made Himself worldly for the world's sake or not? (p. 196).

God chooses condescension. He chooses humiliation, lowliness and obedience (p. 199).

. . . in giving Himself up to this alien life in His Son God did not evade the cause of man's fall and destruction, but exposed Himself to and withstood the temptation which man suffers and in which he becomes a sinner and the enemy of God (p. 215).[23]

To speak about God and to know him means, therefore, to shape everything that we say and pray into the pattern of Jesus the humiliated Lord. Can we do this in a pure way? Can we do it so perfectly that all the problems of "belief in the time of the death of God" magically disappear? Is there, for the man in Jesus the Lord, no sense of God's withdrawal and hounding presence, no waiting for God? I cannot believe that a decision for Jesus as Lord will so simply make irrelevant the situation that we described. . . . The God of the time of the death of God and the God coming in Jesus the Lord are somehow both with us, and as yet no conceptual way has offered itself that will permit us to assign each an appropriate place. A decision for Jesus as Lord is the way we face our difficulties, the way we turn the corner, the way we put off the threat of unbelief in, or rebellion against, that other kind of divinity. Perhaps some new formulation of the doctrine of the Trinity would be a way to fit the two themes together. But now they are both present; each striking, correcting, and violating the other.

One thing is true. We have chosen to live with the dangers of the impotence or weakness of God rather than with the dangers of his power, for we believe that this was God's choice in the crucifixion. We have gained something, and we have lost something. We have gained the power to say:

[23] The page references are to *Church Dogmatics*, Vol. IV, Part 1. It should be pointed out that this note is sounded in the first part of Barth's three-part study of the person and work of Christ. He would doubtless consider the position being suggested here woefully incomplete without the parallel emphasis on the exaltation of man to God alongside the condescension of God to man. The weakness of my position that I indicate just below is not weakness in Barth.

"because of Jesus the Lord, God is always emptying himself to meet us where we are. In joy and in despair, he will never let us go." But if we have one kind of confidence along these lines, we have deprived ourselves of another kind, that kind which can say: "God's rule cannot be violated, his purposes for his creation are sure, his power stands sure over all earthly powers." We have chosen to stand with his lowly presence, but we have so defined power as weakness, that our life in that presence has lost much of the protection and serenity other Christians have known.

PHILOSOPHICAL
CONCEPTS
OF ATHEISM

Ernest Nagel

Ernest Nagel (1901–   ), *American philosopher chiefly
concerned with issues in logic and the philosophy of science. His writings
include* An Introduction to Logic and Scientific Method (1934, *with
Morris Cohen*), Logic without Metaphysics (1957), *and* The Structure
of Science: Problems in the Logic of Scientific Explanation (1961).

1

I must begin by stating what sense I am attaching to the word "atheism," and how I am construing the theme of this paper. I shall understand by "atheism" a critique and a denial of the major claims of all varieties of theism. And by theism I shall mean the view which holds, as one writer has expressed it, "that the heavens and the earth and all that they contain owe their existence and continuance in existence to the wisdom and will of a supreme, self-consistent, omnipotent, omniscient, righteous, and benevolent being, who is distinct from, and independent of, what he has created." Several things immediately follow from these definitions.

In the first place, atheism is not necessarily an irreligious concept, for theism is just one among many views concerning the nature and origin of the world. The denial of theism is logically compatible with a religious outlook upon life, and is in fact characteristic of some of the great historical religions. For as readers of this volume will know, early Buddhism is a religion which does not subscribe to any doctrine about a god; and there are pantheistic religions and philosophies which, because they deny that God is a being separate from and independent of the world, are not theistic in the sense of the word explained above.

The second point to note is that atheism is not to be identified with sheer unbelief, or with disbelief in some particular creed of a religious group. Thus, a child who has received no religious instruction and has never heard about God, is not an atheist—for he is not denying any theistic claims. Similarly in the case of an adult who, if he has withdrawn from the faith of his fathers without reflection or because of frank indifference to any theological issue, is also not an atheist—for such an adult is not challenging theism and is not professing any views on the subject. Moreover, though the term "atheist" has been used historically as an abusive label for those who do not happen to subscribe to some regnant orthodoxy (for example, the ancient Romans called the early Christians atheists, because the latter denied the Roman divinities), or for those who engage in conduct regarded as immoral it is not in this sense that I am discussing atheism.

One final word of preliminary explanation. I propose to examine some *philosophic* concepts of atheism, and I am not interested in the slightest in the many considerations atheists have advanced against the evidences for some particular religious and theological doctrine—for example, against the truth of the Christian story. What I mean by "philosophical" in the present context is that the views I shall consider are directed against any form of theism, and have their origin and basis in a logical analysis of the theistic position, and in a comprehensive account of the world believed to be wholly intelligible without the adoption of a theistic hypothesis.

Theism as I conceive it is a theological proposition, not a statement of a position that belongs primarily to religion. On my view, religion as a historical and social phenomenon is primarily an institutionalized *cultus* or practice, which possesses identifiable social functions and which expresses certain attitudes men take toward their world. Although it is doubtful whether men ever engage in religious practices or assume religious attitudes without some more or less explicit interpretation of their ritual or some rationale for their attitude, it is still the case that it is possible to distinguish religion as a social and personal phenomenon from the theological doctrines which may be developed as justifications for religious practices. Indeed, in some of the great religions of the world the profession of a creed plays a relatively minor role. In short, religion is a form of social communion, a participation in certain kinds of ritual (whether it be a dance, worship, prayer, or the like), and a form of experience (sometimes, though not invariably, directed to a personal confrontation with divine and holy things). Theology is an articulated and, at its best, a rational attempt at understanding these feelings and practices, in the light of their relation to other parts of human experience, and in terms of some hypothesis concerning the nature of things entire.

2

As I see it, atheistic philosophies fall into two major groups: 1) those which hold that the theistic doctrine is meaningful, but reject it either on the ground that, (a) the positive evidence for it is insufficient, or (b) the negative evidence is quite overwhelming; and 2) those who hold that the theistic thesis is not even meaningful, and reject it (a) as just nonsense or (b) as literally meaningless but interpreting it as a symbolic rendering of human ideals, thus reading the theistic thesis in a sense that most believers in theism would disavow. It will not be possible in the limited space at my disposal to discuss the second category of atheistic critiques; and in any event, most of the traditional atheistic critiques of theism belong to the first group.

But before turning to the philosophical examination of the major classical arguments for theism, it is well to note that such philosophical critiques do not quite convey the passion with which atheists have often carried on their analyses of theistic views. For historically, atheism has been, and indeed continues to be, a form of social and political protest, directed as much against institutionalized religion as against theistic doctrine. Atheism has been, in effect, a moral revulsion against the undoubted abuses of the secular power exercised by religious leaders and religious institutions.

Religious authorities have opposed the correction of glaring injustices, and encouraged politically and socially reactionary policies. Religious institutions have been havens of obscurantist thought and centers for the dissemination of intolerance. Religious creeds have been used to set limits to free inquiry, to perpetuate inhumane treatment of the ill and the underprivileged, and to support moral doctrines insensitive to human suffering.

These indictments may not tell the whole story about the historical significance of religion; but they are at least an important part of the story. The refutation of theism has thus seemed to many as an indispensable step not only towards liberating men's minds from superstition, but also towards achieving a more equitable reordering of society. And no account of even the more philosophical aspects of atheistic thought is adequate, which does not give proper recognition to the powerful social motives that actuate many atheistic arguments.

But however this may be, I want now to discuss three classical arguments for the existence of God, arguments which have constituted at least a partial basis for theistic commitments. As long as theism is defended simply as dogma, asserted as a matter of direct revelation or as the deliverance of authority, belief in the dogma is impregnable to rational argument. In fact, however, reasons are frequently advanced in support of the theistic creed, and these reasons have been the subject of acute philosophical critiques.

One of the oldest intellectual defenses of theism is the cosmological argument, also known as the argument from a first cause. Briefly put, the argument runs as follows. Every event must have a cause. Hence an event A must have as cause some event B, which in turn must have a cause C, and so on. But if there is no end to this backward progression of causes, the progression will be infinite; and in the opinion of those who use this argument, an infinite series of actual events is unintelligible and absurb. Hence there must be a first cause, and this first cause is God, the initiator of all change in the universe.

The argument is an ancient one, and is especially effective when stated within the framework of assumptions of Aristotelian physics; and it has impressed many generations of exceptionally keen minds. The argument is nonetheless a weak reed on which to rest the theistic thesis. Let us waive any question concerning the validity of the principle that every event has a cause, for though the question is important its discussion would lead us far afield. However, if the principle is assumed, it is surely incongruous to postulate a first cause as a way of escaping from the coils of an infinite series. For if everything must have a cause, why does not God require one for His own existence? The standard answer is that He does not need any, because He is self-caused. But if God can be self-caused, why cannot the world be self-caused? Why do we require a God transcending the world to bring the world into existence and to initiate changes in it? On the other hand, the supposed inconceivability and absurdity of an infinite series of regressive causes will be admitted by no one who has competent familiarity with the modern mathematical analysis of infinity. The cosmological argument does not stand up under scrutiny.

The second "proof" of God's existence is usually called the ontological argument. It too has a long history going back to early Christian days, though it acquired great prominence only in medieval times. The argument can be stated in several ways, one of which is the following. Since God is conceived to be omnipotent, he is a perfect being. A perfect being is defined as one whose essence or nature lacks no attributes (or properties) whatsoever, one whose nature is complete in every respect. But it is evident that we have an idea of a perfect being, for we have just defined the idea; and since this is so, the argument continues, God who is the perfect being must exist. Why must he? Because his existence follows from his defined nature. For if God lacked the attribute of existence, he would be lacking at least one attribute, and would therefore not be perfect. To sum up, since we have an idea of God as a perfect being, God must exist.

There are several ways of approaching this argument, but I shall consider only one. The argument was exploded by the 18th century philosopher Immanuel Kant. The substance of Kant's criticism is that it is just a confusion to say that existence is an attribute, and that though the *word* "existence" may occur as the grammatical predicate in a sentence no attribute is being predicated of a thing when we say that the thing exists or has existence. Thus, to use Kant's example, when we think of $100 we are thinking of the nature of this sum of money; but the nature of $100 remains the same whether we have $100 in our pockets or not. Accordingly, we are confounding grammar with logic if we suppose that some characteristic is being attributed to the nature of $100 when we say that a hundred dollar bill exists in someone's pocket.

To make the point clearer, consider another example. When we say that a lion has a tawny color, we are predicating a certain attribute of the animal, and similarly when we say that the lion is fierce or is hungry. But when we say the lion exists, all that we are saying is that something is (or has the nature of) a lion; we are not specifying an attribute which belongs to the nature of anything that is a lion. In short, the word "existence" does not signify any attribute, and in consequence no attribute that belongs to the nature of anything. Accordingly, it does not follow from the assumption that we have an idea of a perfect being that such a being exists. For the idea of a perfect being does not involve the attribute of existence as a constituent of that idea, since there is no such attribute. The ontological argument thus has a serious leak, and it can hold no water.

3

The two arguments discussed thus far are purely dialectical, and attempt to establish God's existence without any appeal to empirical data. The next argument, called the argument from design, is different in character, for it is based on what purports to be empirical evidence. I wish to examine two forms of this argument.

One variant of it calls attention to the remarkable way in which different things and processes in the world are integrated with each other, and concludes that this mutual "fitness" of things can be explained only by the assumption of a divine architect who planned the world and everything in it. For example, living organisms can maintain themselves in a variety of environments, and do so in virtue of their delicate mechanisms which adapt the organisms to all sorts of environmental changes. There is thus an intricate pattern of means and ends throughout the animate world. But the existence of this pattern is unintelligible, so the argument runs, except on the hypothesis that the pattern has been deliberately instituted by a Supreme Designer. If we find a watch in some deserted spot, we do not think it came into existence by chance, and we do not hesitate to conclude that an intelligent creature designed and made it. But the world and all its contents exhibit mechanisms and mutual adjustments that are far more complicated and subtle than are those of a watch. Must we not therefore conclude that these things too have a Creator?

The conclusion of this argument is based on an inference from analogy: the watch and the world are alike in possessing a congruence of parts and an adjustment of means to ends; the watch has a watch-maker; hence the world has a world-maker. But is the analogy a good one? Let us once more waive some important issues, in particular the issue whether the universe is the unified system such as the watch admittedly is. And let us concentrate on the question what is the ground for our assurance that watches do not come into existence except through the operations of intelligent manufacturers. The answer is plain. We have never run across a watch which has not been deliberately made by someone. But the situation is nothing like this in the case of the innumerable animate and inanimate systems with which we are familiar. Even in the case of living organisms, though they are generated by their parent organisms, the parents do not "make" their progeny in the same sense in which watch-makers make watches. And once this point is clear, the inference from the existence of living organisms to the existence of a supreme designer no longer appears credible.

Moreover, the argument loses all its force if the facts which the hypothesis of a divine designer is supposed to explain can be understood on the basis of a better supported assumption. And indeed, such an alternative explanation is one of the achievements of Darwinian biology. For Darwin showed that one can account for the variety of biological species, as well as for their adaptations to their environments, without invoking a divine creator and acts of special creation. The Darwinian theory explains the diversity of biological species in terms of chance variations in the structure of organisms, and of a mechanism of selection which retains those variant forms that possess some advantages for survival. The evidence for these assumptions is considerable; and developments subsequent to Darwin have only strengthened the case for a thoroughly naturalistic explanation of the facts of biological adaptation. In any event, this version of the argument from design has nothing to recommend it.

A second form of this argument has been recently revived in the speculations of some modern physicists. No one who is familiar with the facts, can fail to be impressed by the success with which the use of mathematical methods has enabled us to obtain intellectual mastery of many parts of nature. But some thinkers have therefore concluded that since the book of nature is ostensibly written in mathematical language, nature must be the creation of a divine mathematician. However, the argument is most dubious. For it rests, among other things, on the assumption that mathematical tools can be successfully used only if the events of nature exhibit some *special* kind of order, and on the further assumption that if the structure of things were different from what they are mathematical language would be inadequate for describing such structure. But it can be shown that no matter what the world were like—even if it impressed us as being utterly chaotic—it would still possess some order, and would in principle be amenable to a mathematical description. In point of fact, it makes no sense to say that there is absolutely *no* pattern in any conceivable subject matter. To be sure, there are differences in complexities of structure, and if the patterns of events were sufficiently complex we might not be able to unravel them. But however that may be, the success of mathematical physics in giving us some understanding of the world around us does not yield the conclusion that only a mathematician could have devised the patterns of order we have discovered in nature.

4

The inconclusiveness of the three classical arguments for the existence of God was already made evident by Kant, in a manner substantially not different from the above discussion. There are, however, other types of arguments for theism that have been influential in the history of thought, two of which I wish to consider, even if only briefly.

Indeed, though Kant destroyed the classical intellectual foundations for theism, he himself invented a fresh argument for it. Kant's attempted proof is not intended to be a purely theoretical demonstration, and is based on the supposed facts of our moral nature. It has exerted an enormous influence on subsequent theological speculation. In barest outline, the argument is as follows. According to Kant, we are subject not only to physical laws like the rest of nature, but also to moral ones. These moral laws are categorical imperatives, which we must heed not because of their utilitarian consequences, but simply because as autonomous moral agents it is our duty to accept them as binding. However, Kant was keenly aware that though virtue may be its reward, the virtuous man (that is, the man who acts out of a sense of duty and in conformity with the moral law) does not always receive his just desserts in this world; nor did he shut his eyes to the fact that evil men frequently enjoy the best things this world has to offer. In short, virtue does not always reap happiness. Nevertheless, the highest human good is the realization of happiness commensurate with one's virtue; and Kant believed that it is a practical postulate of the moral life to promote this good. But what can guarantee that the highest good is realizable? Such a guarantee can be found only in God, who must therefore exist if the highest good is not to be a fatuous ideal. The existence of an omnipotent, omniscient, and omnibenevolent God is thus postulated as a necessary condition for the possibility of a moral life.

Despite the prestige this argument has acquired, it is difficult to grant it any force. It is enough to postulate God's existence. But as Bertrand

Russell observed in another connection, postulation has all the advantages of theft over honest toil. No postulation carries with it any assurance that what is postulated is actually the case. And though we may postulate God's existence as a means to guaranteeing the possibility of realizing happiness together with virtue, the postulation establishes neither the actual realizability of this ideal nor the fact of his existence. Moreover, the argument is not made more cogent when we recognize that it is based squarely on the highly dubious conception that considerations of utility and human happiness must not enter into the determination of what is morally obligatory. Having built his moral theory on a radical separation of means from ends, Kant was driven to the desperate postulation of God's existence in order to relate them again. The argument is thus at best a *tour de force*, contrived to remedy a fatal flaw in Kant's initial moral assumptions. It carries no conviction to anyone who does not commit Kant's initial blunder.

One further type of argument, pervasive in much Protestant theological literature, deserves brief mention. Arguments of this type take their point of departure from the psychology of religious and mystical experience. Those who have undergone such experiences, often report that during the experience they feel themselves to be in the presence of the divine and holy, that they lose their sense of self-identity and become merged with some fundamental reality, or that they enjoy a feeling of total dependence upon some ultimate power. The overwhelming sense of transcending one's finitude which characterizes such vivid periods of life, and of coalescing with some ultimate source of all existence, is then taken to be compelling evidence for the existence of a supreme being. In a variant form of this argument, other theologians have identified God as the object which satisfies the commonly experienced need for integrating one's scattered and conflicting impulses into a coherent unity, or as the subject which is of ultimate concern to us. In short, a proof of God's existence is found in the occurrence of certain distinctive experiences.

It would be flying in the face of well-attested facts were one to deny that such experiences frequently occur. But do these facts constitute evidence for the conclusion based on them? Does the fact, for example, that an individual experiences a profound sense of direct contact with an alleged transcendent ground of all reality, constitute competent evidence for the claim that there is such a ground and that it is the immediate cause of the experience? If well-established canons for evaluating evidence are accepted, the answer is surely negative. No one will dispute that many men do have vivid experiences in which such things as ghosts or pink elephants appear before them; but only the hopelessly credulous will without further ado count such experiences as establishing the existence of ghosts and pink elephants. To establish the existence of such things, evidence is required that is obtained under controlled conditions and that can be confirmed by independent inquirers. Again, though a man's report that he is suffering pain may be taken at face value, one cannot take at face value the claim, were he to make it, that it is the food he ate which is the cause (or a contributory cause) of his felt pain—not even if the man were to report a vivid feeling of abdominal disturbance. And similarly, an overwhelming feeling of being in the presence of the Divine is evidence enough for admitting the genuineness of such feeling; it is no evidence for the claim that a supreme being with a substantial existence independent of the experience is the cause of the experience.

5

Thus far the discussion has been concerned with noting inadequacies in various arguments widely used to support theism. However, much atheistic criticism is also directed toward exposing incoherencies in the very thesis of theism. I want therefore to consider this aspect of the atheistic critique, though I will restrict myself to the central difficulty in the theistic position which arises from the simultaneous attribution of omnipotence, omniscience, and omnibenevolence to the Deity. The difficulty is that of reconciling these attributes with the occurrence of evil in the world. Accordingly, the question to which I now turn is whether, despite the existence of evil, it is possible to construct a theodicy which will justify the ways of an infinitely powerful and just God to man.

Two main types of solutions have been proposed for this problem. One way that is frequently used is to maintain that what is commonly called evil is only an illusion, or at worst only the "privation" or absence of good. Accordingly, evil is not "really real," it is only the "negative" side of God's beneficence, it is only the product of our limited intelligence which fails to plumb the true character of God's creative bounty. A sufficient comment on this proposed solution is that facts are not altered or abolished by rebaptizing them. Evil may indeed be only an appearance and not genuine. But this does not eliminate from the realm of appearance the tragedies, the sufferings, and the iniquities which men so frequently endure. And it raises once more, though on another level, the problem of reconciling the fact that there is evil in the realm of appearance with God's alleged omnibenevolence. In any event, it is small comfort to anyone suffering a cruel misfortune for which he is in no way responsible, to be told that what he is undergoing is only the absence of good. It is a gratuitous insult to mankind, a symptom of insensitivity and indifference to human suffering, to be assured that all the miseries and agonies men experience are only illusory.

Another gambit often played in attempting to justify the ways of God to man is to argue that the things called evil are evil only because they are viewed in isolation; they are not evil when viewed in proper perspective and in relation to the rest of creation. Thus, if one attends to but a single instrument in an orchestra, the sounds issuing from it may indeed be harsh and discordant. But if one is placed at a proper distance from the whole orchestra, the sounds of that single instrument will mingle with the sounds issuing from the other players to produce a marvellous bit of symphonic music. Analogously, experiences we call painful undoubtedly occur and are real enough. But the pain is judged to be an evil only because it is experienced in a limited perspective—the pain is there for the sake of a more inclusive good, whose reality eludes us because our intelligences are too weak to apprehend things in their entirety.

It is an appropriate retort to this argument that of course we judge things to be evil in a human perspective, but that since we are not God this is the only proper perspective in which to judge them. It may indeed be the case that what is evil for us is not evil for some other part of creation. However, we are not this other part of creation, and it is irrelevant to argue that were we something other than what we are, our evaluations of what is good and bad would be different. Moreover, the worthlessness of the argument becomes even more evident if we remind ourselves that it is unsupported speculation to suppose that whatever is evil in a finite perspective is good from the purported perspective of the totality of things. For the argument can be turned around: what we judge to be a good is a good only because it is viewed in isolation; when it is viewed in proper perspective, and in relation to the entire scheme of things, it is an evil. This is in fact a standard form of the argument for a universal pessimism. Is it any worse than the similar argument for a universal optimism? The very raising of this question is a *reductio ad absurdum* of the proposed solution to the ancient problem of evil.

I do not believe it is possible to reconcile the alleged omnipotence and omnibenevolence of God with the unvarnished facts of human existence. In point of fact, many theologians have concurred in this conclusion; for in order to escape from the difficulty which the traditional attributes of God present, they have assumed that God is not all powerful, and that there are limits as to what He can do in his efforts to establish a righteous order in the universe. But whether such a modified theology is better off, is doubtful; and in any event, the question still remains whether the facts of human life support the claim that an omnibenevolent Deity, though limited in power, is revealed in the ordering of human history. It is pertinent to note in this connection that though there have been many historians who have made the effort, no historian has yet succeeded in showing to the satisfaction of his professional colleagues that the hypothesis of a Divine Providence is capable of explaining anything which cannot be explained just as well without this hypothesis.

6

This last remark naturally leads to the question whether, apart from their polemics against theism, philosophical atheists have not shared a common set of positive views, a common set of philosophical convictions which set them off from other groups of thinkers. In one very clear sense of this query the answer is indubitably negative. For there never has been what one might call a "school of atheism," in the way in which there has been a Platonic school or even a Kantian school. In point of fact, atheistic critics of theism can be found among many of the conventional groupings of philosophical thinkers—even, I venture to add, among professional theologians in recent years who in effect preach atheism in the guise of language taken bodily from the Christian tradition.

Nevertheless, despite the variety of philosophic positions to which at one time or another in the history of thought atheists have subscribed, it seems to me that atheism is not simply a negative standpoint. At any rate, there is a certain quality of intellectual temper that has characterized, and continues to characterize, many philosophical atheists. (I am excluding from consideration the so-called "village atheist," whose primary concern is to twit and ridicule those who accept some form of theism, or for that matter those who have any religious convictions.) Moreover, their rejection of theism is based not only on the inadequacies they have found in the arguments for theism, but often also on the positive ground that atheism is a corollary to a better supported general outlook upon the nature of things. I want therefore to conclude this discussion with a brief enumeration of some points of positive doctrine to which by and large philosophical atheists seem to me to subscribe. These points fall into three major groups.

In the first place, philosophical atheists reject the assumption that there are disembodied spirits, or that incorporeal entities of any sort can exercise a causal agency. On the contrary, atheists are generally agreed that if we wish to achieve any understanding of what takes place in the universe, we must look to the operations of organized bodies. Accordingly, the various processes taking place in nature, whether animate or inanimate, are to be explained in terms of the properties and structures of identifiable and spatio-temporally located objects. Moreover, the present variety of systems and activities found in the universe is to be accounted for on the basis of the transformations things undergo when they enter into different relations with one another—transformations which often result in the emergence of novel kinds of objects. On the other hand, though things are in flux and undergo alteration, there is no all-encompassing unitary pattern of change. Nature is ineradicably plural, both in respect to the individuals occurring in it as well as in respect to the processes in which things become involved. Accordingly, the human scene and the human perspective are not illusory; and man and his works are no less and no more "real" than are other parts or phases of the cosmos. At the risk of using a possibly misleading characterization, all of this can be summarized by saying that an atheistic view of things is a form of materialism.

In the second place, atheists generally manifest a marked empirical temper, and often take as their ideal the intellectual methods employed in the contemporaneous empirical sciences. Philosophical atheists differ considerably on important points of detail in their account of how responsible claims to knowledge are to be established. But there is substantial agreement among them that controlled sensory observation is the court of final appeal in issues concerning matters of fact. It is indeed this commitment to the use of an empirical method which is the final basis of the atheistic critique of theism. For at bottom this critique seeks to show that we can understand whatever a theistic assumption is alleged to explain, through the use of the proved methods of the positive sciences and without the introduction of empirically unsupported *ad hoc* hypotheses about a Deity. It is pertinent in this connection to recall a familiar legend about the French mathematical physicist Laplace. According to the story, Laplace made a personal presentation of a copy of his now famous book on celestial mechanics to Napoleon. Napoleon glanced through the volume, and finding no reference to the Deity asked Laplace whether God's existence played any role in the analysis. "Sire, I have no need for that hypothesis," Laplace is reported to have replied. The dismissal of sterile hypotheses characterizes not only the work of Laplace; it is the uniform rule in scientific inquiry. The sterility of the theistic assumption is one of the main burdens of the literature of atheism both ancient and modern.

And finally, atheistic thinkers have generally accepted a utilitarian basis for judging moral issues, and they have exhibited a libertarian attitude toward human needs and impulses. The conceptions of the human good they have advocated are conceptions which are commensurate with the actual capacities of mortal men, so that it is the satisfaction of the complex needs of the human creature which is the final standard for evaluating the validity of a moral ideal or moral prescription.

In consequence, the emphasis of atheistic moral reflection has been this-worldly rather than other-worldly, individualistic rather than authoritarian. The stress upon a good life that must be consummated in this world, has made atheists vigorous opponents of moral codes which seek to repress human impulses in the name of some unrealizable other-worldly ideal. The individualism that is so pronounced a strain in many philosophical atheists has made them tolerant of human limitations and sensitive to the plurality of legitimate moral goals. On the other hand, this individualism has certainly not prevented many of them from recognizing the crucial role which institutional arrangements can play in achieving desirable patterns of human living. In consequence, atheists have made important contributions to the development of a climate of opinion favorable to pursuing the values of a liberal civilization and they have played effective roles in attempts to rectify social injustices.

Atheists cannot build their moral outlook on foundations upon which so many men conduct their lives. In particular, atheism cannot offer the incentives to conduct and the consolations for misfortune which theistic religions supply to their adherents. It can offer no hope of personal immortality, no threats of Divine chastisement, no promise of eventual recompense for injustices suffered, no blueprints to sure salvation. For on its view of the place of man in nature, human excellence and human dignity must be achieved within a finite life-span, or not at all, so that the rewards of moral endeavor must come from the quality of civilized living, and not from some source of disbursement that dwells outside of time. Accordingly, atheistic moral reflection at its best does not culminate in a quiescent ideal of human perfection, but is a vigorous call to intelligent activity—activity for the sake of realizing human potentialities and for eliminating whatever stands in the way of such realization. Nevertheless, though slavish resignation to remediable ills is not characteristic of atheistic thought, responsible atheists have never pretended that human effort can invariably achieve the heart's every legitimate desire. A tragic view of life is thus an uneliminable ingredient in atheistic thought. This ingredient does not invite or generally produce lugubrious lamentation. But it does touch the atheist's view of man and his place in nature with an emotion that makes the philosophical atheist a kindred spirit to those who, within the framework of various religious traditions, have developed a serenely resigned attitude toward the inevitable tragedies of the human estate.

A FREE MAN'S WORSHIP
Bertrand Russell

Bertrand Russell (1872–1970), one of the foremost philosophers of the twentieth century, celebrated both for his work in epistemology and mathematical logic and his more general philosophic investigations in ethics, politics, morality, and religion. Among his sixty books are Principia Mathematica (1910–1913, *with Alfred North Whitehead*), Philosophical Essays (1910), The Analysis of Matter (1927), Marriage and Morals (1929), Education and the Social Order (1932), Power: A New Social Analysis (1938), The Impact of Science on Society (1952), *and* Fact and Fiction (1962).

To Dr. Faustus in his study Mephistopheles told the history of the Creation, saying:

> The endless praises of the choirs of angels had begun to grow wearisome; for, after all, did he not deserve their praise? Had he not given them endless joy? Would it not be more amusing to obtain undeserved praise, to be worshiped by beings whom he tortured? He smiled inwardly, and resolved that the great drama should be performed.
>
> For countless ages the hot nebula whirled aimlessly through space. At length it began to take shape, the central mass threw off planets, the planets cooled, boiling seas and burning mountains heaved and tossed, from black masses of cloud hot sheets of rain deluged the barely solid crust. And now the first germ of life grew in the depths of the ocean, and developed rapidly in the fructifying warmth into vast forest trees, huge ferns springing from the damp mold, sea monsters breeding, fighting, devouring, and passing away. And from the monsters, as the play unfolded itself, Man was born, with the power of thought, the knowledge of good and evil, and the cruel thirst for worship. And Man saw that all is passing in this mad, monstrous world, that all is struggling to snatch, at any cost, a few brief moments of life before Death's inexorable decree. And Man said: "There is a hidden purpose, could we but fathom it, and the purpose is good; for we must reverence something, and in the visible world there is nothing worthy of reverence." And Man stood aside from the struggle, resolving that God intended harmony to come out of chaos by human efforts. And when he followed the instincts which God had transmitted to him from his ancestry of beasts of prey, he called it Sin, and asked God to forgive him. But he doubted whether

he could be justly forgiven, until he invented a divine Plan by which God's wrath was to have been appeased. And seeing the present was bad, he made it yet worse, that thereby the future might be better. And he gave God thanks for the strength that enabled him to forgo even the joys that were possible. And God smiled; and when he saw that Man had become perfect in renunciation and worship, he sent another sun through the sky, which crashed into Man's sun; and all returned again to nebula.

"Yes," he murmured, "It was a good play; I will have it performed again."

Such, in outline, but even more purposeless, more void of meaning, is the world which Science presents for our belief. Amid such a world, if anywhere, our ideals henceforth must find a home. That Man is the product of causes which had no prevision of the end they were achieving; that his origin, his growth, his hopes and fears, his loves and his beliefs, are but the outcome of accidental collocations of atoms; that no fire, no heroism, no intensity of thought and feeling, can preserve an individual life beyond the grave; that all the labors of the ages, all the devotion, all the inspiration, all the noonday brightness of human genius, are destined to extinction in the vast death of the solar system, and that the whole temple of Man's achievement must inevitably be buried beneath the débris of a universe in ruins—all these things, if not quite beyond dispute, are yet so nearly certain, that no philosophy which rejects them can hope to stand. Only within the scaffolding of these truths, only on the firm foundation of unyielding despair, can the soul's habitation henceforth be safely built.

How, in such an alien and inhuman world, can so powerless a creature as Man preserve his aspirations untarnished? A strange mystery it is that Nature, omnipotent but blind, in the revolutions of her secular hurryings through the abysses of space, has brought forth at last a child, subject still to her power, but gifted with sight, with knowledge of good and evil, with the capacity of judging all the works of his unthinking Mother. In spite of Death, the mark and seal of the parental control, Man is yet free, during his brief years, to examine, to criticize, to know, and in imagination to create. To him alone, in the world with which he is acquainted, this freedom belongs; and in this lies his superiority to the resistless forces that control his outward life.

The savage, like ourselves, feels the oppression of his impotence before the powers of Nature; but having in himself nothing that he respects more than Power, he is willing to prostate himself before his gods, without inquiring whether they are worthy of his worship. Pathetic and very terrible is the long history of cruelty and torture, of degradation and human sacrifice, endured in the hope of placating the jealous gods: surely, the trembling believer thinks, when what is most precious has been freely given, their lust for blood must be appeased, and more will not be required. The religion of Moloch—as such creeds may be generically called

—is in essence the cringing submission of the slave, who dare not, even in his heart, allow the thought that his master deserves no adulation. Since the independence of ideals is not yet acknowledged, Power may be freely worshiped, and receive an unlimited respect, despite its wanton infliction of pain.

But gradually, as morality grows bolder, the claim of the ideal world begins to be felt; and worship, if it is not to cease, must be given to gods of another kind than those created by the savage. Some, though they feel the demands of the ideal, will still consciously reject them, still urging that naked Power is worthy of worship. Such is the attitude inculcated in God's answer to Job out of the whirlwind: the divine power and knowledge are paraded, but of the divine goodness there is no hint. Such also is the attitude of those who, in our own day, base their morality upon the struggle for survival, maintaining that the survivors are necessarily the fittest. But others, not content with an answer so repugnant to the moral sense, will adopt the position which we have become accustomed to regard as specially religious, maintaining that, in some hidden manner the world of fact is really harmonious with the world of ideals. Thus Man creates God, all-powerful and all-good, the mystic unity of what is and what should be.

But the world of fact, after all, is not good; and, in submitting our judgment to it, there is an element of slavishness from which our thoughts must be purged. For in all things it is well to exalt the dignity of Man, by freeing him as far as possible from the tyranny of non-human Power. When we have realized that Power is largely bad, that man, with his knowledge of good and evil, is but a helpless atom in a world which has no such knowledge, the choice is again presented to us: Shall we worship Force, or shall we worship Goodness? Shall our God exist and be evil or shall he be recognized as the creation of our own conscience?

The answer to this question is very momentous, and affects profoundly our whole morality. The worship of Force, to which Carlyle and Nietzsche and the creed of Militarism have accustomed us, is the result of failure to maintain our own ideals against a hostile universe: it is itself a prostrate submission to evil, a sacrifice of our best to Moloch. If strength indeed is to be respected, let us respect rather the strength of those who refuse that false "recognition of facts" which fails to recognize that facts are often bad. Let us admit that, in the world we know, there are many things that would be better otherwise, and that the ideals to which we do and must adhere are not realized in the realm of matter. Let us preserve our respect for truth, for beauty, for the ideal of perfection which life does not permit us to attain, though none of these things meet with the approval of the unconscious universe. If Power is bad, as it seems to be, let us reject it from our hearts. In this lies Man's true freedom: in determination to worship only the God created by our own love of the good, to respect only the heaven which inspires the insight of our best moments.

In action, in desire, we must submit perpetually to the tyranny of out-side forces; but in thought, in aspiration, we are free, free from our fellow-men, free from the petty planet on which our bodies impotently crawl, free even, while we live, from the tyranny of death. Let us learn, then, that energy of faith which enables us to live constantly in the vision of the good; and let us descend, in action, into the world of fact, with that vision always before us.

When first the opposition of fact and ideal grows fully visible, a spirit of fiery revolt, of fierce hatred of the gods, seems necessary to the assertion of freedom. To defy with Promethean constancy a hostile universe, to keep its evil always in view, always actively hated, to refuse no pain that the malice of Power can invent, appears to be the duty of all who will not bow before the inevitable. But indignation is still a bondage, for it com-pels our thoughts to be occupied with an evil world; and in the fierceness of desire from which rebellion springs there is a kind of self-assertion which it is necessary for the wise to overcome. Indignation is a submission of our thoughts, but not of our desires; the Stoic freedom in which wis-dom consists is found in the submission of our desires, but not of our thoughts. From the submission of our desires springs the virtue of resigna-tion; from the freedom of our thoughts springs the whole world of art and philosophy, and the vision of beauty by which, at last, we half re-conquer the reluctant world. But the vision of beauty is possible only to unfettered contemplation, to thoughts not weighted by the load of eager wishes; and thus Freedom comes only to those who no longer ask of life that it shall yield them any of those personal goods that are subject to the mutations of Time.

Although the necessity of renunciation is evidence of the existence of evil, yet Christianity, in preaching it, has shown a wisdom exceeding that of the Promethean philosophy of rebellion. It must be admitted that, of the things we desire, some, though they prove impossible, are yet real goods; others, however, as ardently longed for, do not form part of a fully purified ideal. The belief that what must be renounced is bad, though sometimes false, is far less often false than untamed passion supposes; and the creed of religion, by providing a reason for proving that it is never false, has been the means of purifying our hopes by the discovery of many austere truths.

But there is in resignation a further good element: even real goods, when they are unattainable, ought not to be fretfully desired. To every man comes, sooner or later, the great renunciation. For the young, there is nothing unattainable; a good thing desired with the whole force of a passionate will, and yet impossible, is to them not credible. Yet, by death, by illness, by poverty, or by the voice of duty, we must learn, each one of us, that the world was not made for us, and that, however beauti-ful may be the things we crave, Fate may nevertheless forbid them. It is the part of courage, when misfortune comes, to bear without repining the ruin of our hopes, to turn away our thoughts from vain regrets. This degree of submission to Power is not only just and right: it is the very gate of wisdom.

But passive renunciation is not the whole of wisdom; for not by renunciation alone can we build a temple for the worship of our own ideals. Haunting foreshadowings of the temple appear in the realm of imagination, in music, in architecture, in the untroubled kingdom of reason, and in the golden sunset magic of lyrics, where beauty shines and glows, remote from the touch of sorrow, remote from the fear of change, remote from the failures and disenchantments of the world of fact. In the contemplation of these things the vision of heaven will shape itself in our hearts, giving at once a touchstone to judge the world about us, and an inspiration by which to fashion to our needs whatever is not incapable of serving as a stone in the sacred temple.

Except for those rare spirits that are born without sin, there is a cavern of darkness to be traversed before that temple can be entered. The gate of the cavern is despair, and its floor is paved with the gravestones of abandoned hopes. There Self must die; there the eagerness, the greed of untamed desire must be slain, for only so can the soul be freed from the empire of Fate. But out of the cavern the Gate of Renunciation leads again to the daylight of wisdom, by whose radiance a new insight, a new joy, a new tenderness, shine forth to gladden the pilgrim's heart.

When, without the bitterness of impotent rebellion, we have learnt both to resign ourselves to the outward rule of Fate and to recognize that the nonhuman world is unworthy of our worship, it becomes possible at last so to transform and refashion the unconscious universe, so to transmute it in the crucible of imagination, that a new image of shining gold replaces the old idol of clay. In all the multiform facts of the world—in the visual shapes of trees and mountains and clouds, in the events of the life of man, even in the very omnipotence of Death—the insight of creative idealism can find the reflection of a beauty which its own thoughts first made. In this way mind asserts its subtle mastery over the thoughtless forces of Nature. The more evil the material with which it deals, the more thwarting to untrained desire, the greater is its achievement in inducing the reluctant rock to yield up its hidden treasures, the prouder its victory in compelling the opposing forces to swell the pageant of its triumph. Of all the arts, Tragedy is the proudest, the most triumphant; for it builds its shining citadel in the very center of the enemy's country, on the very summit of his highest mountain; from its impregnable watchtowers, his camps and arsenals, his columns and forts, are all revealed; within its walls the free life continues, while the legions of Death and Pain and Despair, and all the servile captains of tyrant Fate, afford the burghers of that dauntless city new spectacles of beauty. Happy those sacred ramparts, thrice happy the dwellers on the all-seeing eminence. Honor to those brave warriors who, through countless ages of warfare,

have preserved for us the priceless heritage of liberty, and have kept undefiled by sacrilegious invaders the home of the unsubdued.

But the beauty of Tragedy does but make visible a quality which, in
more or less obvious shapes, is present always and everywhere in life. In
the spectacle of Death, in the endurance of intolerable pain, and in the
irrevocableness of a vanished past, there is a sacredness, an overpowering
awe, a feeling of the vastness, the depth, the inexhaustible mystery of
existence, in which, as by some strange marriage of pain, the sufferer is
bound to the world by bonds of sorrow. In these moments of insight, we
lose all eagerness of temporary desire, all struggling and striving for petty
ends, all care for the little trivial things that, to a superficial view, make
up the common life of day by day; we see, surrounding the narrow raft
illumined by the flickering light of human comradeship, the dark ocean
on whose rolling waves we toss for a brief hour; from the great night without, a chill blast breaks in upon our refuge; all the loneliness of humanity
amid hostile forces is concentrated upon the individual soul, which must
struggle alone, with what of courage it can command, against the whole
weight of a universe that cares nothing for its hopes and fears. Victory,
in this struggle with the powers of darkness, is the true baptism into the
glorious company of heroes, the true initiation into the overmastering
beauty of human existence. From that awful encounter of the soul with
the outer world, renunciation, wisdom, and charity are born; and with
their birth a new life begins. To take into the inmost shrine of the soul
the irresistible forces whose puppets we seem to be—Death and change,
the irrevocableness of the past and the powerlessness of man before the
blind hurry of the universe from vanity to vanity—to feel these things and
know them is to conquer them.

This is the reason why the Past has such magical power. The beauty
of its motionless and silent pictures is like the enchanted purity of late
autumn, when the leaves, though one breath would make them fall, still
glow against the sky in golden glory. The Past does not change or strive;
like Duncan, after life's fitful fever it sleeps well; what was eager and
grasping, what was petty and transitory, has faded away, the things that
were beautiful and eternal shine out of it like stars in the night. Its beauty,
to a soul not worthy of it, is unendurable; but to a soul which has conquered Fate it is the key of religion.

The life of Man, viewed outwardly, is but a small thing in comparison
with the forces of Nature. The slave is doomed to worship Time and Fate
and Death, because they are greater than anything he finds in himself,
and because all his thoughts are of things which they devour. But, great
as they are, to think of them greatly, to feel their passionless splendor,
is greater still. And such thought makes us free men; we no longer bow
before the inevitable in Oriental subjection, but we absorb it, and make it
a part of ourselves. To abandon the struggle for private happiness, to ex-
pel all eagerness of temporary desire, to burn with passion for eternal

things—this is emancipation, and this is the free man's worship. And this liberation is effected by a contemplation of Fate; for Fate itself is subdued by the mind which leaves nothing to be purged by the purifying fire of Time.

United with his fellow-men by the strongest of all ties, the tie of common doom, the free man finds that a new vision is with him always, shedding over every daily task the light of love. The life of Man is a long march through the night, surrounded by invisible foes, tortured by weariness and pain, towards a goal that few can hope to reach, and where none may tarry long. One by one, as they march, our comrades vanish from our sight, seized by the silent orders of omnipotent Death. Very brief is the time in which we can help them, in which their happiness or misery is decided. Be it ours to shed sunshine on their path, to lighten their sorrows by the balm of sympathy, to give them the pure joy of a never-tiring affection, to strengthen failing courage, to instill faith in hours of despair. Let us not weigh in grudging scales their merits and demerits, but let us think only of their need—of the sorrows, the difficulties, perhaps the blindnesses, that make the misery of their lives; let us remember that they are fellow-sufferers in the same darkness, actors in the same tragedy with ourselves. And so, when their day is over, when their good and their evil have become eternal by the immortality of the past, be it ours to feel that, where they suffered, where they failed, no deed of ours was the cause; but wherever a spark of the divine fire kindled in their hearts, we were ready with encouragement, with sympathy, with brave words in which high courage glowed.

Brief and powerless is Man's life; on him and all his race the slow, sure doom falls pitiless and dark. Blind to good and evil, reckless of destruction, omnipotent matter rolls on its relentless way; for Man, condemned to-day to lose his dearest, to-morrow himself to pass through the gate of darkness, it remains only to cherish, ere yet the blow falls, the lofty thoughts that ennoble his little day; disdaining the coward terrors of the slave of Fate, to worship at the shrine that his own hands have built; undismayed by the empire of chance, to preserve a mind free from the wanton tyranny that rules his outward life; proudly defiant of the irresistible forces that tolerate, for a moment, his knowledge and his condemnation, to sustain alone, a weary but unyielding Atlas, the world that his own ideals have fashioned despite the trampling march of unconscious power.

Selected bibliography

Eastern Beliefs

Arnold, Sir Edwin. *The Light of Asia*. London: Routledge & Kegan Paul, 1909.
Aurobindo, Sri. *Future Evolution of Man: The Divine Life Upon Earth*. New York: Humanities Press, 1971.

————. *Mind of Light*. New York: Dutton, 1971.

Bouquet, A. C. *Comparative Religion*. New York: Penguin Books, 1950.

————. *Hinduism*. London: Hutchinson, 1949.

Briggs, William A., ed. *Anthology of Zen*. New York: Grove Press, 1961.

Carus, Paul. *The Gospel of the Buddha*. LaSalle, Ill.: Open Court, 1917.

Chinmoy, Sri. *Yoga and Spiritual Life*. New York: Aum Publications, 1974.

Conze, Edward. *Buddhism, Its Essence and Development*. New York: Philosophical Library, 1954.

Coomaraswamy, Ananda. *Hinduism and Buddhism*. New York: Philosophical Library, 1943.

Eliade, Mircea. *Yoga: Immortality and Freedom*. Princeton: Princeton University Press, 1970.

Eliot, Sir Charles. *Hinduism and Buddhism*. Boston: Routledge & Kegan Paul, 1954.

Fromm, Erich, et al. *Zen Buddhism and Psychoanalysis*. New York: Harper & Row, 1970.

Hamilton, C. H., ed. *Buddhism*. New York: Liberal Arts Press, 1952.

Hiriyanna, M. *Essentials of Indian Philosophy*. London: Allen & Unwin, 1949.

Johnston, William. *Christian Zen*. New York: Harper & Row, 1974.

Jurji, Edward, ed. *The Great Religions of the Modern World*. Princeton: Princeton University Press, 1946.

Keith, A. B. *Buddhist Philosophy in India and Ceylon*. Oxford: Oxford University Press, 1923.

Macnicol, N., ed. *Hindu Scriptures*. London: J. M. Dent, 1938.

Noss, J. B. *Man's Religions*. New York: Macmillan, 1956.

Pratt, J. B. *The Pilgrimage of Buddhism*. New York: Macmillan, 1928.

Radhakrishnan, S. *Indian Philosophy*. London: Allen & Unwin, 1927.

Reischauer, A. K. *Studies in Japanese Buddhism*. New York: Macmillan, 1917.

Suzuki, D. T. *Essays in Zen Buddhism*. London: Luzac, 1934.

Watts, Alan W. *The Way of Zen*. New York: Pantheon Books, 1957.

Zimmer, Heinrich. *Philosophies of India*. New York: Pantheon Books, 1951.

Contemporary Christianity

Barth, Karl. *The Word of God and Man*. Gloucester: Peter Smith, 1958.

Bennett, John C. *Christianity and Our World*. New York: Association Press, 1943.

Bonhoeffer, Dietrich. *Ethics*. New York: Macmillan, 1955.

Brown, C. R., et al. *Christianity and Modern Thought*. Plainview, N.Y.: Books for Libraries, 1973.

Brunner, Emil. *The Divine Imperative*. London: Westminster Press, 1947.

Bultmann, Rudolf. *Theology of the New Testament*. New York: Charles Scribner's, 1951.

Cave, Sidney. *The Christian Way*. New York: Philosophical Library, 1951.

Cooper, John C. *Radical Christianity and its Sources*. London: Westminster Press, 1968.

Fletcher, Joseph. *Situation Ethics: The New Morality*. Philadelphia: Westminster Press, 1966.

Flew, Anthony, and MacIntyre, Alasdair, eds. *New Essays in Philosophical Theology*. New York: Macmillan, 1955.

Fuller, Reginald H., and Rice, Brian. *Christianity and the Affluent Society*. Grand Rapids: Eerdmans, 1967.

Gill, Eric. *Christianity and the Machine Age*. New York: Gordon Press, 1959.

Heim, Karl. *Christian Faith and Natural Science*. New York: Harper Brothers, 1957.

Latourette, Kenneth S. *Christianity in a Revolutionary Age.* 5 vols. Grand Rapids: Zondervan, 1973.

Lewis, C. S. *The Screwtape Letters.* New York: Macmillan, 1967.

Niebuhr, H. Richard. *Christ and Culture.* Gloucester: Peter Smith, 1952.

Niebuhr, Reinhold. *The Nature and Destiny of Man.* New York: Charles Scribner's, 1951.

Novak, V. M., et al. *Christianity Today.* New York: Holt, Rinehart & Winston, 1966.

Otto, Rudolf. *The Idea of the Holy.* Oxford: Clarendon Press, 1926.

Phillips, John B. *God Our Contemporary.* New York: Macmillan, 1960.

Rahner, Karl, et al. *Christian and the World.* New York: Kenedy, 1965.

Robinson, John A. T. *Honest to God.* London: S. C. M. Press, 1963.

Royce, Josiah. *Problem of Christianity.* Chicago: University of Chicago Press, 1968.

Tennant, F. R. *Philosophical Theology.* New York: Cambridge University Press, 1930.

Tillich, Paul. *The Courage to Be.* New Haven: Yale University Press, 1952.

————. *Theology of Culture.* Oxford: Oxford University Press, 1964.

Death of God

Altizer, Thomas J. J. *The Gospel of Christian Atheism.* Philadelphia: Westminster Press, 1966.

Altizer, Thomas J. J., and Hamilton, William. *Radical Theology and the Death of God.* New York: Bobbs-Merrill, 1966.

Bloch, Ernst. *Atheism in Christianity.* New York: Seabury Press, 1972.

Buren, Paul van. *The Secular Meaning of the Gospel.* New York: Macmillan, 1963.

Fabro, Cornelio. *God in Exile: Modern Atheism.* Paramus: Paulist-Newman, 1968.

Feuerbach, L. *The Essence of Christianity.* New York: Frederick Ungar, 1957.

Freud, S. *The Future of an Illusion.* New York: Liveright, 1953.

Gurdavsky, Vitezslav. *God Is Not Yet Dead.* Harmondsworth, England: Penguin Books, 1973.

Hamilton, William. *The Christian Man.* Philadelphia: Westminster Press, 1956.

————. *The New Essence of Christianity.* New York: Association Press, 1961.

Ice, Jackson L., and Carey, John J., eds. *Death of God Debate.* Philadelphia: Westminster Press, 1965.

Kaufmann, Walter. *The Faith of a Heretic.* New York: Doubleday, 1961.

Kliever, Lonnie D., and Hayes, John H. *Radical Christianity: The New Theologies in Perspective.* Anderson: Droke-Hallux, 1968.

MacIntyre, Alasdair, and Ricoeur, Paul. *Religious Significance of Atheism.* New York: Columbia University Press, 1969.

Marx, Karl, and Engels, Frederick. *On Religion.* London: Lawrence & Wishart, 1958.

Nietzsche, F. *The Antichrist* and *The Joyful Wisdom* in *The Portable Nietzsche.* New York: Viking Press, 1954.

O'Hair, Madalyn M., ed. *The Atheist Viewpoint.* 25 vols. New York: Arno, 1972.

Robinson, Richard. *Atheist's Values.* Oxford: Oxford University Press, 1964.

Russell, Bertrand. *Atheism: Collected Essays.* New York: Arno, 1972.

Vahanian, Gabriel. *The Death of God.* New York: Braziller, 1961.

————. *Wait Without Idols.* New York: Braziller, 1964.

EXPLAINING HOW YOU KNOW

IV

T HE PROBLEM WITH which we are concerned in this section is that of establishing a standard for determining what constitutes reliable knowledge. For we must decide the conditions under which a claim is well-founded before making any statements about religious truth, moral ideals, or the nature of the external world. Genuine knowledge can only be differentiated from that which is bogus by establishing some criterion for judgment which is decisive.

In philosophic terminology, the problem is considered under the label of epistemology, or theory of knowledge, and it is basic to philosophy because it is the foundation of all philosophic assertions and systems of thought. On the personal level, it concerns us because each of us has to reach some conclusion as to how we know what we claim to know and thereby establish our individual epistemological position.

It is especially difficult to do this today because there are so many divergent ideas presented to us as true, and we are extremely uncertain as to whether any standards can be discovered for deciding between them. We know what others thought before us, but we lack a basis for deciding what *we* ought to think, and when we look around us at the views of educated people, we find opinion so fragmented that the whole makes little sense. Fields of knowledge differ in their explanations of the same phenomenon, and the experts in a given field will disagree among themselves and organize into schools of thought that can hardly communicate with each other, much less reach common answers to their problems. Not only is the physicist unable to talk to the historian, but the Freudian psychologist cannot converse with the existential psychologist, and the behaviorist has little sympathy with the Gestalt approach.

In these circumstances, we are tempted to renounce all hope of finding any criteria with which to measure conflicting claims and to simply rely on our personal feelings about what is real and which statements are true; and without any objective basis for assessment, we can become extremely broad-minded, refusing to call anything false if it seems true to someone. But subjective feelings are notoriously undependable, and reliance on them makes us liable to be swept up by every form of superstition, every charismatic leader, and every intellectual fashion of the times.

Therefore, before we give in to the subjectivist view let us look at the epistemological tradition in philosophy and the theories of genuine knowledge that have been proposed.

The prevalent epistemological theory today is empiricism, in which verification by means of sense experience is considered to be adequate proof that knowledge of reality has been obtained. The sense experience can be of a casual kind, as when we observe and report the weather, or of a deliberate and formally disciplined kind, as in scientific investigation, and our senses can be trusted in their customary natural state or we can extend the abilities of sense perception through instruments such as microscopes, telescopes, stethoscopes, and so forth. However widely we may wish to interpret sense experience, the empiricist maintains that it is the primary channel to reality. In order to establish the truth of any statement about the world we must show the "empirical" evidence on which it is based.

The demand for empirical validation certainly characterizes the epistemological climate of our age, and the advances made by the empirical sciences are among the most outstanding accomplishments of mankind. Nevertheless, empiricism is not the only possible theory of knowledge (as it is sometimes claimed to be), and not only is it challenged by other theories but it suffers from certain problems within itself.

For one thing, conflicts can occur between the evidence supplied by raw sense experience and the data obtained from experiments using technical instruments. For example, the world looks very different when viewed by the naked eye than it does when viewed through a microscope, and the greater the magnification the more radical the difference is, so that we never really know when we have arrived at reality. We can attempt to reconcile the discrepancy by claiming that there are various levels of reality, but this violates our customary assumption that reality is One and leaves us fundamentally unsatisfied.[1]

Another problem arises with regard to the limitations of the senses (whether or not they are used in conjunction with instruments), for there are areas of human experience that are inaccessible to sense verification and yet are important enough for us to want to know the actual truth about them. For instance, a system of mathematical thought need not have any reference to empirical fact, but mathematicians take their work seriously, nonetheless, and declare certain proofs to be correct and others incorrect. The same can be said of the fields of ethics, religion, literature, aesthetics, and other liberal-arts subjects; empirical facts are certainly used, but they do not form the essence of these fields. The ethical principle in Christianity that one should love one's enemies may be right, but it is not empirically verifiable.

Another criticism frequently made against empiricism is the common observation that sense perception is highly unreliable: we perceive the world as flat and motionless when it is round and rotating, and we watch the sun rise when it is actually the earth that turns; we see mirages in the desert, have illusions of purple mountains, and perceive railroad tracks converging and objects decreasing in size as they recede in the distance; we think we see the stars as they are when, in fact, because of the time the light takes to reach us, we are actually seeing the stars as they were, and in some cases, we are looking at a ghostly image from the past because the stars we see no longer exist. The examples could be compounded, but the

---

[1] The same type of problem exists when two or more of our senses do not report the same facts, as when a substance looks solid but feels liquid, or a stick in water looks bent but feels straight.

point is that the senses are extremely fallible instruments, and yet they are the basis for the empiricist's knowledge claims.

In scientific method, the empirical approach reaches its highest state and attempts are made to minimize the problems of sense perception just described. Scientists incorporate into their methodology the strictest procedures possible, so as to maximize the probability of arriving at sound conclusions. In fact, science does not mean particular subjects so much as it means a type of rigorous method; astrology and astronomy both deal with the same subject, but only one is a science.

In the essays that follow, by C. S. Peirce,[2] T. H. Huxley, and J. Bronowski, the nature of scientific method is described from different perspectives, and a good understanding and appreciation of the empirical approach of science can be gained.

But many people have found that empiricism, even when it employs the refinements of scientific method, can still be criticized in basic ways and that by its very nature it will always leave significant areas of life untouched. As an alternative, intuitionism has been proposed as our fundamental means of knowing, with intuition defined as an immediate awareness or sudden understanding of reality without the prior operation of sense perception. Not only is intuition claimed to be the "faculty" whereby the import of empirical findings is grasped but it is said to make accessible the more subtle and profound truths of the emotional part of our being. In particular, in the form of mystical awareness it enables us to grasp religious reality, an area beyond the province of hard science.

To concentrate on mysticism alone, mystics believe that we possess the ability to apprehend extraordinary or supernatural knowledge which is transmitted in heightened moments of revelation. They do not deny that ordinary knowledge is obtained through sense experience, but they insist that through the mystical experience insight is gained into the essence of reality; therefore, mystical knowledge has priority over any other type of knowledge and in cases of conflict must be held supreme.

With regard to the nature and content of mystical experience, here we are on difficult ground because mystics claim that their experience is indescribable; it utterly transcends the normal categories of thought and cannot be translated into words, for language merely serves to express the conventional understanding of reality. Nevertheless, from the oblique remarks made about the central experience in the writings of the mystics, certain features can be described. The firsthand experience, of course, is far better than any indirect description, and this may be obtained through meditation, the study of Scripture, yoga, drugs, privations (such as extreme hunger or lack of sleep), or aesthetic contemplation: it can even

---

[2] Peirce is generally associated with the philosophic movement of Pragmatism, which shares essential features with empiricism but has its own emphasis; it stresses securing "anticipated results" as a test of truth. See the other writings of C. S. Peirce (especially "How To Make Our Ideas Clear") and the work of William James and John Dewey.

occur during the most ordinary moments of consciousness, when no attempt has been made to induce the experience.

People who undergo a mystical experience apparently feel inundated by a spiritual power (sometimes accompanied by radiant light) which overwhelms them and renders them passive spectators of the forces moving within them. They become aware of the fundamental unity of all things and of the meaningful pattern to all existence. Sometimes the Oneness is identified as God or it can be felt as the totality of existence made manifest in a sublime, intense moment. The mystic state is usually brief, and afterward mystics regard the experience as undeniably authentic and profoundly important; their subsequent lives are often radically changed as a consequence.

Although the mystic feels absolutely certain that genuine knowledge has been revealed, it is difficult for others to judge the authenticity of the experience because it is totally private, inexpressible, and immune to empirical or rational considerations. We cannot assume that mystics must be mistaken simply because they cannot present publicly verifiable proof of their beliefs, but at the same time we find it difficult to accept their claims at face value, without any external verification. The outward change in the individual's life, which may follow the mystical experience, only indicates that he or she believes something profound occurred, it does not guarantee that anything real did occur; self-deception can have the same effect as a genuine experience.

And just as illusions (misinterpretations of sense data) count against empiricism, hallucinations (imaginary perceptions arising from internal disorders) militate against the credibility of the reports of mystics. We know that food deprivation can cause trances and visions, that excessive consumption of alcohol can result in the projection of images, that mental disturbances can produce vivid fantasies—all of which are overwhelmingly convincing to the person involved. How are we to separate the hallucinations of people in extraordinary states of consciousness from the allegedly authentic experiences of religious mystics which yield reliable knowledge? To paraphrase Bertrand Russell, there seems little difference between the person who drinks much and sees snakes, and the person who eats little and sees saints.

The selections by Evelyn Underhill and Bertrand Russell in this section will greatly expand the foregoing remarks, but we may well find that the validity of mysticism must be left an open question—a theory for which no evidence is conclusive, not even the personal experience itself. For a powerful advocacy of "subjective knowledge," which lies at the heart of the mystic's claim, the reader is urged to examine Sören Kierkegaard's *Concluding Unscientific Postscript* (Chapters II and III).

As a third possible source of knowledge, reason has been endorsed by a great many epistemologists as having a much higher degree of reliability than either the intuitive apprehensions of mysticism or the sensory experiences of empiricism. The reliance upon reason usually assumes two forms: the acceptance of rationalism as our primary theory of knowledge and reasoning as our basic methodology.[3]

Rationalists maintain that the mind can discern various self-evident truths which are not derived from ordinary sense experience (or extraordinary mystical experience), but are understood and acknowledged by any reflective person. The most obvious examples occur in mathematics, especially geometry, where certain indubitable axioms are accepted at the outset and other propositions are deduced from them. For example, the axioms "equals added to equals give equals" and "a straight line is the shortest distance between two points" are taken as self-evident truths, not because the senses have verified them but because our ability to reason assures us that they are true. The same rational certainty operates in other areas of thought and enables us to begin with *a priori* principles and, from that solid base, to infer additional reliable truths. The most famous case is the *principle of non-contradiction*, which is a general law of thought stating that two contradictory statements cannot both be true; that is, we cannot rationally maintain that something exists and does not exist, is blue and not blue, square and not square.[4]

Reasoning is the process whereby we think in a sound and orderly way so as to arrive at valid conclusions; when reasoning is done formally in strict accordance with the laws of valid inference it is termed logic. We may begin our process of reasoning from self-evident principles of rationalism or from mystical or empirical experience, but whatever material is used, we must be sure to avoid fallacies in our thinking, so that our conclusions follow strictly from the premises.

Obviously, rationalism makes use of reasoning in developing its first principles, and in reasoning we can begin with the first principles asserted by rationalism, nevertheless, the two are distinguishable and can be separately criticized.

The main problem with rationalism lies in the claim of self-evident truths. Upon analysis, most allegedly rational truths are found to be either derived from experience or not universally accepted as self-evident. The ones that remain are so few and so broad that they are of limited practical help in gathering reliable knowledge. With regard to reasoning, the principal or exclusive concern of the reasoner is the consistency and coherence of his or her system of thought, but little attention is paid to the truth or falsity of the content of the argument. A system of thought can be valid, in the sense of rigorously following the rules of logic, but fictitious and absurd as a description of reality; in short, valid conclusions are not necessarily true.

---

[3] In the latter form it plays a large part in scientific method, although empiricism still constitutes the main emphasis.

[4] Sometimes the claim is made that the self-evident truths of rationalism are equivalent to intuitive certainties, and that intuitionism underlies rationalism.

A related criticism is that what is true may not be logically valid, which is to claim that life is wider than logic. The real world may be irrational in character and therefore not amenable to the operations of reason. But here we seem to be returning to a more mystical theory of knowledge.

If the reader is tempted at this point to dismiss reason altogether, it would be wise to suspend judgement, at least until reading the selections by Roger Trigg and C. E. M. Joad, who both present a very persuasive case in its favor.

When we review the three theories of knowledge, we may feel that the various objections can be avoided and a sound epistemological position attained by combining all three into a composite set of criteria. That is, we might argue that genuine knowledge has been gained if there is confirmation by sense experience, immediate and inward certainty, and logical consistency within a system of thought.

Certainly if all three standards can be satisfied, we have greater protection than if we relied on just one. However, occasions can arise when the several theories are in conflict, mysticism assuring us of truths that empiricism denies, reason demanding a logical explanation which mysticism disdains, and so forth. In these circumstances, we cannot avoid making a decision between the competing epistemological positions, and this requires a reexamination of the alternatives to determine which is the most defensible and the most dependable way of knowing.

Before ending the discussion, one final, teasing thought should be interjected: Which epistemological standard should one use—the empirical, mystical, or rational—in determining whether empiricism, mysticism, or rationalism is most reliable?

10

SCIENTIFIC METHOD

THE FIXATION OF BELIEF
C. S. Peirce

C. S. Peirce (1839–1914), American philosopher and founder of the Pragmatic theory (or Pragmaticism, as he termed it), which was later expounded by John Dewey and William James. His essays on Pragmatism, as well as on logic and the philosophy of science, were published posthumously under the title Collected Papers (1931–33).

The object of reasoning is to find out, from the consideration of what we already know, something else which we do not know. Consequently, reasoning is good if it be such as to give a true conclusion from true premises, and not otherwise. Thus, the question of validity is purely one of fact and not of thinking. A being the premises and B being the conclusion, the question is, whether these facts are really so related that if A is B is. If so, the inference is valid; if not, not. It is not in the least the question whether, when the premises are accepted by the mind, we feel an impulse to accept the conclusion also. It is true that we do generally reason correctly by nature. But that is an accident; the true conclusion would remain true if we had no impulse to accept it; and the false one would remain false, though we could not resist the tendency to believe in it.

We are doubtless, in the main logical animals, but we are not perfectly so. Most of us, for example, are naturally more sanguine and hopeful than logic would justify. We seem to be so constituted that in the absence of any facts to go upon we are happy and self-satisfied; so that the effect of experience is continually to counteract our hopes and aspirations. Yet a lifetime of the application of this corrective does not usually eradicate sanguine disposition. Where hope is unchecked by any experience, it is likely that our optimism is extravagant. Logicality in regard to practical matters is the most useful quality an animal can possess, and might, therefore, result from the action of natural selection; but outside of these it is probably of more advantage to the animal to have his mind filled with pleasing and encouraging visions, independently of their truth; and thus, upon unpractical subjects, natural selection might occasion a fallacious tendency of thought.

That which determines us, from given premises, to draw one inference rather than another is some habit of mind, whether it be constitutional or acquired. The habit is good or otherwise, according as it produces true conclusions from true premises or not; and an inference is regarded as valid or not, without reference to the truth or falsity of its conclusion specially, but according as the habit which determines it is such as to produce true conclusions in general or not. The particular habit of mind which governs this or that inference may be formulated in a proposition whose truth depends on the validity of the inferences which the habit determines; and such a formula is called a *guiding principle of* inference. Suppose, for example, that we observe that a rotating disk of copper quickly comes to rest when placed between the poles of a magnet, and we infer that this will happen with every disk of copper. The guiding principle is that what is true of one piece of copper is true of another. Such a guiding principle with regard to copper would be much safer than with regard to many other substances—brass, for example.

A book might be written to signalize all the most important of these guiding principles of reasoning. It would problably be, we must confess, of no service to a person whose thought is directed wholly to practical subjects, and whose activity moves along thoroughly beaten paths. The problems which present themselves to such a mind are matters of routine which he has learned once for all to handle in learning his business. But let a man venture into an unfamiliar field, or where his results are not continually checked by experience, and all history shows that the most masculine intellect will ofttimes lose his orientation and waste his efforts in directions which bring him no nearer to his goal, or even carry him entirely astray. He is like a ship on the open sea, with no one on board who understands the rules of navigation. And in such a case some general study of the guiding principles of reasoning would be sure to be found useful.

The subject could hardly be treated, however, without being first limited; since almost any fact may serve as a guiding principle. But it so happens that there exists a division among facts, such that in one class are all those which are absolutely essential as guiding principles, while in the other are all those which have any other interest as objects of research. This division is between those which are necessarily taken for granted in asking whether a certain conclusion follows from certain premises, and those which are not implied in that question. A moment's thought will show that a variety of facts are already assumed when the logical question is first asked. It is implied, for instance, that there are such states of mind as doubt and belief—that a passage from one to the other is possible, the object of thought remaining the same, and that this transition is subject to some rules which all minds are alike bound by. As these are facts which we must already know before we can have any clear conception of reasoning at all, it cannot be supposed to be any longer of much interest to inquire into their truth or falsity. On the other hand, it is easy to believe that those rules of reasoning which are deduced from the very idea of the process are the ones which are the most essential; and, indeed, that so long as it conforms to these it will, at least, not lead to false conclusions from true premises. In point of fact, the importance of what may be deduced from the assumptions involved in the logical question turns out to be greater than might be supposed, and this for reasons which it is difficult to exhibit at the outset. The only one which I shall here mention is that conceptions which are really products of logical reflections, without being readily seen to be so, mingle with our ordinary thoughts, and are frequently the causes of great confusion. This is the case, for example, with the conception of quality. A quality as such is never an object of observation. We can see that a thing is blue or green, but the quality of being blue and the quality of being green are not things which we see; they are products of logical reflections. The truth is that common sense, or thought as it first emerges above the level of the narrowly practical, is deeply imbued with that bad logical quality to which the epithet *metaphysical* is commonly applied; and nothing can clear it up but a severe course of logic.

We generally know when we wish to ask a question and when we wish to pronounce a judgment, for there is a dissimilarity between the sensation of doubting and that of believing.

But this is not all which distinguishes doubt from belief. There is a practical difference. Our beliefs guide our desires and shape our actions. The Assassins, or followers of the Old Man of the Mountain, used to rush into death at his least command, because they believed that obedience to him would insure everlasting felicity. Had they doubted this, they would not have acted as they did. So it is with every belief, according to its degree. The feeling of believing is a more or less sure indication of there being established in our nature some habit which will determine our actions. Doubt never has such an effect.

Nor must we overlook a third point of difference. Doubt is an uneasy and dissatisfied state from which we struggle to free ourselves and pass into the state of belief, while the latter is a calm and satisfactory state which we do not wish to avoid, or to change to a belief in anything else. On the contrary, we cling tenaciously, not merely to believing, but to believing just what we do believe.

Thus, both doubt and belief have positive effects upon us, though very different ones. Belief does not make us act at once, but puts us into such a condition that we shall behave in a certain way, when the occasion arises. Doubt has not the least effect of this sort, but stimulates us to action until it is destroyed. This reminds us of the irritation of a nerve and the reflex action produced thereby; while for the analogue of belief, in the nervous system, we must look to what are called nervous associations —for example, to that habit of the nerves in consequence of which the smell of a peach will make the mouth water.

The irritation of doubt causes a struggle to attain a state of belief. I shall term this struggle *inquiry*, though it must be admitted that this is sometimes not a very apt designation.

The irritation of doubt is the only immediate motive for the struggle to attain belief. It is certainly best for us that our beliefs should be such as may truly guide our actions so as to satisfy our desires; and this reflection will make us reject any belief which does not seem to have been so formed as to insure this result. But it will only do so by creating a doubt in the place of that belief. With the doubt, therefore, the struggle begins, and with the cessation of doubt it ends. Hence, the sole object of inquiry is the settlement of opinion. We may fancy that this is not enough for us, and that we seek not merely an opinion, but a true opinion. But put this fancy to the test, and it proves groundless; for as soon as a firm belief is reached we are entirely satisfied, whether the belief be false or true. And it is clear that nothing out of the sphere of our knowledge can be our object, for nothing which does not affect the mind can be a motive for a mental effort. The most that can be maintained is that we seek for a belief that we shall *think* to be true. But we think each one of our beliefs to be true, and, indeed, it is mere tautology to say so.

That the settlement of opinion is the sole end of inquiry is a very important proposition. It sweeps away, at once, various vague and erroneous conceptions of proof. A few of these may be noticed here.

1. Some philosophers have imagined that to start an inquiry it was only necessary to utter a question or set it down on paper, and have even recommended us to begin our studies with questioning everything! But the mere putting of a proposition into the interrogative form does not stimulate the mind to any struggle after belief. There must be a real and living doubt, and without all this, discussion is idle.

2. It is a very common idea that a demonstration must rest on some

ultimate and absolutely indubitable propositions. These, according to one school, are first principles of a general nature; according to another, are first sensations. But, in point of fact, an inquiry, to have that completely satisfactory result called demonstration, has only to start with propositions perfectly free from all actual doubt. If the premises are not in fact doubted at all, they cannot be more satisfactory than they are.

3. Some people seem to love to argue a point after all the world is fully convinced of it. But no further advance can be made. When doubt ceases mental action of the subject comes to an end; and, if it did go on, it would be without a purpose, except that of self-criticism.

If the settlement of opinion is the sole object of inquiry, and if belief is of the nature of a habit, why should we not attain the desired end, by taking any answer to a question which we may fancy, and constantly reiterating it to ourselves, dwelling on all which may conduct to that belief, and learning to turn with contempt and hatred from anything which might disturb it? This simple and direct method is really pursued by many men. I remember once being entreated not to read a certain newspaper lest it might change my opinion upon free-trade. "Lest I might be entrapped by its fallacies and misstatements" was the form of expression. "You are not," my friend said, "a special student of political economy. You might, therefore, easily be deceived by fallacious arguments upon the subject. You might, then, if you read this paper, be led to believe in protection. But you admit that free-trade is the true doctrine; and you do not wish to believe what is not true." I have often known this system to be deliberately adopted. Still oftener, the instinctive dislike of an undecided state of mind, exaggerated into a vague dread of doubt, makes men cling spasmodically to the views they already take. The man feels that if he only holds to his belief without wavering, it will be entirely satisfactory. Nor can it be denied that a steady and immovable faith yields great peace of mind. It may, indeed, give rise to inconveniences, as if a man should resolutely continue to believe that fire would not burn him, or that he would be eternally damned if he received his *ingesta* otherwise than through a stomach-pump. But then the man who adopts this method will not allow that its inconveniences are greater than its advantages. He will say, "I hold steadfastly to the truth and the truth is always wholesome." And in many cases it may very well be that the pleasure he derives from his calm faith overbalances any inconveniences resulting from its deceptive character. Thus, if it be true that death is annihilation, then the man who believes that he will certainly go straight to heaven when he dies, provided he have fulfilled certain simple observances in this life, has a cheap pleasure which will not be followed by the least disappointment. A similar consideration seems to have weight with many persons in religious topics, for we frequently hear it said, "Oh, I could not believe so-and-so, because I should be wretched if I did." When an ostrich buries its head in the sand as danger approaches, it very likely takes the happiest course. It hides the danger, and then calmly says there is no danger; and if it feels perfectly sure there is none, why should it raise its head to see? A man may go through life, systematically keeping out of view all that might cause a change in his opinions, and if he only succeeds—basing his method, as he does, on two fundamental psychological laws—I do not see what can be said against his doing so. It would be an egotistical impertinence to object that his procedure is irrational, for that only amounts to saying that his method of settling belief is not ours. He does not propose to himself to be rational, and indeed, will often talk with scorn of man's weak and illusive reason. So let him think as he pleases.

But this method of fixing belief, which may be called the method of tenacity, will be unable to hold its ground in practice. The social impulse is against it. The man who adopts it will find that other men think differently from him, and it will be apt to occur to him in some saner moment that their opinions are quite as good as his own, and this will shake his confidence in his belief. This conception, that another man's thought or sentiment may be equivalent to one's own, is a distinctly new step, and a highly important one. It arises from an impulse too strong in man to be suppressed, without danger of destroying the human species. Unless we make ourselves hermits, we shall necessarily influence each other's opinions; so that the problem becomes how to fix belief, not in the individual merely, but in the community.

Let the will of the state act, then, instead of that of the individual. Let an institution be created which shall have for its object to keep correct doctrines before the attention of the people, to reiterate them perpetually, and to teach them to the young; having at the same time power to prevent contrary doctrines from being taught, advocated, or expressed. Let all possible causes of a change of mind be removed from men's apprehensions. Let them be kept ignorant, lest they should learn of some reason to think otherwise than they do. Let their passions be enlisted, so that they may regard private and unusual opinions with hatred and horror. Then, let all men who reject the established belief be terrified into silence. Let the people turn out and tar-and-feather such men, or let inquisitions be made into the manner of thinking of suspected persons, and, when they are found guilty of forbidden beliefs, let them be subjected to some signal punishment. When complete agreement could not otherwise be reached, a general massacre of all who have not thought in a certain way has proved a very effective means of settling opinion in a country. If the power to do this be wanted, let a list of opinions be drawn up, to which no man of the least independence of thought can assent, and let the faithful be required to accept all these propositions, in order to segregate them as radically as possible from the influence of the rest of the world.

This method has, from the earliest times, been one of the chief means of upholding correct theological and political doctrines, and of preserving their universal or catholic character. In Rome, especially, it has been practiced from the days of Numa Pompilius to those of Pius Nonus. This is the most perfect example in history; but wherever there is a priesthood—and no religion has been without one—this method has been more or less made use of. Wherever there is aristocracy, or a guild, or any association of a class of men whose interests depend or are supposed to depend on certain propositions, there will be inevitably found some traces of this natural product of social feeling. Cruelties always accompany this system; and when it is consistently carried out, they become atrocities of the most horrible kind in the eyes of any rational man. Nor should this occasion surprise, for the officer of a society does not feel justified in surrendering the interests of that society for the sake of mercy, as he might his own private interests. It is natural, therefore, that sympathy and fellowship should thus produce a most ruthless power.

In judging this method of fixing belief, which may be called the method of authority, we must, in the first place, allow its immeasurable mental and moral superiority to the method of tenacity. Its success is proportionally greater; and in fact it has over and over again worked the most majestic results. The mere structures of stone which it has caused to be put together—in Siam, for example, in Egypt, and in Europe—have many of them a sublimity hardly more than rivaled by the greatest works of nature. And, except the geological epochs, there are no periods of time so vast as those which are measured by some of these organized faiths. If we scrutinize the matter closely, we shall find that there has not been one of their creeds which has remained always the same; yet the change is so slow as to be imperceptible during one person's life, so that individual belief remains sensibly fixed. For the most of mankind, then, there is perhaps no better method than this. If it is their highest impulse to be intellectual slaves, then slaves they ought to remain.

But no institution can undertake to regulate opinions upon every subject. Only the most important ones can be attended to, and on the rest men's minds must be left to the action of natural causes. This imperfection will be no source of weakness so long as men are in such a state of culture that one opinion does not influence another—that is, so long as they cannot put two and two together. But in the most priest-ridden states some individuals will be found who are raised above that condition. These men possess a wider sort of social feeling; they see that men in other countries and in other ages have held to very different doctrines from those which they themselves have been brought up to believe; and they cannot help seeing that it is the mere accident of their having been taught as they have, and of their having been surrounded with the manners and associations they have, that has caused them to believe as they do and not far differently. And their candor cannot resist the reflection that there is no reason to rate their own views at a higher value than those of other nations and other centuries; and this gives rise to doubts in their minds.

They will further perceive that such doubts as these must exist in their minds with reference to every belief which seems to be determined by the caprice either of themselves or of those who originated the popular opinions. The willful adherence to a belief, and the arbitrary forcing of it upon others, must, therefore, both be given up and a new method of settling opinions must be adopted, which shall not only produce an impulse to believe, but shall also decide what proposition it is which is to be believed. Let the action of natural preferences be unimpeded, then, and under their influence let men conversing together and regarding matters in different lights, gradually develop beliefs in harmony with natural causes. This method resembles that by which conceptions of art have been brought to maturity. The most perfect example of it is to be found in the history of metaphysical philosophy. Systems of this sort have not usually rested upon observed facts, at least not in any great degree. They have been chiefly adopted because their fundamental propositions seemed "agreeable to reason." This is an apt expression; it does not mean that which agrees with experience, but that which we find ourselves inclined to believe. Plato, for example, finds it agreeable to reason that the distances of the celestial spheres from one another should be proportional to the different lengths of strings which produce harmonious chords. Many philosophers have been led to their main conclusions by considerations like this; but this is the lowest and least developed form which the method takes, for it is clear that another man might find Kepler's [earlier] theory, that the celestial spheres are proportional to the inscribed and circumscribed spheres of the different regular solids, more agreeable to *his* reason. But the shock of opinions will soon lead men to rest on preferences of a far more universal nature. Take, for example, the doctrine that man only acts selfishly—that is, from the consideration that acting in one way will afford him more pleasure than acting in another. This rests on no fact in the world, but it has had a wide acceptance as being the only reasonable theory.

This method is far more intellectual and respectable from the point of view of reason than either of the others which we have noticed. But its failure has been the most manifest. It makes of inquiry something similar to the development of taste; but taste, unfortunately, is always more or less a matter of fashion, and accordingly, metaphysicians have never come to any fixed agreement, but the pendulum has swung backward and forward between a more material and a more spiritual philosophy, from the earliest times to the latest. And so from this, which has been called the *a priori* method, we are driven, in Lord Bacon's phrase, to a true induction. We have examined into this *a priori* method as something which promised to deliver our opinions from their accidental and capricious element. But development, while it is a process which eliminates the effect of some casual circumstances, only magnifies that of others. This method, therefore, does not differ in a very essential way from that of authority. The government may not have lifted its finger to influence my convictions; I may have been left outwardly quite free to choose, we will say, between monogamy and polygamy, and appealing to my conscience only, I may have concluded that the latter practice is in itself licentious. But when I come to see that the chief obstacle to the spread of Christianity among a people of as high culture as the Hindoos has been a conviction of the immorality of our way of treating women, I cannot help seeing that, though governments do not interfere, sentiments in their development will be very greatly determined by accidental causes. Now, there are some people, among whom I must suppose that my reader is to be found, who, when they see that any belief of theirs is determined by any circumstance extraneous to the facts, will from that moment not merely admit in words that that belief is doubtful, but will experience a real doubt of it, so that it ceases in some degree at least to be a belief.

To satisfy our doubts, therefore, it is necessary that a method should be found by which our beliefs may be caused by nothing human, but by some external permanency—by something upon which our thinking has no effect. Some mystics imagine that they have such a method in a private inspiration from on high. But that is only a form of the method of tenacity, in which the conception of truth as something public is not yet developed. Our external permanency would not be external, in our sense, if it was restricted in its influence to one individual. It must be something which affects, or might affect, every man. And, though these affections are necessarily as various as are individual conditions, yet the method must be such that the ultimate conclusion of every man shall be the same, or would be the same if inquiry were sufficiently persisted in. Such is the method of science. Its fundamental hypothesis, restated in more familiar language, is this: There are real things, whose characters are entirely independent of our opinions about them; those realities affect our senses according to regular laws, and, though our sensations are as different as our relations to the objects, yet, by taking advantage of the laws of perception, we can ascertain by reasoning how things really are, and any man, if he have sufficient experience and reason enough about it, will be led to the one true conclusion. The new conception here involved is that of reality. It may be asked how I know that there are any realities. If this hypothesis is the sole support of my method of inquiry, my method of inquiry must not be used to support my hypothesis. The reply is this: (1) If investigation cannot be regarded as proving that there are real things, it at least does not lead to a contrary conclusion; but the method and the conception on which it is based remain ever in harmony. No doubts of the method, therefore, necessarily arise from its practice, as is the case with all the others. (2) The feeling which gives rise to any method of fixing belief is a dissatisfaction at two repugnant propositions. But here already is a vague concession that there is some *one* thing to which a proposition should conform. Nobody, therefore, can really doubt that there are realities, or, if he did, doubt would not be a source of dissatisfaction. The hypothesis, therefore, is one which every mind admits. So that the social impulse does not cause men to doubt it. (3) Everybody uses the scientific method about a great many things, and only ceases to use it when he does not know how to apply it. (4) Experience of the method has not led us to doubt it, but, on the contrary, scientific investigation has had the most wonderful triumphs in the way of settling opinion. These afford the explanation of my not doubting the method or the hypothesis which it supposes; and not having any doubt, nor believing that anybody else whom I could influence has, it would be the merest babble for me to say more about it. If there be anybody with a living doubt upon the subject, let him consider it.

To describe the method of scientific investigation is the object of this series of papers. At present I have only room to notice some points of contrast between it and other methods of fixing belief.

This is the only one of the four methods which presents any distinction of a right and a wrong way. If I adopt the method of tenacity and shut myself out from all influences, whatever I think necessary to doing this is necessary according to that method. So with the method of authority; the state may try to put down heresy by means which, from a scientific point of view, seem very ill-calculated to accomplish its purposes; but the only test on that method is what the state thinks, so that it cannot pursue the method wrongly. So with the *a priori* method. The very essence of it is to think as one is inclined to think. All metaphysicians will be sure to do that, however they may be inclined to judge each other to be perversely wrong. The Hegelian system recognizes every natural tendency of thought as logical, although it is certain to be abolished by counter-tendencies. Hegel thinks there is a regular system in the succession of these tendencies, in consequence of which, after drifting one way and the other for a long time, opinion will at last go right. And it is true that metaphysicians get the right ideas at last; one may be sure that whatever scientific investigation has put out of doubt will presently receive *a priori* demonstration on the part of the metaphysicians.

It is not to be supposed that the first three methods of settling opinion present no advantage whatever over the scientific method. On the contrary, each has some peculiar convenience of its own. The *a priori* method is distinguished for its comfortable conclusions. It is the nature of the process to adopt whatever belief we are inclined to, and there are certain flatteries to one's vanities which we all believe by nature, until we are awakened from our pleasing dream by rough facts. The method of authority will always govern the mass of mankind; and those who wield the various forms of organized force in the state will never be convinced that dangerous reasoning ought not to be suppressed in some way. If liberty of speech is to be untrammeled from the grosser forms of constraint, then uniformity of opinion will be secured by a moral terrorism to which the respectability of society will give its thorough approval. Following the method of authority is the path of peace. Certain non-conformities are permitted: certain others (considered unsafe) are forbidden. These are different in different countries and in different ages; but, wherever you are, let it be known that you seriously hold a tabooed belief, and you may be perfectly sure of being treated with a cruelty no less brutal but more refined than hunting you like a wolf. Thus, the greatest intellectual benefactors of mankind have never dared, and dare not now, to utter the whole of their thought; and thus a shade of *prima facie* doubt is cast upon every proposition which is considered essential to the security of society. Singularly enough, the persecution does not all come from without; but a man torments himself and is oftentimes most distressed at finding himself believing propositions which he has been brought up to regard with aversion. The peaceful and sympathetic man will, therefore, find it hard to resist the temptation to submit his opinions to authority. But most of all I admire the method of tenacity for its strength, simplicity, and directness. Men who pursue it are distinguished for their decision of character, which becomes very easy with such a mental rule. They do not waste time in trying to make up their minds to what they want, but, fastening like lightning upon whatever alternative comes first, they hold to it to the end, whatever happens, without an instant's irresolution. This is one of the splendid qualities which generally accompany brilliant, unlasting success. It is impossible not to envy the man who can dismiss reason, although we know how it must turn out at last.

Such are the advantages which the other methods of settling opinions have over scientific investigation. A man should consider well of them; and then he should consider that, after all, he wishes his opinions to coincide with the fact, that there is no reason why the results of those first three methods should do so. To bring about this effect is the prerogative of the method of science. Upon such considerations he has to make his choice —a choice which is far more than the adoption of any intellectual opinion, which is one of the ruling decisions of his life, to which when once made he is bound to adhere. The force of habit will sometimes cause a man to hold on to old beliefs after he is in a condition to see that they have no sound basis. But reflection upon the state of the case will overcome these habits, and he ought to allow reflection full weight. People sometimes shrink from doing this, having an idea that beliefs are wholesome which they cannot help feeling rest on nothing. But let such persons suppose an analogous though different case from their own. Let them ask themselves what they would say to a reformed Mussulman who should hesitate to give up his old notions in regard to the relations of the sexes; or to a reformed Catholic who should still shrink from the Bible. Would they not say that these persons ought to consider the matter fully, and clearly understand the new doctrine, and then ought to embrace it in its entirety? But, above all, let it be considered that what is more wholesome than any particular belief is integrity of belief; and that to avoid looking into the support of any belief from a fear that it may turn out rotten is quite as immoral as it is disadvantageous. The person who confesses that there is such a thing as truth, which is distinguished from falsehood simply by this, that if acted on it should, on full consideration, carry us to the point we aim at and not astray, and then, though convinced of this, dares not know the truth and seeks to avoid it, is in a sorry state of mind, indeed.

Yes, the other methods do have their merits: a clear logical conscience does cost something—just as any virtue, just as all that we cherish, costs us dear. But, we should not desire it to be otherwise. The genius of a man's logical method should be loved and reverenced as his bride, whom he has chosen from all the world. He need not condemn the others; on the contrary, he may honor them deeply, and in doing so he only honors her the more. But she is the one that he has chosen, and he knows that he was right in making that choice. And having made it, he will work and fight for her, and will not complain that there are blows to take, hoping that there may be as many and as hard to give, and will strive to be the worthy knight and champion of her from the blaze of whose splendors he draws his inspiration and his courage.

THE METHOD
OF SCIENTIFIC
INVESTIGATION
T. H. Huxley

*T. H. Huxley (1825–1895), English scientist and human-
ist renowned for his defense of Darwinism and his educational reforms in
the teaching of science and the humanities.* His publications include
Zoological Evidence as to Man's Place in Nature (1863), Lay Sermons
(1870), Science and Culture (1881), *and* Evolution and Ethics (1893).

. . . You have all heard it repeated, I dare say, that men of science work
by means of induction and deduction, and that by the help of these
operations, they, in a sort of sense, wring from Nature certain other things,
which are called natural laws, and causes, and that out of these, by some
cunning skill of their own, they build up hypotheses and theories. And it
is imagined by many, that the operations of the common mind can be by
no means compared with these processes, and that they have to be
acquired by a sort of special apprenticeship to the craft. To hear all these
large words, you would think that the mind of a man of science must be
constituted differently from that of his fellow men; but if you will not be
frightened by terms, you will discover that you are quite wrong, and that
all these terrible apparatus are being used by yourselves every day and
every hour of your lives.

There is a well-known incident in one of Molière's plays,[1] where the
author makes the hero express unbounded delight on being told that he
had been talking prose during the whole of his life. In the same way, I
trust, that you will take comfort, and be delighted with yourselves, on the
discovery that you have been acting on the principles of inductive and
deductive philosophy during the same period. Probably there is not one
here who has not in the course of the day had occasion to set in motion a
complex train of reasoning, of the very same kind, though differing of
course in degree, as that which a scientific man goes through in tracing the
causes of natural phenomena.

A very trivial circumstance will serve to exemplify this. Suppose you

[1] *Le Bourgeois Gentilhomme.*

go into a fruiterer's shop, wanting an apple,—you take up one, and, on biting it, you find it is sour; you look at it, and see that it is hard and green. You take up another one, and that too is hard, green, and sour. The shopman offers you a third; but, before biting it, you examine it, and find that it is hard and green, and you immediately say that you will not have it, as it must be sour, like those that you have already tried.

Nothing can be more simple than that, you think; but if you will take the trouble to analyze and trace out into its logical elements what has been done by the mind, you will be greatly surprised. In the first place, you have performed the operation of induction. You found that, in two experiences, hardness and greenness in apples went together with sourness. It was so in the first case, and it was confirmed by the second. True, it is a very small basis, but still it is enough to make an induction from; you generalize the facts, and you expect to find sourness in apples where you get hardness and greenness. You found upon that a general law, that all hard and green apples are sour; and that, so far as it goes, is a perfect induction. Well, having got your natural law in this way, when you are offered another apple which you find is hard and green, you say, "All hard and green apples are sour; this apple is hard and green, therefore this apple is sour." That train of reasoning is what logicians call a syllogism, and has all its various parts and terms—its major premise, its minor premise, and its conclusion, and, by the help of further reasoning, which, if drawn out, would have to be exhibited in two or three other syllogisms, you arrive at your final determination, "I will not have that apple." So that, you see, you have, in the first place, established a law by induction, and upon that you have founded a deduction, and reasoned out the special conclusion of the particular case. Well now, suppose, having got your law, that at some time afterwards, you are discussing the qualities of apples with a friend: you will say to him, "It is a very curious thing,—but I find that all hard and green apples are sour!" Your friend says to you, "But how do you know that?" You at once reply, "Oh, because I have tried them over and over again, and have always found them to be so." Well, if we were taking science instead of common sense, we should call that an experimental verification. And, if still opposed, you go further, and say, "I have heard from the people in Somersetshire and Devonshire, where a large number of apples are grown, that they have observed the same thing. It is also found to be the case in Normandy, and in North America. In short, I find it to be the universal experience of mankind wherever attention has been directed to the subject." Whereupon, your friend, unless he is a very unreasonable man, agrees with you, and is convinced that you are quite right in the conclusion you have drawn. He believes, although perhaps he does not know he believes it, that the more extensive verifications are,— that the more frequently experiments have been made, and results of the same kind arrived at,—that the more varied the conditions under which the same results are obtained the more certain is the ultimate conclusion, and he disputes the question no further. He sees that the experiment has been tried under all sorts of conditions, as to time, place, and people, with the same result; and he says with you, therefore, that the law you have laid down must be a good one, and he must believe it.

In science we do the same thing;—the philosopher exercises precisely the same faculties, though in a much more delicate manner. In scientific inquiry it becomes a matter of duty to expose a supposed law to every possible kind of verification, and to take care, moreover, that this is done intentionally, and not left to a mere accident, as in the case of the apples. And in science, as in common life, our confidence in a law is in exact proportion to the absence of variation in the result of our experimental verifications. For instance, if you let go your grasp of an article you may have in your hand, it will immediately fall to the ground. That is a very common verification of one of the best established laws of nature—that of gravitation. The method by which men of science establish the existence of that law is exactly the same as that by which we have established the trivial proposition about the sourness of hard and green apples. But we believe it in such an extensive, thorough, and unhesitating manner because the universal experience of mankind verifies it, and we can verify it ourselves at any time; and that is the strongest possible foundation on which any natural law can rest.

So much, then, by way of proof that the method of establishing laws in science is exactly the same as that pursued in common life. Let us now turn to another matter (though really it is but another phase of the same question), and that is, the method by which, from the relations of certain phenomena, we prove that some stand in the position of causes towards the others.

I want to put the case clearly before you, and will therefore show you what I mean by another familiar example. I will suppose that one of you, on coming down in the morning to the parlor of your house, finds that a tea-pot and some spoons which had been left in the room on the previous evening are gone,—the window is open, and you observe the mark of a dirty hand on the window-frame, and perhaps, in addition to that, you notice the impress of a hob-nailed shoe on the gravel outside. All these phenomena have struck your attention instantly, and before two seconds have passed you say, "Oh, somebody has broken open the window, entered the room, and run off with the spoons and the tea-pot!" That speech is out of your mouth in a moment. And you will probably add, "I know there has; I am quite sure of it!" You mean to say exactly what you know; but in reality you are giving expression to what is, in all essential particulars, an hypothesis. You do not *know* it at all; it is nothing but an hypothesis founded on a long train of inductions and deductions.

What are those inductions and deductions, and how have you got at this hypothesis? You have observed, in the first place, that the window is open; but by a train of reasoning involving many inductions and deductions, you have probably arrived long before at the general law—and a very good one it is—that windows do not open of themselves; and you therefore conclude that something has opened the window. A second general law that you have arrived at in the same way is, that tea-pots and spoons do not go out of a window spontaneously, and you are satisfied that, as they are not now where you left them, they have been removed. In the third place, you look at the marks on the window-sill, and the shoe-marks outside, and you say that in all previous experience the former kind of mark had never been produced by anything else but the hand of a human being; and the same experience shows that no other animal but man at present wears shoes with hob-nails in them such as would produce the marks in the gravel. I do not know, even if we could discover any of those "missing links" that are talked about, that they would help us to any other conclusion! At any rate the law which states our present experience is strong enough for my present purpose. You next reach the conclusion that, as these kinds of marks have not been left by any other animal than man, or are liable to be formed in any other way than by a man's hand and shoe, the marks in question have been formed by a man in that way. You have, further, a general law, founded on observation and experience, and that, too, is, I am sorry to say, a very universal and unimpeachable one—that some men are thieves; and you assume at once from all these premises—and that is what constitutes your hypothesis—that the man who made the marks outside and on the window-sill, opened the window, got into the room, and stole your tea-pot and spoons. You have now arrived at a *vera causa*;—you have assumed a cause which, it is plain, is competent to produce all the phenomena you have observed. You can explain all these phenomena only by the hypothesis of a thief. But that is an hypothetical conclusion, of the justice of which you have no absolute proof at all; it is only rendered highly probable by a series of inductive and deductive reasonings.

I suppose your first action, assuming that you are a man of ordinary common sense, and that you have established this hypothesis to your own satisfaction, will very likely be to go off for the police, and set them on the track of the burglar, with the view to the recovery of your property. But just as you are starting with this object, some person comes in, and on learning what you are about, says, "My good friend, you are going on a great deal too fast. How do you know that the man who really made the marks took the spoons? It might have been a monkey that took them, and the man may have merely looked in afterwards." You would probably reply, "Well, that is all very well, but you see it is contrary to all experience of the way tea-pots and spoons are abstracted; so that, at any rate, your hypothesis is less probable than mine." While you are talking the thing over in this way, another friend arrives, one of the good kind of people that I was talking of a little while ago. And he might say, "Oh, my dear sir, you are certainly going on a great deal too fast. You are most presumptuous. You admit that all these occurrences took place when you were fast asleep, at a time when you could not possibly have known anything about what was taking place. How do you know that the laws of Nature are not suspended during the night? It may be that there has been some kind of supernatural interference in this case." In point of fact, he declares that your hypothesis is one of which you cannot at all demonstrate the truth, and that you are by no means sure that the laws of Nature are the same when you are asleep as when you are awake.

Well, now, you cannot at the moment answer that kind of reasoning. You feel that your worthy friend has you somewhat at a disadvantage. You will feel perfectly convinced in your own mind, however, that you are quite right, and you say to him, "My good friend, I can only be guided by the natural probabilities of the case, and if you will be kind enough to stand aside and permit me to pass, I will go and fetch the police." Well, we will suppose that your journey is successful, and that by good luck you meet with a policeman; that eventually the burglar is found with your property on his person, and the marks correspond to his hand and to his boots. Probably any jury would consider those facts a very good experimental verification of your hypothesis, touching the cause of the abnormal phenomena observed in your parlor, and would act accordingly.

Now, in this supposititious case, I have taken phenomena of a very common kind, in order that you might see what are the different steps in an ordinary process of reasoning, if you will only take the trouble to analyze it carefully. All the operations I have described, you will see, are involved in the mind of any man of sense in leading him to a conclusion as to the course he should take in order to make good a robbery and punish the offender. I say that you are led, in that case, to your conclusion by exactly the same train of reasoning as that which a man of science pursues when he is endeavoring to discover the origin and laws of the most occult phenomena. The process is, and always must be, the same; and precisely the same mode of reasoning was employed by Newton and Laplace in their endeavors to discover and define the causes of the movements of the heavenly bodies, as you, with your own common sense, would employ to detect a burglar. The only difference is, that the nature of the inquiry being more abstruse, every step has to be most carefully watched, so that there may not be a single crack or flaw in your hypothesis. A flaw or crack in many of the hypotheses of daily life may be of little or no moment as affecting the general correctness of the conclusions at which we may arrive; but, in a scientific inquiry, a fallacy, great or small, is always of importance, and is sure to be in the long run constantly productive of mischievous, if not fatal results.

Do not allow yourselves to be misled by the common notion that an hypothesis is untrustworthy simply because it is an hypothesis. It is often urged, in respect to some scientific conclusion that, after all, it is only an hypothesis. But what more have we to guide us in nine-tenths of the most important affairs of daily life than hypotheses, and often very ill-based ones? So that in science, where the evidence of an hypothesis is subjected to the most rigid examination, we may rightly pursue the same course. You may have hypotheses and hypotheses. A man may say, if he likes, that the moon is made of green cheese: that is an hypothesis. But another man, who has devoted a great deal of time and attention to the subject, and availed himself of the powerful telescopes and the results of the observations of others, declares that in his opinion it is probably composed of materials very similar to those of which our own earth is made up: and that is also only an hypothesis. But I need not tell you that there is an enormous difference in the value of the two hypotheses. That one which is based on sound scientific knowledge is sure to have a corresponding value; and that which is a mere hasty random guess is likely to have but little value. Every great step in our progress in discovering causes has been made in exactly the same way as that which I have detailed to you. A person observing the occurrence of certain facts and phenomena asks, naturally enough, what process, what kind of operation known to occur in Nature, applied to the particular case, will unravel and explain the mystery? Hence you have the scientific hypothesis; and its value will be proportionate to the care and completeness with which its basis had been tested and verified. It is in these matters as in the commonest affairs of practical life: the guess of the fool will be folly, while the guess of the wise man will contain wisdom. In all cases, you see that the value of the result depends on the patience and faithfulness with which the investigator applies to his hypothesis every possible kind of verification.

Wherever there are complex masses of phenomena to be inquired into, whether they be phenomena of the affairs of daily life, or whether they belong to the more abstruse and difficult problems laid before the philosopher, our course of proceeding in unravelling that complex chain of phenomena with a view to get at its cause, is always the same; in all cases we must invent an hypothesis; we must place before ourselves some more or less likely supposition respecting that cause; and then, having assumed an hypothesis, having supposed a cause for the phenomena in question, we must endeavor, on the one hand, to demonstrate our hypothesis, or, on the other, to upset and reject it altogether, by testing it in three ways. We must, in the first place, be prepared to prove that the supposed causes of the phenomena exist in nature; that they are what the logicians call *veræ causæ*—true causes; in the next place, we should be prepared to show that the assumed causes of the phenomena are competent to produce such as those we wish to explain by them; and in the last place, we ought to be able to show that no other known causes are competent to produce these phenomena. If we can succeed in satisfying these three conditions, we shall have demonstrated our hypothesis; or rather I ought to say, we shall have proved it as far as certainty is possible for us; for, after all, there is no one of our surest convictions which may not be upset, or at any rate modified by a further accession of knowledge. It was because it satisfied these conditions that we accepted the hypothesis as to the disappearance of the tea-pot and spoons in the case I supposed; we found that our hypothesis on that subject was tenable and valid, because the supposed cause existed in nature, because it was competent to account for the phenomena, and because no other known cause was competent to account for them; and it is upon similar grounds that any hypothesis you choose to name is accepted in science as tenable and valid.

SCIENCE AND
HUMAN VALUES
J. Bronowski

J. Bronowski (1908–1975), British mathematician and humanist known principally for rendering science intelligible to the layman and for analyzing the role of science in society. In works such as The Common Sense of Science *(1951)* and Science and Human Values *(1956), Bronowski maintains that science teaches us not only techniques but a spirit of "independence and originality, dissent and freedom and tolerance."*

There is a likeness between the creative acts of the mind in art and in science. Yet, when a man uses the word science in such a sentence, it may be suspected that he does not mean what the headlines mean by science. Am I about to sidle away to those riddles in the Theory of Numbers which Hardy loved, or to the heady speculations of astrophysicists, in order to make claims for abstract science which have no bearing on its daily practice?

I have no such design. My purpose is to talk about science as it is, practical and theoretical. I define science as the organization of our knowledge in such a way that it commands more of the hidden potential in nature. What I have in mind therefore is both deep and matter of fact; it reaches from the kinetic theory of gases to the telephone and the suspension bridge and medicated toothpaste. It admits no sharp boundary between knowledge and use. There are of course people who like to draw a line between pure and applied science; and oddly, they are often the same people who find art unreal. To them, the word useful is a final arbiter, either for or against a work; and they use this word as if it can mean only what makes a man feel heavier after meals.

There is no sanction for confining the practice of science in this or another way. True, science is full of useful inventions. And its theories have often been made by men whose imagination was directed by the uses to which their age looked. Newton turned naturally to astronomy because it was the subject of his day; and it was so because finding one's way at sea had long been a practical preoccupation of the society into which he was born. It should be added, mischievously, that astronomy also had some standing because it was used very practically to cast horoscopes. (Kepler used it for this purpose; in the Thirty Years' War, he cast the horoscope of Wallenstein which wonderfully told his character, and he predicted a universal disaster for 1634 which proved to be the murder of Wallenstein.)

In a setting which is more familiar, Faraday worked all his life to link electricity with magnetism because this was the glittering problem of his day; and it was so because his society, like ours, was on the lookout for new sources of power. Consider a more modest example today: the new mathematical methods of automatic control, a subject sometimes called cybernetics, have been developed now because this is a time when communication and control have in effect become forms of power. These inventions have been directed by social needs, and they are useful inventions; yet it was not their usefulness which dominated and set light to the minds of those who made them. Neither Newton nor Faraday, nor yet Professor Norbert Wiener, spent their time in a scramble for patents.

What a scientist does is compounded of two interests: the interest of his time and his own interest. In this his behavior is no different from any other man's. The need of the age gives its shape to scientific progress as a whole. But it is not the need of the age which gives the individual scientist his sense of pleasure and of adventure and that excitement which keeps him working late into the night when all the useful typists have gone home at five o'clock. He is personally involved in his work, as the poet is in his and as the artist is in the painting. Paints and painting, too, must have been made for useful ends; and language was developed, from whatever beginnings, for practical communication. Yet you cannot have a man handle paints or language or the symbolic concepts of physics, you cannot even have him stain a microscope slide, without instantly waking in him a pleasure in the very language, a sense of exploring his own activity. This sense lies at the heart of creation.

The sense of personal exploration is as urgent, and as delightful, to the practical scientist as to the theoretical. Those who think otherwise are confusing what is practical with what is humdrum. Good humdrum work without originality is done every day by every one, theoretical scientists as well as practical, and writers and painters too, as well as truck drivers and bank clerks. Of course the unoriginal work keeps the world going; but it is not therefore the monopoly of practical men. And neither need the practical man be unoriginal. If he is to break out of what has been done before, he must bring to his own tools the same sense of pride and discovery which the poet brings to words. He cannot afford to be less radical in conceiving and less creative in designing a new turbine than a new world system.

And this is why in turn practical discoveries are not made only by practical man. As the world's interest has shifted, since the Industrial Revolution, to the tapping of new springs of power, the theoretical scientist has shifted his interests too. His speculations about energy have been as abstract as once they were about astronomy; and they have been profound now as they were then, because the man loved to think. The Carnot cycle and the dynamo grew equally from this love, and so did nuclear physics and the German V weapons and Kelvin's interest in low temperatures. Man does not invent by following either use or tradition; he does not invent even a new form of communication by calling a conference of communication engineers. Who invented the television set? In any deep sense, it was Clark Maxwell who foresaw the existence of radio waves, and Heinrich Hertz who proved it, and J. J. Thomson who discovered the electron. This is not said in order to rob any practical man of the invention, but from a sad sense of justice; for neither Maxwell nor Hertz nor J. J. Thomson would take pride in television just now.

Man masters nature not by force but by understanding. This is why science has succeeded where magic failed: because it has looked for no spell to cast on nature. The alchemist and the magician in the Middle Ages thought, and the addict of comic strips is still encouraged to think, that nature must be mastered by a device which outrages her laws. But in four hundred years since the Scientific Revolution we have learned that we gain our ends only *with* the laws of nature; we control her only by understanding her laws. We cannot even bully nature by any insistence that our work shall be designed to give power over her. We must be content that power is the by-product of understanding. So the Greeks said that Orpheus played the lyre with such sympathy that wild beasts were tamed by the hand on the strings. They did not suggest that he got this gift by setting out to be a lion tamer.

What is the insight with which the scientist tries to see into nature? Can it indeed be called either imaginative or creative? To the literary man the question may seem merely silly. He has been taught that science is a large collection of facts; and if this is true, then the only seeing which scientists need do is, he supposes, seeing the facts. He pictures them, the colorless professionals of science, going off to work in the morning into the universe in a neutral, unexposed state. They then expose themselves like a photographic plate. And then in the darkroom or laboratory they develop the image, so that suddenly and startlingly it appears, printed in capital letters, as a new formula for atomic energy.

Men who have read Balzac and Zola are not deceived by the claims of these writers that they do no more than record the facts. The readers of Christopher Isherwood do not take him literally when he writes: "I am a camera." Yet the same readers solemnly carry with them from their school days this foolish picture of the scientist fixing by some mechanical process the facts of nature. I have had, of all people, a historian tell me that science is a collection of facts, and his voice had not even the irony of one filing cabinet reproving another.

It seems impossible that this historian had ever studied the beginnings of a scientific discovery. The Scientific Revolution can be held to begin in the year 1543 when there was brought to Copernicus, perhaps on his deathbed, the first printed copy of the book he had written about a dozen years earlier. The thesis of this book is that the earth moves around the sun. When did Copernicus go out and record this fact with his camera? What appearance in nature prompted his outrageous guess? And in what odd sense is this guess to be called a neutral record of fact?

Less than a hundred years after Copernicus, Kepler published (between 1609 and 1619) the three laws which describe the paths of the planets. The work of Newton and with it most of our mechanics spring from these laws. They have a solid, matter-of-fact sound. For example, Kepler says that if one squares the year of a planet, one gets a number which is proportional to the cube of its average distance from the sun. Does any one think that such a law is found by taking enough readings and then squaring and cubing everything in sight? If he does then, as a scientist, he is doomed to a wasted life; he has as little prospect of making a scientific discovery as an electronic brain has.

It was not this way that Copernicus and Kepler thought, or that scientists think today. Copernicus found that the orbits of the planets would look simpler if they were looked at from the sun and not from the earth. But he did not in the first place find this by routine calculation. His first step was a leap of imagination—to lift himself from the earth, and put himself wildly, speculatively into the sun. "The earth conceives from the sun," he wrote; and "the sun rules the family of stars." We catch in his mind an image, the gesture of the virile man standing in the sun, with arms out-stretched, overlooking the planets. Perhaps Copernicus took the picture from the drawings of the youth with outstretched arms which the Renaissance teachers put into their books on the proportions of the body. Perhaps he knew Leonardo's drawings of his loved pupil Salai. I do not know. To me, the gesture of Copernicus, the shining youth looking outward from the sun, is still vivid in a drawing which William Blake about 1800 based on all these: the drawing which is usually called *Glad Day*.

Kepler's mind, we know, was filled with just such fanciful analogies; and we know what they were. Kepler wanted to relate the speeds of the planets to the musical intervals. He tried to fit the five regular solids into their orbits. None of these likenesses worked, and they have been forgotten; yet they have been and they remain the stepping stones of every creative mind. Kepler felt for his laws by way of metaphors, he searched mystically for likenesses with what he knew in every strange corner of nature. And when among these guesses he hit upon his laws, he did not think of their numbers as the balancing of a cosmic bank account, but as a revelation of the unity in all nature. To us, the analogies by which Kepler listened for the movement of the planets in the music of the spheres are far-fetched; but are they more so than the wild leap by which Rutherford and Bohr found a model for the atom in, of all places, the planetary system?

No scientific theory is a collection of facts. It will not even do to call a theory true or false in the simple sense in which every fact is either so or not so. The Epicureans held that matter is made of atoms two thousand years ago and we are now tempted to say that their theory was true. But if we do so, we confuse their notion of matter with our own. John Dalton in 1808 first saw the structure of matter as we do today, and what he took from the ancients was not their theory but something richer, their image: the atom. Much of what was in Dalton's mind was as vague as the Greek notion, and quite as mistaken. But he suddenly gave life to the new facts of chemistry and the ancient theory together, by fusing them to give what neither had: a coherent picture of how matter is linked and built up from different kinds of atoms. The act of fusion is the creative act.

All science is the search for unity in hidden likenesses. The search may be on a grand scale, as in the modern theories which try to link the fields of gravitation and electro-magnetism. But we do not need to be browbeaten by the scale of science. There are discoveries to be made by snatching a small likeness from the air too, if it is bold enough. In 1932 the Japanese physicist Yukawa wrote a paper which can still give heart to a young scientist. He took as his starting point the known fact that waves of light can sometimes behave as if they were separate pellets. From this he reasoned that the forces which hold the nucleus of an atom together might sometimes also be observed as if they were solid pellets. A schoolboy can see how thin Yukawa's analogy is, and his teacher would be severe with it. Yet Yukawa without a blush calculated the mass of the pellet he expected to see, and waited. He was right; his meson was found, and a range of other mesons, neither the existence nor the nature of which had been suspected before. The likeness had borne fruit.

The scientist looks for order in the appearances of nature by exploring such likenesses. For order does not display itself of itself; if it can be said to be there at all, it is not there for the mere looking. There is no way of pointing a finger or a camera at it; order must be discovered and, in a deep sense, it must be created. What we see, as we see it, is mere disorder.

This point has been put trenchantly in a fable by Professor Karl Popper. Suppose that someone wished to give his whole life to science. Suppose that he therefore sat down, pencil in hand, and for the next twenty, thirty, forty years recorded in notebook after notebook everything that he could observe. He may be supposed to leave out nothing: today's humidity, the racing results, the level of cosmic radiation and the stock market prices and the look of Mars, all would be there. He would have compiled the most careful record of nature that has ever been made; and, dying in the calm certainty of a life well spent, he would of course leave his notebooks to the Royal Society. Would the Royal Society thank him for the treasure of a lifetime of observation? It would not. It would refuse to open his notebooks at all, because it would know without looking that they contain only a jumble of disorderly and meaningless items.

Science finds order and meaning in our experience, and sets about this in quite a different way. It sets about it as Newton did in the story which he himself told in his old age, and of which the schoolbooks give only a caricature. In the year 1665, when Newton was twenty-two, the plauge broke out in southern England, and the University of Cambridge was closed. Newton therefore spent the next eighteen months at home, removed from traditional learning, at a time when he was impatient for knowledge and, in his own phrase: "I was in the prime of my age for invention." In this eager, boyish mood, sitting one day in the garden of his widowed mother, he saw an apple fall. So far the books have the story right; we think we even know the kind of apple; tradition has it that it was a Flower of Kent. But now they miss the crux of the story. For what struck the young Newton at the sight was not the thought that the apple must be drawn to the earth by gravity; that conception was older than Newton. What struck him was the conjecture that the same force of gravity, which reaches to the top of the tree, might go on reaching out beyond the earth and its air, endlessly into space. Gravity might reach the moon: this was Newton's new thought; and it might be gravity which holds the moon in her orbit. There and then he calculated what force from the earth would hold the moon, and compared it with the known force of gravity at tree height. The forces agreed; Newton says laconically: "I found them answer pretty nearly." Yet they agreed only nearly: the likeness and the approximation go together, for no likeness is exact. In Newton's sentence modern science is full grown.

It grows from a comparison. It has seized a likeness between two unlike appearances; for the apple in the summer garden and the grave moon overhead are surely as unlike in their movements as two things can be. Newton traced in them two expressions of a single concept, gravitation: and the concept (and the unity) are in that sense his free creation. The progress of science is the discovery at each step of a new order which gives unity to what had long seemed unlike. Faraday did this when he closed the link between electricity and magnetism. Clerk Maxwell did it when he linked both with light. Einstein linked time with space, mass with energy, and the path of light past the sun with the flight of a bullet; and spent his dying years in trying to add to these likenesses another, which would find a single imaginative order between the equations of Clerk Maxwell and his own geometry of gravitation.

When Coleridge tried to define beauty, he returned always to one deep thought: beauty, he said, is "unity in variety." Science is nothing else than the search to discover unity in the wild variety of nature—or more exactly, in the variety of our experience. Poetry, painting, the arts are the same search, in Coleridge's phrase, for unity in variety. Each in its own way looks for likenesses under the variety of human experience. What is a poetic image but the seizing and the exploration of a hidden likeness, in holding together two parts of a comparison which are to give depth each to the other? When Romeo finds Juliet in the tomb, and thinks her dead, he uses in his heartbreaking speech the words:

Death that hath suckt the honey of thy breath.

The critic can only haltingly take to pieces the single shock which this image carries. The young Shakespeare admired Marlowe, and Marlowe's Faustus had said of the ghostly kiss of Helen of Troy that it sucked forth his soul. But that is a pale image; what Shakespeare has done is to fire it with the single word honey. Death is a bee at the lips of Juliet, and the bee is an insect that stings; the sting of death was a commonplace phrase when Shakespeare wrote. The sting is there, under the image; Shakespeare has packed it into the word honey; but the very word rides powerfully over its own undertones. Death is a bee that stings other people, but it comes to Juliet as if she were a flower; this is the moving thought under the instant image. The creative mind speaks in such thoughts.

The poetic image here is also, and accidentally, heightened by the tenderness which town dwellers now feel for country ways. But it need not be; there are likenesses to conjure with, and images as powerful, within the man-made world. The poems of Alexander Pope belong to this world. They are not countrified, and therefore readers today find them unemotional and often artificial. Let me then quote Pope: here he is in a formal satire face to face, towards the end of his life, with his own gifts. In eight lines he looks poignantly forward towards death and back to the laborious years which made him famous.

> *Years foll'wing Years, steal something ev'ry day,*
> *At last they steal us from our selves away;*
> *In one our Frolicks, one Amusements end,*
> *In one a Mistress drops, in one a Friend:*
> *This subtle Thief of Life, this paltry Time,*
> *What will it leave me, if it snatch my Rhime?*
> *If ev'ry Wheel of that unweary'd Mill*
> *That turn'd ten thousand Verses, now stands still.*

The human mind had been compared to what the eighteenth century called a mill, that is to a machine, before; Pope's own idol Bolingbroke had compared it to a clockwork. In these lines the likeness goes deeper, for Pope is thinking of the ten thousand Verses which he had translated from Homer: what he says is sad and just at the same time, because this really had been a mechanical and at times a grinding task. Yet the clockwork is present in the image too; when the wheels stand still, time for Pope will stand still for ever; we feel that we already hear, over the horizon, the defiance of Faust which Goethe had not yet written—let the clock strike and stop, let the hand fall, and time be at an end.

> *Werd ich zum Augenblicke sagen:*
> *Verweile doch! du bist so schön!*
> *Dann magst du mich in Fesseln schlagen,*
> *Dann will ich gern zugrunde gehn!*
> *Dann mag die Totenglocke schallen,*
> *Dann bist du deines Dienstes frei,*
> *Die Uhr mag stehn, der Zeiger fallen,*
> *Es sei die Zeit für mich vorbei!**

I have quoted Pope and Goethe because their metaphor here is not poetic; it is rather a hand reaching straight into experience and arranging it with new meaning. Metaphors of this kind need not always be written in words. The most powerful of them all is simply the presence of King Lear and his Fool in the hut of a man who is shamming madness, while lightning rages outside. Or let me quote another clash of two conceptions of life, from a modern poet. In his later poems, W. B. Yeats was troubled by the feeling that in shutting himself up to write, he was missing the active pleasures of life; and yet it seemed to him certain that the man who lives for these pleasures will leave no lasting work behind him. He said this at times very simply, too:

> *The intellect of man is forced to choose*
> *Perfection of the life, or of the work.*

This problem, whether man fulfills himself in work or in play, is of course more common than Yeats allowed; and it may be more commonplace. But it is given breadth and force by the images in which Yeats pondered it.

> *Get all the gold and silver that you can,*
> *Satisfy ambition, or animate*
> *The trivial days and ram them with the sun,*

* The translation by Anna Swanwick in *The Dramatic Works of Goethe* (London: Dell & Daldy, 1867) runs thus:

> If ever to the passing hour I say
> "So beautiful thou art! thy flight delay!"
> Then round my soul thy fetters throw,
> then to perdition let me go!
> Then may the solemn death-bell sound,
> Then from thy service thou art free,
> The index-hand may cease its round,
> And time be never more for me!

And yet upon these maxims meditate:
All women dote upon an idle man
Although their children need a rich estate;
No man has ever lived that had enough
Of children's gratitude or woman's love.

The love of women, the gratitude of children: the images fix two philosophies as nothing else can. They are tools of creative thought, as coherent and as exact as the conceptual images with which science works: as time and space, or as the proton and the neutron.

The discoveries of science, the works of art are explorations—more, are explosions, of a hidden likeness. The discoverer or the artist presents in them two aspects of nature and fuses them into one. This is the act of creation, in which an original thought is born, and it is the same act in original science and original art. But it is not therefore the monopoly of the man who wrote the poem or who made the discovery. On the contrary, I believe this view of the creative act to be right because it alone gives a meaning to the act of appreciation. The poem or the discovery exists in two moments of vision: the moment of appreciation as much as that of creation; for the appreciator must see the movement, wake to the echo which was started in the creation of the work. In the moment of appreciation we live again the moment when the creator saw and held the hidden likeness. When a simile takes us aback and persuades us together, when we find a juxtaposition in a picture both odd and intriguing, when a theory is at once fresh and convincing, we do not merely nod over someone else's work. We re-enact the creative act, and we ourselves make the discovery again. At bottom, there is no unifying likeness there until we too have seized it, we too have made it for ourselves.

How slipshod by comparison is the notion that either art or science sets out to copy nature. If the task of the painter were to copy for men what they see, the critic could make only a single judgement: either that the copy is right or that it is wrong. And if science were a copy of fact, then every theory would be either right or wrong, and would be so forever. There would be nothing left for us to say but this is so or is not so. No one who has read a page by a good critic or a speculative scientist can ever again think that this barren choice of yes or no is all that the mind offers.

Reality is not an exhibit for man's inspection, labeled: "Do not touch." There are no appearances to be photographed, no experiences to be copied, in which we do not take part. We re-make nature by the act of discovery, in the poem or in the theorem. And the great poem and the deep theorem are new to every reader, and yet are his own experiences, because he himself re-creates them. They are the marks of unity in variety; and in the instant when the mind seizes this for itself, in art or in science, the heart misses a beat.

11
MYSTICAL AWARENESS

MYSTICISM
Evelyn Underhill

Evelyn Underhill (1875–1941), British mystical poet and author of such works as Mysticism *(1911),* The Mystic Way *(1913),* Man and the Supernatural *(1927), and* Worship *(1936). Her lucid and lyrical writings helped establish mysticism as a theologically respectable discipline in the twentieth century.*

The most highly developed branches of the human family have in common one peculiar characteristic. They tend to produce—sporadically it is true, and usually in the teeth of adverse external circumstances—a curious and definite type of personality; a type which refuses to be satisfied with that which other men call experience, and is inclined, in the words of its enemies, to "deny the world in order that it may find reality." We meet these persons in the east and the west; in the ancient, mediaeval, and modern worlds. Their one passion appears to be the prosecution of a certain spiritual and intangible quest: the finding of a "way out" or a "way back" to some desirable state in which alone they can satisfy their craving for absolute truth. This quest, for them, has constituted the whole meaning of life: they have made for it without effort sacrifices which have appeared enormous to other men: and it is an indirect testimony to its objective actuality, that whatever the place or period in which they have arisen, their aims, doctrines and methods have been substantially the same. Their experience, therefore, forms a body of evidence, curiously self-consistent and often mutually explanatory, which must be taken into account before we can add up the sum of the energies and potentialities of the human spirit, or reasonably speculate on its relations to the unknown world which lies outside the boundaries of sense.

All men, at one time or another, have fallen in love with the veiled Isis whom they call Truth. With most, this has been but a passing passion: they have early seen its hopelessness and turned to more practical things. But there are others who remain all their lives the devout lovers of reality: though the manner of their love, the vision which they make unto themselves of the beloved object, varies enormously. Some see Truth as Dante saw Beatrice: a figure adorable yet intangible, found in this world yet revealing the next. To others she seems rather an evil yet an irresistible enchantress: enticing, demanding payment and betraying her lover at the last. Some have seen her in a test tube, and some in a poet's dream: some before the altar, others in the slime. The extreme pragmatists have even sought her in the kitchen; declaring that she may best be recognized by her utility. Last stage of all, the philosophic sceptic has comforted an unsuccessful courtship by assuring himself that his mistress is not really there.

Under whatsoever symbols they may have objectified their quest, none of these seekers have ever been able to assure the world that they have found, seen face to face, the Reality behind the veil. But if we may trust the reports of the mystics—and they are reports given with a strange accent of certainty and good faith—they have succeded where all these others have failed, in establishing immediate communication between the spirit of man, entangled as they declare amongst material things, and that "only Reality," that immaterial and final Being, which some philosophers call the Absolute, and most theologians call God. This, they say—and here many who are not mystics agree with them—is the hidden Truth which is the object of man's craving; the only satisfying goal of his quest. Hence, they should claim from us the same attention that we give to other explorers of countries in which we are not competent to adventure ourselves; for the mystics are the pioneers of the spiritual world, and we have no right to deny validity to their discoveries, merely because we lack the opportunity or the courage necessary to those who would prosecute such explorations for themselves.

It is the object of this book to attempt a description, and also—though this is needless for those who read that description in good faith—a justification of these experiences and the conclusions which have been drawn from them. So remote, however, are these matters from our ordinary habits of thought, that their investigation entails, in all those who would attempt to understand them, a certain definite preparation: a purging of the intellect. As with those who came of old to the Mysteries, purification is here the gate of knowledge. We must come to this encounter with minds cleared of prejudice and convention, must deliberately break with our inveterate habit of taking the "visible world" for granted; our lazy assumption that somehow science is "real" and metaphysics is not. We must pull down our own card houses—descend, as the mystics say, "into our nothing-ness"—and examine for ourselves the foundations of all possible human experience, before we are in a position to criticize the buildings of the visionaries, the poets, and the saints. We must not begin to talk of the unreal world of these dreamers until we have discovered—if we can—a real world with which it may be compared.

Such a criticism of reality is of course the business of philosophy. I need hardly say that this book is not written by a philosopher, nor is it addressed to students of that imperial science. Nevertheless, amateurs though we be, we cannot reach our proper starting-point without tres-passing to some extent on philosophic ground. That ground covers the whole area of first principles: and it is to first principles that we must go, if we would understand the true significance of the mystic type.

Let us then begin at the beginning: and remind ourselves of a few of the trite and primary facts which all practical persons agree to ignore. That beginning, for human thought, is of course the I, the Ego, the self-conscious subject which is writing this book, or the other self-conscious subject which is reading it; and which declares, in the teeth of all argu-ments, I AM.[1] Here is a point as to which we all feel quite sure. No meta-physician has yet shaken the ordinary individual's belief in his own exis-tence. The uncertainties only begin for most of us when we ask what else *is*.

To this I, this conscious self "imprisoned in the body like an oyster in his shell,"[2] come, as we know, a constant stream of messages and exper-iences. Chief amongst these are the stimulation of the tactile nerves whose result we call touch, the vibrations taken up by the optic nerve which we call light, and those taken up by the ear and perceived as sound.

What do these experiences mean? The first answer of the unsophis-ticated Self of course is, that they indicate the nature of the external world: it is to the "evidence of her senses" that she turns, when she is asked what that world is like. From the messages received through those senses, which pour in on her whether she will or no, batter upon her gate-ways at every instant and from every side, she constructs that "sense-world" which is the "real and solid world" of normal men. As the impres-sions come in—or rather those interpretations of the original impressions which her nervous system supplies—she pounces on them, much as players in the spelling-game pounce on the separate letters dealt out to them. She

---

[1] Even this I AM, which has seemed safe ground to most metaphysicians, is of course combated by certain schools of philosophy. "The word *Sum*," said Eckhart long ago, "can be spoken by no creature but by God only: for it becomes the creature to testify of itself *Non Sum*." In a less mystical strain Lotze, and after him Bradley and other modern writers, have devoted much destructive criticism to the concept of the Ego as the starting-point of philosophy: looking upon it as a large, and logically unwar-rantable, assumption.

[2] Plato, Phaedrus, § 250.

sorts, accepts, rejects, combines: and then triumphantly produces from them a "concept" which *is*, she says, the external world. With an enviable and amazing simplicity she attributes her own sensations to the unknown universe. The stars, she says, *are* bright; the grass *is* green. For her, as for the philosopher Hume, "reality consists in impressions and ideas."

It is immediately apparent, however, that this sense-world, this seemingly real external universe—though it may be useful and valid in other respects—cannot be *the* external world, but only the Self's projected picture of it.[3] It is a work of art, not a scientific fact; and, whilst it may well possess the profound significance proper to great works of art, is dangerous if treated as a subject of analysis. Very slight investigation will be enough to suggest that it is a picture whose relation to reality is at best symbolic and approximate, and which would have no meaning for selves whose senses, or channels of communication, happened to be arranged upon a different plan. The evidence of the senses, then, cannot safely be accepted as evidence of the nature of ultimate reality: useful servants, they are dangerous guides. Nor can their testimony disconcert those seekers whose reports they appear to contradict.

The conscious self sits, so to speak, at the receiving end of a telegraph wire. On any other theory than that of mysticism, it is her one channel of communication with the hypothetical "external world." The receiving instrument registers certain messages. She does not know, and—so long as she remains dependent on that instrument—never can know, the object, the reality at the other end of the wire, by which those messages are sent; neither can the messages truly disclose the nature of that object. But she is justified on the whole in accepting them as evidence that something exists beyond herself and her receiving instrument. It is obvious that the structural peculiarities of the telegraphic instrument will have exerted a modifying effect upon the message. That which is conveyed as dash and dot, colour and shape, may have been received in a very different form. Therefore this message, though it may in a partial sense be relevant to the supposed reality at the other end, can never be adequate to it. There will be fine vibrations which it fails to take up, others which it confuses together. Hence a portion of the message is always lost; or, in other language, there are aspects of the world which we can never know.

The sphere of our possible intellectual knowledge is thus strictly con-

---

[3] Thus Eckhart, "Every time that the powers of the soul come into contact with created things, they receive and *create* images and likenesses from the created thing and absorb them. In this way arises the soul's knowledge of created things. Created things cannot come nearer to the soul than this, and the soul can only approach created things by the voluntary reception of images. And it is through the presence of the image that the soul approaches the created world: for *the image is a Thing, which the soul creates* with her own powers. Does the soul want to know the nature of a stone—a horse—a man? She forms an image."—Meister Eckhart, Pred. i. ("Mystische Schriften," p. 15).

ditioned by the limits of our own personality. On this basis, not the ends of the earth, but the external termini of our own sensory nerves, are the termini of our explorations: and to "know oneself" is really to know one's universe. We are locked up with our receiving instruments: we cannot get up and walk away in the hope of seeing whither the lines lead. Eckhart's words are still final for us: "the soul can only approach created things by the voluntary reception of images." Did some mischievous Demiurge choose to tickle our sensory apparatus in a new way, we should receive by this act a new universe.

The late Professor James once suggested as a useful exercise for young idealists a consideration of the changes which would be worked in our ordinary world if the various branches of our receiving instruments happened to exchange duties; if, for instance, we heard all colours and saw all sounds. Such a remark as this throws a sudden light on the strange and apparently insane statement of the visionary Saint-Martin, "I heard flowers that sounded, and saw notes that shone"; and on the reports of certain other mystics concerning a rare moment of consciousness in which the senses are fused into a single and ineffable act of perception; and colour and sound are known as aspects of the same thing.[4]

Since music is but an interpretation of certain vibrations undertaken by the ear, and colour an interpretation of other vibrations performed by the eye, all this is less mad than it sounds. Were such an alteration of our senses to take place the world would still be sending us the same messages—that strange unknown world from which, on this hypothesis, we are hermetically sealed—but we should have interpreted them differently. Beauty would still be ours, though speaking another tongue. The bird's song would then strike our retina as a pageant of colour: we should see all the magical tones of the wind, hear as a great fugue the repeated and harmonized greens of the forest, the cadences of stormy skies. Did we realize how slight an adjustment of our own organs is needed to initiate us into such a world, we should perhaps be less contemptuous of those mystics who tell us that they apprehended the Absolute as "heavenly music" or "Uncreated Light": less fanatical in our determination to make the "real and solid world of common sense" the only standard of reality. This "world of common sense" is a conceptual world. It may represent an external universe: it certainly does represent the activity of the human mind. Within that mind it is built up: and there most of us are content "at ease for aye to dwell," like the soul in the Palace of Art.

A direct encounter with absolute truth, then, appears to be impossible for normal non-mystical consciousness. We cannot know the reality, or even prove the existence, of the simplest object: though this is a limitation which few people realize acutely and most would strenuously deny. But

---

[4] Thus Edward Carpenter says of his own experience of the onset of mystical consciousness, "The perception seems to be one in which all the senses unite into one sense" (quoted in Bucke's "Cosmic Consciousness," p. 198).

there persists in the race a type of personality which does realize this limitation: and cannot be content with the sham realities that furnish the universe of normal men. It is necessary, as it seems, to the comfort of persons of this type to form for themselves some image of the Something or Nothing which is at the end of their telegraph lines: some "conception of being," some "theory of knowledge." They are tormented by the Unknowable, ache for first principles, demand some background to the shadow show of things. In so far as man possesses this temperament, he hungers for reality, and must satisfy that hunger as best he can: staving off starvation, though he may not be filled.

. . .

In answer to the "Why? Why?" of the bewildered and eternal child in us, philosophy, though always ready to postulate the unknown if she can, is bound to reply only, *"Nescio! Nescio!"* In spite of all her busy map-making, she cannot reach the goal which she points out to us: cannot explain the curious conditions under which we imagine that we know; cannot even divide with a sure hand the subject and object of thought. Science, whose business is with phenomena and our knowledge of them, though she too is an idealist at heart, has been accustomed to explain that all our ideas and instincts, the pictured world that we take so seriously, the oddly limited and illusory nature of our experience, appear to minister to one great end: the preservation of life, and consequent fulfilment of that highly mystical hypothesis, the Cosmic Idea. Each perception, she assures us, serves a useful purpose in this evolutionary scheme: a scheme, by the way, which has been invented—we know not why—by the human mind, and imposed upon an obedient universe.

By vision, hearing, smell, and touch, says Science, we find our way about, are warned of danger, obtain our food. The male perceives beauty in the female in order that the species may be propagated. It is true that this primitive instinct has given birth to higher and purer emotions; but these too fulfil a social purpose and are not so useless as they seem. Man must eat to live, therefore many foods give us agreeable sensations. If he overeats, he dies; therefore indigestion is an unpleasant pain. Certain facts of which too keen a perception would act detrimentally to the life-force are, for most men, impossible of realization: *i.e.*, the uncertainty of life, the decay of the body, the vanity of all things under the sun. When we are in good health, we all feel very real, solid, and permanent; and this is of all our illusions the most ridiculous, and also the most obviously useful from the point of view of the efficiency and preservation of the race.

But when we look a little closer, we see that this brisk generalization does not cover all the ground—not even that little tract of ground of which our senses make us free; indeed, that it is more remarkable for its omissions than for its inclusions. Récéjac has well said that "from the moment in which man is no longer content to devise things useful for his existence under the exclusive action of the will-to-live, the principle of (physical) evolution has been violated."[5] Nothing can be more certain than that man is not so content. He has been called by utilitarian philosophers a tool-making animal—the highest praise they knew how to bestow. More surely he is a vision-making animal;[6] a creature of perverse and unpractical ideals, dominated by dreams no less than by appetites—dreams which can only be justified upon the theory that he moves towards some other goal than that of physical perfection or intellectual supremacy, is controlled by some higher and more vital reality than that of the determinists. One is driven to the conclusion that if the theory of evolution is to include or explain the facts of artistic and spiritual experience—and it cannot be accepted by any serious thinker if these great tracts of consciousness remain outside its range—it must be rebuilt on a mental rather than a physical basis.

Even the most normal, most ordinary human life includes in its range fundamental experiences—violent and unforgettable sensations—forced on us as it were against our will, for which science finds it hard to account. These experiences and sensations, and the hours of exalted emotion which they bring with them—often recognized by us as the greatest, most significant hours of our lives—fulfil no office in relation to her pet "functions of nutrition and reproduction." It is true that they are far-reaching in their effects on character; but they do little or nothing to assist that character in its struggle for physical life. To the unprejudiced eye many of them seem hopelessly out of place in a universe constructed on strictly physico-chemical lines—look almost as though nature, left to herself, tended to contradict her own beautifully logical laws. Their presence, more, the large place which they fill in the human world of appearance, is a puzzling circumstance for deterministic philosophers; who can only escape from the dilemma here presented to them by calling these things illusions, and dignifying their own more manageable illusions with the title of facts.

Amongst the more intractable of these groups of perceptions and experiences are those which we connect with religion, with pain, and with beauty. All three, for those selves which are capable of receiving their messages, possess a mysterious authority far in excess of those feelings, arguments, or appearances which they may happen to contradict. All three, were the universe of the naturalists true, would be absurd; all three have ever been treated with the reverence due to vital matters by the best minds of the race.

A. I need not point out the hopelessly irrational character of all great religions, which rest, one and all, on a primary assumption that can never be intellectually demonstrated, much less proved; the assumption that the supra-sensible is somehow important and real, and can be influenced by

---

[5] "Fondements de la Connaissance Mystique," p. 15.
[6] Or, as St. Thomas Aquinas suggests, a contemplative animal, since "this act alone in man is proper to him, and is in no way shared by any other being in this world" ("Summa Contra Gentiles," I. iii. cap. xxxvii., Rickaby's translation).

the activities of man. This fact has been incessantly dwelt upon by their critics, and has provoked many a misplaced exercise of ingenuity on the part of their intelligent friends. Yet religion—emphasizing and pushing to extremes that general dependence on faith which we saw to be an inevitable condition of our lives—is one of the most universal and ineradicable functions of man, and this although it constantly acts detrimentally to the interests of his merely physical existence, opposes "the exclusive action of the will-to-live," except in so far as that will aspires to eternal life. Strictly utilitarian, almost logical in the savage, religion becomes more and more transcendental with the upward progress of the race. It begins as black magic; it ends as Pure Love. Why did the Cosmic Idea elaborate this religious instinct, if the construction put upon its intentions by the determinists be true?

B. Consider again the whole group of phenomena which are known as "the problem of suffering": the mental anguish and physical pain which appear to be the inevitable result of the steady operation of "natural law" and its voluntary assistants, the cruelty, greed, and injustice of man. Here, it is true, the naturalist seems at first sight to make a little more headway, and is able to point to some amongst the cruder forms of suffering which are clearly useful to the race: punishing us for past follies, spurring to new efforts, warning against future infringements of "law." But he forgets the many others which refuse to be resumed under this simple formula: forgets to explain how it is that the Cosmic Idea involves the long torments of the incurable, the tortures of the innocent, the deep anguish of the bereaved, the existence of so many gratuitously agonizing forms of death. He forgets, too, the strange fact that man's capacity for suffering tends to increase in depth and subtlety with the increase of culture and civilization; ignores the still more mysterious, perhaps most significant circumstance that the highest types have accepted it eagerly and willingly, have found in Pain the grave but kindly teacher of immortal secrets, the conferrer of liberty even the initiator into amazing joys.

Those who "explain" suffering as the result of nature's immense fecundity—a by-product of that overcrowding and stress through which the fittest tend to survive—forget that even were this demonstration valid and complete it would leave the real problem untouched. The question is not, whence come those conditions which provoke in the self the experiences called sorrow, anxiety, pain: but, why do these conditions *hurt* the self? The pain is mental; a little chloroform, and though the conditions continue unabated the suffering is gone. Why does full consciousness always include the mysterious capacity for misery as well as for happiness —a capacity which seems at first sight to invalidate any conception of the Absolute as Beautiful and Good? Why does evolution, as we ascend the ladder of life, foster instead of diminishing the capacity for useless mental anguish, for long, dull torment, bitter grief? Why, when so much lies outside our limited powers of perception, when so many of our own most vital functions are unperceived by consciousness, does suffering of some sort form an integral part of the experience of man? For utilitarian purposes acute discomfort would be quite enough; the Cosmic Idea, as the determinists explain it, did not really need an apparatus which felt all the throes of cancer, the horrors of neurasthenia, the pangs of birth. Still less did it need the torments of impotent sympathy for other people's irremediable pain, the dreadful power of feeling the world's woe. We are hopelessly over-sensitized for the part science calls us to play.

Pain, however we may look at it, indicates a profound disharmony between the sense-world and the human self. If it is to be vanquished, either the disharmony must be resolved by a deliberate and careful adjustment of the self to the world of sense, or, that self must turn from the sense-world to some other with which it is in tune.[7] Pessimist and optimist here join hands. But whilst the pessimist, resting in appearance, only sees "nature red in tooth and claw" offering him little hope of escape, the optimist thinks that pain and anguish—which may in their lower forms be life's harsh guides on the path of physical evolution—in their higher and apparently "useless" developments are her leaders and teachers in the upper school of Supra-sensible Reality. He believes that they press the self towards another world, still "natural" for him, though "super-natural" for his antagonist, in which it will be more at home. Watching life, he sees in Pain the complement of Love: and is inclined to call these the wings on which man's spirit can best take flight towards the Absolute. Hence he can say with A Kempis, "Gloriari in tribulatione non est grave amanti,"[8] and needs not to speak of morbid folly when he sees the Christian saints run eagerly and merrily to the Cross.[9]

He calls suffering the "gymnastic of eternity," the "terrible initiative caress of God"; recognizing in it a quality for which the disagreeable rearrangement of nerve molecules cannot account. Sometimes, in the excess of his optimism, he puts to the test of practice this theory with all its implications. Refusing to be deluded by the pleasures of the sense world, he accepts instead of avoiding pain, and becomes an ascetic; a puzzling type for the convinced naturalist, who, falling back upon contempt —that favourite resource of the frustrated reason—can only regard him as diseased.

Pain, then, which plunges like a sword through creation, leaving on the one side cringing and degraded animals and on the other side heroes

---

[7] All the healing arts, from Æsculapius and Galen to Metchnikoff and Mrs. Eddy, have virtually accepted and worked upon these two principles.

[8] "De Imitatione Christi," l. ii. cap. vi.

[9] "Such as these, I say, as if enamoured of My honour and famished for the food of souls, run to the table of the Most holy Cross, willing to suffer pain. . . . To these, My most dear sons, trouble is a pleasure, and pleasure and every consolation that the world would offer them are a toil" (St. Catherine of Siena, Dialogo, cap. xxviii). Here and throughout I have used Thorold's translation.

and saints, is one of those facts of universal experience which are peculiarly intractable from the point of view of a merely materialistic philosophy.

C. From this same point of view the existence of music and poetry, the qualities of beauty and of rhythm, the evoked sensations of awe, reverence, and rapture, are almost as difficult to account for. The question *why* an apparent corrugation of the Earth's surface, called for convenience' sake an Alp, coated with congealed water, and perceived by us as a snowy peak, should produce in certain natures acute sensations of ecstasy and adoration, why the skylark's song should catch us up to heaven, and wonder and mystery speak to us alike in "the little speedwell's darling blue" and in the cadence of the wind, is a problem that seems to be merely absurd, until it is seen to be insoluble. Here Madam How and Lady Why alike are silent. With all our busy seeking, we have not found the sorting house where loveliness is extracted from the flux of things. We know not why "great" poetry should move us to unspeakable emotion, or a stream of notes, arranged in a peculiar sequence, catch us up to heightened levels of vitality: nor can we guess how a passionate admiration of that which we call "best" in art or letters can possibly contribute to the physical evolution of the race. In spite of many lengthy disquisitions on æsthetics, Beauty's secret is still her own. A shadowy companion, half seen, half guessed at, she keeps step with the upward march of life: and we receive her message and respond to it, not because we understand it but because we *must*.

Here it is that we approach that attitude of the self, that point of view, which is loosely and generally called *mystical*. Here, instead of those broad blind alleys which philosophy showed us, a certain type of mind has always discerned three strait and narrow ways going out towards the Absolute. In religion, in pain, in beauty, and the ecstasy of artistic satisfaction—and not only in these, but in many other apparently useless peculiarities of the empirical world and of the perceiving conciousness—these persons insist that they recognize at any rate the fringe of the real. Down these three paths, as well as by many another secret way, they claim that news comes to the self concerning levels of reality which in their wholeness are inaccessible to the senses: worlds wondrous and immortal, whose existence is not conditioned by the "given" world which those senses report. "Beauty," said Hegel, who, though he was no mystic, had a touch of that mystical intuition which no philosopher can afford to be without, "is merely the Spiritual making itself known sensuously."[10] "In the good, the beautiful, the true," says Rudolph Eucken, "we see Reality revealing its personal character. They are parts of a coherent and substantial spiritual world."[11] Here, some of the veils of that substantial world are stripped off: Reality peeps through, and is recognized dimly, or acutely, by the imprisoned self.

[10] "Philosophy of Religion," vol. ii. p. 8.
[11] "Der Sinn und Wert des Lebens," p. 148.

Récéjac only develops this idea when he says,[12] "If the mind pene-trates deeply into the facts of æsthetics, it will find more and more, that these facts are based upon an ideal identity between the mind itself and things. At a certain point the harmony becomes so complete, and the finality so close that it gives us actual emotion. The Beautiful then be-comes the sublime; brief apparition, by which the soul is caught up into the true mystic state, and touches the Absolute. It is scarcely possible to persist in this æsthetic perception without feeling lifted up by it above things and above ourselves, in an ontological vision which closely resem-bles the Absolute of the Mystics."

It was of this underlying reality—this truth of things—that St. Augus-tine cried in a moment of lucid vision, "Oh, Beauty so old and so new, too late have I loved thee!"[13] It is in this sense also that "beauty is truth, truth beauty": and as regards the knowledge of ultimate things which is possible to ordinary men, it may well be that

> *"That is all*
> *Ye know on earth, and all ye need to know."*

"Of Beauty," says Plato in an immortal passage, "I repeat again that we saw her there shining in company with the celestial forms; and coming to earth we find her here too shining in clearness through the clearest aperture of sense. For sight is the most piercing of our bodily senses: though not by that is wisdom seen; her loveliness would have been trans-porting if there had been a visible image of her, and the other ideas, if they had visible counterparts, would be equally lovely. But this is the privilege of Beauty, that being the loveliest she is also the most palpable to sight. Now he who is not newly initiated, or who has been corrupted, does not easily rise out of this world to the sight of true beauty in the other. . . . But he whose initiation is recent, and who has been the spec-tator of many glories in the other world, is amazed when he sees anyone having a godlike face or form, which is the expression of Divine Beauty; and at first a shudder runs through him, and again the old awe steals over him. . . ."[14]

Most men in the course of their lives have known such Platonic hours of initiation, when the sense of beauty has risen from a pleasant feeling to

---

[12] "Fondements de la Connaissance Mystique," p. 74.
[13] Aug. Conf., bk. x. cap. xxvii.
[14] Phaedrus, § 250 (Jowett's translation). The reference in the phrase "he whose initiation is recent" is to the rite of admission into the Greek Mysteries. It is believed by some authorities that the neophyte was then cast into an hypnotic sleep by his "initiator," and whilst in this condition a vision of the "glories of the other world" was suggested to him. The main phenomena of "conversion" were thus artificially produced: but the point of attack being the mind rather than the heart, the results, as would appear from the context, were usually transient. See for matter bearing on this point, Rudolf Steiner, "Das Christenthum als mystiche Thatsache."

a passion, and an element of strangeness and terror has been mingled with their joy. In those hours the world has seemed charged with a new vitality; with a splendour which does not belong to it but is poured through it, as light through a coloured window, grace through a sacrament, from that Perfect Beauty which "shines in company with the celestial forms" beyond the pale of appearance. In such moods of heightened consciousness each blade of grass seems fierce with meaning, and becomes a well of wondrous light: a "little emerald set in the City of God." The seeing self is indeed an initiate thrust suddenly into the sanctuary of the mysteries: and feels the "old awe and amazement" with which man encounters the Real. In such experiences as these, a new factor of the eternal calculus appears to be thrust in on us, a factor which no honest seeker for truth can afford to neglect; since, if it be dangerous to say that any two systems of knowledge are mutually exclusive, it is still more dangerous to give uncritical priority to any one system. We are bound, then, to examine this path to reality as closely and seriously as we should investigate the most neatly finished safety-ladder of solid ash which offered a *salita alle stelle*.

Why, after all, take as our standard a material world whose existence is affirmed by nothing more trustworthy than the sense-impressions of "normal men"; those imperfect and easily cheated channels of communication? The mystics, those adventurers of whom we spoke upon the first page of this book, have always declared, implicitly or explicitly, their distrust in these channels of communication. They have never for an instant been deceived by phenomena, nor by the careful logic of the industrious intellect. One after another, with extraordinary unanimity, they have rejected that appeal to the unreal world of appearance which is the standard of all sensible men: affirming that there is another way, another secret, by which the conscious self may reach the actuality which it seeks. More complete in their grasp of experience than the votaries of intellect or of sense, they accept as central for life those spiritual messages which are mediated to the self by religion, by beauty, and by pain. More reasonable than the rationalists, they find in that very hunger for reality which is the mother of all metaphysics, an implicit proof that such reality exists; that there is something else, some final satisfaction, beyond the ceaseless stream of sensation which besieges consciousness. "In that thou hast sought me, thou hast already found me," says the voice of Absolute Truth in their ears. This is the first doctrine of mysticism. Its next is that only in so far as the self is real can it hope to *know* Reality: like to like: *Cor ad cor loquitur*. Upon the propositions implicit in these two laws the whole claim and practice of the mystic life depends.

"Finite as we are," they say—and here they speak not for themselves, but for the race—"lost though we seem to be in the woods or in the wide air's wilderness, in this world of time and of chance, we have still, like the strayed animals or like the migrating birds, our homing instinct. . . . We seek. That is a fact. We seek a city still out of sight. In the contrast with this goal, we live. But if this be so, then already we possess something of Being even in our finite seeking. For the readiness to seek is already something of an attainment, even if a poor one."[15]

Further, in this our finite seeking we are not wholly dependent on that homing instinct. For some, who have climbed to the hill-tops, that city is not really out of sight. The mystics see it clearly. They report to us concerning it. Science and metaphysics may do their best and their worst: but these pathfinders of the spirit never falter in their statements concerning that independent spiritual world which is the only goal of "pilgrim man." They say that messages come to him from that spiritual world, that complete reality which we call Absolute: that we are not, after all, hermetically sealed from it. To all selves who will receive it, news comes every hour of the day of a world of Absolute Life, Absolute Beauty, Absolute Truth, beyond the bourne of time and place: news that most of us translate—and inevitably distort in the process—into the language of religion, of beauty, of love, or of pain.

Of all those forms of life and thought with which humanity has fed its craving for truth, mysticism alone postulates, and in the persons of its great initiates proves, not only the existence of the Absolute, but also this link: this possibility first of knowing, finally of attaining it. It denies that possible knowledge is to be limited (a) to sense impressions, (b) to any process of intellectation, (c) to the unfolding of the content of normal consciousness. Such diagrams of experience, it says, are hopelessly incomplete. The mystics find the basis of their method not in logic but in life: in the existence of a discoverable "real," a spark of true being, within the seeking subject which can, in that ineffable experience which they call the "act of union," fuse itself with and thus apprehend the reality of the sought Object. In theological language, their theory of knowledge is that the spirit of man, itself essentially divine, is capable of immediate communion with God, the One Reality.[16]

In mysticism that love of truth which we saw as the beginning of all philosophy leaves the merely intellectual sphere, and takes on the assured aspect of a personal passion. Where the philosopher guesses and argues, the mystic lives and looks; and speaks, consequently, the disconcerting language of first-hand experience, not the neat dialectic of the schools. Hence whilst the Absolute of the metaphysicians remains a diagram—impersonal and unattainable—the Absolute of the mystics is lovable, attainable, alive.

15 Royce, "The World and the Individual," vol. i. p. 181.
16 The idea of Divine Union as man's true end is of course of immeasurable antiquity. Its first definite appearance in the religious consciousness of Europe seems to coincide with the establishment of the Orphic Mysteries in Greece and Southern Italy in the sixth century B.C. See Adam, "The Religious Teachers of Greece," p. 92. It is also found in the Hermetic writings, which vary between the fifth and second century B.C. Compare Petrie, "Personal Religion in Egypt before Christianity," p. 102, and Rhode, "Psyche" (1898).

"Oh, taste and see!" they cry, in accents of astounding certainty and joy. "Ours is an experimental science. We can but communicate our system, never its result. We come to you not as thinkers, but as doers. Leave your deep and absurd trust in the senses, with their language of dot and dash, which may possibly report fact but can never communicate personality. If philosophy has taught you anything, she has surely taught you the length of her tether, and the impossibility of attaining to the doubtless admirable grazing land which lies beyond it. One after another, idealists have arisen who, straining frantically at the rope, have announced to the world their approaching liberty; only to be flung back at last into the little circle of sensation. But here we are, a small family, it is true, yet one that refuses to die out, assuring you that we have slipped the knot and are free of those grazing grounds. This is evidence which you are bound to bring into account before you can add up the sum total of possible knowledge; for you will find it impossible to prove that the world as seen by the mystics, 'unimaginable, formless, dark with excess of bright,' is less real than that which is expounded by the youngest and most promising demonstrator of a physico-chemical universe. We will be quite candid with you. Examine us as much as you like: our machinery, our veracity, our results. We cannot promise that you shall see what we have seen, for here each man must adventure for himself; but we defy you to stigmatize our experiences as impossible or invalid. Is your world of experience so well and logically founded that you dare make of it a standard? Philosophy tells you that it is founded on nothing better than the reports of your sensory apparatus and the traditional concepts of the race. Certainly it is imperfect, probably it is illusion; in any event, it never touches the foundation of things. Whereas "what the world, which truly knows *nothing*, calls 'mysticism,' is the science of *ultimates* . . . the science of self-evident Reality, which cannot be 'reasoned about,' because it is the object of pure reason or perception."[17]

[17] Coventry Patmore, "The Rod, the Root, and the Flower," "Aurea Dicta," cxxviii.

MYSTICISM
AND LOGIC
Bertrand Russell

Bertrand Russell (1872–1970). For notes on Russell see the article "A Free Man's Worship" on page 311.

Mystical philosophy, in all ages and in all parts of the world, is characterised by certain beliefs. . . .

There is, first, the belief in insight as against discursive analytic knowledge: the belief in a way of wisdom, sudden, penetrating, coercive, which is contrasted with the slow and fallible study of outward appearance by a science relying wholly upon the senses. All who are capable of absorption in an inward passion must have experienced at times the strange feeling of unreality in common objects, the loss of contact with daily things, in which the solidity of the outer world is lost, and the soul seems, in utter loneliness, to bring forth, out of its own depths, the mad dance of fantastic phantoms which have hitherto appeared as independently real and living. This is the negative side of the mystic's initiation: the doubt concerning common knowledge, preparing the way for the reception of what seems a higher wisdom. Many men to whom this negative experience is familiar do not pass beyond it, but for the mystic it is merely the gateway to an ampler world.

The mystic insight begins with the sense of a mystery unveiled, of a hidden wisdom now suddenly become certain beyond the possibility of a doubt. The sense of certainty and revelation comes earlier than any definite belief. The definite beliefs at which mystics arrive are the result of reflection upon the inarticulate experience gained in the moment of insight. Often, beliefs which have no real connection with this moment become subsequently attracted into the central nucleus; thus in addition to the convictions which all mystics share, we find, in many of them, other convictions of a more local and temporary character, which no doubt become amalgamated with what was essentially mystical in virtue of their subjective certainty. We may ignore such inessential accretions, and confine ourselves to the beliefs which all mystics share.

The first and most direct outcome of the moment of illumination is belief in the possibility of a way of knowledge which may be called revelation or insight or intuition, as contrasted with sense, reason, and analysis, which are regarded as blind guides leading to the morass of illusion. Closely connected with this belief is the conception of a Reality behind the world of appearance and utterly different from it. This Reality is regarded with an admiration often amounting to worship; it is felt to be always and everywhere close at hand, thinly veiled by the shows of sense, ready, for the receptive mind, to shine in its glory even through the apparent folly and wickedness of Man. The poet, the artist, and the lover are seekers after that glory: the haunting beauty that they pursue is the faint reflection of its sun. But the mystic lives in the full light of the vision: what others dimly seek he knows, with a knowledge beside which all other knowledge is ignorance.

The second characteristic of mysticism is its belief in unity, and its refusal to admit opposition or division anywhere. We found Heraclitus saying "good and ill are one"; and again he says, "the way up and the way down is one and the same." The same attitude appears in the simultaneous assertion of contradictory propositions, such as: "We step and do not step into the same rivers; we are and are not." The assertion of Parmenides, that reality is one and indivisible, comes from the same impulse towards unity. In Plato, this impulse is less prominent, being held in check by his theory of ideas; but it reappears, so far as his logic permits, in the doctrine of the primacy of the Good.

A third mark of almost all mystical metaphysics is the denial of the reality of Time. This is an outcome of the denial of division; if all is one, the distinction of past and future must be illusory. We have seen this doctrine prominent in Parmenides; and among moderns it is fundamental in the systems of Spinoza and Hegel.

The last of the doctrines of mysticism which we have to consider is its belief that all evil is mere appearance, an illusion produced by the divisions and oppositions of the analytic intellect. Mysticism does not maintain that such things as cruelty, for example, are good, but it denies that they are real: they belong to that lower world of phantoms from which we are to be liberated by the insight of the vision. Sometimes—for example in Hegel, and at least verbally in Spinoza—not only evil, but good also, is regarded as illusory, though nevertheless the emotional attitude towards what is held to be Reality is such as would naturally be associated with the belief that Reality is good. What is, in all cases, ethically characteristic of mysticism is absence of indignation or protest, acceptance with joy, disbelief in the ultimate truth of the division into two hostile camps, the good and the bad. This attitude is a direct outcome of the nature of the mystical experience: with its sense of unity is associated a feeling of infinite peace. Indeed it may be suspected that the feeling of peace produces, as feelings do in dreams, the whole system of associated beliefs which make up the body of mystic doctrine. But this is a difficult question, and one on which it cannot be hoped that mankind will reach agreement.

Four questions thus arise in considering the truth or falsehood of mysticism, namely:

> I. Are there two ways of knowing, which may be called respectively reason and intuition? And if so, is either to be preferred to the other?
>
> II. Is all plurality and division illusory?
>
> III. Is time unreal?
>
> IV. What kind of reality belongs to good and evil?

On all four of these questions, while fully developed mysticism seems to me mistaken, I yet believe that, by sufficient restraint, there is an element of wisdom to be learned from the mystical way of feeling, which does not seem to be attainable in any other manner. If this is the truth, mysticism is to be commended as an attitude towards life, not as a creed about the world. The metaphysical creed, I shall maintain, is a mistaken outcome of the emotion, although this emotion, as colouring and informing all other thoughts and feelings, is the inspirer of whatever is best in Man. Even the cautious and patient investigation of truth by science, which seems the very antithesis of the mystic's swift certainty, may be fostered and nourished by that very spirit of reverence in which mysticism lives and moves.

I. REASON AND INTUITION

Of the reality or unreality of the mystic's world I know nothing. I have no wish to deny it, nor even to declare that the insight which reveals it is not a genuine insight. What I do wish to maintain—and it is here that the scientific attitude becomes imperative—is that insight, untested and unsupported, is an insufficient guarantee of truth, in spite of the fact that much of the most important truth is first suggested by its means. It is common to speak of an opposition between instinct and reason; in the eighteenth century, the opposition was drawn in favour of reason, but under the influence of Rousseau and the romantic movement instinct was given the preference, first by those who rebelled against artificial forms of government and thought, and then, as the purely rationalistic defence of traditional theology became increasingly difficult, by all who felt in science a menace to creeds which they associated with a spiritual outlook on life and the world. Bergson, under the name of "intuition," has raised instinct to the position of sole arbiter of metaphysical truth. But in fact the opposition of instinct and reason is mainly illusory. Instinct, intuition, or insight is what first leads to the beliefs which subsequent reason confirms or confutes; but the confirmation, where it is possible, consists, in the last analysis, of agreement with other beliefs no less instinctive. Reason is a harmonising, controlling force rather than a creative one. Even in the most purely logical realm, it is insight that first arrives at what is new.

Where instinct and reason do sometimes conflict is in regard to single beliefs, held instinctively, and held with such determination that no degree of inconsistency with other beliefs leads to their abandonment. Instinct, like all human faculties, is liable to error. Those in whom reason is weak are often unwilling to admit this as regards themselves, though all admit it in regard to others. Where instinct is least liable to error is in practical matters as to which right judgment is a help to survival: friendship and hostility in others, for instance, are often felt with extraordinary discrimination through very careful disguises. But even in such matters a wrong impression may be given by reserve or flattery; and in matters less directly practical, such as philosophy deals with, very strong instinctive beliefs are sometimes wholly mistaken, as we may come to know through their perceived inconsistency with other equally strong beliefs. It is such considerations that necessitate the harmonising mediation of reason, which tests our beliefs by their mutual compatibility, and examines, in doubtful cases, the possible sources of error on the one side and on the other. In this there is no opposition to instinct as a whole, but only to blind reliance upon some one interesting aspect of instinct to the exclusion of other more commonplace but not less trustworthy aspects. It is such one-sidedness, not instinct itself, that reason aims at correcting.

.   .   .

II. UNITY AND PLURALITY

One of the most convincing aspects of the mystic illumination is the apparent revelation of the oneness of all things, giving rise to pantheism in religion and to monism in philosophy. An elaborate logic, beginning with Parmenides, and culminating in Hegel and his followers, has been gradually developed, to prove that the universe is one indivisible Whole, and that what seem to be its parts, if considered as substantial and self-existing, are mere illusion. The conception of a Reality quite other than the world of appearance, a reality one, indivisible, and unchanging, was introduced into Western philosophy by Parmenides, not, nominally at least, for mystical or religious reasons, but on the basis of a logical argument as to the impossibility of not-being, and most subsequent meta-physical systems are the outcome of this fundamental idea.

The logic used in defence of mysticism seems to be faulty as logic, and open to technical criticisms, which I have explained elsewhere. I shall not here repeat these criticisms, since they are lengthy and difficult, but shall instead attempt an analysis of the state of mind from which mystical logic has arisen.

Belief in a reality quite different from what appears to the senses arises with irresistible force in certain moods, which are the source of most mysticism, and of most metaphysics. While such a mood is dominant, the need of logic is not felt, and accordingly the more thoroughgoing mystics do not employ logic, but appeal directly to the immediate deliverance of their insight. But such fully developed mysticism is rare in the West. When the intensity of emotional conviction subsides, a man who is in the habit of reasoning will search for logical grounds in favour of the belief which he finds in himself. But since the belief already exists, he will be very hospitable to any ground that suggests itself. The paradoxes appar-ently proved by his logic are really the paradoxes of mysticism, and are the goal which he feels his logic must reach if it is to be in accordance with insight. The resulting logic has rendered most philosophers incapable of giving any account of the world of science and daily life. If they had been anxious to give such an account, they would probably have discovered the errors of their logic; but most of them were less anxious to understand the world of science and daily life than to convict it of unreality in the interests of a super-sensible "real" world.

It is in this way that logic has been pursued by those of the great philosophers who were mystics. But since they usually took for granted the supposed insight of the mystic emotion, their logical doctrines were pre-sented with a certain dryness, and were believed by their disciples to be quite independent of the sudden illumination from which they sprang. Nevertheless their origin clung to them, and they remained—to borrow a useful word from Mr. Santayana—"malicious" in regard to the world of science and common sense. It is only so that we can account for the com-placency with which philosophers have accepted the inconsistency of their doctrines with all the common and scientific facts which seem best estab-lished and most worthy of belief.

The logic of mysticism shows, as is natural, the defects which are inherent in anything malicious. The impulse to logic, not felt while the mystic mood is dominant, reasserts itself as the mood fades, but with a desire to retain the vanishing insight, or at least to prove that it *was* in-sight, and that what seems to contradict it is illusion. The logic which thus arises is not quite disinterested or candid, and is inspired by a certain hatred of the daily world to which it is to be applied. Such an attitude naturally does not tend to the best results. Everyone knows that to read an author simply in order to refute him is not the way to understand him;

and to read the book of Nature with a conviction that it is all illusion is just as unlikely to lead to understanding. If our logic is to find the common world intelligible, it must not be hostile, but must be inspired by a genuine acceptance such as is not usually to be found among metaphysicians.

III. TIME

The unreality of time is a cardinal doctrine of many metaphysical systems, often nominally based, as already by Parmenides, upon logical arguments, but originally derived, at any rate in the founders of new systems, from the certainty which is born in the moment of mystic insight. As a Persian Sufi poet says:

> "Past and future are what veil God from our sight.
> Burn up both of them with fire! How long
> Wilt thou be partitioned by these segments as a reed?"[1]

The belief that what is ultimately real must be immutable is a very common one: it gave rise to the metaphysical notion of substance, and finds, even now, a wholly illegitimate satisfaction in such scientific doctrines as the conservation of energy and mass.

It is difficult to disentangle the truth and the error in this view. The arguments for the contention that time is unreal and that the world of sense is illusory must, I think, be regarded as fallacious. Nevertheless there is some sense—easier to feel than to state—in which time is an unimportant and superficial characteristic of reality. Past and future must be acknowledged to be as real as the present, and a certain emancipation from slavery to time is essential to philosophic thought. The importance of time is rather practical than theoretical, rather in relation to our desires than in relation to truth. A truer image of the world, I think, is obtained by picturing things as entering into the stream of time from an eternal world outside, than from a view which regards time as the devouring tyrant of all that is. Both in thought and in feeling, even though time be real, to realise the unimportance of time is the gate of wisdom.

That this is the case may be seen at once by asking ourselves why our feelings towards the past are so different from our feelings towards the future. The reason for this difference is wholly practical: our wishes can affect the future but not the past, the future is to some extent subject to our power, while the past is unalterably fixed. But every future will some day be past: if we see the past truly now, it must, when it was still future,

[1] Whinfield's translation of the *Masnavi* (Trübner, 1887), p. 34.

have been just what we now see it to be, and what is now future must be just what we shall see it to be when it has become past. The felt difference of quality between past and future, therefore, is not an intrinsic difference, but only a difference in relation to us: to impartial contemplation, it ceases to exist. And impartiality of contemplation is, in the intellectual sphere, that very same virtue of disinterestedness which, in the sphere of action, appears as justice and unselfishness. Whoever wishes to see the world truly, to rise in thought above the tyranny of practical desires, must learn to overcome the difference of attitude towards past and future, and to survey the whole stream of time in one comprehensive vision.

The kind of way in which, as it seems to me, time ought not to enter into our theoretic philosophical thought, may be illustrated by the philosophy which has become associated with the idea of evolution, and which is exemplified by Nietzsche, pragmatism, and Bergson. This philosophy, on the basis of the development which has led from the lowest forms of life up to man, sees in *progress* the fundamental law of the universe, and thus admits the difference between *earlier* and *later* into the very citadel of its contemplative outlook. With its past and future history of the world, conjectural as it is, I do not wish to quarrel. But I think that, in the intoxication of a quick success, much that is required for a true understanding of the universe has been forgotten. Something of Hellenism, something, too, of Oriental resignation, must be combined with its hurrying Western self-assertion before it can emerge from the ardour of youth into the mature wisdom of manhood. In spite of its appeals to science, the true scientific philosophy, I think, is something more arduous and more aloof, appealing to less mundane hopes, and requiring a severer discipline for its successful practice.

Darwin's *Origin of Species* persuaded the world that the difference between different species of animals and plants is not the fixed immutable difference that it appears to be. The doctrine of natural kinds, which had rendered classification easy and definite, which was enshrined in the Aristotelian tradition, and protected by its supposed necessity for orthodox dogma, was suddenly swept away for ever out of the biological world. The difference between man and the lower animals, which to our human conceit appears enormous, was shown to be a gradual achievement, involving intermediate being who could not with certainty be placed either within or without the human family. The sun and the planets had already been shown by Laplace to be very probably derived from a primitive more or less undifferentiated nebula. Thus the old fixed landmarks became wavering and indistinct, and all sharp outlines were blurred. Things and species lost their boundaries, and none could say where they began or where they ended.

But if human conceit was staggered for a moment by its kinship with the ape, it soon found a way to reassert itself, and that way is the "philosophy" of evolution. A process which led from the amœba to Man appeared to the philosophers to be obviously a progress—though whether the amœba would agree with this opinion is not known. Hence the cycle of changes which science had shown to be the probable history of the past was welcomed as revealing a law of development towards good in the universe—an evolution or unfolding of an idea slowly embodying itself in the actual. But such a view, though it might satisfy Spencer and those whom we may call Hegelian evolutionists, could not be accepted as adequate by the more whole-hearted votaries of change. An ideal to which the world continuously approaches is, to these minds, too dead and static to be inspiring. Not only the aspiration, but the ideal too, must change and develop with the course of evolution: there must be no fixed goal, but a continual fashioning of fresh needs by the impulse which is life and which alone gives unity to the process.

Life, in this philosophy, is a continuous stream, in which all divisions are artificial and unreal. Separate things, beginnings and endings, are mere convenient fictions: there is only smooth unbroken transition. The beliefs of to-day may count as true to-day, if they carry us along the stream; but to-morrow they will be false, and must be replaced by new beliefs to meet the new situation. All our thinking consists of convenient fictions, imaginary congealings of the stream: reality flows on in spite of all our fictions, and though it can be lived, it cannot be conceived in thought. Somehow, without explicit statement, the assurance is slipped in that the future, though we cannot foresee it, will be better than the past or the present: the reader is like the child which expects a sweet because it has been told to open its mouth and shut its eyes. Logic, mathematics, physics disappear in this philosophy, because they are too "static"; what is real is no impulse and movement towards a goal which, like the rainbow, recedes as we advance, and makes every place different when it reaches it from what it appeared to be at a distance.

I do not propose to enter upon a technical examination of this philosophy. I wish only to maintain that the motives and interests which inspire it are so exclusively practical, and the problems with which it deals are so special, that it can hardly be regarded as touching any of the questions that, to my mind, constitute genuine philosophy.

The predominant interest of evolutionism is in the question of human destiny, or at least of the destiny of Life. It is more interested in morality and happiness than in knowledge for its own sake. It must be admitted that the same may be said of many other philosophies, and that a desire for the kind of knowledge which philosophy can give is very rare. But if philosophy is to attain truth, it is necessary first and foremost that philosophers should acquire the disinterested intellectual curiosity which characterises the genuine man of science. Knowledge concerning the future— which is the kind of knowledge that must be sought if we are to know about human destiny—is possible within certain narrow limits. It is impossible to say how much the limits may be enlarged with the progress of

science. But what is evident is that any proposition about the future belongs by its subject-matter to some particular science, and is to be ascer-
tained, if at all, by the methods of that science. Philosophy is not a short
cut to the same kind of results as those of the other sciences: if it is to be
a genuine study, it must have a province of its own, and aim at results
which the other sciences can neither prove nor disprove.

Evolutionism, in basing itself upon the notion of *progress*, which is
change from the worse to the better, allows the notion of time, as it seems
to me, to become its tyrant rather than its servant, and thereby loses that
impartiality of contemplation which is the source of all that is best in
philosophic thought and feeling. Metaphysicians, as we saw, have frequently denied altogether the reality of time. I do not wish to do this; I
wish only to preserve the mental outlook which inspired the denial, the
attitude which, in thought, regards the past as having the same reality as
the present and the same importance as the future. "In so far," says
Spinoza, "as the mind conceives a thing according to the dictate of reason,
it will be equally affected whether the idea is that of a future, past, or
present thing."[2] It is this "conceiving according to the dictate of reason"
that I find lacking in the philosophy which is based on evolution.

IV. GOOD AND EVIL

Mysticism maintains that all evil is illusory, and sometimes maintains
the same view as regards good, but more often holds that all Reality is
good. Both views are to be found in Heraclitus: "Good and ill are one,"
he says, but again, "To God all things are fair and good and right, but
men hold some things wrong and some right." A similar twofold position
is to be found in Spinoza, but he uses the word "perfection" when he
means to speak of the good that is not merely human. "By reality and
perfection I mean the same thing," he says;[3] but elsewhere we find the
definition: "By *good* I shall mean that which we certainly know to be
useful to us."[4] Thus perfection belongs to Reality in its own nature, but
goodness is relative to ourselves and our needs, and disappears in an
impartial survey. Some such distinction, I think, is necessary in order to
understand the ethical outlook of mysticism: there is a lower mundane
kind of good and evil, which divides the world of appearance into what
seem to be conflicting parts; but there is also a higher, mystical kind of
good, which belongs to Reality and is not opposed by any correlative kind
of evil.

[2] *Ethics*, Bk. IV, Prop. LXII.
[3] *Ethics*, Pt. II, Df. VI.
[4] Ib., Pt. IV, Df. I.

It is difficult to give a logically tenable account of this position without recognising that good and evil are subjective, that what is good is merely that towards which we have one kind of feeling, and what is evil is merely that towards which we have another kind of feeling. In our active life, where we have to exercise choice, and to prefer this to that of two possible acts, it is necessary to have a distinction of good and evil, or at least of better and worse. But this distinction, like everything pertaining to action, belongs to what mysticism regards as the world of illusion, if only because it is essentially concerned with time. In our contemplative life, where action is not called for, it is possible to be impartial, and to overcome the ethical dualism which action requires. So long as we remain *merely* impartial, we may be content to say that both the good and the evil of action are illusions. But if, as we must do if we have the mystic vision, we find the whole world worthy of love and worship, if we see

> *"The earth, and every common sight. . . .*
> *Apparell'd in celestial light,"*

we shall say that there is a higher good than that of action, and that this higher good belongs to the whole world as it is in reality. In this way the twofold attitude and the apparent vacillation of mysticism are explained and justified.

The possibility of this universal love and joy in all that exists is of supreme importance for the conduct and happiness of life, and gives inestimable value to the mystic emotion, apart from any creeds which may be built upon it. But if we are not to be led into false beliefs, it is necessary to realise exactly *what* the mystic emotion reveals. It reveals a possibility of human nature—a possibility of a nobler, happier, freer life than any that can be otherwise achieved. But it does not reveal anything about the non-human, or about the nature of the universe in general. Good and bad, and even the higher good that mysticism finds everywhere, are the reflections of our own emotions on other things, not part of the substance of things as they are in themselves. And therefore an impartial contemplation, freed from all pre-occupation with Self, will not judge things good or bad, although it is very easily combined with that feeling of universal love which leads the mystic to say that the whole world is good.

The philosophy of evolution, through the notion of progress, is bound up with the ethical dualism of the worse and the better, and is thus shut out, not only from the kind of survey which discards good and evil altogether from its view, but also from the mystical belief in the goodness of everything. In this way the distinction of good and evil, like time, becomes a tyrant in this philosophy, and introduces into thought the restless selectiveness of action. Good and evil, like time, are, it would seem, not general or fundamental in the world of thought, but late and highly specialised members of the intellectual hierarchy.

Although, as we saw, mysticism can be interpreted so as to agree with the view that good and evil are not intellectually fundamental, it must be admitted that here we are no longer in verbal agreement with most of the great philosophers and religious teachers of the past. I believe, however, that the elimination of ethical considerations from philosophy is both scientifically necessary and—though this may seem a paradox—an ethical advance. Both these contentions must be briefly defended.

The hope of satisfaction to our more human desires—the hope of demonstrating that the world has this or that desirable ethical characteristic—is not one which, so far as I can see, a scientific philosophy can do anything whatever to satisfy. The difference between a good world and a bad one is a difference in the particular characteristics of the particular things that exist in these worlds: it is not a sufficiently abstract difference to come within the province of philosophy. Love and hate, for example, are ethical opposites, but to philosophy they are closely analogous attitudes towards objects. The general form and structure of those attitudes towards objects which constitute mental phenomena is a problem for philosophy, but the difference between love and hate is not a difference of form or structure, and therefore belongs rather to the special science of psychology than to philosophy. Thus the ethical interests which have often inspired philosophers must remain in the background: some kind of ethical interest may inspire the whole study, but none must obtrude in the detail or be expected in the special results which are sought.

If this view seems at first slight disappointing, we may remind ourselves that a similar change has been found necessary in all the other sciences. The physicist or chemist is not now required to prove the ethical importance of his ions or atoms; the biologist is not expected to prove the utility of the plants or animals which he dissects. In pre-scientific ages this was not the case. Astronomy, for example, was studied because men believed in astrology: it was thought that the movements of the planets had the most direct and important bearing upon the lives of human beings. Presumably, when this belief decayed and the disinterested study of astronomy began, many who had found astrology absorbingly interesting decided that astronomy had too little human interest to be worthy of study. Physics, as it appears in Plato's Timæus for example, is full of ethical notions: it is an essential part of its purpose to show that the earth is worthy of admiration. The modern physicist, on the contrary, though he has no wish to deny that the earth is admirable, is not concerned, as physicist, with its ethical attributes: he is merely concerned to find out facts, not to consider whether they are good or bad. In psychology, the scientific attitude is even more recent and more difficult than in the physical sciences: it is natural to consider that human nature is either good or bad, and to suppose that the difference between good and bad, so all-important in practice, must be important in theory also. It is only during the last century that an ethically neutral psychology has grown up; and here too, ethical neutrality has been essential to scientific success.

In philosophy, hitherto, ethical neutrality has been seldom sought and hardly ever achieved. Men have remembered their wishes, and have judged philosophies in relation to their wishes. Driven from the particular sciences, the belief that the notions of good and evil must afford a key to the understanding of the world has sought a refuge in philosophy. But even from this last refuge, if philosophy is not to remain a set of pleasing dreams, this belief must be driven forth. It is a commonplace that happiness is not best achieved by those who seek it directly; and it would seem that the same is true of the good. In thought, at any rate, those who forget good and evil and seek only to know the facts are more likely to achieve good than those who view the world through the distorting medium of their own desires.

We are thus brought back to our seeming paradox, that a philosophy which does not seek to impose upon the world its own conceptions of good and evil is not only more likely to achieve truth, but is also the outcome of a higher ethical standpoint than one which, like evolutionism and most traditional systems, is perpetually appraising the universe and seeking to find in it an embodiment of present ideals. In religion, and in every deeply serious view of the world and of human destiny, there is an element of submission, a realisation of the limits of human power, which is somewhat lacking in the modern world, with its quick material successes and its insolent belief in the boundless possibilities of progress. "He that loveth his life shall lose it"; and there is danger lest, through a too confident love of life, life itself should lose much of what gives it its highest worth. The submission which religion inculcates in action is essentially the same in spirit as that which science teaches in thought; and the ethical neutrality by which its victories have been achieved is the outcome of that submission.

The good which it concerns us to remember is the good which it lies in our power to create—the good in our own lives and in our attitude towards the world. Insistence on belief in an external realisation of the good is a form of self-assertion, which, while it cannot secure the external good which it desires, can seriously impair the inward good which lies within our power, and destroy that reverence towards fact which constitutes both what is valuable in humility and what is fruitful in the scientific temper.

Human beings cannot, of course, wholly transcend human nature; something subjective, if only the interest that determines the direction of our attention, must remain in all our thought. But scientific philosophy comes nearer to objectivity than any other human pursuit, and gives us, therefore, the closest constant and the most intimate relation with the outer world that it is possible to achieve. To the primitive mind, everything is either friendly or hostile; but experience has shown that friendliness and hostility are not the conceptions by which the world is to be understood. Scientific philosophy thus represents, though as yet only in a nascent condition, a higher form of thought than any pre-scientific belief or imagination, and, like every approach to self-transcendence, it brings with it a rich reward in increase of scope and breadth and comprehension. Evolutionism, in spite of its appeals to particular scientific facts, fails to be a truly scientific philosophy because of its slavery to time, its ethical preoccupations, and its predominant interest in our mundane concerns and destiny. A truly scientific philosophy will be more humble, more piecemeal, more arduous, offering less glitter of outward mirage to flatter fallacious hopes, but more indifferent to fate, and more capable of accepting the world without the tyrannous imposition of our human and temporary demands.

12

REASONING

REASON AND COMMITMENT

Roger Trigg

Roger Trigg (1941–   ), *Lecturer in Philosophy at the University of* W*arwick in England. In addition to* Reason and Commitment (1973), *a selection from which appears below, he is the author of* Pain and Emotions (1970).

A fundamental distinction must be drawn between the way the world is and what we say about it, even if we all happen to agree. We could all be wrong. Some of the most important commitments we make in our life could be based on error. What is true and what we think is true need not coincide. This simple statement seems self-evident, since it merely draws attention to human fallibility in general, and our own in particular.

It might be salutary to remind ourselves of our fallibility if we felt certain about what to believe. In fact, however, many now would not only doubt that we can ever arrive at truth, but would doubt whether there is such a thing. We are faced with fundamental human disagreement not merely over what to believe, but over what would count in the first place as an adequate reason for belief. Morality and religion are notoriously areas where humanity seems to speak with many voices. Science seems by contrast to provide an example of a discipline where there are settled methods for ending disputes, and there exists an impressive unanimity of belief. Even here, however, the same problem can arise. What are we to say to somebody who will not accept the assumptions of Western science in the first place? And even the unanimity of scientists disappears when we approach the frontiers of knowledge and encounter the controversies of contemporary research.

Perhaps, then, it is not surprising that it is currently fashionable to decry the notion that certain thnigs are simply *true*, and are therefore valid for all men whether they recognise the fact or not. Many people shrink from claiming that their moral or religious beliefs have this kind of truth and that those who reject the beliefs are mistaken. This hesitation may arise from a desire to be tolerant, from the fact of persistent disagreement in these areas, and also from the truism that no one has a monopoly of truth. It can slip imperceptibly into the view that while one set of things may be true in one religion or one society, a different set may hold in another. Truth is then made to depend on what groups of people happen to believe. The possibility of false beliefs is ruled out, so that a whole community could not be judged mistaken. What its members believe is true for them, just as what we believe is true for us. Facts are then dependent on the way people think, and no room is left for the idea that things can be the case whether anyone thinks they are or not. In other words, the possibility of something being objectively the case is ruled out. Truth must always be considered *relative* to a society, whether it consists of the believers in a particular religion, the holders of a certain scientific theory, the members of one tribe, or any other identifiable grouping.

All this means that it is impossible to conceive of any kind of independent reality. Reality becomes merely what people think it is, and as different people have different conceptions of it, there must be different realities. However, to hold that there is no such thing as 'reality' but only realities seems itself to be an incoherent position. It is in effect to claim that it is objectively true that there are different realities and that they exist whether each person concerned with his particular world realises it or not. Thus the very denial of the possibility of something being independently or objectively real itself rests on the view that the various realities are objectively real. The incoherence can be shown in another way. If someone declares that truth is not objective but only relative to societies, he may very well claim 'there is no such thing as "objective truth"' or 'truth is relative to societies.' Both assertions, however, clearly purport to be objectively true, and are intended as truths about all societies. There would not be much point in the relativist uttering them if he did not wish to convince someone else of them. He thus has to accept that sentences which state his thesis are apparently inconsistent with it. He can always claim that the truth of his words is only relative to his own society, but as their whole point is to describe other societies as well, this just serves to emphasise the incoherence in the position.

The difficulty of stating relativism without lapsing into self-contradiction is not enough to counterbalance its undeniable attractions, and different versions of the theory will be forced on our attention in the course of this book. The term 'relativism' often seems to be used without any great precision, and it sometimes appears to be no more than a synonym of 'subjectivism.' The subjectivist holds that what I think is true is

true for me and what you think is true is true for you. He is making truth
relative to individuals rather than to groups of people. Protagoras is usually
thought to have made the classic statement of the relativist position, but
the views which he put forward in Athens in the fifth century b.c. seem
to be much more those of the subjectivist as we have defined him. Protagoras maintained that man is the measure of all things. Plato quotes him
as holding that anything 'is to me as it appears to me and is to you as it
appears to you.'[1] This makes it clear that Protagoras is thinking in terms
of each individual, rather than of societies. He is not saying that what
is true in Egypt may not be true in Athens, but that what is true for
Protagoras may not be true for Socrates or someone else.

Both relativism as applied to societies and subjectivism as applied to
individuals are alike in what they deny, and this is presumably why the
two are sometimes not distinguished. Neither allows for the logical possibility that the beliefs of an individual in the one case, or of a society in
the other, can be judged by measuring them against anything external to
the beliefs. The conception of something being the case apart from either
a community or an individual thinking it is, is ruled out by both. Man
effectively decides what is to count as true and what is to count as false.
Truth is in the mind of the thinker, according to the subjectivist, or arises
from the collective agreement of a society, according to the relativist. The
objectivist, on the other hand, holds that truth is a goal which we aim at
but do not necessarily reach.

By talking in terms of societies, the relativist does seem to allow some
scope for beliefs to be mistaken or wrong, since *individuals* may be mistaken. They may make judgments which happen to go against the views
of their society, and which as such may be false for that society. The
individual would thus be subject to the standards of the society. Presumably the man who is out of step with his society has come to hold beliefs
which are not shared by others in his community. This means that there
is a disagreement in the society, which must be resolved by deciding what
the majority thinks. There is clearly an oddity in deciding by ballot or
similar means what is to be true, even if it is to be merely truth relative to
a society. It may be said that it only appears odd because we are still be-
witched by an objectivist view of truth. The point of the ballot, however,
would be to ask what each man believes, or in other words what he thinks
is *true* and it is obviously circular to use this as a basis for the definition of
truth.

We could avoid this by asking people to predict in the ballot what
the result of the ballot would be. This is not circular, although it may be
idiotic. Even here, however, the incoherence of the situation is brought
out when we consider what precisely we are supposed to predict. The only
possible answer is that we must predict our own and other people's predic-

<hr>

[1] Plato, *Theaetetus* 152 A.

tions. This must involve predicting our own and other people's predictions of our predictions . . . and so on. It is certainly possible to predict the result of a ballot on a definite issue, but this merely emphasises that people have to have beliefs *before* the ballot.

The conclusion must be that once it is allowed that different people believe different things in a society, truth cannot be defined in terms of what that society thinks. Everyone in a society may unthinkingly accept the same beliefs, and this is particularly liable to happen in an unsophisticated society immune from outside influences. If, however, they begin to consider consciously what to believe, they cannot all look at each other simultaneously to see what the majority thinks. It must therefore be assumed that individual judgments about what is true precede questions about what most people think. Each individual must have some prior conception of what it is for something to be true, which is totally independent of what others happen to think. A relativistic view of truth appears to collapse at this point.

. . .

The absurdities which result from the relativistic views we have been considering clearly indicate that the views must be mistaken. Where have they gone wrong? Why does it seem so attractive to some philosophers to deny that any resolution of basic conflicts is even in principle possible? Clearly they start by observing that in fact it is very difficult to gain any wide agreement in matters of fundamental importance. Ethics and religion provide examples of this. It is a fact of life that there are competing moral systems and competing religions, each making claims to truth. The members of one seem unable to convince the members of another. It is natural, therefore, to conclude that there is no such thing as objective truth. To assert that there is would not be to change anything. Men would still disagree.

Wittgenstein notes that what men consider reasonable and unreasonable varies. He sees that this might indicate there is no 'objective character' here and comments: '*Very* intelligent and well-educated people believe in the story of creation in the Bible, while others hold it as proven false, and the grounds of the latter are well known to the former.'[2] The fact that the same grounds convince some and fail to convince others suggests that it is impossible to lay down standards for what is to be considered reasonable.

In other words the main impetus to relativistic theories comes from the fact of human disagreement. Even basic changes of view are then explained as being the product of causal factors. All this, however, is to concentrate too much on the psychology of individual men. What they do in fact accept or reject ought to be a different question from what is worthy of acceptance or rejection. Why men first became committed to

[2] Wittgenstein, *On Certainty*, § 336.

some system may be totally irrelevant to the question of the validity of the system as such. The way someone happens to arrive at a particular view may not be the way the view might be justified. What might make a scientist suddenly relate experimental findings which he had not previously related may have nothing to do with the validity or otherwise of his insight. What makes someone suddenly become converted to a particular religion could be totally irrelevant to general questions about the truth of that religion. The fact, for instance, that a choir sang in an inspiring way at a critical moment could easily be a major cause of a conversion. But one would not suppose that this could justify the new commitment.

Without these basic distinctions, the inevitable result is an obsession with what men do in fact accept and reject. Unless some common denominator is discovered in their beliefs, it will be concluded that the same standards cannot be expected to apply to everyone. If I do not apply the normal standards of rationality to my own thinking, then they cannot be understood to apply to me. The temptation might then well be to say that I am a member of a different 'system' of thought, or 'form of life.' The truth might be that I am obstinate, stupid, or irrational, but on the view under consideration, such concepts could have no application. If there are no standards other than those I accept, then clearly there is no legitimate way in which any adverse judgment could be passed on me.

Important consequences follow from the distinction between an individual's psychology and the justification for his beliefs. Reference to one must be seen as irrelevant to the other. MacIntyre refers to the fact of Wordsworth being driven into the Church of England by his brother's death, and quite rightly points out that any experience can provide an occasion for conversion.[3] . . .

MacIntyre says: 'Religious belief is a matter not of argument but of conversion . . . There are no reasons to which one can appeal to evade the burden of decision.'[4] The fact, however, that an argument may not convince someone does not necessarily reflect on its validity. Conversion is a matter of psychology: the question of rational justification has to be dealt with on another plane altogether. Just because men do not always think or behave in a rational way, it does not follow that their thoughts and actions cannot be judged against rational standards. Why someone has come to hold certain religious beliefs must be a totally different issue from the question whether what he believes is true. . . .

· · ·

There is a . . . fallacy that any recognition of objective standards will inevitably lead to arrogance and intolerance, and eventually to the persecution of those who reject them. Nowell-Smith expresses what is at the back of many philosophers' minds when he maintains that the 'objectivist'

[3] MacIntyre, 'The Logical Status of Religious Beliefs,' *Metaphysical Beliefs*, p. 210.
[4] *Ibid.*, p. 209.

is in an even worse position than the subjectivist in solving moral conflicts. He says of the objectivist:

> He necessarily attributes his opponent's denial of the truth to wilful perversity, and, holding as he does that in spite of his denials his opponent must really see the truth all the time, he realises that what his opponent needs is not argument but castigation . . . It is no accident that religious persecutions are the monopoly of objective theorists.[5]

Nowell-Smith is writing about intuitionism in particular, but he might have levelled the same charges at any objectivist theory. If someone claims to be right and others do not agree with him, may not he be tempted to enforce what he believes to be right? The answer is of course that he may be. In the same way, a subjectivist may want to make everyone accept what he says, and he may resort to force precisely because he believes rational argument is impossible. Non-objectivist theories cannot distinguish between different methods of conversion. The objectivist, however, does believe that rational argument can at least in principle establish what is true; and there is no reason why someone who believes that basic disagreement *can* admit of solution firstly should arrogantly assume that he himself has a monopoly of truth, and secondly should then make others accept his views by force. The mere fact that a disagreement is capable of solution does not of itself suggest which side is right. When two sides flatly contradict each other, whether in the fields of morality, religion or any other area, each will recognise (if they are objectivists) that at least one side must be mistaken. It could logically be *either*. To be consistent, therefore, an objectivist should recognise the possibility that he himself is mistaken. There need be no contradiction between strongly believing that one is right and yet realising that one could be wrong. Arrogance is not entailed by any objectivist theory. Certainly Nowell-Smith is wrong in thinking that any objectivist must consider that his opponent is disagreeing with him out of wilful perversity. An intuitionist theory which held that certain moral truths were self-evident might find itself in the position of having to say that everyone *must* see what is true. There are, however, other objectivist theories besides intuitionism, and it is no contradiction both to assert that truth is attainable in moral and religious matters and that it is often far from easy to arrive at it. It follows that sincere and reasonable men may find themselves disagreeing. The point, however, according to the objectivist is that they would be *disagreeing*. One would be asserting something which the other denied. They would be arguing about what was true.

Even if an objectivist were convinced that he was right and that others would benefit from his insight, it does not follow that he should impose his views on others by force. Indeed the toleration of views which are

[5] Nowell-Smith, *Ethics*, pp. 46–7.

different from and even opposed to one's own is itself something which either admits of rational justification or does not. If it does, it is clear that the objectivist is right after all since there is at least one moral principle (that of toleration) which has objective validity. It follows that the objectivist would be mistaken not to adopt it. If it cannot be justified rationally, it is not very obvious what the critics of the objectivist are doing when they complain that his theory leads to intolerance. They may happen to think intolerance is a bad thing, but they cannot consistently say that anyone else should also think it is, without themselves adopting an objectivist position.

There is nothing intrinsic in non-objectivist views which promotes tolerance. Someone who thinks that although something is right or wrong for him or his society, he cannot speak for other people or other societies may *seem* to be very tolerant. He appears to be championing the right of everyone to make up his own mind. He cannot, however, uphold this as a *right*. The fact that he supports it does not on his view mean that others should. To put it round the other way, there can be no reason why he should be tolerant of opposing viewpoints. Talk of a 'reason' must suggest something which can be assessed by others and has some general validity, and he is denying the possibility of such a thing. Similarly, anyone who criticises any objectivist view in the name of freedom is immediately setting up at least one objective standard by which others may be judged, namely that of freedom.

We have been reasserting the possibility of giving rational justification for a commitment to a moral practice, a scientific theory, a religion, or any other 'form of life.' Relativists do not agree amongst themselves what kind of commitment could count as ultimate and unjustifiable. Commitments to Roman Catholicism, Christianity, and religion have all been held to set the standards of rationality in the appropriate area. Western science, physics, and particular scientific theories have each been mentioned as comprising self-contained conceptual systems.

However confusing the details of these theories may be, the basic claims are clear enough. It is held that there are separate, although possibly overlapping, systems of thought, which can be judged only by the standards they themselves create. Either one is an adherent of a system and grasps its concepts or one is outside and as a result must find it incomprehensible. One's commitment determines what is a reason, and one cannot give reasons for the commitment. Beliefs about what is the case can form no basis for this kind of commitment, since the commitment itself determines what is to count as a fact, or as 'reality.' Any decision to join or opt out of a 'system' or 'form of life' must be outside the scope of reason.

When truth is divided into watertight compartments, so that what is true for one group may not be true for another, and may not even be intelligible to them, the notion of an all-embracing rationality must be completely abandoned. If I am barred from thinking of what is true as a first step towards deciding what to commit myself to, there will be no firm basis for making the commitment. It will either be totally arbitrary, or caused. The connection between commitment and propositional belief, which I have previously insisted upon, must be ruled out by conceptual relativism, for the simple reason that what will count as a proposition will depend on the system of which it is a part. Propositional belief already presupposes a system, according to the conceptual relativist. It cannot therefore be used to justify one (except, possibly, as a part of a wider whole).

The notion of an ultimate arbitrary commitment from which everything springs is in many ways an unsatisfactory one, although popular in some quarters. Some of those who have faced the problems which result from versions of conceptual relativism have not surprisingly felt the need to show that explanations for the ultimate commitments which people make individually or collectively are still available. We have seen how Kuhn thought the explanation of scientific progress 'must, in the final analysis, be psychological or sociological.'[6] Whether others putting forward similar views have realised it or not, the undermining of the role of reason and the emphasis that truth is relative to systems has paved the way to this conclusion. If reasons cannot be given to justify men committing themselves to one system rather than another, it is a fairly obvious step to say that we must look for causes to explain the existence of different 'systems' or forms of life. If the holding of concepts is essentially a social matter, then the sociologists can provide causal explanations as to why particular communities should be as they are. The problem why an individual stays in or out of a particular community, when there can be no good reason for his leaving or joining, can be passed over to the psychologist. Between them, the two specialists would seem to be able to answer all the questions which can be intelligibly asked about the situation. All that we can do is to look for causes why things are as they are.

Even though conceptual relativism seems to lead to deterministic explanations, there does remain the question whether it should in fact do so. The explanations which sociologists and psychologists give can no more be regarded as *true* by conceptual relativists than the beliefs of the system under scrutiny. The explanations must themselves only be valid within sociology or psychology. Even this is probably too large a claim. Since sociologists or psychologists may well fundamentally disagree amongst themselves about what counts as an adequate explanation in their discipline, the various explanations may well have only to be regarded as valid within a particular school of sociologists or psychologists.

The very considerations which apparently make people turn to psychology and sociology for enlightenment would also ensure that these

[6] Kuhn, 'Reflections on my Critics,' p. 21.

disciplines could give no help in explaining why men have certain commitments. The commitments just exist and some men happen to be committed to the standards of psychology or of sociology. Once it is denied that there can be any standards which are valid for everyone, it is open to anyone to reject these disciplines, just as others have rejected other commitments. If it is argued that their explanations fit the facts as no others do, that they provide the possibility of making successful predictions and so on, the conceptual relativist can give the familiar reply that all this merely begs the question. Why, he might say, should *these* be counted as relevant facts, or why should such-and-such a prediction be thought to be successful? The answer he would give is that we think like this as a result of our prior commitment to psychology or sociology (or at least to the procedures of modern science of which they form a part). The disciplines themselves decide what is relevant, and even what is to count as a fact. Kuhn's faith in them is merely evidence of his own commitment to science as it is understood in the contemporary Western world. If conceptual relativism were correct, one could dismiss psychology and sociology out of hand, for no scientific explanations could be regarded as having objective validity.

But paradoxically a belief in determinism may itself lead to conceptual relativism. If we hold that all our beliefs and commitments are causally explicable, rationality and questions of truth and falsity become irrelevant. In these circumstances the commitment of a Marxist or a Christian cannot be affected by reason. He is what he is because of his upbringing, his environment, his genetic make-up or whatever other causal explanation may be given. The fact that one set of beliefs might be true and another false could not possibly affect him. He will only take to be true what he is caused to believe and will only think something a good reason if he is caused to. Determinism makes all disagreement a matter for causal explanation, and as a result makes it impossible in principle to conceive of the rational solution of any disagreement. Whether the two parties to a dispute eventually agree is determined by the causal influences at work. Reason can have no independent role, according to determinism, because it must itself be merely the product of a chain of causes. Indeed because *all* reasoning must for a determinist be caused, this raises difficulties about his belief in determinism. As has often been pointed out, it seems to be self-defeating to maintain that determinism is true, since one's belief in determinism could also be causally explained. Determinism does not deny the possibility of objective truth. It is just that what is actually true, as opposed to what we are caused to believe is true, becomes an impossible goal.

.   .   .

If what I am committed to can be stated, my commitment must be subject to the presuppositions which make language possible. It will be based on beliefs which are objectively true or false and which are not merely valid for me and those who agree with me. Whether it is easy or difficult to establish the truth of a belief will clearly depend on its nature. The important point is that if it is a genuine belief, it is in principle within the scope of truth and falsity, it can be understood by those who do not hold it, and can therefore be rationally scrutinised. When someone is committed to Christianity, he shares the beliefs which themselves constitute Christianity, and if they are true, they are true for everyone, including atheists. If they are false, they are false even for Christians, even though they do not recognise it. If this were not so, there would be no clash between Christians and atheists, since they could not be disagreeing. Christianity is therefore not something very different from the way Christians conceive it. If it is saying anything at all, it must be making claims about what is objectively the case. Since the fact that these claims may be true also means that they could be false, Christianity is put at risk in a way which is uncongenial to some. At the same time as it is clear that since its claims are of far-reaching significance and could be true, they cannot be ignored by anyone concerned, as rationality demands, with what is true.

It is fashionable to fix one's attention on the fact of commitment. This is understandable. If our commitment determines what we regard as true, all that matters is whether a commitment is sincere, and it is perhaps significant that in some people's eyes sincerity is the only virtue, and hypocrisy the only vice. As we have seen, however, commitments involve claims to truth which are logically prior to the commitment. It follows that what ought to be of fundamental interest is whether the claims are true and the commitments justifiable.

Closely linked with questions about commitment are questions concerning concepts. Since we live in one world with which our beliefs may or may not correspond, the interesting question should not merely be what concepts we have, but also whether they properly reflect reality. In recent years the preoccupation of philosophers with conceptual analysis has sometimes blinded them to problems about the adequacy of our concepts. If there are different ways of conceiving reality, it is not enough to describe them. We cannot avoid choosing between them. To deny that this can be done on a rational basis involves us in the incoherence of conceptual relativism.

. . . This kind of point is particularly important for the philosophy of religion. The fact that some men have a concept of God does not mean that He does exist, any more than the fact that no-one had a concept of God would mean that He did not exist. Confusion about this may be one of the reasons why in a sceptical age it has become fashionable to talk of 'the death of God.' Even if men have stopped thinking of God and the concept of God has 'died,' it is nonsense to say that God has died. If an eternal being such as God ever existed, by definition He could not die.

Whether He does exist is a separate issue from questions about the concepts men may or may not have.

What reality is like and how we conceive it are always separate questions. We ourselves cannot say what it is like independently of our conceptions of it. Our concepts provide as it were a window on the world which may well distort it. This does not mean that we cannot recognise the possibility that we are mistaken and we may even be able to discover our mistake for ourselves. Other concepts may prove more adequate, as when someone is converted to a religion or adopts a new scientific theory.

What in fact has been missing from so much recent controversy in religion, science and other fields, is the notion of objectivity—of things being the case whether people recognise them or not. This gives point to arguments which otherwise, if they were possible at all, would merely appear to result from clashes of different personalities or different social structures. Its role is more vital still, since it is indispensable for the existence of language. Without it there could be no criteria to distinguish knowledge from ignorance, and human reason becomes impotent. With it the claims of religion, the discoveries of science, the assumptions of moral argument, and much else, take on the importance they deserve.

DEFENCE OF REASON
C. E. M. Joad

C. E. M. Joad (1891–1953), philosopher and author of Introduction to Modern Philosophy *(1924),* Return to Philosophy *(1935),* Guide to Philosophy *(1936), and* Philosophical Aspects of Modern Science *(1948). In* Return to Philosophy *(from which the following selection is drawn) Joad offers a "defence of reason," an "affirmation of values," and a general "plea for philosophy."*

. . .

I. ATTACK ON REASON

Reason the tool of impulse and desire. I propose to begin . . . the defence of reason to which I committed myself. . . . The contemporary disparagement takes two main forms. There are those who assert that in the realm of thought reason does not and cannot give us the truth and those who in the realm of conduct declare that reason should not, even if it can, guide our lives. Both forms of attack have in recent years derived considerable impetus from the growth of psycho-analysis and the popularization of the notions which psycho-analysts have made familiar. The animal origin of human nature is emphasized and the fact that our roots stretch back to a remote pre-human past. It is from these roots, it is said, that the continuous stream of impulses and desires which is the driving force of our actions takes its rise. Impulses and desires are the springs not only of conduct but also of thought. The energy with which we think, no less than the energy with which we act is, therefore, non-rational in origin. And not only the energy, but also the incentive. For thinking no less than acting is undertaken with a purpose; it is prompted by the desire to reach a conclusion. The desire for a conolusion determines the character and trend of our thinking. Hence, the goal which attracts, no less than the energy which inspires our apparently rational activities is irrational. If impulse is the motive force which drives reason from behind, it is difficult not to suppose that reason will march to the tune that impulse pipes her. If goals and ends are the prizes that pull reason from in front, it is difficult not to believe that she will reach only those conclusions which are compatible with their achievement. Thus reason comes increasingly to be represented not as a free activity, moving disinterestedly in accordance with the laws which she herself has dictated to the dispassionate contemplation of ends which only she can conceive, but as a servant of irrational forces suborned by them to reach the goal, whether of action or belief, that will afford them the greatest instinctive satisfaction.

In pursuance of this role, reason invents arguments for what we instinctively wish to believe and pretexts for what we instinctively wish to do. Morality itself may be, and frequently is, interpreted in this way. Laws and codes, conventions and prohibitions are screens erected by society to disguise from its members the real nature of their motives. Englishmen, it is said, have brought the use of reason to an unusual degree of efficiency in the performance of this office, and are never at a loss for an argument to convince themselves that they are only doing their duty, whenever they want an excuse for making themselves disagreeable. Thus Samuel Butler tells us of his father that he never would admit that he did anything because he wanted to; he was always able to persuade himself that what he wanted to do was also what he ought to do.

Impotence of reason in action and thought. The fisherman who persuades himself that fish being cold-blooded animals do not really feel the pain of having their throats dragged out of them by a hook, the parent who believes that he flogs his child for its good and not for his pleasure, the smoker who assures us that tobacco ash is good for the carpet, no less than the nation which pretends that it is fighting to maintain the integrity of treaties, to make the world safe for democracy, to preserve its honour, its place in the sun, its wives, children, firesides, religion or what not, whenever it wants an excuse to indulge its impulses of aggression and destruction, are all it is said, in their own ways utilizing their reasons to justify them in indulging their passions. It is, indeed, the chief difference between the civilized man and the savage, that the former is under the necessity of invoking his reason to assure himself that he is doing his individual or civic duty by judicially murdering criminals, patriotically hating foreigners, or 'lynching' negroes in a passion of moral indignation, whenever he wants an excuse for gratifying instincts which savages indulge without hypocrisy.

As in action, so in thought. 'Metaphysics,' said F. H. Bradley, may be 'the finding of bad reasons for what we believe upon instinct'; but 'to find these reasons is no less an instinct.' Science is represented as the product of the impulse of curiosity, philosophy of that of wonder, art of that of play. As for religion, it is simply a contrivance on the part of reason for satisfying our unconscious need to think that the universe is at heart friendly to human nature, and that the spiritual, the minded and the akin condition and underly the brutal, the mindless and the alien. Thus reason,

together with conscience and will, together in fact with all the more conscious and lately acquired faculties of the race, is regarded as a screen for
our instincts, an apologist for our passions and a tool of our needs. It is a
cork bobbing about on the waves of unconscious impulses whose direction
is determined by the currents that run below the surface.

Reason as the cancer of the soul.   Impotent in the sphere of thought,
reason is represented as deleterious in that of practice. The life of the
philosopher or the scholar which men in the past have consented to admire even when they could not hope to emulate, is today decried because
it does not give scope to our passions and impulses. Under the influence
of D. H. Lawrence and similar writers, men have come to think that
thinking is almost a crime. Not only must we not pass our lives reading
in the library or observing in the laboratory; we must not even permit
reason to guide them in the home or the market place. To do so is to do
violence to our 'real' nature by damming up the stream of impulses and
desires in which it resides. Upon this 'real' nature reason is treated as a
sort of excrescence, which has grown and spread until it has sucked into
itself all the energies of our being. It is represented as absorbing for its
own nourishment the generous forces of man's passional nature, thus depriving the organism as a whole of the primitive energy which alone can
give zest and love of living. Reason has in fact become a cancer preying
upon the tissues of the soul. Hence, the life according to reason comes
to be regarded as a kind of bloodless abstraction from life proper, and we
are asked in the interests of full, free and fruitful living to restrain not the
passions but the reason.

The cult of the primitive.   In contemporary literature this attack upon
the reason takes two rather different forms. At Huxley's intellectual anti-
rationalism we have already glanced. There remains the romantic anti-
rationalism of Lawrence.

     One of the outstanding developments of the post-war years has been
a revolt against sophistication and a romantic cult of the primitive. The
post-war repudiation of the traditional disciplines in conduct has been accompanied by a repudiation of traditional disciplines in art. Negroes and
jazz, the emanation of negroes; the jungle and the Ju-Ju and Epstein's
statues, the emanation of the jungle and the Ju-Ju; the music of Stravinsky
and the pictures of the *Surréalistes* are acclaimed just because they are *not*
in the classical tradition, because they do *not* embody the traditional
æsthetic virtues, the virtues of clarity and poise and studied beauty of
form. M. Breton writing in *This Quarter*, an American review which has
devoted a whole number to the exposition of *Surréalisme*, expresses his
belief 'in the higher reality of certain forms of association hitherto neglected in the omnipotence of dreaming, in the unbiased play of thought.'
To this unexplored territory he welcomes artists and creative writers, sug-

gesting that it is the matrix of all true art. 'Artists and creative writers' are not slow to accept the invitation. Roy Campbell gives us poems whose exploration of the vague territories of the subliminal issues via a fabric of unconscious association in phrases and rhythms that derive their meaning, if any, from the forgotten past, and apparently make their appearance on the poet's writing paper as unaccountably as spirit messages, which, indeed, they often resemble, while Salvadore Dali offers us pictures in which, against a predominating background of grand pianos, the skulls of animals, entrails, fœtuses and alarmingly distorted human beings jostle one another in their efforts to portray the enigmatic pulsings of the subliminal self.

.   .   .

Indictment of reason summarized.   Pride of intellect is censured; spiritual humility approved. The heart has its reasons of which the reason knows nothing; and they are good reasons. Logic is a bad guide, feeling is a good one. Let us, therefore, at all costs stop thinking and try to feel. As Chesterton has told us, 'It is better to talk wisdom foolishly like a saint, than to babble folly wisely like a don.'

Again, I am not sure how far Huxley would approve this particular form of the current anti-rationalism. That slighting reference to 'greed of experience,' for example, seems to traverse one of his favourite doctrines. One can almost see him wince, as that favourite corn, 'Give them all a show,' is trodden on. But with the general trend of the indictment of reason, he would, as we have seen in previous chapters, find little to quarrel. And since he is at once the most lucid and the most influential of the anti-rationalists, it will be as well to return for a summary and succinct statement of the modern anti-rationalist case to his writings.

The indictment might, then, read somewhat as follows. First, reason never gives us theoretical truth—'Science,' it will be remembered, is 'no truer than common sense or lunacy, than art or religion,' since 'even if one should correspond to things in themselves as perceived by some hypothetical non-human being, it would be impossible for us to discover which it was.' Secondly, to allow reason to rule the soul is to commit an offence against life: 'To live, the soul must be in intimate contact with the world; must assimilate it through all the channels of sense and desire, thought and feeling, which nature has provided for the purpose.'

The pitiable intellectual.   Now this precisely is what, according to Huxley, the intellectual does not do. The scholar, the philosopher, the recluse, even the scientist, are men who have chosen to go through the world halt and maimed. In choosing reason as their guide, knowledge as their goal, they have definitely abjured some of 'the channels of sense and desire,' and have scorned delights in order the better to live laborious days. And they are condemned for their pains as pitiable human abstractions. Huxley quotes with appropriate comments the famous passage from the

Phaedo in which Socrates describes the characteristic austerities of the philosopher. ' "Do you think it like a philosopher to take very seriously what are called pleasures such as eating and drinking?" "Certainly not, Socrates," said Simmias. (How one's feet itch to kick the bottoms of these imbeciles who always agree with the old sophist, whatever nonsense he talks! They deserved the hemlock even more richly than their master.) "Or sex?" Socrates goes on. "No." "Or the whole business of looking after the body? Will the philosopher rate that highly?" Of course he won't— the fool! The philosopher's soul "withdraws itself as far as it can from all association and contact with the body and reaches out after truth by itself." With what results? Deprived of its nourishment, the soul grows thin and mangy, like the starved lion.'

Nor do the other philosophers fare better. Kant, Newton and Descartes are treated with pitying contempt because, in greater or less measure, they chose to withdraw themselves from the ordinary avocations of life in order to pursue truth. They are stigmatized as 'extraordinary and lamentable souls.' ' "Poor brutes," we cry at the sight of them.' ' "Why aren't they given enough to eat?" ' A little hard this on men who devoted their lives to trying to penetrate the secrets of the universe! Hard, and in the case of Descartes unjust; Descartes, who voluntarily enlisted as a soldier in order to see the world; saw it and saw, too, fighting in the Low Countries; incurred the displeasure of the Church, was threatened with the fate of Galileo, and ultimately died of inflammation of the lungs caught through getting up at five in the morning to teach the Queen of Sweden philosophy. I wonder how often Huxley gets up at five in the morning!

Attitude of my students.   Waiving the somewhat unfortunate illustration of Descartes, we may state Huxley's case as follows. All sides of our nature must be given free and equal play, because all sides of our nature have equal value. To guide one's life by reason and to cultivate one's intelligence, either for its own sake or in order that one may the better guide one's life, is to forgo the development of certain important sides of one's nature. It is in fact to starve oneself, and such starvation is an offence against life. Reasoning and reflecting, we lose contact with the earth and, as Lawrence would add, with our own entrails. Cut off from the natural source of its being, the soul becomes parched and thin, like a plant whose taproot has been severed. The intellectual, in short, lives and thinks in a watertight compartment which his reason has made for him. So isolated, he is precluded both from living happily and from thinking fruitfully.

This criticism of reason has become part of the intellectual climate of our time. It is implicit in the thought of the age. And, inevitably, the great Victorians are its particular targets. How emphatically my students in their essays denounce such men as Spencer and Mill. How pitiably they depict their lives! They did not get drunk; they were not notorious for the quantity or the exuberance of their affairs with women; they did not set or cultivate new æsthetic fashions; they had no taste in wines; it is most improbable they even overrate. Also they did not rush about in cars, go to cocktail parties, play games, thrill at the movies, or consort with young women in beach pyjamas. They only wrote books. What starved, what miserable lives!

.   .   .

II. DEFENCE OF REASON

Distinction between theoretical and practical reason.   Let us adopt for the purposes of discussion the distinction between the theoretical and the practical reason which the critics of reason employ. The function of the theoretical reason, we will assume, is to discover truth; that of the practical reason, to guide our conduct, to teach us, in a word, how to live. The distinction, which is Aristotle's, prescribes an ideal, the ideal of reason's ultimate performance. For the theoretical reason the ideal is the discovery and contemplation of truth; for the practical, the right conduct of life. That reason does not think or live up to these ideals is obvious; it is obvious too that we must judge it by its actual, not its ideal, performance. How far, then, does the actual performance of reason judged in relation to these ideals, justify the contemporary strictures at which I have glanced?

Emergence of disinterested reasoning.   It is not denied that the operations of reason in the theoretical sphere are frequently biased by our desires and distorted by our prejudices; that we embrace conclusions not because they are true, but because we wish to think them true; and that, finding the universe as it appears unamenable to our wishes and antagonistic to our desires, we employ our reasons to persuade us that, in its real as opposed to its apparent nature, it is such as we should desire. We may even consider that most of what passes for religion and philosophy is the outcome of precisely this kind of reasoning, for which the modern world has coined the word 'rationalizing.' Does it, therefore, follow that reason can never operate freely, can never reach conclusions solely as a result of the compulsive force of the evidence?

If we look at the history of human thought, we can trace the gradual emergence of disinterested reason, and a gradual increase in the scope of its operations. Initially, it would seem, men used their reasons to justify their wishes or to further their desires, and for no other purpose at all.

They certainly did not use them disinterestedly in order to acquire knowledge for its own sake.

As the mind of man develops and the employment of reason extends,
a process can be discerned which the historians of human thought have
traced in some detail. It is the process whereby mythology becomes religion, superstition science, alchemy chemistry, and astrology astronomy.

Let us take one or two examples of the process at work. The credit for
originating it must surely belong to the Greeks. It is, indeed, their greatest
achievement. Thales, travelling in the East, found that the Egyptians
possessed certain rough rules of land measurement. Every year the inunda-
tion of the Nile obliterated the landmarks, and the peasants' fields had to
be marked out afresh. The Egyptians had invented a method of dividing
up the land into rectangular areas, by means of which they contrived to
cope with the floods. Thales was not interested in marking out fields. He
saw that the method could be detached from the particular purpose for
which it had been used, and generalized into a method for calculating
areas of any shape. So the rules of land measurement were converted into
the science of geometry. The use of reason to achieve a practical end, the
furtherance of human desires, had given way to the use of reason in disinterested contemplation. The disinterested contemplative reason discovered, and delighted to discover, that the angles at the base of an
isosceles triangle are always equal; discovered too why they must be equal.
The land surveyor still makes use of this truth in constructing maps; reason is content to enjoy it because it is true. In the same way the Greeks
turned the art of astrology into the science of astronomy. For many centuries the Babylonian priests had recorded the movements of the planets,
in order to predict human events which the stars were believed to govern.
The Greeks borrowed the results of their observation, and Thales predicted an eclipse which occurred in Asia Minor in 585 B.C. But they
ignored the whole fabric of astrological superstition which had hitherto
provided the sole, the practical motive for observing the heavens.

The movement of which Thales is so eminent an example is the beginning of science. Natural phenomena had previously been ascribed to
the agency of supernatural forces. These forces had been personified into
gods and devils, owning fragmentary or complete personalities accessible
by prayer and sacrifice, amenable to magical compulsion, corruptible by
what was known as propitiation. Thunder and lightning, for example, were
the acts of these beings. It was left to Anaximander to propound the view
that thunder and lightning were caused by the blast of the wind. Shut up
in a thick cloud, the wind, he said, bursts forth; the tearing of the cloud
makes the noise, and the rift gives the appearance of a flash in contrast
with the blackness of the cloud. This is a typically *scientific* explanation.

From superstition to science.   Now it seems to me that there is an important distinction between the uses of reason to persuade us that thunder

and lightning are caused by beings like ourselves, who are often angry but may be propitiated, and to discover exactly how thunder and lightning are in fact caused. The former, the method of superstition, is rationalizing; it interprets the unknown in terms of the human, and arrives at explanations of phenomena which are pre-eminently gratifying, inasmuch as they represent phenomena as controllable by the human. The latter, the method of science, interprets phenomena in terms of the non-human, and propounds explanations which are ethically neutral.

It is this distinction which the wholesale disparagement of reason on the ground that it cannot be disinterested in its search for truth culpably ignores. Science has not legislated to the universe; it has been content to catalogue it. Its triumphs have been gained as the result of an impartial outlook upon the world which has sought to maintain a modest attitude towards objective fact. Instead of prescribing to things what they must be, it has been the object of the scientific method to discover what things are. It was only when science divorced itself from ethical preoccupations that it advanced. The early sciences, for example astrology and alchemy, were dominated by utilitarian considerations. It was thought that the movements of the stars had an important influence on human beings, and that certain combinations of elements would bring untold material benefits to human lives; for these reasons the movements of the stars and the nature of the chemical combinations were studied. The early physicists were dominated by the desire to prove that the universe had a purpose and was, therefore, ethically admirable, and psychology is still to some extent influenced by the need to arrive at similar conclusions about human nature. It was only when astrology and alchemy divested themselves of utilitarian considerations, that they developed into astronomy and chemistry; only when physics emancipated itself from the need to show that the universe it studied possessed this or that ethical characteristic, that it was found possible to discover how the physical universe worked. Psychology is only now beginning to reach a certitude of result as it emancipates itself from the necessity of illustrating preconceived notions about the rationality or ethical desirability of human nature.

To reflect upon this process, the process which leads from superstition to science, as it has historically taken place, is to realize a certain highly significant fact. The victory of reason has been won first in those spheres in which both the subject matter studied and the conclusions reached are furthest removed from the sphere of the human, which are, therefore most remote from human wishes.

Ethical neutrality of mathematics.   The first victories are achieved in mathematics. Now, so far as I can see, the relations of numbers have no bearing whatever upon human aspirations or emotions. So far as I am concerned, seven times seven might just as well make forty-eight as forty-nine. Why, then, do I think that it makes forty-nine? Only, I imagine, be-

cause I can see that it does; at any rate, after the most careful inspection
of my conscious, and a painstaking effort to acquaint myself with all that
analysts tell me about my unconscious self, I can find no other reason for
my belief. A poultry farmer once a week goes to market with ten dozen
eggs which he sells for twopence each; he sells so many eggs every year;
the upkeep of his poultry farm cost him £700 a year. How much profit
does he make on every egg? I don't know; nor, I expect, does the farmer.
He ought to know, you say, and he would be a more successful farmer if
he did. Certainly! Therefore, you conclude arithmetic does concern human
interests. And that is where you are wrong; for the farmer's concerns are
not arithmetic. They are arithmetic made easy for children by the introduction of a little not very successful local colouring. Arithmetic as such
has not heard of farmers, has no cognizance of eggs or of the means by
which they are produced, and is sublimely indifferent as to whether there
is a profit or not. When a problem in the arithmetic book begins 'A
poultry farmer goes to market,' it is not strictly telling the truth. What it
ought to say is: 'If there were a poultry farmer who sold weekly ten dozen
egg for twopence each, and if the upkeep of his poultry farm cost him
£700 a year, then . . . what would be the profit on each egg?' Or, more
austerely still: 'What is the relation expressed in pounds, shillings and
pence between 120 twopences, seven hundred pounds and twelve months,
in the circumstances in which . . . etc.?' Arithmetic, in other words, is
concerned not with facts but with relations; with the relations not between things but between quantities. No doubt the matters upon which
the discovery of these relations between quantities throws light interest
us enormously. Arithmetic, in fact, can be applied. It can enable us to
calculate, to predict, to cheat. But the relations themselves are matters
completely indifferent.

As for the fact that the product of $(a + b)$ and $(a - b)$ is $a^2 - b^2$, I
can see absolutely nothing to be said for it except that it is a fact: it is
neither beautiful, holy, helpful, consoling nor useful. It just is; and mankind by a process of apparently disinterested reason has discovered that it
is. It is because of its remoteness that it is in mathematics that reason first
wins its triumphs, exploring the relations between numbers and mapping
what it has discovered without fear or favour, and, so far as I can see, with
no purpose except the desire to find out.

It is, of course, the case that even in mathematics in its early stages
human wishes made their influence felt. Men anthropomorphized numbers and humanized geometrical shapes. Thus the Pythagoreans invested
the number 10 with a nimbus of sanctity—it was the perfect number—and
the regular pentagon with mystical significance. And all sorts of mysterious
meanings have been read by cabalists into the numbers three and seven.
But numbers are unsatisfactory subjects for anthropomorphization, nor is
it easy to read hidden messages between the lines of an addition sum.
Consequently the human element is banished quite early in civilized his-

tory from the mathematical field, and men arrive at conclusions which there is no reason for holding except that they are true. Even Aldous Huxley, so far as I know, has never been disposed to question the objective truth of mathematics, or to doubt that two and two make four, not because he wishes them to make four and has carefully chosen or cooked the evidence that favours this view, but because they do, because in fact the universe is like that.

.   .   .

Objective truth attainable.   The conclusion of the foregoing seems to be that reason can reach objective truth; or, more precisely, the implications that underlie the process I have briefly sketched, and the assumption which the distinction between superstition and science entails are that objective truth is at least humanly attainable. Now it is, of course, the case that human beings may be wrong to draw these implications, to make this assumption. They may be wrong, that is to say, in holding, as they undoubtedly do hold, that the methods of astronomy are scientifically fruitful and the conclusions of astronomers valid in some sense in which the methods and conclusions of astrology were neither fruitful nor valid, and that the judgment that three and two make five is true in some sense in which the judgments that the English are the thirteen lost tribes of Israel, or that the great pyramid contains information as to the precise date and manner of the destruction of the world are not. Human minds may, I say, be wrong in drawing these implications and in making these assumptions; but it is certainly a fact that all intelligent human minds, including those of Huxley, Lawrence and Richards, do draw them and do make them.

And to make them is to make also by implication the admissions (a) that the human intellect can on occasion discover objective fact unbiased by prejudice and undistracted by desire; (b) that although it may begin by mistaking wishes for judgments and being the dupe of its hopes, the harder it tries and the more it develops, the more likely it is to reach conclusions in the formation of which hopes and wishes have had no part; and (c) that it is possible sometimes to distinguish between those cases in which reason is functioning freely, and those in which it is a mere puppet twitched into the appropriate conclusions by instincts that pull the strings. I should wish to add a fourth conclusion, although it is more than doubtful whether the above-mentioned writers would be willing to subscribe to it, and, unlike the others, it does not follow from what has been said, namely, (d) that the emancipation of reason from the play of instinct and the pull of desire is a good, and that in the increase of this good lies the chief hope of our race.

This fourth conclusion is, I say, less likely to win assent. It is not so much that it is inconsistent with the explicit pronouncements of Lawrence and Huxley, of whom the former would subordinate reason to the solar plexus and the latter submerge it in life as a whole; for, so far as concerns consistency, the other three conclusions, which nobody in his senses would wish to deny, are equally at variance with some of their utterances. It is rather that in men's hearts to-day there is, I believe, a deep-seated distrust of reason and a desire to see its operations curtailed.

Reason the prop of social justice.   Yet apart altogether from theoretical considerations touching the advance of pure knowledge, as to whether it is desirable or not that men should know things, the practical advantages of the increasing application of reason to human affairs are universally acclaimed. Consider justice, for example. Justice is a word that covers a multitude of meanings; one of them is that an innocent man should not suffer for the fault of another. Hence it is a corollary of justice that no step should be left untaken to discover the guilty. I will now suppose that a criminal lunatic, or, if you prefer, a private enemy with a grudge of malice and a taste for sadism breaks into my house, assaults my wife and slits the stomach of my baby. As soon as I who, we will suppose, am writing at the bottom of the garden, hear screams, I rush into the house but am too late to catch the lunatic sadist. I rush out into the street and see a man running at a rapid pace down the road. I catch him up and threaten him with a revolver. 'Hands up' I say and shout for the police, when my wife comes running up and tells me that this is the wrong man. Her assailant had lost the fore and little fingers of his right hand; the hands which are now being held up are, she observes, intact. Now the fact that I am beside myself with anger and excitement, that my emotions are violently aroused, that instinct, the instinct for revenge, that desire, the desire to capture and to punish, dominate my whole being, do not prevent my reason from operating to tell me that I have made a mistake, with the result that I lower my revolver and apologize. I am sufficiently just not to wish that an innocent man should suffer for another's crime, and it is my ability to reason that enables my sentiment of justice to take effect. Now nobody, so far as I am aware, thinks that it would be a good thing for me to attack the wrong man. I infer (a) that it is reason refusing to be biased by instinct or desire that also refuses to allow me to give way to either; (b) that it is regarded as a good thing that reason should have achieved this degree of emancipation. The point is, indeed, so obvious that it is incredible that it should be overlooked. Yet it is, I think, quite certainly the case that it is overlooked by the writers to whom I have referred, or, more precisely, its neglect is a necessary corollary of the attitude to reason which they have both engendered and expressed. Hence, though I hesitate to labour the point, I cannot deny myself the pleasure of asking them whether, when they have every reason to believe that X, whom they loathe, has ravished their wives, and they are, therefore, thirsting for the punishment, and, unless they are eccentrically humanitarian, for the strangulation by hanging of X, they would, nevertheless, refuse to listen to the arguments of the detective who, after an elaborate accumulation of evidence finds himself in a position to demonstrate that the murderer was not in fact X but Y, Y being uncaught and not, therefore, in immediate danger of being hanged. As good readers of detective stories, in which category I confidently include both Mr. Huxley and Mr. Richards, they would, I feel sure, find themselves constrained to bow to the exegesis of the demonstrating detective. In other words, in spite of the fact that their instincts were clamouring for vengeance on X, they would obey the dictates of reason which pointed not to X but to Y. Why would they obey them? Only, so far as I can see, because of their implicit trust in the ability of reason, dispassionately considering evidence without regard to wishes, instincts or desires to reach objectively true conclusions.

Emancipation of reason a good. Now, I suggest again that this emancipation of reason from the predisposing bias of non-rational factors, which has resulted in the establishment of impartial justice, is a good. I think further that a similar emancipation of reason in other spheres would also be a good, and I contend that what has been achieved in logic and mathematics, is at least theoretically achievable in biology, psychology and sociology, and that it is the hope of achieving it that inspires the work of biologists, psychologists and sociologists.

Reason, emancipated from desire in mathematics, has still, it is agreed, to achieve objectivity in psychology. Reason, which operates freely to reach just decisions in disputes between individuals, has still to achieve a similar objectivity in its application to disputes between nations. Already, indeed, it does on occasion operate impartially even in this sphere,[1] but the communal will to implement its deliverances is lacking. Hence the advance, which took place when astrology became astronomy and alchemy chemistry, has still to be made from the law of the jungle, based upon fear and force, which still regulates international affairs, to the law of impartial justice administered by disinterested parties, which already prevails in disputes between individuals.

Truth and verifiability. There is a further application of these conclusions. The school of thought I have described is, as we have seen in previous essays, scornful of philosophy and religion. Both, it holds, are forms of wish fulfilment, projections of the desires of the human heart or the fantasies of the human mind upon the empty canvas of the universe. Neither can claim truth. It is not my intention here to defend philosophy, which is later to be accorded a couple of chapters in its exclusive honour. It is sufficient for my purpose to point out that, if I am right in supposing that the achievement of objective truth by the human mind is at last pos-

[1] E.g., in the admirable pronouncements of the Bank for International Settlements or the International Labour Office.

sible in other spheres, there is no reason why it should be impossible in those of philosophy and religion.

The difference between astronomy or geology, let us say, and philosophy is not a difference between spheres in which truth is possible and achievable and a sphere in which it is not; it is a difference between spheres in which truth *can be known* to have been achieved and one in which no such knowledge is possible. The difference between the conclusions of science and of philosophy is, in a word, not one of truth but of verifiability. If I believe that the attraction between two bodies in empty space varies inversely with the square of the distance between them, I can by suitable apparatus establish the fact that my belief is correct. If I believe with Bradley that judgment is an act which ascribes an ideal content to reality, there is no available means of verification which will tell me whether my belief is correct or not. But it does not, therefore, follow that it cannot be correct; nor does it follow in the case of judgments of value.

If five people are asked to guess the temperature of a room, two things will happen: first they will all guess differently; secondly, their estimates will be relative to and determined by subjective, physiological conditions prevailing in themselves. It does not follow, however, that the room has not got a temperature. What is more, we can by using a thermometer find out what it is; we can also find out which of the guesses is nearest the truth. Similarly, if five people are asked to pronounce upon the æsthetic value of a picture, or a quartet, it is probable that all will estimate it differently; moreover, the varying estimates will be relative to and determined by subjective circumstances of training, environment and taste, that is, by the æsthetic experience, the age and culture of the judges. It does not, therefore, follow either that the work of art has no æsthetic value in its own right, or that some of the judgments will not be nearer the mark than others. The only difference from the preceding instance is that in the present case there is no instrument analogous to the thermometer, by reference to which we can test the respective accuracies of the differing judgments. It is for this reason that art criticism is a battle of *ipse-dixitisms* and that there is no disputing about anything but tastes.

Conclusions.   I conclude, first, that reason can sometimes reach results which are objectively and absolutely true. This is notably the case in the sphere of mathematics; it is frequently the case in that of the sciences; it is also the case in human affairs in the degree to which we are prepared to hang a man who is rich and respected by eminent persons in preference to one who is poor and a known Communist, merely because the evidence shows that he and not the Communist committed the crime. Secondly, that this capacity of reason is in practice recognized by those whose doctrine requires them to deny it, since they no more doubt that three and two make five and that a man ought to be and sometimes is hanged in accordance with evidence and not political prejudice or personal dislike, than I do. Thirdly, that we can trace as an historical process the spread of reason and its gradual invasion of new spheres. Fourthly, that in its success in bringing under its ægis spheres which have hitherto been the province of emotion and feeling lies the chief hope of the race.

Selected bibliography

Scientific Method

Aristotle. *Prior and Post Analytics*. Oxford: Oxford University Press, 1949.

Ayer, A. J. *Language, Truth and Logic*. New York: Dover, 1936.

Bacon, Francis. *Novum Organum*. The Great Books, vol. 30. Chicago: Encyclopaedia Brittanica, 1952.

Bernal, J. D. *The Social Function of Science*. Cambridge: M.I.T. Press, 1939.

Braithwaite, Richard B. *Scientific Explanation*. Cambridge: Cambridge University Press, 1953.

Broad, C. D. *Scientific Thought*. London: Routledge & Kegan Paul, 1923.

Carnap, Rudolf. *The Unity of Science*. London: Routledge & Kegan Paul, 1934.

Conant, James B. *Science and Common Sense*. New Haven: Yale University Press, 1951.

Eddington, Arthur. *Philosophy of Physical Science*. Ann Arbor: University of Michigan Press, 1958.

Feibleman, James K. *Scientific Method*. New York: Humanities Press, 1972.

Korner, Stephan. *Experience and Theory*. New York: Humanities Press, 1972.

Lenzen, Victor F. *Procedures of Empirical Sciences*. Chicago: University of Chicago Press, 1938.

Mandelbaum, Maurice. *Philosophy, Science and Sense Perception*. Baltimore: Johns Hopkins University Press, 1964.

Mill, John Stuart. *Philosophy of Scientific Method*. New York: Hafner, 1950.

Nagel, E. *Sovereign Reason, and Other Studies in the Philosophy of Science*. Glencoe, Ill.: The Free Press, 1954.

Northrop, F. S. C. *The Logic of the Sciences and the Humanities*. New York: Macmillan, 1947.

Poincaré, H. *The Foundations of Science*. New York: The Science Press, 1913.

Polanyi, Michael. *Personal Knowledge*. Chicago: University of Chicago Press, 1958.

Popper, Karl. *Conjectures and Refutations: The Growth of Scientific Knowledge*. New York: Harper & Row, 1968.

Suppes, P. *Studies in the Methodology and Foundations of Science*. Boston: Reidel Publications, 1969.

Whitehead, A. N. *Science and the Modern World*. New York: Macmillan, 1930.

Mystical Awareness

Bergson, Henri. *The Creative Mind*. New York: Philosophical Library, 1946.

Besant, Annie. *Esoteric Christianity*. Wheaton: Theosophical Publishing House, 1966.

Boehme, Jacob. *Six Theosophic Points and Other Writings*. Ann Arbor: University of Michigan Press, 1958.

Bruner, Jerome S. *On Knowing: Essays for the Left Hand*. Cambridge: Harvard University Press, 1962.

Butler, Dom. C. *Western Mysticism*. London: Constable, 1927.
Castaneda, Carlos. *The Teachings of Don Juan: A Yaqui Way of Knowledge*. New York: Ballantine, 1969.
Cordelier, J. *The Spiral Way*. London: John M. Watkins, 1922.
Dasgupta, S. *Hindu Mysticism*. LaSalle, Ill.: Open Court, 1927.
Fairweather, William. *Among the Mystics*. Plainview, N.Y.: Books for Libraries, 1936.
Fleming, W. K. *Mysticism in Christianity*. London: Robert Scott, 1933.
Gerling, Helene. *Intuition Through the Ages*. Jericho, N.Y.: Exposition, 1972.
Greeley, Andrew M. *Ecstasy: A Way of Knowing*. Englewood Cliffs, N.J.: Prentice-Hall, 1974.
Huxley, Aldous. *The Doors of Perception* and *Heaven and Hell*. New York: Harper & Row, 1956.
Inge, William R. *Studies of English Mystics*. Plainview, N.Y.: Books for Libraries, 1906.
James, William. *Varieties of Religious Experience*. New York: Longmans Green, 1923.
Jones, Rufus M. *Studies in Mystical Religion*. London: Macmillan, 1923.
Montague, W. P. *Ways of Knowing*. New York: Macmillan, 1925.
Otto, Rudolf. *Mysticism East and West*. Oxford: Oxford University Press, 1924.
Peers, E. A. *Studies of the Spanish Mystics*. London: Sheldon Press, 1927.
Stutfield, H. E. M. *Mysticism and Catholicism*. London: Allen & Unwin, 1925.
Underhill, E. *The Mystic Way*. London: J. M. Dent, 1913.
Waite, Arthur E. *Lamps of Western Mysticism*. Blauvelt, N.Y.: Multimedia, 1973.
Watkin, Edward I. *The Philosophy of Mysticism*. London: Grant Richards, 1920.
Zaehner, Robert C. *Mysticism: Sacred and Profane*. Oxford: Oxford University Press, 1961.

*Reasoning**

Aaron, Richard I. *Knowing and the Function of Reason*. Oxford: Oxford University Press, 1971.
Armstrong, Allen. *Belief, Truth and Knowledge*. Cambridge: Cambridge University Press, 1973.
Austin, John L. *Sense and Sensibilia*. Oxford: Oxford University Press, 1962.
Blanshard, B. *The Nature of Thought*. 2 vols. New York: Humanities Press, 1964.
Carnap, Rudolf. *The Logical Structure of the World*. Berkeley: University of California Press, 1967.
Descartes, René. *Discourse on Method* and *Meditations*. New York: Dutton, 1951.
Dewey, John. *Logic: The Theory of Inquiry*. New York: Henry Holt, 1938.
Johnstone, Henry W. *Philosophy and Argument*. University Park: Pennsylvania State University Press, 1959.
Kant, I. *Critique of Pure Reason*. New York: Dutton, 1972.
Kemp, John. *Reason, Action and Morality*. New York: Humanities Press, 1964.
MacMurray, John. *Reason and Emotion*. New York: Humanities Press, 1972.
Passmore, John. *Philosophical Reasoning*. New York: Basic Books, 1969.

* For examples of philosophic reasoning (specifically the dialectic method), see the *Dialogues* of Plato, B. Jowett translation, especially the *Meno*, *Euthyphro*, and *Republic*.

Quine, W. V. *From a Logical Point of View*. Cambridge: Harvard University Press, 1953.

Russell, Bertrand. *Human Knowledge: Its Scope and Limitations*. New York: Simon & Schuster, 1948.

Slote, Michael A. *Reason and Scepticism*. New York: Humanities Press, 1970.

Toulmin, S. *The Uses of Argument*. Cambridge: Cambridge University Press, 1958.

Whitehead, A. N. *The Function of Reason*. Boston: Beacon Press, 1958.

Wilson, Brian, ed. *Rationality*. New York: Harper & Row, 1971.

Wilson, John. *Reason and Morals*. New York: Cambridge University Press, 1961.

Wolff, Robert P. *The Autonomy of Reason*. New York: Harper & Row, 1974.

DECIDING
WHAT TO
LIVE FOR

V

W E WANT TO LIVE our lives as well as possible, and this means selecting a dominant purpose to serve as the pivot of our daily activities. We can, of course, live from day to day without an overall direction, but knowing what we desire and consciously pursuing it seems to be a more promising approach for living a satisfying life as a whole. As Aristotle pointed out, if we know the target we are more likely to hit the mark. And if we deliberately aim at our ideal existence we stand a better chance of attaining it. Those who lead a thoughtless, drifting life will often frustrate themselves through shortsightedness, choosing what is immediately gratifying but ultimately self-defeating.

One obvious answer to the question of what to live for is that people should strive to achieve happiness. Common sense and conventional wisdom certainly support this view, for it is difficult to regard an unhappy life as a good one, and we are inclined to say of someone who has been happy that he or she lived well. But happiness is so broad a concept that it must be broken down to more specific parts and defined in terms that make it practically accessible to us as a goal. And when happiness is defined more precisely, it often appears rather vulnerable to criticism and not sufficiently dignified to constitute the primary purpose of human existence.

For example, we may mean by happiness the maximum amount of physical pleasure in our lifetime, from the enjoyment of sense experiences, such as eating flavorful meals, lying on the beach in the sun, skiing, and dancing, to the sensual satisfaction of lovemaking. But a life that treats these types of acts as central tends to be fundamentally unsatisfying and to yield diminishing returns. The happiness it provides is extremely brief, and a feeling of vacuousness and despondency often follows the moments of joy. In fact, the greater the intensity of the pleasure the more likely it is to be followed by disagreeable sensations as, for example, the heavy drinker and the drug addict discover. Above all, we find it difficult to justify a life of pleasure seeking because it engages only a small portion of our total being—the portion that lies closest to the surface. The happiness we experience is never profound, long lasting, or pervasive, and we feel cheated ultimately if we base our lives upon it. Pleasure may be a necessary ingredient in a worthwhile life, but it does not lie at the core.

Alternately, we may define happiness in more mental and less physical terms, identifying it with tranquil modes of enjoyment, such as the appreciation of fine music, good conversation with friends, the satisfactions that accompany creative efforts and the solution of intellectual problems, the religious emotion of communion with the sacred, thoughts in solitude, and so forth. But this interpretation, while refining the idea of happiness, may be too adult and precious to impart much vibrancy to life. It appears too careful and contrived, and to lack the important quality of spontaneity. The happiness that is offered may be of long duration, but it seldom carries enough vividness and intensity to be considered supremely valuable.

Both views are deficient in concern for other people, except as instruments for personal happiness,[1] and both fall prey to the hedonistic paradox. This paradox states that happiness is least likely to be attained when it is directly sought and most likely to occur as a concomitant to the attainment of other values. In brief, happiness seems to come when we do not look for it and therefore cannot be pursued as a goal.

If the hedonistic paradox is a valid criticism, then it becomes necessary to seek other aims in life even if we believe in the value of happiness. And if the other criticisms are valid and happiness is discredited, we would then be led to a different purpose for living, not as an indirect means of achieving happiness but as an alternative direction for our lives.

Three of these alternatives are presented in this chapter: self-realization, humanism, and existentialism. Each appears to be a more sophisticated notion than happiness, and they all speak more immediately to the consciousness of our age.

Self-realization has a long philosophic history behind it, stemming from the ancient Greeks, but its most forcible expression today is in the writings of psychologists such as Erich Fromm, Carl Rogers, and A. H. Maslow. In its philosophic form it was presented by Aristotle, and later by G. W. F. Hegel, T. H. Green, F. H. Bradley, J. H. Muirhead, Josiah Royce, and W. E. Hocking.

The central idea of self-realization as a philosophic theory is that the individual should strive to fully realize his or her capacities so that no significant talent, interest, ability, or desire is neglected or stunted in its development. We should try to fulfill ourselves as completely as possible through the realization of our potentialities and ultimately become all that we are capable of being.

Obviously, all of our capacities cannot be realized in our lifetime, and even if they could, it would be undesirable to be that diversified, sacrificing depth for breadth. Therefore, the self-realizationist advocates the subordination of our less inclusive capacities to our more inclusive ones so that, utilizing this ordering principle, we will be able to develop ourselves in a harmonious and beneficial way. It would be wrong, according to the self-realizationist, to try to become everything, for if we were everything in general we would be nothing in particular and thus lack individuality. It would also be misguided to allow our lesser interests to take precedence over our greater interests, for then we would be distorted in our development.

Some self-realizationists emphasize the fulfillment of each individual's self and some stress the development of our common human nature.

---

[1] Other theories of happiness, most notably Utilitarianism, present a more altruistic approach to life, but it would take us too far afield to discuss them here. See J. Bentham, *Introduction to the Principles of Morals and Legislation*, and J. S. Mill, *Utilitarianism*.

These two concepts are by no means identical, since a person can be closer or farther away from the ideal of humanness in his or her individual self, and the question then is whether to develop one's unique talents or to aim for the ideal development for a human being.

When the *self* is emphasized, it is never the self at any given moment in time that is significant, but the ideal self—that self that would exist if the major potentialities of our nature were realized. The task, then, becomes that of gaining an awareness of the principal capacities inherent in our present self, and, with this knowledge in mind, to work toward the actualization of these potentialities and the creation of our ideal self.

When our *human nature* is considered to be most important, the self-realizationist tries to uncover common human factors present in every individual which we are then urged to maximize in a harmonious manner; the goal is for each person to become as fully human as possible. For example, one analysis of human nature stresses three common human factors: (1) the drive toward physical well-being, including food, sex, and property, (2) the social tendencies, which incorporate the capacity for sympathy and the desire to win approval, and (3) the spiritual capacity, which includes the need for knowledge, the ability to appreciate beauty, and a religious nature. Being human involves all these characteristics, it is alleged, and each must be developed with proper emphasis so that a unified and complete human being will result. Our physical drives, for instance, must be expressed in such a way that the organism as a whole is enhanced: a proper amount and kind of food should be consumed, sex should enrich rather than demean the person, and property should not encumber but enlarge our being.

One obvious criticism of the self-realization ethic is that little attention is paid to the well-being of other people. That is, it appears to be extremely selfish in its concentration upon the realization of the individual's capacities. Attempts have been made by self-realizationists to show that one cannot develop oneself without having concern for others (as in 2 above), but the logical connection is questionable. Certainly we need be only minimally sensitive to other people's welfare in following the ideal of self-realization, and perhaps if we focus upon the development of our individual selves, rather than our humanness, we hardly need to be concerned at all, for compassion may not be one of our dominant characteristics.

This last point leads to a related criticism of both forms of the self-realization theory. If we say that people should develop their individual talents and capacities, then the miser, drunkard, or gangster can be justified in their ways of living provided they are developing those characteristics that are dominant and peculiar to themselves. Even Hitler, Atilla the Hun, and Ghengis Khan may be said to have lived "good" lives. But there is something odd about this which makes us question the general value of individual self-realization. Some selves should never be fully realized, or at least the minor tendencies should take precedence over the major ones; in many cases suppression, not expression, may be called for.

In the same way, we are not at all sure that realizing our humanness is a worthwhile goal, for human beings are not completely admirable. Aggression, malice, envy, and spite seem as much a part of human nature as peace, love, creativity, and generosity. Therefore, to be fully human may not be desirable.

To all of these criticisms we are tempted to respond that the actual goal of self-realization is to develop our *real* self, not a distortion, and that we want to be genuinely human, not animal, in our reactions. But descriptively speaking, our awful tendencies are just as real and human as our worthwhile ones and cannot legitimately be excluded if we aim at complete self-realization.

Perhaps we should say that self-realization in the general sense is not absolutely desirable, but that it does seem valuable to realize our capacities insofar as they are worth realizing. That is, we should select from among our potentialities those that promise to produce a rich and worthwhile person and reject for development those tendencies that appear negative—even if they are major parts of ourselves or definite characteristics of humanness. But the matter must be left there for the reader's consideration, and, hopefully, some personal conclusions can be reached following the reading of Erich Fromm, Carl Rogers, and A. H. Maslow in this section.

An alternative but complementary conception of the good life is offered by the philosophy of humanism. Humanists too would like to see us develop our potentialities, but they stress other values as being equally important or instrumental to this goal.

Humanists believe, first of all, that we should commit ourselves to the welfare of mankind, that we have a moral obligation to be humanitarian in outlook and continually improve the conditions of human life. Since, the humanist maintains, our own good is bound up with that of others, we will necessarily profit from our dedication to the human race. But that is only a fortunate consequence and not the reason for our commitment; rather, we have a primary moral responsibility to promote the highest possible life for all people.

To most humanists this means engaging in practical actions that create the conditions for a just and equitable society and working to solve the social problems of one's age. For example, contemporary humanists concern themselves with urban violence and international tension, poverty and starvation, overpopulation and the waste of natural resources, racial and sex discrimination, energy consumption and the pollution of the environment, and so forth. There is not complete unanimity among humanists with regard to the means for achieving justice and social harmony, but most humanists support a democratic program in which the individual is accorded maximum dignity and change occurs through peaceful processes, that is, by moral persuasion rather than violent confrontation.

In keeping with humanitarian concerns, humanists also stress that all moral values are derived from human experience, rather than from supposed divine laws of right and wrong, and are measured by their contribution to the improvement of man's life on earth. Humanists, in fact, reject the existence of God or of a supernatural realm stretching beyond the natural one and refuse to base human life on alleged cosmic purposes and the authoritarian commandments of religion. Man is alone in the universe without divine support or protection, and all values are created by human beings and are relative to human welfare.

Rather than being depressed at the prospect of an empty universe, indifferent to human aspiration and suffering, the humanist sees this fact as hopeful and liberating. For man need not be demeaned any longer, cowering in dependency and sinfulness before a cosmic father figure, denying bodily passions and feeling guilty over materialistic improvements in life. Human beings are freed to attain the status of adults responsible for themselves and the world they create. Without the fear of eternal damnation or the hope of immortal salvation, we can concentrate our energies on improving human existence here and now.

Humanists, then, are essentially optimistic in their attitude. The earth need not be filled with suffering—a testing ground for the life to come—and the human race is not inherently corrupt. Through reason and intelligence, and especially the human employment of science and technology, genuine progress can be made. Reason is capable of discerning ethical standards, unaided by divine revelation, and can identify the features of an ennobling and enriching life for the individual and the best social conditions for the human community.[2]

Now the altruistic character of humanism certainly seems greater than that of self-realization, and many people today find the ideal of service to mankind extremely compelling. But when we examine the ethic more closely, we wonder whether the humanists aren't championing a list of moral platitudes: they are in favor of peace, freedom, dignity, equality, and universal brotherhood. There is little to criticize in such a list, but that in itself may be an indictment. In brief, humanism may be right in what it advocates, but at the same time rather too full of clichés and banalities to serve as our life purpose.

The religious person, of course, criticizes the atheistic character of humanism, claiming that it makes a god of man, who is hardly worthy of worship, and puts its trust in human reason and goodness, both of which have (historically) proven disappointing. Above all, the religious person rejects the possibility of a compelling secular ethic. When man is

[2] For a concise statement of the humanist position, see the *Humanist Manifestos I and II*, ed. Paul Kurtz (Buffalo: Prometheus Books, 1973).

declared the measure of all things and God is deposed as the source of values, then moral anarchy must prevail. Without God as a fixed point, it is alleged, we can have no standard against which divergent moral claims may be measured.

Whether or not humanism is clichéd and platitudinous and whether it can provide an independent ethic are questions that readers must answer for themselves, along with other issues that will arise in reading the essays by Corliss Lamont and H. J. Blackham. But before we leave humanism let me draw the question of the independence of ethics into sharper focus.

It does seem that if God does not exist to authenticate moral principles, then all values become arbitrary and subjective, mere matters of preference and taste. But some philosophers have argued (most notably Plato in the *Euthyphro*) that moral principles do not come from God in any case; that God cannot make something good by willing it, but rather that He wills something because it is good. That is, goodness is something God cannot impart, but only recognize as intrinsic to an act such as loving one's neighbor. He cannot make that which is good into something bad by disapproving of it or transform the bad into the good by condoning it. In short, morality is autonomous and does not depend upon the commands of a divine being.

The issue turns on whether goodness is intrinsic to God (or, perhaps, coextensive with Him) or whether the realm of God and the realm of morals are separate.[3] But at this point the problem must be left for the reader to investigate.

Existentialism, the third theory of the good life that concerns us in this section, is a twentieth-century philosophic movement with nineteenth-century origins and is associated with the names Friedrich Nietzsche, Søren Kierkegaard, Karl Jaspers, Gabriel Marcel, Miguel de Unamuno, Ortega y Gasset, Martin Buber, Jean-Paul Sartre, Albert Camus, Martin Heidegger, and many others. According to most accounts, it arose between the world wars in conditions of uncertainty, devastation, and uprootedness, and although it is European in origin and character, it quickly became assimilated into American thought.

Because existentialism encompasses so many diverse philosophers and is explicitly opposed to strict formulation it is extremely difficult to define. Nevertheless, certain features do appear quite consistently in existential literature and can be said to characterize the movement.

Existentialists seem united, for one thing, in concentrating on the actual concrete conditions of human existence. Rather than beginning at an abstract level and subsequently deducing what existence should entail (as in a Platonic or Thomistic scheme), the existentialist asks "What is it like to be a conscious existent being in the twentieth century?"

---

[3] See Kai Nielsen, "Ethics Without Religion," *The Ohio University Review* II (1964), 48–62, and my book *Deity and Morality* (New York: Humanities Press, 1968), Ch. I, IV, and VIII.

The existentialist answers this question by identifying several pervasive psychological states of modern man which are thought to have philosophic significance. The contemporary consciousness, the existentialist asserts, is overburdened with feelings of dread, estrangement and alienation, boredom, forlornness, displacement, anxiety, and despair. These states arise from the human condition and are an outgrowth of our unique awareness of our mortality and aloneness, but they have also been greatly exacerbated by the conditions of life in this century.

To take just one of these states as illustration, the existentialist analyzes the phenomenon of anxiety and sees it as something essentially different from fear.[4] In fear there exists a determinate object of one's fear, something that can be perceived and labeled (such as a competitive exam, a wild animal, the threat of nuclear warfare), whereas in the case of anxiety, nothing can be specified as the cause. The source of our anxiety always remains indeterminate and we are inclined to say to anyone who expresses concern about our state "It is really nothing"; anxiety and "nothing" regularly correspond to one another. But in this connection lies the clue to its understanding. We are basically anxious about nothingness, or non-being, the prospect of ultimate annihilation. As human beings, conscious of our temporary and precarious hold on life, we necessarily exist in a perpetual state of anxiety which cannot be eliminated, only reduced; it is part of the meaning of being human.

The task, then, according to the existentialists, is not to avoid but to confront our situation of being finite creatures condemned to death and to use our anxiety as a catalyst for maximizing our existence. Instead of living our days as though we lived forever, we should maintain a constant awareness of our mortality and live as fully and meaningfully as possible.

Through analyses of this kind the existentialist hopes to illuminate the nature of the human condition and to enliven and intensify human existence.

A second feature of existentialism is its insistence upon the self-creating character of human beings. There is no such thing as human nature, the existentialist maintains, for every generalization about man is proven false as he changes through history. Unlike the self-realizationist, the existentialist refuses to draw up a list of the characteristics of human nature since man is constantly transcending himself through time. An object can be described in its finality, but human beings continually develop their essences by free actions and commitments. As Sartre says, in the case of man "existence precedes essence," whereas for objects "essence precedes existence." That is, man first exists and then fills out his essence by what he does in his lifetime; he does not come into existence with his essence already formed as objects do. Human beings are therefore the

---

[4] Several psychologists, including Sigmund Freud and Harry Stack Sullivan, have made a similar distinction.

ensemble of their actions and, most existentialists feel, do not lead lives predetermined by a God who created them to fulfill a certain purpose.

Obviously, then, one must be an active participant in life, rather than a spectator, since it is only through engagement that one develops an essence at all and is truly human; existentialism, therefore, is a philosophy of activism. It is presupposed that human beings possess the free will necessary to choose their courses of action and can become whatever they intend to be. One becomes what one does and does what one freely chooses. Consequently, our responsibility for ourselves is total; what we become is not the result of social or psychological forces beyond our control, but the outcome of our free choice.

A third point made by the existentialists is that human beings should transcend both rationality and morality. Rationality suppresses our freedom by limiting us to the realm of reasonable thoughts and actions. Unless we are free to be irrational, even perverse and self-destructive if we desire, then we are not at liberty to conduct our lives as we please. As Dostoyevsky phrased it, "Twice two makes four without my will; as if free will meant that!"

Morality, to the existentialist, consists of mere mores which society uses to control people by persuading them that objective and universal values are involved. But there are no values intrinsic to the universe, and for the sake of maximizing one's existence and creating new ideals for mankind, one should free oneself from society's rules. Nietzsche, in particular, stresses the need for transcending conventional morality, which stifles the creativity and joy of life for the individual and the race. He urges us to be self-assertive and to create original and personal systems of morality.

As a final point, the existentialist says that since we live in a universe devoid of external values and without a God to provide direction and purpose,[5] life in itself is meaningless. But we can invest human life with meaning through our projects and commitments, choosing those undertakings that are personally satisfying and lead to experiential richness. With full lucidity about the human condition, in integrity and authenticity, we can project meaning into life and find existence worthwhile.

The critics of existentialism generally point out its preoccupation with the sordid and pathological aspects of human nature and maintain that such states as anxiety, dread, anguish, and despair are neither basic nor revealing. In addition, it is often charged that existentialism overestimates the amount of freedom that individuals possess and underestimates the role of social, political, and psychological conditioning.

Sometimes the existentialists are charged with inconsistency in claiming, on the one hand, that man is essentially free and, on the other, that

[5] Existentialists are usually atheistic, but there are notable exceptions, for example Søren Kierkegaard and Gabriel Marcel.

he does not have an essence, for isn't the possession of free will part of man's essence? Finally, questions have been raised as to the possibility of creating values through choices, that is, making an act or mode of life valuable by choosing it. For surely a murderer's life is not made valuable by virtue of his having chosen it.

Some of these objections can be met, but again the reader must now consider the criticisms and claims of this philosophy and decide whether it is a suitable basis for life. The essays that follow by Jean-Paul Sartre, Friedrich Nietzsche, and Miguel de Unamuno will present the existential position much more fully and richly.

It should be noted that self-realization, humanism, and existentialism while being separate theories also share some common ground. In realizing one's self one would necessarily explore the humanistic dimension, but primarily for the sake of one's own development. In the following selection, Erich Fromm speaks of self-realization as humanistic in this sense. Humanists likewise believe in the realization of potentialities, but place the potentialities of mankind above those of their own individual selves.

Existentialism is obviously concerned with self-realization, and vice versa (Rogers, for example, speaks of existential living), and our humanistic obligation is also emphasized. In fact, Sartre's essay *Existentialism* is sometimes titled *Existentialism Is a Humanism*. Nevertheless, existentialism and self-realization are not identical. For instance, the existentialist does not think individuals possess selves that can be "unpacked" through time, but rather that the self is the product of actions; we are nothing other than what we have done. And although existentialism has a humanistic component, particularly in Sartre and Camus, much greater stress is placed on enlivening the individual to the terms of his or her personal existence.

Various similarities and differences could be described, but let it suffice to say that the reader should not expect three utterly distinct theories of the good life. Overlapping will occur here and elsewhere, for philosophy is all of a piece.

One further word of warning. In evaluating the three theories of what to live for, it is relatively easy to find criticisms. But the task is to find a way of life that is essentially worthwhile despite its various weaknesses. Many people make the mistake of treating philosophy as an intellectual game in which the discovery of theoretical defects becomes a form of entertainment. The serious intent of doing philosophy is to reach conclusions, however tentative, about the basic problems of human existence —problems that each individual must resolve in order to live a worthwhile life.

13

SELF-
REALIZATION

MAN FOR HIMSELF
Erich Fromm

Erich Fromm (1900–   ), psychotherapist and social philosopher who analyzes in his writings the emotional problems common to a democratic society in the present age and outlines the principles of a sane social order. Fromm has presented his ideas in highly readable, semipopular works such as Escape from Freedom (1941), Man for Himself (1947), The Art of Loving (1956), *and* The Anatomy of Human Destructiveness (1975).

. . .

HUMANISTIC VS. AUTHORITARIAN ETHICS

Humanistic ethics, in contrast to authoritarian ethics, may . . . be distinguished by formal and material criteria. *Formally*, it is based on the principle that only man himself can determine the criterion for virtue and sin, and not an authority transcending him. *Materially*, it is based on the principle that "good" is what is good for man and "evil" what is detrimental to man; *the sole criterion of ethical value being man's welfare.*

The difference between humanistic and authoritarian ethics is illustrated in the different meanings attached to the word "virtue." Aristotle uses "virtue" to mean "excellence"—excellence of the activity by which the potentialities peculiar to man are realized. "Virtue" is used, e.g., by Paracelsus as synonymous with the individual characteristics of each thing —that is, its peculiarity. A stone or a flower each has its virtue, its combination of specific qualities. Man's virtue, likewise, is that precise set of qualities which is characteristic of the human species, while each person's virtue is his unique individuality. He is "virtuous" if he unfolds his "virtue." In contrast, "virtue" in the modern sense is a concept of authoritarian ethics. To be virtuous signifies self-denial and obedience, suppression of individuality rather than its fullest realization.

Humanistic ethics is anthropocentric; not, of course, in the sense that man is the center of the universe but in the sense that his value judgments, like all other judgments and even perceptions, are rooted in the peculiarities of his existence and are meaningful only with reference to it; man, indeed, is the "measure of all things." The humanistic position is that there is nothing higher and nothing more dignified than human existence. Against this position it has been argued that it is in the very nature of ethical behavior to be related to something *transcending* man, and hence that a system which recognizes man and his interest alone cannot be truly moral, that its object would be merely the isolated, egotistical individual.

This argument, usually offered in order to disprove man's ability—and right—to postulate and to judge the norms valid for his life, is based on a fallacy, for the principle that good is what is *good for man* does not imply that man's nature is such that egotism or isolation are good for him. It does not mean that man's purpose can be fulfilled in a state of unrelatedness to the world outside him. In fact, as many advocates of humanistic ethics have suggested, it is one of the characteristics of human nature that man finds his fulfillment and happiness only in relatedness to and solidarity with his fellow men. However, to love one's neighbor is not a phenomenon *transcending* man; it is something inherent in and *radiating from* him. Love is not a higher power which descends upon man nor a duty which is imposed upon him; it is his own power by which he relates himself to the world and makes it truly his.

SUBJECTIVISTIC VS. OBJECTIVISTIC ETHICS

If we accept the principle of humanistic ethics, what are we to answer those who deny man's capacity to arrive at normative principles which are *objectively* valid?

Indeed, one school of humanistic ethics accepts this challenge and agrees that value judgments have no objective validity and are nothing but arbitrary preferences or dislikes of an individual. From this point of view the statement, for instance, that "freedom is better than slavery" describes nothing but a difference in taste but is of no objective validity.

Value in this sense is defined as "any desired good" and desire is the test of value, not value the test of desire. Such radical subjectivism is by its very nature incompatible with the idea that ethical norms should be universal and applicable to all men. If this subjectivism were the only kind of humanistic ethics then, indeed, we would be left with the choice between ethical authoritarianism and the abandonment of all claims for generally valid norms.

Ethical hedonism is the first concession made to the principle of objectivity: in assuming that pleasure is good for man and that pain is bad, it provides a principle according to which desires are rated: only those desires whose fulfillment causes pleasure are valuable; others are not. However, despite Herbert Spencer's argument that pleasure has an objective function in the process of biological evolution, pleasure can not be a criterion of value. For there are people who enjoy submission and not freedom, who derive pleasure from hate and not from love, from exploitation and not from productive work. This phenomenon of pleasure derived from what is objectively harmful is typical of the neurotic character and has been studied extensively by psychoanalysis. . . .

An important step in the direction of a more objective criterion of value was the modification of the hedonistic principle introduced by Epicurus, who attempted to solve the difficulty by differentiating between "higher" and "lower" orders of pleasure. But while the intrinsic difficulty of hedonism was thus recognized, the attempted solution remained abstract and dogmatic. Nevertheless, hedonism has one great merit: by making man's own experience of pleasure and happiness the sole criterion of value it shuts the door to all attempts to have an authority determine "what is best for man" without so much as giving man a chance to consider what he feels about that which is said to be best for him. It is not surprising, therefore, to find that hedonistic ethics in Greece, in Rome, and in modern European and American culture has been advocated by progressive thinkers who were genuinely and ardently concerned with the happiness of man.

But in spite of its merits hedonism could not establish the basis for objectively valid ethical judgments. Must we then give up objectivity if we choose humanism? Or is it possible to establish norms of conduct and value judgments which are objectively valid for all men and yet postulated by man himself and not by an authority transcending him? I believe, indeed, that this is possible and shall attempt now to demonstrate this possibility.

At the outset, let us not forget that "objectively valid" is not identical with "absolute." For instance, a statement of probability, of approximation, or any hypothesis can be valid and at the same time "relative" in the sense of having been established on limited evidence and being subject to future refinement if facts or procedures warrant it. The whole concept of relative vs. absolute is rooted in theological thinking in which a divine realm, as the "absolute," is separated from the imperfect realm of man. Except for this theological context the concept of absolute is meaningless and has as little place in ethics as in scientific thinking in general.

But even if we are agreed on this point, the main objection to the possibility of objectively valid statements in ethics remains to be answered: it is the objection that "facts" must be clearly distinguished from "values." Since Kant, it has been widely maintained that objectively valid statements can be made only about facts and not about values, and that one test of being scientific is the exclusion of value statements.

However, in the arts we are accustomed to lay down objectively valid norms, deduced from scientific principles which are themselves established by observation of fact and/or extensive mathematico-deductive procedures. The pure or "theoretical" sciences concern themselves with the discovery of facts and principles, although even in the physical and biological sciences a normative element enters which does not vitiate their objectivity. The applied sciences concern themselves primarily with practical norms according to which things ought to be *done*—where "ought" is determined by scientific knowledge of facts and principles. Arts are activities calling for specific knowledge and skill. While some of them demand only common-sense knowledge, others, such as the art of engineering or medicine, require an extensive body of theoretical knowledge. If I want to build a railroad track, for instance, I must build it according to certain principles of physics. *In all arts a system of objectively valid norms constitutes the theory of practice (applied science) based on the theoretical science.* While there may be different ways of achieving excellent results in any art, norms are by no means arbitrary; their violation is penalized by poor results or even by complete failure to accomplish the desired end.

But not only medicine, engineering, and painting are arts; *living itself is an art*[1]—in fact, the most important and at the same time the most difficult and complex art to be practiced by man. Its object is not this or that specialized performance, but the performance of living, the process of developing into that which one is potentially. In the art of living, *man is both the artist and the object of his art*; he is the sculptor *and* the marble; the physician *and* the patient.

Humanistic ethics, for which "good" is synonymous with good for man and "bad" with bad for man, proposes that in order to know *what* is good for man we have to know his nature. *Humanistic ethics is the applied science of the "art of living" based upon the theoretical "science of man."* Here as in other arts, the excellence of one's achievement ("virtus") is proportional to the knowledge one has of the science of man and to one's skill and practice. But one can deduce norms from theories only on the premise that a certain activity is chosen and a certain aim is desired. The premise for medical science is that it is desirable to cure

---

[1] This use of "art," though, is in contrast to the terminology of Aristotle who differentiates between "making" and "doing."

disease and to prolong life; if this were not the case, all the rules of medical science would be irrelevant. Every applied science is based on an axiom which results from an act of choice: namely, that the end of the activity is desirable. There is, however, a difference between the axiom underlying ethics and that of other arts. We can imagine a hypothetical culture where people do not want paintings or bridges, but not one in which people do not want to live. The drive to live is inherent in every organism, and man can not help wanting to live regardless of what he would like to think about it.[2] The choice between life and death is more apparent than real; man's real choice is that between a good life and a bad life.

It is interesting at this point to ask why our time has lost the concept of *life as an art*. Modern man seems to believe that reading and writing are arts to be learned, that to become an architect, an engineer, or a skilled worker warrants considerable study, but that *living* is something so simple that no particular effort is required to learn how to do it. Just because everyone "lives" in some fashion, life is considered a matter in which everyone qualifies as an expert. But it is not because of the fact that man has mastered the art of living to such a degree that he has lost the sense of its difficulty. The prevailing lack of genuine joy and happiness in the process of living obviously excludes such an explanation. Modern society, in spite of all the emphasis it puts upon happiness, individuality, and self-interest, has taught man to feel that not his happiness (or if we were to use a theological term, his salvation) is the aim of life, but the fulfillment of his duty to work, or his success. Money, prestige, and power have become his incentives and ends. He acts under the illusion that his actions benefit his self-interest, though he actually serves everything else *but* the interests of his real self. Everything is important to him except his life and the art of living. He is for everything except for himself.

If ethics constitutes the body of norms for achieving excellence in performing the art of living, its most general principles must follow from the nature of life in general and of human existence in particular. In most general terms, the nature of all life is to preserve and affirm its own existence. All organisms have an inherent tendency to preserve their existence: it is from this fact that psychologists have postulated an "instinct" of self-preservation. The first "duty" of an organism is to be alive.

"To be alive" is a dynamic, not a static, concept. *Existence and the unfolding of the specific powers of an organism are one and the same.* All organisms have an inherent tendency to actualize their specific potentialities. *The aim of man's life*, therefore, is to be understood as *the unfolding of his powers according to the laws of his nature.*

Man, however, does not exist "in general." While sharing the core of human qualities with all members of his species, he is always an individual, a unique entity, different from everybody else. He differs by his

2 Suicide as a pathological phenomenon does not contradict this general principle.

particular blending of character, temperament, talents, dispositions, just as he differs at his fingertips. He can affirm his human potentialities only by realizing his individuality. The duty to be alive is the same as the duty to become oneself, to develop into the individual one potentially is.

To sum up, *good in humanistic ethics is the affirmation of life, the unfolding of man's powers. Virtue is responsibility toward his own existence.* Evil constitutes the crippling of man's powers; *vice is irresponsibility toward himself.*

.   .   .

SELFISHNESS, SELF-LOVE, AND SELF-INTEREST[3]

Thou shalt love thy neighbour as thyself.
—Bible

Modern culture is pervaded by a tabu on selfishness. We are taught that to be selfish is sinful and that to love others is virtuous. To be sure, this doctrine is in flagrant contradiction to the practice of modern society, which holds the doctrine that the most powerful and legitimate drive in man is selfishness and that by following this imperative drive the individual makes his best contribution to the common good. But the doctrine which declares selfishness to be the arch evil and love for others to be the greatest virtue is still powerful. Selfishness is used here almost synonymously with self-love. The alternative is to love others, which is a virtue, or to love oneself, which is a sin.

This principle has found its classic expression in Calvin's theology, according to which man is essentially evil and powerless. Man can achieve absolutely nothing that is good on the basis of his own strength or merit. "We are not our own," says Calvin. "Therefore neither our reason nor our will should predominate in our deliberations and actions. We are not our own; therefore let us not propose it as our end to seek what may be expedient for us according to the flesh. We are not our own; therefore, let us, as far as possible, forget ourselves and all things that are ours. On the contrary, we are God's; for Him, therefore, let us live and die. For, as it is the most devastating pestilence which ruins people if they obey themselves, it is the only haven of salvation not to know or to want anything

---

[3] Cf. Erich Fromm, "Selfishness and Self-Love," *Psychiatry* (November, 1939). The following discussion of selfishness and self-love is a partial repetition of the earlier paper.

by oneself but to be guided by God Who walks before us."[4] Man should have not only the conviction of his absolute nothingness but he should do everything to humiliate himself. "For I do not call it humility if you suppose that we have anything left. . . . We cannot think of ourselves as we ought to think without utterly despising everything that may be supposed an excellence in us. This humility is unfeigned submission of a mind overwhelmed with a weighty sense of its own misery and poverty; for such is the uniform description of it in the word of God."[5]

This emphasis on the nothingness and wickedness of the individual implies that there is nothing he should like and respect about himself. The doctrine is rooted in self-contempt and self-hatred. Calvin makes this point very clear: he speaks of self-love as "a pest."[6] If the individual finds something "on the strength of which he finds pleasure in himself," he betrays this sinful self-love. This fondness for himself will make him sit in judgment over others and despise them. Therefore, to be fond of oneself or to like anything in oneself is one of the greatest sins. It is supposed to exclude love for others[7] and to be identical with selfishness.[8]

. . .

The doctrine that selfishness is the arch-evil and that to love oneself excludes loving others is by no means restricted to theology and philosophy, but it became one of the stock ideas promulgated in home, school, motion pictures, books; indeed in all instruments of social suggestion as well. "Don't be selfish" is a sentence which has been impressed upon millions of children, generation after generation. Its meaning is somewhat vague. Most people would say that it means not to be egotistical, inconsiderate, without any concern for others. Actually, it generally means more than that. Not to be selfish implies not to do what one wishes, to give up one's own wishes for the sake of those in authority. "Don't be selfish," in the last analysis, has the same ambiguity that it has in Calvinism. Aside from its obvious implication, it means, "don't love yourself," "don't be yourself," but submit yourself to something more important

---

[4] Johannes Calvin, *Institutes of the Christian Religion*, trans. by John Allen (Philadelphia: Presbyterian Board of Christian Education, 1928), in particular Book III, Chap. 7, p. 619. From "For, as it is . . ." the translation is mine from the Latin original (Johannes Calvini, *Institutio Christianae Religionis. Editionem curavit*, A. Tholuk, Berolini, 1935, par. 1, p. 445).

[5] *Ibid.*, Chap. 12, par. 6, p. 681.

[6] *Ibid.*, Chap. 7, par. 4, p. 622.

[7] It should be noted, however, that even love for one's neighbor, while it is one of the fundamental doctrines of the New Testament, has not been given a corresponding weight by Calvin. In blatant contradiction to the New Testament, Calvin says: "For what the schoolmen advance concerning the priority of charity to faith and hope, is a mere reverie of a distempered imagination. . . ."—Chap. 24, par. 1, p. 531.

[8] Despite Luther's emphasis on the spiritual freedom of the individual, his theology, different as it is in many ways from Calvin's, is pervaded by the same conviction of man's basic powerlessness and nothingness.

than yourself, to an outside power or its internalization, "duty." "Don't be selfish" becomes one of the most powerful ideological tools in suppressing spontaneity and the free development of personality. Under the pressure of this slogan one is asked for every sacrifice and for complete submission: only those acts are "unselfish" which do not serve the individual but somebody or something outside himself.

This picture, we must repeat, is in a certain sense one-sided. For besides the doctrine that one should not be selfish, the opposite is also propagandized in modern society: keep your own advantage in mind, act according to what is best for you; by so doing you will also be acting for the greatest advantage of all others. As a matter of fact, the idea that egotism is the basis of the general welfare is the principle on which competitive society has been built. It is puzzling that two such seemingly contradictory principles could be taught side by side in one culture; of the fact, however, there is no doubt. One result of this contradiction is confusion in the individual. Torn between the two doctrines, he is seriously blocked in the process of integrating his personality. This confusion is one of the most significant sources of the bewilderment and helplessness of modern man.[9]

The doctrine that love for oneself is identical with "selfishness" and an alternative to love for others has pervaded theology, philosophy, and popular thought; the same doctrine has been rationalized in scientific language in Freud's theory of narcissism. Freud's concept presupposes a fixed amount of libido. In the infant, all of the libido has the child's own person as its objective, the stage of "primary narcissism," as Freud calls it. During the individual's development, the libido is shifted from one's own person toward other objects. If a person is blocked in his "object-relationships," the libido is withdrawn from the objects and returned to his own person; this is called "secondary narcissism." According to Freud, the more love I turn toward the outside world the less love is left for myself, and vice versa. He thus describes the phenomenon of love as an impoverishment of one's self-love because all libido is turned to an object outside oneself.

These questions arise: Does psychological observation support the thesis that there is a basic contradiction and a state of alternation between love for oneself and love for others? Is love for oneself the same phenomenon as selfishness, or are they opposites? Furthermore, is the selfishness of modern man really a *concern for himself* as an individual, with all his intellectual, emotional, and sensual potentialities? Has "he" not become an appendage of his socioeconomic role? *Is his selfishness identical with self-love or is it not caused by the very lack of it?*

Before we start the discussion of the psychological aspect of selfish-

---

[9] This point has been emphasized by Karen Horney, *The Neurotic Personality of Our Time* (New York: W. W. Norton & Company, 1937), and by Robert S. Lynd, *Knowledge for What?* (Princeton: Princeton University Press, 1939).

ness and self-love, the logical fallacy in the notion that love for others and love for oneself are mutually exclusive should be stressed. If it is a virtue to love my neighbor as a human being, it must be a virtue—and not a vice—to love myself since I am a human being too. There is no concept of man in which I myself am not included. A doctrine which proclaims such an exclusion proves itself to be intrinsically contradictory. The idea expressed in the Biblical "Love thy neighbor as thyself!" implies that respect for one's own integrity and uniqueness, love for and understanding of one's own self, can not be separated from respect for and love and understanding of another individual. The love for my self is inseparably connected with the love for any other self.

We have come now to the basic psychological premises on which the conclusions of our argument are built. Generally, these premises are as follows: not only others, but we ourselves are the "object" of our feelings and attitudes; the attitudes toward others and toward ourselves, far from being contradictory, are basically *conjunctive*. With regard to the problem under discussion this means: Love of others and love of ourselves are not alternatives. On the contrary, an attitude of love toward themselves will be found in all those who are capable of loving others. *Love, in principle, is indivisible as far as the connection between "objects" and one's own self is concerned.* Genuine love is an expression of productiveness and implies care, respect, responsibility, and knowledge. It is not an "affect" in the sense of being affected by somebody, but an active striving for the growth and happiness of the loved person, rooted in one's own capacity to love.

To love is an expression of one's power to love, and to love somebody is the actualization and concentration of this power with regard to one person. It is not true, as the idea of romantic love would have it, that there is only *the* one person in the world whom one could love and that it is the great chance of one's life to find that one person. Nor is it true, if that person be found that love for him (or her) results in a withdrawal of love from others. Love which can only be experienced with regard to one person demonstrates by this very fact that it is not love, but a symbiotic attachment. The basic affirmation contained in love is directed toward the beloved person as an incarnation of essentially human qualities. Love of one person implies love of man as such. The kind of "division of labor" as William James calls it, by which one loves one's family but is without feeling for the "stranger," is a sign of a basic inability to love. Love of man is not, as is frequently supposed, an abstraction coming after the love for a specific person, but it is its premise, although, genetically, it is acquired in loving specific individuals.

From this it follows that my own self, in principle, must be as much an object of my love as another person. *The affirmation of one's own life, happiness, growth, freedom, is rooted in one's capacity to love,* i.e., in care, respect, responsibility, and knowledge. If an individual is able to love productively, he loves himself too; if he can love *only* others, he can not love at all.

Granted that love for oneself and for others in principle is conjunctive, how do we explain selfishness, which obviously excludes any genuine concern for others? The *selfish* person is interested only in himself, wants everything for himself, feels no pleasure in giving, but only in taking. The world outside is looked at only from the standpoint of what he can get out of it; he lacks interest in the needs of others, and respect for their dignity and integrity. He can see nothing but himself; he judges everyone and everything from its usefulness to him; he is basically unable to love. Does not this prove that concern for others and concern for oneself are unavoidable alternatives? This would be so if selfishness and self-love were identical. But that assumption is the very fallacy which has led to so many mistaken conclusions concerning our problem. *Selfishness and self-love, far from being identical, are actually opposites.* The selfish person does not love himself too much but too little; in fact he hates himself. This lack of fondness and care for himself, which is only one expression of his lack of productiveness, leaves him empty and frustrated. He is necessarily unhappy and anxiously concerned to snatch from life the satisfactions which he blocks himself from attaining. He seems to care too much for himself but actually he only makes an unsuccessful attempt to cover up and compensate for his failure to care for his real self. Freud holds that the selfish person is narcissistic, as if he had withdrawn his love from others and turned it toward his own person. *It is true that selfish persons are incapable of loving others, but they are not capable of loving themselves either.*

It is easier to understand selfishness by comparing it with greedy concern for others, as we find it, for instance, in an oversolicitous, dominating mother. While she consciously believes that she is particularly fond of her child, she has actually a deeply repressed hostility toward the object of her concern. She is overconcerned not because she loves the child too much, but because she has to compensate for her lack of capacity to love him at all.

This theory of the nature of selfishness is borne out by psychoanalytic experience with neurotic "unselfishness," a symptom of neurosis observed in not a few people who usually are troubled not by this symptom but by others connected with it, like depression, tiredness, inability to work, failure in love relationships, and so on. Not only is unselfishness not felt as a "symptom"; it is often the one redeeming character trait on which such people pride themselves. The "unselfish" person "does not want anything for himself"; he "lives only for others," is proud that he does not consider himself important. He is puzzled to find that in spite of his unselfishness he is unhappy, and that his relationships to those closest to him are unsatisfactory. He wants to have what he considers are his symptoms removed—but not his unselfishness. Analytic work shows that his unselfishness is not something apart from his other symptoms but one of them; in fact often the most important one; that he is paralyzed in his capacity to love or to enjoy anything; that he is pervaded by hostility against life and that behind the façade of unselfishness a subtle but not less intense self-centeredness is hidden. This person can be cured only if his unselfishness too is interpreted as a symptom along with the others so that his lack of productiveness, which is at the root of both his unselfishness *and* his other troubles, can be corrected.

The nature of unselfishness becomes particularly apparent in its effect on others and most frequently, in our culture, in the effect the "unselfish" mother has on her children. She believes that by her unselfishness her children will experience what it means to be loved and to learn, in turn, what it means to love. The effect of her unselfishness, however, does not at all correspond to her expectations. The children do not show the happiness of persons who are convinced that they are loved; they are anxious, tense, afraid of the mother's disapproval and anxious to live up to her expectations. Usually, they are affected by their mother's hidden hostility against life, which they sense rather than recognize, and eventually become imbued with it themselves. Altogether, the effect of the "unselfish" mother is not too different from that of the selfish one; indeed, it is often worse because the mother's unselfishness prevents the children from criticizing her. They are put under the obligation not to disappoint her; they are taught, under the mask of virtue, dislike for life. If one has a chance to study the effect of a mother with genuine self-love, one can see that there is nothing more conducive to giving a child the experience of what love, joy, and happiness are than being loved by a mother who loves herself.

Having analyzed selfishness and self-love we can now proceed to discuss the concept of *self-interest,* which has become one of the key symbols in modern society. . . .

The modern concept of self-interest is a strange blend of two contradictory concepts: that of Calvin and Luther on the one hand, and on the other, that of the progressive thinkers since Spinoza. Calvin and Luther had taught that man must suppress his self-interest and consider himself only an instrument for God's purposes. Progressive thinkers, on the contrary, have taught that man ought to be only an end for himself and not a means for any purpose transcending him. What happened was that man has accepted the contents of the Calvinistic doctrine while rejecting its religious formulation. He has made himself an instrument, not of God's will but of the economic machine or the state. He has accepted the role of a tool, not for God but for industrial progress; he has worked and amassed money but essentially not for the pleasure of spending it and of enjoying life but in order to save, to invest, to be successful. Monastic asceticism has been, as Max Weber has pointed out, replaced by an *inner-*

worldly asceticism where personal happiness and enjoyment are no longer the real aims of life. But this attitude was increasingly divorced from the one expressed in Calvin's concept and blended with that expressed in the progressive concept of self-interest, which taught that man had the right —and the obligation—to make the pursuit of his self-interest the supreme norm of life. The result is that modern man *lives* according to the principles of self-denial and *thinks* in terms of self-interest. He believes that he is acting in behalf of *his* interest when actually his paramount concern is money and success; he deceives himself about the fact that his most important human potentialities remain unfulfilled and that he loses himself in the process of seeking what is supposed to be best for him.

The deterioration of the meaning of the concept of self-interest is closely related to the change in the concept of self. In the Middle Ages man felt himself to be an intrinsic part of the social and religious community in reference to which he conceived his own self when he as an individual had not yet fully emerged from his group. Since the beginning of the modern era, when man as an individual was faced with the task of experiencing himself as an independent entity, his own identity became a problem. In the eighteenth and nineteenth centuries the concept of self was narrowed down increasingly; the self was felt to be constituted by the property one had. The formula for this concept of self was no longer "I am what I think" but "I am what I have," "what I possess."[10]

In the last few generations, under the growing influence of the market, the concept of self has shifted from meaning "I am what I possess" to meaning "I am as you desire me."[11] Man, living in a market

---

[10] William James expressed this concept very clearly. "To have," he says, "a self that I can care for, Nature must first present me with some object interesting enough to make me instinctively wish to appropriate it for its own sake. . . . My own body and what ministers to its needs are thus the primitive object, instinctively determined, of my egoistic interests. Other objects may become interesting derivatively, through association with any of these things, either as means or as habitual concomitants; and so, in a thousand ways, the primitive sphere of the egoistic emotions may enlarge and change its boundaries. This sort of interest is really the meaning of the word *mine*. Whatever has it, is, *eo ipso*, a part of me!"—*Principles of Psychology* (New York: Henry Holt and Company, 2 vols., 1896), I, 319, 324. Elsewhere James writes: "It is clear that between what a man calls *me* and what he simply calls *mine*, the line is difficult to draw. We feel and act about certain things that are ours very much as we feel and act about ourselves. Our fame, our children, the work of our hands, may be as dear to us as our bodies are, and arouse the same feelings and the same acts of reprisal if attacked. . . . In its widest possible sense, however, a man's Self is the sum-total of all that he can call his, not only his body, and his psychic powers, but his clothes and his house, his wife and children, his ancestors and friends, his reputation and works, his land and horses and yacht and bank account. All these things give him the same emotions. If they wax or prosper, he feels triumphant, if they dwindle and die away, he feels cast down—not necessarily in the same degree for each thing, but in much the same way for all."—*Ibid.*, I, 291–292.

[11] Pirandello in his plays has expressed this concept of self and the self-doubt resulting from it.

economy, feels himself to be a commodity. He is divorced from himself, as the seller of a commodity is divorced from what he wants to sell. To be sure, he is interested in himself, immensely interested in his success on the market, but "he" is the manager, the employer, the seller—and the commodity. His self-interest turns out to be the interest of "him" as the subject who employs "himself," as the commodity which should obtain the optimal price on the personality market.

The "fallacy of self-interest" in modern man has never been described better than by Ibsen in *Peer Gynt*. Peer Gynt believes that his whole life is devoted to the attainment of the interests of his *self*. He describes this self as:

> "The Gyntian Self!
> —An army, that, of wishes, appetites, desires!
> The Gyntian Self!
> It is a sea of fancies, claims and aspirations;
> In fact, it's all that swells within my breast
> And makes it come about that I am I and live as such."[12]

At the end of his life he recognizes that he had deceived himself; that while following the principle of "self-interest" he had failed to recognize what the interests of his real self were, and had lost the very self he sought to preserve. He is told that he never had been himself and that therefore he is to be thrown back into the melting pot to be dealt with as raw material. He discovers that he has lived according to the Troll principle: "To thyself be enough"—which is the opposite of the human principle: "To thyself be true." He is seized by the horror of nothingness to which he, who has no self, can not help succumbing when the props of pseudo self, success, and possessions are taken away or seriously questioned. He is forced to recognize that in trying to gain all the wealth of the world, in relentlessly pursuing what seemed to be his interest, he had lost his soul—or, as I would rather say, his self.

The deteriorated meaning of the concept of self-interest which pervades modern society has given rise to attacks on democracy from the various types of totalitarian ideologies. These claim that capitalism is *morally* wrong because it is governed by the principle of selfishness, and commend the moral superiority of their own systems by pointing to their principle of the unselfish subordination of the individual to the "higher" purposes of the state, the "race," or the "socialist fatherland." They impress not a few with this criticism because many feel that there is no happiness in the pursuit of selfish interest, and are imbued with a striving, vague though it may be, for a greater solidarity and mutual responsibility among men.

[12] Act V. Scene I.

We need not waste much time arguing against the totalitarian claims. In the first place, they are insincere since they only disguise the extreme selfishness of an "elite" that wishes to conquer and retain power over the majority of the population. Their ideology of unselfishness has the purpose of deceiving those subject to the control of the elite and of facilitating their exploitation and manipulation. Furthermore, the totalitarian ideologies confuse the issue by making it appear that they represent the principle of unselfishness when they apply to the state as a whole the principle of ruthless pursuit of selfishness. Each citizen ought to be devoted to the common welfare, but the state is permitted to pursue its own interest without regard to the welfare of other nations. But quite aside from the fact that the doctrines of totalitarianism are disguises for the most extreme selfishness, they are a revival—in secular language—of the religious idea of intrinsic human powerlessness and impotence and the resulting need for submission, to overcome which was the essence of modern spiritual and political progress. Not only do the authoritarian ideologies threaten the most precious achievement of Western culture, the respect for the uniqueness and dignity of the individual; they also tend to block the way to constructive criticism of modern society, and thereby to necessary changes. The failure of modern culture lies not in its principle of individualism, not in the idea that moral virtue is the same as the pursuit of self-interest, but in the deterioration of the meaning of self-interest; not in the fact that people are *too much concerned with their self-interest*, but that they are *not concerned enough with the interest of their real self; not in the fact that they are too selfish, but that they do not love themselves.*

If the causes for persevering in the pursuit of a fictitious idea of self-interest are as deeply rooted in the contemporary social structure as indicated above, the chances for a change in the meaning of self-interest would seem to be remote indeed, unless one can point to specific factors operating in the direction of change.

Perhaps the most important factor is the inner dissatisfaction of modern man with the results of his pursuit of "self-interest." The religion of success is crumbling and becoming a façade itself. The social "open spaces" grow narrower; the failure of the hopes for a better world after the First World War, the depression at the end of the twenties, the threat of a new and immensely destructive war so shortly after the Second World War, and the boundless insecurity resulting from this threat, shake the faith in the pursuit of this form of self-interest. Aside from these factors, the worship of success itself has failed to satisfy man's ineradicable striving to be himself. Like so many fantasies and daydreams, this one too fulfilled its function only for a time, as long as it was new, as long as the excitement connected with it was strong enough to keep man from considering it soberly. There is an increasing number of people to whom everything they are doing seems futile. They are still under the spell of the slogans which preach faith in the secular paradise of success and glamour.

But doubt, the fertile condition of all progress, has begun to besest them and has made them ready to ask what their real self-interest as human beings is.

This inner disillusionment and the readiness for a revaluation of self-interest could hardly become effective unless the economic conditions of our culture permitted it. I have pointed out that while the canalizing of all human energy into work and the striving for success was one of the indispensable conditions of the enormous achievement of modern capitalism, a stage has been reached where the problem of *production* has been virtually solved and where the problem of the *organization* of social life has become the paramount task of mankind. Man has created such sources of mechanical energy that he has freed himself from the task of putting all his human energy into work in order to produce the material conditions for living. He could spend a considerable part of his energy on the task of living itself.

Only if these two conditions, the subjective dissatisfaction with a culturally patterned aim and the socioeconomic basis for a change, are present, can an indispensable third factor, rational insight, become effective. This holds true as a principle of social and psychological change in general and of the change in the meaning of self-interest in particular. The time has come when the anesthetized striving for the pursuit of man's real interest is coming to life again. Once man knows what his self-interest is, the first, and the most difficult, step to its realization has been taken.

A THERAPIST'S VIEW OF THE GOOD LIFE: THE FULLY FUNCTIONING PERSON

Carl Rogers

Carl Rogers (1902–   ), psychotherapist and educator known primarily for his nondirective, "client centered" theory of therapy in which a personal relationship is established with the client (patient), who controls the course, pace, and length of treatment. Among his publications are Counseling and Psychotherapy *(1942),* Client Centered Therapy *(1951),* Psychotherapy and Personality Change *(1954, with others), and* On Becoming a Person *(1961).*

My views regarding the meaning of the good life are largely based upon my experience in working with people in the very close and intimate relationship which is called psychotherapy. These views thus have an empirical or experiential foundation, as contrasted perhaps with a scholarly or philosophical foundation. I have learned what the good life seems to be by observing and participating in the struggle of disturbed and troubled people to achieve that life.

. . .

. . . The good life, from the point of view of my experience, is the process of movement in a direction which the human organism selects when it is inwardly free to move in any direction, and the general qualities of this selected direction appear to have a certain universality.

THE CHARACTERISTICS OF THE PROCESS

Let me now try to specify what appear to be the characteristic qualities of this process of movement, as they crop up in person after person in therapy.

436

An increasing openness to experience

In the first place, the process seems to involve an increasing openness to experience. This phrase has come to have more and more meaning for me. It is the polar opposite of defensiveness. Defensiveness I have described in the past as being the organism's response to experiences which are perceived or anticipated as threatening, as incongruent with the individual's existing picture of himself, or of himself in relationship to the world. These threatening experiences are temporarily rendered harmless by being distorted in awareness, or being denied to awareness. I quite literally cannot see, with accuracy, those experiences, feelings, reactions in myself which are significantly at variance with the picture of myself which I already possess. A large part of the process of therapy is the continuing discovery by the client that he is experiencing feelings and attitudes which heretofore he has not been able to be aware of, which he has not been able to "own" as being a part of himself.

If a person could be fully open to his experience, however, every stimulus—whether originating within the organism or in the environment —would be freely relayed through the nervous system without being distorted by any defensive mechanism. There would be no need of the mechanism of "subception" whereby the organism is forewarned of any experience threatening to the self. On the contrary, whether the stimulus was the impact of a configuration of form, color, or sound in the environment on the sensory nerves, or a memory trace from the past, or a visceral sensation of fear or pleasure or disgust, the person would be "living" it, would have it completely available to awareness.

Thus, one aspect of this process which I am naming "the good life" appears to be a movement away from the pole of defensiveness toward the pole of openness to experience. The individual is becoming more able to listen to himself, to experience what is going on within himself. He is more open to his feelings of fear and discouragement and pain. He is also more open to his feelings of courage, and tenderness, and awe. He is free to live his feelings subjectively, as they exist in him, and also free to be aware of these feelings. He is more able fully to live the experiences of his organism rather than shutting them out of awareness.

Increasingly existential living

A second characteristic of the process which for me is the good life, is that it involves an increasing tendency to live fully in each moment. This is a thought which can easily be misunderstood, and which is perhaps vague in my own thinking. Let me try to explain what I mean.

I believe it would be evident that for the person who was fully open to his new experience, completely without defensiveness, each moment would be new. The complex configuration of inner and outer stimuli which exists in this moment has never existed before in just this fashion. Consequently such a person would realize that "What I will be in the next moment, and what I will do, grows out of that moment, and cannot be predicted in advance either by me or by others." Not infrequently we find clients expressing exactly this sort of feeling.

One way of expressing the fluidity which is present in such existential living is to say that the self and personality emerge *from* experience, rather than experience being translated or twisted to fit preconceived self-structure. It means that one becomes a participant in and an observer of the ongoing process of organismic experience, rather than being in control of it.

Such living in the moment means an absence of rigidity, of tight organization, of the imposition of structure on experience. It means instead a maximum of adaptability, a discovery of structure *in* experience, a flowing, changing organization of self and personality.

It is this tendency toward existential living which appears to me very evident in people who are involved in the process of the good life. One might almost say that it is the most essential quality of it. It involves discovering the structure of experience in the process of living the experience. Most of us, on the other hand, bring a preformed structure and evaluation to our experience and never relinquish it, but cram and twist the experience to fit our preconceptions, annoyed at the fluid qualities which make it so unruly in fitting our carefully constructed pigeonholes. To open one's spirit to what is going on *now*, and to discover in that present process whatever structure it appears to have—this to me is one of the qualities of the good life, the mature life, as I see clients approach it.

An increasing trust in his organism

Still another characteristic of the person who is living the process of the good life appears to be an increasing trust in his organism as a means of arriving at the most satisfying behavior in each existential situation. Again let me try to explain what I mean.

In choosing what course of action to take in any situation, many people rely upon guiding principles, upon a code of action laid down by some group or institution, upon the judgment of others (from wife and friends to Emily Post), or upon the way they have behaved in some similar past situation. Yet as I observe the clients whose experiences in living have taught me so much, I find that increasingly such individuals are able to trust their total organismic reaction to a new situation because they discover to an ever-increasing degree that if they are open to their experience, doing what "feels right" proves to be a competent and trust-worthy guide to behavior which is truly satisfying.

As I try to understand the reason for this, I find myself following this line of thought. The person who is fully open to his experience would have access to all of the available data in the situation, on which to base his behavior; the social demands, his own complex and possibly conflicting needs, his memories of similar situations, his perception of the uniqueness of this situation, etc., etc. The data would be very complex indeed. But he could permit his total organism, his consciousness participating, to con-sider each stimulus, need, and demand, its relative intensity and impor-tance, and out of this complex weighing and balancing, discover that course of action which would come closest to satisfying all his needs in the situa-tion. An analogy which might come close to a description would be to compare this person to a giant electronic computing machine. Since he is open to his experience, all of the data from his sense impressions, from his memory, from previous learning, from his visceral and internal states, is fed into the machine. The machine takes all of these multitudinous pulls and forces which are fed in as data, and quickly computes the course of action which would be the most economical vector of need satisfaction in this existential situation. This is the behavior of our hypothetical person.

The defects which in most of us make this process untrustworthy are the inclusion of information which does *not* belong to this present situa-tion, or the exclusion of information which *does*. It is when memories and previous learnings are fed into the computations as if they were *this* reality, and not memories and learnings, that erroneous behavioral answers arise. Or when certain threatening experiences are inhibited from aware-ness, and hence are withheld from the computation or fed into it in dis-torted form, this too produces error. But our hypothetical person would find his organism thoroughly trustworthy, because all of the available data would be used, and it would be present in accurate rather than distorted form. Hence his behavior would come as close as possible to satisfying all his needs—for enhancement, for affiliation with others, and the like.

In this weighing, balancing, and computation, his organism would not by any means be infallible. It would always give the best possible answer for the available data, but sometimes data would be missing. Be-cause of the element of openness to experience, however, any errors, any following of behavior which was not satisfying, would be quickly cor-rected. The computations, as it were, would always be in process of being corrected, because they would be continually checked in behavior.

Perhaps you will not like my analogy of an electronic computing machine. Let me return to the clients I know. As they become more open to all of their experiences, they find it increasingly possible to trust their reactions. If they "feel like" expressing anger they do so and find that this comes out satisfactorily, because they are equally alive to all of their other desires for affection, affiliation, and relationship. They are surprised at their own intuitive skill in finding behavioral solutions to complex and troubling human relationships. It is only afterward that they realize how surprisingly trustworthy their inner reactions have been in bringing about satisfactory behavior.

The process of functioning more fully

I should like to draw together these three threads describing the process of the good life into a more coherent picture. It appears that the person who is psychologically free moves in the direction of becoming a more fully functioning person. He is more able to live fully in and with each and all of his feelings and reactions. He makes increasing use of all his organic equipment to sense, as accurately as possible, the existential situation within and without. He makes use of all of the information his nervous system can thus supply, using it in awareness, but recognizing that his total organism may be, and often is, wiser than his awareness. He is more able to permit his total organism to function freely in all its complexity in selecting, from the multitude of possibilities, that behavior which in this moment of time will be most generally and genuinely satisfying. He is able to put more trust in his organism in this functioning, not because it is infallible, but because he can be fully open to the consequences of each of his actions and correct them if they prove to be less than satisfying.

He is more able to experience all of his feelings, and is less afraid of any of his feelings; he is his own sifter of evidence, and is more open to evidence from all sources; he is completely engaged in the process of being and becoming himself, and thus discovers that he is soundly and realistically social; he lives more completely in this moment, but learns that this is the soundest living for all time. He is becoming a more fully functioning organism, and because of the awareness of himself which flows freely in and through his experience, he is becoming a more fully functioning person.

SOME IMPLICATIONS

Any view of what constitutes the good life carries with it many implications, and the view I have presented is no exception. I hope that these implications may be food for thought. There are two or three of these about which I would like to comment.

A new perspective on freedom vs determinism

The first of these implications may not immediately be evident. It has to do with the age-old issue of "free will." Let me endeavor to spell out the way in which this issue now appears to me in a new light.

For some time I have been perplexed over the living paradox which exists in psychotherapy between freedom and determinism. In the therapeutic relationship some of the most compelling subjective experiences are those in which the client feels within himself the power of naked choice. He is *free*—to become himself or to hide behind a façade; to move forward or to retrogress; to behave in ways which are destructive of self and others, or in ways which are enhancing; quite literally free to live or die, in both the physiological and psychological meaning of those terms. Yet as we enter this field of psychotherapy with objective research methods, we are, like any other scientist, committed to a complete determinism. From this point of view every thought, feeling, and action of the client is determined by what preceded it. There can be no such thing as freedom. The dilemma I am trying to describe is no different than that found in other fields—it is simply brought to sharper focus, and appears more insoluble.

This dilemma can be seen in a fresh perspective, however, when we consider it in terms of the definition I have given of the fully functioning person. We could say that in the optimum of therapy the person rightfully experiences the most complete and absolute freedom. He wills or chooses to follow the course of action which is the most economical vector in relationship to all the internal and external stimuli, because it is that behavior which will be most deeply satisfying. But this is the same course of action which from another vantage point may be said to be determined by all the factors in the existential situation. Let us contrast this with the picture of the person who is defensively organized. He wills or chooses to follow a given course of action, but finds that he *cannot* behave in the fashion that he chooses. He is determined by the factors in the existential situation, but these factors include his defensiveness, his denial or distortion of some of the relevant data. Hence it is certain that his behavior will be less than fully satisfying. His behavior is determined, but he is not free to make an effective choice. The fully functioning person, on the other hand, not only experiences, but utilizes, the most absolute freedom when he spontaneously, freely, and voluntarily chooses and wills that which is also absolutely determined.

I am not so naive as to suppose that this fully resolves the issue between subjective and objective, between freedom and necessity. Nevertheless it has meaning for me that the more the person is living the good life, the more he will experience a freedom of choice, and the more his choices will be effectively implemented in his behavior.

Creativity as an element of the good life

I believe it will be clear that a person who is involved in the directional process which I have termed "the good life" is a creative person. With his sensitive openness to his world, his trust of his own ability to form new relationships with his environment, he would be the type of person from whom creative products and creative living emerge. He would not necessarily be "adjusted" to his culture, and he would almost certainly not be a conformist. But at any time and in any culture he would live constructively, in as much harmony with his culture as a balanced satisfaction of needs demanded. In some cultural situations he might in some ways be very unhappy, but he would continue to move toward becoming himself, and to behave in such a way as to provide the maximum satisfaction of his deepest needs.

Such a person would, I believe, be recognized by the student of evolution as the type most likely to adapt and survive under changing environmental conditions. He would be able creatively to make sound adjustments to new as well as old conditions. He would be a fit vanguard of human evolution.

Basic trustworthiness of human nature

It will be evident that another implication of the view I have been presenting is that the basic nature of the human being, when functioning freely, is constructive and trustworthy. For me this is an inescapable conclusion from a quarter-century of experience in psychotherapy. When we are able to free the individual from defensiveness, so that he is open to the wide range of his own needs, as well as the wide range of environmental and social demands, his reactions may be trusted to be positive, forward-moving, constructive. We do not need to ask who will socialize him, for one of his own deepest needs is for affiliation and communication with others. As he becomes more fully himself, he will become more realistically socialized. We do not need to ask who will control his aggressive impulses; for as he becomes more open to all of his impulses, his need to be liked by others and his tendency to give affection will be as strong as his impulses to strike out or to seize for himself. He will be aggressive in situations in which aggression is realistically appropriate, but there will be no runaway need for aggression. His total behavior, in these and other areas, as he moves toward being open to all his experience, will be more balanced and realistic, behavior which is appropriate to the survival and enhancement of a highly social animal.

I have little sympathy with the rather prevalent concept that man is basically irrational, and that his impulses, if not controlled, will lead to destruction of others and self. Man's behavior is exquisitely rational, moving with subtle and ordered complexity toward the goals his organism is endeavoring to achieve. The tragedy for most of us is that our defenses keep us from being aware of this rationality, so that consciously we are moving in one direction, while organismically we are moving in another. But in our person who is living the process of the good life, there would be a decreasing number of such barriers, and he would be increasingly a participant in the rationality of his organism. The only control of impulses which would exist, or which would prove necessary, is the natural and internal balancing of one need against another, and the discovery of behaviors which follow the vector most closely approximating the satisfaction of all needs. The experience of extreme satisfaction of one need (for aggression, or sex, etc.) in such a way as to do violence to the satisfaction of other needs (for companionship, tender relationship, etc.)—an experience very common in the defensively organized person—would be greatly decreased. He would participate in the vastly complex self-regulatory activities of his organism—the psychological as well as physiological thermostatic controls—in such a fashion as to live in increasing harmony with himself and with others.

The greater richness of life

One last implication I should like to mention is that this process of living in the good life involves a wider range, a greater richness, than the constricted living in which most of us find ourselves. To be a part of this process means that one is involved in the frequently frightening and frequently satisfying experience of a more sensitive living, with greater range, greater variety, greater richness. It seems to me that clients who have moved significantly in therapy live more intimately with their feelings of pain, but also more vividly with their feelings of ecstasy; that anger is more clearly felt, but so also is love; that fear is an experience they know more deeply, but so is courage. And the reason they can thus live fully in a wider range is that they have this underlying confidence in themselves as trustworthy instruments for encountering life.

I believe it will have become evident why, for me, adjectives such as happy, contented, blissful, enjoyable, do not seem quite appropriate to any general description of this process I have called the good life, even though the person in this process would experience each one of these feelings at appropriate times. But the adjectives which seem more generally fitting are adjectives such as enriching, exciting, rewarding, challenging, meaningful. This process of the good life is not, I am convinced, a life for the faint-hearted. It involves the stretching and growing of becoming more and more of one's potentialities. It involves the courage to be. It means launching oneself fully into the stream of life. Yet the deeply exciting thing about human beings is that when the individual is inwardly free, he chooses as the good life this process of becoming.

THE GOOD LIFE
OF THE
SELF-ACTUALIZING
PERSON
A. H. Maslow

A. H. Maslow (1908–1970), American psychologist cele-brated for his hierarchical theory of motives in which physiological needs are placed at the bottom of the scale and self-actualization is placed at the top as the ultimate and most desirable goal. In addition to some ninety papers contributed to professional journals, Maslow also wrote Motivation and Personality (1954), New Knowledge in Human Values (1959, ed.), and Toward a Psychology of Being (1962).

Self-actualizing people are gratified in all their basic needs embracing affection, respect, and self-esteem. They have a feeling of belongingness and rootedness. They are satisfied in their love needs, because they have friends, feel loved and love-worthy. They have status, place in life, and respect from other people, and they have a reasonable feeling of worth and self-respect.

Self-actualizing people do not for any length of time feel anxiety-ridden, insecure, unsafe; do not feel alone, ostracized, rootless, or isolated; do not feel unlovable, rejected, or unwanted; do not feel despised and looked down upon; and do not feel unworthy nor do they have crippling feelings of inferiority or worthlessness.

Since the basic needs had been assumed to be the only motivations for human beings, it was possible, and in certain contexts useful, to say of self-actualizing people that they were "unmotivated." This aligned these people with the Eastern philosophical view of health as the transcendence of striving or desiring or wanting.

It is also possible to say and to describe self-actualizing people as expressing rather than coping. They are spontaneous, natural, and more easily themselves than other people.

What motivates the self-actualizing person? What are the psycho-dynamics in self-actualization? What makes him move and act and struggle? What drives or pulls such a person? What attracts him? For what does he hope? What makes him angry, or dedicated, or self-sacrificing? What does he feel loyal to? Devoted to? What does he aspire to and yearn for? What would he die or live for?

These questions ask for an answer to the question: What are the motivations of self-actualizing people? Clearly we must make an immediate distinction between the ordinary motives of those people who are below the level of self-actualization and motivated by the basic needs, and the motivations of people who are sufficiently gratified in all their basic needs and are no longer primarily motivated by them. For convenience, call these motives and needs of self-actualizing persons "meta-needs." This also differentiates the category of motivation from the category of "meta-motivation."

Examining self-actualizing people, I find that they are dedicated people, devoted to some task outside themselves, some vocation, or duty, or job. Generally the devotion and dedication is so marked that one can correctly use the old words vocation, calling, or mission to describe their passionate, selfless, and profound feeling for their "work." We could even use the words destiny or fate in the sense of biological or temperamental or constitutional destiny or fate. Sometimes I have gone so far as to speak of oblation in the religious sense of dedicating oneself upon some altar for a particular task, some cause outside oneself and bigger than oneself, something not merely selfish, something impersonal. This is one way of putting into adequate words the feeling that one gets when one listens to self-actualizing people talking about their work or task. One gets the feeling of a beloved job, and further, of something for which the person is "a natural," that he is suited for, that is right for him, even something for which he was born.

In this kind of a situation, it is easy to sense something like a pre-established harmony or a good match like a perfect love affair in which it seems that people belong to each other and were meant for each other. In the best instances the person and his job fit together and belong together perfectly like a key and a lock, or resonate together like a sung note which sets into sympathetic resonance a particular string in the piano keyboard.

Often I get the feeling that I can tease apart two kinds of determinants from this fusion which has created a unity out of a duality, and that these two sets of determinants can, and sometimes do, vary independently. One can be spoken of as the responses to forces relatively within the person: e.g., "I love babies (or painting, or research, or political power) more than anything in the world." "It fascinates me." "I am inexorably drawn to . . ." "I need to . . ." This we may call "inner requiredness" and it is felt as a kind of self-indulgence rather than as a duty. It is different from and separable from "external requiredness," which is felt as a response to what the environment, the situation, the problem, or the external world calls for and requires of the person. A fire "calls for" putting out, or a helpless baby demands that one take care of it, or some obvious injustice calls for righting. Here one feels more the element of duty, of obligation, of responsibility, of being compelled helplessly to respond no matter what one was planning to do, or wished to do. It is more "I must," "I have to," "I am compelled" than "I want to."

In the ideal instance, "I want to" coincides with "I must." There is a good matching of inner with outer requirements. The observer is over-awed by the degree of compellingness, of inexorability, or preordained destiny, necessity, and harmony that he perceives. Furthermore, the observer, as well as the person involved, feels not only that "it has to be" but also that "it ought to be, it is right, it is suitable, appropriate, fitting, and proper." I have often felt a gestaltlike quality about this kind of belonging together, the formation of a "one" out of "two." I hesitate to call this simply "purposefulness" because that may imply that it happens only out of will, purpose, decision, or calculation; the word doesn't give enough weight to the subjective feeling of being swept along, of willing and eager surrender, or yielding to fate and happily embracing it at the same time. Ideally, one discovers one's fate; it is not made or constructed or decided upon. It is recognized as if one had been unwittingly waiting for it. Perhaps the better phrase would be "Spinozistic" or "Taoistic" choice or decision or purpose.

The best way to explain these feelings is to use the example of "falling in love." It is clearly different from doing one's duty, or doing what is sensible or logical. Also "will," if mentioned at all, is used in a very special sense. When two people fall in love with each other fully, each one knows what it feels like to be a magnet and what it feels like to be iron filings, and what it feels like to be both simultaneously. Very useful, also, is the parallel with the happy abandon of the ideal sexual situation. Here people resist and delay the inevitable climax, in a kind of fond self- and other-teasing, holding off as long as possible. Suddenly, in a single instant they can change to the opposite course of embracing eagerly and totally the end which they were moments ago delaying, as the tides suddenly change from going north to going south.

This example also helps convey what is difficult to communicate in words; the lovers' sense of good fortune, of luck, of gratuitous grace, of gratitude, of awe that this miracle should have occurred, of wonder that they should have been chosen, and of the peculiar mixture of pride fused with humility, of arrogance shot through with the pity-for-the-less-fortunate that one finds in lovers.

It can be said of the self-actualizing person that he is being his own kind of person, or being himself, or actualizing his real self. Observation would lead one to understand that "This person is the best one in the whole world for this particular job, and this particular job is the best job in the whole world for this particular person and his talents, capacities, and tastes. He was meant for it, and it was meant for him."

Accepting this premise, we move into another realm of discourse—the realm of being, of transcendence. Now we can speak meaningfully only in the language of being (the "B-language," communication at the mystical level described in my book *Toward a Psychology of Being*). It is quite obvious with such people that the ordinary or conventional dichotomy between work and play is transcended totally. Such a person's work is his play and his play is his work. If a person loves his work and enjoys it more than any other activity in the whole world and is eager to get to it, to get back to it, after any interruption, then how can we speak about "labor" in the sense of something one is forced to do against one's wishes?

What sense, for instance, is left to the concept "vacation"? For such individuals it is often observed that during the periods in which they are totally free to choose whatever they wish to do and in which they have no external obligations to anyone else, they devote themselves happily and totally to their "work." What does it mean "to have some fun"? What is the meaning of the word "entertainment"? How does such a person "rest"? What are his "duties," responsibilities, obligations?

What sense does money or pay or salary make in such a situation? Obviously the most beautiful fate, the most wonderful good luck, the most marvelous good fortune that can happen to any human being is to be paid for doing that which he passionately loves to do. This is exactly the situation, or almost the situation, with many self-actualizing persons. Of course, money is welcome, and in certain amounts is even needed. It is certainly not the finality, the end, the goal, however. The check such a man gets is only a small part of his "pay." Self-actualizing work or B-work, being its own intrinsic reward, transforms the money or paycheck into a by-product, an epiphenomenon. This is different from the situation of less fortunate human beings who do something that they do not want to do in order to get money, which they then use to get what they really want. The role of money in the realm of being is certainly different from the role of money in the realm of deficiencies.

These are scientific questions, and can be investigated in scientific ways. They have been investigated in monkeys and apes to a degree. The most obvious example, of course, is the rich research literature on monkey curiosity and other precursors of the human yearning for and satisfaction with the truth. But it will be just as easy in principle to explore the aesthetic choices of these and other animals under conditions of fear and of lack of fear, by healthy specimens or by unhealthy ones, under good choice conditions or bad ones, etc.

If one asks the fortunate, work-loving, self-actualizing person, "Who are you?" or "What are you?" he tends to answer in terms of his "call" . . . "I am a lawyer." "I am a mother." "I am a psychiatrist." "I am an artist." He tells you that he identifies his call with his identity, his Self. It is a label for the whole of him and it becomes a defining characteristic of the person.

If one confronts him with the question, "Supposing you were not a scientist (or a teacher, or a pilot), then what would you be?" or "Supposing you were not a psychologist, then what?" his response is apt to be one of puzzlement, thoughtfulness. He does not have a ready answer. Or the response can be one of amusement. It strikes him funny. In effect, the answer is, "If I were not a mother (lover, anthopologist, industrialist) then I wouldn't be *me*. I would be someone else, and I can't imagine being someone else."

A tentative conclusion is, then, that in self-actualizing subjects, their beloved calling tends to be perceived as a defining characteristic of the self, to be identified with, incorporated, introjected. It becomes an inextricable aspect of one's Being.

When asked why they love their work, which are the moments of higher satisfaction in their work, which moments of reward make all the necessary chores worthwhile or acceptable, which are the peak-experiences, self-actualizing people give many specific and *ad hoc* answers which to them are instrinsic reinforcers.

As I classified these moments of reward, it became apparent that the best and most natural categories of classification were mostly or entirely values of an ultimate and irreducible kind! Call them "B-values": truth, goodness, beauty, unity, aliveness, uniqueness, perfection, completion, justice, simplicity, totality, effortlessness, playfulness, self-sufficiency, meaningfulness.

For these people the profession seems to be not functionally autonomous, but to be a carrier of ultimate values. I could say, if I were not afraid of being misunderstood, that for example, the profession of law, is a means to the end of justice, and not a law to itself in which justice might get lost. For one man the law is loved because it is justice, while another man, the pure value-free technologist, might love the law simply as an intrinsically lovable set of rules, precedents, procedures without regard to the ends or products of their use.

B-values or meta-motives are not only intrapsychic or organismic. They are equally inner and outer. The meta-needs, insofar as they are inner, and the requiredness of all that is outside the person are each stimulus and response to each other. And they move toward becoming indistinguishable, toward fusion.

This means that the distinction between self and not-self has broken down or has been transcended. There is less differentiation between the world and the person because he has incorporated into himself part of the world and defines himself thereby. He becames an enlarged self. If justice or truth or lawfulness have now become so important to him that he identifies his self with them, then where are they? Inside his skin or outside his skin? This distinction comes close to being meaningless at this point because his self no longer has his skin as its boundary.

Certainly simple selfishness is transcended here and has to be defined at higher levels. For instance, we know that it is possible for a person to get more pleasure out of food through having his child eat it than through eating it with his own mouth. His self has enlarged enough to include his child. Hurt his child and you hurt him. Clearly the self can no longer be identified with the biological entity which is supplied with blood from his heart along his blood vessels. The psychological self can obviously be bigger than his own body.

Just as beloved people can be incorporated into the self, thereby becoming defining characteristics of it, so also can causes and values be similarly incorporated into a person's self. Many people are so passionately identified with trying to prevent war, racial injustices, slums, or poverty that they are quite willing to make great sacrifices, even to the point of risking death. Very clearly, they do not mean justice for their own biological bodies alone. They mean justice as a general value, justice for everyone, justice as a principle.

There are other important consequences of this incorporation of values into the self. For instance, you can love justice and truth in the world or in a person out there. You can be made happier as your friends move toward truth and justice, and sadder as they move away from it. That's easy to understand. However, suppose you see yourself moving successfully toward truth, justice, beauty, and virtue? Then you may find that, in a peculiar kind of detachment and objectivity toward oneself, for which our culture has no place, you will be loving and admiring yourself in the kind of healthy self-love that Fromm has described. You can respect yourself, admire yourself, take tender care of yourself, reward yourself, feel virtuous, love-worthy, respect-worthy. You may then treat yourself with the responsibility and otherness that a pregnant woman does whose self now has to be defined to overlap with not-self. So may a person with a great talent protect it and himself as if he were a carrier of something which is simultaneously himself and not himself. He may become his own friend.

These people, although concretely working for, motivated by, and loyal to some conventional category of work, are transparently motivated by the intrinsic or ultimate values or aspects of reality for which the profession is only a vehicle.

This is my impression from observing them, interviewing them, and asking them why they like doctoring, or just which are the most rewarding moments in running a home, or chairing a committee, or having a baby, or writing. They may meaningfully be said to be working for truth, for beauty, for goodness, for law and for order, for justice, for perfection, if I boil down to a dozen or so intrinsic values (or values of Being) all the hundreds of specific reports of what is yearned for, what gratifies, what is valued, what they work for from day to day, and why they work.

It is at this point in my theory that, quite fairly, both methodology and validity can be called into question. I have not deliberately worked with an *ad hoc* control group of non-self-actualizing people. I could say that most of humanity is a control group. I have a considerable fund of experience with the attitudes toward work of average people, immature people, neurotic and borderline people, psychopaths, and others. There is no question that their attitudes cluster around money, basic-need gratification rather than B-values, sheer habit, stimulus-binding, convention, and the inertia of the unexamined and nonquestioned life, and from doing what other people expect or demand. However, this intuitive or naturalistic conclusion is susceptible to more careful and more controlled and pre-designed examination.

Secondly, it is my strong impression that there is not a sharp line between my subjects chosen as self-actualizing and other people. I believe that each self-actualizing subject more or less fits the description I have given, but it seems also true that some percentage of other, less healthy people are meta-motivated by the B-values also; especially individuals with special talents and people placed in especially fortunate circumstances. Perhaps all people are meta-motivated to some degree.

The conventional categories of career, profession, or work many serve as channels of many other kinds of motivations, not to mention sheer habit or convention or functional autonomy. They may satisfy or seek vainly to satisfy any or all of the basic needs as well as various neurotic needs. They may be a channel for "acting out" or for "defensive" activities rather than for real gratifications.

My guess, supported by both my "empirical" impressions and by general psychodynamic theory, is that we will find it ultimately most true and most useful to say that all these various habits, determinants, motives, and meta-motives are acting simultaneously in a very complex pattern which is centered more toward one kind of motivation or de-terminedness than the others.

If we can try to define the deepest, most authentic, most constitutionally based aspects of the real self, of the identity, or of the authentic person, we find that in order to be comprehensive, we must include not only the person's constitution and temperament, not only anatomy, physiology, neurology, and endocrinology, not only his capacities, his biological style, not only his basic instinctoid needs, but also *the* B-values which are also *his* B-values. They are equally a part of his "nature," or definition, or essence, along with his "lower" needs. They must be included in any definition of the human being, or of full-humanness, or of a person. It is true that they are not fully evident or actualized in most people. Yet, so far as I can see at this time, they are not excluded as potentials in any human being born into the world.

Thus, a fully inclusive definition of a fully developed self or person includes a value system by which he is meta-motivated.

What all of this means is that the so-called spiritual or "higher" life is on the same continuum (is the same kind of quality or thing) with the life of the flesh, or of the body, i.e., the animal life, the "lower" life. The spiritual life is part of our biological life. It is the "highest" part of it, but yet part of it. The spiritual life is part of the human essence. It is a defining-characteristic of human nature, without which human nature is not full human nature. It is part of the real self, of one's identity, of one's inner core, or one's specieshood, of full-humanness.

To the extent that pure expressing of oneself, or pure spontaneity is possible, to that extent will the meta-needs be expressed. "Uncovering" or Taoistic therapeutic or "Ontogogic" techniques should uncover and strengthen the meta-needs as well as the basic needs. Depth-diagnostic and therapeutic techniques should ultimately also uncover these same meta-needs because, paradoxically, our highest nature is also our deepest nature. They are not in two separate realms as most religions and philosophies have assumed, and as classical science has also assumed. The spiritual life (the contemplative, "religious," philosophical, or value-life) is within the jurisdiction of human thought and is attainable in principle by man's own efforts. Even though it has been cast out of the realm of reality by the classical, value-free science which models itself upon physics, it is now being reclaimed as an object of study and technology by humanistic science. Such an expanded science will consider the eternal verities, the ultimate truths, the final values, to be "real" and natural, fact-based rather than wish-based, legitimate scientific problems calling for research.

The so-called spiritual, transcendent, or axiological life is clearly rooted in the biological nature of the species. It is a kind of "higher" animality whose precondition is a healthy "lower" animality and the two are hierarchically integrated rather than mutually exclusive. However, the higher, spiritual "animality" is timid and weak. It is so easily lost, easily crushed by stronger cultural forces, that it can become widely actualized *only* in a culture which approves of human nature and, therefore, fosters its fullest growth.

14

HUMANISTIC PURPOSE

THE PHILOSOPHY OF HUMANISM

Corliss Lamont

> *Corliss Lamont (1902–   ), humanistic philosopher who has greatly promoted the understanding and propagation of humanism through such writings as* The Illusions of Immortality (1950), The Philosophy of Humanism (1965), *and* Freedom of Choice Affirmed (1967).

Since the earliest days of philosophic reflection in ancient times in both East and West thinkers of depth and acumen have advanced the simple proposition that the chief end of human life is to work for the happiness of man upon this earth and within the confines of the Nature that is his home. This philosophy of enjoying, developing, and making available to everyone the abundant material, cultural, and spiritual goods of this natural world is profound in its implications, yet easy to understand and congenial to common sense. This man-centered theory of life has remained relatively unheeded during long periods of history. While it has gone under a variety of names, it is a philosophy that I believe is most accurately designated as *Humanism*.

Humanism as a philosophy has ever competed with other philosophic viewpoints for the allegiance of men. But however far-reaching its disagreements with rival philosophies of the past and present, Humanism at least agrees with them on the importance of philosophy as such. That importance stems from the perennial need of human beings to find significance in their lives, to integrate their personalities around some clear, consistent and compelling view of existence, and to seek definite and reliable methods in the solution of their problems. Philosophy brings clarity and meaning into the careers of individuals, nations, and civilizations.

As Aristotle once remarked, everyone adheres to a philosophy whether he is aware of it or not. Every adult conducts his life according to some general pattern of behavior that is more or less conscious, more or less consistent, more or less adequate, to cope with the everyday affairs and inevitable crises of the human scene. This guiding pattern in the life of every person *is* his philosophy, even though it be implicit in his actions rather than explicit in his mind; "his inarticulate major premise," as Justice Oliver Wendell Holmes put it. Such is the strength of tradition that men have always tended to accept the particular philosophy or religion prevailing in the group into which they were born. In any case, human beings, primitive or civilized, educated or uneducated, plodding or brilliant, simply cannot escape from philosophy. Philosophy is everybody's business.

As a developed study and discipline, philosophy has for its purpose the analysis and clarification of human aims and actions, problems and ideals. It brings into the light of intelligence the half-conscious, half-expressed gropings of men and of peoples. It teaches us to say what we mean and to mean what we say. It is the tenacious attempt of reasoning men to think through the most fundamental issues of life, to reach reasoned conclusions on first and last things, to suggest worthwhile goals that can command the loyalty of individuals and groups. . . .

.   .   .

There can be no doubt that if a philosophy of life is to fulfill its proper role, it must be a philosophy of living, a philosophy to live by, a philosophy of action. Philosophy at its best is not simply an interpretation or explanation of things. It is also a dynamic enterprise that aims to stimulate men in the direction of those ends and values that are supremely worthwhile and desirable; to bring mankind closer to those standards of truth and methods of truth-seeking that are most reliable. All this implies the working out of effective methods for the application of tried and tested philosophic wisdom. Hence philosophy has the task, not only of attaining the truth, but also of showing how that truth can become operative in the affairs of men, of helping to bridge the age-long gap between thinkers and doers, between theory and practice. Philosophy could well recommend as a universal motto Henri Bergson's striking epigram: "*Act* as men of thought; *think* as men of action."

The old phrase "taking things philosophically" has come to have a connotation of acquiescence and defeatism that Humanists cannot possibly accept. As Professor Ralph Barton Perry of Harvard remarked, philosophers who emphasize "the cult of resignation . . . have made philosophy the opium of the intelligentsia."

Philosophy's constant involvement in the issues that mean most to men and in the defense of truth is dramatically brought out in the career of Socrates. Just as in the Western tradition the great martyr-death in religion was that of Jesus, so in philosophy it was that of Socrates. And just as the New Testament tells in simple and beautiful language the unforgettable story of Jesus, so the *Dialogues* of Plato permanently enshrine the memory of Socrates. The powers that were in ancient Athens accused Socrates of corrupting the minds of youth by raising too many thought-provoking questions and giving those questions unorthodox answers. Rather than remain silent or compromise, Socrates defied the authorities and drank the hemlock. "The unexamined life is not worth living," said Socrates in his final remarks to the judges, as recounted in the *Apology*. "I would rather die," he continued, "having spoken after my manner, than speak in your manner and live. . . . The difficulty, my friends, is not to avoid death, but to avoid unrighteousness. . . . No evil can happen to a good man, either in life or after death."[1]

Then and there, in the year 399 B.C., Socrates once and for all established a moral imperative for philosophers: that no matter what the personal consequences, it is necessary for them to exercise their freedom of speech and stand firm for what they consider the truth and the right. Indeed, no man has a philosophy worthy of the name or has achieved full stature as a human being unless he is willing to lay down his life for his ultimate principles.

In addition to Socrates, there have been other outstanding heroes in the philosophic pantheon, such as Giordano Bruno, the Italian Pantheist, burned at the stake by the Catholic Inquisition in 1600, together with his books, after he refused to recant; and Benedict Spinoza, a Dutch Jew of the seventeenth century, ostracized and excommunicated at an early age by the Amsterdam Synagogue and hounded throughout life because of his opinions in philosophy.

But since philosophers are, after all, only human and are subject to most of the same pressures as other men, they do not always demonstrate intellectual and moral courage of the highest order. It is not surprising that some of them should be intellectually timorous, out of touch with the everyday world, and fearful of becoming embroiled in those deep-reaching disputes that are the heart of the philosophic quest. One familiar way of evading fundamental issues is to throw around them an intricate net of unintelligible verbiage, to redefine ordinary words in such an extraordinary manner that utter confusion is the result. Another favorite method is to assume an attitude of noble impartiality toward those recurring controversies that mean most to the common man, or to turn aside every question of consequence by asking another question in return. Yet it is precisely the business of philosophers to do their best to give answers to honest inquiries.

One of the chief troubles with philosophy has been that most of the

[1] Plato, *Apology*, trans. Benjamin Jowett, Sections 38, 39, 41.

works on the subject have been written *by* professional philosophers *for* professional philosophers or have been addressed to an intellectual elite. There are of course technical problems in philosophy, as in other spheres of knowledge, that only specialists can understand and fruitfully pursue, but there is no reason under the sun why the basic ideas in this field should not be presented in a simple, concise, and understandable fashion. Philosophy has always been both in need of and susceptible to such humanization. Again, Socrates, by making philosophy an absorbing and exciting thing to the young men of Athens, set an excellent example that philosophers have rarely taken seriously enough.

Socrates lived and taught in Greece during a time of far-reaching social turmoil and disintegration. This leads me to say that important as philosophy always is, it assumes even greater significance during periods of crisis. If philosophy is worth anything, it should be able to bring to men and nations some measure of poise, steadfastness, and wisdom in exactly such a tumultuous epoch of world history as that of the twentieth century. A people without a clear and recognized philosophy is likely to falter in a serious crisis because it is confused about the central issues or has no supreme loyalty for which it is willing to make supreme sacrifices.

America and all mankind continue to live through critical days. Philosophy should have much to say on why the human race, despite all its much-vaunted progress, fought two devastating world wars within the space of thirty years, and still faces the awful possibility of the Great Nuclear War. Indubitably philosophers possess the right and duty to pass some severe moral judgments on modern man. And their broad perspectives may well lead us to regard with a good deal of skepticism the widespread prophecies about civilization collapsing or coming to an end; or to realize that if our civilization does perish, another and perhaps better one may succeed it.

The fact is that the entire world is in want of a sound and dynamic philosophy adequate to the spirit and needs of this twentieth century; a generalized view of human life and all existence that will give the peoples of every continent and country a total and integrated perspective; a universal goal, method, and hope that will lift mortal men above their personal limitations and provincial interests to a vision of the magnificent possibilities of humanity as a whole. In my judgment the philosophy best calculated to liberate the creative energies of mankind and to serve as a common bond between the different peoples of the earth is that way of life most precisely described as Humanism.

Humanism has had a long and notable career, with roots reaching far back into the past and deep into the life of civilizations supreme in their day. It has had eminent representatives in all the great nations of the world. As the American historian Professor Edward P. Cheyney says, Humanism has meant many things: "It may be the reasonable balance of life that the early Humanists discovered in the Greeks; it may be merely the study of the humanities or polite letters; it may be the freedom from religiosity and the vivid interest in all sides of life of a Queen Elizabeth or a Benjamin Franklin; it may be the responsiveness to all human passions of a Shakespeare or a Goethe; or it may be a philosophy of which man is the center and sanction. It is in the last sense, elusive as it is, that Humanism has had perhaps its greatest significance since the sixteenth century."[2]

It is with this last sense of Humanism that this book is mainly concerned. And I shall endeavor to the best of my ability to remove any elusiveness or ambiguity from this meaning of the word. The philosophy of Humanism represents a specific and forthright view of the universe, the nature of man, and the treatment of human problems. The term *Humanist* first came into use in the early sixteenth century to designate the writers and scholars of the European Renaissance. Contemporary Humanism includes the most enduring values of Renaissance Humanism, but in philosophic scope and significance goes far beyond it.

To define twentieth-century humanism briefly, I would say that it is a philosophy of joyous service for the greater good of all humanity in this natural world and advocating the methods of reason, science, and democracy. While this statement has many profound implications, it is not difficult to grasp. Humanism in general is not a way of thinking merely for professional philosophers, but is also a credo for average men and women seeking to lead happy and useful lives. It does not try to appeal to intellectuals by laying claim to great originality, or to the multitude by promising the easy fulfillment of human desires either upon this earth or in some supernatural dream world. But Humanism does make room for the various aspects of human nature. Though it looks upon reason as the final arbiter of what is true and good and beautiful, it insists that reason should fully recognize the emotional side of man. Indeed, one of Humanism's main functions is to set free the emotions from cramping and irrational restrictions.

Humanism is a many-faceted philosophy, congenial to this modern age, yet fully aware of the lessons of history and the richness of the philosophic tradition. Its task is to organize into a consistent and intelligible whole the chief elements of philosophic truth and to make that synthesis a powerful force and reality in the minds and actions of living men. What, then, are the basic principles of Humanism that define its position and distinguish it from other philosophic viewpoints? There are, as I see it, ten central propositions in the Humanist philosophy:

First, Humanism believes in a naturalistic metaphysics or attitude toward the universe that considers all forms of the supernatural as myth; and that regards Nature as the totality of being and as a constantly

[2] *Encyclopaedia of the Social Sciences* (New York: Macmillan, 1937), Vol. IV, p. 541.

changing system of matter and energy which exists independently of any mind or consciousness.

Second, Humanism, drawing especially upon the laws and facts of science that man is an evolutionary product of the Nature of which he is part; that his mind is indivisibly conjoined with the functioning of his brain; and that as an inseparable unity of body and personality he can have no conscious survival after death.

Third, Humanism, having its ultimate faith in man, believes that human beings possess the power or potentiality of solving their own problems, through reliance primarily upon reason and scientific method applied with courage and vision.

Fourth, Humanism, in opposition to all theories of universal determinism, fatalism, or predestination, believes that human beings, while conditioned by the past, possess genuine freedom of creative choice and action, and are, within certain objective limits, the masters of their own destiny.

Fifth, Humanism believes in an ethics or morality that grounds all human values in this-earthly experiences and relationships and that holds as its highest goal the this-wordly happiness, freedom, and progress— economic, cultural, and ethical—of all mankind, irrespective of nation, race, or religion.

Sixth, Humanism believes that the individual attains the good life by harmoniously combining personal satisfactions and continuous self-development with significant work and other activities that contribute to the welfare of the community.

Seventh, Humanism believes in the widest possible development of art and the awareness of beauty, including the appreciation of Nature's loveliness and splendor, so that the aesthetic experience may become a pervasive reality in the life of men.

Eighth, Humanism believes in a far-reaching social program that stands for the establishment throughout the world of democracy, peace, and a high standard of living on the foundations of a flourishing economic order, both national and international.

Ninth, Humanism believes in the complete social implementation of reason and scientific method; and thereby in the use of democratic procedures, including full freedom of expression and civil liberties, throughout all areas of economic, political, and cultural life.

Tenth, Humanism, in accordance with scientific method, believes in the unending questioning of basic assumptions and convictions, including its own. Humanism is not a new dogma, but is a developing philosophy ever open to experimental testing, newly discovered facts, and more rigorous reasoning.

I think that these ten points embody Humanism in its most acceptable modern form. This philosophy can be more explicitly characterized as scientific Humanism, secular Humanism, naturalistic Humanism, or democratic Humanism, depending on the emphasis that one wishes to give. Whatever it be called, Humanism is the viewpoint that men have but one life to lead and should make the most of it in terms of creative work and happiness; that human happiness is its own justification and requires no sanction or support from supernatural sources; that in any case the supernatural, usually conceived of in the form of heavenly gods or immortal heavens, does not exist; and that human beings, using their own intelligence and cooperating liberally with one another, can build an enduring citadel of peace and beauty upon this earth.

It is true that no people has yet come near to establishing the ideal society. Yet Humanism asserts that man's own reason and efforts are man's best and, indeed, only hope; and that man's refusal to recognize this point is one of the chief causes of his failures throughout history. The Christian West has been confused and corrupted for almost 2,000 years by the idea so succinctly expressed by St. Augustine, "Cursed is everyone who places his hope in man."

In an era of continuing crisis and disintegration like that of the twentieth century, men face the temptation of fleeing to some compensatory realm of make-believe or supernatural solace. Humanism stands uncompromisingly against this tendency, which both expresses and encourages defeatism. The Humanist philosophy persistently strives to remind men that their only home is in this mundane world. There is no use in our searching elsewhere for happiness and fulfillment, for there is no place else to go. We human beings must find our destiny and our promised land in the here and now, or not at all. And Humanism is interested in a future life, not in the sense of some fabulous paradise in the skies, but as the on-going enjoyment of earthly existence by generation after generation through eternities of time.

On the ethical and social side Humanism sets up service to one's fellowmen as the ultimate moral ideal. It holds that the individual can find his own highest good in working for the good of all, which of course includes himself and his family. In this sophisticated and disillusioned era Humanism emphatically rejects, as psychologically naïve and scientifically unsound, the widespread notion that human beings are moved merely by self-interest. It repudiates the constant rationalization of brute egoism into pretentious schemes on behalf of individuals or groups bent on self-aggrandizement. It refuses to accept the reduction of human motivation to economic terms, to sexual terms, to pleasure-seeking terms, or to *any* one limited set of human desires. It insists on the reality of genuine altruism as one of the moving forces in the affairs of men.

Since we live during a time of nationalism run wild, of terrible world wars, of hate and misunderstanding between peoples and governments, I want to underscore at the start Humanism's goal of the welfare of *all* mankind. In its primary connotation Humanism means simply human-being-ism, that is, devotion to the interests of human beings, wherever they live and whatever their status. Though certain groups in certain countries have in the past put themselves beyond the pale of human decency, and though this could happen again, Humanism cannot tolerate discrimination against any people or nation as such. And it reaffirms the spirit of cosmopolitanism, of international friendship, and of the essential brotherhood of man. Humanists feel *compassionate concern* for their fellowmen throughout the globe.

An English bishop recently asserted that "50 per cent of the intelligent people of the modern world are Humanists."[3] Most of the individuals to whom he refers probably do not call themselves Humanists and may never have taken the trouble to find out to what precise school of philosophy they belong. It is important, however, that all those who actually are Humanists should come to recognize in the word *Humanism* the symbol of their central purpose in life, their community of interests and their sense of fellowship. As Walter Lippmann has written in his Humanist book, *A Preface to Morals*, "If civilization is to be coherent and confident it must be *known* in that civilization what its ideals are."[4] This implies that those ideals shall be given a habitation and a name in some philosophy.

. . .

In the Humanist ethics the chief end of thought and action is to further this-earthly human interests on behalf of the greater glory of man. The watchword of Humanism is happiness for all humanity in this existence as contrasted with salvation for the individual soul in a future existence and the glorification of a supernatural Supreme Being. Humanism urges men to accept freely and joyously the great boon of life and to realize that life in its own right and for its own sake can be as beautiful and splendid as any dream of immortality.

The philosophy of Humanism constitutes a profound and passionate affirmation of the joys and beauties, the braveries and idealisms, of existence upon this earth. It heartily welcomes all life-enhancing and healthy pleasures, from the vigorous enjoyments of youth to the contemplative delights of mellowed age, from the simple gratifications of food and drink, sunshine and sports, to the more complex appreciation of art and literature, friendship and social communion. Humanism believes in the beauty of love and the love of beauty. It exults in the pure magnificence of external Nature. All the many-sided possibilities for good in human living the Humanist would weave into a sustained pattern of happiness under the guidance of reason.

In this Humanist affirmation of life the monistic psychology again plays a most significant role. For this view means that in whatever he

---

[3] Quoted by Willard L. Sperry (ed.), *Religion and Our Divided Denominations* (Cambridge: Harvard University Press, 1945), p. viii.
[4] Walter Lippmann, *A Preface to Morals* (New York: Macmillan, 1929), p. 322.

does man is a living unity of body and personality, an interfunctioning oneness of mental, emotional, and physical qualities. Humanism adheres to the highest ethical ideals and fosters the so-called goods of the spirit, such as those of culture and art and responsible citizenship. At the same time it insists that all ideals and values are grounded in this world of human experience and natural forms. As Santayana put it in summing up his conception of human nature, "everything ideal has a natural basis and everything natural an ideal development."[5]

Much of the emphasis in supernaturalist ethics has been negative, calling on men continually to deny many of their most wholesome impulses in order to keep their souls pure and undefiled for that life after death which is so very much more important than life before death. In this ethics the prospect of supernatural rewards and punishments in the future overshadows present conduct; the values decreed by supernatural authority override those of the natural and temporal order in which man actually lives.

By contrast, the emphasis of Humanist and naturalistic ethics is *positive*.[6] It is an ethics in which conscience does not merely play the role of a vetoing censor, but is creative in the sense of bringing to the fore new and higher values. This system of morality recommends the greater and more frequent enjoyment of earthly goods on the part of all men everywhere; it repudiates ascetic other-worldliness in favor of buoyant this-worldliness; it is against all defeatist systems which either postpone happiness to an after-existence or recommend acquiescence to social injustice in this existence.

An excellent example of the typical religious defeatism that Humanism decries is the following consolation offered by Pope Pius XI in his encyclical of 1932, at the height of the Great Depression: "Let the poor and all those who at this time are facing the hard trial of want of work and scarcity of food, let them in a like spirit of penance suffer with greater resignation the privations imposed upon them by these hard times and the state of society, which Divine Providence in an ever-loving but inscrutable plan has assigned them. Let them accept with a humble and trustful heart from the hand of God the effects of poverty, rendered harder by the distress in which mankind now is struggling. . . . Let them take comfort in the certainty that their sacrifices and troubles borne in a Christian spirit will concur efficaciously to hasten the hour of mercy and peace."[7]

Humanism sweeps aside the confusing and corrupting Dualism of the past in which "the natural life of man with its desires and pleasures

---

[5] Santayana, *Reason in Common Sense*, p. 21.
[6] Whereas eight of the Old Testament's Ten Commandments, for instance, are phrased in negative terms.
[7] It is only fair to note that, since this statement was made, the Roman Catholic Church has become liberalized to some extent, particularly under the stimulus of John XXIII, Pope from 1958 until 1963, and of Paul VI, who succeeded him.

became something to be shunned as evil and degraded, something to be forsaken for higher things. Man's true nature was of a different quality, his destiny lay in another realm. . . . It is this dualism running through all of man's actions that has left its impress on the commonly accepted moral codes of the West to this day, and seems even yet to make impossible that wholehearted and simply enjoyment of the goods of a natural existence that men now envy in the Greeks of old. It is not that men have ever refrained from action or from these pleasures, but that they have never been able to rid themselves of the notion that there is something essentially wrong about them."[8]

Humanist ethics is opposed to the puritanical prejudice against pleasure and desire that marks the Western tradition of morality. Men and women have profound wants and needs of an emotional and physical character, the fulfillment of which is an essential ingredient in the good life. Contempt for or suppression of normal desires may result in their discharge in surreptitious, coarse, or abnormal ways. While it is true that uncontrolled human desires are a prime cause of evil in the world, it is equally true that human desires directed by reason toward socially useful goals are a prime foundation of the good. They provide the drive and energy that eventuate in individual and group achievement.

.   .   .

The realm of ethics is pre-eminently social in scope and application; within its sphere lies all human conduct in which socially significant alternatives are possible. Many small everyday acts have no ethical significance, though any type of action may under certain circumstances carry such significance. In origin and development ethics is likewise social, the term itself coming from the Greek word *ethos,* meaning custom or usages. Ethical values and standards evolve in the interaction between individual and individual, between the individual and the group, and between group and group. The sympathetic impulses in human nature, such as the parental, the sexual, and the gregarious, become socially transformed and broadened in human association.

The advantages of mutual cooperation, support, and protection lead to the social functioning and utilization of basic instincts such as those of self-preservation and reproduction. Conscience, the sense of right and wrong and the insistent call of one's better, more idealistic, more social-minded self, is a social product. Feelings of right and wrong that at first have their locus within the family gradually develop into a pattern for the tribe or city, then spread to the much larger unit of the nation, and finally from the nation to mankind as a whole. Humanism sees no need for resorting to supernatural explanations or sanctions at any point in the ethical process. A divine First Cause or Sustaining Principle is no more

[8] Randall, *The Making of the Modern Mind,* pp. 48–49.

necessary in the sphere of ethics than in that of physics or metaphysics. Human beings can and do behave decently toward one another without depending on the intercession of a third party known as God.

. . .

Humanism does not for a moment imply that *any* social goal which evokes loyalty in an individual is worthwhile, because then allegiance to an evil cause would have to be considered good. To guard against such confusion and to know what we really mean we must always assign concrete content to our social aims. While it is needful to use a shorthand term such as *the social good* or *the general welfare* to sum up Humanism's ultimate ethical objective, it is equally needful to break down that objective in terms of specific goods. Thus the social good surely entails such values for the individual as health, significant work, economic security, friendship, sex, love, community recognition, educational opportunity, a developed intelligence, freedom of speech, cultural enjoyment, a sense of beauty, and opportunity for recreation. Here are twelve major goods that any rational society would presumably attempt to encourage and establish; and an inclusive list would contain many more. A knowledge of how different goods or values of this sort are interrelated is an indispensable factor in ethical analysis.

There often occurs a clash between acknowledged values in which one good must be temporarily sacrificed for another. Frequently tragedy turns out to be the conflict, not between right and wrong, but between right and right. Our interest in human progress may at times be at variance with our concern for the present happiness of men. And sacrifices in the immediate present by both the individual and the community are sometimes required for the sake of achieving a future goal. Conflicts between two compelling goods we must resolve as best we can by way of the broadest and most permanent synthesis of values that is possible.

Turning now to a more detailed analysis of individual human happiness, we can state that happiness is not properly definable in terms of the glorified heavenly rest home or passive contemplation so common to the supernaturalist tradition. Nor is it to be defined as withdrawal from the world in this life and retreat to some ivory tower of art or reflection. Such ideals of happiness are escapist dreams originating to a large extent in bad social conditions where most work is drudgery, where human living lacks aesthetic quality, and where in general the struggle to maintain life at a decent level is heartbreakingly difficult.

The fact is that men are inherently active beings and can therefore discover happiness only in some form of activity. The most pathetic sight on earth is not the tired businessman, but the *retired* businessman. He is restive and dissatisfied because suddenly he finds himself with nothing to do. No one can long remain content merely in contemplating past successes. As we know, the entire universe, from atoms to stars, is naturally and eternally active. Likewise the human character can never stand still, because continual change is part of its own nature and resides in the very constitution of things.

Happiness, however, does not consist in activity as such or simply in the attainment of one object of desire after another. This is why we so often have that empty feeling after accomplishing some difficult end upon which we have set our hearts; why the thrill of achievement can give way so quickly to the blankness of boredom. The Humanist conclusion is that the final goal of human striving is unity, satisfaction, equilibrium *in* activity. The path to happiness for the personality lies in harmony in worthwhile action; not a static, but a dynamic harmony that is achieved under the guidance of wisdom. In this way the mind, which is in essence a problem-solving instrument, keeps on meeting the challenges of the environment and stays alert to the end instead of sinking into semisomnolent quiescence.

Modern men may find "peace of mind" or "peace of soul" in calmly and successfully coping with problems as they arise, but not in imagining that they can eradicate all personal discontents. Dr. Karl Menninger, one of America's most eminent psychiatrists, asserts: *"Unrest of spirit is a mark of life*; one problem after another presents itself and in the solving of them we can find our greatest pleasure. The continuous encounter with continually changing conditions is the very substance of living. From an acute awareness of the surging effort we have the periodic relief of seeing one task finished and another begun. . . . A querulous search for a premature permanent 'peace' seems to me a thinly disguised wish to die."[9]

It is the Humanist view that if the individual pursues activities that are healthy, socially useful, and in accordance with reason, pleasure will generally accompany them; and happiness, the supreme good, will be the eventual result. . . .

.   .   .

In the meaningful perspectives of the Humanist philosophy man, although no longer the darling of the universe or even of the earth, stands out as a far more heroic figure than in any of the supernaturalist creeds, old or new. He has become truly a Prometheus Unbound with almost infinite powers and potentialities. For his great achievements man, utilizing the resources and the laws of Nature, yet without Divine aid, can take full credit. Similarly, for his shortcomings he must take full responsibility. Humanism assigns to man nothing less than the task of being his own saviour and redeemer.

[9] Bernard H. Hall (ed.), *A Psychiatrist's World* (New York: Viking, 1959), p. 5.

THE HUMAN PROGRAMME

H. J. Blackham

H. J. Blackham (1903–　　), British philosopher and active exponent of humanism through his writings and his executive positions in the Ethical Union and the International Humanist and Ethical Union. Among his publications are Living as a Humanist *(1950, with others),* Six Existentialist Thinkers *(1952), and* The Human Tradition *(1953).*

THE WAY THINGS ARE

Before deciding how to live, one wants to know how things are; at any rate, this is a question that comes first logically. It is not a question that is simply answered by taking thought; a fully reliable answer is the delayed outcome of persistently trying to find out, and learning thereby how to find out. Meanwhile, life goes on, generations come and go, and make do with traditional assumptions, the body of established knowledge, and some current speculations.

In the European tradition, for some dozen centuries after the fall of Rome, thought was dominated by Christian theology, an amalgam of Platonic and Aristotelian ways of thinking with Judaistic concepts and Christian claims. Three component ideas in this product are relevant to Humanist thinking. (1) The universe is purposive throughout; purpose is built into the structure of everything. (2) Men are free to conform to or defy this purpose, but not to alter it; and they doom themselves to futility and nullity, or worse, by failing to conform. (3) The temporal order of nature is in some sense inferior and illusory, secondary to an eternal order that is ultimate reality.

The relevance to Humanist thinking of these three ideas of the way things are is that Humanists hold their contraries to be true: (i) they believe that the order discovered in nature is not properly teleological; (ii) that men are free to introduce valid purposes of their own, and to multiply the possibilities of purpose by exploring the uses of things; (iii) that there is no reason for thinking that the temporal order of nature is not, first and last, the condition of all human experience and achievement. How are these affirmations and the consequent rejection of the traditional ideas justified? The answer is, first, that tradition can be matched with tradition, and, secondly, that the Humanist affirmations stand or fall with reliance on the rational methods of learning from experience.

On the first point, although Christian theology, taking up the main strand of Greek philosophical thought, was dominant in the European tradition for so many centuries, there was an alternative and contrary tradition derived from the Greeks. This began to come into its own in the seventeenth century when its renascence assisted the nascent scientific movement by helping the pioneers of science to find their way.[1] This alternative tradition was based on the materialism of Democritus, the most alternative tradition was based on the materialism of Democritus, the most learned man of his time and the great rival of Plato, a philosophy made popular by the Epicureans who rivalled the Stoics for nearly six centuries as guides to thinking and living in the Roman world. Democritus, 'the greatest investigator of nature in antiquity,' was free from the preoccupation with purpose of Socrates, the greatest investigator of human opinion in antiquity.[2] He posited self-subsistent, self-moving atoms, whose union and separation by mechanical necessity was the ground for the explanation of all phenomena. This natural causal model for thinking, in place of the human purposive model, was the neglected clue to learning from nature.

THE GLOBAL FRAME

If Humanists are fully justified, then, in holding that there is no evidence of a divine purpose, revealed in history or at work in nature, to which one ought to try to conform, how does this view of the way things are affect the way of living? When God is dead, are all things permissible? Having rejected the traditional theistic, not to say Christian, basis and framework (which gives a destined perfection as the highest reality and the goal of striving), are Humanists thrown into the chaos of ethical relativism or must they logically lapse into the ethical solipsism of some existentialist philosophies?[3] No, not merely because they know that they are human only because they are social (and society requires rules as

[1] Hall, A. R. *The Scientific Revolution* 1500–1800. New York: Longmans, 1954.
[2] Windelband, W. *History of Ancient Philosophy*. New York: Dover Publications, 1957.
[3] For an understanding of what is true and what is false in ethical relativism, see M. Ginsburg, 'On the Diversity of Morals' in the volume with that title. New York: Macmillan, 1957, and A. MacBeath, *Experiments in Living*. New York: St. Martin's Press, 1952.

thinking requires rules), but also because, as Humanists, they stand upon the continent of history; their ethical thinking has historical concreteness and historical direction towards definite achievements if no goal of history.

What does this mean? Mainly two things: (i) the ethical thinking of Humanists is empirically at grips with the great social alternatives of better and worse possibilities which history poses in every age and to every generation; (ii) whether or not there is a constant called 'human nature,' there is a variable called 'human behaviour,' and Humanists have learned from history that human behaviour is a response to social conditions; they have seen that institutions, situations, education, devices, and techniques have made it better or worse.

These statements of course raise severe questions. How does one distinguish between 'better' and 'worse' possibilities? If human behaviour is socially determined, what becomes of personal responsibility? If one sets about controlling and 'improving' human behaviour, why not employ the most efficient totalitarian methods, up to and including "brain-washing'? Before going on to develop the argument in a way that will meet such questions, I must indicate where the Humanist stands in relation to the position of the Marxist, who also claims that his ethical thinking is historical.[4]

That human thought and behaviour are socially conditioned is a fact. If one decides to have nothing to do with this fact, out of a scrupulous regard for individual dignity and personal responsibility, there is that much less chance of providing the necessary conditions of individual dignity and personal responsibility. It works both ways: free institutions are as deliberate an attempt at social conditioning as totalitarian methods. Free institutions are necessary, though not sufficient, conditions for maximizing spontaneity and diversity in a society. The human person, as the maker of value by his creative activities, and as the marker of standards by his enjoyments and his critical activities, is given the greatest practicable scope, stimulus, and protection in a developed political democracy. Thus, other things being equal, just because Humanists cherish human values, including of course the human personality which is their source, seat, and seal, they want and uphold a society based on agreed rules and agreed rules for changing the rules.

Other things *are* more or less equal in modern industrial societies, in the sense that economic plenty is widely available, and therefore the Marxist argument of the mid-nineteenth century that plenty could never be made available to all so long as the economic machine (and the political and military machines) remained effectively in the hands of a few owners, has lost its power to force the issue.

The eighteenth-century Humanists supposed that the accumulation of capital, the expansion of trade and industry, and the development of the arts and sciences would, with the spread of enlightenment and emanci-

[4] Blackham, H. J. *The Human Tradition*. New York: Beacon Press, 1954.

pation, benefit mankind universally.[5] They were right in principle, except in so far as they did not reckon seriously enough with the exclusiveness of possessing classes and nation-states. The distinction of Marx is that he saw this exclusiveness as a total obstruction that could not and would not be tolerated. Although the exclusiveness of classes and nations has been greatly relaxed since the Second World War, and is everywhere under challenge, it is now clear that it is only by enlightened, deliberate, and sustained policies and plans that the benefits of civilization can be made universal. They will not become universal in the eighteenth-century manner by a natural expansion and diffusion. There is of course an element of natural expansion and diffusion, today reinforced by the impatient demands of underdeveloped peoples for these benefits, inadequately met by responsive efforts on the part of the most advanced industrial nations. If the haphazard and hazardous working of these three elements could be superseded by a world development project, initiated jointly by the advanced industrial powers, both Communist states and political democracies, the dangerous and widening gap between rich and poor peoples could be reduced, and the hopeless and helpless masses made capable of participating by their own efforts in the growing wealth of the world.[6] This is the 'better possibility' of our time, to set against the worse possibilities of rivalry in exploiting the needs and demands of the underdeveloped peoples, local resistance to them, or inadequate response. If one completes the outline of better and worse possibilities by bringing in the danger of total war, of mounting populations, of dwindling resources, one is not likely to start an *ethical* argument. The whole ethical landscape is dominated by what is plainly good or bad, right or wrong, to most thinking people not plainly prejudiced.

The idea of a world development project is not utopian, because the need, the incentives, and the means are present. The moral unity and responsibility of mankind are the results of advances in knowledge and technology. Ethical thinking today gets its universality not merely from abstract principles but mainly from the pressure of a universal concrete situation which constrains mankind to decide its own fate.

THE DISTRIBUTION
OF MORAL RESPONSIBILITY

To speak of the responsibility of mankind is vast and vague. Who is responsible to whom for what? The men and women of the generations

[5] Condorcet, A.–N. de. *The Progress of the Human Mind*, 1795. Tr. June Barraclough, ed. Stuart Hampshire. New York: Noonday Press, 1955.
[6] Myrdal, Gunnar. *Rich Lands and Poor*, World Perspectives Series. New York: Harper & Brothers, 1957.

adult today are responsible to their children and to posterity for taking the necessary steps to create a universal human civilization, a human providence. This is of course a moral responsibility; it cannot be enforced. What makes it a moral responsibility is a situation which demands it (and in default threatens the worse possibilities of the age) and the availability of the technological and institutional means for doing it. This still leaves vast and vague what the responsibilities are and who is to shoulder them.

Three overriding problems about which all thinking people are worried define the responsibility more closely: the prevention of war, the control of population, the conservation of resources. These are problems that can be resolved only on a global scale, and the beginnings of a definite, if not definitive, solution of them would be the foundation of a universal civilization and a human providence. On the other hand, everybody who has thought about it knows that failure to deal with them adequately will bring general disaster. The clear recognition of this situation constitutes the awakening of mankind to its collective responsibility and necessary solidarity, the condition of a universal ethics.

How is this general responsibility of mankind for human fate at the present time divided? Thought of as responsibility for decisions, policies, and programmes in connection with the three major problems just mentioned, the responsibility falls inevitably most heavily on those, persons and powers, who are in a position to make effective decisions, form policies, and initiate and sustain programmes. The great problem of organizing world security and preventing war, for example, is mainly the joint responsibility of those who control the policy of NATO and of the USSR. It takes two to make a bargain, and without agreement the arms race cannot be halted and the first step taken in the reverse direction of controlled general disarmament and the institution of a World Security Authority.[7] Three related points are relevant to this stubborn difficulty, and they are of the first importance.

(1) Human thought and behaviour are largely socially determined. This has nowhere been seen more conspicuously than in the case of war. Nations of course have been aggressive, and have sought and gained aggrandizement. They have done so partly because otherwise they were liable to become victims. Even a purely defensive policy was bound to prove provocative. In this situation of inescapable rivalry, war is a further step in politics which sooner or later will have to be taken. That is to say, war is a product not simply of human iniquity but necessarily of the situation of international anarchy. Neither peace-loving peoples nor diplomatic skill can permanently keep the sovereign nation-state out of war. The situation calls for an institutional solution. Better behaviour

---

[7] Noel-Baker, Philip. *The Arms Race*. New York: Oceana Publications, 1958.

will follow because it will have been made possible, as well as because the old patterns of behaviour will have become inexcusable and would be universally censured.

(2) An institutional solution requires the agreement in the first place of the main parties, the nuclear powers. How can those on one side make the other side agree? The side which, whilst continuing to make itself efficient in defence, ceases to rely on its own armed power as a solution of the security problem, and therefore genuinely seeks controlled general disarmament and an institutional solution as necessary to its defence, is likely to succeed if it persists. At least it is true that to negotiate disarmament for advantage, whilst continuing to rely for security on armed power and diplomatic skill, is fatal to success in disarmament—and ultimately to security—and is ethically indefensible now that the destructive power of weapons has nullified the political justifications of war.

(3) Although the responsibility rests finally on those who have the power to act decisively, their responsibility is brought home to them by those to whom they are accountable, those whose interests are affected by their decisions. In democratic states this accountability is formally organized, and democratic peoples therefore have a heavy share of responsibility; but all peoples in some measure, and by whatever means are available to them, are responsible for the responsibility of their leaders. Only the pressure of expectation and demand make moral responsibility, as distinct from political accountability, more than a matter of conscience; and there is a responsibility for making this expectation and demand lively and exigent, a responsibility for responsibility. In turn, only in so far as it is organized is this responsibility for responsibility more than a matter of conscience. In this many agencies play their parts, but it is obvious that they have greatest scope in a society which enjoys free institutions. Again, the political democracies bear a heavy share of this secondary responsibility. To seek the costly security of graduated defence by deterrence *in order to be able to exchange it* for the security of agreed and tested international control (the professed policy of NATO) is so extraordinarily difficult a policy that an exceptionally alert and informed public opinion is needed to insist that neither form of security shall be sacrificed to an illusion of the other.

In sum, the general responsibility of mankind for these global matters cannot be neatly divided. It is shared and shaded, and levies specific demands on everybody. As moral demands, these are demands of an enlightened conscience, and that requires organized enlightenment and organized pressures. The history of all social achievement exemplifies this, and history calls now to those who have ears to hear.

PROGRESS
WITHIN THE
AFFLUENT SOCIETY

The big world problems of organizing security, controlling population, conserving resources, developing backward regions, intrude into national affairs and private lives, and demand a concerted world project with due priorities and an institutional organization of power and responsibility for dealing with them. Otherwise they continue to threaten the foundations of human existence. If and when peace and plenty are assured, social problems will not vanish, however. Better and worse possibilities are evident within affluent societies today. Human prospects are to be judged very largely by what happens on this front.

The worse possibilities of social organization in our time have been horribly delineated in *Nineteen Eighty Four* and *Brave New World*. With the prospect of affluence in the USSR, it is *Brave New World* that raises questions for modern highly organized mass industrial societies. Its author has recently pointed out that his fable has been documented by the sociologists since it was first written.[8] Human problems can be solved on these inhuman terms. What better possibilities are there, and what social conditions do they require?

The vision of human progress which the eighteenth-century Humanists had was comprehensive and not fundamentally mistaken. They relied on four main agencies. (1) Progressive knowledge by scientific enquiry was the key that opened every door. Bacon had written the great manifesto of human advance in the treatise (*Novum Organum*, 1620) which pleaded for empirical enquiry as the source of human confidence, freedom, and power. The practical arts were linked with the sciences, because they promoted the sciences and were in turn promoted by them. (2) The organization of mass-production by the accumulation and investment of capital and the division of labour was seen to be the means of progressive wealth. (3) If anarchy was the worst of social evils, tyrannical government was hardly less bad and worse than natural calamities, but the remedy was in the hands of the governed, who could adopt devices by which capable and trustworthy rulers were selected and kept under control. If the social rules were agreed rules they would be upheld by all and could be equally enforced on each, and there were rules by which rules could be agreed, and changed to keep them agreed. (4) Education was a primary public interest, not only because it furnished the trained

[8] Huxley, Aldous. *Brave New World Revisited*. New York: Harper & Brothers, 1959.

ability which promoted the arts and sciences and industrial enterprise and
supplied the public service, but also because it made men self-dependent
and responsible. Therefore it should be available to all, and not merely
to the mentally gifted.

All these fundamentals of human progress were argued out in the
eighteenth century. Not one of them can be seriously challenged in the
light of experience since that time. Of course, under each head the formula of that day was far too simple for the needs and problems of ours,
but the general orientation and commitments remain the same. We are
still governed by the ideals set by the tasks under each of these heads, and
there can be no serious question of turning away from them in any other
direction. One ought to discuss present problems and trends under each of
them. I have space to say something only about education.

Every culture propagates itself by means of its pattern of child-rearing
and education. Except in advanced cultures, this is not based on child
study, but on immemorial customs. Even modern sophisticated societies
reproduce themselves largely in their own image through the family and
through the schools, but child study has had a say as well as social
exigencies in most modern educational policy and practice, and in some
places has gone so far as to transform the content of the curriculum and
the methods of teaching. At any rate, where child study is allowed a
continuous influence upon educational policy and practice, in a society of
free institutions, there are the optimum social conditions of human
development.

The earliest years are of proved importance for character and personality, in determining whether the child will be able to accept and
deal with reality, within and without, or will helplessly impose upon it his
own fantasies. For instance, every child is normally and necessarily
checked and corrected. In being frustrated by correction the child is made
to feel hostile and aggressive against the adult who checks him, and he
projects this hatred and aggressiveness on to the adult, that is, he cannot
help feeling that the adult hates him and wants to hurt him. At the same
time, the adult is, or may be, the one on whom he is utterly dependent,
the source of all good. Thus a conflict is set up within the child which
may become an unbearable tension, resulting in a total repression of the
hostility and aggressiveness and a total submission to adult authority.
Thereafter, the child is either impaired in his vitality by the repressed
conflict, or he projects the repressed guilt on to some object in the world
which he treats as wholly evil and pursues with hatred. He tends to see
and to seek in the world what is wholly good which he can worship and
with which he can be identified and what is wholly bad which he is justified in pursuing with hate and harm and on which he can project his
buried guilty self. Here is the authoritarian (who is also the submissive)

personality in the making, e.g. the Hitler who deifies the Aryan-Nordic-Teuton and projects his guilt upon the Jew and imposes these fantasies on his countrymen when frustrations of their social situation have made them responsive.[9]

On the other hand, if the child is enabled to come to terms with his conflict, his ambivalent feelings of love and hate, because he is assured in the act of correction that he is also loved, he learns to tolerate his own guilt and that of others, that is to say, to meet reality, within and without, with sane discrimination.[10]

If the child's vitality and sanity are well founded in this way, he can be enabled to become self-dependent, that is to say, to acquire required competence and to accomplish recognized achievements within the range of his own abilities and aptitudes. With his interests thus initiated and given scope and encouragement, he can be socialized, that is to say, learn to recognize and accept and respect the 'other' and to participate and play his part in a co-operative world, as one among many. At adolescence, he can be shown how to make up his mind, how to solve his problems, how to overcome his failures, by being put into possession of appropriate techniques. In such ways he can be made capable of a life of his own. Meanwhile, through the subjects of the curriculum and the activities of the school he has been introduced to the great themes of human living, so that in the manifold interests brought within his experience he finds congenial soil in which to strike root and thrive.

Whatever on these lines is done to good purpose in the home and the school is after all to no purpose if society at large faces the school-leaver with the Big-Brotherly features of Ad-mass and Organization-Man.[11] If he is drafted and routed and required to conform to prescribed procedures and practices, if his wife has to keep up with the Joneses, if he has to buy what the advertisers want, and if the entertainment which is laid on for all hours of the day fills in the time which should be his own, then there is no point in preparing him for a life of his own; he might as well be left to the 'other-directed' pattern of life which the structure of contemporary society tends to impose upon him.[12] This is the kind of dilemma which, it is widely supposed, vitiates the hope of progress within the affluent society.

[9] Adorno, T. W. (ed.) et al. The Authoritarian Personality. New York: Harper & Brothers, 1958; and J. C. Flugel, Man, Morals and Society. London: Duckworth, 1955, especially Chapter IX.

[10] In his Romanes Lecture, Section III, printed in Touchstone for Ethics (New York: Harper & Brothers, 1947), Sir Julian Huxley stresses the ethical superiority of this internal ethical realism—it is the primary ethical standard—and therefore the ethical importance of educational disciplines which enable the child to achieve it.

[11] Whyte, William H. The Organization Man. New York: Simon & Schuster, 1956.

[12] Potter, D. M. People of Plenty. University of Chicago Press, 1954.

The dilemma is probably false, but the problem is certainly real. Of course our mass-industrial societies are shaped into general patterns of conformity one way or another by massive social and commerical influences. It is the price that is paid for the productive power of highly populated and highly organized societies. These powerful influences, however, although they may destroy individual initiative and taste, do not necessarily do so. If people in the formative phases of their lives are made capable of living lives of their own, they will normally want to do so. Much that is made available by commercial means or by social policy is excellently to their purpose and can be selectively used. It is by means of standardization that standards have been raised; and if one may judge by the amazing vagaries of individual style in young men's dress in Britain, standardization of products does not entail uniformity in use and enjoyment.

The standard of living is rising in the affluent society not only in terms of income and expenditure but also in real terms: physical and mental health, personal relations, taste, and achievement. How can one say this when it is about this that so many people have depressing doubts and fears supported by the evidence of adolescent discontent and delinquency in all the affluent societies? From some things, of course, there are figures, health for example, but general assurance can be drawn from argument on these lines: there are many social services and other agencies besides the schools which are engaged in raising the standard of living in these real terms; the workers in these services will not utterly fail, and their skill and their techniques will improve with experience and practice, and some of this improvement will be funded in training and transmitted, just as the beneficiaries of these services, as parents, as husbands and wives, as employers (benefiting from industrial management studies and institutes) will transmit benefits through their own improved standards. If the rise of real standards is not cumulative in this way (as knowledge and wealth are progressive), this will be the first case in which effort based on study and improved by experience is not rewarded. We live and move and have our being in a material organized world which is dependable and improvable because it is material and organized. This is the foundation of the Humanist's faith in man. The affluent society is one that can afford to invest in society continuously knowledge, capital, and service. These valuable commodities are not being laid out to no purpose, and they will be increasingly laid out to better purpose, like successful investments in industry. The faith in man that has confidence in this kind of argument is a faith inspired by history. It is not daunted by two world wars, by Nazi enormities, by the crime-rate, nor by the extent of juvenile delinquency, not because these are not serious and shocking matters, but because they have causes that can be understood and because reasonable human behaviour also has causes and can be achieved.

SECULAR FAITH

It is reasonable, then, to think that it is not beyond the wit of man to bring about situations and conditions everywhere in which it will be reasonable for men to behave reasonably. Irrational behaviour is not a wanton manifestation of an original evil; it is understandable, and its drives and goals are the common drives and goals of men. If the social situation between nations and within nations can be made conducive to reasonable and reliable behavior, so also can the situation within the human person and within the family, the root sources of tension and of destructive passions. Deliberate decisions and policies and programmes will be necessary at all levels, and most urgently at the international level; but the need for them is evident and the means are at hand.

The high Baconian confidence of the eighteenth-century Humanists has flagged; it can be renewed at the source, for Bacon rallied his contemporaries to the standard of method, a method of that time undeveloped and imperfectly understood. We are in a better position to see what method can do, applied by man to himself for his own orderly fulfilment in freedom and responsibility. Faith in progress on the road to a universal high civilization can be restored if it can be shown to be a reasonable faith.[13] Is this secular faith in conflict with the older faiths of traditional religion, particularly the Christian faith? Yes, if it belongs to the Christian faith to 'sit loose to civilization.' That is the test. The Humanist is reconciled to reality and makes his home there, and has a horror of the black-and-white fantasy of heaven and hell. Of course reality is tolerable only in so far as it is being transcended. But that is the human vocation.

The Decalogue, the Sermon on the Mount, the ethics of the Stoics or of Kant, the ethics of Aristotle, and not less the ethics of the Epicureans and of the Utilitarians, have all had an immense formative influence in the moral tradition of Western peoples, and no doubt they will continue to do so and will not be simply superseded. All the same, a new Humanist ethic is needed, to create in the climate of modern ideals and in the context of new possibilities an ethos of personal excellence and public spirit worthy of the human vocation, the ethos of an enlightened universal civilization.

Such an ethic is not likely to be couched in the language either of abstract principle or of moral codes. On the private side, it is likely to be

---

13 Frankel, Charles. *The Case for Modern Man.* New York: Harper & Brothers, 1956. For the grounds of a reasonable faith, see my *Political Discipline in a Free Society.* London: Allen & Unwin, 1961.

evocative rather than repressive, exemplary rather than prohibitive. On the public side, it is likely to be more definite, pointing to particular practical imperatives which govern the preventive and constructive work peremptorily required on behalf of mankind.

Justice and morality between equals may be left to take care of themselves. The moral responsibility that tends to fail and requires to be reinforced is a responsibility of the strong for the weak, or a responsibility that arises from new knowledge, or a responsibility for the future and the unborn, or a responsibility due to relevant considerations not usually taken into account. In such cases, Humanists have been conspicuously forward in reinforcing moral responsibility; they have ever been an *avant-garde* in morals, because of their concern for human welfare and their eagerness for the advancement of knowledge and the use and enjoyment of its fruits.

To reinforce moral responsibility where it is weak does not mean to lay down the law in enlightened codes of ethics to govern the great departments of human activity—an international code, an economic code, an educational code. Such codes have been drafted. Their rudiments have even been subscribed by the nations in the Universal Declaration of Human Rights of 1948. They have their uses. They ought not to give the satisfaction of duty done. To get an informed and exigent public opinion to operate as an effective sanction on all who bear any share of any given moral responsibility is an altogether bigger and longer affair, an always unfinished campaign on many fronts of thought and action. This practical reinforcement of moral responsibility where it is weak is the unending matter of daily excursions and encounters in the public arena and within the precincts of private and professional gardens. Humanists, by their acceptance of human responsibility for establishing the conditions of human fulfilment, are committed to exceptional efforts to raise the standard of behaviour in this way. Theirs is the dedication of an order. They ought to be in modest anonymity the unacknowledged legislators of the world. They are a cadre of activists who insistently and persistently make high expectations the measure of man.

15

ENGAGEMENT EXISTENTIAL

EXISTENTIALISM

Jean-Paul Sartre

(*Trans. by Bernard Frechtman*)

Jean-Paul Sartre (1905–   ), French philosopher, novelist, and playwright generally considered the dean of contemporary existentialism. His massive Being and Nothingness (1943) *presents a definitive account of his metaphysics, while his literary works, such as* No Exit, Nausea, *and* The Wall, *dramatize various aspects of the existentialist ethic.*

.   .   .

. . . There are two kinds of existentialist; first, those who are Christian, among whom I would include Jaspers and Gabriel Marcel, both Catholic; and on the other hand the atheistic existentialists, among whom I class Heidegger, and then the French existentialists and myself. What they have in common is that they think that existence precedes essence, or, if you prefer, that subjectivity must be the starting point.

Just what does that mean? Let us consider some object that is manufactured, for example, a book or a paper-cutter: here is an object which has been made by an artisan whose inspiration came from a concept. He referred to the concept of what a paper-cutter is and likewise to a known method of production, which is part of the concept, something which is, by and large, a routine. Thus, the paper-cutter is at once an object produced in a certain way and, on the other hand, one having a specific use; and one can not postulate a man who produces a paper-cutter but does not know what it is used for. Therefore, let us say that, for the paper-cutter, essence—that is, the ensemble of both the production routines and the properties which enable it to be both produced and defined—precedes existence. Thus, the presence of the paper-cutter or book in front of me is determined. Therefore, we have here a technical view of the world whereby it can be said that production precedes existence.

When we conceive God as the Creator, He is generally thought of as a superior sort of artisan. Whatever doctrine we may be considering, whether one like that of Descartes or that of Leibnitz, we always grant that will more or less follows understanding or, at the very least, accompanies it, and that when God creates He knows exactly what He is creating. Thus, the concept of man in the mind of God is comparable to the concept of paper-cutter in the mind of the manufacturer, and, following certain techniques and a conception, God produces man, just as the artisan, following a definition and a technique, makes a paper-cutter. Thus, the individual man is the realisation of a certain concept in the divine intelligence.

In the eighteenth century, the atheism of the *philosophes* discarded the idea of God, but not so much for the notion that essence precedes existence. To a certain extent, this idea is found everywhere; we find it in Diderot, in Voltaire, and even in Kant. Man has a human nature; this human nature, which is the concept of the human, is found in all men, which means that each man is a particular example of a universal concept, man. In Kant, the result of this universality is that the wild-man, the natural man, as well as the bourgeois, are circumscribed by the same definition and have the same basic qualities. Thus, here too the essence of man precedes the historical existence that we find in nature.

Atheistic existentialism, which I represent, is more coherent. It states that if God does not exist, there is at least one being in whom existence precedes essence, a being who exists before he can be defined by any concept, and that this being is man, or, as Heidegger says, human reality. What is meant here by saying that existence precedes essence? It means that, first of all, man exists, turns up, appears on the scene, and, only afterwards, defines himself. If man, as the existentialist conceives him, is indefinable, it is because at first he is nothing. Only afterward will he be something, and he himself will have made what he will be. Thus, there is no human nature, since there is no God to conceive it. Not only is man what he conceives himself to be, but he is also only what he wills himself to be after this thrust toward existence.

Man is nothing else but what he makes of himself. Such is the first principle of existentialism. It is also what is called subjectivity, the name we are labeled with when charges are brought against us. But what do we mean by this, if not that man has a greater dignity than a stone or table? For we mean that man first exists, that is, that man first of all is the being who hurls himself toward a future and who is conscious of imagining himself as being in the future. Man is at the start a plan which is aware of itself, rather than a patch of moss, a piece of garbage, or a cauliflower; nothing exists prior to this plan; there is nothing in heaven; man will be what he will have planned to be. Not what he will want to be. Because by the word "will" we generally mean a conscious decision, which is subsequent to what we have already made of ourselves. I may want to belong to a political party, write a book, get married; but all that is only a manifestation of an earlier, more spontaneous choice that is called "will." But if existence really does precede essence, man is responsible for what he is. Thus, existentialism's first move is to make every man aware of what he is and to make the full responsibility of his existence rest on him. And when we say that a man is responsible for himself, we do not only mean that he is responsible for his own individuality, but that he is responsible for all men.

The word subjectivism has two meanings, and our opponents play on the two. Subjectivism means, on the one hand, that an individual chooses and makes himself; and, on the other, that it is impossible for man to transcend human subjectivity. The second of these is the essential meaning of existentialism. When we say that man chooses his own self, we mean that every one of us does likewise; but we also mean by that that in making this choice he also chooses all men. In fact, in creating the man that we want to be, there is not a single one of our acts which does not at the same time create an image of man as we think he ought to be. To choose to be this or that is to affirm at the same time the value of what we choose, because we can never choose evil. We always choose the good, and nothing can be good for us without being good for all.

If, on the other hand, existence precedes essence, and if we grant that we exist and fashion our image at one and the same time, the image is valid for everybody and for our whole age. Thus, our responsibility is much greater than we might have supposed, because it involves all mankind. If I am a workingman and choose to join a Christian trade-union rather than be a communist, and if by being a member I want to show that the best thing for man is resignation, that the kingdom of man is not of this world, I am not only involving my own case—I want to be resigned for everyone. As a result, my action has involved all humanity. To take a more individual matter, if I want to marry, to have children; even if this marriage depends solely on my own circumstances or passion or wish, I am involving all humanity in monogamy and not merely myself. Therefore, I am responsible for myself and for everyone else. I am creating a certain image of man of my own choosing. In choosing myself, I choose man.

This helps us understand what the actual content is of such rather grandiloquent words as anguish, forlornness, despair. As you will see, it's all quite simple.

First, what is meant by anguish? The existentialists say at once that man is anguish. What that means is this: the man who involves himself and who realizes that he is not only the person he chooses to be, but also a law-maker who is, at the same time, choosing all mankind as well as himself, can not help escape the feeling of his total and deep responsibility. Of course, there are many people who are not anxious; but we claim that they are hiding their anxiety, that they are fleeing from it. Certainly, many people believe that when they do something, they themselves are the only ones involved, and when someone says to them, "What if everyone acted that way?" they shrug their shoulders and answer, "Everyone doesn't act that way." But really, one should always ask himself, "What would happen if everybody looked at things that way?" There is no escaping this disturbing thought except by a kind of double-dealing. A man who lies and makes excuses for himself by saying "not everybody does that," is someone with an uneasy conscience, because the act of lying implies that a universal value is conferred upon the lie.

Anguish is evident even when it conceals itself. This is the anguish that Kierkegaard called the anguish of Abraham. You know the story: an angel has ordered Abraham to sacrifice his son; if it really were an angel who has come and said, "You are Abraham, you shall sacrifice your son," everything would be all right. But everyone might first wonder, "Is it really an angel, and am I really Abraham? What proof do I have?"

There was a madwoman who had hallucinations; someone used to speak to her on the telephone and give her orders. Her doctor asked her, "Who is it who talks to you?" She answered, "He says it's God." What proof did she really have that it was God? If an angel comes to me, what proof is there that it's an angel? And if I hear voices, what proof is there that they come from heaven and not from hell, or from the subconscious, or a pathological condition? What proves that they are addressed to me? What proof is there that I have been appointed to impose my choice and my conception of man on humanity? I'll never find any proof or sign to convince me of that. If a voice addresses me, it is always for me to decide that this is the angel's voice; if I consider that such an act is a good one, it is I who will choose to say that it is good rather than bad.

Now, I'm not being singled out as an Abraham, and yet at every moment I'm obliged to perform exemplary acts. For every man, everything happens as if all mankind had its eyes fixed on him and were guiding itself by what he does. And every man ought to say to himself, "Am I really the kind of man who has the right to act in such a way that humanity might guide itself by my actions?" And if he does not say that to himself, he is making his anguish.

There is no question here of the kind of anguish which would lead to quietism, to inaction. It is a matter of a simple sort of anguish that anybody who has had responsibilities is familiar with. For example, when a military officer takes the responsibility for an attack and sends a certain number of men to death, he chooses to do so, and in the main he alone makes the choice. Doubtless, orders come from above, but they are too broad; he interprets them, and on this interpretation depend the lives of ten or fourteen or twenty men. In making a decision he can not help having a certain anguish. All leaders know this anguish. That doesn't keep them from acting; on the contrary, it is the very condition of their action. For it implies that they envisage a number of possibilities, and when they choose one, they realize that it has value only because it is chosen. We shall see this kind of anguish, which is the kind that existentialism describes, is explained, in addition, by a direct responsibility to the other men whom it involves. It is not a curtain separating us from action, but is part of action itself.

When we speak of forlornness, a term Heidegger was fond of, we mean only that God does not exist and that we have to face all the consequences of this. The existentialist is strongly opposed to a certain kind of secular ethics which would like to abolish God with the least possible expense. About 1880, some French teachers tried to set up a secular ethics which went something like this: God is a useless and costly hypothesis; we are discarding it; but, meanwhile, in order for there to be an ethics, a society, a civilization, it is essential that certain values be taken seriously and that they be considered as having an *a priori* existence. It must be obligatory, *a priori*, to be honest, not to lie, not to beat your wife, to have children, etc., etc. So we're going to try a little device which will make it possible to show that values exist all the same, inscribed in a heaven of ideas, though otherwise God does not exist. In other words—and this, I believe, is the tendency of everything called reformism in France—nothing will be changed if God does not exist. We shall find ourselves with the same norms of honesty, progress, and humanism, and we shall have made of God an outdated hypothesis which will peacefully die off by itself.

The existentialist, on the contrary, thinks it very distressing that God does not exist, because all possibility of finding values in a heaven of ideas disappears along with Him; there can no longer be an *a priori* Good, since there is no infinite and perfect consciousness to think it. Nowhere is it written that the Good exists, that we must be honest, that we must not lie; because the fact is we are on a plane where there are only men. Dostoievsky said, "If God didn't exist, everything would be possible." That is the very starting point of existentialism. Indeed, everything is permissible if God does not exist, and as a result man is forlorn, because neither within him nor without does he find anything to cling to. He can't start making excuses for himself.

If existence really does precede essence, there is no explaining things away by reference to a fixed and given human nature. In other words, there is no determinism, man is free, man is freedom. On the other hand, if God does not exist, we find no values or commands to turn to which legitimize our conduct. So, in the bright realm of values, we have no excuse behind us, nor justification before us. We are alone, with no excuses.

That is the idea I shall try to convey when I say that man is condemned to be free. Condemned, because he did not create himself, yet, in other respects is free; because, once thrown into the world, he is responsible for everything he does. The existentialist does not believe in the power of passion. He will never agree that a sweeping passion is a ravaging torrent which fatally leads a man to certain acts and is therefore an excuse. He thinks that man is responsible for his passion.

The existentialist does not think that man is going to help himself by finding in the world some omen by which to orient himself. Because he thinks that man will interpret the omen to suit himself. Therefore, he thinks that man, with no support and no aid, is condemned every moment to invent man. Ponge, in a very fine article, has said, "Man is the future of man." That's exactly it. But if it is taken to mean that this future is recorded in heaven, that God sees it, then it is false, because it would really no longer be a future. If it is taken to mean that, whatever a man may be, there is a future to be forged, a virgin future before him, then this remark is sound. But then we are forlorn.

To give you an example which will enable you to understand forlornness better, I shall cite the case of one of my students who came to see me under the following circumstances: his father was on bad terms with his mother, and, moreover, was inclined to be a collaborationist; his older brother had been killed in the German offensive of 1940, and the young man, with somewhat immature but generous feelings, wanted to avenge him. His mother lived alone with him, very much upset by the half-treason of her husband and the death of her older son; the boy was her only consolation.

The boy was faced with the choice of leaving for England and joining the Free French Forces—that is, leaving his mother behind—or remaining with his mother and helping her to carry on. He was fully aware that the woman lived only for him and that his going-off—and perhaps his death—would plunge her into despair. He was also aware that every act that he did for his mother's sake was a sure thing, in the sense that it was helping her to carry on, whereas every effort he made toward going off and fighting was an uncertain move which might run aground and prove completely useless; for example, on his way to England he might, while passing through Spain, be detained indefinitely in a Spanish camp; he might reach England or Algiers and be stuck in an office at a desk job. As a result, he was faced with two very different kinds of action: one, concrete, immediate, but concerning only one individual; the other concerned an incomparably vaster group, a national collectivity, but for that very reason was dubious, and might be interrupted en route. And, at the same time, he was wavering between two kinds of ethics. On the one hand, an ethics of sympathy, of personal devotion; on the other, a broader ethics, but one whose efficacy was more dubious. He had to choose between the two.

Who could help him choose? Christian doctrine? No. Christian doctrine says, "Be charitable, love your neighbor, take the more rugged path, etc., etc." But which is the more rugged path? Whom should he love as a brother? The fighting man or his mother? Which does the greater good, the vague act of fighting in a group, or the concrete one of helping a particular human being to go on living? Who can decide *a priori*? Nobody. No book of ethics can tell him. The Kantian ethics says, "Never treat any person as a means, but as an end." Very well, if I stay with my mother, I'll treat her as an end and not as a means; but by virtue of this very fact, I'm running the risk of treating the people around me who are fighting, as means; and, conversely, if I go to join those who are fighting, I'll be treating them as an end, and, by doing that, I run the risk of treating my mother as a means.

If values are vague, and if they are always too broad for the concrete and specific case that we are considering, the only thing left for us is to trust our instincts. That's what this young man tried to do; and when I saw him, he said, "In the end, feeling is what counts. I ought to choose whichever pushes me in one direction. If I feel that I love my mother enough to sacrifice everything else for her—my desire for vengeance, for action, for adventure—then I'll stay with her. If, on the contrary, I feel that my love for my mother isn't enough, I'll leave."

But how is the value of a feeling determined? What gives his feeling for his mother value? Precisely the fact that he remained with her. I may say that I like so-and-so well enough to sacrifice a certain amount of money for him, but I may say so only if I've done it. I may say "I love my mother well enough to remain with her" if I have remained with her. The only way to determine the value of this affection is, precisely, to perform an act which confirms and defines it. But, since I require this affection to justify my act, I find myself caught in a vicious circle.

On the other hand, Gide has well said that a mock feeling and a true feeling are almost indistinguishable; to decide that I love my mother and will remain with her, or to remain with her by putting on an act, amount somewhat to the same thing. In other words, the feeling is formed by the acts one performs; so, I can not refer to it in order to act upon it. Which means that I can neither seek within myself the true condition which will impel me to act, nor apply to a system of ethics for concepts which will permit me to act. You will say, "At least, he did go to a teacher for advice." But if you seek advice from a priest, for example, you have chosen this priest; you already knew, more or less, just about what advice he was going to give you. In other words, choosing your adviser is involving yourself. The proof of this is that if you are a Christian, you will say, "Consult a priest." But some priests are collaborating, some are just marking time, some are resisting. Which to choose? If the young man chooses a priest who is resisting or collaborating, he has already decided on the kind of advice he's going to get. Therefore, in coming to see me he knew the answer I was going to give him, and I had only one answer to give:

"You're free, choose, that is, invent." No general ethics can show you what is to be done; there are no omens in the world. The Catholics will reply, "But there are." Granted—but, in any case, I myself choose the meaning they have.

.   .   .

As for despair, the term has a very simple meaning. It means that we shall confine ourselves to reckoning only with what depends upon our will, or on the ensemble of probabilities which make our action possible. When we want something, we always have to reckon with probabilities. I may be counting on the arrival of a friend. The friend is coming by rail or street-car; this supposes that the train will arrive on schedule, or that the street-car will not jump the track. I am left in the realm of possibility; but possibilities are to be reckoned with only to the point where my action comports with the ensemble of these possibilities, and no further. The moment the possibilities I am considering are not rigorously involved by my action, I ought to disengage myself from them, because no God, no scheme, can adapt the world and its possibilities to my will. When Descartes said, "Conquer yourself rather than the world," he meant essentially the same thing.

The Marxists to whom I have spoken reply, "You can rely on the support of others in your action, which obviously has certain limits because you're not going to live forever. That means: rely on both what others are doing elsewhere to help you, in China, in Russia, and what they will do later on, after your death, to carry on the action and lead it to its fulfillment, which will be the revolution. You even *have* to rely upon that, otherwise you're immoral." I reply at once that I will always rely on fellow-fighters insofar as these comrades are involved with me in a common struggle, in the unity of a party or a group in which I can more or less make my weight felt; that is, one whose ranks I am in as a fighter and whose movements I am aware of at every moment. In such a situation, relying on the unity and will of the party is exactly like counting on the fact that the train will arrive on time or that the car won't jump the track. But, given that man is free and that there is no human nature for me to depend on, I can not count on men whom I do not know by relying on human goodness or man's concern for the good of society. I don't know what will become of the Russian revolution; I may make an example of it to the extent that at the present time it is apparent that the proletariat plays a part in Russia that it plays in no other nation. But I can't swear that this will inevitably lead to a triumph of the proletariat. I've got to limit myself to what I see.

Given that men are free and that tomorrow they will freely decide what man will be, I can not be sure that, after my death, fellow-fighters will carry on my work to bring it to its maximum perfection. Tomorrow, after my death, some men may decide to set up Fascism, and the others may be cowardly and muddled enough to let them do it. Fascism will then be the human reality, so much the worse for us.

Actually, things will be as man will have decided they are to be. Does that mean that I should abandon myself to quietism? No. First, I should involve myself; then, act on the old saw, "Nothing ventured, nothing gained." Nor does it mean that I shouldn't belong to a party, but rather that I shall have no illusions and shall do what I can. For example, suppose I ask myself, "Will socialization, as such, ever come about?" I know nothing about it. All I know is that I'm going to do everything in my power to bring it about. Beyond that, I can't count on anything. Quietism is the attitude of people who say, "Let others do what I can't do." The doctrine I am presenting is the very opposite of quietism, since it declares, "There is no reality except in action." Moreover, it goes further, since it adds, "Man is nothing else than his plan; he exists only to the extent that he fulfills himself; he is therefore nothing else than the ensemble of his acts, nothing else than his life."

According to this, we can understand why our doctrine horrifies certain people. Because often the only way they can bear their wretchedness is to think, "Circumstances have been against me. What I've been and done doesn't show my true worth. To be sure, I've had no great love, no great friendship, but that's because I haven't met a man or woman who was worthy. The books I've written haven't been very good because I haven't had the proper leisure. I haven't had children to devote myself to because I didn't find a man with whom I could have spent my life. So there remains within me, unused and quite viable, a host of propensities, inclinations, possibilities, that one wouldn't guess from, the mere series of things I've done."

Now, for the existentialist there is really no love other than one which manifests itself in a person's being in love. There is no genius other than one which is expressed in works of art; the genius of Proust is the sum of Proust's works; the genius of Racine is his series of tragedies. Outside of that, there is nothing. Why say that Racine could have written another tragedy, when he didn't write it? A man is involved in life, leaves his impress on it, and outside of that there is nothing. To be sure, this may seem a harsh thought to someone whose life hasn't been a success. But, on the other hand, it prompts people to understand that reality alone is what counts, that dreams, expectations, and hopes warrant no more than to define a man as a disappointed dream, as miscarried hopes, as vain expectations. In other words, to define him negatively and not positively. However, when we say, "You are nothing else than your life," that does not imply that the artist will be judged solely on the basis of his works of art; a thousand other things will contribute toward summing him up. What we mean is that a man is nothing else than a series of undertakings, that he is the sum, the organization, the ensemble of the relationships which make up these undertakings.

BEYOND
GOOD AND EVIL
Friedrich Nietzsche
(*Trans. by Helen Zimmern*)

Friedrich Nietzsche (1844–1900), German philosopher whose theory that every individual seeks a richer, more powerful state of being greatly influenced literature, psychoanalysis, and existential philosophy. His ideas—often disjointed, yet remarkably insightful—are contained in a variety of forceful works such as The Birth of Tragedy (1872), Human, All-too-Human (1878), The Joyful Wisdom (1882), Thus Spoke Zarathustra (1884), *and* Beyond Good and Evil (1886).

WHAT IS NOBLE?

257.

Every elevation of the type "man," has hitherto been the work of an aristocratic society—and so will it always be—a society believing in a long scale of gradations of rank and differences of worth among human beings, and requiring slavery in some form or other. Without the *pathos of distance,* such as grows out of the incarnated difference of classes, out of the constant outlooking and downlooking of the ruling caste on subordinates and instruments, and out of their equally constant practice of obeying and commanding, of keeping down and keeping at a distance—that other more mysterious pathos could never have arisen, the longing for an ever new widening of distance within the soul itself, the formation of ever higher, rarer, further, more extended, more comprehensive states, in short, just the elevation of the type "man," the continued "self-surmounting of man," to use a moral formula in a supermoral sense. To be sure, one must not resign oneself to any humanitarian illusions about the history of the origin of an aristocratic society (that is to say, of the preliminary condition for the elevation of the type "man"): the truth is hard. Let us acknowledge unprejudicedly how every higher civilisation hitherto has *originated!* Men with a still natural nature, barbarians in every terrible sense of the word, men of prey, still in possession of unbroken strength of will and desire for power, threw themselves upon weaker, more moral, more peaceful races (perhaps trading or cattle-rearing communities), or upon old mellow civilisations in which the final vital force was flickering out in brilliant fireworks of wit and depravity. At the commencement, the noble caste was always the barbarian caste: their superiority did not consist first of all in their physical, but in their psychical power—they were more *complete* men (which at every point also implies the same as "more complete beasts").

.   .   .

259.

To refrain mutually from injury, from violence, from exploitation, and put one's will on a par with that of others: this may result in a certain rough sense in good conduct among individuals when the necessary conditions are given (namely, the actual similarity of the individuals in amount of force and degree of worth, and their co-relation within one organisation). As soon, however, as one wished to take this principle more generally, and if possible even as *the fundamental principle of society*, it would immediately disclose what it really is—namely, a will to the *denial* of life, a principle of dissolution and decay. Here one must think profoundly to the very basis and resist all sentimental weakness: life itself is *essentially* appropriation, injury, conquest of the strange and weak, suppression, severity, obtrusion of its own forms, incorporation, and at the least, putting it mildest, exploitation;—but why should one for ever use precisely these words on which for ages a disparaging purpose has been stamped? Even the organisation within which, as was previously supposed, the individuals treat each other as equal—it takes place in every healthy aristocracy —must itself, if it be a living and not a dying organisation, do all that towards other bodies, which the individuals within it refrain from doing to each other: it will have to be the incarnated Will to Power, it will endeavour to grow, to gain ground, attract to itself and acquire ascendency —not owing to any morality or immorality, but because it *lives*, and because life *is* precisely Will to Power. On no point, however, is the ordinary consciousness of Europeans more unwilling to be corrected than on this matter; people now rave everywhere, even under the guise of science, about coming conditions of society in which "the exploiting character" is to be absent:—that sounds to my ears as if they promised to invent a mode of life which should refrain from all organic functions. "Exploitation" does not belong to a depraved, or imperfect and primitive society: it belongs to the *nature* of the living being as a primary organic function; it is a consequence of the intrinsic Will to Power, which is precisely the Will to Life.—Granting that as a theory this is a novelty—as a reality it is the *fundamental fact* of all history: let us be so far honest towards ourselves!

260.

In a tour through the many finer and coarser moralities which have hitherto prevailed or still prevail on the earth, I found certain traits recurring regularly together, and connected with one another, until finally two primary types revealed themselves to me, and a radical distinction was brought to light. There is *master-morality* and *slave-morality;*—I would at once add, however, that in all higher and mixed civilisations, there are also attempts at the reconciliation of the two moralities; but one finds still oftener the confusion and mutual misunderstanding of them, indeed, sometimes their close juxtaposition—even in the same man, within one soul. The distinctions of moral values have either originated in a ruling caste, pleasantly conscious of being different from the ruled—or among the ruled class, the slaves and dependents of all sorts. In the first case, when it is the rulers who determine the conception "good," it is the exalted, proud disposition which is regarded as the distinguishing feature, and that which determines the order of rank. The noble type of man separates from himself the beings in whom the opposite of this exalted, proud disposition displays itself: he despises them. Let it at once be noted that in this first kind of morality the antithesis "good" and "bad" means practically the same as "noble" and "despicable";—the antithesis "good" and *"evil"* is of a different·origin. The cowardly, the timid, the insignificant, and those thinking merely of narrow utility are despised; moreover, also, the distrustful, with their constrained glances, the self-abasing, the dog-like kind of men who let themselves be abused, the mendicant flatterers, and above all the liars:—it is a fundamental belief of all aristocrats that the common people are untruthful. "We truthful ones"—the nobility in ancient Greece called themselves. It is obvious that everywhere the designations of moral value were at first applied to *men,* and were only derivatively and at a later period applied to *actions;* it is a gross mistake, therefore, when historians of morals start with questions like, "Why have sympathetic actions been praised?" The noble type of man regards *himself* as a determiner of values; he does not require to be approved of; he passes the judgment: "What is injurious to me is injurious in itself"; he knows that it is he himself only who confers honour on things; he is a *creator of values.* He honours whatever he recognises in himself: such morality is self-glorification. In the foreground there is the feeling of plenitude, of power, which seeks to overflow, the happiness of high tension, the consciousness of a wealth which would fain give and bestow:—the noble man also helps the unfortunate, but not—or scarcely

—out of pity, but rather from an impulse generated by the superabundance of power. The noble man honours in himself the powerful one, him also who has power over himself, who knows how to speak and how to keep silence, who takes pleasure in subjecting himself to severity and hardness, and has reverence for all that is severe and hard. "Wotan placed a hard heart in my breast," says an old Scandinavian Saga: it is thus rightly expressed from the soul of a proud Viking. Such a type of man is even proud of *not* being made for sympathy; the hero of the Saga therefore adds warningly: "He who has not a hard heart when young, will never have one." The noble and brave who think thus are the furthest removed from the morality which sees precisely in sympathy, or in acting for the good of others, or in *désintéressement*, the characteristic of the moral; faith in oneself, pride in oneself, a radical enmity and irony towards "selflessness," belong as definitely to noble morality, as do a careless scorn and precaution in presence of sympathy and the "warm heart."—It is the powerful who *know* how to honour, it is their art, their domain for invention. The profound reverence for age and for tradition—all law rests on this double reverence,—the belief and prejudice in favour of ancestors and unfavourable to newcomers, is typical in the morality of the powerful; and if, reversely, men of "modern ideas" believe almost instinctively in "progress" and the "future," and are more and more lacking in respect for old age, the ignoble origin of these "ideas" has complacently betrayed itself thereby. A morality of the ruling class, however, is more especially foreign and irritating to present-day taste in the sternness of its principle that one has duties only to one's equals; that one may act towards beings of a lower rank, towards all that is foreign, just as seems good to one, or "as the heart desires," and in any case "beyond good and evil"; it is here that sympathy and similar sentiments can have a place. The ability and obligation to exercise prolonged gratitude and prolonged revenge—both only within the circle of equals,—artfulness in retaliation, *raffinement* of the idea in friendship, a certain necessity to have enemies (as outlets for the emotions of envy, quarrelsomeness, arrogance—in fact, in order to be a good *friend*): all these are typical characteristics of the noble morality, which, as has been pointed out, is not the morality of "modern ideas," and is therefore at present difficult to realise, and also to unearth and disclose.—It is otherwise with the second type of morality, *slave-morality*. Supposing that the abused, the oppressed, the suffering, the unemancipated, the weary, and those uncertain of themselves, should moralise, what will be the common element in their moral estimates? Probably a pessimistic suspicion with regard to the entire situation of man will find expression, perhaps a condemnation of man, together with his situation. The slave has an unfavourable eye for the virtues of the powerful; he has a scepticism and distrust, a *refinement* of distrust of everything "good" that is there honoured—he would fain persuade himself that the very happiness there is not genuine. On the other hand, *those* qualities

which serve to alleviate the existence of sufferers are brought into prominence and flooded with light; it is here that sympathy, the kind, helping
hand, the warm heart, patience, diligence, humility, and friendliness attain
to honour; for here these are the most useful qualities, and almost the
only means of supporting the burden of existence. Slave-morality is essentially the morality of utility. Here is the seat of the origin of the famous
antithesis "good" and "*evil*":—power and dangerousness are assumed to
reside in the evil, a certain dreadfulness, subtlety, and strength, which do
not admit of being despised. According to slave-morality, therefore, the
"evil" man arouses fear; according to master-morality, it is precisely the
"good" man who arouses fear and seeks to arouse it, while the bad man
is regarded as the despicable being. The contrast attains its maximum
when, in accordance with the logical consequences of slave-morality, a
shade of depreciation—it may be slight and well-intentioned—at last at-
taches itself even to the "good" man of this morality; because, according to
the servile mode of thought, the good man must in any case be the *safe*
man: he is good-natured, easily deceived, perhaps a little stupid, *un
bonhomme*. Everywhere that slave-morality gains the ascendency, language
shows a tendency to approximate the significations of the words "good"
and "stupid."—A last fundamental difference: the desire for *freedom*, the
instinct for happiness and the refinements of the feeling of liberty belong
as necessarily to slave-morals and morality, as artifice and enthusiasm in
reverence and devotion are the regular symptoms of an aristocratic mode
of thinking and estimating.—Hence we can understand without further
detail why love *as a passion*—it is our European specialty—must absolutely
be of noble origin; as is well known, its invention is due to the Provençal
poet-cavaliers, those brilliant ingenious men of the "*gai saber*," to whom
Europe owes so much, and almost owes itself.

261.

Vanity is one of the things which are perhaps most difficult for a noble
man to understand: he will be tempted to deny it, where another kind
of man thinks he sees it self-evidently. The problem for him is to represent
to his mind beings who seek to arouse a good opinion of themselves which
they themselves do not possess and consequently also do not "deserve,"—
and who yet *believe* in this good opinion afterwards. This seems to him
on the one hand such bad taste and so self-disrespectful, and on the other
hand so grotesquely unreasonable, that he would like to consider vanity
an exception, and is doubtful about it in most cases when it is spoken of.
He will say, for instance: "I may be mistaken about my value, and on the
other hand may nevertheless demand that my value should be acknowledged by others precisely as I rate it:—that, however, is not vanity (but
self-conceit, or, in most cases, that which is called 'humility,' and also

'modesty')." Or he will even say: "For many reasons I can delight in the good opinion of others, perhaps because I love and honour them, and rejoice in all their joys, perhaps also because their good opinion endorses and strengthens my belief in my own good opinion, perhaps because the good opinion of others, even in cases where I do not share it, is useful to me, or gives promise of usefulness:—all this, however, is not vanity." The man of noble character must first bring it home forcibly to his mind, especially with the aid of history, that, from time immemorial, in all social strata in any way dependent, the ordinary man *was* only that which he *passed for*:—not being at all accustomed to fix values, he did not assign even to himself any other value than that which his master assigned to him (it is the peculiar *right of masters* to create values). It may be looked upon as the result of an extraordinary atavism, that the ordinary man, even at present, is still always *waiting* for an opinion about himself, and then instinctively submitting himself to it; yet by no means only to a "good" opinion, but also to a bad and unjust one (think, for instance, of the greater part of the self-appreciations and self-depreciations which believing women learn from their confessors, and which in general the believing Christian learns from his Church). In fact, conformably to the slow rise of the democratic social order (and its cause, the blending of the blood of masters and slaves), the originally noble and rare impulse of the masters to assign a value to themselves and to "think well" of themselves, will now be more and more encouraged and extended; but it has at all times an older, ampler, and more radically ingrained propensity opposed to it— and in the phenomenon of "vanity" this older propensity overmasters the younger. The vain person rejoices over *every* good opinion which he hears about himself (quite apart from the point of view of its usefulness, and equally regardless of its truth or falsehood), just as he suffers from every bad opinion: for he subjects himself to both, he *feels* himself subjected to both, by that oldest instinct of subjection which breaks forth in him.—It is "the slave" in the vain man's blood, the remains of the slave's craftiness —and how much of the "slave" is still left in woman, for instance!—which seeks to *seduce* to good opinions of itself; it is the slave, too, who immediately afterwards falls prostrate himself before these opinions, as though he had not called them forth.—And to repeat it again: vanity is an atavism.

262.

A *species* originates, and a type becomes established and strong in the long struggle with essentially constant *unfavourable* conditions. On the other hand, it is known by the experience of breeders that species which receive superabundant nourishment, and in general a surplus of protection and care, immediately tend in the most marked way to develop variations, and are fertile in prodigies and monstrosities (also in monstrous vices).

Now look at an aristocratic commonwealth, say an ancient Greek *polis,* or Venice, as a voluntary or involuntary contrivance for the purpose of *rearing* human beings; there are three men beside one another, thrown upon their own resources, who want to make their species prevail, chiefly because they *must* prevail, or else run the terrible danger of being exterminated. The favour, the superabundance, the protection are there lacking under which variations are fostered; the species needs itself as species, as something which, precisely by virtue of its hardness, its uniformity, and simplicity of structure, can in general prevail and make itself permanent in constant struggle with its neighbours, or with rebellious or rebellion-threatening vassals. The most varied experience teaches it what are the qualities to which it principally owes the fact that it still exists, in spite of all Gods and men, and has hitherto been victorious: these qualities it calls virtues, and these virtues alone it develops to maturity. It does so with severity, indeed it desires severity; ever aristocratic morality is intolerant in the education of youth, in the control of women, in the marriage customs, in the relations of old and young, in the penal laws (which have an eye only for the degenerating): it counts intolerance itself among the virtues, under the name of "justice." A type with few, but very marked features, a species of severe, warlike, wisely silent, reserved and reticent men (and as such, with the most delicate sensibility for the charm and *nuances* of society) is thus established, unaffected by the vicissitudes of generations; the constant struggle with uniform *unfavourable* conditions is, as already remarked, the cause of a type becoming stable and hard. Finally, however, a happy state of things results, the enormous tension is relaxed; there are perhaps no more enemies among the neighbouring people, and the means of life, even of the enjoyment of life, are present in superabundance. With one stroke the bond and constraint of the old discipline severs: it is no longer regarded as necessary, as a condition of existence—if it would continue, it can only do so as a form of *luxury,* as an archaïsing *taste.* Variations, whether they be deviations (into the higher, finer, and rarer), or deteriorations and monstrosities, appear suddenly on the scene in the greatest exuberance and splendour; the individual dares to be individual and detach himself. At this turning-point of history there manifest themselves, side by side, and often mixed and entangled together, a magnificent, manifold, virgin-forest-like up-growth and up-striving, a kind of *tropical tempo* in the rivalry of growth, and an extraordinary decay and self-destruction, owing to the savagely opposing and seemingly exploding egoisms, which strive with one another "for sun and light," and can no longer assign any limit, restraint, or forbearance for themselves by means of the hitherto existing morality. It was this morality itself which piled up the strength so enormously, which bent the bow in so threatening a manner: —it is now "out of date," it is getting "out of date." The dangerous and disquieting point has been reached when the greater, more manifold, more comprehensive life *is lived beyond* the old morality; the "individual" stands out, and is obliged to have recourse to his own law-giving, his own arts and artifices for self-preservation, self-elevation, and self-deliverance. Nothing but new "Whys," nothing but new "Hows," no common formulas any longer, misunderstanding and disregard in league with each other, decay, deterioration, and the loftiest desires frightfully entangled, the genius of the race overflowing from all the cornucopias of good and bad, a portentous simultaneousness of Spring and Autumn, full of new charms and mysteries peculiar to the fresh, still inexhausted, still unwearied corruption. Danger is again present, the mother of morality, great danger; this time shifted into the individual, into the neighbour and friend, into the street, into their own child, into their own heart, into all the most personal and secret recesses of their desires and volitions. What will the moral philosophers who appear at this time have to preach? They discover, these sharp onlookers and loafers, that the end is quickly approaching, that everything around them decays and produces decay, that nothing will endure until the day after to-morrow, except one species of man, the incurably *mediocre*. The mediocre alone have a prospect of continuing and propagating themselves—they will be the men of the future, the sole survivors; "be like them! become mediocre!" is now the only morality which has still a significance, which still obtains a hearing. —But it is difficult to preach this morality of mediocrity! it can never avow what it is and what it desires! it has to talk of moderation and dignity and duty and brotherly love—it will have difficulty *in concealing its irony!*

263.

There is an *instinct for rank*, which more than anything else is already the sign of a *high* rank; there is a *delight* in the *nuances* of reverence which leads one to infer noble origin and habits. The refinement, goodness, and loftiness of a soul are put to a perilous test when something passes by that is of the highest rank, but is not yet protected by the awe of authority from obtrusive touches and incivilities: something that goes its way like a living touchstone, undistinguished, undiscovered, and tentative, perhaps voluntarily veiled and disguised. He whose task and practice it is to investigate souls, will avail himself of many varieties of this very art to determine the ultimate value of a soul, the unalterable, innate order of rank to which it belongs: he will test it by its *instinct for reverence*. *Différence engendre haine*: the vulgarity of many a nature spurts up suddenly like dirty water, when any holy vessel, any jewel from closed shrines, any look bearing the marks of great destiny, is brought before it; while on the other hand, there is an involuntary silence, a hesitation of the eye, a cessation of all gestures, by which it is indicated that a soul *feels* the nearness of what is worthiest of respect. The way in which, on the whole, the reverence for the *Bible* has hitherto been maintained in Europe, is perhaps the best example of discipline and refinement of manners which Europe owes to Christianity: books of such profoundness and supreme significance require for their protection an external tyranny of authority, in order to acquire the *period* of thousands of years which is necessary to exhaust and unriddle them. Much has been achieved when the sentiment has been at last instilled into the masses (the shallow-pates and the boobies of every kind) that they are not allowed to touch everything, that there are holy experiences before which they must take off their shoes and keep away the unclean hand—it is almost their highest advance towards humanity. On the contrary, in the so-called cultured classes, the believers in "modern ideas," nothing is perhaps so repulsive as their lack of shame, the easy insolence of eye and hand with which they touch, taste, and finger everything; and it is possible that even yet there is more *relative* nobility of taste, and more tact for reverence among the people, among the lower classes of the people, especially among peasants, than among the newspaper-reading *demi-monde* of intellect, the cultured class.

.   .   .

287.

—What is noble? What does the word "noble" still mean for us nowadays? How does the noble man betray himself, how is he recognised under this heavy overcast sky of the commencing plebeianism, by which everything is rendered opaque and leaden?—It is not his actions which establish his claim—actions are always ambiguous, always inscrutable; neither is it his "works." One finds nowadays among artists and scholars plenty of those who betray by their works that a profound longing for nobleness impels them; but this very *need of* nobleness is radically different from the needs of the noble soul itself, and is in fact the eloquent and dangerous sign of the lack thereof. It is not the works, but the *belief* which is here decisive and determines the order of rank—to employ once more an old relig·ous formula with a new and deeper meaning,—it is some fundamental certainty which a noble soul has about itself, something which is not to be sought, is not to be found, and perhaps, also, is not to be lost. —*The noble soul has reverence for itself.*—

THE TRAGIC SENSE OF LIFE

Miguel de Unamuno

(*Trans. by J. E. Crawford Flitch*)

Miguel de Unamuno (1864–1936), Spanish writer, philosopher, and educator best known for his book The Tragic Sense of Life *(1921) and his short novel* St. Emmanuel the Good, Martyr *(1954). In his writings he was principally concerned with the themes of unbelief, the longing for immortality, and the significance of the individual.*

. . .

The man we have to do with is the man of flesh and bone—I, you, reader of mine, the other man yonder, all of us who walk solidly on the earth.

And this concrete man, this man of flesh and bone, is at once the subject and the supreme object of all philosophy, whether certain self-styled philosophers like it or not.

In most of the histories of philosophy that I know, philosophic systems are presented to us as if growing out of one another spontaneously, and their authors, the philosophers, appear only as mere pretexts. The inner biography of the philosophers, of the men who philosophized, occupies a secondary place. And yet it is precisely this inner biography that explains for us most things.

It behoves us to say, before all, that philosophy lies closer to poetry than to science. All philosophic systems which have been constructed as a supreme concord of the final results of the individual sciences have in every age possessed much less consistency and life than those which expressed the integral spiritual yearning of their authors.

And, though they concern us so greatly, and are, indeed, indispensable for our life and thought, the sciences are in a certain sense more foreign to us than philosophy. They fulfil a more objective end—that is to say, an end more external to ourselves. They are fundamentally a matter of economics. A new scientific discovery, of the kind called theoretical, is, like a mechanical discovery—that of the steam-engine, the telephone, the phonograph, or the aeroplane—a thing which is useful for something else. Thus the telephone may be useful to us in enabling us to communicate at a distance with the woman we love. But she, wherefore is she useful to us? A man takes an electric tram to go to hear an opera, and asks himself, Which, in this case, is the more useful, the tram or the opera?

Philosophy answers to our need of forming a complete and unitary conception of the world and of life, and as a result of this conception, a feeling which gives birth to an inward attitude and even to outward action. But the fact is that this feeling, instead of being a consequence of this conception, is the cause of it. Our philosophy—that is, our mode of understanding or not understanding the world and life—springs from our feeling towards life itself. And life, like everything affective, has roots in subconsciousness, perhaps in unconsciousness.

It is not usually our ideas that make us optimists or pessimists, but it is our optimism or our pessimism, of physiological or perhaps pathological origin, as much the one as the other, that makes our ideas.

Man is said to be a reasoning animal. I do not know why he has not been defined as an affective or feeling animal. Perhaps that which differentiates him from other animals is feeling rather than reason. More often I have seen a cat reason than laugh or weep. Perhaps it weeps or laughs inwardly—but then perhaps, also inwardly, the crab resolves equations of the second degree.

And thus, in a philosopher, what must needs most concern us is the man.

Take Kant, the man Immanuel Kant, who was born and lived at Königsberg, in the latter part of the eighteenth century and the beginning of the nineteenth. In the philosophy of this man Kant, a man of heart and head—that is to say, man—there is a significant somersault, as Kierkegaard, another man—and what a man!—would have said, the somersault from the *Critique of Pure Reason* to the *Critique of Practical Reason*. He reconstructs in the latter what he destroyed in the former, in spite of what those may say who do not see the man himself. After having examined and pulverized with his analysis the traditional proofs of the existence of God, of the Aristotelian God, who is the God corresponding to the ζῷον πολιτικόν, the abstract God, the unmoved prime Mover, he reconstructs God anew; but the God of the conscience, the Author of the moral order —the Lutheran God, in short. This transition of Kant exists already in embryo in the Lutheran notion of faith.

The first God, the rational God, is the projection to the outward infinite of man as he is by definition—that is to say, of the abstract man, of the man no-man; the other God, the God of feeling and volition, is the projection to the inward infinite of man as he is by life, of the concrete man, the man of flesh and bone.

Kant reconstructed with the heart that which with the head he had overthrown. And we know, from the testimony of those who knew him and from his testimony in his letters and private declarations, that the man Kant, the more or less selfish old bachelor who professed philosophy at Königsberg at the end of the century of the Encyclopedia and the goddess of Reason, was a man much preoccupied with the problem—I mean with the only real vital problem, the problem that strikes at the very root of our being, the problem of our individual and personal destiny, of the immortality of the soul. The man Kant was not resigned to die utterly. And because he was not resigned to die utterly he made that leap, that immortal somersault, from the one Critique to the other.

Whosoever reads the *Critique of Practical Reason* carefully and without blinkers will see that, in strict fact, the existence of God is therein deduced from the immortality of the soul, and not the immortality of the soul from the existence of God. The categorical imperative leads us to a moral postulate which necessitates in its turn, in the teleological or rather eschatological order, the immortality of the soul, and in order to sustain this immortality God is introduced. All the rest is the jugglery of the professional of philosophy.

The man Kant felt that morality was the basis of eschatology, but the professor of philosophy inverted the terms.

Another professor, the professor and man William James, has somewhere said that for the generality of men God is the provider of immortality. Yes, for the generality of men, including the man Kant, the man James, and the man who writes these lines which you, reader, are reading.

Talking to a peasant one day, I proposed to him the hypothesis that there might indeed be a God who governs heaven and earth, a Consciousness[1] of the Universe, but that for all that the soul of every man may not be immortal in the traditional and concrete sense. He replied: "Then wherefore God?" So answered, in the secret tribunal of their consciousness, the man Kant and the man James. Only in their capacity as professors they were compelled to justify rationally an attitude in itself so little rational. Which does not mean, of course, that the attitude is absurd.

Hegel made famous his aphorism that all the rational is real and all the real rational; but there are many of us who, unconvinced by Hegel, continue to believe that the real, the really real, is irrational, that reason builds upon irrationalities. Hegel, a great framer of definitions, attempted with definitions to reconstruct the universe, like that artillery sergeant who said that cannon were made by taking a hole and enclosing it with steel.

. . .

That which determines a man, that which makes him one man, one and not another, the man he is and not the man he is not, is a principle of unity and a principle of continuity. A principle of unity firstly in space, thanks to the body, and next in action and intention. When we walk, one

---

[1] "*Conciencia.*" The same word is used in Spanish to denote both consciousness and conscience. If the latter is specifically intended, the qualifying adjective "*moral*" or "*religiosa*" is commonly added.—J. E. C. F.

foot does not go forward and the other backward, nor, when we look, if we are normal, does one eye look towards the north and the other towards the south. In each moment of our life we entertain some purpose, and to this purpose the synergy of our actions is directed. Notwithstanding the next moment we may change our purpose. And in a certain sense a man is so much the more a man the more unitary his action. Some there are who throughout their whole life follow but one single purpose, be it what it may.

Also a principle of continuity in time. Without entering upon a discussion—an unprofitable discussion—as to whether I am or am not he who I was twenty years ago, it appears to me to be indisputable that he who I am to-day derives, by a continuous series of states of consciousness, from him who was in my body twenty years ago. Memory is the basis of individual personality, just as tradition is the basis of the collective personality of a people. We live in memory and by memory, and our spiritual life is at bottom simply the effort of our memory to persist, to transform itself into hope, the effort of our past to transform itself into our future.

All this, I know well, is sheer platitude; but in going about in the world one meets men who seem to have no feeling of their own personality. One of my best friends with whom I have walked and talked every day for many years, whenever I spoke to him of this sense of one's own personality, used to say: "But I have no sense of myself; I don't know what that is."

On a certain occasion this friend remarked to me: "I should like to be So-and-so" (naming someone), and I said: "That is what I shall never be able to understand—that one should want to be someone else. To want to be someone else is to want to cease to be he who one is. I understand that one should wish to have what someone else has, his wealth or his knowledge; but to be someone else, that is a thing I cannot comprehend." It has often been said that every man who has suffered misfortunes prefers to be himself, even with his misfortunes, rather than to be someone else without them. For unfortunate men, when they preserve their normality in their misfortune—that is to say, when they endeavour to persist in their own being—prefer misfortune to non-existence. For myself I can say that as a youth, and even as a child, I remained unmoved when shown the most moving pictures of hell, for even then nothing appeared to me quite so horrible as nothingness itself. It was a furious hunger of being that possessed me, an appetite for divinity, as one of our ascetics has put it.[2]

To propose to a man that he should be someone else, that he should become someone else, is to propose to him that he should cease to be himself. Everyone defends his own personality, and only consents to a change in his mode of thinking or of feeling in so far as this change is able to enter into the unity of his spirit and become involved in its continuity; in

---

[2] San Juan de los Angeles.

so far as this change can harmonize and integrate itself with all the rest of his mode of being, thinking and feeling, and can at the same time knit itself with his memories. Neither of a man nor of a people—which is, in a certain sense, also a man—can a change be demanded which breaks the unity and continuity of the person. A man can change greatly, almost completely even, but the change must take place within his continuity.

It is true that in certain individuals there occur what are called changes of personality; but these are pathological cases, and as such are studied by alienists. In these changes of personality, memory, the basis of consciousness, is completely destroyed, and all that is left to the sufferer as the substratum of his individual continuity, which has now ceased to be personal, is the physical organism. For the subject who suffers it, such an infirmity is equivalent to death—it is not equivalent to death only for those who expect to inherit his fortune, if he possesses one! And this infirmity is nothing less than a revolution, a veritable revolution.

A disease is, in a certain sense, an organic dissociation; it is a rebellion of some element or organ of the living body which breaks the vital synergy and seeks an end distinct from that which the other elements coordinated with it seek. Its end, considered in itself—that is to say, in the abstract— may be more elevated, more noble, more anything you like; but it is different. To fly and breathe in the air may be better than to swim and breathe in the water; but if the fins of a fish aimed at converting themselves into wings, the fish, as a fish, would perish. And it is useless to say that it would end by becoming a bird, if in this becoming there was not a process of continuity. I do not precisely know, but perhaps it may be possible for a fish to engender a bird, or another fish more akin to a bird than itself; but a fish, this fish, cannot itself and during its own lifetime become a bird.

Everything in me that conspires to break the unity and continuity of my life conspires to destroy me and consequently to destroy itself. Every individual in a people who conspires to break the spiritual unity and continuity of that people tends to destroy it and to destroy himself as a part of that people. What if some other people is better than our own? Very possibly, although perhaps we do not clearly understand what is meant by better or worse. Richer? Granted. More cultured? Granted likewise. Happier? Well, happiness . . . but still, let it pass! A conquering people (or what is called conquering) while we are conquered? Well and good. All this is good—but it is something different. And that is enough. Because for me the becoming other than I am, the breaking of the unity and continuity of my life, is to cease to be he who I am—that is to say, it is simply to cease to be. And that—no! Anything rather than that!

Another, you say, might play the part that I play as well or better? Another might fulfil my function in society? Yes, but it would not be I.

"I, I, I, always I!" some reader will exclaim; "and who are you?" I might reply in the words of Obermann, that tremendous man Obermann: "For the universe, nothing—for myself, everything"; but no, I would rather remind him of a doctrine of the man Kant—to wit, that we ought to think of our fellow-men not as means but as ends. For the question does not touch me alone, it touches you also, grumbling reader, it touches each and all. Singular judgments have the value of universal judgments, the logicians say. The singular is not particular, it is universal.

Man is an end, not a means. All civilization addresses itself to man, to each man, to each I. What is that idol, call it Humanity or call it what you like, to which all men and each individual man must be sacrificed? For I sacrifice myself for my neighbours, for my fellow-countrymen, for my children, and these sacrifice themselves in their turn for theirs, and theirs again for those that come after them, and so on in a never-ending series of generations. And who receives the fruit of this sacrifice?

Those who talk to us about this fantastic sacrifice, this dedication without an object, are wont to talk to us also about the right to live. What is this right to live? They tell me I am here to realize I know not what social end; but I feel that I, like each one of my fellows, am here to realize myself, to live.

Yes, yes, I see it all!—an enormous social activity, a mighty civilization, a profuseness of science, of art, of industry, of morality, and afterwards, when we have filled the world with industrial marvels, with great factories, with roads, museums, and libraries, we shall fall exhausted at the foot of it all, and it will subsist—for whom? Was man made for science or was science made for man?

"Why!" the reader will exclaim again, "we are coming back to what the Catechism says: 'Q. For whom did God create the world? A. For man.' " Well, why not?—so ought the man who is a man to reply. The ant, if it took account of these matters and were a person, would reply "For the ant," and it would reply rightly. The world is made for consciousness, for each consciousness.

A human soul is worth all the universe, someone—I know not whom— has said and said magnificently. A human soul, mind you! Not a human life. Not this life. And it happens that the less a man believes in the soul —that is to say in his conscious immortality, personal and concrete—the more he will exaggerate the worth of this poor transitory life. This is the source from which springs all that effeminate, sentimental ebullition against war. True, a man ought not to wish to die, but the death to be renounced is the death of the soul. "Whosoever will save his life shall lose it," says the Gospel; but it does not say "whosoever will save his soul," the immortal soul—or, at any rate, which we believe and wish to be immortal.

And what all the objectivists do not see, or rather do not wish to see, is that when a man affirms his "I," his personal consciousness, he affirms man, man concrete and real, affirms the true humanism—the humanism of man, not of the things of man—and in affirming man he affirms consciousness. For the only consciousness of which we have consciousness is that of man.

The world is for consciousness. Or rather this *for*, this notion of finality, and feeling rather than notion, this teleological feeling, is born only where there is consciousness. Consciousness and finality are fundamentally the same thing.

If the sun possessed consciosuness it would think, no doubt, that it lived in order to give light to the worlds; but it would also and above all think that the worlds existed in order that it might give them light and enjoy itself in giving them light and so live. And it would think well.

And all this tragic fight of man to save himself, this immortal craving for immortality which caused the man Kant to make that immortal leap of which I have spoken, all this is simply a fight for consciousness. If consciousness is, as some inhuman thinker has said, nothing more than a flash of light between two eternities of darkness, then there is nothing more execrable than existence.

Some may espy a fundamental contradiction in everything that I am saying, now expressing a longing for unending life, now affirming that this earthly life does not possess the value that is given to it. Contradiction? To be sure! The contradiction of my heart that says Yes and of my head that says No! Of course there is contradiction. Who does not recollect those words of the Gospel, "Lord, I believe, help thou my unbelief"? Contradiction! Of course! Since we only live in and by contradictions, since life is tragedy and the tragedy is perpetual struggle, without victory or the hope of victory, life is contradiction.

The values we are discussing are, as you see, values of the heart, and against values of the heart reasons do not avail. For reasons are only reasons—that is to say, they are not even truths. There is a class of pedantic labelmongers, pedants by nature and by grace, who remind me of that man who, purposing to console a father whose son has suddenly died in the flower of his years, says to him, "Patience, my friend, we all must die!" Would you think it strange if this father were offended at such an impertinence? For it is an impertinence. There are times when even an axiom can become an impertinence. How many times may it not be said—

> *Para pensar cual tú, sólo es preciso*
> *no tener nada mas que inteligencia.*[3]

There are, in fact, people who appear to think only with the brain, or with whatever may be the specific thinking organ; while others think with all the body and all the soul, with the blood, with the marrow of the bones, with the heart, with the lungs, with the belly, with the life. And

---

[3] To be lacking in everything but intelligence is the necessary qualification for thinking like you.

the people who think only with the brain develop into definition-mongers; they become the professionals of thought. And you know what a professional is? You know what a product of the differentiation of labour is?

Take a professional boxer. He has learnt to hit with such economy of effort that, while concentrating all his strength in the blow, he only brings into play just those muscles that are required for the immediate and definite object of his action—to knock out his opponent. A blow given by a non-professional will not have so much immediate, objective efficiency; but it will more greatly vitalize the striker, causing him to bring into play almost the whole of his body. The one is the blow of a boxer, the other that of a man. And it is notorious that the Hercules of the circus, the athletes of the ring, are not, as a rule, healthy. They knock out their opponents, they lift enormous weights, but they die of phthisis or dyspepsia.

If a philosopher is not a man, he is anything but a philosopher; he is above all a pedant, and a pedant is a caricature of a man. The cultivation of any branch of science—of chemistry, of physics, of geometry, of philology—may be a work of differentiated specialization, and even so only within very narrow limits and restrictions; but philosophy, like poetry, is a work of integration and synthesis, or else it is merely pseudophilosophical erudition.

All knowledge has an ultimate object. Knowledge for the sake of knowledge is, say what you will, nothing but a dismal begging of the question. We learn something either for an immediate practical end, or in order to complete the rest of our knowledge. Even the knowledge that appears to us to be most theoretical—that is to say, of least immediate application to the non-intellectual necessities of life—answers to a necessity which is no less real because it is intellectual, to a reason of economy in thinking, to a principle of unity and continuity of consciousness. But just as a scientific fact has its finality in the rest of knowledge, so the philosophy that we would make our own has also its extrinsic object—it refers to our whole destiny, to our attitude in face of life and the universe. And the most tragic problem of philosophy is to reconcile intellectual necessities with the necessities of the heart and the will. For it is on this rock that every philosophy that pretends to resolve the eternal and tragic contradiction, the basis of our existence, breaks to pieces. But do all men face this contradiction squarely?

Little can be hoped from a ruler, for example, who has not at some time or other been preoccupied, even if only confusedly, with the first beginning and the ultimate end of all things, and above all of man, with the "why" of his origin and the "wherefore" of his destiny.

And this supreme preoccupation cannot be purely rational, it must involve the heart. It is not enough to think about our destiny: it must be felt. And the would-be leader of men who affirms and proclaims that he pays no heed to the things of the spirit, is not worthy to lead them. By which I do not mean, of course, that any ready-made solution is to be required of him. Solution? Is there indeed any?

So far as I am concerned, I will never willingly yield myself, nor entrust my confidence, to any popular leader who is not penetrated with the feeling that he who orders a people orders men, men of flesh and bone, men who are born, suffer, and, although they do not wish to die, die; men who are ends in themselves, not merely means; men who must be themselves and not others; men, in fine, who seek that which we call happiness. It is inhuman, for example, to sacrifice one generation of men to the generation which follows, without having any feeling for the destiny of those who are sacrificed, without having any regard, not for their memory, not for their names, but for them themselves.

All this talk of a man surviving in his children, or in his works, or in the universal consciousness, is but vague verbiage which satisfies only those who suffer from affective stupidity, and who, for the rest, may be persons of a certain cerebral distinction. For it is possible to possess great talent, or what we call great talent, and yet to be stupid as regards the feelings and even morally imbecile. There have been instances.

These clever-witted, affectively stupid persons are wont to say that it is useless to delve in the unknowable or to kick against the pricks. It is as if one should say to a man whose leg has had to be amputated that it does not help him at all to think about it. And we all lack something; only some of us feel the lack and others do not. Or they pretend not to feel the lack, and then they are hypocrites.

A pedant who beheld Solon weeping for the death of a son said to him, "Why do you weep thus, if weeping avails nothing?" And the sage answered him, "Precisely for that reason—because it does not avail." It is manifest that weeping avails something, even if only the alleviation of distress; but the deep sense of Solon's reply to the impertinent questioner is plainly seen. And I am convinced that we should solve many things if we all went out into the streets and uncovered our griefs, which perhaps would prove to be but one sole common grief, and joined together in beweeping them and crying aloud to the heavens and calling upon God. And this, even though God should hear us not; but He would hear us. The chiefest sanctity of a temple is that it is a place to which men go to weep in common. A *miserere* sung in common by a multitude tormented by destiny has as much value as a philosophy. It is not enough to cure the plague: we must learn to weep for it. Yes, we must learn to weep! Perhaps that is the supreme wisdom. Why? Ask Solon.

There is something which, for lack of a better name, we will call the tragic sense of life, which carries with it a whole conception of life itself and of the universe, a whole philosophy more or less formulated, more or less conscious. And this sense may be possessed, and is possessed, not only by individual men but by whole peoples. And this sense does not so much flow from ideas as determine them, even though afterwards, as is manifest, these ideas react upon it and confirm it. Sometimes it may originate in a chance illness—dyspepsia, for example; but at other times it is constitutional. And it is useless to speak, as we shall see, of men who are healthy and men who are not healthy. Apart from the fact there is no normal standard of health, nobody has proved that man is necessarily cheerful by nature. And further, man, by the very fact of being man, of possessing consciousness, is, in comparison with the ass or the crab, a diseased animal. Consciousness is a disease.

.   .   .

Philosophy and religion are enemies, and because they are enemies they have need of one another. There is no religion without some philosophic basis, no philosophy without roots in religion. Each lives by its contrary. The history of philosophy is, strictly speaking, a history of religion. And the attacks which are directed against religion from a presumed scientific or philosophical point of view are merely attacks from another but opposing religious point of view. "The opposition which professedly exists between natural science and Christianity really exists between an impulse derived from natural religion blended with the scientific investigation of nature, and the validity of the Christian view of the world, which assures to spirit its pre-eminence over the entire world of nature," says Ritschl (*Rechtfertgung und Versöhnung*, iii. chap. iv. § 28). Now this instinct is the instinct of rationality itself. And the critical idealism of Kant is of religious origin, and it is in order to save religion that Kant enlarged the limits of reason after having in a certain sense dissolved it in scepticism. The system of antitheses, contradictions, and antinomies, upon which Hegel constructed his absolute idealism, has its root and germ in Kant himself, and this root is an irrational root.

.   .   .

Every position of permanent agreement or harmony between reason and life, between philosophy and religion, becomes impossible. And the tragic history of human thought is simply the history of a struggle between reason and life—reason bent on rationalizing life and forcing it to submit to the inevitable, to mortality; life bent on vitalizing reason and forcing it to serve as a support for its own vital desires. And this is the history of philosophy, inseparable from the history of religion.

Our sense of the world of objective reality is necessarily subjective, human, anthropomorphic. And vitalism will always rise up against rationalism; reason will always find itself confronted by will. Hence the rhythm of the history of philosophy and the alteration of periods in which life imposes itself, giving birth to spiritual forms, with those in which reason imposes itself, giving birth to materialist forms, although both of these classes of forms of belief may be disguised by other names. Neither reason nor life ever acknowledges itself vanquished. But we will return to this in the next chapter.

The vital consequence of rationalism would be suicide. Kierkegaard puts it very well: "The consequence for existence[4] of pure thought is suicide. . . . We do not praise suicide but passion. The thinker, on the contrary, is a curious animal—for a few spells during the day he is very intelligent, but, for the rest, he has nothing in common with man" (*Afsluttende uvidenskabelig Efterskrift*, chap iii., § 1).

As the thinker, in spite of all, does not cease to be a man, he employs reason in the interests of life, whether he knows it or not. Life cheats reason and reason cheats life. Scholastic-Aristotelian philosophy fabricated in the interest of life a teleologic-evolutionist system, rational in appearance, which might serve as a support for our vital longing. This philosophy, the basis of the orthodox Christian supernaturalism, whether Catholic or Protestant, was, in its essence, merely a trick on the part of life to force reason to lend it its support. But reason supported it with such pressure that it ended by pulverizing it.

I have read that the ex-Carmelite, Hyacinthe Loyson, declared that he could present himself before God with tranquillity, for he was at peace with his conscience and with his reason. With what conscience? If with his religious conscience, then I do not understand. For it is a truth that no man can serve two masters, and least of all when, though they may sign truces and armistices and compromises, these two are enemies because of their conflicting interests.

To all this someone is sure to object that life ought to subject itself to reason, to which we will reply that nobody ought to do what he is unable to do, and life cannot subject itself to reason. "Ought, therefore can," some Kantian will retort. To which we shall demur: "Cannot, therefore ought not." And life cannot submit itself to reason, because the end of life is living and not understanding.

Again, there are those who talk of the religious duty of resignation to mortality. This is indeed the very summit of aberration and insincerity. But someone is sure to oppose the idea of veracity to that of sincerity. Granted, and yet the two may well be reconciled. Veracity, the homage I owe to what I believe to be rational, to what logically we call truth, moves me to affirm, in this case, that the immortality of the individual soul is a contradiction in terms, that it is something, not only irrational, but contra-rational; but sincerity leads me to affirm also my refusal to resign myself to this previous affirmation and my protest against its validity. What I feel is a truth, at any rate as much a truth as what I see, touch, hear, or what is demonstrated to me—nay, I believe it is more of a truth—and sincerity obliges me to hide what I feel.

---

[4] I have left the original expression here, almost without translating it—*Existents-Consequents*. It means the existential or practical, not the purely rational or logical, consequence. (Author's note.)

And life, quick to defend itself, searches for the weak point in reason and finds it in scepticism, which it straightway fastens upon, seeking to save itself by means of this stranglehold. It needs the weakness of its adversary.

Nothing is sure. Everything is elusive and in the air. In an outburst of passion Lamennais exclaims: "But what! Shall we, losing all hope, shut our eyes and plunge into the voiceless depths of a universal scepticism? Shall we doubt that we think, that we feel, that we are? Nature does not allow it; she forces us to believe even when our reason is not convinced. Absolute certainty and absolute doubt are both alike forbidden to us. We hover in a vague mean between these two extremes, as between being and nothingness; for complete scepticism would be the extinction of the intelligence and the total death of man. But it is not given to man to annihilate himself; there is in him something which invincibly resists destruction, I know not what vital faith, indomitable even by his will. Whether he likes it or not, he must believe, because he must act, because he must preserve himself. His reason, if he listened only to that, teaching him to doubt everything, itself included, would reduce him to a state of absolute inaction; he would perish before even he had been able to prove to himself that he existed" (*Essai sur l'indifférence en matière de religion,* iiie partie, chap. lxvii.).

Reason, however, does not actually lead us to absolute scepticism. No! Reason does not lead me and cannot lead me to doubt that I exist. Whither reason does lead me is to vital scepticism, or more properly, to vital negation—not merely to doubt, but to deny, that my consciousness survives my death. Scepticism is produced by the clash between reason and desire. And from this clash, from this embrace between despair and scepticism, is born that holy, that sweet, that saving incertitude, which is our supreme consolation.

The absolute and complete certainty, on the one hand, that death is a complete, definite, irrevocable annihilation of personal consciousness, a certainty of the same order as the certainty that the three angles of a triangle are equal to two right angles, or, on the other hand, the absolute and complete certainty that our personal consciousness is prolonged beyond death in these present or in other conditions, and above all including in itself that strange and adventitious addition of eternal rewards and punishments—both of these certainties alike would make life impossible for us. In the most secret chamber of the spirit of him who believes himself convinced that death puts an end to his personal consciousness, his memory, for ever, and all unknown to him perhaps, there lurks a shadow, a vague shadow, a shadow of shadow, of uncertainty, and while he says within himself, "Well, let us live this life that passes away, for there is no other!" the silence of this secret chamber speaks to him and murmurs, "Who knows! . . ." He may not think he hears it, but he hears it nevertheless. And likewise in some secret place of the soul of the believer who most firmly holds the belief in a future life, there is a muffled voice, a voice of uncertainty, which whispers in the ear of his spirit, "Who knows! . . ." These voices are like the humming of a mosquito when the south-west wind roars through the trees in the wood; we cannot distinguish this faint humming, yet nevertheless, merged in the clamour of the storm, it reaches the ear. Otherwise, without this uncertainty, how could we live?

"*Is there?*" "*Is there not?*"—these are the bases of our inner life. There may be a rationalist who has never wavered in his conviction of the mortality of the soul, and there may be a vitalist who has never wavered in his faith in immortality; but at the most this would only prove that just as there are natural monstrosities, so there are those who are stupid as regards heart and feeling, however great their intelligence, and those who are stupid intellectually, however great their virtue. But, in normal cases, I cannot believe those who assure me that never, not in a fleeting moment, not in the hours of direst loneliness and grief, has this murmur of uncertainty breathed upon their consciousness. I do not understand those men who tell men that the prospect of the yonder side of death has never tormented them, that the thought of their own annihilation never disquiets them. For my part I do not wish to make peace between my heart and my head, between my faith and my reason—I wish rather that there should be war between them!

. . .

Do you remember the end of that *Song of the Wild Cock* which Leopardi wrote in prose?—the despairing Leopardi, the victim of reason, who never succeeded in achieving belief. "A time will come," he says, "when this Universe and Nature itself will be extinguished. And just as of the grandest kingdoms and empires of mankind and the marvellous things achieved therein, very famous in their own time, no vestige or memory remains to-day, so, in like manner, of the entire world and of the vicissitudes and calamities of all created things, there will remain not a single trace, but a naked silence and a most profound stillness will fill the immensity of space. And so before ever it has been uttered or understood, this admirable and fearful secret of universal existence will be obliterated and lost." And this they now describe by a scientific and very rationalistic term—namely, *entropia*. Very pretty, is it not? Spencer invented the notion of a primordial homogeneity, from which it is impossible to conceive how any heterogeneity could originate. Well now, this *entropia* is a kind of ultimate homogeneity, a state of perfect equilibrium. For a soul avid of life, it is the most like nothingness that the mind can conceive.

. . .

Several times in the devious course of these essays I have defined, in spite of my horror of definitions, my own position with regard to the problem that I have been examining; but I know there will always be some dissatisfied reader, educated in some dogmatism or other, who will say: "This man comes to no conclusion, he vacillates—now he seems to affirm one thing and then its contrary—he is full of contradictions—I can't label him. What is he?" Just this—one who affirms contraries, a man of contradiction and strife, as Jeremiah said of himself; one who says one thing with his heart and the contrary with his head, and for whom this conflict is the very stuff of life. And that is as clear as the water that flows from the melted snow upon the mountain tops.

I shall be told that this is an untenable position, that a foundation must be laid upon which to build our action and our works, that it is impossible to live by contradictions, that unity and clarity are essential conditions of life and thought, and that it is necessary to unify thought. And this leaves us as we were before. For it is precisely this inner contradiction that unifies my life and gives it its practical purpose.

Or rather it is the conflict itself, it is this self-same passionate uncertainty, that unifies my action and makes me live and work.

We think in order that we may live, I have said; but perhaps it were more correct to say that we think because we live, and the form of our thought corresponds with that of our life. Once more I must repeat that our ethical and philosophical doctrines in general are usually merely the justification *a posteriori* of our conduct, of our actions. Our doctrines are usually the means we seek in order to explain and justify to others and to ourselves our own mode of action. And this, be it observed, not merely for others, but for ourselves. The man who does not really know why he acts as he does and not otherwise, feels the necessity of explaining to himself the motive of his action and so he forges a motive. What we believe to be the motives of our conduct are usually but the pretexts for it. The very same reason which one man may regard as a motive for taking care to prolong his life may be regarded by another man as a motive for shooting himself.

Nevertheless it cannot be denied that reasons, ideas, have an influence upon human actions, and sometimes even determine them, by a process analogous to that of suggestion upon a hypnotized person, and this is so because of the tendency in every idea to resolve itself into action—an idea being simply an inchoate or abortive act. It was this notion that suggested to Fouillée his theory of idea-forces. But ordinarily ideas are forces which we accommodate to other forces, deeper and much less conscious.

But putting all this aside for the present, what I wish to establish is that uncertainty, doubt, perpetual wrestling with the mystery of our final destiny, mental despair, and the lack of any solid and stable dogmatic foundation, may be the basis of an ethic.

He who bases or thinks that he bases his conduct—his inward or his outward conduct, his feeling or his action—upon a dogma or theoretical principle which he deems incontrovertible, runs the risk of becoming a fanatic, and moreover, the moment that this dogma is weakened or shat-

tered, the morality based upon it gives way. If the earth that he thought
firm begins to rock, he himself trembles at the earthquake, for we do not
come up to the standard of the ideal Stoic who remains undaunted among
the ruins of a world shattered into atoms. Happily the stuff that is underneath a man's ideas will save him. For if a man should tell you that he
does not defraud or cuckold his best friend only because he is afraid of
hell, you may depend upon it that neither would he do so even if he were
to cease to believe in hell, but that he would invent some other excuse
instead. And this is all to the honour of the human race.

But he who believes that he is sailing, perhaps without a set course,
on an unstable and sinkable raft, must not be dismayed if the raft gives
way beneath his feet and threatens to sink. Such a one thinks that he acts,
not because he deems his principle of action to be true, but in order to
make it true, in order to prove its truth, in order to create his own spiritual
world.

My conduct must be the best proof, the moral proof, of my supreme
desire; and if I do not end by convincing myself, within the bonds of the
ultimate and irremediable uncertainty, of the truth of what I hope for,
it is because my conduct is not sufficiently pure. Virtue, therefore, is not
based upon dogma, but dogma upon virtue, and it is not faith that creates
martyrs but martyrs who create faith. There is no security or repose—so far
as security and repose are obtainable in this life, so essentially insecure and
unreposeful—save in conduct that is passionately good.

Conduct, practice, is the proof of doctrine, theory. "If any man will
do His will—the will of Him that sent me," said Jesus, "he shall know of
the doctrine, whether it be of God or whether I speak of myself" (John
vii. 17); and there is a well-known saying of Pascal: "Begin by taking holy
water and you will end by becoming a believer." And pursuing a similar
train of thought, Johann Jakob Moser, the pietist, was of the opinion that
no atheist or naturalist had the right to regard the Christian religion as
void of truth so long as he had not put it to the proof by keeping its
precepts and commandments (Ritschl, *Geschichte des Pietismus,* book
vii., 43).

What is our heart's truth, anti-rational though it be? The immortality
of the human soul, the truth of the persistence of our consciousness without any termination whatsoever, the truth of the human finality of the
Universe. And what is its moral proof? We may formulate it thus: Act
so that in your own judgement and in the judgement of others you may
merit eternity, act so that you may become irreplaceable, act so that you
may not merit death. Or perhaps thus: Act as if you were to die to-
morrow, but to die in order to survive and be eternalized. The end of
morality is to give personal, human finality to the Universe; to discover
the finality that belongs to it—if indeed it has any finality—and to discover it by acting.

More than a century ago, in 1804, in Letter XC of that series that constitutes the immense monody of his *Obermann,* Sénancour wrote the words which I have put at the head of this chapter[5]—and of all the spiritual descendants of the patriarchal Rousseau, Sénancour was the most profound and the most intense; of all the men of heart and feeling that France has produced, not excluding Pascal, he was the most tragic. "Man is perishable. That may be; but let us perish resisting, and if it is nothingness that awaits us, do not let us so act that it shall be a just fate." Change this sentence from its negative to the positive form—"And if it is nothingness that awaits us, let us so act that it shall be an unjust fate"—and you get the firmest basis of action for the man who cannot or will not be a dogmatist.

[5] L'homme est périssable. Il se peut; mais périssons en résistant, et, si le néant nous est reservé, ne faisons pas que ce soit une justice.—SÉNANCOUR: *Obermann,* lettre xc.

Selected bibliography

Self-realization
Aristotle. *The Nicomachean Ethics.* Cambridge: Harvard University Press, 1968.
Bradley, F. H. *Ethical Studies.* New York: Liberal Arts Press, 1951.
Fromm, Erich. *Escape From Freedom.* New York: Farrar & Rinehart, 1941.
Green, T. H. *Prolegomena to Ethics.* Oxford: Clarendon Press, 1924.
Hegel, G. W. F. *Philosophy of Right.* Oxford: Clarendon Press, 1958.
Hocking, W. E. *Human Nature and Its Remaking.* New Haven: Yale University Press, 1932.
Johnson, David W. *Reaching Out: Interpersonal Effectiveness and Self-Actualization.* Englewood Cliffs, N.J.: Prentice-Hall, 1972.
Maslow, Abraham H., ed. *Motivation and Personality.* New York: Harper & Row, 1970.
May, Rollo. *Man's Search for Himself.* New York: Dell, 1973.
Muirhead, J. H. *Elements of Ethics.* New York: Charles Scribner's, 1932.
Naranjo, Claudio. *The One Quest.* New York: Viking, 1972.
Ostrovsky, Everett. *Self Discovery and Social Awareness.* New York: Wiley, 1974.
Paton, H. J. *The Good Will.* New York: Macmillan, 1927.
Plato. *Republic* in *Dialogues of Plato.* Oxford: Clarendon Press, 1920.
Roberts, Jane. *The Nature of Personal Reality.* Englewood Cliffs, N.J.: Prentice-Hall, 1974.
Rogers, Carl. *On Becoming a Person.* Boston: Houghton Mifflin, 1961.
Royce, Josiah. *The World and the Individual.* New York: Macmillan, 1927.
Seth, James. *A Study of Ethical Principles.* New York: Charles Scribner's, 1926.
Shostrom, Everett L. *Man the Manipulator: The Inner Journey From Manipulation to Actualization.* Nashville: Abingdon Press, 1967.
Tournier, Paul. *Adventures of Living.* New York: Harper & Row, 1965.
Wheelis, Allen. *How People Change.* New York: Harper & Row, 1973.

Humanism
Ayer, A. J., ed. *The Humanist Outlook.* London: Pemberton, 1968.

Blackham, H. J. *Humanism.* Harmondsworth, England: Penguin Books, 1968.
————, ed. *Objections to Humanism.* Harmondsworth, England: Penguin Books, 1963.
Dakin, Arthur H. *Man the Measure.* Princeton: Princeton University Press, 1939.
Hawton, Hector. *The Humanist Revolution.* London: Barrie Books, 1963.
Huxley, Julian, ed. *The Humanist Frame.* London: Allen & Unwin, 1961.
————. *Religion Without Revelation.* London: Ernest Benn, 1927.
Jaeger, Werner W. *Humanism and Theology.* Milwaukee: Marquette University Press, 1967.
Jones, Howard M. *American Humanism.* New York: Harper & Row, 1957.
Kurtz, Paul, ed. *Humanist Manifestos One and Two.* Buffalo: Prometheus Books, 1973.
————, ed. *Moral Problems in Contemporary Society.* Englewood Cliffs, N.J.: Prentice-Hall, 1969.
Lamont, Corliss. *The Philosophy of Humanism.* New York: Ungar, 1965.
Liat, Kwee Swan. *Bibliography of Humanism.* Utrecht: The Humanist League, 1957.
Mouat, Kit. *What Humanism Is About.* London: Barrie Books, 1963.
Potter, C. F. *Humanism: A New Religion.* New York: Simon & Schuster, 1930.
Reese, Curtis W. *The Meaning of Humanism.* Boston: Beacon Press, 1945.
Robinson, Richard. *An Atheist's Values.* London: Oxford University Press, 1964.

Existentialism
Barnes, Hazel. *An Existentialist Ethic.* New York: Knopf, 1967.
Barrett, William. *What Is Existentialism?* New York: Grove Press, 1964.
Berdyaev, Nicolas. *The Fate of Man in the Modern World.* Ann Arbor: University of Michigan Press, 1961.
Buber, Martin. *I and Thou.* New York: Charles Scribner's, 1958.
Camus, Albert. *The Myth of Sisyphus and Other Essays.* New York: Vintage Books, 1955.
Heidegger, Martin. *Being and Time.* New York: Harper & Row, 1962.
————. *An Introduction to Metaphysics.* New York: Doubleday, 1961.
Heinemann, F. H. *Existentialism and the Modern Predicament.* New York: Harper & Brothers, 1958.
Jaspers, Karl. *Man in the Modern Age.* New York: Doubleday, 1957.
Kierkegaard, S. *Concluding Unscientific Postscript.* Princeton: Princeton University Press, 1944.
————. *Fear and Trembling* and *Sickness Unto Death.* New York: Doubleday, 1954.
Marcel, Gabriel. *Being and Having.* New York: Harper & Row, 1965.
————. *The Philosophy of Existence.* New York: Citadel Press, 1961.
Maritain, Jacques. *Existence and the Existent.* New York: Pantheon Books, 1948.
Nietzsche, F. *Beyond Good and Evil.* New York: Vintage Books, 1966.
Reinhardt, Kurt F. *The Existentialist Revolt.* Milwaukee: Bruce, 1952.
Sanborn, Patricia. *Existentialism.* New York: Pegasus Books, 1968.
Sartre, Jean-Paul. *Being and Nothingness.* New York: Philosophical Library, 1956.

EPILOGUE

CONTEMPLATION AND ACTION

THE YOGI AND THE COMMISSAR

Arthur Koestler

> *Arthur Koestler (1905–   ), novelist, journalist, and political philosopher of international reputation whose interests range from Marxist philosophy to contemporary science. His most widely read novel is* Darkness at Noon *(1940), but he has published numerous other outstanding works, including* The Gladiators *(1939),* The God that Failed *(1950, with others),* The Sleepwalkers *(1958),* The Lotus and the Robot *(1960), and* The Act of Creation *(1963).*

I. THE STATIC SPECTRUM

I like to imagine an instrument which would enable us to break up patterns of social behaviour as the physicist breaks up a beam of rays. Looking through this sociological spectroscope we would see spread out under the diffraction grating the rainbow-coloured spectrum of all possible human attitudes to life. The whole distressing muddle would become neat, clear and comprehensive.

On one end of the spectrum, obviously on the infra-red end, we would see the Commissar. The Commissar believes in Change from Without. He believes that all the pests of humanity, including constipation and the

Oedipus complex, can and will be cured by Revolution, that is, by a radical reorganization of the system of production and distribution of goods; that this end justifies the use of all means, including violence, ruse, treachery and poison; that logical reasoning is an unfailing compass and the Universe a kind of very large clockwork in which a very large number of electrons once set into motion will forever revolve in their predictable orbits; and that whosoever believes in anything else is an escapist. This end of the spectrum has the lowest frequency of vibrations and is, in a way, the coarsest component of the beam; but it conveys the maximum amount of heat.

On the other end of the spectrum, where the waves become so short and of such high frequency that the eye no longer sees them, colourless, warmthless but all-penetrating, crouches the Yogi, melting away in the ultra-violet. He has no objection to calling the universe a clockwork, but he thinks that it could be called, with about the same amount of truth, a musical-box or a fishpond. He believes that the End is unpredictable and that the Means alone count. He rejects violence under any circumstances. He believes that logical reasoning gradually loses its compass value as the mind approaches the magnetic pole of Truth or the Absolute, which alone matters. He believes that nothing can be improved by exterior organisation and everything by the individual effort from within; and what whosoever believes in anything else is an escapist. He believes that the debt-servitude imposed upon the peasants of India by the money lenders should be abolished not by financial legislation but by spiritual means. He believes that each individual is alone, but attached to the all-one by an invisible umbilical cord; that his creative forces, his goodness, trueness and usefulness can alone be nourished by the sap which reaches him through this cord; and that his only task during his earthly life is to avoid any action, emotion or thought which might lead to a breaking of the cord. This avoidance has to be maintained by a difficult, elaborate technique, the only kind of technique which he accepts.

Between these two extremes are spread out in a continuous sequence the spectral lines of the more sedate human attitudes. The more we approach its centre, the more does the spectrum become blurred and woolly. On the other hand, this increase of wool on the naked spectral bodies makes them look more decent, and intercourse with them more civilised. You cannot argue with a naked Commissar—he starts at once to beat his chest and next he strangles you, whether you be friend or foe, in his deadly embrace. You cannot argue with the ultra-violet skeleton either, because words mean nothing to him. You can argue with post-war planners, Fabians, Quakers, liberals and philanthropists. But the argument will lead nowhere, for the real issue remains between the Yogi and the Commissar, between the fundamental conceptions of Change from Without and Change from Within.

It is easy to say that all that is wanted is a synthesis—the synthesis between saint and revolutionary; but so far this has never been achieved. What has been achieved are various motley forms of compromise—the blurred intermediary bands of the spectrum—compromise but not synthesis. Apparently the two elements do not mix, and this may be one of the reasons why we have made such a mess of our History. The Commissar's emotional energies are fixed on the relation between individual and society, the Yogi's on the relation between the individual and the universe. Again it is easy to say that all that is wanted is a little mutual effort. One might as well ask a homosexual to make a little effort towards the opposite sex, and vice versa.

All attempts to change the nature of man by Commissar methods have so far failed, from Spartacus's Sun State through Inquisition and Reformation to Soviet Russia. . . .

The attempts to produce Change from Within on a mass-scale were equally unsuccessful. Whenever an attempt was made to organise saintliness by exterior means, the organisers were caught in the same dilemmas. The Inquisition flew off at a tangent; the Churches in the liberal era circle round and round the peak without gaining height. To subordinate the End to the Means leads to a slope as fatal as the inverse one. Gandhi's slope started with non-violence and made him gradually slide down to his present position of non-resistance to Japanese conquest: the Japanese might kill a few million Indians but some day they would get tired of it, and thus the moral integrity of India would be saved.

Obviously the prospects for the masses of common people are not brighter under this inverted Machiavellianism than under the leadership of the Commissars. One slope leads to the Inquisition and the Purges; the other to passive submission to bayoneting and raping; to villages without sewerage, septic childbeds and trachoma. The Yogi and the Commissar may call it quits.

II. THE SPECTRUM IN MOTION

But they don't. Unable to form a synthesis and unsatisfied by the patched-up compromises in the medium bands of the spectrum, they attract and repel each other in rhythmical intervals. This strange minuet is one of the more exciting aspects of History which Marxism, otherwise the most serviceable guide, falls short of explaining.

Under certain historic climates mass-migrations start from one end of the spectrum to the other, general displacements from infra-red to ultra-violet or vice versa, like mighty trade winds travelling over the seas. The nineteenth century brought such a general displacement towards the

Commissar or infra-red end. The present climate favours the opposite direction. Since the early 'thirties we are all travelling, more or less consciously, more or less willingly, towards the ultra-violet end.

The less consciously we drift with the wind the more willingly we do it; the more consciously the less willingly. Personally I belong to the latter type; I wish one could still write an honest infra-red novel without an ultra-violet ending. But one can't, just as no honest scientist can now publish a book on physics without a metaphysical epilogue, no honest Socialist can write a survey of the Left's defeats without accounting for the irrational factor in mass-psychology. He who clings blindly to the past will be left behind; but he who abandons himself too readily will be carried away like a dry leaf; all one can do is to travel even more consciously and even less willingly.

But again, is such intentional readaptation possible? Are those who survive the great spectral displacements the fittest or merely the glibbest? Thinking of some fellow-writers who achieved the journey from the pink decade to the Yogi decade with such monkey-like agility one is tempted to say, "Let the dead bury their dead." They answer, "But we mean it"—and there is no doubt that, at least, they believe that they mean it. Yet what writer has ever written a line without at least meaning to mean it? Hence one first feels disgust with them; then one finds out that one was disgusted for the wrong reasons; and after that one is still disgusted because they were so quick to find the right reasons for their expatriation from the infra-red to the ultra-violet. In these matters clumsiness is respectable and glibness abject. They never seriously attempted to sail against the wind; they abandoned themselves to its first breeze, which broke them gently from their stems, and whirled them round and dropped them gently at the other end; that is perhaps why, when you hear their whisper, it sounds so much like the rattling of dead leaves.

· · ·

There is one definite profiteer of the spectral displacement: the Scientist. In a certain sense it was he who started the movement; then its momentum carried him further than he probably liked. One should remember that the irrational or ultra-violet element which so strongly taints present-day physics, biology, and psychology was not a philosophical fashion smuggled into the laboratories, but grew out of the laboratories themselves and created the new philosophical climate. The most striking example is the development of physics which was an enormously successful rational Commissar-science up to the closing years of the last century and has since become more and more of a Yogi-science. Matter, substance, time, space, causality, precision of measurement and the belief in the predictability of behaviour of the Measured have run like sand through the physicist's fingers until nothing remained but a group of formal statements of this type: "If a small poker-die is so constructed that we have no reason to assume a preference on its part for falling on the ace-side, then we are entitled to expect that, in the course of a great number of casts, it will show no preference for falling on the ace-side."

This is undeniably a precise statement, but a rather modest one in relation to our hunger for the mysteries of the Universe explained to us. The modern physicist of course denies that his task should be to "explain" anything, and he takes a masochistic delight in producing formulae which establish with precision the degree of imprecision in his statements, i.e., the inadequacy of physics not only to explain but even to describe what exactly is going on in the physical world. . . .

· · ·

III. THE PENDULUM

The Commissar, the Artist, the vague Man of Goodwill, the Scientist, not only seem to react in different ways to the great spectral displacement, but their motives for participating in it seem also different in nature. Is there a common reason for this pilgrimage? To a certain extent the revolution in psychology has influenced political outlook, and similar cross-influences are easy to discover. They form a pattern of diagonal lines of forces, but this pattern is that of a network, not of a causal chain. There is no causal chain running from Quantum Mechanics to the self-accusations of Bucharin, but in an indirect way they are all linked together by diagonals. We cannot ask for a common reason, we can only ask for a common denominator in the variety of reasons.

In the critical years of the Weimar Republic, when a communist or fascist revolution seemed equally possible and the only impossibility the continuation of the worn-out regime, a certain Ernst Juenger coined the phrase of the "anti-capitalistic nostalgia of the masses." This vague but violent longing was indeed shared by groups of people of otherwise very different tendencies. Perhaps the common denominator we are looking for can best be described as an "anti-materialistic nostalgia." It is allergic to the rationalism, the shallow optimism, the ruthless logic, the arrogant self-assurance, the Promethean attitude of the nineteenth century; it is attracted by mysticism, romanticism, the irrational ethical values, by mediaeval twilight. In short it is moving towards the very things from which the last-but-one great spectral displacement towards the infra-red has moved away. Apparently these movements have a pendular rhythm.

The swinging of this pendulum from rationalistic to romantic periods and back is not contradictory to the conception of a basic dialectic movement of history. They are like the tidal waves on a river which yet flows into the sea. . . .

Perhaps it is not too hazardous to assume that these pendular changes in the mass-psychological spectrum are a process analogous to the rhythmical change of waking and sleep in the individual. The irrational or romantic periods of mass-psychology are periods of sleep and dream. The dreams are not necessarily peaceful; more often they are nightmares; but without these periodic plunges into the subconscious the vital juices would not be provided for the next wideawake Promethean or Commissar period. Perhaps every Gothic period is followed by a Renaissance period and they are but the succession of Yoga-nights and Commissar-days in the curriculum of the race. And perhaps this, our present civilisation, is not dying, only sleepy.

Copyrights and Acknowledgments

For permission to use the selections reprinted in this book, the author is grateful to the following publishers and copyright holders:

ASSOCIATION PRESS For the excerpts from "Belief in a Time of the Death of God" by William Hamilton. From *The New Essence of Christianity* by William Hamilton. Reprinted by permission of Association Press.

ATHENEUM PUBLISHERS, INC. For the excerpts from *Privacy and Freedom* by Alan F. Westin. Copyright © 1967 by The Association of the Bar of the City of New York. Reprinted by permission of Atheneum Publishers.

BEACON PRESS For "What Is the Value of Life?" by Herbert W. Richardson. From *Updating Life and Death*, edited by Donald R. Cutler. Copyright © 1969 by Beacon Press. Reprinted by permission of Beacon Press.

H. J. BLACKHAM For "The Human Programme" by H. J. Blackham. From *The Humanist Frame*, edited by Julian Huxley. Reprinted by permission of H. J. Blackham.

CAMBRIDGE UNIVERSITY PRESS For the excerpts from *Reason and Commitment* by Roger Trigg. Reprinted by permission of Cambridge University Press.

COLUMBIA UNIVERSITY PRESS For "A Liberal Catholic's View" by J. F. Donceel. From R. E. Hall (ed.): *Abortion in a Changing World*, Volume I, New York: Columbia University Press, 1970, © 1970 The Association for the Study of Abortion, pp. 38–45, by permission of the publisher and the editor.

E. P. DUTTON & CO., INC. For "Zen Buddhism" by D. T. Suzuki. From *The Essentials of Zen Buddhism*, an anthology of the writings of Daisetz T. Suzuki, edited by Bernard Phillips. Copyright © 1962 by Bernard Phillips. Reprinted by permission of the publishers, E. P. Dutton & Co., Inc.

FABER & FABER LTD. For the excerpts from "Defence of Reason" by C. E. M. Joad. From *Return to Philosophy* by C. E. M. Joad. Reprinted by permission of Faber & Faber Ltd.

HARPER & ROW, PUBLISHERS, INC. For the excerpt, pp. 572–85, from "Philosophical Ideas and World Peace" by A. Campbell Garnett in *Approaches to World Peace*, edited by Lyman Bryson et al. Copyright © 1944 by Conference on Science, Philosophy & Religion In Their Relation To The Democratic Way Of Life, Inc. By permission of Harper & Row, Publishers, Inc. For "A Free Man's Worship" and "Mysticism and Logic" from *Mysticism and Logic* by Bertrand Russell; © George Allen & Unwin Ltd., 1963. By permission of Harper & Row, Publishers, Inc., Barnes & Nobel Import Division. And for the excerpts (abridged from pp. 1–22, 105–07, 126–07) from *Dynamics of Faith* by Paul Tillich. Volume 10 in *World Perspectives*, planned and edited by Ruth Nanda Anshen. Copyright © 1957 by Paul Tillich. By permission of Harper & Row, Publishers, Inc.

HARVARD UNIVERSITY PRESS For pp. 64–79 from "Reference Points in Deciding About Abortion" by Paul Ramsey. Reprinted by permission of the publishers from John T. Noonan, Jr., ed., *The Morality of Abortion: Legal and Historical Perspectives*, Cambridge, Mass.: Harvard University Press, Copyright 1970 by the President and Fellows of Harvard College.

Pantheon Books, Inc. Reprinted by permission of Pantheon Books, a division of Random House, Inc.

PHILOSOPHICAL LIBRARY, INC. For the excerpts from *Existentialism* by Jean-Paul Sartre. Reprinted by permission of Philosophical Library, Inc.

THE PHILOSOPHICAL QUARTERLY For an excerpt from "The Political Ideal of Privacy" by H. J. McCloskey. First appeared in *The Philosophical Quarterly*, Vol. 21 (October 1971) pp. 303–14. Reprinted by permission of The Philosophical Quarterly and H. J. McCloskey.

PRINCETON UNIVERSITY PRESS For the selections from "Euthanasia: Our Right to Die," in Joseph Fletcher, *Morals and Medicine* (copyright 1954 by Princeton University Press), pp. 172–76 and 189–210. Reprinted by permission of Princeton University Press.

RANDOM HOUSE, INC. For the excerpt from *The Age of Anxiety* by W. H. Auden. Copyright 1946, 1947 by W. H. Auden. Reprinted by permission of Random House, Inc.

SHERIDAN HOUSE, INC. For "Philosophical Concepts of Atheism" by Ernest Nagel. From *Basic Beliefs* edited by J. E. Fairchild. Copyright 1959 by Sheridan House, Inc. Reprinted by permission of Sheridan House, Inc.

FREDERICK UNGAR PUBLISHING CO., INC. For the excerpts from *The Philosophy of Humanism* by Corliss Lamont. Copyright © 1949, 1957, 1965 by Corliss Lamont. Reprinted by permission of Frederick Ungar Publishing Company, Inc.

ALEXANDER R. JAMES. For "The Moral Equivalent of War" by William James. From *Pragmatism and Other Essays* by William James. Copyright 1901 by William James. Reprinted by permission of Alexander R. James. First appeared in *Popular Science Monthly* (October 1910).

A 5
B 6
C 7
D 8
E 9
F 0
G 1
H 2
I 3
J 4